John Hodgson

# A MEMOIR

OF

# THE REV. JOHN HODGSON,

M.A., M.R.S.L., F.S.A.N.

VICAR OF HARTBURN,

AND AUTHOR OF A HISTORY OF NORTHUMBERLAND, &c.

BY THE

## REV. JAMES RAINE, D.C.L. F.S.A.N.

RECTOR OF MELDON,

AUTHOR OF A HISTORY OF NORTH DURHAM, ETC.

IN TWO VOLUMES.

VOL. II.

---

" Historia præstat, ut qui ævo priore vixerant, vivere adhuc nostra
videantur ætate."—*Salmas. Præf. in Aug. Hist. Scriptores.*

LONDON:

LONGMAN, BROWN, GREEN, LONGMANS, AND ROBERTS,

PATERNOSTER ROW.

M.DCCC.LVIII.

WESTMINSTER :

J. B. NICHOLS AND SONS, PRINTERS,

PARLIAMENT STREET.

# CONTENTS.

# MEMOIR

OF THE

# REV. JOHN HODGSON, M.A.

---

### CHAPTER I.—1823.

Those of my readers who have pictured to themselves the painful circumstances detailed in the latter part of the preceding volume, and have a heart of humanity, will readily comprehend the joy with which the following letter would be received at Heworth. Mr. Hodgson's eldest son, then in his eleventh year, was its bearer from the post office, and he informs me that when he saw the frank of the Bishop of Durham he had a presentiment that it contained good news for his father. And so it did.

FROM THE BISHOP OF DURHAM.

"REV. SIR, Cavendish Square, Mar. 22, 1823.

"The same post which brought me the information of the vacancy of the Vicarage of Kirk Whelpington, by the death of the Rev. Mr. Gardner, would have conveyed to you an offer of the living had I known its real value. I still remain ignorant on that subject; yet I feel unwilling to delay any longer assuring you of my intentions, in the event of your thinking it worthy of your acceptance. As soon as you have determined you will inform me, and in the event of your acceptance, I will order the necessary instruments to be made out. I am, with much regard, your sincere friend and brother,

" S. Dunelm."

### From the BISHOP of DURHAM.

" Dear Sir,       Cavendish Square, Mar. 24, 1823.

" You will not feel more pleasure in receiving than I have in transmitting the inclosed authentic valuation of the Vicarage of Kirk Whelpington.* As there does not now remain a doubt of your acceptance, I shall give directions for preparing the instruments for collating you by commission at Durham. I am, with much regard, your sincere friend and brother,

" S. Dunelm."

### From Sir J. E. SWINBURNE, Bart.

" My dear Sir,      Grosvenor Place, 29 March, 1823.

" I had my pen in my hand when I got your kind note, to congratulate you on your preferment, that Mr. Ellison had just informed me of; and to express the great pleasure and satisfaction it has afforded myself and all my family. No appointment could be more gratifying to us; and I hope the society of Capheaton and the use of my library will compensate for the remoteness of the situation from the more active occupations of Newcastle and its neighbourhood; and afford you more leisure for your literary pursuits.

" My worthy friend Mr. Redman has long managed all the concerns of the living, and I am sure will afford you every information you can require.

" Looking forward with much pleasure to our future meeting, and with the best wishes and congratulations of all my family, believe me, my dear Sir, very sincerely yours,

" J. E. Swinburne."

---

* A valuation of the vicarage by the Rev. Thomas Redman, Vicar of Kirkharle, the adjoining parish, making the income about 354l. 15s. per annum, all outgoings except agent's salary deducted. To Hodgson, of course, a curate would be unnecessary. Mr. Redman's valuation, however, could not be maintained. See a letter to the author in December of the year before us.

But Hodgson's connection with the cure of Jarrow-with-Heworth was not severed by his collation to the vicarage of Whelpington. He had for some time generally enjoyed the assistance of a curate upon such a small stipend, under the bishop's sanction, as the living would allow of, and therefore had been instrumental in securing the performance of full duty in both places; he had built a new chapel at Heworth, for the cost of which a final settlement remained to be made; he had schools, which required much of personal superintendence; and there was a fear that the patron, in whose turn it was to present to the benefice in the event of its being declared vacant, would not adopt measures to separate the two places of divine worship from each other, but appoint a sole incumbent, as had previously been the case. Under these circumstances, there being at that time no law against it, it was arranged that Hodgson should continue to hold the benefice, and nominate two curates as his representatives; allowing to each such a salary as to leave to himself a sum not more than sufficient to defray the expenses of his periodical visits and general superintendence. The following letters afford all the information which is necessary, in explanation of this arrangement, into which, from after circumstances, Hodgson had great reason to regret that he had ever entered. But it is needless to detail here the annoyances which Jarrow and Heworth occasioned to him in after years until his connection with the parish finally ceased in 1833. The quiet of Whelpington during this period must have been his consolation. The gentle murmur of the Wansbeck soothed the noise arising from the swelling turbulence of the Tyne.

FROM C. ELLISON, Esq.

"MY DEAR SIR,                                     Beckenham, Mar. 31, 1823.

"Upon the best consideration I am of opinion that it would be very much for the interest of your present parishioners that you should retain the care of them, although you will not hereafter be at liberty to give them your personal attention, inasmuch as the duties will be more

B 2

effectually done by a curate at each place, under your controul, than by any one individual nominated by the patron, who might not be disposed, out of so small a stipend as belongs to the preferment, to spare a curate's salary; for want of whom, as you well know, the duties of some portion of the parish must be totally neglected. If the Bishop objects to your keeping it in perpetuity, I then think he should be asked to allow you to retain it for a limited time, till the objects you had in view for the good of the parish are matured, and particularly till the concerns of the new chapel are wound up. Let me hear from you again; and consider yourself at liberty to refer the Bishop to me in confirmation of the advantages which you conceive will be secured to the parish, either by his permitting you to keep it altogether, or by allowing you to retain it for a limited period.

" Our weather has at last improved a little, and we may hope for the return of spring.

" My grateful acknowledgements are due to you for the exemplary manner in which you have discharged your duties in the important trust committed to you; and I earnestly hope that you may long enjoy in health, happiness, and ease, the lighter cares the Bishop has entrusted to you. Yours, very truly,

" CUTHBERT ELLISON."

FROM THE BISHOP OF DURHAM.

" DEAR SIR,                                        Cavendish Square, April 5, 1823.

" From the fullest conviction that your removal from all control over the parishes of Heworth and Jarrow would materially injure the best interests of both, I readily consent to the plan you propose of appointing two curates with a stipend of 70*l.* each. By retaining the controul, and by such occasional visits from Kirk Whelpington as you shall judge necessary, the affairs of all the three parishes will be conducted as they should. I am, with much regard, your sincere friend,

" S. DUNELM."

The parish of Whelpington is situated in the heart of Northumberland, at a distance from Newcastle of about twenty-one miles in a north-westerly direction.

According to the census of 1821, it was sub-divided into ten townships, containing in all 154 houses, and a population of 743 pèrsons. It is described as being five miles from east to west, and six miles from north to south. These measurements do not include the detached township of Capheaton, which is separated from the bulk of the parish by portions of not fewer than four intervening ecclesiastical districts.

The parish of Whelpington occupies upon the map of Northumberland precisely that situation in which, like similar districts in Yorkshire, Durham, and other counties touching upon either side of the great line of hills, commonly called the Back-bone of England, there is not only a great, but also almost invariably a beautiful variety of surface—hills gradually sloping downwards, and dying away in level ground; and streams in general extremely picturesque in themselves and in their accompaniments, struggling to escape from rocks and cliffs and natural woods, to flow on at ease through pastures and meadows and arable land, which they frequently overflow and enrich by their fertilizing contributions. "A broad belt of heathy moors," as Hodgson informs us, "lies on the west and north sides of the parish, and the soil of the other parts of it is very various," as is always the case in such localities. "On the whinstone range the soil is generally thin, and easily affected by drought; on the sandstone cold and heavy; but on the limestone a rich dry mould. The greatest part of it is in sheep farms or used in grazing or dairy purposes, the climate being too high and unsteady to allow much of it to be advantageously employed in agriculture."* Of timber, with the exception of that, if it may be so called, which naturally and therefore gracefully fringes the banks of its streamlets, such as alder, birch, hazle, mountain ash, willows, &c., the parish has not much to boast, except upon the estate of Little Harle, then one of its component parts, but now, as we believe, severed from it and attached by the Church Commissioners to the parish of Kirkharle, to which it is closely contiguous.

Here there is no smoke from coal-pits or chemical works, as on the Tyne, and none of the pestilential effluvia from crowded towns with which Hodgson had been to his cost and sorrow but too long familiar. With respect to the population of the parish, and its

* Hist. vol. i. p. ii. 189, &c.

character and occupations, the change from Heworth to Whel-·
pington, was still more remarkable and advantageous.  In Northumberland the people of a parish so situated are almost entirely
occupied in agricultural pursuits.    They are strong, intelligent,
and independent; and in general, as the result of their mode of
life, living to an extreme old age.   The pale look of the artizan,
or the stunted and bending figure of the collier is here unknown.
Even to old age the men are active and vigorous, and their Saxon
or Danish origin, as the case may be, is in general most manifest
in their external appearance.

The village of Whelpington itself stands upon high and dry
ground, and is of the usual character of Northumbrian hamlets;
its houses mean and straggling, picturesque from their thatch of
ling, and giving no external indication of what they seldom possess
—internal comfort.   The church, of which somewhat more will be
said hereafter, is placed upon a sunny elevation in front; and
abutting upon the west side of the churchyard are the vicarage
house and garden, the latter terminated on the south-west by a
rugged precipice, finely fringed with timber, beneath which flows
the Wansbeck, that lively streamlet of which Akenside sung, and
with which, here or at Hartburn, it was Hodgson's fate to be
closely and pleasantly connected during the remainder of his life.
It may be well to give a description of the Wansbeck and its
devious course in his own words.*

" This charming stream rises in a bog between Airdlaw and the Great
and Little Wayney-house Crags; runs in pools as black and reflective
as polished obsidian down Russell dene, and thence through Sweethope
Lough, and takes in the Rayburn at Whelpington, the Hart at Hartburn,
and the Font at Mitford, and enters the sea at Cambois.  From its rise to
Sweethope its course is through moors; but there it begins to be
hemmed with brushwood or grassy turf.   From the ruins of the old
ville of West Whelpington, and especially about Whelpington and to
Little Harle, its banks are beautifully formed and rich in soil, but naked,
and growing rushes where they should be producing corn, or covered
with fine sward.    In passing the Little Harle and Wallington grounds
it has a woody country on each side of it, and takes in the Kirkharle burn;

* Hist. part. ii. vol. ii. 467, under Morpeth.

which rises in Our Lady's Well near Bavington, and the Swilder burn, which through a considerable part of its course is a boundary between the Capheaton and Kirkharle estates. From Middleton Bridge to its junction with the Hart, it has a slow and sedgy course through flat and fertile pastures; and from its entrance into Meldon Park to where it becomes an estuary it passes a succession of scenes of great variety and beauty."

But at Whelpington Hodgson was affected by other circumstances of a still happier kind.

Here, by one of those fortunate coincidences which Divine Providence is continually throwing in our way, he found, as one of his parishioners, the earliest and latest of his friends, and a large estate under his spiritual superintendence and care of which that friend was the owner. Sir John Edward Swinburne and Capheaton were names which had been long deeply written upon his mindful heart; and tears glistened in his eyes when he told the writer of these pages, soon after he had taken possession of his preferment, of the joy which it had given him to settle near such a friend. Besides, at Capheaton there in general resided Sir John's brother, Edward Swinburne, Esq., and with this gentleman, to whom, as Hodgson acknowledges,[*] he owed " the highest obligation for his masterly and beautiful drawings, from which the greater part of the engravings in his History were taken," he came into immediate neighbourhood. I have already placed before my readers numerous proofs of the deep interest which Mr. Swinburne took in Hodgson and his literary proceedings. More remain in infinite abundance.

Another family, to Hodgson's great comfort, was also near at hand with which he had become acquainted in 1819, and which from that time had taken an active interest in his pursuits, and had favoured him with its friendship. On the eastern verge of his new parish, at no great distance beyond its boundary line, stood Wallington, the seat of Sir John Trevelyan. With Walter Calverley Trevelyan, Esq., the eldest son of Sir John, (now Sir W. C. Trevelyan, Bart.) he had been in active correspondence for some time; not only on subjects of Natural History, a science

* Hist. pt. ii. vol. i. p. 234.

with which Mr. Trevelyan was intimately acquainted, but also on the local history of the county, in which he took an equal interest. He had, in fact, already begun to devote a considerable portion of his time during his frequent visits to London and Oxford to the gathering together from the British Museum, or the Bodleian Library, historical matter of great value to be placed at Hodgson's disposal for his Northumberland.* In all these respects Hodgson's change of residence was a fortunate one. Seldom can it have happened that a man going to settle in a new locality has found himself so completely at home.

And then, in an antiquarian point of view, Hodgson was once more singularly fortunate in subjects to engage his attention and exercise his thoughtful mind.

It does not appear that the Romans have left behind them in this parish any remains of their handiwork, military or domestic; but of their predecessors the Britons there are camps and earthworks in abundance. On the summit of almost every hill there is a fortification, and among them Hodgson would walk and muse, and think of the rise and fall of nations and of the people by whom the district had been once inhabited of whom now so little is known.

In his church, sadly defaced by modern rashness and folly, there was much remaining of good old Norman workmanship; in his vicarage house were embodied portions of an old border place of strength, in which his predecessors had resided for seven centuries, in times of turmoil and insecurity; and in the village there was a peel-house of the usual character, for the protection of the village against Scotch marauders. Of these various subjects of interest he has left a minute account in his History; and of the Natural History of his parish, he has also in the same volume given a full description. In this latter department of science in particular he found much to engage the attention of one, who, like himself, had made no inconsiderable progress in such inquiries whilst resident in other places.

Of two localities in the parish of Whelpington of considerable

* The reader has been already introduced to Mr. Trevelyan. See p. 302 in our first volume.

interest, I feel tempted to give an account in Hodgson's own
words.    I remember walking with him in the summer of 1824,
over the grass-grown lines and hillocks of the latter, and listening
with profound attention to his moralizing reflections upon a plot
of ground, then so still and quiet, which had not much more than
a century before been the scene of life and animation on village
feast-days and rejoicings, or of joy or sorrow, as the bridal-band
or the funeral procession was descending from its now silent hill
to that common object of sacred interest in rural districts the
parish church.

"CATCHERSIDE. This place, now so still and lonely, seems in former
ages to have known something of life.  The Scotch street ran through
it, and it had an ale-house, where the carriers and cadgers in the bell-
horse times baited, and the neighbouring villagers used to meet, so late
as the beginning of the last century, to shoot through long duck-guns
at the bull's-eye for buck's skins.   Forty years since there was an old
oaken door here, all battered and bored with shot expended in these
contentions.  But it was not merely with carousals of the carriers and
the thunder of duck-guns that Catcherside formerly resounded.  [He
proceeds to detail the particulars of the execution of a deed there in
1274 before two knights, &c.]  Tradition says there was a mill here—the
water by which it was supplied now falls into a bed of limestone, and
is supposed to rise again in the large spring a mile or more westward,
in Heestone Bank.  On the Camp-Hill in Catcherside Park was a large
camp, which the tenant improved by ploughing and ridding it of stones.
The floors of a great many *shields* or *circular huts*, which had been in
it, were rudely paved, and had strong marks of fire upon them.   In
one of the old fir plantations to the north of Catcherside, the beautiful
trailing shrub *Linnæa borealis* was discovered wild, in a large patch, in
Sept. 1820, for the first time in England, by Miss E. Trevelyan. (*Edin.
Philos. Jour. iv.* 206.)  *Trientalis Europæa* and *Pyrola Minor* also
occur in the same locality.

" The village of WEST WHELPINGTON stood proudly on the northern
margin of the Wansbeck, on an elevated plain, which slopes gently
towards the east, and is defended on all sides, and especially on the
south, by a whinstone precipice.  It was of an oblong form, about 440
yards long, and consisted of two rows of houses inclosing a large town-
green, near the centre of which a small circle probably points out the
site of its cock-pit; near which has stood a peel-house, having very

thick walls and a sort of yard or barmekin in front, apparently the
only little fortified habitation which the place could ever boast of.    Its
name occurs in the parish registers up to 1715, in connection, among
other names, with those of Harle and Stote, one of which last family,
when he took the whole of it to rent, " put out 15 farmers " here, according to the phrase and account of a person who was his servant, and
is still living at the age of 86.    No person, however, remembers any
one residing here; and the place is now only remarkable for the dis-
tinctness of its ruins, the beautiful verdure of its site, and especially for
having been one of the numerous places in the North where a long line
of ancient tenantry had toiled and gamboled, but were forced by a new
order of things to quit the only spot upon earth which was dear to
them, and find employment in some of the populous places where, in
the language of The Deserted Village,

> ————" Trade's unfeeling train
> Usurp the land, and dispossess the swain."

" Ray, too, with respect to its building and population has nearly met
with the same fate as West Whelpington, for it now consists only of one
principal house, in a very ruinous state, occupied by one family, a peel-
house unoccupied, and traces of numerous dwellings."

Of the accessories to the happiness of my friend of an external
kind, if I may use the term, arising out of his change of residence, and the fortunate combinations with which it was connected, enough has been said.    Let me briefly touch upon a few
circumstances of a domestic and private nature which at the
same time added to his joy and brightened his hearth by bringing
along with them comforts and facilities with which he had previously been unacquainted.

His family now consisted of seven children, four boys and
three girls, the eldest of whom, a daughter, was now twelve years
of age.    He had long felt and regretted his incompetence to give to
his family such an education as might be of use to them in after
life.    He had himself of necessity hitherto been their instructor,
with the occasional assistance of the son of his clerk and schoolmaster, an intelligent youth, who, when not so employed, acted
as his amanuensis on subjects connected with his History.    This
happy change in his circumstances enabled him in due time to

send his eldest son and daughter to school, and to engage the
services of a governess for his younger girls, and for his boys a
young man of education, who was not, however, above the
humbler duty of acting as his copyist in time of need. And then,
again, to the children themselves how beneficial, and delightful to
boot, must have been the change! For those of them who had
suffered so much from illness a while before, there was the healthy
and bracing air of the Northumbrian hills in all its uncontaminated
purity, and for all of them there were new scenes and new subjects to engage their attention at a most interesting period of their
lives—for the boys the Wansbeck, alive with trout, and green
fields, and birds-nests and wild moors and an unlimited range in
safety, and for the girls a garden for flowers, out of the reach of
smoke and its withering effects, and the freedom of enjoying
without the restraints of a populous neighbourhood the sports and
amusements and rambles of their brothers. I well remember my
drawing Hodgson's attention to these gratifying subjects for
thankfulness, soon after his removal to Whelpington, and my
making the discovery that they had been duly thought of and
appreciated. The " tacitum pertentant gaudia pectus " of the
poet was most manifest in his demeanour during our conversation.*

Hodgson was inducted into the vicarage of Whelpington by
the Rev. Thomas Redman, Vicar of Kirkharle, his now nearest
clerical neighbour, and, what was still more agreeable to him, a
native of his own Westmerland and well acquainted with the
localities and beauties of that interesting county. Mr. Redman
had, moreover, been in his younger days curate of Whelpington,
and his knowledge of the parish and its people must have been
peculiarly valuable to its new incumbent. Of this gentleman I
shall have much to say hereafter, in proof of the kindness of his
heart and of the sincere regard which he entertained for the sub-

* In this enumeration of circumstances of an agreeable nature which presented
themselves at Whelpington, one great inconvenience must be mentioned which pressed
hard upon Hodgson for some time after his settlement in his new parish—his distance
from a post town and his consequent want of frequent communication with his distant friends and the press. This subject of regret will often present itself in the
following pages.

ject of our memoir in after years, when domestic affliction and long-continued personal ill-health required the prop and stay of sympathy and consolation.

The taking possession of a living is an event of considerable interest to the new incumbent and his friends. Of a similar event at Whelpington, in an earlier day, there has been preserved a very unusual but pleasing record which deserves to be placed before my readers.

In the year 1786, there was presented to this benefice a gentleman of the name of Clarkson, at that time Vicar of Kirkharle; a man who had studied at St. John's College in Cambridge; had afterwards been second master in the Grammar School of Newcastle; next Vicar of Kirkharle, and, lastly, of Whelpington, which benefice he held along with his former living. Archdeacon Paley, Bishop Law, and Dr. Ekins, Dean of Carlisle, and, at the same time, Rector of Morpeth and Sedgfield, were among Clarkson's friends; and upon his dying suddenly in 1788, Law wrote his epitaph, in which he is described as " sacris humanisque literis ornatissimus." These brief notices may serve as an introduction to the following admirable poetical address to Clarkson by his friend and neighbour Ekins, upon his taking possession of the living of Whelpington. The verses were communicated to Mr. Hodgson in 1831, by the late Mr. Ekins, the successor of his father in the Rectory of Morpeth; and, as they have not been printed before, they may not be out of place in our account of another induction after a lapse of fifty years. Hodgson would most assuredly have found a niche for them in his History, if the volume containing the account of his parish had not been published before they came into his hands.

AD AMICUM G[ALFRIDUM] C[LARKSON] ÆDES APUD VELPINGTONIAM JAM PRIMUM INCOLENTEM.

Dum me tarda tenet vexatque podagra jacentem,
  Quamque negat somnus musa ministrat, opem;
Tu vacuus latos spatiaris, amice, per agros,
  Velpingteoa novas quâ tibi pandit opes.

En! rupes circum horrescunt, latèque patentes
  Saxoso campos aggere murus obit.
Quid memorem quod rara apparet in æquore vasto
  Arbor; Hyperboreis et strepit aura sonis ?
Nec procul hinc summas libat celer attagen oras
  Quà fera muscoso floret erica solo;
(Ah! miseram Augusti jam designata calendis,
  Undique per gentem mos sine lege furet ?)
At tibi sunt flavis ridentia messibus arva;
  Sunt pecorum crebro gramina trita pede.
Sunt tibi secretæ valles, atque ædibus umbram
  Sylva frequens gaudet consociare tuis;
Rivus ubi vitreis circumdat flexibus hortum,
  Et prono in scopulis flumine rumpit iter.
Stat prope conjunctumque domo præsepe, nitentem
  Quo manus assidue plaudat herilis equum;
Hic, stabuli ante fores, pulli pascuntur; et illic
  Stramineum noctu vacca cubile petit.
Murorum hic surgit moles, ne forte viretis
  Insiliant nitidis, turba molesta, sues.
Hic domus, haud altis si conspicienda columnis,
  Ast humili ac mundâ simplicitate nitet.

E.   "Intima sit tecum fas visere claustra, novosque,
    "Dum novitatis adest gratia, inire lares ? "

Ostia panduntur, camera hinc atque inde notatur.

E.   "Quos petat hæc usus, quos petat illa suos ? "

C.   "Omnia conveniunt mirè, placet apta culinæ
    "Hæc bene, convivis aptior illa placet."

Nec mora, scrutamur cellam, laqueataque tecta,
  Quéis sequa inclusum temperet aura merum;
Ne forte æstivo nimium sub sole tepescat,
  Nec tenera hyberno frigeat uva gelu.
Inde superveniat si quis jucundior hospes

E.   "Quadrimo expromis vina notata cado.
    "Jam scalas liceat mihi tecum ascendere—præbet
    "En! solum innupto triste cubile torum :
    "Attamen hic justo stipantur in ordine, pauci,
    "Qui totum rapiunt te, tua vita, libri.
    "Hic arctum Ciceronis opus, Flaccusque, Maroque
    "Scriptaque Foulisiis Græca notata typis ;"
    "Queis procul interpres Latius, qui ludat ocellos,
    "Et ferat infidam, non bene certus, opem.
    "Hic noctu invigilas, gaudesque ediscere quicquid
    "Antiqui sapiunt desipiuntve sophi.

" Parte aliâ famulo sedes, aliâque ministris
   " Virgineis—famulo non adeunda proco.
" Est quoque bina locus quo sternas tegmina, amicos
   " Si simul accipiant tecta referta duos.
" Quin age; restat adhuc nobis conclave tuendum
   " Indica quà lautas præbeat herba dapes."
Intramus, laquearque placet, spatiumque, situsque,
   Quo medium æstivo sol regit axe diem.
Area lata placet, pulchro obducenda tapete,
   Mœniaque auleo lauta futura novo;
Artificique manu curvata fenestra placeret,
   Ni foret opposito non satis apta foco.

O,    " Stat cito protrusos muros divellere, servet
   " Ut focus hic justos, illa fenestra, locos."
Non tamen intereà camera est intranda, vetârunt
   Ædificatorum lex geniusque loci.

E.    " I, perge, ut libet, ædifica, vel dirue; acerbet
   Nec cura his placidos tristior ulla dies.

Mr. Hodgson did not take up his residence at Whelpington till July in the year of his presentation, having, as is generally the case, found it necessary to make many repairs and alterations in the vicarage house, in which his predecessor had been long non-resident. He received, however, a reasonable sum of money for dilapidations to assist in defraying the outlay which he was obliged to incur in making such repairs as time and neglect had rendered necessary. At first he seemed somewhat disinclined to give himself much trouble on this subject, but the compiler of these pages prevailed upon him to employ as the valuer of the dilapidations on his part Mr. Edward Fairclough, clerk of the works to the Dean and Chapter of Durham, who made a report accordingly. The executors of the former incumbent made their valuation also, which somewhat exceeded that of Fairclough, and they honourably insisted upon paying this latter sum instead of that named by Hodgson's own valuer.

We have already seen the value of the vicarage itself. The rectorial tithes had been appropriated at an early period to the Abbey of Newminster, and a layman was in possession of that upon which the monks had been suffered by authority to lay their hands. On the subject of appropriations more may be said in a subsequent page.

"With this you will receive a tract which I will thank you to get forwarded to Mr. Surtees. I have not indulged in the Mithraic paper in any attempts at fine writing; because I think such flourishes perfectly unsuited to the dignity and sobriety which should always accompany either philosophical or antiquarian inquiries. The metaphor contrasting paganism with the produce of seeds of the same plant was introduced merely as an illustration, scarcely as an embellishment. Most truly, dear Sir, yours,

"JOHN HODGSON."


To the Rev. JAMES TATE.

"MY DEAR SIR,                    Upper Heworth, 26 May, 1823.

"I send with this a copy of my paper on Mithras, &c. of which I beg your acceptance. It is printed in the Archæologia Æliana; and I had a few copies thrown off for my friends who are not members of our Antiquarian Society. The apologies made in it for its roughness are bonâ fide true. I see that some of the translations from the Greek are very stiff. Much matter for a new impression has accumulated since it went to press, which I shall print as soon as I have leisure to put the old and new materials into proper method; of which the paper in its present condition is altogether deficient. Indeed it grew greatly in size between the time of its being read and its delivery from the press.

"I sometimes see poor Dawes's monument in the marble-cutter's show-room as I go past, but dare not go in; as I scolded the man roundly some six weeks since about not getting forward with the work. Pray let me hear something from you.* The Parian marble is still a *tabula rasa*, and seems to implore some prophet's hand to touch it with Promethean fire, and give it language and an utterance. You will do me the greatest kindness by putting life into it. There is nobody here who has had the oracular mantle falling upon him, and consequently that dare venture to take a brand from Apollo's altar to light a perennial fire at the tomb of Richard Dawes.

"I had agreed with a gentleman to take my cure at Heworth; but as soon as our bishop's sanction was got to the arrangement he declined coming, because he could have a much better situation; which was very unhandsomely offered to him immediately after he had agreed with

---

* Of the memoir and monument of Dawes much will be said in a subsequent page. Mr. Tate had undertaken to write an inscription for the latter.

mie, though the party who engaged him knew that he was in treaty with me.

"Do you know of any gentleman who would take the situation? The salary is 70*l.* a year, with some small perquisites; exactly the same as I give to the curate of Jarrow. There is full Sunday duty at the chapel, in the morning and evening; and 4000 people in the chapelry, which extends no way more than 1½ mile from the chapel; and Heworth is only 2½ miles from Newcastle. It requires a person who has a sound, clear, and audible voice, and is naturally industrious, but withal gentle, and of unblameable life. I would not look for much learning, if I could be recommended to one who had, with moderate talents, sincerity and discretion; though, with these requisites, good talents, that have been well improved, are very desirable. If you could serve me in this my necessity, you would confer a lasting benefit on, my dear Sir, yours faithfully,

John Hodgson."

From THOMAS THOMSON, Esq.

" My dear Sir,       Charlotte Square, Edinb., July 16, 1823.

"A few days ago I had the pleasure of receiving your valuable present of the second part of *Archæologia Æliana*, from which, and more especially from your own contributions, I expect a great deal of instruction.

"As I observe that you have placed your copy of the new edition of the Acts of the Parliaments of Scotland, &c. in the Library of the Society of Antiquaries of Newcastle, I have thought it might not be unacceptable to the members to have a set of another of our Record works, which I believe was not sent to you. It is an abridgement of Retours of Services down to the close of the 17th century (" Inquisitionum Retornatarum Abbreviatio "), and may chance to be useful in some genealogical investigations. I shall probably take the liberty of sending some other publications, or rather prints, in which I have been concerned; particularly a set of my Annual Reports as Deputy Clerk Register of Scotland, Sir George Mackenzie's History, and one or two antiquarian fragments. To save you trouble I shall order the parcel to be sent to Mr. Adamson, leaving it to you to explain from whom it comes.

"I feel tempted to take this opportunity of inquiring after the welfare of your History of Northumberland. Your fifth volume, which is all I have yet seen, afforded me great satisfaction; particularly the Swinburne Charters. On a few of them I made some trifling remarks at the time, which I may now take the liberty of sending you, though they cannot be of much use.

"I long to have possession of Mr. Raine's Appendix of Coldingham Muniments; though I fear he has despised some that I should have found interesting. I remain, with sincere respect, my dear Sir, your very faithful servant,

"THO. THOMSON."

To the Rev. JAMES TATE.

"DEAR SIR,                              Upper Heworth, 30 July, 1823.

"I am to-day employed in packing up all my goods and chattels here, in order to have them sent to-morrow to Kirkwhelpington; and finding, among other stray and lost articles, a duplicate of the inscription which I put upon Dawes's basalt *tomb* stone, I venture to send it to you to melt down to pay for the carriage of it, or to put it up in your study, as you please.

"My residence in about ten days or a fortnight will be wholly at Whelpington, during which time I get lodgings for my family in a house of my own at Heworth Shore, and till that at Whelpington get into some order: but after that time I shall be so seldom at Newcastle that I trust you will not fail to give me forthwith some few words for the monument in memory of Dawes. I dare not venture near the marble-cutter's shop, it is now so long since he had the monument, a *tabula rasa*, exhibited in his show-rooms.

"By drilling a nail-hole at each end of the bronze plate it may be let into any piece of strong furniture—under the end of a book-case, or other stationary article; but let it not be inferred that (should the plate be honoured with a place in your book-case) the said case is a burial-place for the intellectual remains of Richard Dawes.

"Surrounded with as much disorder as if I was writing in a sale-room, I am, dear Sir, most truly yours,

"JOHN HODGSON."

Hodgson had not been long settled in his new habitation before he sent his eldest son Richard Wellington Hodgson to a school then in considerable repute at Stamfordham, a village at no great distance from Whelpington on the south. The master of the school was the Rev. John Rawes, a member of the numerous Westmerland family of that name so often already mentioned, to which he was related on the side of his mother. The removal of the boy from home introduces us to a new series of letters, from which I select a few, as pleasing indications of paternal kindness and anxiety.

To RICHARD WELLINGTON HODGSON.

"MY DEAR BOY,                    Carr Hill, Gateshead, Aug. 23, 1823.

"I promised to write to you very soon, and you must not be disappointed. How matters are going on at home I am unacquainted. I came hither on Wednesday morning and shall return on Tuesday. When I write from Kirkwhelpington I will endeavour to relate to you everything which I think will be interesting to you. At present I have no leisure to enter into particulars. Your uncle and aunts are all well. I am staying with Mr. Atkinson, and Mr. Leonard * is at Kirkwhelpington. I hope all your tears are dried up long before this. Endeavour by all means to spend your time usefully, to be gentle and kind amongst the other boys, and to learn obedience and gratitude to Mr. Rawes for all his attention to you. Adieu, my dear boy, and God bless you! From your ever affectionate father,

"JOHN HODGSON."

To R. W. HODGSON.

"MY DEAR RICHARD,               Whelpington, 9 Sept., 1823.

"I learnt at nine o'clock yesterday morning that Ord the tailor here was going this morning to Stamfordham, and cannot omit the opportunity I have of writing to you: but when you know that Joe and John Fenwick are come to help Philipson to stack the hay you will not expect a long letter.

"I could not, when I returned a week since on Friday, have come by Stamfordham, as it was nearly three o'clock before I left Newcastle: and I do assure you I had no fine time of it, as you imagine, while I

* The curate of Heworth.

c 2

was at Heworth. Be very careful in writing your letters not to omit any words, but, lest the pen should slip any, read your letters once or twice carefully over; and any points, letters, or words that may be wanting, supply them with a caret or otherwise. Your grandmother is still with us. While I was at Heworth, and for some days after, she was very unwell, but she is quite recovered, and is now up at half-past six. Some of the people here have finished winning their hay: but not all. I see none to mow. There are several patches of barley cut, and one large field at the Three Farms.

"Be so good as say to Mr. Rawes that our cousin Mr. Robert Rawes of Bromley is in want of a *clever* classical scholar above 24 years old, to undertake the higher classes of his school in Greek and Latin. The salary 70*l*. or 75*l*. a-year with board and lodging.

"You left your watch. Was it intentionally continued here, or must it be sent, or remain till your cousin John Rawes and you come over?

"I can think of no news. John is very busy about the stack, and William and the rest are rioting finely about the lower part of the house. We are all very well, and send our affectionate love to you, and kind compliments and regard to Mr. and Mrs. Rawes and family.

"Poor Codling has not got his hay stacked, but it is some days since he got it into pike, which set him at ease. God bless you, my dear child.

"JOHN HODGSON."

"P.S. We have had a small cow for the last fortnight: and you will be glad to hear that the ass continues in good health; though it will be matter of regret to you to be told that the horse is not quite recovered from his cold. Adieu."

To R. W. HODGSON.

"MY DEAR BOY,                              Whelpington, 27 Sept. 1823.

"I got your letter of the      inst. by Carr last night; and, as Charleton the butcher tells me he intends being at Stamfordham to-morrow, I take the earliest opportunity of sending you a Bible and a Prayer Book, which indeed ought to have been among the number of books which you took with you. I could not make a more interesting request to you than to beg that at your leisure moments, between this time and Christmas, you would read over the book of Genesis with great care, and endeavour to impress upon your memory the succession of events and characters which it records. It forms the foundation of all authentic history; and there is one thing in its own history which is very curious, but very little known; namely, that Moses was not the Author of it but only the Editor; that is, he did not compose the facts of which it consists into a narrative in his own words, but merely collected several distinct ancient narratives into one. I could in a conversation with you show you that the first chapter, and the 1st, 2nd, and 3rd verses of the second, were written by one person, and the remaining part of the second to the end of the third by another; while the story of Cain and Abel is in a style very different from the former two. The fifth chapter has all the character of a distinct table of Genealogy; and the chapters from the beginning of the sixth to the end of the ninth are remarkable for brevity of diction, but at the same time for breadth and comprehensiveness of language. The same observations may be applied to the remaining parts of the book: some parts of which are evidently a translation from hieroglyphics (i.e. sacred engravings—figures of animals which each stood for a word or idea) into alphabetical language. I say these things to awaken your curiosity, which is the mine out of which all knowledge and truth are derived, provided its inquiries be rightly directed at first. Curiosity every day enlarges the mind with new discoveries of truth—fills it with genuine light; but if at the outset curiosity fixes itself upon certain dazzling fictions, and embraces doctrines which allure and charm the imagination without satisfying the reason, then the light which the mind thinks it receives is only darkness. Take heed, therefore, my dear child, as the Scriptures advise, ' that the light which is in thee be not darkness.' We are all very well. From your most affectionate father,

"JOHN HODGSON."

Soon after Hodgson's removal to Whelpington, he received a kind letter from T. W. Beaumont, Esq., offering him the perpetual curacy of Hexham, then vacant, the value of which was about 150l. per annum, personal residence being required. This small benefice he of course declined. Mr. Beaumont's letter is dated on the 6th of October in this year.

To the Rev. J. RAINE.

Whelpington, 7 Dec. 1823.

" —————— Have you ever sought for the original instrument which gave the rectory of my parish to Newminster Abbey? You will remember that the record of it has been cut out of the Bishop's register.

" I am still at war with the Radicals at Jarrow, and feel a determination to withstand them: for, if the Easter dues be given up, all my plans for double duty at Jarrow and Heworth will fall to the ground, because the remaining revenues will be inadequate to the support of two curates. It grieves me much too that I have had no answer to my last application through Mr. Darnell, whether, since my removal hither, I might expect that the piece of ground adjoining Heworth Chapel-yard would be enfranchised by the Dean and Chapter, for the purpose of building a parsonage-house there. I bought the lessee's interest in it in the full expectation that it would be conceded to the living.

" You will see by the Durham Chronicle that, if radicalism should once prevail, I am foredoomed to destruction. I have not been more than once in Newcastle these two months, but the last time I was there I had the honour to see the bill-sticker posting me on the walls of the Exchange in a very conspicuous manner. But, as the defamation of the clergy is the only source which the Radicals have now left to make a livelihood out of, I must submit to take my share of their bespattering.

" I got last week the third volume of Mr. Surtees's book, the splendour of which will certainly be enough for the eyes of the Newcastle critics. Sir John Swinburne is in raptures with it. I have not seen his brother. I do not know how to write to Surtees about it. Will you do me the favour to say that I have received it, and that I am very greatly his debtor, not only for it, but for favours which I can never repay him or be too grateful for? I really find it the most arduous of all tasks to write to my friends about productions of their own brain with which they may favour me; because mere dry thanks for a book which has real intrinsic excellence in it are but mean and sordid stuff as returns for such a favour as Mr. Surtees has conferred upon me, and I know him too well to sit down and con over words and sentences for fine phrases and expressions about the labour and genius that have been expended on the work.

" Mr. Taylor too has been here from Sunderland not long since, and

he said something about Mr. Surtees having had some communications
with me respecting the embellishments of my book, which, at the time,
I did not understand rightly, and answered in a negative manner; for
which I was heartily vexed when I was left here alone to reflect upon
what he had meant; as Mr. Surtees certainly not only gave me ten
pounds towards them, but mentioned other assistance that would be
given when it began to show itself again *sub die.**

"I have been long wishing to write to you, and have far more to say
than I can recollect now. Of dilapidations I have pocketed about 144*l.*
and expect the remainder soon. Mr. Gardener's executors sent a
surveyor from Newcastle, who saddled them with a little more than Mr.
Fairclough had charged.

"There is a mighty mass of papers in the Tower, which were brought
from Whitehall about seven years since, concerning the Great and the
Scotch Rebellions: but when Mr. Lysons shewed them to me they were
unsorted: possibly they may contain the information you are in quest
of. But does not the pedigree tell against your supposition? or, if the
place in question was sequestered, did it not pass by consent of Government to the Dilston family? Was not the estate restored with the
Restoration? The date of the first Lord Derwentwater's marriage with
Katherine Fenwick may possibly lead you to some conclusions on the
subject. Look into Dugdale and such other authorities. I will not be
idle, but will call at Capheaton to-morrow and try what Sir J. S. can
furnish me with; but I cannot write to you again on the subject till our
next post-day after to-morrow, which is Thursday. This is a dull, wild,
and dreary place in winter, and you will be disappointed to hear a worse
account of it, viz., that the living turns out to be at the least 100*l.* a
year less than it was represented to the bishop. The account sent him
was taken from the agent's accounts for 1820, when lamb and wool as
well as the land were at much higher rates than now. The land then
was 170*l.*, now 130*l.* But I am not complaining; only telling you how
things are. Most truly yours,

"JOHN HODGSON."

"Mr. Tate has never sent me the Επιγραμμα for Dawes's monument,
which has been ready for it since May. Shall you see him at Christmas? I am ashamed to teaze him about it.

* See vol. i. p. 381.

"To the Rev. J. Raine.—Whelpington, 27 Dec. 1823.—Plenty of shells but no pearls. I went to Lapminston on Monday, and spent all day in rummaging the Record closets there in quest of information de Meldon; but, though I met with large Pipe Rolls and bundles of papers labelled 'Sequestrations,' I met with nothing that bore directly upon the point to which you directed me to steer. You must not take it for granted that Sir William Fenwick's estates were sold merely because they were ordered to be surveyed and disposed of. Nothing was more frequent than for estates to lie long under sequestration and with the hammer lifted over them, and yet at be at length allowed to the families they in truth belonged to, after heavy bribes had taught the Commissioners justice. This is everywhere apparent in the petitions and correspondence respecting the property of the Swinburnes, concerning which the Record closets at Capheaston afford armfuls of proofs.———

To W. C. TREVELYAN, Esq.

"My dear Sir,                                        Whelpington, 27 Dec. 1823.

"I am very much obliged by the loan of the MSS., which I return; and which have afforded me much useful information for my work. You will not, I know, be surprised to hear that the Whelpington lava rests upon a *flagged floor*. I opened the spot yesterday. Around the outsides the floor was thickly covered with charcoal, and above it with broken pieces of whinstone and about five inches of clay, which contained a few bones. The place is certainly very curious; but I have been so far wrong in supposing it to have had its origin in natural causes that I dare not attempt to say whether it has been an unsuccessful attempt to burn whin into lime, or to roast it previous to subjecting it to fusion into iron. Believe me to be always most truly yours,
<br>"JOHN HODGSON."

To W. C. TREVELYAN, Esq.

"My dear Sir,                                        Whelpington, 30 Dec. 1823.

"I have sent as many impressions of vegetables as the basket will hold, and any of those that are left, excepting a very few, you are most perfectly welcome to. Should you wish for more, or better impressions, Mr. Hill, of Kenton, will, I am sure, be most happy to order them to be collected for you in Fawdon Colliery; and if you do not like to apply to him yourself I shall be glad to do so for you. The specimens on the top of the basket are from Jarrow Colliery; the rest from Fawdon. Those figured thus [*a sketch*], appear to me to have belonged to a very large plant, consisting of numerous branches, lessening in thickness very gradually, but very sensibly. Some of them I have seen have a sort of leaf or arm growing from the under-angle of each quarry, thus [*a sketch*]. The leaves where the quarries are of this size [*a sketch*] are about three inches long, ridged on the outer side, and sulcated on the lower surface, [*a sketch*].

" I did not ever suppose the spot I opened last Friday was of the same active volcanic nature as those mountains which throw out lava; but that the contents of the place had been melted and retained in their original situation; in the same manner as the old red sandstone on Little Mellfell, in Cumberland, certainly has been at its *junction* with the trap-rock, on the east side of that hill. The unfused stones around the outside of the bottom of the kiln and those in the fused mass are all of about the same sizes as are usually broken for lime, and of about the same size as the masses of iron subjected to the roasting-ovens before they are put into the furnace to smelt. The flags were much too thin and too loosely laid to justify the supposition that the place had ever been a dwelling-house. But I will talk to you more upon this subject when I have the pleasure of seeing you, which I will certainly do on Thursday if I possibly can; but, as I have my amanuensis here at present, I must not indulge myself with staying at Wallington all night, but be at home to see him at work by daylight on Friday morning. Most truly yours,

" JOHN HODGSON."

# CHAPTER II.—1824.

Correspondence—Preaches a Visitation Sermon at Morpeth—Further Correspondence—Expedition into Scotland—A Smuggler—An Itinerant Poet—Correspondence.

"To the Revd. J. Raine.—Whelpington, 7 Jan. 1824.—As you cannot now possibly have any use for the papers I last sent you, pray return me them as early as possible. I would not have troubled you with them but from experience that a very distant hint is often of great use in inquiries like that in which you have been engaged respecting Meldon. But you must go on, and say, give me back my lands, and my tithes of Rivergreen, &c.

"Whelpington Appropriation in particular I wish for, and still hope you will meet with it in the Treasury. Then anything more about that parish, or about Elsdon, Corsenside, Kirkharle, Hartburn, Netherwitton, Bolam, and Whalton parishes, I am now particularly engaged with, would be of great service. I ask for few, because much work before me is sickening, and I wish to make ready returns. Meldon I of course expect cut and dry. You might add Mitford, about which I copied several charters about tofts and crofts, but none about chapels or charities.                                                                "J. H."

## To R. W. HODGSON.

"My dear Richard,                                        Whelpington, 11 February, 1824.

"Your mamma has a parcel to send to you, and requests me to say that we are all well. I returned from Heworth on Saturday last. The horse's eye is better, but he grew quite lame before I got to Kenton, on my way to Hebburn on the day I wrote to you, and is not quite sound yet. He had been slightly pricked in shoeing, and had got a piece of dry gravel in his hoof.

"My dear boy, pray attend to your books, and especially to Latin; founding yourself well in its elements: work at it late and soon; but be not inattentive to the History of England and to geography—for, though in learning Latin the mind is chiefly occupied in contemplating the properties of words and sentences, and thus engaged in one of the most useful and beautiful of all the sciences with which we are acquainted, yet it is always to be dreaded that if the thoughts fasten too exclusively upon the study of grammar their range will become very limited, and, therefore, that the circle they move in should be continually enlarging by extending it into the history of the various families of mankind and over the countries which they have and do at present occupy. Above all things, however, don't neglect the frequent perusal of your Bible, and of forming the words of your *duty to God* and your *duty to man* in the church catechism into prayers. Mamma and your brothers and sisters send their kind love to you, and best respects to Mr. and Mrs. Rawes and family. Miss Sedgewick * has sent you a book. From your most affectionate father,

"JOHN HODGSON."

" P.S. On looking at the book which Miss Sedgewick wished to send you, I find it so silly and childish that I cannot think you would be amused with it."


FROM THE REV. A. HEDLEY.

"MY DEAR SIR,                                        Bensham, 23 Feb. 1824.

" I went up to Whitfield,* as I wrote to you I should, on Friday, and was very much pleased with my visit. Mr. Scott received me in the kindest and most cordial manner possible, and evinced every desire to make everything connected with my appointment agreeable to me. The stipend is 200l. per annum, with the house, garden, and church-yard, and all taxes paid, and repairs of every kind kept up. It is indeed quite the bishopric of curacies. The house, notwithstanding all Mr. Scott has expended upon it, is not yet quite comfortable; but he has promised to make it so. It is more compact and will afford more accommodation than yours. As we intend to keep a governess for our little girls, we shall stand in need of all the room that can be made. A glebe of 40 acres, all in grass, and sloping down very prettily in front of the house towards the West Allen, is likewise offered to me, if I like to farm it, and I think I shall do so; for with so few professional cares I shall want occupation.————I like everything about the place but the *newish* church. I had much rather it had been 700 years old; but this, even you will say, is an idle fancy.———— A. H."

* The governess of his daughters.
† Mr. Scott, the rector of Whitfield, was leaving England as Archdeacon of Nova Scotia, and had appointed Mr. Hedley to act as his curate at Whitfield in his absence.

### To R. W. HODGSON.

" MY DEAR RICHARD,                          Whelpington, 23 March, 1824.

" George Carr allows me a moment before he sets out for Stamfordham, to say to you that we are all well, and that we shall be glad
to send the gig for you on Maundy Thursday, and to take you back
any day in the following week which Mr. Rawes may appoint, if he has
no objection to your coming over.  I have nothing new to tell you.
You would see by the newspapers that Robert Lee is dead.  We have
had eight funerals here this year, and the united ages of seven of them
is 433 years.  You wrote for some fishing tackle, but unfortunately I
am almost as ill provided with such things as yourself.  When you come
over at Easter (and that will be quite soon enough) I shall see what
you want and get you supplied.  John Thornhill is here writing for
me: and I am going forward with printing.

" While you were here at Christmas, I quite forgot to ask you if you
had read the Book of Genesis in the manner I requested you would do.
It is the foundation of all history and of all in religion that we ought to
love and reverence, and I trust that you will make yourself very intimately acquainted with it.  With our united love and affection to yourself and kind regard to Mr. and Mrs. Rawes and family, believe me to
be your ever affectionate father,

" JOHN HODGSON."

### To THE REV. J. RAINE.

" MY DEAR SIR,                              Kirk Whelpington, 30 Ap. 1824.

" The compositors are treading on my heels, and there is a chasm
before me which I cannot get over, unless you can find a few minutes
to put me the article " Appropriatio Ecclesiæ de Horsley Prioratui de
Brinkburne " into printing fettle; which done, I shall have a bridge
that will enable me to pursue my journey without being tormented by
the caterers for Walker's hungry presses.  You must also contrive to
send me de Meldon et Whelpington.  Wooler will not be wanted for
some time.  Pray consult your Magnum Repertorium for Kirkharle
and Woodhorn.  I have not a syllable about either place.  Randal
says nothing about the appropriation of Woodhorn; though it was given
to Tynemouth before 1119, as appears from Paris's Lives of the Abbots
of St. Alban's.

"I shall not forget my promise to get you half a dozen copies of Meldon printed off with distinct titles, paging, &c.

"Last week I was at Elsdon for a few days. It is a very curious outlandish sort of place. I have been often at it, but never before saw it in its winter's garb. When you come to see me we must take a ride into Redesdale. You must have a sight of it. Wild and bare it seems to me as if made on purpose for such a race as figured in it during the border raiding. The *Mote Hill* at Elsdon is also very curious. It is something in this manner [*a neat drawing with his pen*].

"The spring is very cold still and my garden quite bare. The very sycamores are still leafless, and .I have not seen a swallow or heard a cuckoo this year.

"The Appropriation of Bolam describes Blanchland well: ' possessiones, super quibus monasterium fundatum fuit, pro magna parte in loco quasi solitudinis sterili et minus fructifero in respectu existunt; quæ propter carentiam incolarum—qui—loca fertiliora pro eorum habitatione et mora elegerunt, inculta remanent et quasi deserta," &c. &c. words very descriptive of the country which I see out of my study window; lands still remaining blanched by the hand of winter or black with ling. We have had five months of winter here. The place, however, is very quiet and well situated for my present pursuits.

"This 12th of May sermon * is a terrible thing to me. I cannot get it begun. There is nothing I dislike so much as to make an exhibition. Many a time I have thought, if it ever fell to my lot to preach a Visitation Sermon I would say this and that—dash all the dust out of the cushion, and turn the rosy cheeks of the personæ ecclesiarum hujusce dioceseos into fearful paleness. But as the day approaches, and I go about considering who I am, and to whom I am to preach, all this vapour of courage and self-sufficiency begins to melt away.

"11 Jas. I. Theophilus Lord Howard, who was afterwards second Earl of Suffolk, and who married Lady Elizabeth Hume, daughter of George Earl of Dunbar, had a grant of the manors of Redesdale and Coketdale; and the heirs of Charles Howard of Overacres, in the parish of Elsdon, sold that estate, with the seigniory of Redesdale and the advowson of Elsdon, to the late Duke of Northumberland. This Charles Howard was said to be a descendant of the Carlisle branch of the Howards, and the present Earl, I am told, procured a commission for Charles the last of the Overacres family. Can you by any-means put

* To be preached at the Archdeacon's visitation to be held at Morpeth on that day.

me right in this matter. The early part of the Howard pedigree stands thus———

"When you come to this place you may give me a few days' notice, and I will send my gig to Newcastle for you. Very faithfully yours,

"JOHN HODGSON."

To THE REV. J. RAINE.

"MY DEAR SIR,                  Whelpington, 7th May, 1824.

"You have undertaken to befriend me in the article I am now printing respecting Northumberland churches, from the Hunter MSS. and I must not permit you to flag in your assistance. The press is standing at *Horsley*, and Meldon and Whelpington will be wanted in a few days after Horsley is in the compositors' hands.

"The new type for my parochial history has arrived, and I am very anxious to get forward with it, which I cannot do till I have printed off the article in the 6th vol. with which I am at present engaged.

"Have you written to Nicholson? because the Meldon seals you mentioned will take some time to cut; and the printers grow very impatient when they are stopped, either for want of copy or by the engraver.

"We have had delightful weather, and I begin to enjoy Whelpington much.

"You will think me impatient, but I am anxious to get my work done, and to do it well; and, therefore, begin to find I must not neglect to ask the willing and the able to assist me. When I am able to make proper returns and acknowledgements for the trouble I give, I hope I shall not be found ungrateful. But, to you, oil and incense are not offerings I can honestly make. Shall I see you at Morpeth? Wednesday unnerves me. Most truly yours,

"JOHN HODGSON."

The dreaded day of the visitation sermon arrived, and Hodgson preached before Archdeacon Bouyer and the clergy of the deanery of Morpeth, on the 17th of May, an excellent discourse on the grand ecclesiastical canon: "Let all things be done decently and in order"—1 Cor. xiv. 40. Natural Decency, Natural Order, Disorder of the Fall, Order restored by Christ; the Commissions of the Clergy, their Recreations and Studies; Church Presentments; the Rubrics; Liberality and Charity, were the high subjects upon which he treated, with the above text before him; and his sermon was remarkable for its earnestness and simplicity of speech. It was printed at the special request of the Archdeacon and clergy, but not published. As not more than fifty copies issued from the press, one for each clergyman within the deanery, and a few for private distribution, this sermon is now rarely met with, and therefore a few extracts may not be out of place:

"The temple in which Almighty God dwells is the Universe. And are not all things in it formed and conducted with decency? Look at the beauty and magnificence of its vaulted walls and roof; and listen to the everlasting service that is performing in it, with the same harmony as in the dawn of the creation, 'when the morning stars sang together, and all the sons of God shouted for 'joy.' Look at our earth, the floor of this temple, and all the goodly furniture with which it is adorned! how magnificent, yet how decent! how becoming! The Greeks called the world *cosmos*, and the Latins *mundus*, *i. e.*, the *decent*, the simply elegant. And shall not all that enters, and all that is done in Christian temples, be distinguished by decency,*——?

"In almost all other matters which fall within our province as pastors to perform, discretion is the law that should guide us. However our characters be aspersed, our intentions misrepresented, ourselves and our office made a jest of, mocked and treated with contumely and scorn by the united and unanimous voice of all that dissent from us and differ from each other, still, it is our duty to treat all that name the name of Christ with kindness and respect. We must do no violence to their feelings, understanding, or judgment; we must not ourselves waver between the Church and the conventicle. It is no part of our liberality to unite our labours with theirs in promoting objects and opinions discordant to the doctrines, maxims, and discipline of our own Church. Want of firmness, indeed, and vacillating opinions in churchmen, are as fertile sources of dissent and eventual alienation from our Church, as that harsh, high, and bigoted adherence to our own tenets which

* The above striking paragraph had not met my eye when I made my remarks in a preceding page (vol. i. p. 395) upon the subject of that grand temple of the Almighty the Universe, of which He himself was the architect. But the idea must of very necessity be as old as the Creation.

neither time, place, nor expediency can bend from the strictest observance of ritual discipline; which rebukes every departure from our forms and ceremonies with angry asperity, and which, in preaching against dissent, imagines that strength of argument consists in bitterness of censure.  Our duty is to ' preach the Word,' fearlessly and at all times, ' in season and out of season, to be ready to reprove, rebuke, and exhort;' but we are to do it ' with all long suffering and instruction,' ' endeavouring to keep the unity of the spirit in the bond of peace'— We may brandish over the sinner's head ' the sword of the Spirit, which is the Word of God,' but we are not permitted to lift up against him the sword of human power.——

" Respecting the recreations which a clergyman may engage in, consistently with the self-denying doctrines which he has to preach, I dare not take upon me to determine; but I can have no hesitation in saying, that, if we enter into the world, enjoy its gaieties, be charmed with its amusements, move on with its joyous multitudes in pastimes and pleasures, we shall soon become like the companies with whom we associate, soon deserve the discreditable title of men of the world, soon be objects of grief among the serious, and of contempt among that crowd which bears us along with it.  But oh! what is that contempt to the feelings which a clergyman ought to have, when he comes from the feverish pleasures of the world to perform his duties on the Sabbath-day—to the contempt which he cannot fly from—to the cries of his injured conscience, which he cannot silence—to pangs which he cannot soothe?——

" And it is not only in pure theological studies that our time is to be consumed.  We live in times which require us to rise with zeal, industry, and activity, to the study of all those sciences and subjects, the powerful artillery of which are constantly directed against our holy religion. Physiology, the doctrine of the constitution of the works of nature, that mighty weapon in the hands of the atheist and the materialist, it is our bounden duty to search into with intensity and care.  And who that suffers himself to be ignorant of the numerous discoveries which have been made respecting the history, the manners, the customs, and the religions of the several nations connected with the Hebrews, from the patriarchal ages down to the time when the canon of the Christian Scriptures was completed can pretend to interpret the Word of God rightly, or stand up in defence of revelation against the libels and blasphemy of learned infidels ?

" Let it be our duties, while knowledge is employing its mighty energies around us, to labour to keep before that knowledge; to watch over its tendencies, to prepare the minds of the children and people of our parishes for receiving it, by imbuing them deeply with the art of thinking and judging clearly, with simplicity of understanding; for to them that which is called learning is unintelligible. It is to no purpose that we go deep after knowledge for them; for the mass of mankind, when it is brought to daylight, cannot understand it. But the fortress which is to be erected around their minds is that liberty of thinking which sets the mind free from the thraldom of sin, which quickens in it all the good qualities that were dead, which casts all devils out of it, and which illuminates and fills it with that most valuable of all attainments, with Christian love."

### To W. C. TREVELYAN, Esq.

"MY DEAR SIR, Whelpington, 18th May, 1824.

"I congratulate you most sincerely on your being able to get from home, and beg your acceptance of my warmest thanks for the papers you have sent me. Pray, too, do me the favour to convey to your sister, Miss Emma, my most grateful acknowledgments of obligation for the trouble she has taken. I ought to have mentioned the page of the volume, Cott. MSS. Calig. B. VIII. 10, to prevent any mistake and consequently needless trouble. I have a manuscript catalogue of the contents of all the Cotton Records respecting the Borders, but it is very brief. Your hint about the derivation of Fawns is good. The parity between Elves and Fairies, and Fauns and Satyrs, often struck me when my noddle was on the subject of accounting for the names the *Fawns* and the Elf-hills; but I never could find any way of fairly accounting for the one being Saxon and the other Latin, till you hint to me that Fauni is good latin for Elves. I have no book I can think of to turn to on the subject; but had always thought that fairies were *benevolent*, elves *wicked* sprites. Will you have the goodness to see in the B. M. or in the Oxford library, if any Glossary of Chaucer contains the word *faun*, and in what sense; for if it can be found in connection with Scandinavian theogony, as well as Roman, there is an end of the important difficulty, the derivation of the Fawns. This celebrated place in the Testa de Neville is classed with Cambo and Farnilawe, as a member of the manor of Wallington, and parcel of the barony of Bolbeck. In 1420 it belonged to Gilbert de Umfreville, and passed by his female heir to Wm. Emeldon, whose daughter married Tempest, whose heir sold to Haggerston, 1497, 'le ffawnys' near Kirkwhelpington, and he to Thomas

Swinburne, his kinsman, with whose descendants it still continues. This is the history of its fee simple; but I apprehend it was let off to the Fenwicks of Wallington in leases for lives: as it certainly was to one Michael Fenwicke and three of his sons in 1611.  *Lawnes* can be no other place than *Fawnes.*

"Now respecting my wants, which you must begin to find are none of the moderate kind.  The parts of the Survey of the waste lands in the East and Middle Marches, Caligula B. vIII. 63, which relate to places in *Morpeth Ward*, and copies of such parts of the letters Cal. C. v. from p. 33 to 61 as are interesting, are most urgent.  I have the letters numbered 16, 17, and 18, in the Cat. of the Cot. Lib. and which conclude fol. 326 of Cal. C. v.    Everything about Redesdale is of moment now; but, fearing that you have not time, and that the hand-writings are so bad that your sister will not venture upon them, I have written to Mr. Singleton, begging that what you cannot do for me he will get done; as I am sure he will have great pleasure in seeing justice done to his parish; and justice must have something to say about theft and affray under his parish, or it will not be even-handed justice.

"I have gone through Julius D. III. Aug. I. vol. 2, which is plans, &c., Calig. B. III. and v. and p. 31 and 32 of Cal. C. v.; and have only minutes of all the rest in the Cottonian Library that relates to Northumberland.  If therefore Miss Emma would do me the favour, when her antiquarian spirit triumphs over the other amiable spirits that are her familiars, to cull me out a few of such anecdotes of plunder and blood and burning, as the catalogue of the Cottonian Library, especially under the head Caligula, will readily lead her to, she will lay me under irredeemable obligations.

"I have sometimes thought that the Lansdowne MS. 326. is only a transcript of the vol. Northd. 49, 50, 51, and of vol. 45 of the Dodsworth MSS., in the Bodleian Library.  I have a fortnight since written to Dr. Bandinel to get me a copy of the Rawlinson MS. B. 894, which I will thank you to inquire about, as I am anxious to see it before I begin to print my parochial history, the types for which are now ready.    I examined all the prints in Gough's room, and took minutes of its contents concerning Northumberland, but nothing further.  When you have got me transcripts of the article ' In Cartis Johannis Fenwyke *de* Wallington,' you will have executed all the commissions I have to trouble you with at Oxford.  Most truly, but in haste, yours

" JOHN HODGSON."

## To W. C. TREVELYAN, Esq.

" MY DEAR SIR,                                    At Stamfordham, 26 May, 1824.

" I have received your last kind packet while I am making some observations here; and, having to write under cover to a friend in London, cannot forego the opportunity of thanking you for the papers you have sent.

" There is no need to make a literatim copy of any of the Dodsworth MSS., excepting it be any very old one where you see he has been careful to preserve the orthography of the original, and the form of the *ets*, for the sake of shewing to what time the writing belongs, when it is without date. I *have* a copy of the MS. respecting 'the habyllitie' of the Northumberland gentry, given to Henry VIII. by his Secretary A. Browne.

" While you are at Oxford you will oblige me by copying out of the Dodsworth MSS. in Gough's Room, I think vol. 45, anything there may be about the Swinburnes from the Witherington papers. It will be at fol. 89. In the Lansdowne MSS. there are I know several deeds from the ' Haughton and Humsaugh Box.' I did not think of troubling any friend for copies of them till I came to write about that neighbourhood; but, as I hope they will be useful in giving some authorities to the Swinburne pedigree, you will oblige me much by taking the trouble of transcribing them for me; and if you cannot have a frank in Oxford, I have written to Mr. Ellison saying that you will send them under cover to him, 79, Pall Mall, and he will forward them to me. Most truly yours

" JOHN HODGSON."

## To W. C. TREVELYAN, Esq.

" MY DEAR SIR,                                    Whelpington, 23rd June, 1824.

" I have heard that you were confined to your room; but am much gratified to conjecture from your note of the 18th inst., that my information has been incorrect. Thank you a thousand times for the copy of Dodsworth's extracts from the Wallington Deeds. But pray do nothing more with the Cottonian MS. Caligula B. VIII. 10, 65, a Survey, &c. 2 Decr. 1542; as I expect Mr. Grey, the amanuensis in the Museum, is making me a full copy of it, at the expense of the Duke of Northumberland—a circumstance I mention to you, though I do not

feel myself authorised to say so generally.     But if your health and
leisure will permit you, you will oblige me by making such extracts
from the Cott. MS. Cal. C. v., from the beginning of folio 33 to folio 60,
as are of a local nature, and describe the force, &c. at the affray of the
Redeswire.     I have copies of the letters on folios 31 and 32.     You will
oblige me by engaging Mr. Grey, who is generally in the reading-room,
to copy me Dodsworth's extracts from the Charters of William Wyther-
ington, Knight, respecting Humsaugh and Haughton, or rather those
from the Box of Haughton and Houmsaugh, Lansdowne MS. 326, folio
146.    I will write some time next week to Mr. Grey and direct him to
send me the copies he is making.    Pray look into Lansdowne 326, folio
98, where Wm. Reed of Troughwhen is mentioned, and copy anything there either about him or that place.    I have somewhere an
extract, but whether made by yourself or me I cannot tell, from the
same page respecting Julian, the widow of Michael Bayflet, granting
lands in Trowen to Robert de Insula: but I can no where, after diligent
search, meet with it.    There is much about the Whelp or Welp you
mention in Burn and Nicholson's History of Westmerland.    In the
Brinkburn Cartulary I find a place called ' Whelpesticroke,' and a son
of Ligurd Earl of the Orknies was in 996 baptised by the name Hwœlpr,
or, as it is in Latin, Hoelpum.

" My boys are at home from school, and wish me much to go with
them to Sweethope on Saturday, ' to troll for pike, despoilers of the
lake.'    Should Mr. Trevelyan hear of a poaching excursion thither, and
my name be handed to him as one of the party, I hope he will not scold
when I have the pleasure of seeing him.    We have had above a week of
very dull weather, with the wind from the north and east.    I am, ——
                                        " JOHN HODGSON."

In the end of June 1824, the author of this memoir was invited
by Mr. Hodgson to accompany him in a short expedition into
Scotland.    The line chosen was from Whelpington over the
Harwood moors to Elsdon, and so up the vale of Reedwater by
Otterburne and the Roman Station of Bremenium, or Rochester,
over Carter Fell into Scotland, and down that most romantic
and beautiful stream the Jed to Jedburgh, and thence to Melrose.    On our road down the Jed we were anxious to obtain
a sight of the old border tower of Fernihirst, the stronghold of
the Carrs, a famous family in the history of the Border; and we

were not disappointed. Here it was that the prince of darkness was believed to have manifested himself to the English army, six times in one night, in 1523, duly attended by a train of goblins; and in all probability from this reported occurrence the place had been long looked upon with terror by the neighbourhood. Whether any tradition of these infernal manifestations still lingers on the Jed I know not. The story, which seems to be worthy of a short notice, is contained in a letter from the Earl of Surrey to Cardinal Wolsey, dated at Berwick on the 27th Sept. 1523, from which it appears that Lord Dacre, aided by Sir Arthur Darcy, Sir Marmaduke Constable, and a stout English army, after having taken much spoil in the neighbourhood, and set fire to Jedburgh, marched to Fernihirst, " the lord whereof was his mortall enemye." Tye tower, as the letter goes on to state, " stode mervelous strongly within a great woode." It was however soon " thrown downe:" and now comes the tale of spirits and fearful sights, and of the " devill " himself, which doubtless at the time made every one who heard it tremble with awe.

" After that, my said Lord (Dacre) retorning to the campe, wold in no wyse be lodged in the same, but where he laye the furst night; and he being with me (Lord Surrey) at souper, about viii a clock, the horses of his company brake lowse, and sodenly ran out of his feld in suche numbre that it caused a marvelouse alarome in our feld, and our standinge watch being set the horses cam ronnyng along the campe, at whome were shot above one hundred shief of arrowes and dyvers gonnys, thinking they had ben Scotts that wold have saulted the campe. Fynally, the horses were soo madde that they ran like wilde dere into the feld, above 1500 at the leest, in dyvers companys —— and in one place above 50 fell downe a great rok and slew themself, and above 200 ran into the town, being on fyre, and by the women taken and carried away right evil brent, and many were taken agayne; but, fynally, by that I can esteme by the nombre of theym that I saw goo on foote the next daye, I thinke there is lost above 800 horses, and all with foly for lak of not lying within the campe. I dare not write the wondres that my Lord Dacre and all his company doo saye they sawe that nyght 6 tymes of sprits and fereful sights; and universally, all their company saye playnly the devill was that nyght amongs them 6 tymes.—— There is noo

herdier nor better knyght (than Lord Dacre) but often tymes he doth
not use the most sure ordre, which he hath now payed derely for.——
" T. Surrey."

From Melrose we descended the Tweed, by Dryburgh and
Kelso and Wark Castle to Coldstream, from which place we
turned southwards to Whelpington by Floddon Field, Wooler,
and Rothbury. The weather was favourable, and Hodgson was
in high health, an unusual thing; and in excellent spirits. He
knew well every hill and stream and village by the way, especially
on the English side of the Border, and talked of the castles and
peels on the road in a manner which proved his intimate acquaintance with their history. The expedition was made in his
own little carriage, drawn by one horse, of which he was the
driver and the friend, and, as the progress was intentionally slow,
to consult the comfort of the animal in such roads, there was
abundance of time and no lack of memory or inclination on his
part for the recital of one wild legendary tale after another, connected with the district. Otterburne and its conflict, the Chevy
Chase of old, was a glorious subject. Bremenium came in for its
share of his attention, and in short every turn of the road, romantic enough in itself to have engaged the mind in the
absence of more stirring matter, furnished a subject for its future
historian. Hodgson's history of that part of the county was then
deeply occupying his thoughts, and three years afterwards, when
it made its appearance, I failed not to recognise in it many of the
legendary tales which had contributed to my amusement whilst
sitting by the side of my friend. One of those stories, as told
afterwards by Hodgson in his history, deserves a place in these
pages. It had previously engaged the attention of Sir Walter
Scott, and is mentioned in his " Rokeby."

" A little to the north of Otterburne, and on the east side of the Otter,
on a plot of rich green sward, stood Girsonfield, a farm-house which
since the time of Queen Elizabeth had belonged to the proprietors of
Otterburne Castle. Some parts of its walls still remain, and a new house
of the same name has been built on the hill-side to the east of it, in a
much more exposed, poor, and inconvenient situation. There it was that

'the false-hearted Ha' resided, whose treachery bred a long and bitter
feud between the clans of Hall and Reed. The occupier of Girsonfield
had been enjoying the confidence and friendship of Percival Reed; but
when the latter, as keeper of Redesdale, was leading out a party of his
neighbours against an inroad of the clan of Crozier from the opposite
border, Hall betrayed him into the hands of the enemy, who slew him
at Batenshope on the Whitelee ground. Some say that Hall secretly
damped the inside of Mr. Reed's musket after it was loaded, and that it
burst at the first fire and killed him. All agree that he came to his
death by the circumvention of Hall, whose clan were privy to his plot
and ever after holden in the greatest detestation. They say too that
the spirit of Reed, even after it was disembodied, could find no rest, but
was seen wandering far and near, in trouble, and in various forms, till
one gifted with words to lay it to rest summoned it to his presence, and
offered it the place and form it might wish to have. It chose the banks
of the Rede, between Todlawhaugh and Pringlehaugh, and there

'Oft by the Pringle's haunted side
The shepherd sees his spectre glide.'—*Rokeby.*

"It had five miles of river side scenery to range along, in which it
flitted about by night, or roosted on some stone or tree by day. One
of its favourite haunts was about the Todlaw Mill, now in ruins, where
the people as they went to the meeting-house at Birdhope Cragg often
saw it, uncovered their heads as they passed and bowed, and the
courteous phantom bowed again, till its 'certain time' was expired;
on the last day of which, as the conjurer who laid him was following
his ordinary occupation of a thatcher at the Woodlaw, he felt something
touch him like the wing of a bird whisking by, came down the ladder,
was seized with a cold trembling, shivered and died."—Hist. Vol. i., p.
II. p. 110, 111.

One part of the tale, as told by Hodgson, is here omitted.
The spectre was more frequently seen sitting in an elder tree and
grinning at the passers by, than in any other place or attitude.

In our ascent towards the summit of Carter Fell, from the top
of which the road begins to decline into Scotland, we had an
amusing adventure. Whilst we were slowly walking up the hill
by the side of the vehicle, we observed a man on horseback

approaching.    As he came nearer he appeared to scan us both
with an inquisitive eye; till, having apparently come to the conclusion that he had nothing to fear from two such sedate-looking
personages, he pulled in his rein, and came to a stand beside us.
The man was dressed in a humble manner; and over his unsaddled
horse, of which any one might have told all the bones, there was
slung a short sack with something of a bulky nature in each of its
ends.  " Sars, ye wad na like a drap o' new melk the morn?" was
his greeting.  "New milk, my good man," said my companion in
his usual grave way, "new milk is a very good thing: I am very
fond of it at home.   Where do you bring it from, and whither are
you going?"  The man began to be more assured, and after another
scrutinizing glance, became apparently satisfied that we were not
excisemen in disguise. " Sars," said he, "its jist a drap o' whusky,
an' ye may pat i' your machine," pointing to the gig, " an' nae
body 'll know naething about it."    To my great amusement
Hodgson began to give the smuggler a long lecture on obedience to
the law, to which of course he paid no attention, and so we parted.
We had only a very short time before been amused with a
grotesque caricature over the fireplace, in a little room at the
toll-bar at the foot of the hill, a picture of " the De'il runnin
awa wi' the exciseman," the subject of one of Burns's most
characteristic songs.    Whilst the duty upon whisky was low in
Scotland and high in England, the law against border smuggling
was evaded in a thousand ways.    Our friend above called his
contraband article *new milk*, a name by which doubtless it was
well known to the intelligent.    Another name for it was *knives
and forks*, under which appellation it frequently found its way
south as far as Durham.    One tale which Hodgson told me on
our road after the above meeting is worthy of being placed upon
record as a sequel to the above.    Once upon a time, not long, I
believe, before the date of our expedition, the young men and
maidens of Coquetdale agreed to celebrate a great meeting for
mirth and jollity on one of the green haughs of that beautiful
river.    The time was, of course, summer.    The afternoon was
appointed; friends far and wide were invited; but most especially
the excisemen and supervisors stationed in the district; and the

gathering was immense. But the smugglers on both sides of the border had been warned. It was in truth for this express purpose that the day had been set, and the country-side cleared of gaugers, every one of whom the young lads contrived to make tipsy and useless for the night before the meeting was brought to a close. The quantity of whisky which found its way into England during this scene of feasting and dancing was enormous.

But we soon afterwards had another adventure of a different kind. As we were driving slowly along the road between Melrose and Dryburgh, and I was reading aloud to my companion from a little book I had purchased at Jedburgh, containing some pleasing border poems and ballads which had been published by a local poet of the name of James Telfer, there started from the hedge by the roadside a figure not soon or easily to be forgotten. The poor man was tall and thin, and wretchedly clad; and his gait and gestures were of a very extraordinary kind. To those who have seen the painted toy resembling a human figure (and who has not) which, when a child pulls a string, throws its legs and arms into all kinds of wild postures and attitudes, no further description of our new friend is necessary, save that the rags in which he was clad performed their part also in aid of the bodily contortions of their wearer. A violent stammering for a while prevented us from understanding what the man had got to say, till at length his words became intelligible, and in the true furor of his profession he exclaimed, "I am the poet of Yatholm." "Poor man," said Hodgson, "a poet! let us stop and talk to him. And so you are a poet; pray let us hear some of your poetry." This was spoken in so kind a way, that the man again became extremely excited, and leapt from one side of the road to the other, and back again, for joy. There had been a short time before erected in the neighbourhood a memorial in honour of the Duke of Wellington. On this subject our poet had composed many stanzas, and these he recited in his broad Scotch dialect; gesticulating and capering at every line to such a degree that it was no easy matter to keep our horse in order. We listened to another composition in honour of a young lady on the Tweed, and at length we left the poet of Yetholm rejoicing over the guerdon

which he had earned.  Seven years afterwards it was my fortune
to meet with this poor man again in a lane near Norham, many
miles down the river, and again I witnessed the same symptoms
of poetic inspiration, and heard the same compositions.  I was
not surprised to hear that much of this apparent excitement was
put on for a purpose.  It appeared that he had a few stanzas on
every gentleman's house upon the Tweed, and gained his bread
by reciting them.  The following extract from the Newcastle
Magazine (for May 1829, p. 226) must conclude my account of
our interview with this son of the muses, who died in the union
workhouse at Wooler on the 3rd of February, 1844, having in
1813 published a few of his poems, which three years afterwards
made their appearance in a second edition.

"Robert Gray of Yetholm, a rhyming, crippled, tipsy itinerant,
chanced to be in Edinburgh, where, being reeling about the streets, he
was picked up and carried to the police office.  'Who are you, or what
account can you give of yourself?' asked a lieutenant of the police.
'I am Robie Gray, sir, the poyet o' Yatholm,' was the answer.  'I
think you are very lame, Robie,' returned the lieutenant, struck with
the oddity of the answer.  'Ay, sir,' said Robie, 'we're a' maistly
cripples, hus poyets: there was Pop, a little wee puir decreepit object;
an' there was Lord Byron, him that's reckon'd sic a grand poyet, he had
a club fit; an' there's Watty Scot, a sair lamiter too; an' there's
mysel'.'  'Well,' interrupted the lieutenant laughing, 'but what are you
after at present?'  'Seekin' subscribers, sir, for the Queen of the Border,
a grand novelle I've written, only three shillings and sax pence, will ye
subscribe, sir?'  'Here,' cried the lieutenant, putting his hand into his
pocket and giving him money, 'Here, and I hope you will not pester us
again with either the Queen or yourself.'"

I find in Hodgson's Note Book a few particulars of our
expedition, especially remarking upon the scenery, &c. of that
beautiful stream the Jed, and upon occurrences at Melrose; at
which place he made a neat sketch with his pen, of an old coffin-
lid-shaped gravestone in the chancel in memory of Ivo de Corbridge, a person, who, from the unmistakeable character of his
monument, must have died about the year 1250.  This monu-

ment Sir Walter Scott erroneously attributed to Lord Eure, a Durham Baron, who was slain in a border battle at Ancrum Edge in the sixteenth century.[*]

"The bold red scared line of porphyric hills lying east and west with the borders, strikes the eye immediately in passing over the line of demarcation. The Jed a charming river; sometimes rocky sandstone, porphyric, stratified, red schisty sand. Planted trees—graceful birch and alder—narrow glens—cleughs—haughs and holms—brooks down narrow dells, hastening along their dingly banks to wed their waters with the Jed. Cottages gay with trained roses, white and red, some the natives of China. Here and there well thatched or slated farmhouses with excellent offices, and the gentlemen's seats thickly girt with thriving woods. The seat of Col. Rutherford. Farnihurst, the tower of the famous border Kers, peeping out of a wood of oak. Jedburgh—nothing remarkable in it but the fineness of the situation. Its new gaol. Its old abbey church neglected and polluted with dirt and a presbyterian church, and its yard with nettles and docks, hemlock and rank fumitory. An old bridge. Ancrum, a neat old tower with very fine old woods about it. Eildon hills like the Mont de S. Michl. le Archangel. Gatenside opposite Melrose. A quarry near the town of soft granite.

"Melrose. Thursday 1 July. Went to bed last night soon after ten —disturbed by disorderly guests till after twelve. Rose after six. Masons going to work at half-past six. Very few people then to be seen. Not a chimney smoking. What a proof of Scotch economy and order! Burning candles and drinking whisky till after midnight in June, and lying snoring in bed till after seven in the morning. Ah Scotch lazybeds!"

### To W. C. TREVELYAN, Esq.

"MY DEAR SIR,                          Whelpington, 6th July, 1824.

"All the extracts you have made for me are very interesting, and after I am sure that you do no injury to your health by labouring for me in the British Museum, your commission to copy is unlimited. In the extract about the Charletons, Calig. B. I. fol. 128, you are, however, treading very closely upon my heels, for I have copied a line or two from the Earl of Northumberland's letter on fol. 127; and that on

[*] See Memoir of Surtees. Ed. Surt. Soc. 8vo. p. 44.

fol. 128, as far as the *Citis of Carlisle*, with the date ' From Newcastle upon Tyne the vijth. daie of April.' There seems to be an error in the indorse, which is, ' 28 Hen. 8. Charleton's Murderers of *John* Fenwicke, Keeper of Tindale.' I have also copied the Letter to the Council on folios 133 and 134; the Letter respecting Sir Humphrey Lisle, B. II. folio 374; an extract from B. II. fol. 2. about ' iiij Roods made into Tividale by *Thomas Dacre ;*' and a Letter from Cal. B. III. (fol. 7, &c.) respecting the apprehension of three Charletons, principal Headsmen, &c. in Tyndale; and also several others, ' at the Bridel of Colwell,' dated Morpeth, xx day May; also the Earl of Northumberland's Letter about the execution of Wm. Lysle and others, Cal. B. III. fol. 146; the half-year's pensions, fol. 237; and also extracts from a paper signed ' Fran. Walsingham' about the War Establishment at Berwick, 1516; also Cal. B. III. p. 125, and I. p. 203, names of Deputy Wardens.

III.   p. 197.   R. Carnaby, about Charletons. Hexham, July vii.

„     158.    Extract from Wm. Franklyn's Letter.

„     150.    Very short extract about breaking Hexham Gaol.

„     239.    Copy of a Letter sent from the Headsmen of Tyndale.

" The above transcripts I have lately found in sorting my papers; and fear that you may have copied more of them than the extract in your last letter.

" I have not the catalogue of the British Museum by me, only extracts from it in MS., but nothing respecting the contents of Titus F. XIII. and therefore cannot say whether any of them have been printed or not, though I can speak with much confidence about the extract you have sent from fol. 160 not being printed.

" I am writing the volume which I at present have in hand, in the following order:—Elsden, Corsenside, Kirkwhelpington, Kirkharle, Hartburn, Bolam, Meldon, &c., and am only delayed going to press by the hope of receiving some contributions from Lord Redesdale, and the papers from the Bodleian Library. Mr. Raine and I had an excursion last week through Redesdale to Melrose, and thence home by Kelso, Wooler, and Rothbury; which has prevented me from answering your letters punctually. The extracts which your sister has made from Cotton. Claud. C. VIII, list of heirs of noble families, is very interesting, and cannot fail of being of great use to me. I have made copious extracts from a MS. in the Museum, intituled " Apparatus Genealogicus sive Breve Abstractum eorum quæ ad Stemmatum Familiarum Anglicarum Series, &c ' but have omitted to notice in which of the libraries it is to be found. I mention this lest either your sister or yourself should meet with it, and begin to go over the ground that I have already surveyed. Pray inquire if there be not in the Museum an *Herbarium* which was made by Turner. I have somewhere been told that such a curiosity is existing, but have forgot my authority. With many thanks to your sister and yourself for your kind and valuable labours, I am, my dear Sir, most truly yours,

"JOHN HODGSON."

### FROM EDWARD SWINBURNE, ESQ.

"MY DEAR SIR,                                    Barnet, July 25, 1824.

"I am well aware that it is not by your wishes, but by your means, that your proceedings in the decorative part of your History must be regulated. Let us do the best we can. I am somewhat *davered* about the vignettes. How they can be turned to account for this second volume of yours I do not know. I wanted to obtain information *ab experto* about the management of vignettes, and I got them done under my eye from my sketches, by my friend Mr. de Wint: what I had in contemplation was making them a substitute for drawings, so as to keep the number of plates up to the six of the first volume; and in point of size and importance they are little inferior to the four in Lewis's hands. I confess that the difficulties attending the printing of vignettes did not in time recur to my mind, though you had formerly pointed them out to me. At present the objection is that they are not only rather too important for the purpose you mention, but are not calculated for wood-cuts; for which I have learnt a totally different management in the effect is required from that which suits the copper, no blending, but sharp oppositions of light upon dark, and *vice versâ*. What is proper also for a vignette, where the work and mass should be in a focus in the centre, does not do for a square plate; so they would require some alteration to adapt them to that, even were they on copper. With respect to wood-cuts, I have been made to observe, in looking over Bewick's work, that both in the birds and vignettes, wherever the *clean* contrast is attended to, the effect is spirited and sparkling, but insipid where blending, as on copper, is attempted. Sometimes the object is all in half-tint, and brought out by a very deep back-ground. This treatment is requisite from the manner in which wood-cuts are executed and printed. I will, however, send you two drawings by Mr. Ellison, who was expected to return from Bognor to Pall Mall, for a few days on his way home, to be left at Mr. Adamson's. I have no topographical sketches by me, or I would try something in the style I allude to for you. I must, however, make one or two observations before I can be *au fait* of the method. I fully understand your point of view of Whelpington; do you want something done there for your present volume? You had better apply to Miss Swinburne, as my return is uncertain; and she will do it better. I will see Lewis to-morrow to know his progress. Having been for some time out of London, except for two or three days, I have not any recent account to give of Mr. Calverley Trevelyan.————The summer is come at last, and most opportunely for saving the greater part, should it continue, of the hay crops: the early ones were spoilt. The corn is looking well and changing colour. The country is quite exquisite, verdant as spring, and with all the richness of summer luxuriance. You must have enjoyed your Border tour. Your topographical knowledge, poetical reminiscences, and utility of object for your History would give additional zest to the scenery. Yours very truly,

"Ed. Swinburne."

"To the Rev. J. Raine. Whelpington, 7 Aug., 1824.—From the time in which I received your letter of the 4th of August (? July) to the 17th of the same month my study was occupied by a constant succession of of way-faring people, and from the 17th to the 21st I was left alone to beat my brains for the sermon which I preached before my Lord 'Size on the 22d,* after which day I was a week employed in doctoring the dry rot in Heworth Chapel, and since I came hither I have been sufficiently taken up in redeeming almost a month of mis-spent time. I have not, however, been inattentive to the subject of your letter.————

" In return for your sketch of Meg of Meldon I send you a very rough one of a portrait which was at Seaton Delaval, but is now either at Doddington or at Constable Melton the seat of Sir Jacob Astley, to which my note book adds ' Meg of Meldon; she was a Fenwick and married a Delaval.' You will see that another Meg, a Middleton, no mighty good name, might set up as a candidate for the honourable character and the famous deeds which tradition attributes to this Meg of ours.

" I dined at Adamson's a week since in company with Mr. Turner of Newcastle, who said that a friend of his in Bristol asked him in a letter to inquire of me where I found in Shakspeare the lines I had quoted in my introductory Essay in the Archæologia Æliana. Now

---

* This Assize Sermon does not appear to have been preserved.

you will recollect me saying in our journey to Scotland that I had repeatedly searched both in Shakspeare himself and in Ayscough's Index for them, and never could find more than 'rank fumitory,' and that I got the lines in question from Brand's Newcastle, who has them under quotations, and says that 'visitants of taste in their walks amongst the extensive and venerable remains of [Tinmouth] Castle will not forbear to exclaim in the language of Shakespear

"'O it pities me,' &c. (Brand, vol. i. p. 126.)

"Now my object in introducing this to your notice a second time, is to beg that when you next write to Messrs. Nichols and Co. you will drop a note into your packet, mentioning that I had told you how the lines got into my essay, and requesting to know if any reader could find them in any edition of Shakspeare, or where Mr. Brand picked them up, for they seem so much beyond his own poor brain's produce, that I think if he had made them he would not have fathered them on Shakspeare. I say for your own information, and not further, that the draught of the essay was written one morning in the vestry of Jarrow without the use of books; that the quotations were corrected the next day in the Philosophical Society's room; and when the essay was first printed it got some polishing as it was transcribed, and some additions were made to it in the second edition as it now stands in the first volume of the Arch. Æliana.* Most truly yours,

"JOHN HODGSON."

FROM EDWARD SWINBURNE, Esq.

"MY DEAR SIR, Aug. 11, 1824, 18, Grosvenor Place.

"I should have written to you by Mr. Ellison to tell you why I did not by that opportunity send you the vignettes of Halton Castle and Chirdon Peel, as I intended, when I wrote to you. Since that I shewed them to Mr. Lewis, and he was so decided in his opinion that they were not calculated for wood-cuts, and that it would be a pity to throw them away upon what would also be the worse for the attempt, that I thought it best not to send them, but will leave them in his hands, to be dealt with as you direct. If you wish to have them, they

* These statements to a certain extent modify the assertion made above from memory (vol. i. p. 120) that the Essay in question was written in the vestry at Jarrow in the interim between a morning marriage and an afternoon funeral.

can be sent in an office frank. He proposes two things: one is to do them in mezzotinto with etching, which he thinks preferable, as more spirited than aquatint, and which could be done, I think he said, for 5 or 6l. a piece, and annex them as sort of head and tail pieces (though printed on separate paper) to the four etchings, if you want to equal the number of the first volume: or to do them on a reduced scale as etchings for vignettes to this volume, printed on fine paper and pasted and pressed on the sheet of the letterpress: to this, however, you objected, as liable to accident from detaching itself, though Lewis says it can be done easily and securely: or thirdly, to keep them for another volume, either changing them to square drawings or preserving them in the vignette form for variety. Yours, very truly,

"ED. SWINBURNE."

To THE REV. J. RAINE.

"MY DEAR RAINE,                    Whelpington, 19 October, 1824.

"I will not keep your MSS. any longer. For the last three weeks the weather has been so bad that I have not ventured to send them; but as it appears more settled at present, I intend to give them to the carrier to-morrow. I have of late printed so much in brevier from them that I have had only a proof once a fortnight, so that I am still no further on than Ellingham in Alnwick Deanery, and the whole of Berwick is still to go through.———— I have printed a great many papers and records which Hunter has not, and which I have either got from you or from London or Oxford.

"My progress with the parochial history is provokingly slow. The documents which I ordered to be written in the British Museum are dribbled in in such miserable portions, and so slowly, that I long to be in London with half a dozen hacks about me, and satisfy my craving wants at once. Added to this, after writing a most urgent letter three weeks ago to Dr. Bandinel, for papers that were copying for me in the Bodleian Library, he tells me that he left the greater part of them and the most important document with Mr. George Andrews, bookseller in Durham, on the 16th of August last—whose only answer to two letters pressing him to send them to me is that he sent them off to me last Friday, and if they be not arrived, if I will write saying so he will inquire of the coaches. ———— The parcel entrusted to him is not mine, but for my use, and after I have done with it to be lodged in the archives at Alnwick.

"Mr. Swinburne, in a letter about three weeks ago, said that Mr. Blore was on his way to explore the Vallum Romanum, for which purpose I suppose he will have letters missive to my fellow-secretary of the N. A. S. If he has been there within the last fortnight, in spite of the good things to be got at Twice Brewed, the keen air that brushes the whin-stone crags over which the Wall runs, will, I apprehend, have abated a little of the antiquarian fervor with which he left the metropolis; at least it will have contrived to take away a little of the limberness of his finger-ends; and it will require even all his fine strokes to make anything like a picture, even in fine weather and with whin-stone crags to boot, of anything that remains of the Wall. He should have chosen summer for such a work, for all the existing parts of the Wall any way worth notice are in very bleak situations.

"Winter has set in here early and sternly. We had hard frosts for three nights together three weeks since. A few days since the ice was half an inch thick over our water-tubs; and on Sunday all was white with snow. The sycamore trees about the vicarage are leafless. It will be May before the cuckoo comes, and no spring till June, so that there is nothing for us now, for six months at least, but to contrive to be ' as humorous as winter,' keep on our hats and shawm our shins, and be, like other Laplanders, happy at home.——

"I shall go soon to the Greenwich Hospital books with authority; but my extracts, if I make any, are to have Hopper Williamson's fiat before they can be printed.* So no more at present, from yours,

"J. H."

To W. C. TREVELYAN, Esq., University College, Oxford.

"MY DEAR SIR,                    N'Castle, Tyne, 14th Dec. 1824.

"Your letter inclosing the Saxon Charter was so very long in getting to me after its date, that I did not venture to write to you in Oxford, as you kindly permitted me, lest you should have left your college before my letter reached you. I had quite lost sight of the ' Ordering of the Vicarage of Kirknewton,' and cannot bring to my recollection how I became possessed of it, as it is not among my Oxford notes. The proof of the imperfect copy and your corrected one reached me by the same post. Dugdale, i. p. 504 of his Baronage, and on the authority of

* See Vol. I. p. 300.

a record which he takes from Dodsworth, says that William the Conqueror gave Redesdale to Robert de Umfreville, and that it had belonged
to Mildred the son of Acman.    Will you be so good as to see if Dodsworth's extract be in his collection, and to ascertain where he got it ?
I certainly have seen Dugdale's account in Latin, but where I cannot tell.
When you get to London you also may fall upon some opportunity of
finding who Sir Charles Howard was who had Redesdale in 1652, and
whose descendants parted with it to Cranstoun, Northumberland, &c.
    The pedigree stands thus:

George Lord Howme, Earl of Dunbar,=......
    had Redesdale from the Crown 1604

Lady Elizabeth Home had also a grant=Theophilus Lord Howard, 1613, afterwards
of Redesdale with her husband          2nd Earl of Suffolk.

1 Susan = Js. H.=2 Barbara   Geo. H. 4 E.   Mary=Hen. H. 5 E.=...widow, &c.
         3 E. of              of Suffolk.         of Suffolk.
         Suff.

Sir Charles Howard, his lady and sons, petition=...
    Parliament 1652; Lord of Redesdale 1658.

Chs. Howard, Esq. son and heir   James Howard, Esq. had Redes-=...
of Sir Chs., occurs 1663, levies a   dale p. m. Charles Howard, Esq.
fine of Redesdale 1667.              described as father of Chs. and
                                     grandfather of Charles Francis
                                     Howard.

Chs. Howard of Bingfield, Esq. 1691, which=? ...Errington, daughter of Errington
place he sold 1705; died in the minority of     of Bingfield.
his son.

Charles Francis=...Hall   James      Charles   William   Eliz.=Richard   Frances
Howard, of Over-          ob. juv.   ob. juv.  ob. juv.  bur.  Hereford.  born 1722.
acres, Esq.; sold                                        in Ex.
estates to Lord                                          Cath.
Cranstoun 1719;                                          M. I.
buried 22 Jan.,
1746.

Wm. Howard, Esq.; sold Overacres,
lordship of Redesdale, and advowson
of Elsden to D. of Northumberland.

    . " Hitherto I have had no information from Lord Redesdale; but as soon
as my papers are in a fit state will send them to him for additions or
corrections, though I apprehend I have not much to learn after I have
added the wives of the Howards, and know whence Sir Charles was.
James Earl of Carlisle and certain others certainly conveyed Redesdale
and other places in 1657 to Charles Howard and others who were his
trustees. I have collected a good deal about them, but can by no means

discover whether they were related to the Howards Earls of Suffolk, or Howards Earls of Carlisle, one of the latter of whom I find once as a trustee for Charles Howard, Esq., son and heir of Sir Charles. There is also a deed enrolled in Chancery, 23 March 164-, by which James Earl of Suffolk and others convey Redesdale and the advowson of Elsdon to Robert Hopper, Esq. and others; I apprehend, in trust for Sir Charles, who with his wife and children petitioned Parliament in 1652 for restoration of property in Northumberland.

" The printers are keeping me sadly back; for three weeks I have only had four pages sent me. When you are in London I will also thank you to mention to Mr. Grey, the amanuensis, that if he has not already sent off the parts of the Survey of 1551, which your sister did not copy for me, he will forward them without delay, as I am intending to print both that survey and the larger one by Bowes and Ellerker in a small type, and immediately (in a week's time) I shall be at a stand if they do not then arrive.

" One other thing and my troublesome commissions are for the present done with. Be so good, if this letter reaches you while you are in Oxford, as to pay *six guineas* to Dr. Bandinel, for a copy of a MS. which he has procured for me; and I will give the money to any of your family here or pay it to yourself when you arrive, as you think best. I am, dear Sir, most truly yours,

" John Hodgson.

" I have not seen the new edition of Warton.* One was greatly wanting, and I rejoice to hear that the editing of that work has for this time fallen into able hands. It has sold of late years so very highly that I think there is not a copy of it in the library of the Lit. Society. The vile Dublin editions may, I believe, be got for a low price; but the quarto of 1774, when I priced it at Priestley's in 1819, was 10*l.* 10*s.*

" The study of Anglo-Saxon has never yet been sufficiently general in England to make that language thoroughly understood; but the publication of the works you name will, I hope, bring it into familiar use among scholars. It is very easy, and, as the foundation of our language, appears very beautiful when it has become easy. I know very little about the pronunciation of it—a loss which I very much wish to supply, though in fact I have not a moment's time for any study but such as bears upon Northumberland."

---

* The History of English Poetry, edited by Mr. Price.

E 2

THE request contained in the following letter has been alluded
to in a preceding page. The church of Gateshead Fell glories in
its spire, but whether Hodgson was the designer of this incon-
gruity or not is unknown to me. From the measurements specified in Mr. Collinson's letter, the architectural reader will know
what to look for. But of all mistakes that of placing a spire,
however perfect in design, in such a naked situation, at such an
elevation above the level of the sea, was perhaps the greatest.
High it may be, but a spire can only look well when it has its
harmonious accompaniments, when it is ' bosomed high in tufted
trees,' or in some other suitable locality.

FROM THE REV. JOHN COLLINSON.

" DEAR SIR,                                    Gateshead, Jan. 29th, 1825.

" The society for the enlarging churches and chapels have
liberally granted us 350*l.* for Gateshead Fell Church. As we are thus
made pretty easy with regard to the funds for the church, we have
turned our thoughts to a spire; for completing which three gentlemen,
laymen, have contributed 20*l.* each.

" The favour I have to beg of you is to ask if you can oblige the
trustees, either by reference or by any plan of your own, with a good
design for a spire. I should perhaps rather say for the upper part of
a tower, as the base of a spire; and for good buttresses with pinnacles
on the top of them. We mean to take Chester-le-Street spire, a plain
octagon building, for our model, on a reduced scale. Chester is 156
feet in height from the ground. Gateshead Fell spire is to be 120 or
130 feet from the ground; that is 60 feet of tower and 60 feet spire.
The tower is already built to the height of 40 feet; and I am anxious
'he remaining 20 feet should be made light, and properly adapted to the

spire, which is to rise from it. The tower is 18 feet square. We propose to have buttresses to the tower from the bottom, as what should be in Gothic architecture.

"Should you be coming to Newcastle, I trust you will favour me with a call. I remain, dear Sir, very truly yours,

" JOHN COLLINSON."

TO THE RIGHT HON. LORD REDESDALE.

" MY LORD,         Whelpington, near Newcastle, 13th Feb. 1825.

" The inclosed account was sent to me on Monday last, and the only observations I have to make upon your lordship's objections to take my work are the following :

" That Mr. Trevelyan, of Wallington, told me that your lordship requested to be put upon the list of subscribers to *the* work—that *Part First*, according to my original proposals published in the Gentleman's Magazine, will be the last in the order of publication—that after the payment of my printer's and engraver's bills I have little left for my expenses, and *nothing* for my labour—that I have never yet solicited any one to ask subscriptions for me—that being a poor man with a large family I feel obliged to those who patronize my work; but that in taking my books, if your lordship thinks you are not likely to get ' value received ' for your money, you will oblige me by returning them, addressed to myself, by some safe and unexpensive conveyance. I print only 300 copies.*

&c. &c.

FROM EDWARD SWINBURNE, Esq.

" MY DEAR SIR,        Linden, April 28th, 1825.

" Mr. Bigge is going to Newcastle on Friday, which will afford me an opportunity (if I do not go with him) of sending you the sketch of the Mote Hill, also the vignette near Woodburn. Shafto Craig's

---

* The following memorandum in Hodgson's Note-book (Y 143,) accounts for the above letter :—" Mr. Murcott, Mr. Walker's agent's report of Lord Redesdale's answer written on Mr. Walker's bill : ' His lordship says he did not order these books

Punch Bowl, the Sheep Bridge over the Lewisburn, and a Fall on the
Oakenshaw burn, will be done for vignettes, and put into your hand to
be disposed of as and when you think proper. The weather is against
adding Edlingham Castle, or anything else to the stock. As I passed
by Wallington I was shewn a letter from Calverley containing a message to you about the engraver (Lizars, I presume), who said he could
judge better of the prices if he could see some of the drawings. He
guessed from two to four guineas. I shall most likely be in Newcastle
myself on Friday. At all events the drawings will be sent to Ord's in
Westgate-street. Yours very truly,

"ED. SWINBURNE."


To W. C. TREVELYAN, Esq. No. 8, St. Andrew's Street, Edinburgh.


"MY DEAR SIR,                          Whelpington, 3rd May, 1825.

    "I have not been able to get a drawing to send to you before
to-day; and now fear it may arrive at Edinburgh too late. The subject
I send is a view of the Rede. On the right bank, where the people and
horse are, you will recollect observing the remains of the house of John
de Lisle de Woodburn. The ground on which it stood is still called the
Hallyards. I will thank you to get this drawing engraved, and to
request that the original may be kept clean and returned to me.[*]
    "On the other side I will give you a slight sketch of the Pedigree of
Umfreville, with the hope that you may get me some additions or illustrations to it. Who was Ingelram de Umfreville, warden of Galway
in 1308, a baron in 1310? His wife's name, Catherine, &c., occurs frequently in the Rotuli Scotiæ.
    "I have been a week from home, and my work has got before me; I
am therefore compelled to write very briefly. Most truly yours,

"JOHN HODGSON."


—that his name was inserted without his knowledge—that he had not had Part I.
—that they are the dearest books he ever saw—that he does not understand the bill,
and that you must send him a letter to explain it.' "

[*] The engraving from this drawing (by Mr. E. Swinburne) appears in Hodgson's
History, Part II. vol. i. p. 172.

To Miss TREVELYAN.

" My dear Madam, Whelpington, 8 May, 1825.

" I annex the arms of Hebburne of Northumberland according to the best authority I have to refer to. I have never met with any ancient deeds or muniments with the seal of that family appended to them. (*A sketch of the arms in the margin.**)

" I shall be very much obliged to your brother by his purchasing me a copy of Douglas's ' Baronage of Scotland.' A copy of any kind, if it be perfect, will serve my purpose; that is, I had rather have a copy with soiled leaves and indifferent binding at a low price than a fair and well-bound copy at a high one.

" Several of the monasteries on the Scotish Borders had possessions in Northumberland (the abbot of Jedborough for instance, in Redes-dale), and it will be very gratifying to me to hear that Mr. Calverley should find any new materials for me in the Cartularies he mentions. I have said in a letter which I wrote to him last week all I can recollect at present about my literary wants which I think there is any likelihood of getting supplied in Edinburgh. I have found by a charter in the pos-session of Sir J. E. Swinburne that Ingelram de Umfreville was a brother of Gilbert de Umfreville, and claimed to have 120 acres of land, 24 of meadow, 300 of wood, and 1000 of pasture in Elsdon, as heir-at-law to the said Gilbert. I only sent one drawing and that of the vig-nette size, to Edinburgh, to get engraved by Lizars, because I have none of the larger size ready. I believe that I have very little about the Riddells, excepting the notices in Wallis, and a short pedigree by Flower, i.e. I have little worked up into form, but great abundance of raw material from the Rotuli Scotiæ, and from numerous unpublished documents. I have taken the address of Mr. Riddell, 111, George Street, Edinburgh, and will not fail to avail myself of the kind assistance which he offers me. I write this in haste, as I have to be at Kirkharle by three o'clock, and suppose you may wish to answer your brother's letter to-day. I have the honour to be, my dear madam, yours very faithfully,

" JOHN HODGSON.

" It is very probable that the Advocates' Library and the Register Office contain much curious matter respecting Northumberland, and if

---

* Party per chevron vert and gules, in chief two mullets, and in base a crescent argent.

your brother should find it so, I would not hesitate to go there for a fortnight or so.  Is it likely that I could find a smart and ingenious boy as
a tutor and amanuensis in Edinburgh?


To W. C. TREVELYAN, Esq.

" MY DEAR SIR,                                    Whelpington, 17 May, 1825.
    " The line over the middle of the distance is a road; but there is no
rock in that part, excepting at the highest point of the farthest hill, just
to the right of the top of the tree, where there is a range of sandstone
which may be very lightly marked.  I will, however, send the proof to
Mr. Swinburne and ask his opinion of it.    It perhaps ought to have
been a little sharper than it is at the roots of the alders on the left side
of the river; and the figures on the right bank not quite so distinctly
made out.  The rock under the two oak trees between the figures and
the river is limestone.  The distance is rather too heavy.
    " It is not possible than I can get from home at present.  Our visita-
tion is to morrow, and Sir J. E. Swinburne returns about Friday; so
that I am expecting that I shall have to do evening service there once a
fortnight at least.*    I wish some such arrangement could be made at
Cambo,† and that I could offer my services to go there now and then in
an evening through the week without the charge of irregularity.  If Mr.
Davison would give his permission to such a measure, I should be most
happy to lend all the aid to it in my power.
    " I should be most happy of a letter to introduce me to the notice of
G. Chalmers: but fear that the collection which you mention as being
made by Bishop Nicholson related to the kingdom of Northumberland.
At present my books are out of the cases—the painters and upholsterers
being in my study; and I am therefore unable to refer to my minutes
on the subject: but suppose that the MS. you mention is the same that
was in the Dean and Chapter's Library at Carlisle, sometime between
1690 and 1700, and then mentioned as ready for the press.  I think its

---

    * The distance of Capheaton foom Whelpington was such (see p. 5) that Divine
service was occasionally performed there in a room duly licensed by the Bishop.
    † Cambo is a hamlet in the parish of Hartburn, and Mr. Davison here spoken of
was the aged vicar of this latter place.  Cambo now has a church of its own.  But see
hereafter.

title was *A Description of the Ancient Kingdom of Northumberland.* Bishop Nicholson also somewhere, probably in his Historical Library, mentions some *collections* as having been made by Mr. Shaftoe and Mr. Clavering, who were contemporaries of his. I most heartily wish that any of those could be procured.

"I do not know O'Connor's Catalogue of the MSS. at Stowe, but I have a copy of a descriptive account of the contents of a Cartulary or Register Book which belonged to Brinkburn Priory, and which formerly belonged to Mr. Astle; but is now in the possession of the Marquis of Buckingham, from whom I have permission to make extracts from it. This Cartulary I suspect to be one of those which were formerly in the possession of Lord William Howard of Naworth; and I wish I could hear where those of Alnwick and Newminster * are, for they were with that of Brinkburn and some more at Naworth in Camden's time.

"The information you have sent me is very curious. I will have the Rot. Scot. consulted: they are in the Newcastle A. S. If you can contrive to get me transcripts of the six charters you have given me extracts of, I shall esteem it a great favour. I have as yet nothing from Scotland. (Indeed I apprehend I have a transcript of the original grant of 40*s.* a year rent out of the Mill of Plessy to the nuns of Coldstream; the original is in the possession of Sir M. W. Ridley.) Sepley is Shepley, *i.e.* Sheepley, as Chipchase was formerly Shepches and Chepches; and Shilbottle Shepeling-bottle. All these deeds will be invaluable to me. My best endeavours shall be given, as soon as I can, to avail myself of the assistance of Mr. Riddell and of being personally acquainted with him.—*(The rest of the letter torn off.)*

### To the Rev. J. RAINE.

"My dear Sir, Whelpington, 25 May, 1825.

"I forgot to ask you when I saw you at Morpeth a week since if you could get me the loan for a few days of Kidd's edition of the Miscellanea Critica (by Dawes), printed in 1817. I cannot procure it in Newcastle, and only want it for a few days; indeed for a few hours.

"And when you find time to answer this first inquiry, say to me

---

* The Chartulary of Newminster was found a few years ago, and now belongs to the Earl of Carlisle. It is about to be printed by the Surtees Society. That of Brinkburne has passed from Stowe into the possession of Lord Ashburnham, and is now inaccessible.

whether you and your brother will visit me this summer, and make a week's tour with me from this place. You know that I shall be most happy to see you. My horse is now getting to his prime and is in excellent condition; and if you will promise me to come I will not turn him out to grass before we have had our tour. What would you say to a jaunt *per lineam Valli* to Carlisle, thence to Penrith, and home by Alston, Whitfield, Hexham, &c.?———Most truly yours,

"JOHN HODGSON."

To W. C. TREVELYAN, Esq. Post Office, Edinburgh.

"MY DEAR SIR,                              Whelpington, 25 May, 1825.

"Your sister Miss Julia favoured me with a note yesterday morning, in which she says that Mr. Thomson has kindly undertaken to get copies of the seven deeds relating to Elsdon and the Umfrevilles from the Kelso Cartulary, and that if I wish for full copies of the deeds respecting Plessy and Shipley, I had better write to you and give you the references to the Cartulary which contains them, as you have no note of them, and she is going from home till Wednesday.

MACFARLANE'S TRANSCRIPT OF THE COLDSTREAM CARTULARY.

"LVI. Carta Donationis terræ in Bamburgh.
"LVI. Carta Donationis molendini de Sepeley.
"LVI. Carta Johannis de Plesseto de lx solidis in Molendino suo.
"1. Odonnell.
"2. Deeds of Rich^d 2 son of O., 'teste tota curia mea apud Whelp-ington.' Confirmation by Wm. W.—Resignatio Rogeri Rectoris de Ellesdon, &c. 1228.
"3. Gilbert de W. grants 10th 'pullanorum . . . . . mei in Cottonshope. Testib. Rob. fil. meo, Petro de Insula, &c., Compositio super quandam litem inter abbatem et conventum de Kalcho et Rogerum Rectorem de Ellisdon, &c. 1228, in which many places in Redesdale are mentioned.
"Charter to Donald Campbell of half the lands of Reed Castle, forfeited by H. Percy and Ingraham de Umfraville. Robert-son's Index, p. 18.
"I have not been able to find in the *Rot. Scot.* any reference to the surrender of the Castle of Dumbarton by Ingelram Umfreville, and his

delivering up his daughters Eva and Isabella as hostages—you refer to
A.D. 1296, and vol. i. p. 212. Nor can I meet with Hailes's History of
Scotland. Harding says Robert Umfreville, Earl of Angus, was taken
prisoner at Strayvelyn Bridge, 25 June, 1814. I have got a great many
particulars respecting Ingelram Umfreville, from *Rymer, Rot. Scot.*,
&c. &c.

"I have not been able to get the proof of the vignette, which you
sent me, transmitted to Edward Swinburne, not knowing where he is;
but with the few alterations which I suggested, and attention to the
keeping and spirit of the original drawing, I have no doubt but the
engraving will be finished very much to his satisfaction. Sir John
returned on Thursday last, and was at church on Sunday, but though
he thought his brother was in Sunderland, he was not certain.

"I have never yet received anything respecting Redesdale from Mr.
Caley, and I fear that the Records respecting that district, which I have
been long expecting from the Tower, will not be forwarded to me till
after Parliament rises.

"Since I wrote the other side I have found in the Scotch Rolls the
record 'Pro Engelramo de Umframvill de terris restituendis,' and
liberating his daughters Eve and Isabella, vol. i. p. 80. The precept
was directed to the Sheriffs of Ayr, and similar letters were forwarded
to the Sheriffs of Berwick, Edinburgh, and Fife, which circumstance
affords probable evidence that he had possessions in these four counties.

"I beg the favour of your presenting my best thanks to Mr. Thomson
for his kindness in offering to procure me copies of Northumberland
charters from the Kelso Cartulary; and am, dear sir, ever very
sincerely yours,

"JOHN HODGSON.

"The index to the Rot. Scot. is very imperfect. I have found
numerous omissions of names, and many mistakes."


FROM EDWARD SWINBURNE, Esq.

"MY DEAR SIR, Newcastle, May 27, 1825.

"You will be somewhat surprised, I hope not indignant, when
you receive what will accompany this note; and you must not grudge
me the pleasure of contributing to your convenience, while you are so
usefully employed for others. It appeared to me that a table you could
write at, and have drawers within reach for your papers, and afford

accommodation for so large and increasing a collection of them, with
space on the top for other matters in request, would be useful to you·
I had some pounds more at the bank than I expected; but I have
restricted myself to the plainest materials, which I thought also would
be most consonant to your feelings. I would have had it of American oak,
but Mr. Watson could neither furnish nor procure me in Newcastle any
that he thought would stand; there being none seasoned. It will therefore be of deal, painted as rosewood; and will be entirely for use and
not ornament. He has promised me that the drawers shall move well,
and the castors for shifting it according to the season be good ones. It is
to be covered with a very nice and well-dried sort of oilcloth, considerably
less expensive than leather, stands work better, and is easily removed;
a lifting desk to write on could not be managed with this covering; a
moveable one will be furnished to supply the place, with a shallow
central drawer for papers, money, &c. It will find its way into your
study by the window, I hope, if not by the door! Yours ever,

"E. SWINBURNE."

The invitation in the letter of the 25th of May above, with the
very pleasing recollection of our visit to Melrose, &c., in the preceding year fresh before me, was gladly accepted; and, accompanied by my brother,* who was then residing in Durham, in a
state of bad health, having been obliged to give up for a while his
studies in Cambridge, I met Hodgson at Newcastle; from which
place we started on the 4th of July on our expedition. My
brother rode on a favourite pony. Hodgson and I sat side by side
in his little carriage; and a few miles to the west of Newcastle
I first became acquainted with the Roman Wall. The day was
fine, and my companion was in better health than usual, and very
communicative and amusing.

Upon reaching Stagshaw Bank, a large open tract of ground,
not far from Corbridge, inclining swiftly from the Roman Wall
to the Tyne, we found ourselves in the midst of a great annual
fair held on this declivity, chiefly for cattle, but in truth for goods
of all kinds, "things," as an old inventory at Durham has it,
"moveable or moving themselves."† At this place, which is a

* Afterwards Fellow of Trinity College, Cambridge, and now Vicar of Blyth in
Nottinghamshire.
† "Inventarium omnium bonorum mobilium et immobilium seseque moventium."
—Here at Stagshaw there was nothing immoveable save the ground.

solitary field, at a distance from any population, there are great
well-known periodical gatherings of buyers and sellers from the
whole north of England, on the western or eastern coast; and the
southern counties of Scotland send forth in abundance their men
and goods to buy, sell, or be sold. Here we met Hodgson's
eldest son, a lively and intelligent lad of thirteen, well mounted
upon a stout Shetland pony, upon which he had ridden across
the country from Whelpington, in the company of a friend, to see
for the first time in his life the humours of this far-famed fair; but
upon which, upon an offer being made to him by his father, he
willingly turned his back and became our companion. Before
our departure, however, we spent an hour in surveying this
scene of bustle and activity, which to myself and my brother, as
well as to the boy, was of a very unusual kind. In a large pasture
upon the slope of a hill, with a wide prospect, extending down
the valley of the Tyne as far as Gateshead Fell, and in every other
direction except on the north, having an almost unlimited view
of a spreading tract of country, there were gathered together,
without the slightest attempt at the order which is of necessity
observed in markets and fairs held within the walls of a town,
horses and cattle, and sheep and swine, and in short every thing
which is bred or of use in farming operations, with thousands of
other things, which it would be no easy task to enumerate; and
then there were people of all ages, from all quarters, and in all
kinds of costume; the Scotchman in his kilt and the Yorkshire-
man in his smockfrock; and every variety of booth or hut for
refreshment or dissipation. That we had stumbled on a fair of
Roman origin may not, I think, be doubted. The situation of
Stagshaw Bank is an extremely convenient one for gathering
together at stated periods of the year the produce of this the
eastern side of the island; and as long as the Romans were in possession of Britain, and there was an immense population along the
line of the Wall from sea to sea, the natives would find a ready
market for the produce of their fields and farmyards. The wall,
which runs at the distance of a mile northwards, would be a protection to the sellers of cattle and wares in that direction; and
from the south they had nothing to fear. There is an annual fair

in all respects of the same character as that of Stagshaw Bank,
held upon Brough Hill, in Westmerland, in the immediate
neighbourhood of Brough, in times of old the site of a great
Roman station; and if the one has been a fair from the time of the
Romans so has the other.  At both there are enormous gatherings
from the whole north of England and the southern counties of
Scotland; and the records of the monks of Durham carry them
both back to the thirteenth century.  From these documents it
would be a very easy matter to supply the price of a fat ox or
sheep at Stagshaw Bank or Brough Hill in any given year during
the period over which they extend.  If it should be suggested
that these fairs may owe their origin to grants from our early
Norman sovereigns, the grant may be admitted, but nothing
more.  In all probability in both cases such a document can be
produced or proof given that it once existed.  But why a grant
for a market in such places, remote for centuries from any considerable population, except that fairs were already held there
at stated periods, and, from having been long kept up, had
gained such great notoriety, that the owner of the soil wished to
become a gainer by the custom in a legal way?  Upon entering
the field at Stagshaw Bank from the public road the vehicle in
which Hodgson and I rode and the ponies of our companions
were called upon to pay a toll to the Lord of the Manor.  After we
had heard and seen enough of the φωναι and απειροκαλιαι * of this
singular scene we took our departure, with much of the day and
Chesters, one of the most interesting stations on the Wall, before us.

On our way to Stagshaw Bank our road had been first on one
side of the Roman Wall and then on the other.  Very frequently
the military way, as it is called, a great public road from Newcastle to Carlisle, along which we were travelling, runs directly
along the line of the Wall itself, the very stones of which were
occasionally visible beneath the wheels of our carriage.  As we
proceeded Hodgson pointed out every turn of the barrier, and its
accompanying works; and very frequently we alighted and made
digressions from the road on foot to see what might otherwise

---

* See Xen. Cyrop. Book 1, § v.  Did the Romans in these extra-mural markets
imitate the Persians?

have passed unnoticed. After leaving Stagshaw Bank we dined at Chollerford Bridge, and slept at a roadside hostel, of a humble character, called Twice Brewed, from the excellence I suppose of its ale, having previously devoted a considerable portion of the afternoon to the examination of Housesteads and its wonders.

Twice Brewed I shall long remember. Until the opening of the rail-road from Newcastle to Carlisle, the military way on which it stands was the main line of communication between the eastern and western coast, and, as it will readily be imagined, the intercourse and traffic between the one and the other, between Carlisle, as the centre of trade in the west, and Newcastle on the east, were very considerable. All communication between the two in the way of trade was by carts, each cart being drawn by one horse, with a man to three. These carriers did not make their journey singly, or at times which best suited their convenience; but for their mutual security, this having been till very modern times a lawless country, they journeyed in bodies on stated days. Now it so happened that when we reached Twice Brewed at a late hour in the evening not fewer than twenty of these men had a short time before put up there for the night, and were enjoying an enormous supper of the most substantial articles of food at the end of their day's work. For us, who were four in number, there was no other accommodation to sit or sleep in than a single bedroom having in it two beds of a very humble character, but the best in the house; and to our still greater annoyance the floor of the room in which we were doomed to sleep abounded with wide chinks between its boards, through which we could not only hear the riotous mirth of the men below us, and smell their savoury dishes, but even see the light of their candles. The carriers feasted and drank and sung till a late hour. Next morning they rose early; and again there was, for a long time, great noise and confusion below us, and we were glad to leave Twice Brewed after a sleepless night in quest of new adventures and fresh air upon the Wall.

During the whole of our expedition, as in that of 1824, Hodgson had a tale or an anecdote for every place we reached or came in sight of. For one only room may be found. I well remember his horrifying us, as we were passing the scene of the outrage,

with the story how two notorious thieves of the name of Armstrong, in the beginning of the last century, by way of vengeance
for his having been instrumental in bringing two of their asso-
ciates to justice, had there cut out the tongue of William Turner
of Cringledykes, and had sliced off part of his cheek and the whole
of his right ear. They had however unintentionally left to the
poor man enough of his tongue to enable him to depose to them
in a court of justice as his mutilators, and bring them to due
punishment.

Our route from Twice Brewed was from one camp to another,
with the Wall in view, till we reached Thirlwall Castle; when
we quitted the barrier and proceeded to Carlisle, turning aside
for a while to Naworth Castle and the Priory of Lanercost. At
this latter place we found in the wall of a stable the shaft of a
cross of the period of King John, on which mention is made of
his name and those of his contemporary sovereigns in Europe. Of
this fragment Hodgson soon afterwards communicated a drawing
and description to the Transactions of the Newcastle Society of
Antiquaries.*

From Carlisle we returned to Thirlwall Castle, and proceeded
by way of Haltwhistle, Langley Castle, &c. to Hexham, where
we parted company—Hodgson and his son for Whelpington, and
my brother and I for Newcastle and Durham.

It is not easy to conceive a person better suited for such an
expedition than Mr. Hodgson. Time spent with such a man,
in such a way, is not soon forgotten. He was communicative,
playful, easily pleased, accommodating, and, what must not be
forgotten, exceedingly attentive to the ease and comfort of his horse,
to which his care was invariably directed in the first instance,
before he thought of himself, upon our arrival at an inn for the
night, or to bait during the day. These extracts from his master's
journal will tell the subsequent history of this faithful and kindly-
treated animal.

"1834, 30 Jul. The night before last my pantry was robbed: and
this morning my horse and cart full of stones went over the bank and
rolled three times over without injury.

* Vol. II. p. 197.

" 1840. 17 Oct. My poor old horse is, I think, dying.

" 1840. 7 Nov. My horse Wylam died on Thursday the 5th instant, and was buried in a pit at the head of the vicarage wood. I purchased him in November 1828, when he was rising four years old. He was upwards of 16 hands high, black, and of fine form and great power. His spirit and temper were also most excellent, and he continued in great health till about two months since. But before that time, for more than a year, he had a stiffness in his right hough; but blistering him to cure the complaint so impaired his appetite that he gradually grew so thin and bad of appetite that he died of mere want of food."

### To the Rev. J. RAINE.

" My dear Sir,                                  Whelpington, 7 July, 1825.

" We arrived at Whelpington about 6 o'clock yesterday evening, all safe and sound; but the bad fish I got to my dinner at Hexham has given me a very sorry night. I have been really very ill with it, but feel recovered.

" The following are dimensions of a great block of whinstone which has been raised (by the Romans) out of the ditch of the Wall, where it takes an acute turn on Low Tipper Moor. Since the block was raised it has fallen into three pieces, probably the action of frost soon after heavy rains. (*Seven sketches, with measurements.*)

" The above are all the notes I have respecting the block of basalt which I requested your brother to try to find the solid contents of, in measure and weight. I have omitted in my Note Book to say whether sketch No. 1 be north or south, side or top, or what; and No. 2 is also imperfectly intituled; but I hope with these hints, and the memoranda which your brother made, he will be able to accomplish the task which I have set him.

" Don't forget the Umfreville charter, or anything to copy which may be materially useful to me. I shall be glad to make you indexes of any MS. volume which has Northumberland matter mixed with your Durham affairs, for the use of such extracts as suit me. If you can make any additions or corrections to the pedigree * pray send them. I have not corrected the clerical mistakes in the proof. Pray contrive to get me some work for my amanuensis. With kind regard to your brother, most truly yours,

" JOHN HODGSON."

* Of the old Lords of Redesdale, for Part II. Vol. i. p. 6.

FROM THE REV. A. HEDLEY.

"MY DEAR HODGSON,       Whitfield Rectory, Aug. 27th, 1825.

" The bearer of this is Mr. John Thompson,* a very worthy neighbour of mine, a miller by profession, and who is going to look at Ray Mill, which he has seen advertised for sale. I am sure you will give him all the assistance in your power. If you can get Joe Fenwick to give him a smatch of the value of the land it will be of great service to him.

" He lives now at Crowhall Mill, opposite Ridley Hall. He is an excellent little fellow; *a very good practical botanist*, very fond of natural history in general, and in every thing perfectly self-taught. In the natural history, and more especially the botanical department, he may be of use to you in this district; and would, I am certain, be quite proud and happy to be employed in this way. He has long been one of Winch's correspondents.

" We have our District Committee Meeting at Chollerford on Wednesday first. After our business we dine together at the inn, and it is generally a very pleasant meeting. I have set my heart on your coming to visit us on this occasion at least. The clergy of the district would take it as a compliment; and you will, as you announce in your work, have to be obliged for their assistance in various ways; so that I think it would be wise in you to cultivate their acquaintance as much as you can. Do come then, and endeavour to bring Redman † with you. You can either return at night, or go to Chester, or with me, either to Mr. Tulip's, or Mr. Ridley's, of Parkend, who would be most happy to see you, and who would show you what papers he has.

" Mr. Hollingsworth,‡ who breakfasted with me yesterday with some south-country friends, requests me to give his best regards to you, and

---

* Hodgson's acquaintance with Mr. Thompson, whom in his journal many years afterwards he calls "the amiable John Thompson," takes its origin from this letter. We shall in the very next letter see how useful Mr. Thompson made himself in the botanical department of the History of Northumberland. He is still alive, and the word Hodgson operates upon him as a charm ; such is his delight in hearing the name of his friend. From my knowledge of his intelligence and modest demeanour he must have been a man after Hodgson's own heart. Other letters from him may perhaps appear in the sequel. Mr. Thompson is in possession of the proof sheets of Hodgson's history of his native parish of Haltwhistle given to him by their author, a present upon which he justly sets a high value.

† Vicar of Kirkharle, Hodgson's nearest clerical neighbour.

‡ Hodgson's old Sedgefield friend, at that time Vicar of Haltwhistle.

wishes to be a subscriber to your work. I have never given you Mr. Ord's name, I believe; who gave me a similar commission before he left the country; but, forgetting to ask him whether he wished a large or small paper copy, I waited to ascertain the point first, which I shall be now enabled to do, as we expect him next week.

" Pray send by Thompson, or bring with you to Chollerford, the form of book according to which you wish me to copy out the neighbouring registers for you. And if your pedigree of the Ridleys be a portable concern, I should like much to see it, as there was about the middle of the seventeenth century an intermarriage between them and the Barrows which I wish to trace more distinctly. Mrs. Hedley joins in best regards to Mrs. Hodgson and yourself, and believe me, my dear H., ever yours most truly,

" ANT. HEDLEY."

FROM MR. THOMPSON.

" REV. SIR,                 Crowhall Mill, Sept. 28, 1825.

" I have sent you a list of such plants as I thought worthy your notice.* I could have made it larger, but thought it unnecessary to send you an account of such as occur in almost every place. I have therefore confined it to such as may be considered rare. I could likewise have mentioned more localities to a great many, but as they are chiefly in this neighbourhood, one or two to each will be sufficient. All those marked * I consider new to the Northumberland Flora, except Mr. Winch has noticed them in the 2nd edition of his essay (just published), as I presented him with specimens. Of the orders Musci, Hepaticæ, Lichens, Algæ, and Fungi, in the class Cryptogamia, though we possess a great number of species in each, I have not sent you an account; yet if you wish it, will send you a list of the rarest species.

" It is with pleasure that I can thus acknowledge my obligation to you for your particular kindness when at your place. I am, Rev. Sir, your obliged humble servant,

" JOHN THOMPSON."

* This List Mr. Hodgson printed under his history of the parish of Haltwhistle in his Part II., vol. iii., p. 360, with due acknowledgment of the obligation. " Besides this," says he, " I am indebted to Mr. Thompson for much information respecting the names of persons and places within the several townships of this parish." On the 3rd Jan. 1839, Mr. Thompson made a further contribution to Hodgson's pages of a list of the *Musci* of his district arranged according to Sir William Hooker's British Flora, printed in p. 361 of the volume above referred to.

F 2

To ROBERT SURTEES, Esq.

" MY DEAR SIR,                              Whelpington, 10 Oct. 1825.

" Mr. W. C. Trevelyan, of Wallington, who is the bearer of this
letter, is very desirous that the interesting work, ' The Fossil Flora of
Great Britain,' projected by our late and much lamented friend Mr.
Brough Taylor, should not be put a stop to by his premature death, and
would therefore be glad to purchase his collection of impressions
of plants for the purpose of carrying on the work himself.   Will you
have the goodness to put him into the best way you can advise of accomplishing his plan?   I know of no person whom talent, previous studies,
and unwearied research into almost every department of natural history
have better qualified for such an undertaking; I am sure that any
labour or interest you may take in furthering his designs will be most
amply remunerated by the gratification you may rest assured of receiving from the able manner in which Mr. Trevelyan will bring out the
work, if he succeed in getting Mr. Taylor's specimens, and in making
arrangements with Mr. Sowerby for conducting the work.*
I have sent you a book of extracts which relate much to the Blackett
family, and out of which you may perhaps get both information and
authorities for the pedigree of that family; but as I am now in almost
daily want of it I will thank you to return it with Mr. Trevelyan.
" Have you done anything at the De-lisle pedigree?   Pray let me
have any genealogical information respecting Northumberland which
comes in your way; for I lie far from the main sources from which it
is to be derived.   I have Tong's and the Visitations of 1575 and 1616,
but very few of Dugdale's pedigrees.—Yours most truly,
                                              " JOHN HODGSON."

To THE REV. J. RAINE.

" MY DEAR RAINE,                            Whelpington, 12 Oct. 1825.

" I have made a copy of the Catalogue of Plants,† and return
you your own transcript.   I fear it is a more difficult subject to write
upon than I had imagined.   Many of the Latin names are quite barbarous, such as I cannot find in Theophrastus, or Pliny, or Matthiolus's

---

* Sir W. C. Trevelyan informs me that he did not become the purchaser of this collection.

† A list of plants in Latin and Saxon, contained in a Norman MS., belonging to
the Dean and Chapter of Durham.

Commentaries on Dioscorides, or even in the Herbal of Turner; and as to the English names, though several of them are both intelligible and curious, yet the same term is so frequently given as a synonym to different Latin names, that in such instances there is no coming to anything like a reconciliation of the contradictions with which the MS. abounds.  For instance *attorlathe* is in Latin atrilla, febrifuga, and gallierus; *banvyrt*, consolda, fila-aurosa, and viola; *eoforthrote*, anta, brotium or boratium, colitus vel colocus, scasa vel scapa vel sisca; and so of many others.

"Pray tell me which of your MSS. it was that I had.——You bade me draw upon you if I wanted anything; and, as it would be very discreditable if I published an imperfect collection of these transcripts, I must beg of you to let me have the volume which I have not perused.

"Let me congratulate you on your appointment to be Chief Surrogate for the diocese.

"My printing goes on most heavily.  If I could get the printers to work I would make my own way rapidly, but I have been and am under obligations which prevent me from commanding, and must therefore be content to advance forward only as I am permitted.  Ever most faithfully yours,

"JOHN HODGSON."


To THE REV. J. RAINE.

"MY DEAR SIR,                              Whelpington, 22 Oct. 1825.

"The printers are pressing hard upon my heels, and by the end of next week will, I fear, be demanding that part of my MS. which I wish to be seasoned with a few extracts of the paper No. 19, in the 23d vol. of the Hunter MSS.  I must be very importunate in begging you to let me have it, and to send it to me *quamprimum*.  Could I at any time be favoured with the perusal of the volume *Reginaldi Monachi*, &c. Appendix No. 101, p. 399, which contains several tales which would I think go down many wondering throats without much seasoning?  Besides it furnishes a few Northumberland names which I have some hopes of getting tacked to a pedigree, especially those of Ede Brane and Eilaf, at No. 108 and 109, p. 408.*

"I have no discoveries or novelties to tell you of that can interest you, excepting that Mr. Singleton has got the altar which Mr. Trevelyan

* This MS. afterwards constituted the first publication of the Surtees Society.

and I met with among the ruins of Risingham last summer, and which contains the two hexameter lines—

SOMNIO PRÆMONITUS MILES HANC PONERE JUSSIT
ARAM QUÆ FABIO, NUPTÆ, ET NYMPHIS VENERANDIS.

" The *o* in *somnio* you must pardon, and consider as an exception very proper to be inserted in the next edition of your Durham Grammar,* under the modern dogma *Obliqui casus in o semper producuntur*, which you see is here contradicted.

" It will however be interesting to your geological friends to know that in our ramble amongst the Cheviot Hills in last month we found a stratum of a magnesian limestone, environed by hills of porphyry, and with fine grained sandstone above it.

" Mr. W. C. Trevelyan is anxious to get Mr. B. Taylor's collection of specimens and his papers for a British Fossil Flora, and Mrs. Taylor, I understand, has left the price he is to give for them to Sir C. Sharp and Mr. Surtees. I sincerely hope that they may fall into Mr. Trevelyan's hands; for I am sure he will carry on the work with very great ability. Most truly yours,

" JOHN HODGSON."

The next letter which I have to present to my readers proves that Mr. Hodgson was still remembered by the venerable Bishop of Durham, then in the 91st year of his age. By such a well-timed and munificent contribution the Bishop laid, not only Mr. Hodgson, but Northumberland itself under deep obligation. Northumberland, however, suffered the example to pass by unheeded. This splendid gift of 200l. might have made a graceful heading to a public acknowledgment of Hodgson's services, gratifying to him and creditable to the county.

FROM THE BISHOP OF DURHAM.

" DEAR SIR,                                    Worthing, Oct. 21, 1825.

" The work in which you are engaged, viz., the History of Northumberland, is of much importance in itself, and still more to those connected with it, as I am, by its constituting a large portion of my diocese.

─────

* A Latin Grammar which I had a while before published for the use of Durham School.

" The work must be attended both with labour and expense. To the former you are equal, to the latter you are not. I have therefore two hundred pounds at your service as my subscription. My most convenient mode of payment will be from my bankers, Messrs. Drummond, to Sir M. W. Ridley, at Newcastle. This transaction will be best arranged by your calling at Sir Matthew's bank and getting it settled there. I am, with much regard, your sincere friend and brother,

" S. DUNELM."

To the BISHOP of DURHAM.

" MY LORD,            Whelpington, 26 October, 1825.

" I shall accept the two hundred pounds. which your Lordship offers me as a subscription towards my History of Northumberland, not only with great thankfulness and gratitude, but as a very splendid and munificent token of your Lordship's approbation of my labours. It will remove many difficulties which have impeded my progress in the undertaking; and it shall act as a new obligation upon me to industry and care in bringing out the work which it is given to promote, in a way to do credit to the distinguished patronage with which your Lordship is honouring me. I am, my Lord, with the highest sentiments of gratitude, your Lordship's most obedient humble servant,

" JOHN HODGSON."

CHAPTER IV.—1826, 1827.

The criticisms in the following letter from Mr. Hedley are
some of them amusing. It appears that he had before him some
of the proof sheets of Hodgson's forth-coming volume of parochial
history, and many of his remarks appear to have been attended to
as far as it was practicable. The volume itself was published in
the course of the following year.

FROM THE REV. A. HEDLEY.

" MY DEAR HODGSON,                    Kirkw—pshaw—Whitfield, 9 Jan. 1826.
    " I received yours on Wednesday last, and was quite delighted
with its accompanying pacquet. I received at the same time my
monthly parcel from Charnley, Gent. Mag., Quarterly Review, &c., &c.,
but all were thrown aside for the History of Redesdale. I need not say
how interesting it was to me; but, to repay you for your etymological
heresies and jibes, I must endeavour to pick a few holes. In the first
place, though I, as a Redesdale man, would not think its history too
long were you to devote a volume to it, I cannot help suspecting the
space you have devoted to it *disproportionably* long. You will have,
you say, 140 pages for the parishes of Elsden and Corsenside, *i.e.* at
the rate of seventy for a parish; but the slightest calculation will shew
that you cannot afford this average; and this kind of calculation you
must not lose sight of, even in the greatest heat and ardour of composition, and in places and subjects even of the greatest interest. I have
always thought that compression and judicious selection from the
immense mass of your valuable materials will be the most difficult task
that you have to perform.
    " P. 85. In most places of Northumberland the trivial name of *pru-
nus padus* is *hag* or rather *hack berry*. I should like the Latin names of
the plants you notice better in italics. In the sentence beginning 'It is
difficult ' there are three '*finds*,' which had been as well avoided. The

construction of the whole sentence, or rather the latter part of it, which is somewhat obscure, is not in your happiest style. P. 86. I fancy I must yield to your torrent of authorities with respect to the derivation of Elsden, and rank with the old women of that ancient city. But, master of mine, why has the *eel* anything more to do with *water* than any other fish? But you might have added, as another buttress to prop up your crazy edifice, *eller*, Anglicè alder, which is strictly an *arbor fluvialis*. If you are right with respect to your Swedish authority *elf*, can it have any reference to *Elf* hills in your neighbourhood? It is odd enough that I never was on the spot, though so near Whelpington; but I believe there had formerly been much marshy ground thereabouts, and a large pond in which a poor girl drowned herself seven or eight years ago. 'But the fair is still, in a small way, in existence,' is, I think, a careless form of expression: at any rate it ought to have been written as I have pointed it: but I fear that you will think that this is criticism 'in a small way.' I am not sure that I like your *brevier* divided into columns by means of rules. P. 88. Nothing, I am sure, can be more technically correct than your description of Elsden—I beg your pardon, Elsden church; but is it not quite elaborate enough for so simple a structure? If you give two pages to Elsden, how many will you find due to Hexham Church? P. 89. I should have liked the succession of incumbents to have appeared in the text—simply their names and the dates of their institution, and all historical notices concerning them in brevier at the bottom. They form an important part of the history of the Church, and ought not to be thrust into foot notes. P. 92. Do you learn that M. Dutens made any arrangement by which the chapel of Birness was to be kept in repair? Though built within my own recollection, it seems, from the want of it, to be fast going to decay. Dutens was a Frenchman, though for a long while he wished to pass for a Swiss; and was distinguished by the affability and politeness, or what some would call the fawning civility, of that nation. Though he was, it is said, continually making liberal promises to his poor parishioners, many of which he never afterwards thought of, he often, to my knowledge, did them substantial acts of kindness. I have now before me a letter of his to my father, dated 'Wetherby, 22 Aug. 1779,' probably when on his road to London, in which he proposes that a poor cousin of my father, the daughter of a deceased innkeeper of Elsdon of the name of Humble, who left his family destitute, should he be brought up 'to wait upon a lady;' and he offers to contribute two guineas towards

sending her to Mrs. Harle (of the Spital) who, he says, ' asks six
guineas for three months, to teach her to mount caps, wash and mend
lace, and such other necessary things.' The idiom is English good
enough, but the spelling in one or two words betrays the Frenchman:
for instance *loge* for lodge: the handwriting very neat and plain, but
French. P. 93. Your Roman capitals for the tomb inscriptions are a
size too large: instead of long primer, which they appear to be, they
would to my fancy have looked better in brevier No. 2. P. 99.* Your
short description of Mr. Ord's park is *excellent:* quite perfect indeed.
Pray write to Mr. Thompson requesting leave for me to search the
Haydon Bridge, Newbrough, and Warden registers, and your red book
shall be returned well filled I trow.—Yours ever most truly,

" ANT. HEDLEY."

## FROM EDWARD SWINBURNE, ESQ.

" MY DEAR SIR,                                    Jedburgh, 12 April, 1826.

"I have not with me the dimensions of the etchings of your
work to regulate the size of Rochester. How would you introduce it?
as one of the principal etchings, or as a head or tail piece? If the
former, as most respectful,† it might be a substitute for one of those
already prepared by Lewis. The morning I was there it was so
tempestuous, wet, and cold, I could not explore; and was moreover
suffering much from the effects of the ride the day before, though but
a short one. A general view of the site would, I think, have been
preferable. If the modern village is to be the type, the Duchess's view
of it is as good as another, and the detail of the cottages sufficient for
the purpose. I was obliged to keep on horseback from the difficulty of
getting on again; but was able to make a few memoranda by which it
might be worked up. In the first place, a wild road winds favourably
in the direction of the houses, and a *midden* is well placed on the opposite side to them, and a break in the green, with stones, &c. On the
green above it I would put some children. Of creatures there was
little display: a boy backing to the storm with his face to the ass's tail
might be taken for a practical pun and retrospect to Bremenium.

---

* These pagings do not correspond with those of the volume as it was published.
The pages which Mr. Hedley had before him were proofs only. The volume itself was
not published till the following year.

† The drawing had been made by the Duchess of Northumberland.

There were two geese and an old woman, of which I could not much avail myself; but I can make some children for you, as they will not be a burden to the parish. I will see Lizars about it when I get to Edinburgh. My stay there will be but short, therefore you must answer this by return of post, especially if I am not in time to-day at the modern Athens for the first mail. Send me also with the dimensions a description of the bairns, &c. I could not make it convenient to diverge to Mr. Singleton's, where I should liked to have passed a day. The Academy dinner, from which I have been several years absent, limits my time narrowly, and there are reasons why I should not make it another year of non-appearance. When the leaves are out, the vale for some miles above Horsley must be very pleasing. I had a very sour ride to Whiteleys. Dodd of Catcleugh is to make great exertions for Liddell in bringing up voters. One sees how the castle inclines. The approach hither is very romantic. Yesterday was the market. What a fine race of beings, and they throw their plaids with dignity. The coach is starting. Yours truly,

" ED. SWINBURNE."

To E. SWINBURNE, Esq.

" MY DEAR SIR,        16 April, 1826.

" It has just struck me that, if you should think fit to put a Roman altar or two in the foreground of the view of Bremenium, sketches of such as have been found upon the spot would be most proper. I have therefore given you a sort of rude notion of those to Minerva. No. 1. DEÆ MINERVÆ ET GENIO COLLEGII OPTATVS TRIBVNVS V. S. L. M. No. 2. DEÆ SANCTÆ MINERVÆ FLAVIVS SEVERINVS TRIBVNVS ARAM DEDIT. No. 3. DEÆ MINERVÆ CARAVTVS S. C. They are in this manner.*

" A great many antiquities have been found here; but these are the most interesting of which I have sketches: that with the lunette or crescent, No. 2, might be introduced with a double meaning, appropriately enough, as the Duchess furnished the drawing.

" I know you will pardon me for sending you this hasty scrawl.

---

* On the sheet of this letter are four neat sketches with pen and ink—distinct elevations of three altars with their inscriptions, and the whole grouped together in the fashion of a vignette in a very elegant way. The hint was not adopted.

The subject you have in hand wants *appliances and means to boot*, and I send this suggestion not to be made use of but as you think fit. Pray do not put the things in if you think that doing so will spoil the simplicity of the design. The lunette is an old Gentile symbol belonging to the moon, Minerva, Diana, and the other female deities, in the character of *Mater Divûm ;* and it is also the Percy badge. I have given the three large rough sketches; not that it would be possible to give a detail of those mouldings, symbols, and inscriptions, but that you may have a true notion of their form if you think it right to use them. Lizars must do it well. Most truly yours,

" JOHN HODGSON."

FROM MISS SWINBURNE.

" DEAR SIR,                    18, Grosvenor Place, May 17, 1826.

"I am ashamed to say how little of your work we have finished,* and now we have so short a time left that I fear we have not a chance of doing all you wished; for being so unused to the kind of thing we go on very slowly. Could you tell us by return of post which you most wish for? Eliz. has looked over and made extracts from Turner's Herbal. The Reveley and Thornton pedigrees, and a small part of the Lansdowne MS. are done. I inclose your own list, that you may mark the most important, without having the trouble of writing it over again. We are all quite well, and beg our compliments to Mrs. Hodgson. Yours sincerely,

" J. SWINBURNE."

FROM EDWARD SWINBURNE, ESQ.

" MY DEAR SIR,                                    1826.

" The Duchess having given me with the twelve guineas the receipt from Lewis, I forwarded it by my niece to the proper hands. Mr. Singleton asked if any passing observation could be introduced that the view in Rochester is a fair specimen of a Northumberland village: I said I thought it was late for anything to be thrown into the text; on the plate it would have a bad effect; and on reflection I do not see what could be said that would be of use. The bearing I apprehend on

* The ladies had undertaken to make transcripts from the British Museum.

his mind is that there should be something of an apology for its introduction, having no local feature of antiquity to recommend it, or merit
as scenery; but such a specification would not be courteous to the
county, as we do not shine in villages. Characteristic fidelity has its
merit on the other hand, and there are ways of doing these things; and
your ingenuity will find one out, if you approve, and the thing is
feasible. It occurs to me, however, that the Duchess should not be the
person to expose in a solitary print from her pencil the nakedness of the
land. To connect her with Bremenium is the object. Yours very truly.

"ED. SWINBURNE."

### FROM THE REV. A. HEDLEY.

MY DEAR HODGSON,                               Whitfield, 22 Decr. 1826.

"I owe a thousand apologies for my delay in congratulating you
on the happy event announced in your last.* You have just tripled
my stock. Nine *bickers* to fill every morning is no joke: but they say
God never sends mouths but he sends meat. And in this season of
good wishes you will permit me to breathe a prayer that He would send
both you and them every other good thing; and that for many many
years nothing but the voice of joy and health may be heard in your
dwelling !

"And now for the proofs. How could Lady Swinburne, Mary,
daughter of Sir H. Bedingfield, married to Sir John S. in 1721,
be, as Lady S., the correspondent of Lord Derwentwater, who died in
1716 ? There are one or two other things, like them very unimportant, which struck me on first perusal, but not having marked them
I have not time to search for them now; neither have I time to combat
your etymological heresies. I will not be driven from the field about
Haltwhistle, without another *tussle*. As you are now in Hartburn, you
know that *Anger*ton is fr. *Anger*, pratum.

"I am delighted to hear that you propose another visit to us in spring,
which will soon be here now; but if you are as lucky in your weather
as Mr. Trevelyan you need not care at what season you come. He left
us on Thursday morning last, professing to be much pleased with our
Whitfield lions, and on his road to get a *snoke* of the Roman dunghill
at Whitley.

"ANT. HEDLEY."

* The birth of his daughter Emma, who afterwards became the wife of the Rev.
B. C. Kennicott, incumbent of the lately erected district church of All Saints, in the
chapelry of Monkwearmouth.

To Miss HODGSON.*

"MY DEAR ELIZABETH,                    Whelpington, 14th Feb. 1827.

"There has been much said about getting a letter written to you
to go in a box by Jacob Carr this morning, and Richard even went so
far as to write a part of one, which was to have been finished before
school hours; but it was found, when Jacob came, as it was left last
night. We have all had colds, but are all got well again. The weather
has been all along since you left home very harsh and unsettled, and I
have never been farther from Whelpington than once to Capheaton, and
once to Morpeth. I am much rejoiced to hear from yourself that you
continue to like school well; and I do trust that you will use all industry and exertion in improving yourself in such common and useful
knowledge as no person can well do without; and in such absolutely
useful Christian knowledge as no person can but do badly without.
Learn, my dear child, all humility of mind, but also learn while you
are young to be *firm* to right principles, and to be orderly and
methodical in the management of your time and duties, and happiness
will be the sure consequence of such conduct.

"Mamma says she hopes to be able to write to you by Curry on
Monday.

"Poor Mrs. Thompson, of Blackhall, since her confinement (a week
since yesterday) has been very dangerously ill; but we have heard this
morning that there is some hope of her recovery.

"The part of Mamma's letter to Miss Kemp which required no
answer, was that I had forgot to say that we did not intend to enter you
for more than half a year.

"With our united and affectionate love and regard, my dear Elizabeth, your most loving father,

"JOHN HODGSON."

FROM THE REV. N. J. HOLLINGSWORTH.

"MY DEAR SIR,                         Haltwhistle, Feb. 19, 1827.

"I have just received the inclosed letter from Mr. Thomas
Lowes, the present proprietor of Ridley Hall, and forward it to you, as
conceiving that you have been engaged to collect materials for the
work mentioned by him.

* His eldest daughter, then about 16 years of age, and at school in Newcastle.
Is is a good letter.

" If this should *still* be the case, and it should not be too late to insert something respecting the endowment and appropriation of Beltingham Chapel, I shall feel obliged by your informing me what notice of it would accord with the nature and style of the History, with a view to which I shall be happy to furnish you with any recent particulars in regard to the chapel in my power. The endowment of it is at present only about to take place, the particulars relating to it not being yet fully settled. The repairs and improvements are nearly completed on an extensive scale for the size of the building; the expense attending which when finished will nearly reach 500*l.*; towards which the Bishop of Durham has kindly contributed 100*l.*, and Mr. Thomas Lowes has 100*l.*, and Sir William Blackett 100*l.* towards the endowment. The chapel will probably be appropriated as a chapel of ease to the parish of Haltwhistle, having been before a private chapel belonging to Sir William Blackett's family. Prior to this you will know the particulars much better than myself. Having to send you this, I have put in a little publication of mine of which I request your acceptance. When you have leisure I shall be glad to hear from you respecting the chapel, and to see you should anything bring you into this neighbourhood.

" Mrs. H. unites with me in compliments to yourself and Mrs. Hodgson, and I remain, dear Sir, yours very sincerely,

" N. J. HOLLINGSWORTH."*

To the Rev. J. RAINE.

" MY DEAR RAINE, Whelpington, 28th March, 1827.

" I forwarded Kidd's Dawes to Mr. Tate immediately after I got your last letter; with which I had also one from Mr. T. which was very brief and tart. Unfortunately I was confined by a bad cold and bilious attack brought on by travelling in quest of information in bad weather, and I had to answer his letter in bed, and did so, I doubt, in much too querulous a tone.†

" I return your Flower's Visitation, which has lain in a drawer since Christmas unopened. There are also some other papers with it, which are your property, and for all which my best thanks are due.

" With this I send our parish book to Mr. Burrell, and will thank you to confirm the rate last entered into, as soon as you possibly can,

* One of Mr. Hodgson's earliest friends. See Sedgefield, Vol. I.

† Hodgson's correspondence with Mr. Tate was chiefly on the subject of the monument in memory of Dawes, of which hereafter.

in order that a little time may be had before Easter to collect it.  I apprehend that your signature will silence the gainsayers.*

" I have this morning finished and sent to press the conclusion of Hartburn parish, and shall to-day begin with Bolam, and then for Meldon! of the church of which I have got a drawing, and Nicholson is making a wood-cut.  Pray let me have as much of your Collectanea Meldoniensia as you think may be useful to me, and do not be long in finding it.  I shall soon be through Bolam.

" As soon as I am through this volume I will not fail to beat up your new quarters.  I wish I was at the Will Office.  Your extracts are of every day use.  They fill 965 octavo pages, and I constantly quote them by the title of (*Raine's Test.*, p. 560, &c.)  But there are many county names of which you have not extracts, but which I could soon complete, if I had leisure to come.

" There were a few copies of my account of Capheaton struck off separately, of which you shall have one as soon as I get them made up.

" Mr. Thos. Shipperdson wrote to me sometime since, saying that I was in a long arrear to the School Society.  I did not answer his letter at the time, because I could not conveniently pay my arrears.  The truth is my tithes this year have been bad, and my family is large.  I have also since I came hither maintained the Sunday School wholly at my own charge, and got the school at the expense of 15l. repaired, without asking any assistance from the society; but I must give over doing such things.  Be so good as to explain this to Mr. S. and say that I really cannot go on subscribing.——

" About 330 pages of my Parochial History are printed; so that 70 more must conclude a volume.——Most truly yours,

" JOHN HODGSON."


To Miss EMMA TREVELYAN.

" DEAR MISS EMMA,                    Whelpington, 26 April, 1827.

" (About paying Dr. Bandinel of the Bodleian Library 6l. 6s. for copying some papers, and Mr. Clayton having paid Dr. Bliss the

* This paragraph refers to his parishioners of Jarrow, who under a pretence of conscience were attempting to commit an act of dishonesty by withholding their church rates.  It is somewhat strange that this self-same conscience has so seldom prompted persons already in possession of what was in times of old dedicated to holy purposes to make restoration.  But to take is one thing, to restore another.

same sum). I will also further trouble you to ask your brother to do me the favour to get for me an amanuensis in the British Museum to copy me as many of the Ogle deeds as relate to Ogle. I am getting fast through Bolam, which will be followed by Whalton, in which parish Ogle is situated. They are at folio 172 of the Lansdowne MS. 326. Perhaps the whole 119 deeds would not be useful at present; but I wish the amanuensis to copy straight forward all that he extracts, in order that I may not have to get them copied again, i.e. I mean that I wish him to begin upon some folio relating to Ogle and copy all respecting it and all other places, as far as there is anything about Ogle; and to mark accurately the beginnings and endings of each folio and their numbers; so that I can refer to it. If he can get them copied in a few days, he may send the whole 119 deeds from Messrs Longman, in two covers.

"Perhaps your brother could contrive while he is in London to ascertain whether or not they have a calendar of the Inquisitiones Post Mortem for Northumberland at the Rolls Chapel, where the records under that title since about Henry the VIII's time are said to be deposited. If I could get such a document it would be a great treasure to me. I believe some of the Libraries about the Temple contain very copious extracts from the Inq P.M.

"Pray also get me from Mr. Trevelyan or Calverley what they know about the great stone by the Statue Pond at Wallington. I certainly have heard that it was brought from Harnham Moor, and made one of the two stones there called the Poind and his Man in the Border-laws: they are also both mentioned as standing when Warburton opened the larger tumulus there in 1748. The flat tumulus has not been opened; but the wall of two concentric circles of flat stones set on edge, which had earth and small stones between them, and which went around it, was removed only a few years since to assist in making a field wall: when perfect it would be in some such manner as this (*a neat drawing with the pen*), only the stones on edge round the lower barrow were higher than here represented. Very respectfully yours,

"J. H."

"It is the most remarkable group of antiquities in Northumberland, when the perfectness of the Roman causeway past it is considered, and that the old salt-way called the Scotch Street passed it on the north side, and went through the Salters' Nick westward, from Newcastle to Scotland. The Salters' Nick is also called *East Shafto-dore* in the Border Laws."

"From the Rev. A. Hedley.—Whitfield, July 7, 1827.  I long very much to see you all and to pass sentence upon your domestic architecture.  Do not be in the slightest degree apprehensive of the sale of every copy of your work.  I am only afraid that from your too modest calculation of the number of your copies, the sale of the whole will not reimburse you: but still I trust you will be paid in one way or another.  A good review in the Gent. Mag. will be of consequence.  Have you any friend at court there?  The mistakes you speak of will elude the general reader, and the antiquarian critic will know how to make allowance for them, as quite inseparable, in a very great degree, from such a work.  The minuteness of your Whelpington details, is, I think, the only thing that can be reasonably carped at in the volume; though, speaking for myself, there is not a word too much, either there or about any other place.  Your account of Whalton and the description of the village is excellent,* and your pedigrees all must admire · who are capable of judging of such things.

"A. H."

From EDWARD SWINBURNE, Esq.

"My dear Sir,                              18 Bury Street, 13 July, 1827.

"I saw yesterday at Lewis's impressions of all the plates he has done for you.  There was some deficiency in the number wanted.  As soon as that shall be made good he will send them altogether to you by sea, to the care of your printer, Newcastle.  They are as follows:—1. Halton Castle.  2. The Chirdon Peel.  3. Haughton Castle.  4. Chipchase Castle.  5. Linnel Bridge.  6. Rochester.  7. Hexham.  He has

---

* This description is worthy of a place in our pages.  "The village of Whalton consists of one street, hangs sweetly on the edge of a southern slope, and contains several well-built houses, which are much enlivened with clusters of trees and old gardens.  The garths and crofts around it have both antiquity and beauty in their form and grouping ; and every village that is girt with small inclosures, where the ground is rich, the hedges of hawthorn scattered here and there with the plum or the bullace tree, or shadowed with timber of larger growth, where the wild and briery lanes leading to it are worn deep into the earth, and where the weaver and the smith work only for the farmer, the mill grinds only corn, the ale-house is not " licensed to let post-horses," and the tailor is not "from London," has something in it that is venerable and lovely, and tells us that it belongs to an ancient race of yeomanry, jealous of seeing their patrimonial lands swallowed up in the vortexes of large estates."  Hist. pt. II. vol. i. p. 374, &c., which was published a few months afterwards, and of which the proof sheets were submitted to Hedley's inspection.

improperly adopted some suggested alterations of the lettering of
Rochester made in Grosvenor-place, when the corrections suggested by
me for the plate were submitted to Miss Swinburne's inspection: he has
got it High Rnchester *or* Bremenium, instead of *o* and *in*.  It is too
late now to alter it: I hope it is not very material.  This plate is much
improved, though everything that I pointed out has not been attended
to.  The same might be said of some of the others; but unless on the
spot, and not even there, are these matters easily accomplished.  I don't
expect to find any body like Miller for that.——Never was the beauty of
the country and promise of crops exceeded.  I had a very interesting
journey to town by the new roads of Haydon Bridge and of Alston and
Hartside to Bowness—had some delicious days with my nephew;
visited the chain-bridge over the Menai, Lichfield Cathedral, Coventry,
and Warwick Castle.  The inside of Lichfield is most beautiful, and
much painted glass! thanks to the French Revolution, and only cost,
repaired, put up, and all, 1000*l.*—worth 10,000*l.* probably.  Warwick
was splendid.  They are, I fear injudiciously, coating both Lichfield
and Coventry Cathedrals with Roman cement.——With assurances of
my unalterable esteem and friendship,

                                        " ED. SWINBURNE."

## CHAPTER V.—1827.

THE year 1827 is memorable in Mr. Hodgson's life for the publication of a second volume of his History of Northumberland. After a lapse of seven years from the date of his first volume he now, after much anxious expectation on the part of his friends and the public, makes his appearance with a portion of his labours of a more popular nature, one entirely and wisely devoted to parochial history.

To this volume is prefixed a very interesting Preface, the whole of which it is my intention to lay before my readers. My plan is, and has been, as I have more than once stated, to make Hodgson become, as far as possible, his own biographer, and, having this object in view, I gladly welcome such a document as this, which so minutely describes its writer's feelings and opinions with respect to his own book and similar undertakings. It has been well said that the mind and character of Mr. Surtees of Mainsforth may be best ascertained from the tenor of the notes in his History of Durham. For Hodgson's mind and character he who looks into his various Prefaces will not look in vain.

" Prefaces are much gone out of fashion; but, as an antiquary, I venture to claim the privilege of making an Address to my Readers; for I am sensible that my book stands much in need of an apology, which, if if I will not be at the trouble of making for it myself, I fear no one else will. For the sake of method, I shall also adopt the old but useful plan of dividing my subjects into heads, and will first speak of the gratitude I owe for obligations; and then put myself upon my defence on the following particulars, viz.—for some alterations in the plan of publishing this work; for the minuteness of my accounts; for my errors and omissions; and lastly, for the long delay that has retarded the publication of this volume.

"On the delightful duty of acknowledging GRATITUDE FOR OBLIGA-TIONS, the only general remark I have to offer is this—that, in the display I have to make of names and favours, I feel a mixture of pride and apprehension. I am proud to mention the many great and excellent personages who have kindly lightened the load of difficulties which this undertaking laid upon me, or condescended to facilitate my researches or to add to my store of materials; but I am apprehensive that I am unequal to perform my own part of the labour in a way to do credit to the distinguished patronage with which I have been honoured, or to satisfy the expectations that may be justly formed of a work that is rising under such able assistance as I have received.

"Besides the gratuity towards the embellishment of this work, which I mentioned at page xiv, in the volume published in 1820, since that time, my acknowledgments of obligation and gratitude, for assistances of every kind, to enable me to go on with the undertaking, are due to many:

"To His Grace the Duke of Northumberland, for a copy of the highly interesting Survey of the Borders between England and Scotland, in 1542, printed between pages 171 and 248 of Part III. Vol. ii.;* and for an historical view of the manors and lands of Henry Percy, the ninth Earl of Northumberland, from of the Rawlinson MSS. in the Bodleian Library.

"To Her Grace the Duchess of Northumberland for the drawing and engraving of the view of Old Rochester, in the ancient Roman fortress of Bremenium, in Redesdale, given at page 140 of this volume.

"To my late revered and munificent patron Dr. Barrington, Bishop of Durham, for the sum of 200l. His lordship's reason for giving me which will be best explained by the following letter to me on the subject.†

"To Sir J. E. Swinburne, of Capheaton, Bart. F.R. and A. SS., &c., &c., for 25l. towards the expense of publishing the Swinburne Charters, between pages 1 and 25 of Part III. Vol. i.; for a copy of the last edition of the Encyclopædia Britannica, and its Supplement, as a book of reference; and for a copy of Dodsworth's Transcript of the Swinburne Charters in the Lansdowne MS. 326; and of various other records from public offices in London.

"To Edward Swinburne, Sen., Esq., of Capheaton, for numerous

* Another volume then in the press, published in 1828.
† For the Bishop's letter here printed see above, p. 70.

drawings for this work; the engraving and impressions of the View of the Old Bridge of Woodburn, at page 167; and for many other valuable favours.

"To Robert Surtees, Esq., of Mainsforth, for 10l. towards the embellishments of this work, and for a copy of his elaborate and splendid History of the County of Durham.

"To the Rev. Archdeacon Singleton, for the engraving of the vignette of Elsdon Castle, and the Mote-hills there, given at page 1, and for much judicious information respecting Redesdale.

"To W. C. Trevelyan, of Wallington, Esq., for three hundred impressions of the view of Wallington, at p. 277; for transcripts of the Ogle and Fenwick Deeds from the Lansdowne MS. 326; for numerous extracts from MSS. in the British Museum, the Bodleian Library in Oxford, the Advocates' Library in Edinburgh; from deeds and papers at Corby Castle, Wallington, and Nether Witton; and for his friendly and unremitting attention to furnish materials, and give interest and accuracy to this work.

"For introductions or access to record offices, public libraries, and collections of historical papers I owe obligations to Richard Grey, Esq., of the Auditor of the Land Revenue's Office; to John Caley, Esq., Keeper of the Records in the Chapter House and Augmentation Office; to J. Bayley, Esq., of the Tower; to Nicholas Carlisle, Esq., Secretary to the Antiquarian Society; to Sir Charles Grey, Lord Chief Justice at Calcutta; and to Dr. Copleston, Provost of Oriel College, Oxford.

"I am also greatly indebted for free access to the libraries at Capheaton and Wallington; for the loan of books from the collection at Little Harle Tower; to the Committees of the Literary and Philosophical and Antiquarian Societies of Newcastle, for leave to keep their books beyond the time allowed to other ordinary members; also for the loan of books by Messrs. John Adamson and John Trotter Brockett, FF.A.S. London, &c.; by Mr. John Murray, Surgeon, Newcastle; and by Mr. Thomas Fenwick of Dipton.

"For the communication of materials to the work and access to private collections of family muniments my obligations are also numerous. To Sir M. W. Ridley, of Blagdon, Bart., M.P., for the loan of a collection of ancient charters respecting Stannington, Plessey, Shotton, and other places in that neighbourhood, referred to in this work under the title of *Cartæ Ridleyana*. To Sir C. M. L. Monck, of Belsay Castle, Bart., for many papers respecting his own family, and for transcripts of the Lisle and Widdrington Charters by Dodsworth, in the Lansdowne MS. No.

326.; and also of the Lisle Muniments from the Harleian MS. No.
2.101; to Sir David Smith, Bart., for permission to make extracts from
his large and curious collection of Delineations and Descriptions of
Camps and of Historical Gleanings of Materials respecting Northumberland; to Cuthbert Ellison, of Hebburn Hall, Esq., M.P. (my earliest
patron and kind benefactor), for access in his record-room to the deeds of
his Northumberland estates; to William Ord, of Whitfield, Esq., M.P., for
permission to copy several charters of the Kings of Scotland, an ancient
chartulary of the Whitfield family, and other curious historical articles,
preserved among the muniments of his estates; to Thomas Purvis, Esq.,
of Lincoln's Inn, barrister-at-law, for several extracts from books and
MSS. in the British Museum.

" To the Rev. James Raine, M.A., Rector of Meldon, &c., my thanks
are especially due for permission to copy a large collection of extracts
from Marriage Bonds, Administrations, and Wills, respecting Northumberland families, made by himself, from the originals in the Registrar's office in Durham. These extracts occupy a volume in my own
collection of nearly 1,000 closely-written demy octavo pages, and are
referred to in this work under the name of *Raine's* TESTAMENTA. Besides
which I have, at different times, enriched my stock of materials with
copies of numerous charters, transcribed by Mr. Raine, from deeds and
other ancient muniments in the Treasury or the Chartularies of the
Cathedral Church of Durham, and with much genealogical information
copied by himself, or the late Mr. Taylor, from MSS. in the British
Museum, and from a variety of other sources.

" To Miss Emma Trevelyan, of Wallington, I owe a great obligation
for copies of various charters from the Lansdowne MS. 326; for extracts
from ' An Alphabetical List of the Heirs of the Noble Families of
England,' in the Cottonian Library, Claudius C. viii.; for the transcript of
Sir Robert Bowes's Survey of the Borders in 1551, in the same collection, Titus F. xiii., and printed in Part III., Vol. ii., between pages 208
and 248; for a chronological index of Northumberland matters in Ho-
linshed's Chronicle of England, and in several volumes of the Year
Books; for copying two volumes of Raine's Testamenta; for putting into
my hands a large and curious collection of original papers respecting
many families and places in this county; and for many curious traditionary tales derived from old people in the neighbourhood of Wallington.

"To Miss Swinburne, of Capheaton, I am also indebted for several
beautiful drawings for this work; for extracts from charters in the

British Museum, and from books in the library at Capheaton; and to Miss Elizabeth Swinburne, for transcribing two volumes of Raine's Testamenta, and several other papers.

" While my gratitude and my thanks are particularly due to my friend the Rev. A. Hedley, M.A., of Whitfield, for copious extracts from the Registers and Parish Books of Warkworth and Edlingham, and for great zeal in promoting the best interest of this work, I stand much in need of his forbearance and pardon for having differed from him in the derivation of the names of a few places, especially because I saw his Etymological paper before it was printed in the Transactions of the Newcastle Antiquarian Society, and was much gratified by its ingenuity and the justness of the rules which it lays down for analysing the origin of the names of places.   The fact is, that many of my own derivations are mere etymological speculations, but such as I have imagined to be founded on rules of just criticism, and have occurred to me in examining the situations of places, and since I began to write this volume.   ' Hoc autem solum malè metuo, ne in etymologiis et conjecturis paulo quibus-dam videar esse audacior: quas tamen, ut scientes medici vulnera, levi et pendente manu tracto; si vero ex Platonis præcepto rei naturam non exprimant, si non sint liquidæ, ex natura ipsa petitæ, explodantur, ejiciantur, exulent.'  (Camden.)

" To Mr. Edward Walker, the proprietor and editor of the Newcastle Courant, I am indebted for the use of the file of that paper, and for many favours and attentions to this work, especially for his liberality in procuring Doomsday and other types, for the especial purpose of printing it.

" My thanks are also due to Mr. Thomas Bell, land-surveyor, New-castle, for access to his extensive collection of pedigrees of North-umberland families; and to his brother, Mr. John Bell, land-surveyor, Windmill Hills, Gateshead, for a volume of Entries of Presentments, &c., at the Visitations of Archdeacon Turner, about the year 1681.

" And, besides this catalogue of acknowledgments, I am indebted for many special obligations which are owned in the body of the work; and am every day, in prosecuting my inquiries, receiving information for the work, or attentions to myself, for which I feel obligations which I can never repay, and gratitude which cannot be extinguished but with my life; but which, on account of the greatness of their number, I have no room to particularize.

" ALTERATION IN THE PLAN OF THE WORK.—The volume of Records, published in 1820, was first printed off with this title-page—'A History of Northumberland, &c., Part III. Vol. i., containing Ancient Records and Historical Papers;' but, the vignette for it being but too finely cut to give a good impression on the kind of paper on which it was printed, the author was induced to cancel it; and, in conformity with the first prospectus of the work, the volume in the new title-page was called 'Vol. V. being the first vol. of part III. and containing, &c.' Since that time, and especially during my experience in writing this volume, I find that Part II., containing the Parochial History, cannot be comprised in three volumes of such size as can be sold without loss, at the prices of two guineas on demy, or three guineas on royal paper. In fulfilling my engagement with the public to complete this work, I therefore began to feel myself in this dilemma—either to omit the mention of many places and subjects altogether, and therefore to write a very imperfect work; or treat them copiously, and suffer loss; or to increase the number of volumes in Part II., and thus throw the expense of getting up the work upon the purchasers of it. In this volume I have combined the two latter plans, as founded most, in my own judgment, upon equity and utility. To suit this new arrangement, a new title-page, table of vignettes, contents, &c. for the volume of records already published, will be given with the second volume of Part III., which is expected to be ready for delivery in the course of this year; and, both in it, and the volume I now submit to the public, it will be seen that this alteration has originated in no sordid views of gain myself; but altogether in a misconception respecting the space which the topographical history of the county would occupy. For, when I sent the first copy of the present volume to press, I expected that all I could have to say about Morpeth Deanery might be comprised in less than one volume; but I had not proceeded far with the history of the franchise of Redesdale, and of the Umfreville family, before I began to find my narrative, in the large type in which it was printed, swelling into so great a bulk, that I must either relinquish the plan I had begun upon, or print in a smaller type. The expedient I fell upon, of weaving family history into the pedigrees, at first seemed so novel, and out of the ordinary way, that I had apprehensions that the cry of innovation against it might silence all considerations in its favour from the advantages it offered of putting much information into small compass; but after about two-thirds of the volume was printed off, I found a precedent for the plan in Sir Richard Heron's Genealogical Tables of the Heron family, which relieved me from all grounds of fear on that head. Want of room also led me to crowd all the minor articles into MISCELLANEA under each general head; by which I was enabled to press three times more matter into a page than could have been done in the pica size, in which I originally proposed to publish the whole work.

When the reader, therefore, knows that the compositor's charge for setting up the types is the same for equal quantities in number, of the smallest kind as the largest, and for the pedigrees and all column work much greater still, I hope he will absolve me from all charges of avarice and deception in deviating from my original plan. Remuneration for my own labour, from the number of copies I have printed, cannot I find be expected. I have, therefore, put it out of my present calculations, and must endeavour to content myself with the hope, that if I can only procure patronage to allow me to go on with the undertaking without loss, and live to see it completed, I shall have reward in the reflection that some portion of my life has been usefully employed, and that I have done something for the age in which I have been permitted to live.

"MINUTENESS OF THE DESCRIPTIONS.—For, though the species of literature which now engages my attention, and to which my mind had an early bias, cannot be ranked high in the scale of letters, I have frequently thought that it deserves, and unobservedly receives, a much higher degree of consideration and attention, from all ranks of persons, than is generally supposed. Let any one reflect, only for a little, how much of the elements of geography, of statistics, of the general and natural history of a country, and especially of the real history of the human race, both as individuals and as families and tribes, is to be found in parochial history, and he will not, I am persuaded, rank it among the inferior and unimportant productions of the human mind; nor condemn me for having introduced so much detail into the portion I have finished.

"I know the cavilling that is frequently made against filling works of this kind with pedigrees, and especially with *pedigrees of extinct families*. But if nothing is to be said but about the living and their ancestors, where are the 'mighty dead' of all nations and tongues, whose titles and race have become extinct, but whose deeds are worthy of remembrance, to be spoken of? It it be thought a thing of credit and importance among some to be skilled in and preserve the pedigrees and characters of horses, and horned cattle, surely it cannot be thought an indifferent matter to keep the genealogies of man clear and distinct, and to record their character and deeds, for the experience of future ages! In this work numerous individuals, whose names had been forgotten, have been brought a second time upon the stage of life—successive generations of whole families come under review—fathers, mothers, children, peaceful possessors of the earth, occupied in useful and ordinary pursuits—with many bold and ambitious characters moving in the host, and statesmen and warriors bidding them do their will, and stirring them up to the temper of their times. Than the genealogies which carry back families into remote apocryphal descents, which had no more existence than Geoffry of Monmouth's Brutus—the Trojan who slew the giant Gog-magog, and established himself and his dynasty of fabulous kings—Ludhudibras, Mulmuchius, and others of harmonious and magical name on the thrones of Britain, nothing can be better subjects of ridicule and contempt. But my own observation among men has led me to this con-clusion—that, however justly they may despise the senile patrician con-sequence that makes a vain-glorious parade of its family tree and armorial insignia, there are none who rise to any distinction in life but would be glad to carry back the line of their ancestors into ancient times; and that people who have fallen into decay, when they had nothing else left to boast of, have had a pride in ancestry. What greater insult can be offered to a person than to remind him of the meanness of his birth? Or what fills a man with more honourable pride than to be told of the worthy deeds of a distinguished progenitor, or to show the history of his forefathers into remote ages, in clear and unbroken con-nection? I therefore hold, that the modesty which treats such honours and distinctions with apparent indifference is all affected, and has as little sincerity in it as hungry bashfulness when it says nay to food, or Cæsar's refusing a crown when ' he would fain have had it.'

With respect to *minuteness in topographical* descriptions, I would ask—What spot of earth is there which has not something re-markable about it, to the eye and the mind that have once been accustomed to examine everything in nature, or connected with the history of man? Civilised man, wherever he goes, sees some-thing to examine, something new to engage his attention; some rock, or mineral, or plant, or colony of microscopic creatures inhabiting that plant; trace of some temple, camp, or grave, that rendered them awful, or powerful, or sacred in some age. While there are some who love to study the heavens—the laws and positions of the worlds, and systems of worlds, that float in the immensity of space, there are others whose genius leads them to the less noble but still interesting study of review-ing, within the neighbourhood in which they live, the evidences which God has written in the rocks of the changes which our globe under-went in its progress to perfection; of tracing the hand of wisdom and

goodness forming its surface and its soils to the infinite purposes to
which they are adapted; from records and remains of their works, of
deducing the history of the several successive tribes and generations of
people that have tenanted it, their laws, manners, customs, and various
fortunes; which of them was distinguished for his virtues, and the
benefits he did to his country and his time; which moved in mischief,
and shook the bulwarks of social order. For what man is there, who
when he hears the place of his birth, and the hills and lands of his forefathers, made the subjects of these various histories and inquiries, does
not glory in them, and feel a love and a veneration for them far above
aught that the dull and incurious people can imagine who hear no such
recitals about the places in which they were born, or the fields that
nurtured them? What is it but this rational and virtuous pride for
one's country, which is the flame and soul of patriotism? 'I know not
what it is,' says Cicero, ' and what the hidden principle in my soul and
senses is, that makes me overjoyed with the place of my birth, if it be
not the same which made the wisest of men exclaim: 'If I could but
see Ithaca I would abandon the hope of immortality;' and then he brings
in Atticus elucidating the theory of this attachment; 'I take none other
but this to be the true cause why you come with greater pleasure here,
and delight so much in this place, but the same which makes me more
attached to this villa and to all this place in which you were born and
bred up; for we are drawn by I know not what bonds to the places
where there are memorials of those whom we love and esteem. For
Athens, the place of my birth, does not so much delight me with the
magnificent works and the fine arts of the ancients, as with the recollection of its great men, where each of them dwelt, where he sat, where he
pleaded; and I wistfully gaze even upon their tombs.'

"When Camden wrote his Britannia, the number of readers was
comparatively few to what they are at present; and his work of course
was of a general nature. Roman remains, fields of battle, castles,
some remarkable seats, persons, or productions were the only objects
that attracted the notice of the topographical historian in those days.
Moderns have introduced more figures into their pictures. And if any
should imagine that I have put many subjects and circumstances into
this work which are unworthy of notice, I would beg them to consider,
that many things in a remote village may be curious and interesting to
its owners, or its old inhabitants, which will fail to interest persons at
a distance: that I judged of the historical value of many subjects by the
anxiety I found to see them noticed; but that I have also rejected great

masses of information that have been put into my hand; and, while I have often had much difficulty in coming at the truth in matters of real importance, I have also lost much time by being taken to great distances to view some reputed camp, or cairn, or standing stone, which I found to be nothing more than an old border night-fold, or heap of stones thrown together at the first ridding or putting a piece of land into cultivation, or perhaps a rough pillar set up for cattle to rub against. With all my antiquarian garrulity, I have however cautiously, and with the best use of my judgment, endeavoured to omit all discussions about rights, and everything of a troublesome and mischievous tendency; and while I may not have been over scrupulously obedient to the poet's injunction, ' nothing extenuate', I am sure I have ' set down naught in malice.'

" ERRORS AND OMISSIONS.—That my prayer for the kind indulgence of scholars has no hypocrisy in it, or affectation of humility in my own performance, the APPENDIX of additions and corrections at page 387 is a proof sufficiently strong; but which candour and the love of truth compel me to make. Many of the *errors* might have been unnoticed, and would thus have been overlooked by general readers. Intelligent antiquarian critics know how difficult it is to keep works of this kind entirely free from mistakes, and will have the sagacity to see that many of those which I have corrected are not of my own making but are to be attributed to wrong information. To the carpings of the petty critics and comma-hunters I am deaf: for, as Cicero asks, ' Quis est qui totum diem jaculans non aliquando collineet ? ' and I may say with Camden, ' Errata possint esse plura ab imperitia—Quis enim tam peritus ut in cæco hoc antiquitatis mari cum Tempore colluctatus scopulis non allidatur?' The *additions* teach me this lesson—that, how long soever I had deferred beginning to print, new researches would have continually been producing new facts and illustrations: for even since the Appendix went to press I have met with several curious papers that might very properly have had a place in it.

" DELAY.—In the preface to the first volume of the third part, the author explained his reasons for publishing that part before the first and second: and in July, 1825, had printed as far as the 248th page of the second and concluding volume of Part III., when he was induced by the representations of friends on whose judgment he places great reliance, to offer to the public a volume of PAROCHIAL HISTORY, before he finally nauseated its taste by another of dry antiquarian records. That the plan he was proceeding upon was calculated to give accuracy and

clearness of arrangement and narrative to the general work, at less expense
and trouble to himself than any other he had been able to think of,
he is well convinced: but he willingly yielded to a temporary interruption of its progress to satisfy a desire which he is persuaded originated
in no intention of increasing his labours or his charges, but in a wish to
see how he was able to illustrate the history of the interesting county,
of which he had ventured upon the difficult and perilous task of becoming the historian.

"The deviation from the plan which he published on the cover of
the Gentleman's Magazine in 1819 will partly account for the long,
and to himself most painful, delay that has occurred between the publication of this volume and of that which came out in the conclusion of
the year 1820. For two years after that time, his leisure hours were
wholly occupied in procuring means for rebuilding the chapel of
Heworth, and in seeing the contract for that purpose carried into effect.
This was followed by a long and afflicting sickness in his family; and
in the spring of 1823 by his removal from Heworth to Whelpington and
by a series of other events, which kept it out of his power to go to press
with a regular supply of copy till the latter end of March 1824; since
which time the press has been uninterruptedly employed, and is still
proceeding with all the dispatch which his time, means, and industry
can supply, in approximating towards the conclusion of the work.

"Besides these causes of delay, he is also willing that the charge of
indolence and irresolution in beginning to work up the materials he had
collected may be brought against him; with this qualification, however,
that few days in the last seven years have passed by without finding
him engaged in some research connected with the subject of this work;
in adding new materials to its stock: in methodising and making
indexes to these 'primordia rerum' as they grew into volumes: or in
some other manner in putting himself, more and more, into a state of
beginning to compose the Parochial History with more ease, and certainty of accuracy, than he could have have done on any preceding
day. That this sin of procrastination is not peculiar to himself, the
numerous collections for county and parochial histories extant in the
libraries of the empire may be mentioned as evidence. The thirst for
collecting materials for works of this kind is often stronger than the
resolution to begin so put them into proper historical form, and prepare
them for press. The amateur artist, in his passion to accumulate
original sketches to compose from, traverses glens and mountains, the
shores of lakes and oceans, visits the palaces of kings, the mansions of

the nobility, the castles of ancient barons, the ruins of monastical edi-fices, tombs, and shrines—he enters temples, senate-houses, theatres, prisons—studies all that is great, or terrible, or lovely in nature, and thus fills his portfolios with designs and details for composition which would take up the age of a planet to colour and to finish. The anti-quary often digs up more of the crude ore of the history of former ages in the zeal of early life, than the study and contemplation of riper years, protracted into extreme old age, can fuse and form into useful, or ornamental, or curious literature. In all arts and sciences it requires much greater courage to begin, and steady perseverance to go on with and to finish any work, than to collect the materials for it. When the lapidary has filled his cabinets with rough specimens of every species of precious stones, and his workshop with wheels and polishing dusts, he may have completed the most expensive part of his establishment; but his skill and the profit of his art can be tested only by the brightness he can bring out of his gems, the beauty of the designs he can put upon them, and by the evenness of the lustre which shines in every distinct series of jewels which he classes together. It is not a seat in parlia-ment, or being called to the bar, that makes a man an eloquent de-fender of his country's rights, or a powerful advocate of the cause of justice. Thousands that enter the threshold of the temple of glory never dare begin to ascend the dangerous way that leads to its summit; and the peril of bringing ruin upon a large and beloved family, and dubiousness in his own powers, were not among the least of the causes which kept the eye of the author of the present work fixed so long upon the floor of that temple, before he could dare to turn them up to the dazzling light that beams over it—or his feet into the dizzy road by which it is ascended. The fate of rashness—to have 'MAGNIS EXCIDIT AUSIS' inscribed on his tomb—may be the only and the empty honour which his children can derive from his labours. His die, however, is cast. Pleas for procrastination can no longer avail him; and whether he has formed a fallacious judgment of his own strength, and shall fail in his arduous undertaking, or he shall have the good fortune to be cheered along his road by the approbation of his readers, he waits the issue of the decision with the hopes and fears of a candidate for their favourable opinion.

"J. H.

"*Whelpington Vicarage House, Aug.* 7, 1827."

Of the embellishments in this volume, which are more numerous and of better execution than those in that of 1820, the following is a list, with the names of their draughtsmen and engravers. Some of the vignettes are peculiarly tasteful and elegant. Not fewer than four ladies appear to have been contributors of drawings. I must be forgiven for including them in the list of *draughtsmen.*

## PLATES, VIGNETTES, ETC. IN THIS VOLUME.

| Page. | Subject. | Designed by | Engraved by |
|---|---|---|---|
| | Elsden Church (on title) | Edw. Swinburne, Esq. . | Isaac Nicholson |
| 1. | Elsden Castle and Mote Hills | ditto . . . . . . | William Collard |
| 96. | Umfreville arms on Elsden Castle | Isaac Nicholson . . . | Isaac Nicholson |
| 149. | High Rochester in Bremenium | Her Grace the Duchess of Northumberland | F. C. Lewis, London |
| 166. | Robin of Risingham . . | The author, and partly from Horsley | Isaac Nicholson |
| 167. | Woodburn Old Bridge * . | Edw. Swinburne, Esq. . | Wm. Miller, Edinburgh |
| 172. | The Rede at the Hall Yards, East Woodburn | ditto . . . . . | W. H. Lizars, ditto |
| 175. | Plan of Habitancum . . | The author . . . . . | Isaac Nicholson |
| 178. | A Roman Tablet . . . | From Horsley and others | Ditto |
| 182 and 183. | Roman Antiquities | Horsley and Gent. Mag. | Ditto |
| 189. | Bolt House, Whelpington | Isaac Nicholson . . . | Ditto |
| 190. | Vicarage Scar, ditto . . | Miss Swinburne . . . | Ditto |
| 203. | Whelpington Church . . | Isaac Nicholson . . . | Ditto |
| 235. | Kirkharle Church . . . | Miss Swinburne . . . | Ditto |
| 277. | Wallington . . . . . | Miss Emma Trevelyan . | W. H. Lizars |
| 282. | Ancient Gravestones at Cambo | Miss Swinburne and the late Miss F. E. Swinburne | Isaac Nicholson |
| 292. | Shaftoe Hall and Punch Bowl Stone | Edw. Swinburne, Esq. . | Ditto |
| 296. | Hartburn Church . . . | Isaac Nicholson . . . | Ditto |
| 338. | Bolam Church . . . . | ditto . . . . . | Ditto |
| 348. | The Poind and his Man . | The author . . . . . | Ditto |
| 377. | Whalton Church . . . | Mr. T. Sopwith, Newcastle | Ditto |
| 410. | Corsenside Church . . . | The author . . . . | Ditto |

* For this elegant engraving the bill paid to Mr. William Miller, the artist by whom it was executed, was as follows : " Engraving Woodburn Bridge 12l. 12s. Copper and lettering 14s. Printing 50 royal and 250 demy 1l. 1s. Paper for ditto 1l. 2s."

The book was dedicated to the Duke of Northumberland.

### FROM ARCHDEACON SINGLETON.

" MY DEAR SIR,                                    Elsdon Castle, Sept. 3, 1827.

" The Duke very readily accepts the compliment you propose to
him, and will feel happy in having his name connected with a work
creditable in itself, and undertaken by a gentleman whose talents and
acquirements he so fully appreciates.

" I remain, my dear Sir, yours very truly,

" THOS. SINGLETON.

" Rev. J. Hodgson."

This volume, as has been remarked above, is exclusively
devoted to parochial history; and, although it be the author's first
attempt at any thing more than a mere cursory topographical view,
like those of his Northumberland and Westmerland in the
Beauties of England and Wales, and his Picture of Newcastle, yet
it gives proofs in abundance that he was in every respect equal to
the more comprehensive task which had long been the subject of
his thoughts and his daily occupation.   His earlier topographical
essays had served as the school in which he had qualified himself
for higher undertakings; and now at length in the year 1827 he
comes forth as a county historian in the true and legitimate sense
of the term.   For four years his body and mind had been comparatively at ease from the laborious occupations, the wear and
tear, of a populous parish.   The very nature and circumstances of
the spiritual duties in which he now found himself engaged had
a direct and wholesome tendency to invigorate his constitution,
and render him less liable to those frequent attacks of ill health
under which he had so often laboured from his youth upwards.
He was at all times an early riser from his bed, and a professional
ramble upon the hills in the clear and bracing atmosphere of a
Northumbrian morning could not fail to send him home in spirits
for the labours of his pen.   Accordingly this portion of his
history gives manifest indications that his mind was at ease, and
his occupation one after his own heart.

And further, as the result of reflection and a due appreciation of the requirements of the period, it will be found upon examination that this volume is not one of mere dry methodical arrangements, according to long-established usage—of names and dates, of abstracts of title or bare pedigrees of families, the names of which not noble or generous deeds, but acres alone, have kept alive and have handed down to posterity.    On the contrary it studiously deals on suitable occasions with real men and their manners, their way of living in private domestic life, their hopes and fears, their joys and sorrows, their successes and disappointments in their journey through the world.    With a few exceptions, and a few only, our county histories till the commencement of the present century were the dullest of all dull publications.    They detail names and facts and dates with great accuracy, but they do nothing more.    Even Dugdale himself is no exception.    Not one flower of taste or imagination or romance sheds its fragrance in their pages.    We look in vain in them for the character of the people who figured from time to time in the districts which they profess to describe, and their general rule is to tell us literally nothing upon which a thoughtful reader might reflect at his leisure, and compare an existing state of society with those of other periods when civilization was in its infancy, and modern discoveries were not even dreamt of.    Sketches of descent of property, church notes which, when ventured upon architecturally, are almost invariably wrong, lists of incumbents, copies of monuments which in design and inscription (upon their veracity I make no remark) are more frequently better suited to a heathen temple than a Christian church, and proofless pedigrees of families who perhaps never conferred one single boon upon the world, " the tenth transmitters of a foolish face," constitute the staple of the books to which I refer.    But with Dr. Whitaker a better period and feeling set in. His example was soon followed by others, and our county histories began to be, not only books of reference, mere epitomes of facts and dates, but repositories abounding with matter for reflection, store-houses of moral information, pictures of men and manners in by-gone times, something to be read and remembered, not merely by the land-owners and lawyers of their respective districts, but by every one whose pleasure it might be to repeople in his imagination the towns and villages, the castles and monasteries of

the land, as they existed at former periods of the history of a
nation making daily discoveries and daily progress for the better
or the worse, in manners and modes of living. With these notions
Hodgson was deeply imbued, and those portions of his book which
are devoted to family or parochial history contain many thoughtful passages which an attentive reader may remember and make
the subject of his meditations. But in nothing has our author
manifested his judgment more than in passing over in silence such
particulars in family history, when they have fallen in his way,
as might have given pain to existing representatives. Feelingly
and creditably to himself has he said, " As I have stood by the stream
of time, I have perhaps collected, in its passage down it, many
an unimportant fact; but I know that I have suffered many a
foul tale of slander and dishonour to glide silently past me, and to
sink in its course."*

The volume before us comprises the history of the parishes of
Elsdon, Corsenside,† Whelpington, Kirkharle, Hartburn with the
chapelry of Netherwitton, Bolam, and Whalton, together with a
long preliminary account of the Franchise of Redesdale, occupying
upwards of eighty pages, and tracing its history and that of its
owners from the Umfrevilles downwards to the present time—the
whole volume containing an immense mass of historical matter
carefully arranged, and exhausting, as it would appear, every
ordinary source of information. That nothing of importance
might be left untold, its author has thrown together, in closely
printed notes, teeming with historical novelty, the stores which he
had been collecting for many years from every quarter, all so
arranged as to cause no confusion in the mind of the reader. It
must not be imagined that these notes are mere vouchers or sup-
plemental after-thoughts and condensations, to fill up an empty
portion of a page, or to give a showy notion of pains-taking,
where in reality but little pains had been bestowed. They are
historical authorities and condensations, especially necessary in
amplification of the narrative beneath which they stand, and they

* Hist. Part II. vol. ii. pref. v.
† Of this name Hodgson attempts no derivation. It is probably *Crossanset*, the *place or situation of the crosses.*

H 2

have in general just as much of novelty and authority in them as
the text itself to which they are appended.    They prove that,
though limited in space, and still· more in purse, Hodgson was
determined to narrate, but in a more economical way both for
himself and his readers, every thing which he had to tell, and
which it might be important for them to know.    These notes are
very striking for their minuteness; and the authorities or sources
from which they are derived are carefully recorded.

Another remarkable novelty must be mentioned, in which, as
he informs us, he imitated the example of Sir Richard Heron in
his genealogical tables of the Heron family.    His pedigrees are
arranged in lines and generations in the ordinary way, but contrary to the usual custom, with the above exception, they consist
of something more than a mere concatenation of names with
nothing more than mere dates of births, marriages and deaths.
In general, under each person, much is given of personal history
—occasionally the additions of this kind extend to a considerable
length, and the whole is so managed, that little or no difficulty
presents itself to the reader.    By this process an immense space
is saved for other purposes.    The technical arrangement of his
pedigrees in this way cost Hodgson much labour.    His copy was
drawn up by his own hand in so precise a manner, so skilfully and
carefully packed, as the term is, according to the size and capabilities of his page, that on the part of the compositor little thought
was required, and to him, to use an expressive phrase, it was all
plain sailing.

To these general remarks another must be added in conclusion.
For one thing this and the preceding, and all his subsequent
volumes, except the last, are most remarkable, for the copious
indexes which they contain of men and places, and even of terms
and things.    Such aids and assistances are of the highest value to
an inquirer.    Hodgson's uniform anxiety in this respect to lighten
the labours of his readers cannot fail to strike every one who has
occasion to consult his volumes.

However reluctant I may be to swell out this memoir with
allusions to Mr. Hodgson's printed works, where they are not of
a personal nature, yet it is but justice to him to draw the attention

of the reader to a few subjects in the present volume which he has treated very happily, and which are in themselves of conꞏderable interest.

The great Roman subjects of attraction in the present portion of the History of Northumberland, are the Camps of Bremenium or Rochester, and Habitancum or Risingham; together with the representation on the face of a rock of that mysterious personage Robin of Risingham, with his Phrygian bonnet and toga and tunic, and dog and hare. These subjects he has approached after the fashion of a *velitatio* in the days of his own Romans, preparatory to a graver attack in an after-year. They served as an exercise for a nobler work, the History of the Wall, in a future volume, which in due time made its appearance. Robin, however, no longer exists as he stands below; or if any portion of him remain it is only from his girdle downwards.

The upper part of his body has been hewn away and converted into gate-posts.*

On the subject of Roman antiquities it may be briefly remarked that, probably after the statements in p. 146 of the volume before us, we shall not hear much more of Richard of Cirencester's Treatise "De Situ Britanniæ" as an authority to be relied on. The conclusion to which Hodgson had arrived after a course of reasoning on the subject, which he takes care to specify, is as follows. "I think it my duty frankly to confess, with all due deference to the able critics who have admired the clearness and sagacity of that work, and have written in defence of its authenticity, that after much reflection on the subject my faith in its credit has entirely given way."——"If Mr. Bertram" (in reality, in Hodgson's opinion, its author) "had employed his time and talents in arranging the information which the Greek and Roman authors contain respecting Britain, in their clear historical light and order, and in illustrating them with his own observations, he could not have failed to confer a considerable benefit upon the literature of his country; but in doing what he did, in our present view of the matter, his time was lost, and Dr. Stukeley's antiquarian glory much sullied by his taking the obstetrical office of bringing the spurious offspring of his friend's labour into the world."

The Franchise of Redesdale is an interesting subject. It was in fact a barony with royal power, resembling the palatinate jurisdiction of the see of Durham; and its possessor was invested with this power for the same purposes for which the Bishops of Durham and the Lords Marchers of Wales exercised a similar authority. In the latter case there was Wales to guard against, and here in the north there was Scotland. Mr. Hodgson has traced the history of this franchise in an elaborate way through a galaxy of illustrious names of its possessors from time to time—the Umfrevilles, the family of Taylboys, the Crown from Henry the Eighth till James the First, the Humes, the Howards, and the Percys. Long however before this franchise was abolished by law, so little had it done to preserve order and obedience, even

---

* See a notice of this emblematical figure in Scott's Rokeby, and also a lamentation for its partial destruction in the preface to his Ivanhoe.

within its own limits, as to lead Hodgson to the conclusion that
"it was the prolific mother of all the disorders, the crimes, and
the peculiarities for which the population here was so long
notorious, and for which there was no certain cure but that
which has at length subdued the malady under which they
laboured, namely, community of interest in all civil matters with
the country around them." (p. 28.)   The most harrowing accounts
of crimes and villanies within this district, even when it was at
peace with Scotland, Englishmen against Englishmen, might be
given from authentic sources.   When, however, there was open
war with Scotland, or a hollow truce, domestic feuds were for a
while laid aside, but not forgotten.   The flame of internal hatred
and malice broke forth with greater violence when there was no
common enemy to withstand.   Restraint and control there were
none.   One lord of the franchise, one whose duty it was to
administer justice and set a good example, Sir Robert de Umfreville, acquired the far-famed name of " Robin Mendmarket " from
the corn and cattle which it was his delight and almost daily habit
to steal from Scotland and sell at a cheap rate in England.   He
even took care to train up his nephew and successor, whilst a
mere boy, in this kind of " military glory."   A Report is preserved in the British Museum from a Warden of the English
Marches in the time of Queen Elizabeth in which the writer
enumerates the horses, oxen, sheep, &c. stolen by Scotland since
his last letter, and gravely proceeds to express his thankfulness in
becoming terms that England had been enabled to steal more
from Scotland during the period in question.

To the Battle of Otterburn, better known by the world-wide
name of Chevy Chase,* Hodgson has devoted not fewer than

* The admirers of the favourite old Ballads of CHEVY CHASE are probably not aware
of the real origin of the name.  The " Forest of Cheviot," and its bucks and does, are
doubtless considered to account for the appellation.  Every thing, however, in these
songs connected with hounds and horns and deer must be rejected as poetical embellishments.  It is most certain from the history of the inroad, by whatever authority,
that military glory, and not the pleasures of the chase, was the object of the invaders,
and it is equally certain that on their way into England the Scots did not even come
near the Cheviot Hills.  Whence then have we the name of Chevy Chase?  An old
French word, familiar in the mouths of En glishmen at the period of the conflict may

seventeen closely printed pages, and has brought together under
one head the great mass of information from manuscript or

perhaps answer the question. The battle of Otterburn was fought in 1388. For
nearly half a century before this date, with few interruptions, an English army had
been as it were domiciled in France, at one time engaged in active warfare, and at
another making hostile inroads into the districts bordering upon its encampments, to
keep alive the spirit of its officers and soldiers. For these expeditions the current name
was " chevauchées," a term thus written by Cotgrave in his Dictionary, and explained
by him to mean " a riding, travelling, journeying, a road or course, a coursing to and
fro on horseback." That the word was used in a warlike sense we have a proof in
Chaucer, and in the self-same passage an instance of its having been introduced into
the English language upon the return of our armies, and a word of known meaning at
the very period of the Battle of Otterburn. Chaucer began to write his Canterbury
Tales in 1382, and in his description of the " Yonge Squier " he tells us—

> " He hadde be somtime in chevachie
> In Flaundres, in Artois, and in Picardie,
> And borne him wel, as of so litel space,
> In hope to stonden in his ladies grace."

Now Tyrwhitt in his edition of Chaucer's Works, in a note upon this passage,
informs us that the word *chevachie* is in French *chevauchée*, and that " it most properly
means an expedition with a small party of cavalry, but is often used generally for any
military expedition. Hollinshed (continues he) calls it *a rode;*" the very term, I
may add, in long and common use upon the Borders for an inroad of the character and
with the object of that which ended in the capture of Percy and the death of Douglas
in the battle before us :—

> " And, by my faith, the gate-ward said,
>    I think 'twill prove a *warden raid*."—*Lay of the Last Minstrel.*

That the word " chivauchée " had become naturalised in England even in a ludi-
crous sense we have a further proof in Chaucer :—

> " And with this speche the coke waxed all wraw,
> And on the manciple he gan nod fast
> For lacke of speche; and doun his hors him cast,
> Wher as he lay, til that men him up toke :
> This was a faire chivachee of a coke."—*The Manciple's Prol.*

I may add that Mr. Wright, in his late admirable edition of Chaucer, explains the
word *chivachie* in the same way as Cotgrave and Tyrwhitt, and suggests its becoming
adopted in England by the process to which I have above referred. He does not
however allude to the term Chevy Chase in confirmation of his statements.

It is admitted that the earlier of the two ballads of Chevy Chase says little of hunting. The second however makes the chase the main object of the invaders. This is
natural. The real origin of the term had been forgotten, and the chase and its exciting allurements were subjects too tempting to the poetical invention of its author to
be passed over in silence with such a name as Chevy Chase before him. The earlier
of the ballads is at least a century and a half later than the battle. I would only add
that to the above origin must, I think, be attributed the *chevy* of the modern school-boy.

printed sources which he had collected on that animating subject.
The Battle of Otterbourn has for a considerable length of time
been engaging the attention of a zealous local antiquary, Mr.
Robert White, of Newcastle, a gentleman whose pen a few years
ago, in verse or prose, gave a character of value to the " Table
Book " of Mr. Richardson; and the result of his historical reading
and personal investigations upon the field of battle, a spot familiar to him from his boyhood, is now happily before the world in
a publication very remarkable for its judicious arrangement and
fidelity of narrative.   The faithful and gentlemanly way in which
Mr. White has executed his undertaking prompts a hope that he
may be inclined to turn his mind and pen to the still more
" dismal tale "—

> " Of the stern strife and carnage drear
>     Of Floddon's fatal field,
>   Where shiver'd was fair Scotland's spear,
>     And broken was her shield."

For such a task the materials are rich and abundant, and well
do they deserve to be sifted and concentrated into a readable
book upon the comprehensive but unpretending plan of " The
Battle of Otterburn."

But Mr. White has a closer connection with the subject of our
memoir than that which arises from his having put a finishing
hand to a subject to which so many pages are devoted in the
volume before us.   He was for many years, and continues to be,
a profound admirer of Hodgson and his character.   So far did he
carry this feeling, that once upon a time (I have it from himself)
he would fain have become the village schoolmaster of Whelpington, that he might be near the object of his admiration, and
help him with his pen in his vacant hours.*   Two sonnets, to be

* I hope I may not be guilty of any breach of confidence when I make the following extract from what in strictness of speech was intended as a private communication.
The feeling which it betrays is too rare and creditable to be kept a secret :—
   " Before coming to Newcastle I was nearly brought into a position that would have
given me many opportunities of being better acquainted with Mr. Hodgson.   In 1825,
about the time when hay-cutting commences, I learned that a teacher was wanted for
the school at Whelpington, and, knowing that Mr. Hodgson was closely occupied in
writing his great work, I felt desirous above all things to be near him; hence I became

presented to the reader in the sequel, evince Mr. White's affectionate regard for the historian of Northumberland at a later
period—his deep sympathy with him in his bodily sufferings, and
with his family after he had been removed from the world.

Hodgson's pages contain the particulars of another Border
quarrel, the "Affray of the Redeswire," a warden-meeting, which
began in ill-suppressed feud and ended in blood, accompanied
with all the usual characteristics of lawless insubordination.

That antiquarian puzzle the Mote-hills of Elsdon is well
described (p. 97); and under the list of rectors we have a few
anecdotes of Lewis Dutens, a well-known literary character in his
day.  Of one in particular let me give another, and I believe a
more correct, version.  Dutens was a Frenchman; and a few of
his leading parishioners complained to the Bishop of Durham
that in his ministrations and parochial communications with his
flock his language was unintelligible.  The Bishop, according to
his custom, sent the complaint to the Rector, who must have
been a man of humour as well as learning.  On the first Sunday
after the Bishop's letter reached him, Dutens sent a message to such
of the complainants as should be at church, stating his wish to have
a few words with them after divine service.  Upon leaving the
church after the sermon, he found them waiting in the porch, and
in his usual mode of addressing them, gave them an invitation to
dinner, which they accepted.  The reader will easily see what
followed after dinner.  " You say you no understand me when I
speak to you in the church, but you understand me vary well
when in the porch I do pray you to dine with me.  I will tell
the Bishop that you do understand me vary well."  And he
heard no more of the complaint.

Hodgson's defence of John Graham, the poverty-stricken Vicar
of Corsenside, is very characteristic of its writer.  Through life it
was his invariable custom to say, if it were possible, a good word
or think a kind and favourable thought of the absent.  The

a candidate for the appointment.  Had I obtained the office I then sought, I cannot
tell you with what alacrity and devotedness I had entered into every kind of work by
which during my leisure hours I could have been of use to that remarkable man.
Copying manuscripts, surveying old camps, &c., would have brought me into my
proper element, and the whole would have been to me a perfect labour of love."

poor man had, as it appears, been reported to the authorities in 1663 as "sordid and scandalous." "At that time," says Hodgson, "he had been forty-six years vicar of the place, and could not be less than seventy years of age. His stipend was 6*l.* 13*s.* 4*d.* a year. We must not therefore consider this record respecting him as hurtful to his character, but as a picture of his abject condition; for when the sordid income on which he existed is considered, can it be matter of wonder that he had 'tattered weeds' and 'overwhelming brows,' and that 'sharp misery' should have so 'worn him to the bone,' as to give him the appearance of being scandalously sordid?" (p. 163.)

The history of the family of Swinburne and of their ancient estate at Capheaton,* is drawn up with considerable care and minuteness of description. That portions of the narrative were submitted to Sir J. E. Swinburne, whilst in the press, appears from the journal of its author; and it further appears from the same authority that certain, doubtless very true, but, as it was conceived, over laudatory passages were requested to be withdrawn. It is perhaps a subject of regret that this request should have been complied with. That they contained nothing more than an expression of the genuine sentiments and grateful feelings of their writer is certain; and men have to come after us who will have a right in us and in our history. However much we may reverence living modesty and delicacy of feeling, nothing in the shape of high desert or good example should be withheld from posterity. Had there been no Sir John Swinburne and no Edward Swinburne, Esq., his brother, there might have been no History of Northumberland by Mr. Hodgson.

In connection with the Swinburne family there is a very romantic tradition, which Hodgson has placed upon record in his pages.† Sir John Swinburne, of Capheaton, the first baronet of the name, "was sent, while a child, to a monastery in France, where a Northumbrian gentleman of the family of Radclyffe, accidentally visiting the place, recognised in his face the features of the Swinburne family. On inquiring of the monks how the boy came thither, the only answer they could give was that he

* P. 213.          † In the pedigree, p. 233.

came from England, and that an annual sum was remitted *for his board and education*. On questioning the boy himself, it was however found that he had been told that his name was Swinburne, which, with the account of his father's death, and his own mysterious disappearance from Northumberland, induced the superior of the house to permit him to return home, where, before a jury specially empannelled for that purpose, he identified himself to be the son of John Swinburne and Ann Blount, by the description he gave of the marks upon a cat and a punch-bowl, which were still in the house." The boy's father, John Swinburne, Esq., who lived in the time of the Grand Rebellion, and was a well-known royalist, was murdered at Meldon in 1643, by Captain John Salkeld of Rock, a notorious rebel; and in the confusion which succeeded, the poor boy, as it appears, had been forgotten except by those whose interest it was to keep him in obscurity.

Of the murder above alluded to a short account may be given, chiefly from Hodgson's pages, in illustration of the unhappy temper of the times, and of the results of political feeling when under excitement from other causes. Hodgson has printed the particulars of the coroner's inquest on the occasion, which terminated in a verdict of wilful murder, but the murderer made his escape, and it does not appear that he was afterwards taken and brought to justice.

The circumstances of this melancholy event, which took place on the 13th February, 1643, are briefly these. Swinburne was a loyalist, Salkeld his assassin a red-hot revolutionist. The two, with several others, among whom were Baron Venables, of Kinderton, a Cheshire gentleman, and a baron of that palatinate by courtesy, the owner also of estates in Northumberland, Sir Nicholas Thornton, of Netherwitton, and Mr. Edward Fenwick, had been feasting with George Heron, Esq., at that time the occupant of Meldon Castle, under Sir William Fenwick its owner, who resided elsewhere. Mrs. Swinburne, the wife of the murdered man, and the sister of Heron their host, had also been present, but at an early hour after dinner had taken her departure for Capheaton, her husband attending her for a short way on horseback; after which he had returned to his friends for half an hour, his servant holding his horse in readiness at the gate that he might overtake her on the road. Upon leaving the castle, however, at his final departure he was, according to the custom of the time, attended to his horse by his friends, and probably by the stirrup-cup, then and long afterwards in use on such occasions. But, before his final departure, Salkeld, who was probably in a state of intoxication, earnestly pressed him to return once more, and "drincke." With this request Swinburne declined to comply, whereupon Salkeld drew his sword, and aimed at him a blow which missed him, but drew blood from his horse. Swinburne instantly alighted to avenge the insult, and letting his cloak fall from him as he was groping for the hilt of his sword, was instantly seized whilst in that attitude by his servant, who grasped him firmly in his arms to prevent further mischief. In the mean time Salkeld availed himself of the advantage afforded by the detention of his opponent, and "came running and thrust him in the belly, which wound was his death." This is the tenor of three out of four of the depositions taken upon the occasion. The fourth, that of Baron Venables, places the affair in a somewhat different light, and gives other particulars.

"Baron Venables said he came to Mr. Swinburne and persuaded him not to be troublesome in that company: then Mr. Swinburne answered him, 'I am houlden till the knave hath slaine me:' whereupon Mr. Swinburne put his hand into his britechesse, and drew forth a part of his hand ful of bloode. Then Barron Venables called Salkeld aside, and caused him to draw forth his sword, whereon he perceaved it to be stained as it had bene in a man's bodie, about an inch and a halfe on the one side of the sword and tow inches or more on the other side of the sword. The Barron his tow men said that Salkeld drew his sword and wounded Mr. Swinburne his horse, Mr. Swinburne rideing upon him: Mr. Swinburne spurred his horse and rode a distance off and lighted from his horse and left him; threw off his cloake and drewe his sworde and walked towards Salkeld; in which time Salkeld had putt up his sword: then Mr. Swinburn his man took his mr. in his armes and there held him; and he and Mr. Edward Fenwick both perswading him to be patient: in the mean while Salkeld drew forth his swoord and came over three or four ridges and did thrust Mr. Swinburne in the bodie: then Mr. Swinburne finding himself wounded proffered to strike

Mr. Fenwick and his owne man for houlding him; and then came Baron Venables and others to perswade Mr. Swinburne to be patient."

In these days this would probably be found to have been a case of manslaughter. The unhappy gentleman lived for two days, and then died in the house of his brother-in-law, Salkeld having in the mean time taken flight. From a note connected with the proceedings it appears that there had been a former quarrel between the two, and those were not times in which wounds of that nature were easily healed. Salkeld is reported to have committed another murder soon afterwards.

The following letter from the host of those unhappy men, addressed to the father of Swinburne, has not yet been made public.

GEORGE HERON, Esq. of Meldon to WILLIAM SWINBURNE, Esq. of Capheaton.

"Sir,                                                   Meldon, Feb. 17, 1642.

"My sorrow for your sonn is as much as any man's, and the more that I cannot come to wait upon his funerall; for my business is of so great concernment that it would much disadvantage the cause if I should stay another day, I haveing comed back with Sr. William Fenwick yesterday (and so past one day) with a resolution to have seen him interred, and to have done my best endevor to have comforted his lady: for I heare have a sharpe censure given of me, which (God willing) I intend (at my coming back) to cleare both to you and my sister: for uppon my credit I was in the hous at that instant, neither do I think there was any gentleman there but would willingly have hazzarded himself to prevent so unhappy an accident. Thus, hopeing you will both excuse my absence, he who desires to serve both you and her rests your sorrowful friend,

"GEORGE HERON."

"For his very loveing cossen William Swinburne, Esq. Capheaton, these present."

In p. 292 there is a beautiful wood engraving from one of Mr. E. Swinburne's happiest drawings of a confused combination of granitic sand-stone rocks called Shaftoe Hall and the Punch Bowl Stone, which Hodgson thus describes.

SHAFTOE HALL, AND THE PUNCHBOWL STONE.

"The rude cavern called Shaftoe Hall is wide and lofty at its entrance, but decreases in width and height to the distance of thirty feet inwards. It is probably the combined work of nature and of art: the mouth having the appearance of being much weather-worn, and marks of tools and holes for wedges of different shapes appearing in several parts of its interior. The rock itself is traversed with layers of pebbles of the size of almonds; and it also contains decayed crystals of felspar, and in some places Mr. W. C. Trevelyan, of Wallington, has found it reddish with minute fragments of garnets. Immediately above the cavern a huge isolated mass of the same kind of rock, called the Punch Bowl Stone, has been on every side undermined by the weather, projects boldly over the brow of the crag, and has its top worn into large holes, some of which are regular hollow hemispheres, around which the wind in rainy weather drives the water they collect in constant eddies. This stone is also traversed with a stratum of large quartz pebbles, and deep gutters are worn from the basins in its top, all over which the country people who have come to visit the place have cut the initials of their names.——Is it not very probable that this cavern and the Punch Bowl Stone were a cave and a rock altar of that primitive heathen worship which prevailed all over the world from India to Britain; that the rock basins on the top of the altar were once consecrated to the Druidical Hu; as modern picnic visitors who have come here according to Whittell 'to carouse and triumph in the joys of wine' have devoted them in latter times to Bacchus?"

Here is an instance of what even a short interval of time can do, and to what surmises it can give rise, after it has erased the once well marked lines of real occurrences. The smaller cavities on the Punch Bowl Stone have doubtless been occasioned by wind and rain and frost, and above all by time, acting upon the softer portions of the rock. For the Punch Bowl itself the Newcastle Courant for the year 1725 (9 October) fully accounts, and at once demolishes the Druids and their rock basin.

It appears from this authority that upon the marriage of Sir William Blackett (a while before) "Shaftoe Vaughan, Esq. caused Shafto Craggs to be illuminated in the night," and "a large Punch Bowl was cut in the most elevated rock, which was filled with such generous liquor as was more than sufficient for the vast crowd of neighbouring inhabitants," &c.

With respect to Whittell above referred to and his poems, some information is given by Hodgson in p. 281.

Of the parish of Hartburn Mr. Hodgson gives a very detailed account—that parish of which in the course of a few years, by the kindness of another Bishop of Durham, he became the vicar. Well would it have been for him, as we gather from himself, if he had remained at Whelpington. But upon this subject more hereafter.

Pope and his history are now engaging the attention of the public. The reader will find in p. 399 a previously unpublished and very characteristic letter written by the poet to Lady Swinburne in 1709, prescribing to her at his mother's request a cure for a malady under which she was labouring. " All this, madam, my mother had written to you herself, but that she does not write at all of late, and commissions one to do it who does nothing else but write: he shall think himself very happy if these directions prove any way serviceable to your ladyship, that he may say he has, once in his life, written to some purpose."

At. p. 105 are some lines of poetry, marked as a quotation, but that they proceeded from Hodgson himself is certain. " About a quarter of a mile (says he) from Ottercops there is a very large cairn—

' Round which the booming bittern flies, and here
In May's sweet morning, amorous and aloft
His wild and high notes o'er the burial pile
The curlew sings: the lark, all life and song
In spiral flight ascends: the lapwing wheels
And wails; the plover plays his mournful pipe.' "

With Hodgson the curlew in particular was a favourite bird; its wild whistle along the edges of the moors or in the rough uncultivated places in which it delights had such charms for him that he would stay his horse and listen to it and watch its rapid motions on the wing with a peculiar pleasure.

FROM MR. EDWARD WALKER (the printer of Mr. Hodgson's History).

" DEAR SIR, Newcastle, Oct. 22, 1827.

" All your books have been some days in the binder's hands, and will be dispersed among the subscribers as fast as possible.

VOL. II. I

"In employing me you have committed an unpardonable sin, and it is already bruited about that the books are all spoiled by the difference of papers used. You must not believe this to the full extent. The fact is, that when we started, I had *royal* sufficient for a volume. Two going on together exhausted the stock. I gave a sheet to the papermaker to match, and I thought he had matched it very fairly. His moulds seem to have been rather larger, and this causes a necessity for the binder to cut the rough edges, as you will see, to bring them to the same size as the old paper. This smoothness of edges gives a whiteness which the rough edges have not, as you will perceive by looking at the top of the book; and I have no doubt that when the paper has gained age, there will be no perceptible difference, as age always mellows the colour of paper; and one batch is probably seven or eight years old, and the other not more than one. I am called into Yorkshire by the alarming illness of my mother, but I hope when I come back to find all the books distributed. Those to Alnwick Castle go to-morrow morning. I am, dear Sir, your most obedient servant,

"EDWD. WALKER."


FROM THE REV. A. HEDLEY.

"MY DEAR HODGSON,                    Rectory Whitfield, 19 Nov. 1827.

"They must be very bad to please who are not delighted with your volume, which is, I think, everything that could be wished for in a work of that kind. The mistake to which you refer in the running title I detected on the foul proof, immediately on receiving it; but it was so glaring and obvious—that I did not think of mentioning it to you, being certain that it would be corrected in the revise: it is vexing, but not of any vital importance. Could you get no friend in Newcastle to look over your proofs? You must not despond about the sale of your copies. I think I for one could get you more subscribers, and if a few more friends use similar exertions, you will not, I should hope, need much warehouse room for your books: but the want of taste and of public spirit in our Northumberland gentry is very deplorable. Pray get Richard to write out a list of your subscribers, to send to me. Is Mr. Thomson of the Register Office one? It strikes me that he said something to me about it, but my recollection on the subject is not very precise.

"Professor Pillans, I believe, subscribes. Did I not give you his name? As four guineas is not quite so formidable a sum as six, I should like to see the whole of the copies subscribed for *before the publication of the third volume.* I hope to be at Newcastle in the first week of December, when I will settle with Walker; and will you drive out to the meeting of the Antiquarian Society, that I may have the pleasure of a *pross* " de omnibus rebus et quibusdam aliis " with yourself? The year 1827 is surely not to pass over our heads without seeing each other face to face. Do try to make an errand to Newcastle. Mrs. H. begs to join in best regards to Mrs. and Miss Hodgson, and believe me, my dear Hodgson, yours ever most truly,

" ANT. HEDLEY."

To the Rev. J. RAINE.

" MY DEAR RAINE,                Whelpington, 10 Dec. 1827.

" Lest you should be sending me a writ to deliver them up without delay, I send you your Meldon papers, and the Theatre of the Greeks; for both of which I am much obliged. You shall see my sketch of Meldon before it goes to press. As yet it wants some sharpening up at home, and additional breadth and correctness given to it *in situ*—something about your little kirk, the woody sides of Wansbeck, Meldon Bridge, Revehow, and the old patriarch Joshua Delaval with his flock of fourscore goats and kids.

" Be so good as say to Mr. Tate that I have sketched out a new life of Dawes, which only waits being sent to press, till I get some facts respecting the real cause of his quarrels with the corporation of Newcastle from the archives of the body. Woodcuts of the marble and basaltic tombs, and of the house in which he lived, are done.

" Meg of Meldon, Sir William Fenwick's wife, resided at Hartington Hall with her husband, before her money ousted the Herons from their old seat at Meldon;* and after her death she had an underground coachway between the two houses, the entrance at Hartington into the subterraneous way was under an enormous block of Whin in the Hart, still used as a battling stone. There was in the memory of several persons living also a picture of her at Hartington Hall, painted on the wall, in a large brimmed hat tied down at the ears, with a ruff round her neck, a riding habit with a long waist: a cat and other hieroglyphics attended, as emblems of her unearthly powers in witching, &c.—I go to Meldon today to get a few sketches of it and Revehow.——Most truly yours,

" JOHN HODGSON."

---

* There is much of error here.—See hereafter.

## CHAPTER VI.—1828.

### To Mr. THOMAS SOPWITH.*

"DEAR SIR,                                        Whelpington, 19 Jan., 1828.

"I shall be delighted to hear that you succeed in etching. You will have no difficulty in the handling, as you can already hatch beautifully with a pen. To a novice in the art the difficulty to encounter is in the management of the acid. I do, however, suppose that the same time expended over the lithographic art, if you could be near a good lithographic press, would be a great deal more usefully employed. Richard does not think of visiting you till the spring has commenced. I have no impressions of my woodcuts separate; but long ago gave directions at Mr. Walker's office for a set to be struck off, and wonder why they have not done so. When they come you shall have a picked set.

* With this gentleman Mr. Hodgson appears to have become personally acquainted in October 1827. Mr. Sopwith was afterwards employed to survey the contemplated line of the new and easier road into Redesdale, to run in the direction of Whelpington, of which mention has been more than once made in the preceding pages; and at the period at which we have arrived he began to make himself singularly useful to Hodgson in furnishing him with sketches of churches and other subjects of interest for his History. Mr. Sopwith's drawings were remarkable for their accuracy, and from being made in general with the pen were peculiarly suited for wood engravings. The author of this Memoir is under a like obligation to Mr. Sopwith for many sketches of the same neat and faithful character for his History of North Durham, and in the last volume of Mr. Surtees's History of Durham there are several embellishments from very characteristic drawings by his pen. Mr. Sopwith is at the present time well known for his scientific pursuits, and for the fidelity and judgment with which he manages the mining concerns on the estates of the Beaumont family at Alston Moor and elsewhere. He was a few years ago employed by Government to survey the Forest of Dean. The author is under further obligation to Mr. Sopwith for the sight of such letters as he received from Mr. Hodgson during their correspondence. Of those several may be found in the following pages.

" Thank you kindly for the shoe sole,* &c., which I have given to Miss Emma Trevelyan. Mr. Henderson had some laid up in store for me. I wonder what has become of them.——Could we get permission to turn over a part of the station of Whitley Castle, subject to the condition of levelling the ground well behind our operations, and cover it with green turf as we went on?——A history of the mines of Alston Moor would be both a very curious and highly interesting work. I hope to be able to give a broad sketch of it. The miners had royal protection granted to them in 1233, and again in 1236 and 1237. In 1282 the king granted to Nicholas de Veteripont the Manor of Aldenston, to hold in fee of the King of Scotland, reserving to himself and the miners there various privileges, especially such as belonged to the Franchise of Tindale, within which Alston was then comprised. These privileges in 7 Ed. III. were confirmed by the Crown to Robert son of Nicholas de Veteripont, and in the following year the coiners (monetarii) of Alston had their liberties confirmed by the king. So that you see Alston in those olden times had not only mines, but a mint. In 24 Edw. III. the crown exemplified some charter of privileges formerly given to the Alston miners; and in 1326 granted them very large privileges: and Henry the Fifth let the manor and mines to William Stapleton, Esq. at an annual fee-farm rent of ten marks, payable at the Exchequer in Carlisle: and the same William Stapleton and his tenants at will had in the same reign large liberties and privileges confirmed to them for the same manor and mines. This is a sketch of what the Patent Rolls in the Tower of London contain on the subject of Aldenston: but the Originalia, Charter Rolls, &c. &c. contain much on the same subject; and I have copied a great part of a volume of ancient charters respecting 'Kirkhalgh' and Aldenston, from original records in the Treasury of the Dean and Chapter of Durham. It is rather expensive to me to get copies of the Records in the Tower, and I suppose there is no one who could afford to get at them about Alston who cares anything about them. I write this note in the greatest haste. Ever thankful for your kind assistance.

" I have looked into a note-book and find there are monumental inscriptions at Kirkhaugh to Albany Featherstonhalgh in English, and to Dr. Richardson in Latin, of which I have no copy. The head of the church-yard cross is used as a gate post for the church-yard. The

---

* A great number of Roman shoes had a while before been found in the camp at Whitley in a state of considerable preservation. This discovery has been already alluded to in p. 77 above. See also Archæolog. Æliana, ii. 205.

church should be drawn so as to get the two rugged but green hills, and the houses near Castle-nook past its west end and past its east, and some houses, thus *(a sketch)*.   Try your hand at another sketch after the weather grows good, and get a little tender distance in.——I could send it to London to get it lithographed in good style.   Very truly yours,
                                        "JOHN HODGSON."


To THE REV. J. RAINE.—12 Feb. 1828.—"I intend to print my account of Dawes in the Transactions of the Newcastle A. S. and have all the woodcuts ready for it, but keep the MS. at home till Adamson sends his writ for it; with the hope of getting some papers out of the archives of the corporation of Newcastle, and some accurate information respecting his books and papers out of Westmerland.*   If you have occasion to write to Mr. Tate, be so good as tell him how the matter stands, and say that I will forward to him a copy of the Memoir separately printed for each subscriber to the monument.


### FROM MR. W. NICHOLSON.

"MY DEAR SIR,                                   Edinburgh, April 10th, 1828.

"I think the best plan for engraving your portrait† would be mezzotinto, as being both cheaper and better.   The expense would be about thirty guineas.   Mr. Hodgetts, the mezzotinto engraver, will return here from London shortly, and I would then get you further particulars, should you think of having it done.   It will not be necessary to have a drawing reduced from the picture.   I have read your last volume of the History of Northumberland with much pleasure: it is full of interesting information, and cannot fail of becoming necessary to any library.   I would certainly avail myself of your kind invitation were I going to Newcastle, but since I became a Benedick I seldom leave home.   Would it not be an agreeable variety for you, to take a trip to Edinburgh by the new conveyance you mention?   If so, Mrs.

---

* On this subject Hodgson made application to his venerable master Mr. Bowstead, but it does not appear that any reply was given to his letter.   For the pen and memory of a man so far advanced in years there are many excuses.

† It would appear that at this period Hodgson was thinking of publishing along with some future volume of his history an engraving from the portrait painted by Nicholson in 1810 or 1811 p. 76, vol 1.   The idea, as we shall see, was abandoned, and an engraving was made for that purpose from a miniature by Miss Mackreth in 1829, of which hereafter.

Nicholson and I would be most happy to see you. I delivered the letter to Miss Morris. Pray make my best respects to Mrs. Hodgson, and believe me, dear Sir, yours most truly,

"WM. NICHOLSON.

"I am indebted to you for the last volume of the History of Northumberland, and would have sent the money by Mr. Trevelyan, but I have forgot the price. Let me know what it is when I next hear from you."

To EDWARD SWINBURNE, Esq.

"MY DEAR SIR,                    Whelpington, 22 April, 1828.

"I got your drawing and notes respecting Mitford Church last night, and have packed them again for Nicholson. But I regret exceedingly that you should have exposed yourself so long to the cold there as to get a return of a sore throat. The weather here still continues very damp and cold, but I hope you are taking much care of yourself and improving every day.

"Since you were here I have had a letter from Mr. Nicholson of Edinburgh, who says that he supposes Mr. Hodgetts, the mezzotinto engraver, would engrave my portrait for about thirty guineas. If you are in the way, you may make any inquiries on the subject that may suggest themselves to you: but as I have so many engravings at present ready, I think it quite useless to be at any more expense with subjects that are not immediately wanted for the work. One of my objects in now writing to you is, to ask the titles of vignettes long ago done, but which I wish to give at the head of the preface and in the colophon of the volume of which the indexes are printing at present. The one I think is a sheep-bridge on Oakenshawburn, North Tindale, the other a linn in Lewisburn. These are the subjects, if you can recognize them by the lines I give. (*Here are two pen-and-ink drawings*). The sheepbridge was done by Collard on copper, the linn by Nicholson on wood. I have got another proof of Keilder Castle, in which all the suggestions given on the former proof are made; especially the stone in the water partly shadowed by alder trees, which is now drawn too much forward.

"I dare not wait your return from Edinburgh for the titles of the two vignettes, though I greatly fear that my indexes may be still a month in the press, as I do not get more than four pages in eight days.

"You will see by the Newcastle papers that the Chevy Chase coach began to run yesterday.——Kirkharle, you will also see, is now regularly advertised in four lots, Kirkharle parish, the Deanhams, Swinburne, and Bavington. They have added six years to Mr. Redman's life (the vicar) and about £60 to his income.——If Mr. Miller gets the remains of the Mitford Manor House done, I should like to have the plate soon, as I think it would come as well in as an ornament to the dry volume of Records, &c. just printing off, as it would in the account of Mitford, which cannot possibly be printed off for twelve months at least. I hope as you will return you will come by the Chevy Chase and let us see you here. I hear nothing about our Alston excursion——

"Our lead-mining operations are going on very briskly. Mill-wrights, masons, miners, knots of labourers at the race and the dam give a life to Whelpington it never saw before, but I am dreading that they will be soon leaving our nice green fields covered with great un-sightly heaps of rubbish, without doing any good to any body.

The Hon. Mrs. Leveson Vernon's lithographic view of Witton Tower by Hullmandell came last night. It is a very stiff performance: the hills on the north side of the Coquet being stuck like a great muck-midden behind a grove of trees, and the house far too bright.

"I trouble you with a long letter about very little, but all the novelties that our quiet neighbourhood afford at present. Mr. Tone has had letters from Sir John, and I have had occasion to write to him since you were here begging him to interest himself to get a model of a machine for breaking stiff and heavy lands, and making them fit to crop, exhibited before the Society of Arts. It is the invention of James Charlton, who was joiner before the late elections at Little Harle. Mr. Redman thinks it very ingenious, and if Sir John can find a way of getting it exhibited it will be immediately forwarded.——We had the mad philosopher Martin * here lecturing last week, and, as he called on me, I went to hear him, but principally with the intention of keeping order; and certainly he was respectfully attended to. His lecture was a jargon of philosophy and religion strangely interspersed with dreams and wild notions respecting Heaven, Hell, the sun, moon, &c. Some of his ideas are bold and original, but very mad and extravagant; but the whole lecture far too seriously handled to be a fit subject for laughter or ridicule, a way it is too frequently treated by his audiences. Yours, dear Sir, ever most truly,

"JOHN HODGSON."

---

* A brother of William Martin the eminent painter, and also of Jonathan Martin the burner of York Minster.

To ROBERT SURTEES, Esq.*

"MY DEAR SIR,

"In my account of Mitford Castle I wish to give a list of the Balliol pedigree for the purpose of shewing the connection between that family and the Strabogies who succeeded Cumin as lords of it. I wish much also to find out who Alianora de Genovre was. A Peter de Genovre and Maud his wife frequently occur. The Placita de Quo Warranto at Newcastle in 1294 represent her as 'formerly Queen of England, mother of Edw. I., widow of Alexander Balliol, and wife of Robert de Stutteville,' but this is evidently a mistake, as Alianora of Provinee, widow of Hen. III., died in the Convent of Amesbury in 1291, and Alianora de Genovre did not die till 1310-11. I am also at a loss to know how Alexander de Balliol who married Isabella de Chilham, as a second husband, was related to the Balliol family. Dugdale makes him brother of John de Balliol, King of Scotland, but does not point out the degree of relationship between them and Alexander de Balliol who died 7 Edw. I. Douglas has nothing about the family. As I know that you were paying attention to the Balliol pedigree some time since, I hope you will be able to put me right. I have two charters about Balliol, one of which mentions Alexander de Balliol as husband of Alianora de Genovre, and the other Robert de Stutteville, who died in Mitford Castle, and who with his wife, the said Alianora, abetted a great riot at Mitford, concerning which there are many records left in the Rolls of Parliament. I have also several scraps and charters shewing the interest the Valentia family had in Mitford after Roger Bertram shattered the fortune of his house in engaging in the Barons wars.

"The Chevy Chase coach has made this part of Northumberland at length accessible. It gets to Cambo (starting from Newcastle at five) at half-past seven in the mornings of Monday, Wednesday and Friday, every week. When will you and Mr. Raine favour my manse with making your appearance at it to breakfast, at eight o'clock some Monday, Wednesday, or Friday and staying a few days with me? I have every accommodation for you, and should be most highly delighted to take you over the moors, a short ride to see Robin of Risingham, or the Field of Otterburn, or the house of the Laird of Trequen, or any of the many things that would interest you either here or in the valley of the Rede. But I beg a day or two's notice, lest I should be in one of my

* From a copy made about the 25th of April, 1828.

parochial rambles. I beg my respectful compliments to Mrs. Surtees, and am, my dear Sir, very faithfully yours,

"JOHN HODGSON."

At this period Mr. Hodgson published another volume of the History of Northumberland. This portion, which followed so quickly upon the heels of that which preceded it, consists, like that published in 1820, of ancient records and historical papers. Its contents and embellishments are as follows.

CONTENTS OF PART III. VOL. II.

"Article I. Extracts from various Ancient Deeds, Royal Grants, and other Records in the possession of Sir J. E. Swinburne, of Capheaton, Baronet, F.R.S., F.A.S., &c.

"Article II. Extracts from Records respecting different Ecclesiastical Institutions in Northumberland.

"Article III. A Book of the State of the Frontiers and Marches betwixt England and Scotland, written by Sir Robert Bowes, Knight, at the request of the Lord Marquis Dorset, the Warden General, 1550, 5° E. 6.—Cotton MSS. Titus F. 13. Also under the text of this article is subjoined—A View and Survey of the East and Middle Marches of England foreanenst Scotland, by Sir Robert Bowes and Sir Rauffe Ellerker, Knights, Commissioners, 2 Dec. 1542, 33 H. 8, Cotton MS. Caligula, B. 8.

"Article IV. The Calendar of Inquisitions after Death, otherwise called Escheats, from the beginning of the reign of Richard the Second to the end of that of Richard the Third, so far as relates to the county of Northumberland.

"Article V. Extracts respecting Northumberland, from the abridgement of the Rolls in the Exchequer called The Originalia.

"Article VI. Extracts from the volume of Public Records, entitled Placitorum in domo capitulari Westmonasteriensi asservatorum Abbreviatio, so far as relates to Northumberland.

"Article VII. Extracts respecting Northumberland from the Calendarium Rotulorum Patentium in Turri Londonensi.

"Article VIII. Extracts relative to Property in Northumberland, from the Calendarium Rotulorum Chartarum.

"Article IX. Extracts respecting Northumberland, from the Calendarium Inquisitionum ad quod Damnum.

" VIGNETTES IN THIS VOLUME.

|  | DESIGNED BY | ENGRAVED BY |
|---|---|---|
| Keilder Castle, | Edw. Swinburne, Esq. | W. Collard New-castle. |
| Sheep Bridge on Lewisburn, North Tindale, some years ago replaced by a stone bridge, built by Sir J. E. Swinburne, bart. | Ditto. | Ditto. |
| Witton Tower, the parsonage house of the Rector of Roth-bury, | The Hon. Mrs Leve-son Vernon. | Lithog. by C. Hull-mandell, London. |
| Little Swinburne Tower, | Edw. Swinburne. Esq. | W. Collard New-castle. |
| Remains of the Manor-house, Mitford, in April, 1828, | Ditto. | W. Millar, Edin-burgh. |
| A Linn on Oakenshawburn, a little above its junction with Lewisburn, North Tin-dale | Ditto. | I. Nicholson." |

The preface by which this valuable volume introduces itself to the reader must also be given at length, as it contains somewhat of explanation, and a further account of its author's feelings and obligations.

#### PREFACE.

" This volume completes, according to the Editor's proposals, the third, and, he is well aware, a very unpopular part of his work. It also concludes much of his labour, inasmuch as it brings a large portion of his material and authority into a digested and methodised form; but, like its predecessor, it is wanting in all that is interesting or attractive to the eye or the mind of the general reader. By the genuine antiquary, the genealogist, and the amateur in county history, he hopes it will be found a productive mine of useful information; and he is persuaded that, as long as the people of Northumberland are permitted to live under the influence of the jurisprudence and customs of their forefathers, it cannot fail to be of frequent use to the lawyers and holders of property in that county.

"Anxiety for the preservation, and a deep sense of the value, of public and family muniments, are feelings that spring out of loyalty and attention to self-preservation, and are characteristic of the high-minded and patriotic people who live upon estates which have descended to them from remote ancestry—have been the reward of valour, or wisdom, or industry, and which especially have been kept unspotted by dishonourable and enthralling incumbrances. How, indeed, can a generous and enlightened progeny look with indifference upon those charters of their rights, liberty, and property, which their ancestors had sealed with their blood, or emblazoned with the glory of great or useful deeds? A conqueror, who wishes to begin a new era in a country, by dividing its property among his adherents, naturally enough desires to destroy all evidences of the achievements and possessions of the people he has vanquished. A remarkable event of this kind occurred in China about 2000 years since, when Chi-Hoang-ti, for the purpose of obliterating every trace of the feudal government that preceded his dynasty, destroyed all its books and writings, excepting such as related to law and medicine, and put to death great numbers of learned men, lest they should relate from memory any portion of the genuine memoirs or established superstitions of their country. Something similar to this may always be expected to happen where neglect or mismanagement permits popular discontent to ripen into hatred, and to bring on a revolution: in the heat of revenge, the actors in a new order of things naturally seek security for themselves, their power, and property, not merely from those whom they had removed from their offices and estates, but from their descendants, by the destruction of such records and papers as might assist the conquered party in the recovery of their rights, in the event of a successful re-action. Prynne asserts, that in several periods of the unsettled state of our country, 'the prevailing king's parties embezzled and suppressed such parliamentary records and proceedings as made most against their interest, power, and prerogative;' and Ayloffe to this quotation adds, that 'it cannot be doubted that in those times the like fate befel many others of our national muniments;' that 'damps, mildew, and vermin have, from time to time, deprived us of many ancient and valuable records.' Dugdale, in his Baronage,* cites the

* Vol. i. p. 525.

Scottish Rolls for the 34th year of Edward the First, which record, as well as similar documents for the preceding and succeeding year of the same reign, were not existing when that copious source of historical evidence was printed by government in 1814.  It is the multiplication of copies of the authentic histories of countries and places, and especially of useful records and papers, which tends to avert these effects of wars, revolutions, and neglect.  It is this process that keeps the most ancient writings in perennial youth.  It preserves the remembrance of such arts and measures as have been found to be useful and good, suitable to the climate in which they have rooted and thriven, and to the genius and habits of the people by whom they have been adopted.  It keeps truth before men's eyes, and consequently gives a relish for histories that are grounded on facts, in preference to works of imagination, fables, and romance.  It prevents the spread of visionary theories, by encouraging us to protect and defend the laws under which our predecessors have long lived happily, rather than venture upon such rash and vain experiments in legislation as usually end in democratical risings and political ruin.  'Records,' indeed, 'are the treasuries and conservators of our laws, and the standard to which we must resort for the resolving and ascertaining all constitutional points; they are the testimonies of our legislation and of all juridical and judicial proceedings, and the perpetual evidence of every man's rights, privileges, and liberties.'  'The same fertile mine likewise offers us a rich vein of materials for improving and illustrating our English topography,' ' and for rendering our local history and antiquities of essential and public use.'*  This then is the object aimed at in the volume now presented to the subscribers to this work, on reference to the first and second parts of which the perpetual use of the third will be observable in almost every page.  Each article, excepting the first, is prefaced with a short account of it, which precludes the necessity of saying more respecting them in this place, than that the first three articles are now printed for the first time, and that the remaining part consists of selections respecting Northumberland, from the Calendars and Abbreviations of the Public Records, printed under the sanction of Parliament.  Every care has been taken to make the Indexes accurate and full; and what is here accomplished may serve to show how much might be done to make the stream of County History flow in a full and clear current, if the provincial Antiquarian Societies of the kingdom would insert similar articles, accom-

* Ayloffe's Calendars, &c. Introd. iv. and v.

panied with good indexes, into their transactions, respecting the counties which lie within the sphere of their researches.

" From the very large and inconvenient size of most of modern deeds, and the great difficulty of keeping them in order and from injury, I cannot here omit this suggestion—that some statutory enactment, making every sort of conveyance of property illegal, unless it were plainly written upon parchment or paper of the foolscap or some other specified size, and the several sheets of each deed were inlaid, might be of considerable individual and national advantage.     Title-deeds would then be easily accessible to the parties they belonged to; and if every deed was paged, and the contents of each clause indexed at its end, it would be rendered still more intelligible and useful.   On this plan, deeds would be all of one size; and might be protected with covers, according to their owner's fancy: series of them belonging to the same estate might be bound into volumes; and copies of the whole much more conveniently made for the purpose of common reference.

" The Editor's special and most grateful thanks are due for contributions to this collection, to His Grace the Duke of Northumberland, Sir J. E. Swinburne, Bart., The Rev. James Raine, A.M., Rector of Meldon, and to Miss Emma Trevelyan, of Wallington; as well as to Edward Swinburne, Esq., for drawings of the vignettes with which the volume is embellished, and the plate of the remains of the Manor House at Mitford; and to the Rev. L. V. Vernon, formerly rector of Rothbury, in Northumberland, and now of Stokesley, in Yorkshire, for several interesting papers respecting the Rectory of Rothbury, acknowledged at p. 139, and for 300 copies of the lithographed view of ' Witton Tower, from an original drawing by the Hon. Mrs Leveson Vernon,' delivered with this volume.

" J. H.

" *Whelpington Vicarage House, March 3, 1828.*"


The second article in the above enumeration contains an immense mass of genuine information relative to the Churches and Chapels of Northumberland, every document in short touching their foundation, or in the case of vicarages of their endowments, which is recorded in the episcopal or capitular archives at Durham, together with some from other sources.   Not the least important of these records are printed in a smaller type at the foot of the page, Hodgson's object being to make the most of the

space to be devoted to such information.* In the initial letter of
the first document, the appropriation of the church of Bolam to
the canons of Blanchland, is inserted a reduced representation of
one of the most beautiful seals in the Treasury of the Dean and
Chapter, that of William de Beverley, who was Archdeacon of
Northumberland in 1369. The design has its historical meaning.
The church standing in water is intended to represent that of
Lindisfarne, the original seat of the see of Durham, which is
twice a day encircled by the German Ocean. On the summit of
one of its turrets stands King Oswald its founder, with his crown
and sceptre, and the letter O, the initial of his name, at his left
side. On the opposite turret is a representation of St. Cuthbert,
with his pastoral staff, and the letter C on his right. The figure
in the doorway is intended to represent the Archdeacon himself.
The selection of this seal to stand at the head of an important
collection of ecclesiastical authorities relative to this district was
made with propriety. It suffers much, however, from its being
reduced to so small a size.

The third article purports to be an historical paper, and so it
is, but one of transcendent interest. In it are embodied two
surveys of the frontiers and marches betwixt England and Scot-

---

* In the *foundation* of the church of Chillingham, by Julius Cæsar, who was kind
enough to endow it with six acres of land by the king's highway (p. 119), there is a
*trifling* anachronism, which I presume not to explain.

land, the first in 1542,* and the second in 1550.   In these two
documents we have a perfect description of the men and manners
of the Borders on both sides at those periods, with a minute
account of the then state of every castle and peel-house on the
side of England.   The picture which they present of the moral
state of the inhabitants is a melancholy one.   If honesty was
known on either side, it was only by name.   Every outrage
which can be conceived, even to the burning alive in their beds
of peaceful families in the dead of the night, was committed by
the one nation against the other, under the plea of retaliation for
injuries received; and, in general, as one of the surveys takes
care to state, the lower class of inhabitants was instigated to these
barbarous acts by idle and lawless young men of rank and
fortune, who went out at the head of their followers to rob and
murder and burn with as much excitement and pleasure as
now-a-days a young Border squire who has nothing better
to do goes out with his hounds.   If these two surveys were reprinted, with well-authenticated proofs of the murders and crimes
to which they refer, and illustrated with a few faithful representations of the present state of the castles and strongholds which
were then the main security of the inhabitants in their neigh-
bourhoods, but now in ruin, the book would be one of great
interest.   The oak is still standing at the gate of Naworth, and
the limb known on which Belted Will Howard, to terrify his
neighbours, used to hang before breakfast such unhappy Scotch-
men as had fallen into his hands.

The remainder of the volume consists of such extracts from
the volumes put forth by the Record Commission as relate to
Northumberland, and are of value to the history of the county;
but it is not easy to understand why in copying from the pages
of these miserably edited books Hodgson should not have thought
it his duty to correct the numerous errors in names of men and
places with which they abound.

Along with this volume, which contains the usual elaborate
index and a few pleasing cuts, &c., chiefly after Mr. Swinburne's
drawings, its author has published a reprint of the preface to that

* 1522, by mistake, in Hodgson.

published in 1820, correcting certain errors and giving amended engravings.

In this year, by the kind recommendation of Sir J. E. Swinburne, Hodgson was elected a Member of the Royal Society of Literature. The following are extracts from Sir John's letters on this subject. It will be seen that Mr. Hodgson was indebted to his friend for a greater favour than the mere proposing his name as a fit person for the honour. The business was managed in a very delicate way, and Hodgson was duly sensible of the obligation.

SIR J. E. SWINBURNE to MR. HODGSON, 25 April, 1828.—Grosvenor Place, London.—" If you have any wish to belong to the Royal Society of Literature, I think upon making them acquainted with your works, viz. the History of Northumberland, the papers you have published on the explosions in and ventilating of Coal Mines, and those in the Transactions of our Society of Antiquaries, which I will have great pleasure in laying before them, it might be accomplished without much difficulty, and I will make proper inquiries, without mentioning your name."

1828, May 11.—" Your name is up as a candidate for admission into the Royal Society of Literature, and the names to your proposal are such as to give me hopes that you will not be disappointed; but in these cases I never trust to probabilities, and shall not consider the thing certain till it is done; and if it does take place I will settle all the business before I leave London."

1829, Feb. 23.—" I am going south about the 5th or 6th March.—I will settle your annual subscription to the Royal Society of Literature when I am in London."

1836, 23 Ap.—Received a receipt from Sir J. E. S. for 30 guineas as a composition for the Royal Society of Literature. Wrote to him to thank him.—*Journal.*

May 1, 1828, Hodgson sends to Mr. Nichols a copy of his new volume of Northumberland, of which he begs his acceptance, and hopes the editor of the Gentleman's Magazine will visit the imperfections of the book in milder terms than he mentioned some mistakes in his papers published in the Transactions of the

Newcastle Antiquarian Society. He acknowledges that there are several typographical errors not noticed in the errata, occasioned in some measure by the very great number of mistakes committed by the compositors, and the impracticability of revises of the proofs being sent to him. As all the royal copies are subscribed for, and the greater part of the demy impression is also engaged, he begins to hope that the undertaking will not eventually be attended with much loss; although with all the industry he can use it may be some years before he can finish it.

Oct. 4, 1828, Hodgson sends to Messrs. Nichols "another volume of his History, (Part III. vol. ii.—Records,) the last of its kind, and certainly a very dull one; but to me, in compiling the rest of my work, of the greatest use, and the law-men of the county are delighted with it. Your reviewer, I hope, will favour me with giving a few extracts from the English parts of it, its preface, and especially from the two Surveys which commence at p. 171."

FROM MR. W. HUTTON.

" DEAR SIR,                    Newcastle-upon-Tyne, 17 May, 1828.

" Some time ago you did me the honour to mention your History of the county as a proper medium of making known any scientific discovery which might be made in the district. As far as my small stock of information goes I shall be very glad to contribute in any way you may point out, and there are one or two minerals which might be worth mention, particularly the Chloropherite, which I found (I believe for the first time in England) about eighteen months ago in a basaltic dyke near to Felton, and since that in one or two places near this town.

" The immediate object of my present letter is to offer you a list of the shells of this district, which has been formed by the joint labours of a club of naturalists, who meet from time to time, and register their information.

" You may depend upon the accuracy of the list, for before a shell is put down the best authorities are consulted, and where books fail a reference is made to Dr. Turton, with whom one of our number (Mr. Josh. Alder) is in frequent communication.

" The list, which contains many rare shells—some that have been found only once before in England—is very precise as to the place, circumstances, and season of finding the shells, and, besides, has the advantage in almost every instance of a reference to specimens in the Newcastle Museum.

" Our museum committee are publishing a list of British shells in the collection at the end of the last year's report, but this is very incomplete as far as regards this district, because it was thought that was not a proper way of making them public; and, although the club have already made some progress in a catalogue for publication, yet they have authorised me to say that all their information is at your service. Our entomologists (of which we have several in the club very zealous) are proceeding in the same way respecting a catalogue of the insects; but, from their immense number, and the obscurity of the subject, it will be long before we can even approximate to a list of them; however, in the meantime, we gradually acquire information, taking care at all times to be correct. Every information I can give is at all times at your service, and I beg you to believe me, dear Sir, yours, with much respect,

" WM. HUTTON."

FROM MR. E. SWINBURNE.

" DEAR SIR,                    Oakwood, Wednesday, May 26, 1828.

" Miss Emma Trevelyan was obliged to return to Wallington on Monday and could not therefore take cognizance of Nafferton. The day was bitter, but, owing to the circumstance of what I thought the best point of view for your purpose being under a dyke (which was the lee side) to the north, I was enabled to bring away a sketch, and after two miles walking restore the circulation to my feet. You shall see it. I get into it a part of the Tower to the east and to the west (the principal front) much foreshortened, with the great ash-trees. I have written to Mr. Losh to beg him to forward to you without delay Carmichael's drawings of Jesmond, and I shall in a few days be in the way to confer with you upon it, and I hope then to have better weather than lately for Mitford, &c. Yours,

" EDW. SWINBURNE."

making an Index to St. Cuthbert.  All the items of relics, jewels, rosaries and such like are noticed.  Could I have had time to have made myself master of the subject I might have been able to improve it considerably; but with the lean assemblage of bones and sinews with which it will reach you, you will be soon able in a short time to put flesh upon it.  The book is exceedingly curious; and I long to see the whole, which I have no doubt will show, in the most decided manner, the connecting link between paganism and christianity.  I am sure I can give your reviewer, when I have seen the concluding part of the book, some very important hints on the subject; and as soon as it reaches me you shall have all the observations which .my leisure will afford or reflections suggest.—Yours,

" JOHN HODGSON."

" 1828.—To THE REV. J. RAINE.—Mr. Walker has printed off the separate account of Meldon, for which he has debited you for sixteen copies according to directions left long ago at the office, but of which I had lost all recollection.  Mr. Affleck, the foreman, says that twelve copies were for yourself and four for me; these sixteen copies each have an Appendix of Records; and besides them I have got a few more copies printed off without the appendix, and will make presents of them to such persons as have assisted me.  You had best send yourself a copy to Mr. Lenox and also to Mr. Wailes.*——

" JOHN HODGSON."

" FROM SIR J. E. SWINBURNE.—Capheaton, July 8, 1828.—If the weather permits, we propose dining between three and four at the Lake to-morrow.——I have likewise had an application that I must consult you about, from an artist engraver in wood, who with Harvey has published a very pretty book that I can shew you.  His name is Jackson, and he has undertaken, under the Duke's auspices, the engraving of a series of illustrations of the poem of Chevy Chase, the Ballad to be given with all notes and matter connected with it.   The publishers therefore wish to have the services of a competent editor, and I am requested to apply to you for that purpose.  How far you can find leisure to do what they want, you alone are the best judge, though I believe nobody could

* The tenants of the two Meldon Farms.

furnish more curious matter or do it better; but you must allow me to suggest that you should not think of doing so without a proper remuneration.*——

" J. E. SWINBURNE."

* I place in a note the following particulars respecting this contemplated publication. On the 21st Nov. 1829, Sir John Swinburne thus writes from Grosvenor Place, London:—" I send you a sort of plan of the form in which Jackson proposes to publish the Chevy Chase. The ten large engravings will be the subjects as numbered and explained in the pages. The introductory preface, in point of length, will depend upon what you think best, as well as the extent of the notes : these he thinks had best be altogether at the end, with numerical references at the bottom of the pages to each respective note. It will be desirable that you should give them some idea of the number of pages that the introduction and notes may consist of. Jackson has been very ill with determination of blood to the head for several months. He seems now very ill with incessant cough, but is able to work. If you want any information or explanation, pray write to me on the subject." On the 9th of March, 1831, Sir John again writes on the business, and informs Hodgson that he " will lose no time in finding out Jackson, and will ascertain what his views are. I suspect (says he) that he is not going on with the work, from what I heard some time ago." The undertaking was abandoned.

IN the year 1829 Hodgson published in the Transactions of the Society of Antiquaries of Newcastle his long promised " Account of the Life and Writings of Richard Dawes," who, after having been Master of the Grammar School in that town from 1738 to 1749, resigned his office, and retired to Heworth Shore, in the chapelry of Heworth, where he died in 1766. " His grave (says Hodgson in his Memoir) in Heworth Chapelyard is still marked with a head-stone of rude workmanship; but said to be the gratuitous offering of a country mason to the memory of a great scholar. The stone bears the following inscription: ' In memory of Richard Dawes, late head master of the grammer school of Newcastle, who died the 21st of March, 1766, aged 57.' Besides noticing the sin of bad spelling, Brand is severe on the ' vile sculpture ' and wretched taste in grouping of a trumpet, sword, and scythe, which are carved above this inscription; but thanks to the intentions and peace to the gentle soul who marked the spot that has the custody of Dawes's ashes ! Before Heworth Chapel was rebuilt (in 1821 and 1822) the incumbent there had the grave carefully marked with a stake, and the stone removed out of the way of injury, and as soon as the building was completed the frail ' memorial ' was moved back to its proper place, a large rolled block of basalt laid lengthways on the grave, and the following inscription, on a plate of bronze, sunk into it:

THE BURIAL PLACE OF RICHARD DAWES, M.A.
AUTHOR OF THE CELEBRATED WORK INTITULED
MISCELLANEA CRITICA.

LET NO MAN MOVE HIS BONES.

So early as the year 1818 Hodgson had contemplated the erection of a more suitable memorial to this eminent scholar, and had in that year thus expressed his wishes to the writer of these pages: " I have seriously resolved to ask for subscriptions to assist me in erecting a plain monument in the Greek style over the grave of Dawes in Heworth Chapel-yard. Will you, therefore, have the goodness, when you are in the company of scholars, to mention the circumstance. I intend to have my design announced in the Classical Journal, if the *digamma* will permit me." The design, however, was abandoned for a while until, the chapel of Heworth having been rebuilt, and an opportunity having presented itself for a suitable monument within the walls of the chapel in a place of greater security, it was resumed, and after much delay carried into execution in 1825.

In raising the necessary funds for carrying the design into execution the Rev. James Tate, at that time the learned master of Richmond School, was chiefly instrumental. The contributors were most of them men of high Greek renown--Dr. Burgess, bishop of Salisbury (Hodgson's examiner in 1802), Emmanuel College, Cambridge; the Rev. Thomas Kidd, the editor of Dawes's Miscellanea Critica; Jonathan Raine, Esq., Q.C., the brother of Dr. Matthew Raine, Master of the Charter House; Professor Musgrave, now Archbishop of York; Dr. Parr; Dr. Maltby, afterwards Bishop of Durham; Dr. Samuel Butler, afterwards Bishop of Lichfield and Coventry; the Rev. G. Butler, (Dean of Peterborough;) the Rev. P. P. Dobree, Professor of Greek in the University of Cambridge; the Rev. H. Drury, of Harrow; the Rev. James Tate; the Rev. E. Moises, Master of Newcastle School; and another contributor who presumed to appear in such an assemblage of learning. I have before me a long correspondence between Mr. Tate and Mr. Hodgson on the subject of the inscription, which the former had kindly undertaken to supply, and which was eventually adopted, after having received the hearty approbation of Dr. Parr. For the letters of the former a more appropriate place may perhaps be found hereafter. The inscription is as follows:—

IN . CŒMETERIO . HVIVS . ECCLESIÆ . SEPVLTVS . IACET .

RICARDUS . DAWES . A. M.

COLL . EMMAN . APVD . CANTABRIGIENSES . OLIM . SOCIVS .

LVDOQVE . LITERARIO . ET . GERONTOCOMIO . APVD . NOVOCASTRENSES .

ANNOS . X . PRÆFECTVS .

ACERRIMO . VIR . INGENIO .

ET . SERMONIS . ATTICI . IVDEX . PERITISSIMVS .

CVI . MISCELLANEA . CRITICA . VNO . LIBRO . EDITA .

ÆTERNVM . HONOREM . APVD . GRAMMATICOS . PEPERERVNT .

NATVS . EST . A. C. MDCCVIII.      DECESSIT . MDCCLXVI.

In addition to his exertions on the subject of the monument, Hodgson promised " to draw up and print a memoir of all that he could collect respecting Dawes and his writings;" and this brings me to the " Account " before me, which occupies thirty quarto pages in the Transactions of the Society, and thus commences:

" Though the subject of this Memoir died only about 61 years since, and, after the death of Bentley, stood pre-eminently at the head of Greek literature in these kingdoms; yet so little is known, or to be gleaned from the publications of his time, respecting him, that to compile an account of his life becomes a matter of difficult antiquarian research. He was one who, in the imaginary maze of lines which the force of ambition and self-interest press in concentric circles towards the throne, like planets of the largest size and dimmest light, moved in the widest of these circles, and was therefore little noticed. In the earlier years of his life he appeared, indeed, for a short time on the stage of human life among the champions of literature, wielding his weapons with the mightiest, and receiving the praises of the wisest; but a cloud of apprehensions came over his mind that he was assailed on every side with the arrows of ingratitude and persecution, and he threw aside his armour and walked gloomily away from the contentions for honour and the post of usefulness, to hold conversation in the obscurity of rural life with unlearned men and his own imagination. The deer which finds itself smitten, fearful of being gored deeper by its own species, rushes to the woods and dies unseen; and the Indian of the New World, when he feels the pestilence of the hot savannahs working in his frame, retires from the companions of his journey into a thicket, and covering his body with his mantle, resigns himself to death. There are no sufferings which neglected and melancholy pride cannot treat with indifference."

With these remarks Hodgson commences his Memoir, and the following is its conclusion:—

" He begs that others may consider this performance in the same light he is constrained to judge of it himself, as a very humble tribute to the memory of Dawes; a series of superficial gleanings from Kippis, and the *Prefaces* to Burgess's and Kidd's editions of the *Miscellanea*, interspersed here and there with a new fact, or with the inferences and reflections of one whose pretensions to sit in judgment on his ' golden book,' the ' decus immortale ' of English learning, Dawes would have treated with merriment, if not with indignation; but whose respect for his memory, admiration of his great critical powers, and sympathy for his sufferings are cordial and intense."

It is well that there is such a record of such a man. Imperfect though it be in many respects, yet it contains every little anecdote with regard to him which could be collected at the time it was compiled, and many of the scraps of information which Hodgson has gathered together might by this time have been forgotten for ever. The labour of his biographer would have been well bestowed if it had done nothing more than disprove the report (which it does effectually) that Dawes died by his own hand. Of his great knowledge of the Greek tongue, and his discriminating powers in the niceties and peculiarities of that language, no doubt whatever can be entertained. His Miscellanea Critica bears testimony to both. The termination of his connection with the Grammar School of Newcastle seems to have originated in two causes—a jealousy in certain persons of his profound learning, and the irascible tendencies of his own peculiarly constructed mind, approaching to insanity when irritated by the snarls and growls of those who were envious of his talents, and unfeeling enough to take delight in goading him on to madness. I may be indulged with a quotation from the Memoir which touches feelingly upon Dawes's mental misfortunes, and is peculiarly illustrative of the kind and gentle heart of its writer:

" In closing the view of Dawes's critical labours it is natural to turn to himself, and observe with what effect upon his own mind he watched their reception in the world. Had he firmness to sit in the complacent
nt of self-approbation, conscious of the benefits he had conferred

upon his own profession, and regardless alike of the approving voice of genuine learning, the detraction of envy, and the commonplace criticisms of the multitude of the wise? There were times when neither admiration, nor envy, nor vulgar wisdom, could find any pleasure in his company; when Mercy and Pity were the only beings that could be gratified by visiting him; when praise fell upon him as cheerlessly as sunshine comes over sorrow. Dr. Kippis has observed that the peculiarities of conduct by which he was distinguished at the universities ' probably arose from a dash of insanity in his constitution.' I wish I could have struck this assertion out of the page of history, and thrown a veil of everlasting oblivion over it. For who is there who does not feel the best and holiest sympathies of his nature afflicted, and shudders, when he recollects how many powerful minds, the sun of whose genius could have dimmed all the intellectual constellations around them, have nevertheless been subjected to have their understandings darkened by ' this heaviest of human afflictions,' and themselves made the sport of ignorance and folly.

> ———— ' From this day forth
> I'll use you for my mirth, yea, for my laughter
> When you are waspish,'

was a threat, the bitterness of which, from the morbid irritability of his mind, poor Dawes too often tasted."

Hodgson's own private copy of the Memoir contains at the end his correspondence with Mr. Tate on the subject of the inscription for Dawes's monument, and various other letters and papers on the subject; and, moreover, the margins of its pages are many of them closely filled with alterations in the narrative, and much additional matter which he seems to have gathered together after its publication.

FROM EDWARD SWINBURNE, Esq. TO R. W. HODGSON.

" DEAR SIR, Capheaton, Thursday, January, 1829.

" I am much obliged to you for your trouble, The wood * may be dear, but it cannot be a great object in so small a concern. I inclose

* For the writing-table above mentioned p. 59.

you by Curry 7*l.*, the bill being 6*l.* 10*s.* 9*d.*    The 9*s.* 3*d.* you can send
back by Curry next post-day with Charleton's receipt.    Your father will,
I hope, excuse the freedom I have taken to get this necessary piece of
furniture for him without any previous intimation to himself: he has so
many of his own to work for, and does so much for others, that one
cannot but be happy to have an opportunity of assisting him, even in a
little way, in his labours.

" This is good weather for studying at home.    My best regards to all
round your fire-side.    Yours very truly,

" EDWD. SWINBURNE."

FROM THE REV. EDW. OTTER.*

" MY DEAR SIR,                              Morpeth, March 16th, 1829.

" For three successive Wednesdays we made inquiries in vain
after your carrier, during which time a letter and a sketch of Bothal
Church were lying in readiness for you.    This was about Christmas.
The sketch was not, however, such as you desired, which made us less
anxious about it; but Mrs. C. Baker has taken a drawing from the
station you described, a copy of which she will most willingly give you
if still acceptable.    I hope that we shall now see you in this quarter, and
that you will take up your abode with me whilst prosecuting your
researches.

" If you did not sign the papers concocted lately at Long Horsley,
perhaps you may think with me, that it may not be unbecoming to dis-
claim, as beneficed clergymen of the Archdeaconry, any participation in
some of the sentiments expressed in the address to the King, more
especially in that which called upon him to dissolve his Parliament, if
it should consent to the removal of the disabilities.    Mr. Hunter will
concur, I know, in such a step, and perhaps others.    My eyes are very
weak and I can only make a sad scrawl, as you will see, but I hope you
will be able to read it.    Yours sincerely,

" E. OTTER."

* What Cambridge man has not read, and does not remember, the unique note
in the Calendar of that university referring to the second, third, and fourth Wranglers
of the year 1786 ?  "Cum inter Dom. Otter, Dm. Hutchinson, et Dm. Lambe nullum
prorsus discrimen in rebus Mathematicis extitisse concedatur, secundum hunc ordinem
disponuntur, hac sola de causa, quia Ds. Otter in dialecticis magis est versatus, et Ds.
Hutchinson in Scholis Sophistarum melius disputavit."    The above is the Dominus
Otter there mentioned, who had the honour of being placed the first of the three, and
after such a senior wrangler as John Bell of the Chancery Bar.    Mr. Otter was
Rector of Bothal near Morpeth, and a most amiable and gentlemanly man.    Of his
learning enough is said in the note referred to.

FROM THE REV. A. HEDLEY.—Whitfield, 5 Ap. 1829.—"All the proofs sent to me are *past mends*.——Your pedigrees in the last parcel were truly interesting to me.——Who will say that such things are not useful? If your pedigree of the Fenwicks of Nunriding, for instance, had been published twenty years ago, or even fifteen, what money and toil and anxiety it would have saved poor Ned Codling of the Dovecot, by clearly proving to him that his claim was not worth a *button*, and that the issue of the sisters of Robert Fenwick (No. 10) was surely before the issue of his aunt! Some foolish people about Hexham are making precisely a similar mistake in a claim they are, at least were, setting up for " the Chief's * estate."

To W. C. TREVELYAN, Esq., University College, Oxford.

" MY DEAR SIR, Whelpington, 23rd April, 1829.

" Your letter of the 14th instant I received late in the evening of last Tuesday; and, having been from home all day yesterday, I found I could not examine my Dodsworth extracts sufficiently that evening to answer your queries by to-day's post.

" The whole of your extracts from the Pipe Rolls are very interesting; and their brevity makes it of the greatest importance that not a letter or figure of them should be omitted. The accounts will be of the greatest use in illustrating *services*, and ascertaining the sizes of estates; as well as showing the duration of various services that fell into disuse long before the abolition of the feudal tenures in the time of Charles the Second.

" In the prospectus of my History I have mentioned that the Natural History of the county will form an article in the introductory volume, and I have one on Botany nearly ready for the press; it only notices rare plants, or such as grow about old castles and villages. I do, however, here and there throw in a sprinkling of natural history into the Parochial department, to give a relish to the insipidity of several subjects treated upon. But the whole that will be found in that part of the book, when finished, if I be permitted to see its conclusion, will be very little as a whole, possibly not more than a couple of pages.

" Respecting Dodsworth's extracts from Northumberland deeds, I have no part of the volume numbered 49, 50, 51, from folio 1 to folio 63, where the extracts ' Ex Cartis prenobilis viri Willelmi Comitis New-

* Mr. Errington of Beaufront, to whom that title had long been given by the courtesy of Hexhamshire. He had died a while before the date of this letter.

castle, 30 Sep. 1641 ' begin, and are contained in the book I gave you to copy into. Then my minutes are, Dodsworth, vol. 45, vol. 1—6, Brinkburn Register 23 Jan. 1638: and folio 15—20; from Alnwick Cartulary 22 Jan. 1638; none of which I seem to have from Lansdowne 326.

[*Here follow two pages describing what extracts he has from the Lansdowne MSS., to show what is wanting from those of Dodsworth.*]

" Besides which, I have from the Lansdowne MS. 326, extracts from the deeds ' Rob'ti Lyell de Felton, Ar. 20 Aug. 1639,' from No. 1 to 30 or 31. The first No. beginning ' Ego Thomas Lyell dominus de Felton, &c.' and the last ' Maria de St. Paul, Contesse de Pembroke,' &c. These extracts from the Lysle Charters I see are contained in the vol. numbered 49, &c. in the Bodleian copy, from folio 33 to folio 37, so that I was wrong in the beginning of this letter in saying that I had no part of that vol. from folio 1 to 63.

" If I had a copy of Dodsworth's transcript of the Pipe Rolls, I would instantly commence with my introductory volume, where I intend to give annals of the county under each sheriff, and these accounts would form a most remarkable feature of the article, especially when translated. But, before such a task is commenced, I must beg of you to let me know how much these rolls for Northumberland contain, and what time they would take to copy; for I cannot expect you to stay at Oxford to go through so arduous an undertaking as to copy the whole. Perhaps Dr. Bliss would tell you for what sum a fair copy of them could be made. Extracts from them, as you mention, the names only, where the account annexed to it does not seem to be interesting, and copies of entries that are more curious, will in the mean time be very useful to me.    They will unravel many difficulties in family history.    If the Pipe Rolls for Cornwall be amongst them, I hope you will look for entries respecting your own family.——I see they are ' Collectiones ex Magnis Rotulis Pipæ,' not copies of the Rolls: they are therefore what Dodsworth considered the marrow of these rolls.    Odardus was sheriff 1 Hen. II., so that it is probable he had continued in that office from the 5 of Stephen to the commencement of the next reign, when William de Vescy succeeded him.    I asked Mr. Riddell of Swinburne Castle, when he was with his regiment at Hounslow, to go to the British Museum to copy me the Chipchase deeds from Lansdowne 326; but do not yet know that he has done so.    Can you find in Dodsworth the grant of Redesdale to Robert de Umfreville, by William the Conqueror?    Yours most truly.

" JOHN HODGSON."

### From Wm. Hutton, Esq.

"Dear Sir,               Newcastle, 24 April, 1829.

"I shall feel particularly obliged by your informing me of the precise situation of the fossil tree you were so good as to describe to me last Saturday. Mr. Witham has been examining some large fossil vegetables at Blanchland, and wishes to see the one you mentioned in his way North, but I am not able to give him the requisite information. Your answer by return of post will be a favour, and, hoping you will excuse the trouble, I am, dear Sir, yours very truly,

"Wm. Hutton."*

### To the Rev. J. RAINE.

"My dear Raine,           .        Whelpington, 1 May, 1829.

"What is the matter? I never hear from you. You would, I hope, get my account of Dawes, and after that a small parcel through Sykes, containing a reprint of a cancelled leaf, and a note, in which I had asked you whether or not you wished for indexes to your North Durham, which my son wished to make for you, having a good deal of time to spare in his new situation in the evenings.†

"I have occasion to write a little about St. Cuthbert under Cawsey Park, and wish to notice your work in the article. But before I commit my account to press I wish to ask you if you are certain that the Feast of the Translation was on the 20th of March, and that of his Deposition on the 4th of September, or that it was *vice versâ*.‡ Nicolas and Hone make his Translation on the 4th September. The two great festivals of the heathens at the equinoxes were, I apprehend, intended to be kept up, and blended with the religious ceremonies of the Church of Durham in the feasts of the Translation and Deposition of their great tutelar idol. On the 4th of September, when nature was preparing to sink into the grave of winter, and the sun to enter the lower hemisphere, the feast

---

* An eminent geologist and naturalist, one of the chief founders of the Newcastle Natural History Society. A very interesting letter from Mr. Hutton on these subjects has been printed above, p. 130.

† Journal, 1829, 16 Feb.—"My son Richard Wellington left me on Monday the 16th, to conduct the books and cash account of the firm of Richard Kell and Co., of which his grandfather left him one-half."

‡ This is the more correct statement, and therefore his inferences are wrong.

of the saint's being committed to the earth was celebrated.  On the
20th of March the sun burst out of the regions of Proserpine and
entered Aries—it was the vernal equinox, the first day of spring, and
the effigy or some symbol of the saint was carried in procession, and
all was joy and gladness.  I do not know what to read for authority on
this subject; but you know so well all about Saint Cuthbert and his
affairs that you can without trouble, I hope, set me right in it.

"I do not get so fast on with printing as I could wish, but hope to
move more quickly as the weather grows better.  Mr. Swinburne and
I in the week before last had a tour to Bothal, Cresswell, Newbiggin, &c.
and had one very beautiful day.  On Thursday I hope to go with my
other draftsman Mr. Sopwith to Woodhorn, Widdrington, Ulgham, &c.
to get sketches of the churches.

"Do you know that Mr. Howard of Corby wrote in a Durham paper
against your Saint Cuthbert?  If the pamphlet published at Newcastle
was by Lingard there is a sad falling off in his style, penetration, and
point.  It is a feeble and powerless thing, and I hope you never re-
garded it.  I have seen Mr. Howard's production also.  Your account
is quite satisfactory against the Benedictine tale.  I write in great haste
because I have to write much.  Ever and most truly yours,

"JOHN HODGSON."

FROM MR. T. SOPWITH.

"DEAR SIR,        Loaning House, near Alston, Cumberland, May 2, 1829.

"I attempted sepia drawings of the views, but having scarcely
done anything that way for some years, except the Morpeth and Stannington sketches, &c. I feel the greatest difficulty in expressing the
ideas I form as to light and shade.  To you, especially, any attempts of
mine in this mode of drawing must seem miserably defective, accustomed as you are to the clearness, transparency, and fine taste of Mr.
Swinburne.  After some abortive attempts at Cresswell and Widdrington, which when nearly finished I committed to the flames, I resolved to
attempt them in pen-and-ink drawings, and in these have succeeded
more to my satisfaction, though I need scarcely observe it seems dearly
enough purchased when the difference between colouring a broad surface
and working it up with lines is considered.

"Cresswell Tower I am compelled by the length of time devoted to
the others to send in a less finished state; but with the original sketch,
shewing the ivy, the engraver will I think be able to manage the broad

dark wall, and to relieve it by a better foreground, which latter I have not attempted, being a horrible delineator of trees. I had a great difficulty with a pen-and-ink drawing of this tower, which, when nearly done, the trees so sorely displeased me that I thrust it into the fire. If, however, the two imperfect sketches of this subject do not afford materials for the engraver to act on, I will willingly attempt once more to make a finished drawing of it.

" I hope Newbiggin and Widdrington will please you. I like the bold and novel perspective of the latter.

" The weather is exceedingly cold and unseasonable. The whole country has twice been covered with snow last week, which of course soon vanishes, leaving only its traces on the furrowed sides of Crossfell. Frequent and violent showers of hail, sleet, and rain, accompanied with cold winds, impede vegetation, and, except for the lengthened days, the season is much more like Christmas than May.

" I have at length seriously commenced with writing a detailed paper on mining records, and think, as I proceed, that there is room for much that is new and interesting on a subject which has been so little handled, and in which I have had considerable opportunities of gaining information. Very respectfully and truly yours,

" THOMAS SOPWITH."

In May 1829 Hodgson paid his third visit to London, and during his stay in town was on the 25th of that month requested by Mr. Bowden, who had married a daughter of Sir John E. Swinburne, to church his wife and baptize his child at St. George's Church. I happened to be in London at the same time; I had travelled with him in fact from Durham, and was glad to lend my friend a helping hand among the MSS. in the British Museum. I was also anxious to have his company to Cambridge and Ely, to which I was going, but he had left home for the purpose of gaining information for his history, and was determined to make the most of his time. In one of his musing fits of abstraction, being in pain from a tight shoe one day as we were walking along Holborn, he suddenly exclaimed, forgetting that he was not at home by the side of the Wansbeck, " Oh my toe !" A mob gathered round us in a moment, and I quietly withdrew the object of their curiosity into a shop hard by to which we were going.

To Mrs. HODGSON.

"MY DEAR JANE,                    British Museum, Thursday, 14th May, 1829.

"I got safely here—but was so tired with walking from place to place yesterday with Raine, that I am good for nothing to-day, and shall therefore be very brief. I breakfasted with Mr. Ellison, whose family are well—and, while I think of it, he says you are to write to me at the Tavistock Hotel, Covent Garden, under cover to him at Whitehall Gardens. From his house I went this morning to Sir John Swinburne's, where I saw nobody but Captain Swinburne. Sir John and Miss Swinburne are in Paris, where they will be for some time. Lady Swinburne is nursing Mrs. Bowden. From Sir John's at Grosvenor Place I came here, and the first opportunity I have had of taking a pen into my hand I employ in writing to Whelpington. My feet are martyred, and my head aches miserably, which I do not expect to get the better of till to-morrow. To-day I got some lunch with Miss Burn and Nina Ellison at half past one, in my way to the anniversary meeting of the Royal Society of Literature. The weather for two days has become more mild than it has been, and the trees are fast bursting into leaf. As we approached London on Tuesday evening, the appearance of Spring was very little better than at Whelpington.

"About 3d. worth of thyme seed, and as much rhubarb seed, should be sent for by Curry at the first opportunity, and sown, as you will find directed in Loudon, on a dry border or plot of ground. Let them be put on some place near where the thyme grew last year. I intend to write to Richard soon. Bessy I hope will be at home as soon as this reaches you. Mrs. Salter and her three pupils will have got fairly to work again, and I hope that Mary and Emma continue to be good girls. I called in the City yesterday, but Mr. Palmer was gone to Bromley. As yet I have not seen Sir John Trevelyan. Yesterday I recognized Lord Wellington in Parliament Street, and knew him, though I had never before seen him. You can have no possible conception of the grandeur of many of the streets and public buildings that have risen up here since I was last in London. It cannot be but this head of this country of ours must ere long suffer some apoplectic shock.

"I hope Edmund by this time has got the potatoes in the field planted, the field itself carefully dressed, the hedge mended, and the cows turned into the pasture. Fenwick must try to find me a pasture

for the cow that has to calve in autumn.  I will write again very soon.
Ever, my dear Jane, thine most truly,

"JOHN HODGSON."


To MRS. HODGSON.

Tavistock Hotel, Covent Garden,

"MY DEAR JANE,                     London, 15th May, 1829.

"I am rejoiced to hear that all things are going on well, but you
must not expect a long letter from me.  I have gone to see no sights,
and am therefore in my lodgings from eight in the evening till nine in
the morning.  On Monday last indeed I walked with Raine around the
Regent's Park, and visited the Gardens of the Zoological Society, for
which I had a ticket.  They are formed for the exhibition of birds and
beasts from all parts of the world.  Some are in water—some in cages,
others in dens, made artificially in the earth, others are seen grazing in
small inclosures with their young.  The collection is not great, as the
gardens are newly formed, but there is no doubt that great additions
will soon be made to it.  For three or four days after I came here the
weather grew warmer, but was wet; since last Sunday it has been fair,
and yesterday was exceedingly hot.  Did I say to you that I dined with
Mr. Nichol at Hackney last Tuesday?  I saw no Mrs. Nichol, and
therefore did not ask after her.  Miss Nichol, a lady of about Hilda's
age, did the honours of the table.  Her eldest brother is upon a tour in
Portugal.  To-morrow by engagement I go to Bromley.  At length I
have seen Mrs. Sedgwick,* at a Mrs. Ray's, No. 1, Wood Street, Cheap-
side; she seems anxious that Margaret may find a situation—but I told
her that so many people of considerable accomplishments were in want of
employment, that I feared Miss E. would have great difficulty in finding
a place.  I am to see her again here on Tuesday.  My feet are a great
deal better; but really I was so much tired yesterday that I went to bed
before nine.  This morning I was up before six; but, as I have a sofa
and a writing-table in my room I do not move out, and the scene and
noise before me would make one imagine that all London was in stir.
I am really most tired of the place—more so because I have got so little
done.  I should have come here by myself.  One thing however I have
got done—an introduction to Mr. Petrie at the Tower; which promises
to be of great use to me.  I have written to Mr. Redman, as he requested

* The mother of his governess.

L 2

a letter from me while I was here. I also wrote one to Mr. Tone, which can go with the Captain on Wednesday. You ought not to have written *London* on my address, but Mr. Ellison had carefully blotted it out. I hope to hear from you in time to buy some things for yourself and bairns. I wish I had known the length of the stairs, to have got carpeting for them. It is now eight o'clock, and I must have a search made for Mr. Swinburne before I go to breakfast at Mr. Ellison's. Give my love to Mrs. Salter in return for hers, and respects to Miss Sedgwick. My whole affection to the dear bairns and thyself. Thine ever, my dear Jane.

" JOHN HODGSON."

To MRS. HODGSON.

" MY DEAR JANE,                                   Bromley, Kent, May 18, 1829.

" Before I came here on Saturday I waited nearly two hours for Raine, whom I had to meet at the Tavistock Hotel at 11 o'clock, but he never came, and I am at a loss to say how I am to arrange about getting home. Of this however I must make myself able to judge when I get to town. Mr. Palmer brought me here on Saturday night in his phaeton and pair. He does not live splendidly, but in a very handsome style. Besides his phaeton he keeps a close carriage, and has two servants in livery to wait at table. He wishes me much to send John and Isaac to school here. Old Mrs. Rawes, my aunt, still enjoys good health. She is sometimes afflicted with gout. I have slept at her house. She was at church yesterday, and went to Mr. Palmer's to dinner, where we stayed till past ten o'clock. We were fifteen to dinner, and all, one way or other, related to each other. Dr. Wilson, an amiable and excellent man, who has considerable preferment in the Church, and with whom I became acquainted in Oxford eight years since, was one of the party. He is related to me by my grandmother Rawes's side. Mr. Richard Rawes, who is my cousin-german, and his wife, were also there. He was sometime a purser to an Indiaman, but has retired at the age of forty-three from business, and resides at Stratford Grove, in Essex, where I am to dine with him to-day. He is to take me in his carriage from Mr. Palmer's office in the city. Captain Richard Rawes, who I told you some time ago has a situation of considerable emolument in the India House, has had a long and severe sickness since the death of his wife; but he is now again able to attend to business, though he has twice said to me with great feeling, ' Things

are not as they used to be with me,' and each time the words were followed with an involuntary effusion of tears. He and his brother
William, who you know visited us, inquired much after Bessy. Wm.
remembers her well, and Miss Rawes, who is most amiable and happy,
in half hinting that we might lose E. ere it were long, says she will not
fail to spend a few days with us in July, during a month's visit she intends to pay to Mrs. Rawes at Houghton-le-Spring. What delightful
weather we have here! I heard the nightingale yesterday night as we
returned from Mr. Palmer's. Our night warbler has not such long or
plaintive or melodious notes, but it is a much more constant and much
merrier songster. The orchards are in full blossom; but I have seen
no appearance of may on the thorns. The pastures are thick with
grass and yellow with flowers. Gooseberries are formed on the trees
about the size of peas, but none yet are fit to pull. This is a most
charming spot. From the point where I am writing I can see Bromley
College and a great part of the village, in which the finest horse-chesnut
trees appear in great abundance, in full leaf, and covered with great
profusion of flowers. The pastures and meadows before Mr. Palmer's
house also appear like a rich carpet of green, bestrewn with the greatest
abundance of flowers, principally yellow. There is before the window
here a sycamore tree, which is also in full leaf, and nearly in full
flower. Pray note when you get this how the sycamore trees in the
churchyard are, as I do not suppose they are much earlier here than
the spring will now be at Whelpington. Before to-morrow at post-
time I shall have made arrangements for coming home, and will finish
this scrawl in London, and get it franked by Mr. Ellison, that you may
receive it by Curry on Thursday evening.

"British Museum, 19 May, 1829.—I hear nothing of Mr. Swinburne. You must get the inclosed letters delivered on Friday morning.
I have not sealed them, that you may know their contents, and thus
spare me writing much. I have not got your letter, but in the expectation of getting away on Thursday have bought you some silk stockings, gloves, &c., and Richard two pairs of trousers and two waistcoats.
I have indeed laid out 6*l*. 15*s*., besides which I have received from Mr.
Richard (Capt.) Rawes a very pretty brilliant and ruby ring for Bessy,
which seems quite new; but which the late Mrs. Captain Rawes wore.
She must consider herself highly honoured. I have this moment been
lunching under this roof with Mrs. Palmer at Mr. Baker's. The boys
*are* to go to Bromley. Let the notice of my not being at home on

Sunday be soon and widely circulated. There will be little time to do it in. You must write a note to Mr. Dodd. Fenwick will tell it at Catcherside. Probably I may never more come here, therefore I wish to do all I can while I am here, and all my friends persuade me to this [*the remainder of the page is torn off*].

To Mrs. HODGSON.

" MY DEAR JANE,                                   Tavistock Hotel, 20 May, 1829.

" I fully expected to have had a letter from you on Monday, and more so this morning, but none has arrived. You would get on Thursday a note written from Bromley, and inclosing a few notes to Mr. Aynsley, Mr. A. Trevelyan, and others. I put the letter into the post-office myself last night, and hope there is no fear of its reaching you. On the method I propose of getting from Newcastle home I will write by Saturday's post, so that you may get my letter on Monday. The inclosed letter was given to me by Mrs. Sedgwick this morning, with a parcel for you, which of course cannot be delivered till I reach home. I have really nothing to write about which can interest you. I slept last night at Stratford, which is near Upton, and Mr. Rawes drove me up this morning. We have been together all the day till about half-past three, when he returned home. I have not heard this week from Mr. Trevelyan. Yesterday I accidentally met with Mrs. Palmer at Mr. Baber's, in the British Museum, and partly promised to spend next Sunday with them at Bromley; though if I can get my job done by Friday evening, and hear that Mr. Trevelyan continues at Oxford, I may possibly go there on Saturday. I doubt that I shall not be able to see my correspondent Mr. Fenwicke at Kempston, near Bedford.*

22d May.—" For the last two days I have been employed in the Museum, and have got each day more done than I had done before in the whole of the time I have been here. To-morrow the Museum is not open, but I shall get three days in it next week. On Thursday I shall set off home, and hope to get to Cambo by the Chevy Chase on Saturday morning. My trunk, which is now rather too heavy with books to bring by the coach, will be put under the care of Mr. Turnbull

* The Rev. G. O. Fenwicke, afterwards Vicar of Aston, near Birmingham, descended from the Fenwickes of Brinkburne Abbey, in Northumberland, and a great promoter and purchaser of topographical publications. His pedigree is given in Hodgson's History, Part II. vol. ii. p. 116.

into the steam-boat on Tuesday, and reach Newcastle on Thursday, in time for Jacob to get it at the Clerk of the Peace's office, which is kept by Mr. Turnbull.  The rest of the things will come with myself in a bag which I have purchased.  Mr. Palmer called here this morning to see if I would be at liberty to go to Bromley, which I consented to do to-morrow afternoon, and stay till Monday morning.  Since I sent my last letter off I have really at times been miserable that I did not set off home yesterday morning; and had I done so, I could never have looked at my small collection of notes without upbraiding myself for doing so little as I have done before the last two days.  The truth is, that if you have anything to do in London, and at distant places, it takes several days to go through it, and I have now only just got fairly set to work. Not having got a second letter from you also makes me uneasy, as I fear one has some way miscarried.  Mr. Adamson is here, and I break-fasted with him at Wills's Coffee Room this morning.  To-morrow I intend to breakfast with Mr. Ellison, whom I have seen only once this week.  His house lies much out of my way.  What shall I buy for William, Mary, and Emma?  You cannot answer me,—but I must con-trive something.  The weather here continues dry, but it is not hot. Grass however is getting plentiful, and in three weeks time the hay harvest will be commencing.  I can give no directions what is to be done about the gardens.  The parcel in my trunk is I see directed to Miss Sedgwick, and not to you.  I really have no subject to fill my letter with.  Mr. Hedley has written twice to me, and I must this evening give him a line.  My evenings are all very dull.  I have nobody to speak with; which is my own fault, as I have not made it known that I am in town, which, indeed, I could not have done without spending more useless time.  There is still above a week to go before I shall see you.  Yesterday I dined with the family in the hotel here: to-day I must seek my dinner elsewhere.  It will I fear be too late in the morning on Friday next, when I get into Newcastle, to ask Richard to meet me, and too soon in the next morning before I set out for Cambo.  The lad had best meet me at the Four Lanes' End, and I can get out there.  This plan you may consider fixed, if I do not write by your Thursday's post to say that I will not start from here till Friday, and that he must meet me at five at Miller's on Sunday morning; a plan which I am not likely to adopt, as I shall have to go to Cap-heaton on the Sunday afternoon.  In the greatest haste, thine, my dear Jane,

"John Hodgson."

To Mrs. HODGSON.

" MY DEAR JANE,                                        Bromley, May 25, 1829.

"I came here yesterday with Mr. Palmer. Mr. Newell, the
clergyman, was indisposed, and while a messenger came to me to ask me
to assist him in his duties, the Bishop of Rochester, whose palace is
here, had sent for his brother for that purpose. I had, however, to
assist at six o'clock in the evening. We had a good deal of rain yesterday afternoon, and this morning the wind is north and the air cold and
cloudy. What a delightful place this of Mr. Palmer's is; and indeed
the country all around Bromley. Mr. Palmer has a great many very
fine oil paintings, several of which I believe were purchased in Italy
during his tour there with Mrs. Palmer and Wm. Rawes. I did not
mention having seen about a fortnight since a most surprising representation, cut in hard sandstone at full length, figures of Tam o' Shanter
and Souter Johnny, now exhibiting in London, and executed by a
common stonemason in Ayr. It is real life—full of animation and
truth. The family here are all well. I keep to my resolution of being
home on Saturday by the Chevy Chase. Let Jacob inquire for my
trunk at Mr. Turnbull's, Clerk of Peace's Office, Newcastle, and if he
does not get it, let Ned call. Ever thine,

                                                              J. H.


To HENRY PETRIE, Esq.

" MY DEAR SIR,                                    Tavistock Hotel, 19th May 1829.

"I mentioned to you that I wanted certain papers respecting the
Middleton family, and will now thank you to let me have an office copy
of the inquest after the death of Christiana de Middleton, 9 Hen. V. and
No. 54 in vol. 4, p. 61, of the printed calendar. Also of the document
Johannes de Middleton, rebellis 4 Edw. III. No. 13, p. 438, of same
volume. I wish to have them on stamped paper and signed by yourself. I am intending to remain here till about the middle of next week.
Should you not be able to have the copies made before that time, you
can inclose them with the copy of the Northumberland Pipe Roll: and
mention the charge of the two Middleton transcripts, which will be
repaid to me. As soon as I get home I will endeavour to embody the
unpublished information I have respecting the Roman History of

Britain, and will also seriously set about some diggings in our northern Roman Stations, the result of which shall be communicated to you. I am, dear Sir, yours truly,

"JOHN HODGSON."

### To MR. SOPWITH.

"MY DEAR SIR,                                    Whelpington, 2nd June, 1829.

"I returned from London on Saturday morning, and found my family visited by the measles. All your drawings have arrived safely, and come up to all my expectations of them. Widdrington and New-biggin are capital, considering the subjects, and on account of their being got up with pen and ink are much better for the engraver than when done in sepia or India ink.——I am glad you have set about the subject of the History of Mining. You should, if you have not done so already, see Sir John Pettus's History of the Chief Mines and Mineral Works in England and Wales. It was printed in London in folio 1670. —— I had heard of, but have not seen, the article in the Quarterly Review respecting Surtees's History of Durham.*——I really do not know what to say about the road through Whelpington. I will remember your offer and talk to Sir John Swinburne about it when he returns from London.——

"JOHN HODGSON."

### To THE REV. J. RAINE.

"MY DEAR RAINE,                                 Whelpington, 6th June, 1829.

"With this I restore you several lost rights; of which I have however not made much use.

"The pamphlet respecting Dawes I promised to Mr. Peacock,† and I send it to you, supposing you may have an opportunity of forwarding it to him free of expense.

"I regret exceedingly that I did not get to Cambridge; but by stay-ing a week longer in London I got through the whole of Dodsworth's volume of Northumberland Extracts, which will be valuable to me. It

* The review here referred to was written by Southey. See the Quarterly Review, vol. xxxiv. p. 360.

† At that time Fellow and Tutor of Trinity College, Cambridge, now Dean of Ely, and Prolocutor of Convocation in the Province of Canterbury.

was great grief to me to come home so soon; for I had obtained access to the Pipe Rolls in the Exchequer Office in Somerset House, and in three weeks could have gathered from them *lots of excellent stuff;* but I could get nobody to do duty for me. I found the accompanying engraving with your Appendix, which Richard saw last Sunday, and was somewhat startled on account of its great length; but I have no doubt he will attack it very soon. Pray have me in view when you come amongst Northumberland Papers; and when you have any at command let me know, and I will ride over to consult with you about them. I hope you found Mrs. Raine and the bairn well. Do not be long in coming to Meldon, and forget not to bring Mr. Peacock with you according to his promise. Ever yours,

"JOHN HODGSON."

"To MR. SOPWITH.—June 27, 1829.—If regular surveys of old workings had been preserved, how many mines would have been re-opened since the invention of the steam-engine that were formerly drowned out with water; and how much needless expense saved in searching for minerals where unsuccessful operations had perhaps very frequently at different forgotten intervals been carried on before! I have not seen any of the new woodcuts yet: they are all under the engraver.

"There was a meeting at Cambo about the much-talked-of new line of road here, but nothing settled about a survey; I, however, strongly recommended that you should be employed to make a general survey with respect to the distance and levels, and the subject is intended to be discussed at a meeting at Ponteland, which will be advertised soon.*—

After the publication of his Volume of Records in 1828, Hodgson again began to make numerous and extended progresses through various parts of the county, to gather together informa-

* On the 26th of July following, Hodgson thus writes to Mr. Sopwith on the same subject: "I am commissioned by Sir John Swinburne to ask you for what sum you could undertake to make a *general* survey of the country between Belsay and Otter-burne, to try if a better line of road between these two places could be got than the one given by McAdam through Cambo.——There is no crop on any part of the line to prevent your beginning the survey at any time ; and you can have a bed and tabling here." The survey was undertaken by Mr. Sopwith, and the new line of road made in due time, to the great convenience of Whelpington and various other places which had long been in a great measure inaccessible.

tion for the future portions of his History. In the autumn of the above year, and in fact until he began to keep a regular Journal in 1832, I find in his Note Books, mixed up with extracts from Title Deeds, surveys of old camps, church notes, &c. more entries than usual of a nature peculiarly suited to these pages. The following extracts may be taken as specimens. We have seen above that in 1814 he paid his first visit to Mounces, the shooting-seat of Sir J. E. Swinburne, situated at the head of the North Tyne on the Scottish border.* Here we have a very interesting account of a second visit to the same place, after an interval of fifteen years, during which there had been time for newly-planted forest trees to grow, and road-making and agriculture to make due progress. Hodgson in this second visit takes care to note the improvement which had taken place in these respects; and he gives a plain but interesting account of the altered appearance of the country. He goes again·at the commencement of grouse shooting, but, as before, he had other game in view.

"1829, 12th August. I got here yesterday with Sir J. E. Swinburne and Mr. Ward. The place is much improved, the plantations much grown, and many kinds of trees and shrubs flourishing beautifully. The parts inclosed grow good crops of hay, where the ground is dry; and by the side of the Tyne, by dividing the land into small inclosures, and even by following the same practice up the sides of many of the becks and bournes that run into it, much land might be reclaimed and rendered fifty times more fruitful. Till, however, capital can be employed to drain a great deal of the land, and divide much of it into small sheltered patches, not much good can be expected to be done here. Butter, cheese, bacon, and grazing, and the rearing of stock, are the things to be principally attended to. Potatoes grow well, but they want an early kind for use in July. They should sow seed and make use of such plants as grow tubers very early. Gardens, too, answer well; and all the way from Bellingham, wherever I saw apple-trees, they were well loaded with fruit; especially the walls on the south of the west wing at Mounces, and the south side of the north wall in the stable yard, have a very full crop of apples. The brooks are very black, from flowing off peat mosses: and the great humidity of the ground is favourable

* Vol. I. p. 137.

to the breed of midges, which are very affectionate to all animals, especially to man: at the entrance to the stables they formed a dense cloud, and they do not fail to salute one very cordially in the house. The inhabitants, whose skins are tormented by their bite, wear black crape sowed to a skullcap before their faces, which, on first coming up into the country, gives one a very unfavourable opinion of them: they seem disguised banditti. The country, however, is capable of much improvement, and in point of climate and produce might be made a paradise of, in comparison to many parts, or indeed all parts, of Norway; for ivy grows well in this dale, which will not bear the winters of Norway. Woods are fast getting up to assist in fencing and building. The valley also abounds in coal, and by the spirited and highly praiseworthy exertions of Sir J. E. Swinburne, a carriage road will this autumn be finished all the way from Bellingham into Liddesdale.

The hedges here should all be made of stake of the sweet-scented willow; each stake about forty inches above ground, and one foot distant from each other; the shoots from them to be cut a year or two after they are planted. Every new cutting may be at a greater distance of time than the preceding: great abundance of fine osiers will be thus produced, but a few of the strongest shoots should be left on each stake, for other stakes and poles and yeathers. If the hedge can be kept from cattle other kinds of willows may be planted, especially such as will grow stakes and shafts for rakes, forks, &c. Where thorns will not grow, mountain-ash may also be planted thickly for hedges; and it endures cutting, and yields hoop and corf rods. It also grows admirably here, and when about thirty years old saws into narrow planks, which will last, especially if the tree has been ringed so as to prevent the rise of its sap the year before it be felled, and so to let it season while standing.

" I rode to-day with Sir John over the Limestone Know, to where the Lewis Burn takes in Okenshaw Burn; and thence by the fine new road he has made over the Border into Scotland, as far as till we had a sight of the Castleton ground, Dinley Bires and Lauriston in Liddesdale, and, between two hills away to the north-west, Hermitage. We could also see, to the south-west, like a great mirror inlaid in land, that fine arm of the Solway frith. Just as we passed the Border, which is nearly a mile on the English side below the summit level of the hill between Scotland and England, I could distinctly see in the south, as we ascended, the smoke of the city of Carlisle, and the tower of St. Mary's there, like a black spot in the sun-illumined smoke. All Liddesdale, as far down as I could see, is much uninclosed, and consists of coarse rushy land in pasture, with here and there along the Lid patches of inclosures, and further up the hill sides light-green spots in the open grounds, where grass has been mown for hay.   Castleton we could not see for the river banks, but its site was marked by its smoke; a number of small inclosures rise up the right bank of the river, and all seem chiefly employed as meadow.   Dinley Bires is the residence of Mr. Oliver, the Deputy Sheriff of Roxburghshire.   It has land in good condition about it.   Mr. Oliver is a spirited and intelligent farmer, and has lately taken a colliery of Sir John on the Lewis Burn, the produce of which he sells to persons who come for it as far as Hawick and Jedburgh: the inferior produce of the mine he employs in burning the lime of a stratum of that kind of stone which runs along the left side of the Liddle, a little above the inclosed ground of Lauriston and Dinley Bires.   The coal is worked by a grove, and of fair quality.   It is found of great use to the inhabitants of Liddesdale.   Sir John is going immediately to open a communication eastward from the colliery to his road, which comes past Mounces from Bellingham, by which the people of Liddesdale will have access to North Tindale with every kind of carriage. The road was laid out by a Mr. Wilson, who lives near Dinley Bires, and as far as he has carried it over Sir John's ground it is exceedingly well planned:   I cannot say as much for the line from the Scotch Border to the west of Liddesdale.

"Okenshaw Burn, as far as the Lodge, is very picturesque.  Just above its junction with the Lewisburn it runs through a narrow and rocky defile.   Sir John's uncle and his father used to take up their residence during the shooting season at the Lodge on Okenshaw Burn, before the house at Mounces was built.   Willow Bog is a good farmhouse, a mile or more above the Lodge, on the left bank of the stream: it was built by Sir John.   The old herd's house here is on the left bank of the burn, and was literally situated in a bog.   In the brook, from this place to its junction with Lewis Burn, I saw large lumps of the black flint, which abounds in this district, and which Sanderson the lapidary in Edinburgh told me, if it could be got in plenty, would be valuable for making mourning ornaments—in plenty, I suppose, to make it fashionable, not common.   As I was riding upon a spirited horse I could not dismount in the rough road to collect specimens; but from the few pieces of it which I took away from Mounces in 1814, and gave to Sanderson to cut next year, I have no doubt but pieces of great beauty might be procured. On the wheel it gives out the odour of lapis lazuli. Sir John had some years since completed a road to the Lodge passable by carts. The waters of all the streams of North Tindale are all *Ale* or *Yall* waters—all a very deep brown, especially in rainy weather.

"After returning from my ride into Scotland I walked through the Hawk Hirst wood north of Mounces, as far as the Lewis Burn, with the intention of fishing, but the day became wet and I returned. Some heaps of iron scoria on the north side of the wood have been employed in making the road. Coals for the use of the estate have been worked in the rising ground, on the west side of the road, north of the Hirst wood, also in the left bank of the Tyne between the Gowan Burn and the Kennel grounds, *i.e.* in the Plashet grounds.

"The park at Mounces is a tract of ground of about 500 acres, inclosed by a stone wall by Sir John's father, who improved ground here and at Rimside moor under an Act of Parliament.

"Liddesdale is a very straight valley, and of gradual ascent from Castleton to the 'Note of the Gate,' which is the name of a toll-bar on the highest ground between the Lid and Rule waters.

"All Liddisdale and Tindale, excepting the little haughs and the corn and foglands, are of an olive green colour; the rushes and bent grass being of a brown tint deepen the green of the grass that rises up amongst them. Where the moors have heather on them, they are now of a beautiful purple colour, the common heath being in flower. The vale of Liddesdale is narrow and wild-looking, with very little wood in it; none but such as has been planted near the river side. The hills about Hermitage seem to be of porphyry.

"13 Aug.—In walking from Lewis Burn yesterday, rain from the east met me, and it continued almost constantly wet from that time till dark. This morning too we have rain from the south-east, and are unable to stir out. Yesterday morning, in our ride over Sir John's new road, we had beautiful weather, a warm and delicious air; but the atmosphere not very clear; we, however, to the west could see the Criffell hills— and to the north-west, in the direction of Edinburgh, could distinguish hills melting in air, as the Eildon hills and those on this side of Selkirk. Yesterday I could see in my ride no where any of the black agate *in situ*. It is plentiful in the round detritus several feet above the bed of the Okenshaw Burn, &c. &c.

To Mr. ROBERT MACRETH, Newcastle.*

"Dear Sir,                                    Whelpington, 5 Sept. 1829.

"Mr. Adamson has again spoken to me about the likeness your sister wished to take. I really cannot say when I can get to Newcastle for the purpose. Could not your sister make it convenient to take it here? Perhaps you could accompany her, and I would send my cabriolet to take you up at Ponteland. My servant says he could not venture my horse in one day further than that place, as he is only in the way of recovery from an over-reach in one of his hoofs; or I would have sent him all the way to Newcastle, to which place, however, on your return he shall re-convey you. Perhaps you could find some employment about this place for your pencil; and I want to talk to you about the views you have in hand for me. You will oblige me by saying how this arrangement will suit you and your sister. If you can come, appoint a day that I may be at home to receive you. I am, dear Sir, yours truly,
                                    " John Hodgson."

The following painful extract will excite a sincere feeling of sympathy in those who like Hodgson have undertaken a fruitless toil in a public cause.

"To the Rev. J. Raine —Whelpington, 7th Sep. 1829.——My work grows a most heavy burden to me; though I work under it cheerfully, and every morning with renewed vigour. But in spite of all my plans and contrivances to get it up cheap but neat, it enthrals and embarrasses me in a pecuniary way. It grows expensive to purchase, and I cannot enter into any tricks to put it off and make it known. I do not know that I ever gave you a list of the subscribers to it, but inclose one which I printed to give a few copies to Archdeacon Singleton, who asked for a MS. copy.——
                                    " John Hodgson."

---

* This is the first of a series of letters on the subject of the Portrait which embellishes a subsequent volume of his history, and for them I am indebted to Mr. Mackreth, who now resides in York. The design of engraving the portrait by Nicholson, spoken of above, had been abandoned. The history, if it may be so called, of that by Miss Mackreth, which was eventually engraved, will be gathered from the letters in their order with which Mr. Mackreth has favoured me.

" TO THE REV. J. RAINE.—Oct. 9, 1829.——Do you know of any boy who could teach Latin, and writes a *goodish* hand, whom I could engage to work for me as my amanuensis, and would for an hour or so in the day teach such of my children as might be at home a lesson in common arithmetic or Latin, qualifications in which our governess does not excel. I have written to Dr. Robinson in Westmerland on the subject, but have not heard from him. A very humble scholar would answer my purpose; but one that was not industrious and tractable I could do nothing with. Forty pounds a year *is all* I could afford to give: I have said to Dr. Robinson only 32*l.* a-year. The situation would be very improving: but the lodgings that could be got here would be very indifferent. Living is very cheap, and a person who could cater for himself, and has been accustomed to plain, frugal living, might, I apprehend, have lodgings and find all his meat for 20*l.* a-year, or indeed for considerably less. Now if you know of any steady lad ' come of a good breed' of folks, however poor, to whom such a situation would be desirable, do me the very great favour to let me know. A lad that has a jem of genius in his cap, and yet could sit down to indexes, transcribe old deeds, read books, copy my rough draughts, and do a thousand other useful things in my study, would be a great blessing to me for a few years, and would find himself as happy as encouragement and kindness and 30*l.* or 40*l.* a year, and lodgings in an old Peelhouse with a canny old tailor and his wife, could make him. 30*l.* a-year is as much as I ought to give."

### To HENRY PETRIE, Esq

"MY DEAR SIR,                               Whelpington, 9th Oct. 1829.

" When I called upon you at the Tower in May last, I promised to go to the Roman Wall, and take some notes respecting the masonry of that celebrated barrier. A few of the members of the Newcastle Antiquarian Society and myself, indeed, had agreed during the course of the summer to examine a considerable part of it, and to dig in some of the Northumberland Stations, and to furnish you with a report of our observations: but the weather hitherto has been so wet and unfavourable for such operations, that we have not been able to fix a day to commence them; and although a friend came hither yesterday for the express purpose of naming a time for our meeting at the station of Little Chesters, which belongs to himself, yet the snow we had in the morning and the hard frost which succeeded in the night, have induced him to return home without coming to any determination when our antiquarian diggings are to commence. I do, however, hope to have leisure before winter sets regularly in to perform my promise to you: but in the mean time I will furnish you with some minutes from my note-books, on the accuracy of which you may rely.

"From a note-book written in the year 1818. 'The Roman Wall is still standing four or five feet high (in one place I counted seven courses of stone) on the west side of Burd-Oswald, but the masonry is of a very common sort—cubical stones with five sides roughly hewn and squared, and the inner end partly tapering from the outward, form the outside casing; and the space between them filled with rough stones laid in bad mortar: the shape of the stones somewhat of this kind. (A sketch.)

"This inscription at Wall Town · VICTORIAE · AVG · COH · VI · NERVIORVM CVI · PRAE · EST · G · IVL · BARBARVS · FEC · V · S · L · M.

"In the station at Great Chesters is a vault full of water to the impost of the arch. The arch itself of the ordinary masonry of the present time. (A neat sketch with the pen.)

"In ascending the basaltic cliffs to the east of Great Chesters and Haltwhistle Burn, the Roman Wall in many places still standing above the surface eight or nine courses high.

"Near the Wall Farm, and eastward of it for half a mile, the top of the remains of the Wall has been partly repaired, and ditches formed on each side of it, out of which the materials have been got for topping it with. (A sketch.)

"On some declivities a little further east the courses of the ashlar work run parallel to the surface of the earth.

"Up the declivity near Craig Lough Castellum parts of the wall of sound masonry and very perfect. The mortar is good, and shews that the wall has been constructed in regular flattings, with layers of basaltic rumlar work between each flatting of the mortar. In many places the inside is of rough masses of basalt. All the outside of hewn sandstone in courses, but at the head of Craig Lough more mortar used in the wall than in any other places. Through all the basaltic range from Tipper Moor to Caervoran limestone is found, either immediately above the basalt or in strata under it, alternating with silicious sandstone, and cropping out to the north of it.

"In ascending the hill east of Craig Lough the wall is very perfect, often above five feet high, and having frequent insets, thus—(a sketch).

VOL. II.                                   M

" A Roman bath at Housesteads built by the side of a brook has of late years been much plundered. The basalt has apparently been levelled for laying the foundations upon, which are formed of large ashlars laid on fine clay. Much limestone tufa found near the foundations of this bath, as indeed about all the Roman baths, probably used to filter and clarify the water through. It has all been squared finely, probaby fictitious, made by strong saturations of water with lime and some earthy impurities, and left to deposit—or from calcareous springs.

" The general appearance of the wall is thus *(a sketch)*, where it has not been disturbed for the purpose of making a fence with it. The inside of it has been filled up with alternate layers of lime and undressed stone. Much basalt in the inside, but generally nearly as much sandstone.

" The following fragment of a Roman mile-pillar was found close adjoining the wall opposite to Walton, where what remains of it is still preserved. *(A drawing, with an inscription.)* This stone was found lying flat, and was cut into several pieces, for the purpose of raising it more conveniently from the ground. The part in dotted letters is wanting. The above notes were made in 1818.

" You will find notices of several Northumberland inscriptions, not given by Horsley, in my account of that county in the Beauties of England and Wales; and of one, *important to your purpose,* I think, in the Archæologia Æliana, vol. i. p. 300. I do not recollect that in my account of the stations Bremenium and Habitancum, in Redesdale, there is anything new: but you will easily see when at the British Museum, by referring to Part II. vol. i. of my work on Northumberland; concerning one copy of which work I long to make some explanation to you, but find I cannot do so consistently with good faith. By the bye, Raine has not yet got a part of his work published, though it was his intention to do so with as much as was printed off in May, as soon as he could have it put up for circulation.

" Now, my dear Sir, the next subject I have to mention is one which of all others I can never talk about, from an apprehension that I might commit some mistake, and give pain in my own presence, but since I have had the pleasure of being introduced to you I can speak on paper freely and without reserve. I have sometimes had papers (all I think since Mr. Lysons's death) from the Tower. To whom, and how much am I indebted for them ? I seek to be in no other footing in asking for copies and extracts of Records than gentlemen engaged in similar works. Mine is certainly thoroughly profitless in a pecuniary point of view; but in the pleasure I have in compiling it I have rich compensation. A family of nine children and a small living confine me indeed within bounds of strict economy in getting up my work; but I expect that the part of the impression which is still to sell will some day or other allow me to pay without eventual loss the whole of the expenses I am at in getting it up.

" You begged me when I had to write to the Tower to write to yourself. I will endeavour not to be a very frequent and importunate beggar; but there is one subject concerning which I may eventually be somewhat unreasonable. I mean the papers respecting the rebellion of Gilbert de Middleton, concerning which I am anxious to give a clear and correct as well as a succinct account; but there is no writing briefly without being in full possession of every fact and bearing of one's subject. At another time I will give you a list of the records I allude to. They are among the Originalia and Patent Rolls. In the mean time allow me to solicit the favour of being furnished with a copy of the Pipe Rolls respecting Northumberland which you shewed me; and of which, if I recollect rightly, you said when I last saw you in the British Museum, you had ordered a copy to be made. I intend them to be printed in the Archæologia Æliana, and it would be a great favour to the Council of the Newcastle Antiquarian Society to have the copy soon, that it might get into this year's Transactions, which will be delivered to the members on the first Wednesday in January next. The transcript might be directed to me under cover to Mr. Charnley, bookseller, Newcastle-upon-Tyne, from Baldwin and Cradock's; or sent as a coach parcel.

" There is a copy of the Archæologia Æliana in the British Museum, and if you have not seen it I particularly recommend you to look at the inscription there, ' Deo Soli, &c. Dominis nostris Gallo et Volusino Consulibus.' From, my dear Sir, yours very faithfully,

" JOHN HODGSON."

### To MR. R. MACKRETH, NEWCASTLE.

" DEAR SIR,                                   Whelpington, 13 October, 1829.

" I like the view of Aydon Castle very much. It is very prettily designed and well printed; and I beg that you will at the first opportunity convey my best thanks for it to Sir Edward Blackett, and say that I will not fail to acknowledge the kindness he has done when my next preface is printed.

" I shall be very glad to receive the miniature from your sister on Thursday, and to shew it to our neighbours, who have asked much for it. We are all sorry, however, to hear of Miss Mackreth's indisposition, and fear it may have been brought on by her staying here or by her journey home: and when I think of it I find that she was most terribly crushed in the gig. As soon as the view of Mr. Lawson's house arrives I will send the whole to my bookbinders, and have them circulated among the subscribers to my work. I should, however, say that I do not expect the last proof-sheet of the part that I am intending to publish till next week. It will be November before I can publish.

" JOHN HODGSON."

To THE REV. JAMES RAINE.—" Featherstone Castle, near Haltwhistle, 26 Oct. 1829. When I was last at Durham I think you said I should find something about Lord Francis Russell, who was murdered at a Border meeting in Queen Elizabeth's time, in your WILLS. I have sought in vain for his name. There is a curious inventory of the goods of his father-in-law, Sir John Forster, of Bamborough, without date. If you have anything respecting him I shall feel very greatly obliged to you for it, because I am writing a short memoir of his life, to accompany some papers out of the Cottonian Library, furnished to the Newcastle Antiquarian Society by Captain Cook, respecting his death. The Indulgence for the pier at Newbigging came in time. I am staying a few days at this place, and shall trudge home by the Roman Wall, to try to make out something for Mr. Petrie. After next Saturday I expect to be pretty stationary at Whelpington for some time.

" Mr. Howard of Corby is come hither. *He says, he has no doubt but you have found the real St. Cuthbert.*\* He is much skilled in legendary lore.

" We have very fine weather, and certainly Featherstonehaugh is one

---

\* And yet in the beginning of this self-same year the same Mr. Howard had communicated to the Durham Chronicle a long review of my book, attempting to disprove this fact by numerous arguments, with but little, however, of plausibility or ingenuity on their side. I rejoiced to learn from the above letter that he had changed his opinion: but would it not have been well that the Durham Chronicle had been informed of the conviction at which he had arrived ?

Thirty years have now come and gone since the discovery was made that that substance which had been passed off as the incorrupt object of veneration, the veritable body of of the most interesting places one can visit. The landscape is excellent. The old tower of Featherstonehaugh remains, and Lord Wallace has built large additions of a useful kind to it in the castellated style, but of common masonry. The drawing-room is hung round, as thick as its extensive walls will allow, with portraits or prints of the most eminent men that have figured on the political scale of Europe for the last forty years.

" JOHN HODGSON."

To HENRY PETRIE, Esq.

" MY DEAR SIR,                          Whelpington, 13th Nov. 1829.

"My friend Mr. Swinburne and I, on leaving Featherstone Castle on the 30th of last month, intended to have measured and made drawings of several parts of the Roman Wall on our way home; but before we reached it the day became rainy, and so cold that it was impossible to do any thing in the way of making minutes and sketching. You perhaps are aware that all the remains of it that are now in any degree of perfection are on the high basaltic ridge of rock which lies between the North Tyne at Chollerford and Thirlwall Castle on the Tippal, and that the situation is so exposed and inhospitable that it is very difficult in a bad season to fall upon a suitable day, especially in winter, for exploring the Stations and Wall itself. Several of my friends are very anxious to be with me for two or three days in a digging excursion, and there is no difficulty in obtaining leave to make sections across any part of the Wall, or to remove rubbish from the walls and gateways of the Stations; which I beg you to rest assured shall be done, as soon as ever I can see fair weather, and muster forces fit for the purpose.

"The copies of the Pipe Rolls came from Raine two or three days

---

St. Cuthbert, wanting only the breath of life, was and had been for centuries nothing more than a well-clothed skeleton, with eyes of wax and other equipments to mislead the beholder. Against the account of this discovery which I published soon afterwards, much has been said and written, in defence of the reputed incorruptibility of the Saint, and against the identity of the human remains then discovered with those of St. Cuthbert. But the time has arrived when somewhat must be said in reply to arguments now in all probability exhausted. In " Saint Cuthbert, a Postscript," now in course of preparation for the press, an attempt will be made to prove that such statements and arguments as have been adduced by my opponents are untenable and worthless.

after I wrote to you. They are very curious, inasmuch as they are amongst the very earliest records respecting this county. I am myself very greatly obliged to you for them; though, as I mentioned to you, I begged for copies of them to be printed in the Antiquarian Society of Newcastle's Transactions.

"I am at present engaged in writing a pedigree of the family of Widdrington of Widdrington, and though I have collected much material for the purpose I find some difficulties in the way. The Lansdowne MS. 826, fol. 131, gives an extract of an Inspeximus of the Inquisitiones post mortem of Adam de Swinburne in 12 Edw. II. No. 28,* and of another Adam de Swinburne in 20 Edw. II. No. 48,† and says that the first Adam died leaving a son and heir Henry, and that the second Adam left three daughters, Barnaba, Christian and Elizabeth. Now Vincent, and I understand from the Inquests themselves, as consulted by Mr. Beltz, gives the following account of the relationship between these two persons and the daughters Barnaba, Christian and Elizabeth.

Johannes de Swinburne ... ...

| Nicholaus de Swinburne. | Dominus Adam de Swinburne miles testis cum patre Johanne A°. 3 Edw. II. ob. 13 Ed. III. Escaet. 13 Ed. III. Tenuit terras de Est Swinburne de Roberto de Swinburne de Gunwarton, &c. | Margareta, jure cujus maritus suus tenuit Laverton in com. Cumb. | Robertus | Willelmus |
|---|---|---|---|---|
| Henricus filius æt. 21 temp. mort. patris. | Adam de Swinburne, dictus Baro, ob. s. p. 20 Edw. II. Esc. eod. an. | Barbara nupta Strivelyn. | Christiana nupta Joh. de Woderington | Elizabetha nupta Heron |
| | Joh. de Strivelyn, Baro, &c. | | Gerardus | Will. Heron. |

Now you will oblige me much by letting me have out of the original Escheats above alluded to such genealogical facts as they may contain. I do not want copies of them. The first of the two Adam de Swinburnes was Sheriff of Northumberland in 9, 10, and 11 Edward II., who imprisoned him for speaking too freely of some Border matters; which proceeding caused the spirited and powerful shock which his kinsman Gilbert de Middleton gave to Edward's power in the North of England

* At this place Mr. Petrie has added a note in pencil, "Ap. Nov. Cast. super Tynam. Henr. fil. et heres, æt. 22."

† Note in pencil by Mr. Petrie: "Barnaba filia Adæ 32 ann. Gerardus de Wooderington filius Xtianæ filiæ Adæ sororis ejusdem Barnabæ 23 ann. Willelmus Heron, filius Elizabethæ filiæ Adæ sororis ejusdem Xtianæ, 22 an. prop. heredes Adæ."

in 1817. As I am writing about the family into which one of his heiresses married, I am anxious to put the conflicting account I have obtained right before it goes to the press, which I cannot do without some kind assistance.

" 23 Nov. Since I wrote the above I have seen Mr. Raine at Durham, and he wishes much to accompany me in making the intended examination of the Wall, but agrees with me that it must be put off till the ensuing spring. I am, dear Sir, very truly yours,

" JOHN HODGSON."

TO THE REV. J. RAINE.—" Ponteland, 7th Dec. 1829.—I came hither this morning to attend a turnpike road meeting.——I write in great haste, and in the confusion of one of the most stormy meetings I was ever at. But we are gaining our point; a Bill for a road through Whelpington is to go to Parliament.

" I have thought much on the subject of reviewing your St. Cuthbert in Blackwood's Magazine, which is a work I never see, and am therefore not acquainted with the genius of its spirit; but as yours is a book of facts, many of which fade off on every side into aerial fictions and superstitions, it cannot I think be unacceptable to the genius of the times to have a little insight into the scenic splendour of the English Roman Catholic Church, during the several centuries it flourished in this country; and especially to have brought before its eyes the shows and pantomimic ceremonies that were constantly exhibiting in the neighbourhood of the Shrine of St. Cuthbert, whom I have in a very short sketch of his wanderings in another place * described as the great idol of the church of Durham, a god neither of wood nor stone, no graven image, nor the likeness of anything in heaven or on the earth or under the earth made by man's hands, but the body of an aged anchoret, who on account of the piety of his life and the reputed miracles which he wrought after his death, became the object of adoration to thousands. Now if your friend Gilly does not get his promise performed to have your book displayed in the Quarterly, I will attempt to get it a conspicuous place in Blackwood. Have you therefore any hints you can give me, any additions or new views, which I could introduce as my own, and weave as a sort of gems and jewels into the hair and embroidery of the robes of the fair literary daughter you have sent into the world? If you have, let me have them.

* History. Part II. vol. ii. p. 132, published in 1832.

"I have not quite recovered from the frightful shock and stunning I got at Sedgefield, which I did not mention to you because it could serve no good purpose for me to publish all the horrible injustices one is forced to become acquainted with.*

"JOHN HODGSON."

* He here refers to a private matter deeply and painfully affecting the interests of his children,—a lease of certain valuable stone quarries on Gateshead Fell held of the see of Durham, the renewal of which at the proper time had been neglected, and which, upon application being made by him for that purpose, was found to have been granted by the bishop as a concurrent lease to another party. The lease had been held by Mr. Kell, Mrs. Hodgson's father.

Correspondence — Mr. Mackay — Extracts from Journal—Wylam — Close House — Corbridge— Healeyside— Cariteth— Tarset Castle— Chirdon— Dalley Castle— Bellingham—Alston—Correspondence—A Fever—Illness of six of his children and death of two—Letters of Condolence.

### To Mr. ROBERT MACKRETH.

" My dear Sir,                                       Whelpington, 13 Feb. (1830).

"Has Mr. Dobson or yourself ever been able to get me any sketches of Horton, Bedlington, or Blyth churches ?   I merely ask on account of intending to go down thither soon, and if you have not been able to do me that kindness, that I may get it done while I am there. I expected Mr. Swinburne the week before last would have gone with me to Hebburn, but the weather was so stormy he did not dare to venture.  As soon, however, as he is able to stir, and your sister is at home, we will do ourselves the pleasure of calling upon her to consult about getting the portrait engraved.  I have heard that she is working hard at Netherwitton.

                                                    " John Hodgson."

Mr. Hodgson's amanuensis, and the tutor of his younger children, had been for some time up to this period Mr. James Holme, a nephew of his friend and neighbour Mr. Redman, vicar of Kirkharle, and afterwards a clergyman of the Church of England; a gentleman of unassuming demeanour and much information.  Upon Mr. Holme leaving Whelpington, to settle upon a curacy, Hodgson, on the 23rd of February in this year, commissioned his friend Professor Pillans to recommend to him a youth duly qualified to act in the above capacities, and the result was an engagement with Mr. P. Mackay, a student in the University of Edinburgh, which was highly satisfactory to both parties.  Mr. Mackay entered with all his heart into Hodgson's pursuits and his own duties, and became as it were a member of the family, receiving the kindest attention from all its members.

His engagement at Whelpington terminated two or three years afterwards, upon his appointment to the mastership of the school of Gifford, near Haddington, but, as the sequel will shew, a friendly intercourse was kept up between Hodgson and him till the death of the former in 1845.

To THE REV. J. RAINE, 3 March, 1830.—" Till I get an amanuensis I cannot get on with observations on your Saint Cuthbert. A review of it might be treated in many different ways. It would be a capital text-book for reflections upon the ancient and present state of the revenues of the Church of Durham, and upon their influence on society. ' Sed in vetita ruebam.'"

1830, 25 March.—" The ground from the steward's house is to the south a long uniform flat, with Painshaw, Warden-Law, and Gateshead Fell in the distance. ——— is attending Parliament, but in his absence I see this morning six grooms and ten horses taking their air in the pleasure grounds. What a curse to the quiet, the prudent, and economical part of mankind is this rage for hunting, for running back into a savage state ! How many families might be employed in useful work at the expense of keeping so many useless dogs, horses, and men ! how much land drained and fenced, how much wood planted!— *Journal.*

In the summer season of the year Hodgson had long been actively engaged in a survey of some particular portion of Northumberland, as he was approaching it in his history. The following are a few extracts from that volume of his Collections which is marked with the letter Z., and which refers to the year before us. They may not be without interest to some of my readers, especially as they relate to localities of which he did not live to write an account for his book. Extracts of this nature and of the same interest might have been made to a great extent, but my space is limited.

1830, 5 May.—" WYLAM.—There is at Wylam an etching of the house, about sixteen inches by ten, drawn and engraved by R. Beilby.* The old house of the Fenwicks is vaulted below, the whole length, which

* An artist employed by Brand in his History of Newcastle.

is sixty feet within. The additions by Blackett, who purchased of Nicholas Fenwick, are apartments added thus [*a sketch*], and fronting the east.

" The farmers are busy washing their sheep,—one whom we saw very like Josceline Percy. In the wood on the banks of the Tyne, just above Wylam wood, hyacinth, stellaria major, lychnis divisa, and chrysosplenium oppositofolium, spartum scoparium, wood strawberry, myositis arvensis, asperula odorata, anemone nemorosa, melampyrum sylvaticum, wood cow-wheat, not in full blossom, but very nearly. About Wylam, by the hedges, sinapis alba very common and in full flower, and about the house the horse-chesnut in full flower and foliage. The terrace walk along the wood, on the right bank of the Tyne, from the house at Wylam to Horsley dene, is very fine; the river broad and noble below it, and the prospect on the opposite banks and up the Tyne broad and beautiful. The walk up Horsley dene might be extended to great advantage, for the woods up the dene both on the Duke's and the Wylam side are very healthy and thick: the dene is broad, and the brook through it constant.

" The situation of CLOSE HOUSE is extremely good. The hill of Heddon rises rapidly behind it on the north, from the rude visitations of which it is also well defended by a very fine grove of trees. .Indeed the trees to a good distance around the house, as well in groves as single in the inclosures, are very beautiful: they are healthy, finely formed, large and luxuriant; but in some places very fine oaks have had larches and other annoyances planted under and beside them, very injudiciously. The prospect from the house down the river is extensive. Gateshead Fell and its cottages and villas glitter and impart life and cheerfulness to the distances, without the inconveniences its population brings to places nearer it. Then the busy traffic on the Tyne, the smoke of various manufactories, and the steam engine, in all directions, *sublimi anhelitu*, performing its stupendous labours, are too distant to be any real abridgment of comfort, while they raise ideas in the mind of the immense wealth and industry to which our country has arrived within the last fifty years. The house was built by the late Mr. Bewick's father from designs by            , but though it is of good masonry, good stone, and I am told very convenient and comfortable within, the style of the exterior of the building is very bald. There are too many windows; the house is nearly square, and too high for its width. But it has near it a         , which has tresses to the earth, and in size and flowing luxuriance has nowhere in the North a rival. It was to-day in full flower: but for May in the North of England this day, and several days that have preceded, were uncommonly fine.    The prospect over the horizon to the south has a bad outline, but nearly to the tops of the high grounds it sparkles with farmhouses and villages.

" CORBRIDGE.—6 May 1830.—The town (for such its antiquity demands that it be styled) is dirty, and in all the streets, except that through which the Newcastle and Carlisle road passes, is filthy with middens and pigsties, with railing before them of split boards, &c.   The population seem half-fed: the women sallow and thin-armed, the men flabby, pot-bellied, and tender-footed: but still the place bears the appearance of ancient.   Many of the houses, even in the back streets, are large, and should be carefully examined for arms, &c.   Rock appears above the bridge (which is of seven arches), and in the gardens above it on the north side.   The river now divides above it into two channels, and runs through two side arches, leaving immense gravel and sand banks above and below.   The valley three quarters of a mile below seems to close, and above forms a fine amphitheatre of an oblong form, and a mile or more in perfectly flat lands in diameter, having Hexham and the hills above Warden at its head, and Dilston, mournful Dilston, and Beaufront, glittering in the sun, on its right.   The church has a dirty doghole of a school on the south side of the steeple, which has had a doorway in its west wall.   The doorway to the nave on the south is ancient and rather of rude simplicity, thus (a drawing); the arch semicircular and zigzagged, and the shaft still remaining.   The whole roof of sandstone, and very ancient, has never been leaded.   Three horrible Venetian windows lately put into the south gable of the south transept, and east end of the chancel, where there had been three lancet-headed windows rather distant from each other (a sketch).   The chapel windows covered with wire grating.   By the road side, on its east end, a Roman funeral head-stone with a figure rudely carved: it has been recently and ignorantly put there.   On the north wall on a panelled stone, probably brought hither as a curious relic, is a cross with ⅭⅮARIA carved upon it somewhat as in the margin (a sketch). The chapel has a tower little higher than its roof, and between the two a small belfry.   A private door in the lower part for a family.   The whole probably built after the Reformation, certainly all at one time, and just as it is at present: it is covered with lead.   In the way from the bridge up the bank, the crown of an arch in the floor of the old gateway still plain.   The outer wall is stripped of its facing stones, and some hewn stones among its fillings. Scandix odorata and arum mac. growing here, and in full flower. The hewn stones parts of former buildings. Remains of the tower or castle 60 feet north and south, and thirty feet east and west on the outside, by stepping. Outside much patched with brick, broken and dilapidated, but venerable. In a haugh above Dilston found one stalk of bracken (Pteris aquilina), exactly three feet long, and with very little feather. All the woods swarming with black ants. Thick with oak. Fine, very fine larch. Allium ursinum thick and in full flower. Vaccinium Myrtillus also abundant, and in flower. Rocks in the burn matted with marcuntia. Three haughs with corn, or in fallow. Little wood-hung amphitheatres. Prunus padus abundant. Wood anemone large, two inches in diameter, and of various colour. The bird-cherry so rich I could adore it with parental piety, as the tree of my native county. The rocks in places grey and bold, and browed with heather, and trees of various kinds. The haughs have different levels, one of them thus (*a sketch*). Large heaps of black ants nestled in small short twigs of birch. Cultivated country seen about two miles above Dilston in the opening of the woods. Old Sandy Armstrong, a cunning buffoon, walking in the woods at Capheaton, and laying his hand upon a large holly-tree, exclaimed, 'Ah, what a muckle thristle!' The left bank finely hung with wood, then wettish inclosed lands, and on the crown of the hill Scotch pine. The private bridge at Dilston was called the Lord's Bridge. Mr. Edward Swinburne and Mr. Christ. Blackett accompanied me to Dilston, and Mr. Swinburne took a sketch of the remains of the castle for a vignette for my book. There is at the Angel Inn at Corbridge a very curious table of oak, inlaid in the frame with other kinds of wood. It is massive and large, and supposed to have been taken out of Dilston after Lord Derwentwater was beheaded. It has slides to make it double the size of which it commonly appears. Mr. Swinburne and I, on May 7, left the kind and hospitable roof of Mr. Blackett, who has promised to send me some dates of births, &c. of his family for the last four generations."

" HESLEYSIDE.—17 May, 1830.—Keming's cross, on Armstrong's map, ought to be Cumin's cross, from Cumins lords of Tarset. There is a strange traditionary story about stealing a silver tankard. The Cumins went into Scotland in the reign of David I. and became powerful." (*From a note by Mr. Ellis of Otterburn.*)

" CARITETH, a farm chiefly of grassland, in ancient inclosure on the west side of Cariteth burn, which slopes up into the moors in two or three streamlets, that join about half a mile above Low Cariteth.  It is wild, and thick with tall alder, birch, hasel, and the property of Mr. Charlton of Hesleyside, who bought it of Colonel Reed.  On the opposite side of the dingle, on a fine high knoll, a group of cottages, called Aldman Shield, one of them occupied as a school (*a sketch*).  The upper part of Cariteth Dene forks off, is broad, and has beautiful oaks and birches, and a rude winding path in it.  A sunny good inclosure of irregular form, on the north side of the dene to where it branches off in the broader part.  Three or four graceful groups of aspen poplar, which sprout up here naturally.  Birch, much of it weeping, and oak not very large, but considerable, and straight and elegant for their kind."  (*A Sketch.*)

"TARSET CASTLE.—18 May.—Orchis conopsea, a common plant on high moist lands, grows plentifully on a knoll on the outskirts of the wood three or four hundred yards above the branching off of the burn.  Much of the North Tindale black flint as far down as Hesleyside; and on the island below the ford Scotch fir spring up naturally and beautifully.  Prospect in a sunny morning from Hesleyside to Bellingham very charming.  A broad glistering reach of the river in it."  (*A ground-plan of Tarset Castle, with measurements.*)

"CHIRDON.  The keep at Chirdon is twenty-seven feet by fifteen within in the vault.  It has a window above the door to the vaulted ground-floor.  The door to the south has no stairs to it.  New stairs put on the outside on the north."

"DALLEY CASTLE is on a green mount formed by cutting across the end of a promontory of rising ground, and throwing the earth of the ditch upon the mount to heighten it (*a ground plan*).  The keep of the castle has been twenty-seven feet by twenty-four, and had some buildings of strong masonry on its west side.  It belongs to Mr. Charlton of Sandhoe, who is a Charlton of the Bower, an ancient seat of that famous family about a mile west of Dalley Castle.  The Chirdon is a broad craggy brook with a very rough bed, and hemmed with alders and other trees.  Dalley Castle was a good barrier against the passage to the Bower, to which place I did not go on account of rain falling and being myself unwell.  Dalley Castle is of strong masonry, as far as it remains, which I apprehend is nothing more than a few feet of the fillings of its foundation walls.  Very little facing stone remains.  Two or three I saw in the inside."

" BELLINGHAM is on a tongue of land between the Tyne and Hareshaw-burn; and looks admirably from the upper windows of Hesleyside in a summer's morning. The hills in the valley from Bellingham to above Mounces are low, and have ling far down them, and in a squally evening look very black and dismal. At the head of the valley they are higher, drier, and more bold. The Plashetts, Kennel, Belling, and Bellingmill, belong to a family of Robsons, and there are abstracts of several deeds respecting them at Hesleyside. Mr. Charlton has a great many very curious grants to Monasteries; and private grants respecting Cumbria: many very old, which would do for the Antiquarian Society's Transactions." *(A ground-plan, and copies notes of Bellingham Church.)*

On the 6th of July he begins to survey the Roman wall at Tepper Moor—reaches Housesteads in the evening, and until the evening of the 9th is engaged in superintending excavations there, of which he has made very copious notes, but, as the substance of these is doubtless incorporated in his History, I make no extracts.

To THE REV. J. RAINE.—JULY 4, 1830.—" I am intending to be at the gates of Housesteads on Wednesday morning. I will not wait of the weather any longer: but make my observations and send them imme-diately to Mr. Petrie. I must brave weather to serve him. Mr. T. Hodgson, I know, wishes to be present at the *houking*, and if you can contrive to get up to Housesteads with him in a gig, it might be con-venient to you both. I should say that Mr. Hodgson is the editor of the Newcastle Chronicle, and preparing a new edition of the Britannia Romana; rouse yourself and come, if Mrs. Raine's health will permit you. I will not visit Surtees till I have finished the volume I am engaged with. Petrie's kindness demands my attention.——

" JOHN HODGSON."

1830, 26 July.—ALSTON.—" I came hither to-day in company with Sir J. E. Swinburne, and his son-in-law Mr. Bowden. I breakfasted at Capheaton. We came in a carriage to Haydon bridge, and thence on horseback. In our way we called on Mr. Hedley, at the parsonage of Whitfield, and at Whitfield, both of which places are in great beauty. Mr. Hedley's garden at any place would be beautiful, but here especially, in a very high and exposed situation, and after a very hard winter, and, till a few days since, a spring and summer very memorable for their wetness. The country here is all in its beauty, the meadows full of grass, which is now cutting. The herbage below the cropping of the great limestone, and especially on the haughs by the river side, rich and various."

"July 27th.—This morning the party I came hither with and myself set off at 7 o'clock for Hartside, and went far enough to see the very glorious sight of the Cumberland and Westmerland hills, and the lake of Ulswater, and the fertile champaign country that laid between us and them. We could not see the Criffell hills, or Solway firth, for a cloud-bank that seemed to rest on the sea.* I went a little further than the rest to get a sight of my native country, and could clearly see the hills above Haweswater and the Knipe scar fir plantations, but could not stay, from the party waiting to return to Alston to breakfast, to particularize and gaze upon many objects dear to me.——We walked with Mr. Pattison to Heleyfield mine, but the day was so excessively hot that we were *sweltered* and tired with a walk of one mile. The people here are good hay-makers; they strew the grass with their hands and work well: they are also leading much of their hay out of windrow, but some small parts of it are put up in pikes. The whinstone, over which Nentforce falls, has a very soft and mouldering stratum of schist under it, and which undermines it both in the bed of the river and on each side, so as to cause it to fall in very huge masses. On the moist sides of these rocky banks, Epylolium parvifl. grows abundantly, and is a very pretty plant. From the nursery garden in the evening the valley looks broad, and Crossfell seems to sweep more boldly the horizon than it does from the higher stations about the inn. The sun set over Knaresdale, and the colours of the hills to the south-west and north were transparent and brilliant. The evening continued so hot till after nine, while I was out, that it was quite a trouble to walk about even by the river side.——July 28. This morning is again excessively hot. The whole atmosphere at half-past six, fervid and breathless."

To ROBERT MACKRETH, Esq. Great Smith Street, Westminster.

"My dear Sir,                      Whelpington, 4 Aug., 1830.

"I am glad you have written to me on the subject of the portrait. You may get it done in the dotted style, and by Deane or any

* See vol. i. p. 13.

other person you may think best. Sir J. Trevelyan showed me two engravings in that manner done by Thompson, whose father was curate of Hartburn, in this county. The size of the engravings for my book is about 7½ inches by 5½, and that of the portrait ought to be nearly the same. I am anxious, on your sister's account, that it should be as well done as possible. Mr. Swinburne has been for some time in London, but the last time I heard of him he was talking about going on a visit to his brother at Milan. He certainly wished to have some alterations made in the tone and drawing of the portrait. One thing only I remember his mentioning about it, which was this: 'There is an expression of sensualism in the lips which yours have not a bit of.' I am no physiognomist, and therefore do not know what that expression is; but if Miss Mackreth can discover it, and rectify what seemed to offend my kind and excellent friend, I will feel obliged to her. Mr. Swinburne indeed may chance to be still in London; and perhaps could be found by inquiring at his brother Sir J. E. Swinburne's house in Grosvenor Place, or of Mr. Howard, the artist, who resides in one of the streets leading out of Oxford Street, and with his brother, I think, who is a lawman.

"You had best purchase the stone of the Mitford Arms, and let it wait being printed till I can find something to add to it, to give it sufficient interest as a plate.

"Will you be so good as to call at the Pipe Office, Exchequer offices, Somerset House, very near the entrance, on the left-hand side, and inquire for Mr. Foxton, junior, and ask him if he is doing anything with copying the Great Roll of the Pipe for Northumberland for me. I wrote to him some time since on this subject; but my letter would cross one of his, which I did not think would require an answer when he received mine.——

"Should I have not been sufficiently explicit about the portrait, do not hesitate to write to me again on the subject.——I know that I need not remind you that I cannot afford to pay any fancy price for the portrait, and that you would oblige me by making the best bargain you can for getting it *well done*.——

"JOHN HODGSON."

To H. PETRIE, Esq.

(In the hand of an amanuensis; post-mark Aug. 13, 1830.)

WHELPINGTON.—" Mr. Hodgson has been at the Roman Wall, and employed four men for three days in clearing away the rubbish of two buildings in Borcovicus, both of which he found to have been granaries, with drying kilns annexed to them. He also opened parts of the Roman Wall near Borcovicus, where it still remains in greater perfection than in any other place. On a high basaltic knoll, called Cuddy's Crag, it is still standing 5 feet 6¼ inches high,* and in another place Mr. Hodgson dug away the soil and rubbish that had accumulated against it, and found it standing eight courses of stone high, three above the surface and five below. The masonry, especially that below the surface, is solid and fresh. It was at the top 6 feet 2 inches thick. The weather was so exceedingly wet that Mr. Hodgson was forced to return home before he had satisfied himself, but as soon as he can again spare a week for the purpose he intends going back again, and will then furnish Mr. Petrie with a full report of his proceedings."

FROM EDWARD SWINBURNE, Esq.

"MY DEAR SIR,                     London, 26 Aug. 1830.

"I wish you had come here. I should have had fine leisure for cruising with you during this protracted stay, which has cut up my humour for the excursions intended. I am, however, proceeding at the eleventh hour southwards. Mr. Howard, my frequent and valuable travelling companion, and I, start for Dieppe from Brighton on Saturday, and by Rouen to Paris, the political wonder of wonders; and I think it very likely when I get so far I shall be disposed to push on for Milan, taking a hurried peep, as I go by, at some of the natural wonders in Switzerland, refreshing my recollections of very early days.

"I wrote to you in my last about the Mackreths. I have since seen Mr. M., who had been to one engraver in the line proposed to have your portrait done in, but he was, we both thought, a long way in price beyond the mark; and he was to look out for another mentioned by Colnaghi, as on a good deal lower scale. He had the portrait with him, still thinking the mouth, though improved, rather coarse in expression. I advised Mr. M., as he said the engraving could not be done for several months, to take some opportunity when he goes again North, of making himself a careful drawing of that part of your face in particular, in order to improve Miss M.'s likeness, for I believe she remains in town. As you must remember what was my opinion of the likeness

---

* The letter contains a sketch with the pen of the structure of the Wall at this place.

I need scarcely say that I much wish it to be improved, more especially now that I understand you are to have it as *the Author's likeness*, intending it for your History. I do not say it to disparage Miss M.'s work, as I have quite a contrary feeling, thinking her very modest and well-behaved, and apparently very industrious in the cultivation of her talents. Mr. Mackreth would do well, as I suggested, to go over to you *per* Chevy Chase, and pass a day in examination of your features, furnishing the result to the engraver in aid of Miss Mackreth's miniature.

" I have thought it best, to save Mr. Cholmley trouble, as he has not the same opportunities as Mr. Ord and Mr. Losh, to advance Lewis for him three guineas more, which will be, within a shilling or two more or less, his share of printing, &c. expenses, and I send Mr. C. Lewis's receipt, with thanks for the plate, on your behalf and mine. He repays me by his York banker. Mr. Ord has already paid me what I advanced for him, viz. eighteen guineas for a plate, as having a great deal of work. Mr. C.'s was fifteen guineas without printing.——Before I concluded this Mr. Mackreth called in again. He had not been able to make out Colnaghi's person, and he is now out of town. He has, however, seen others less high priced than the first he applied to. He will give you all the information necessary when his inquiry is completed. They speak of two months' time for engraving it. When Lewis prints off he must send Mr. Ord a memorandum of his share of remaining expense, and the other to Mr. Losh, as it is settled they are to do so. You had better send him the lettering of all the three plates. I do not know whether Carmichael would like his name to appear to Jesmond: there is not much in it, but I take it it might as well go so.

" EDW. SWINBURNE."

From the year 1823 Hodgson's mind had been comparatively at ease. The preferment which he had received, moderate in value as it was, had kept the privations of Heworth from his door. He had been occupied in parochial duties more suited to his strength and feelings than those in which he had been previously engaged, and consequently he had been assailed by fewer attacks of ill health than in former years. His leisure hours, moreover, had been devoted to a pursuit in which he took a delight, and under such circumstances the occupation itself, his " supervacaneum opus," had been to him not one of pain or trouble, but of a nature invigorating to his spirits, whilst the expeditions from home which it had called upon him to make in quest of information, had been attended with all the wholesome effects which are the result of good bracing air and bodily exercise. His family also had in general been in good health, and upon the whole there had passed over his head seven years remarkably characterised, under Divine Providence, by a freedom from any serious worldly anxiety or distress.

But the hour of affliction was at hand, and hard was the trial which he and his most affectionate wife were called upon to undergo. He now had a family of nine children. Three, his eldest son and two daughters, were in Newcastle, he engaged in business, and of the daughters one was upon a visit and the other at school. The whole of the remaining six were attacked nearly on the self-same day by a virulent fever. John, Isaac, William, Susannah, Mary, and Emma, the oldest sixteen and the youngest four years of age, were all ill at the same time, and objects of fearful anxiety to their father and mother, in a poor country village, far away from good medical advice, with no one to lend a tending hand to them in their peril but their afflicted parents, and the kind-hearted Mr. Mackay, whom I have above mentioned. Of the six two died. John and Susannah were barely beginning to be out of danger when Isaac and Mary sunk under the disease, he on the 26th of September and she on the following day, leaving William and Emma in a state of extreme peril. Happily, however, they had the strength to shake off the malady. I subjoin a few letters referring to this afflicting visitation, and also the following inscription, which Hodgson a while afterwards caused to be engraved upon a plate of brass, and affixed to the stone which covered the remains of his lost son and daughter, and beneath which the body of another daughter found a resting-place in the following year.

ISAAC · ET · MARIA · E · LIBERIS · JOHANNIS · HODGSON · VICARII · IANAEQVE · VXORIS
EIVS · EODEM · DIE · EODEMQVE · SEPVLCHRO · TVMVLATI · SVBTVS · CONDVNTVR · § · FE-
BRIS · VTRIQVE · LETHALIS · § · FILIOLA · VI · KAL · OCT · M·D·CCC·XXX · FILIVS · POSTRIDIE
IN · CHRISTO · OBDORMIVIT · § · ANNO · INSVPER · SEQVENTE . X · KAL · NOV · IANA-BRIGI
DA . FEBRI · ETIAM · TVM · INGRAVESCENTE · APVD . NOVOCASTRENSES · OCCVBVIT · HIC
QVE · GERMANOS · IVXTA · CINERES · OH · TERTIVM · ET · PLANE · ACERBVM · FVNVS · DEPO-
SITA · EST ·§· VIXIT · ANNOS · ISAAC · XI · MARIA · VI . IANA-BRIGIDA · XVI ·§· DESIDERII · ET
AMORIS · ERGO · TABVLAM · HANCCE · MOESTISSIMI · PARENTES . INCIDI . CVRAVERVNT .

·

To Miss HODGSON, Newcastle.

" MY DEAR BESSY,    ·                         Whelpington, Sunday Night.

"John and Susannah are well. Wm. is also recovering better than
any of the others. Isaac has not taken the complaint, and Mary and
Emma would soon be well but for the swellings that the fever has left
under their right ears. Emma's swelling is large, red, and angry, and
must suppurate. Mary's is still larger; but not still so defined. Emma's
appetite is upon the whole good, and Mary drinks plentifully of milk. I
write this at your Mamma's request. She sends with it the things you
request, and is upon the whole pretty well—much thinner, but I hope
not injured in health. Isaac, as I have said, keeps quite well, as well
as your most affectionate father,

" JOHN HODGSON."


" P.S. Your mamma requests me to say that she will send you any
other thing you may stand in need of if you write to her. We send
this to Newcastle; but are uncertain where you are. My dear Bessy,
pray for all here, and for yourself, and for all that is right. I am very
very anxious indeed to have you at home again, and to your mother no
blessing could be greater; you must not, however, come till we send for
you, and we would gladly wish that that will not be long."


To Miss HODGSON.

" MY DEAR DAUGHTER,                    Whelpington, Friday Afternoon.

" John, Susannah, William, and Emma continue to do well: but
Mary has had three very bad days and nights, and is still very restless
and very weak. We hope, however, that the tumour on her neck will

soon suppurate and give her ease. Isaac to-day is also very restless, and talks incoherently. His mouth and throat are exceedingly bad; but we hope his complaint will soon be past its height, and allow him to recover, as John and William are doing.

"Your Mamma, I fear, will not be able to leave Mary to-night, which is, indeed, hard upon her. It would be useless, my dear Bessy, to write more. I wish and pray that God Almighty, of His mercy, would soon permit me to send the joyful tidings that all of us are in the way of recovery, and you could, with some hopes of safety, return home again, after your long absence from us. Your ever affectionate Father,

" JOHN HODGSON."

To R. W. HODGSON, NEWCASTLE.

"MY DEAR RICHARD,                    Whelpington, 29 Sept. 1830.

"By my letter to Mr. Whitehead on Monday you would be apprised of the heavy accumulation of misery and sorrow that has been laid upon us since I wrote to you on Sunday night. Your dear brother and sister are now gone to their long home. I buried them both in one grave, on the right-hand side of the garden door, as you go into the churchyard, and close behind the arbour. Though Isaac did not die till nine o'clock, I interred him that same evening with his sister; to which sudden measure I was urged by a sense of duty to the living, as the fever was most virulently strong upon him; and it was dangerous to keep his martyred frame above the earth. I got Walton to make a wall around the grave, and we covered it with two large free-stone slabs, upon which there is about three feet of earth. No person had ever been buried in the spot before.

"Peace to their lovely souls! Isaac in his devotions was a beautiful model for imitation. John and Susannah continue quite well, but William and Emma are still weak and unable to walk. William's mouth, too, continues sore, which makes him dread to eat anything; but we have them during the day both in the dining-room, William on a sofa and Emma in a cradle. Emma's ear is still at times painful and her neck stiffish, but she likes to be carried about to different parts of the house, and we entertain every hope that in a few days both of them will begin to show symptoms of returning health, and assume their wonted vivacity.

"Your mother bears her affliction admirably. She is full of grief, indeed, but endeavours to conquer affliction by a sense of all the obligations to duty which lie upon her. She has had some refreshing sleep for the two last nights, and is now much revived, and in good health.——Oh! my dear Richard, you will find a great blank made in our domestic circle when we are in a state for you to revisit us. Mr. Mackay has never left the house but in the nights, and has been very good and kind to us. It is, however, useless his staying here at present, for the children cannot for a fortnight or more resume their studies. I have, therefore, recommended him to go for about that time to see his friends in Berwickshire. Your affectionate father,

" JOHN HODGSON."

FROM THE REV. A. HEDLEY.

" MY DEAR HODGSON,                     Whitfield, Oct. 4, 1830.

" It would not be easy to describe the concern I felt at the afflicting intelligence conveyed to me by last Saturday's Chronicle. From Dr. Murray's account of your sick family, given to me through Sopwith, as well, indeed, as your own, I had fondly hoped so different a result. I need not say how sincere is my sympathy, for I have always felt the death of my children as the heaviest of calamities. I have had torn from my side, in the journey of life, father and mother, brother and sister, wife and friend, but nothing ever unmanned me so much as the sufferings and death-bed of my children! But time, and, above all, religion, brought to me, as they will do to you, ' healing on their wings;' and the occupations of your active mind will aid these. Pray, when you have sufficient leisure or freedom of mind for such a thing, give me, if only, a single line, saying how the rest of your family are, and how, above all, Mrs. Hodgson is bearing up under the bereavement. I hope that she, as well as yourself, will be able to look round on those that have been spared to you and be thankful. Mrs. Hedley begs to join in the best and kindest wishes to her and to yourself; and believe me, my dear Hodgson, ever your sincere friend,

" ANT. HEDLEY."

FROM SIR J. E. SWINBURNE.

" MY DEAR SIR,	Post Office, Newport, Isle of Wight, Oct. 8, 1830.

" When we left Capheaton we all participated in one feeling, that of most sincere sorrow and concern for the domestic calamities that have afflicted yourself and Mrs. Hodgson, and we are extremely anxious to have further accounts of your invalids. I fear it will be some time before they recover their wonted health and strength—but I hope neither yourself nor Mrs. Hodgson have suffered materially from your protracted anxieties and afflictions. Pray let us have a line from you when you can write with comfort and convenience. We have heard from my brother, who was sufficiently recovered from his accident, though not quite well, to propose proceeding to Switzerland on the the 16th of last month. Every thing was quiet at Paris; but I fear the present government will have some difficulty in keeping them so—and in Belgium the disorders and outrages are frightful; and an anxiety for change is manifesting itself all over the continent. I look forward with little hope of either peace or tranquillity lasting long. We had a very quick and prosperous journey, and reached this place all well on the fourth day; the surprising improvement in the roads is that you go 100 miles per day without fatigue or inconvenience. We found a great deal of corn out and soaked with wet; as however the weather has been favourable since our arrival, I trust the harvest will be completed in tolerable condition. We found all our friends here in good health, and Mrs. Bennett as brisk and active as ever. Will you take the trouble of letting Mr. Tone know of our safe arrival, as I have nothing particular to write to him about. I was sorry to find that there were grounds for apprehending that money for our new road would not be so easily obtained as we were led to believe. Lady Swinburne and my daughters beg their kind remembrance and good wishes. Believe me, my dear Sir, most truly yours,

" J. E. SWINBURNE."

FROM THE BISHOP OF DURHAM.

" REVEREND SIR,	Auckland Castle, Oct. 11, 1830.

" Within these few days I have received the five copies of your History of Northumberland, which I commissioned Mr. Thorp to bespeak for me: and I now inclose a draft for the amount of them, £40 19*s.*, which I request you to acknowledge when it comes to hand. It gives me pleasure to encourage your valuable labours and researches.

"I fear you are just now under great family affliction. I sincerely condole with you, and beg you will believe me to be, reverend Sir, your very faithful servant,

"W. DUNELM."

### To the Rev. J. RAINE.

" My dear Raine,                Whelpington, Oct. 13, 1830.

" A letter from a friend in time of deep distress is a messenger of consolation. We are bereaved and full of sorrow, but not cast down. We are, however, still prisoners in a fever-house—shunned by all but a few poor neighbours. My eldest son and my two eldest daughters are from home, and forbidden to come near us; and when we may be permitted to see them I cannot tell. Two of the glory of my eyes are in one grave, as near to us in the churchyard as we could find a last habitation for them. Two have, I may say, quite recovered; and two are gradually growing better, but still languid and in need of all our tenderness and care. The Power that does all things in mercy, while he has sent death and pestilence and grief within our doors, has also suffered great kindness and consolation to come to us. You are now a husband and a father; and may the Almighty Father spare you in your own family from seeing the sufferings which I have lately seen and felt! I cannot · write to you on any ordinary subject. Our united and kindest regards both to Mrs. Raine and yourself. Ever, my dear Raine, most truly yours,

"JOHN HODGSON."

### From Sir J. E. SWINBURNE.

" My dear Sir,                Isle of Wight, 18 Oct. 1830.

"It grieves us all to see the low and melancholy tone of your letter to me: there is unfortunately but too much reason for it; but I most earnestly hope time and resignation will restore your spirits and comfort in some degree. I am sure the absence of neighbours proceeds from no other cause than the fear of infection, and the precautions you are still recommended to take, by not allowing your children to return home, and absenting yourself from the presence of young people, shew plainly that those fears are not groundless. I hope and trust a short time will terminate this unpleasant quarantine, and return you to the society of those who I know have a sincere regard and esteem for you. The neglect of others is not worth a thought. As to public affairs, I am scolded every day for croaking, for which, however, I see too much reason; but we must not despair, and hope for the best. That some important change in this country, as in every other part of the world, is not far distant, I am persuaded: if such a revolution, as all good men must deprecate, takes place, I fear you will find the humblest and most retired parish priest will not escape its direful effects any more than the bishop, the rich lord, and the moderate private gentleman. It is a curious fact that after all that France has gone through she is now, after this new revolution, in very great distress; I mean as to poverty and want of employment.

If money is not forthcoming for the new works on the Ponteland road very shortly, I think the trustees are bound to lower the tolls for the present, and I shall certainly propose it. I was always scolded when I expressed my doubts on this very important point, and was always told there was not the least fear of obtaining whatever money we chose as soon as the Act was obtained: for having joined in this measure I see no fair ground of self-reproach: we had an essential public benefit in view, and if that has not been the result, it is from causes over which we had no control, and we are no more to blame than for any other unforeseen failure.

"I left special directions before I left home that you were to have free access to the library at all times; pray go over and look for the Life of Carey. I know I have an account of his journey to Scotland on the death of Queen Elizabeth, but whether it contains more of his life I cannot recollect, as I have not the catalogue with me. If this is not what you want pray let me know, as I hope I shall be able to procure you a copy of the edition of his life that you want, I mean the loan of it, and I shall be much flattered by the dedication. I am sure you will make it both amusing and interesting.* We have here a Major

* It appears from other notices about this period (see p. 192) that Hodgson was meditating a new edition of the Autobiography of Carey Lord Hunsdon, Warden of the Eastern March against Scotland in the latter part of the reign of Elizabeth; a book

————, a friend of Lord Prudhoe's, who was with him in Egypt, and full of hieroglyphic lore, and has an immense number of curious drawings and inscriptions, amongst others, a Greek inscription on the leg of a statue about 7 or 800 years before Christ, and an account of two rocks covered with words in a character entirely unknown—probably ancient Hebrew, as they are on the road Moses went from the Red Sea to Mount Sinai. He says that Dorelli, the French Consul, has made near 50,000*l.* by plundering and selling antiquities from those countries. Blindness is the great scourge of the country—that nearly every fifth person you meet in Cairo is blind.

" Lady S. and my daughters beg to be very kindly remembered to you, and express how much they regret our absence from the North at this period of your affliction. With our best wishes to Mrs. H., believe me ever most sincerely yours,

" J. E. SWINBURNE.

" P.S. We have heard of my brother Edward at Geneva going over immediately to Milan. Pray give the inclosed to Curry."

### FROM CUTHBERT ELLISON, ESQ.

" MY DEAR SIR,  Hebburn Hall, Oct. 23, 1830.

" I heard with deep concern of the heavy affliction that has befallen you and Mrs. Hodgson before I received your letter. I can feel for you, and Mrs. Ellison sympathises in your distress. Our stay here is only for a week from this day, but we shall be at Linden from the 30th till the 4th November. In the interval pray give me a line to this house or to Mr. Bigge's, just to say how your family does. I rejoice to hear that Mr. Thorp thinks as I do of your desire to relinquish this cure. I am convinced that the parish would derive no advantage from the step, and that you ought to satisfy your mind with the conscious-ness of having done all in your power for its advantage.* We intended to have passed the winter at Rome, but in the present unsettled state of

which affords much valuable information respecting the state of the Borders in the time of its writer; and further that the work was intended to be dedicated to Sir John E. Swinburne. Not much progress was made in the undertaking before it was abandoned.

* Hodgson was at this time most anxious to resign his living of Jarrow with Heworth, but his friends prevailed upon him to retain it for the benefit of the parish. He was in deep affliction, and that he should wish to lighten the burden of his cares and responsibilities is not to be wondered at.

Europe I think it prudent to remain in my own country. For Sarah's sake we shall go to some place at the sea-side for the severe months. She is very much better than she was, but still she is not strong, variable in her looks, and very sensible of any weather that permits her taking exercise. I will leave at Akenhead's a paper for you from Mr. G. Vernon, relating I believe to the pedigree, at which he has fagged as at a problem of Euclid. Mrs. Ellison's fear of infection will not allow me to propose a meeting with you whilst we are at home. We therefore unitedly wish you a speedy termination to your present anxieties, and hope to hear a favourable account of you. Very truly yours,

"CUTHBERT ELLISON."

FROM SIR J. SWINBURNE, Nov. 5, 1830, Newport, Isle of Wight.— "We all most cordially rejoice at the returning health of your family, and trust that it will tend to restore (as far as such sad calamities will allow) your mind and spirits to their usual tone. You know we have had our share of similar bitter inflictions, and know well how to feel for others—for none more than yourself."

### FROM EDWARD SWINBURNE, Esq.

"London, Nov. 10, 1830.

——" I have been much concerned, my good friend, for you, on my return to England, hearing of the severe domestic afflictions you have been visited with since last we met. The recent loss you have had cannot fail to press heavily on you and Mrs. Hodgson, and I truly condole with you. I am in hopes it will not be long before I see you, but in such times of present, and of still more threatened calamity, our purposes may be easily thwarted. I have been in countries the account of which may be interesting. I thought of you when in the coal district of St. Etienne de la Forest in France, and was longing that I could see it with you, and have the assistance of all your information; as it was, I only may be said to have passed through it. I am glad to hear that your own health is again better. I will shortly look after Jackson and his Chevy Chase *—he has probably given it up. My best regards to Mrs. Hodgson, and be assured I am your attached friend,

"EDWARD SWINBURNE."

* See above, p. 183.

## To Mr. SOPWITH.

"My dear Sir,       Whelpington, 20 Nov. 1830.

"I was at Morpeth lately, and examined the inside of the gateway of the Castle, which is, as you say, devoid of interest. It is, indeed, a filthy place; but I am told that there is an order for repairing it.* Mr. Collard may etch me the drawings you have made, and he must be as moderate as he can in charging, as I have some most tremendous bills from London for copies of Records I cannot do without.

"My family that are here are now, thank heaven, all quite well; but we were all again plunged into deep distress on Richard's coming hither on last Wednesday, and saying that my daughter Jane was attacked with scarlet fever. Mrs. Hodgson immediately set off to attend upon her. She is at Mrs. Smith's, in Burdon Place, where she is educating, and in the neighbourhood of which place fever is, I understand, very prevalent. We had carefully, ever since the direful malady visited us here, abstained from going to see her; and certainly, after the precautions we had taken, it was very distressing to send Mrs. Hodgson to pay her visit to her while she was suffering under the despoiling malady that robbed us of two of our children.

"I am busy preparing Morpeth for the press, which I fear will be a long article, but it will be the last of the volume I am engaged with. I am glad to hear of Surtees's liberality; but it is his character, which is not only noble but kingly in its way. From me you must expect little more than thanks, which, though they have little feeding in them,

---

* Nothing was done at that time, but the gateway is now under the hands of carpenters and masons. In cases of this kind it is clear what should be done. Suffer the walls to remain in the condition to which time has reduced them, carefully protecting their summit and filling up their chinks with unobtrusive cement, of a durable nature, to keep out the weather, and prevent weeds and the seeds of trees from casting root in their interstices. If an arch is in danger of falling for want of a stone, give it stability by supplying the necessary support; but add nothing which is not absolutely wanted for that purpose. In the next place, remove accumulations of rubbish and every undue pressure from the base of the structure, within and without, and then — do nothing more. Whatever else is done in the way of restoration will be deprecated by true architectural taste and historical feeling: it will be no part of the original fabric, and therefore it will never mislead an experienced eye, but it will infallibly tend to make poor and contemptible the good old workmanship to which it parasitically adheres, and gravely reprehend the judgment of its authors. There is, however, some comfort in the consideration that jobs of this sort seldom last above twenty or thirty years—but, unfortunately, they do not always fall alone.

I must contrive to make as savoury as I can the next time I step before the public in the character of County History cook. What are you painting your cage for ?

" JOHN HODGSON."

To ROBERT MACKRETH, Esq., SEAHAM, NEAR SUNDERLAND.

" MY DEAR SIR,                          Whelpington, 20 Nov. 1830.

"I think there is no chance of the volume with which I am engaged being printed in less than two months. Part of Bedlington and the whole of Morpeth, as well as the Indexes, are still to print. There is no hurry about the miniature. I did not expect you could get it engraved for a less sum than you mention. If I gave £40 for doing it, perhaps some of my friends would take a copy of it who do not take one of my book. When it is done great care should be taken that the engraver and printer do not keep a number of the best proofs themselves, and part with them to the printsellers. Tricks of that kind are very commonly played.

"All my family that are at home are now, thank God, quite well again. But we have still a fearful prospect before us. My second daughter, who is educating with Mrs. Smith of Burdon Place (Newcastle), was attacked with scarlet fever last Tuesday morning. As soon as we heard of it Mrs. Hodgson set off immediately to attend her, and she tells me that the disease affects her much more mildly than it did any of her brothers or sisters. We had none of us been near her; and that she might be in no danger of getting it from us we had avoided even calling where she is, ever since our very heavy sufferings and deprivations. But the frightful disorder is prevalent in the neighbourhood of Newcastle.——I really do not know when I shall be in Newcastle, but when I am permitted to do so I will apprise you of such intention, according to your request.——The prints, as they are ready, had best be forwarded to me. Mr. Dobson said something about a lithographic view of the gaol (of Morpeth). I wish I could get a plan of it to get it engraven on wood, to set up with the letterpress of my book: it should be 5½ inches broad, that is, from north to south, and of proportionate depth, and I think that a foreshortened view of the gateway taken from the north-west, with a little of the bank on the south, if skilfully and sharply drawn, and well engraved on wood and well printed, would have an excellent effect. Such a drawing Mr. Dobson could make me. When you see him pray talk to him on the subject. He should also furnish me with some description of it. I have very little memory of the gaol, but the view of it which I could wish should be something in this way *(a sketch)*. I mean this would give Mr. Dobson an idea in what point of view I wish it to be taken.——Yours,

"JOHN HODGSON."

FROM EDWARD SWINBURNE, Esq.

"MY DEAR SIR,                                    London, 29 Dec. 1830.

"I had some account to wind up with Jackson; and during my stay abroad he has done a vignette from a drawing of mine of the old South Tyne Ferry Boat and South Shore, close to the spot where the Suspension Bridge is built. It was too far advanced when I saw it on my return to admit of several desirable alterations in the light parts of it, the wood being cut away. Something was obtained by working a little on the dark parts. I send you this specimen for the present.

"Yours, E. S."

CHAPTER IX.—1831.

Correspondence—Wallis the Historian—His Portrait by Miss Mackreth—Correspondence—A Printing Press at Whelpington—Excavations at Borcovicus or Housesteads—Visit to the Camp at Piersebridge, &c.—Correspondence—Letter on Westmerland Geology—Illness—Death of another Daughter—University of Durham—Correspondence.

To Mr. WILLIAM WOODMAN, MORPETH.

"MY DEAR SIR,                    Whelpington, 6 Jan., 1831. (1832.)

"I am very much obliged by your kind letter, and will be too happy to avail myself of your kind assistance in London: for I am intending to print in a small press I have here a new edition of the Memoirs of Robert Carey, Earl of Monmouth, and was meditating at my first opportunity to write to Mr. Chambers, one of the amanuenses in the British Museum, to copy for me several letters and papers respecting the Carey family while they had employment on the Borders under their relative Queen Elizabeth. In the accompanying note-book you will find minutes of the papers I am wishful to obtain; and on the reading-room table of the Museum you will be furnished with the different catalogues you will stand in need of. The inclosed letter to Mr. Baber will obtain you an introduction to the Museum. Should he however be absent, any of the North-country Members of Parliament can ask one of the governors of the institution for a ticket for you. .

"You will like to see some of Turner's works, to obtain which you must refer to the printed catalogue of the Museum. Of Turner's Herbal I have extracts by some of the Swinburnes; of the second, a copy of the edition in 1562; of the third, only a description of its contents, the number of leaves of which it consists, &c. Will you skim this third part over, and make extracts of such passages as relate personally to the author, and of such notices of plants as he found growing in Northumberland? The personal notices will be chiefly about his travels, and the masters under whom he studied medicine and natural history; those about Northumberland plants, where he saw them growing, or the uses the people put them to. He often mentions Northumberland in Part II., which I have, and have carefully read over. The extracts Miss Swinburne made for me out of

Part I. are respecting Wormwood, fol. 11; Aconitum, f. 19; Seacole, f. 89; Chiropodium, f. 151; Beane of Egypt, f. 157; Cytisus Tree, f. 196; Dictamnye of Candy, f. 203; of Heth, f. 210.

"I have copies of the following documents out of the Cottonian Library. Caligula, B. I. 26 [&c. &c.].

"All the three libraries of MSS. are full of Border letters, &c., any of which, except these, you may copy that you think curious.

"Perhaps my note-books are too small to copy pedigrees into, though I think you will manage to do so by turning the page sideways and writing into the margin; and, if you have time to do so, I will thank you to get me from Harleian MS. 1448, any of the following pedigrees you have time to copy. Of all the rest I have already made copies. [A list follows ]

"I will thank you to ask Mr. Chambers what I am owing him for the extracts he made me from Turner on Baths, and to let me know when you have an opportunity. My namesake, Mr. Hodgson, M.P., will frank a letter, no doubt. His address is or was 5, Parliament Street. I also inclose you a note to Mr. Petrie, whom you will have opportunity to see frequently at the Museum, if you ask one of the servants when he is there; but I fear he cannot let you have the Morpeth School charter out of his custody. You see I have not stinted you for work, but do no more for me than you can conveniently. Of the letters, &c. respecting the Carey family I stand in the greatest need. I know your ardour in any pursuit you take in hand, and must caution you against over-much exertion. You were looking very thin when I last saw you; and I assure you I had rather see you quite well than receive copies of any of the records I here put you under a profitless commission to make, if you bring them to me with a blanched countenance.

"My volume in the press will soon be out. Morpeth makes a very long affair, a book of itself.——Will you contrive to copy a few interesting Border letters from the Cottonian, Lansdowne, or Harleian MSS. and send them to me, as Secretary to the Newcastle Antiquarian Society; and I will have them read before a meeting, printed in the Archæologia Æliana, or Transactions of the N. A. S., and secure you a few copies of them. If you could do this before the first Wednesday in March you would oblige me.

"There is a most interesting book of the charges of building Wark Castle in 34 Hen. VIII., in the Harleian Library, Cat. vol. ii. p. 187, No. 1724. It is a long affair, being in 180 leaves; but if you could ascertain from Mr. Chambers what it would cost copying, I would consider about having it done.    The MS. is in excellent preservation and well written.    I have eight pages of extracts from it, and I see that it consists of the payments of ten fortnights.    Perhaps it might be greatly abridged by taking one or two fortnights' pays as a specimen of the rest; and from each other fortnight making extracts of such matters contained in it as are curious on account of their locality.    It tells where lime, coal, and timber were procured, as at Carham, Gatherwick, Coldstream, and 'Callowley.'    The prices of labour and material are also curious: '41 women laboreng at caryng of earth for fyllyng of the ramperyng betwixt the new wall that gowith above the house and Castle, at iij d. the day every one.'    If I had a copy of it I would have it presented to the Council of the Antiquarian Society of N. C. to be printed in brevier, a small type, and I would introduce it with a speech about its history, and illustrate it with notes; and in this form *a full and literal copy* of it would not cover much paper in the Society's Transactions.    There are no accounts left, that I have seen, excepting about Dunstanborough, in the Duchy of Lancaster Office, about repairing or rebuilding our Northumberland castles.    In writing in this manner I am far from wishing to excite you to the labour of copying this lengthy document; but it would gratify me to see your name at the head of it as the contributor of it to the first part of the third volume of the Archæologia Æliana.

"My first aim in these commissions is to procure the letters, &c. I have noticed at the beginning of the note-book I send you to copy into, for myself.    My second, to enlist you to labour a little for the Antiquarian Society; in writing anything for which be so good as to put it into a form that will not need transcribing, but be ready, with an introduction and notes, to present to the meeting.

"I have only to add my fervent wish that happiness and health may attend you in your visit to London and return, and dwell long with you.*    Very truly yours,

"JOHN HODGSON."

* From Mr. Woodman, who was then, I believe, starting for London to be admitted as a solicitor, and who afterwards settled in that capacity in his native town of Morpeth, Hodgson received much valuable assistance during the remainder of his life, not merely in his topographical inquiries, but in matters of business.    The History of the Parish of Morpeth, in Part II. vol. ii. gives abundant proof of Mr. Woodman's zeal and judgment.    The youth, however well inclined to make himself useful, must have been not a little astonished upon receiving the above letter, with its extensive commissions.    [The above letter is printed here by mistake.    It belongs to 1852.]

To W. C. TREVELYAN, Esq.

" MY DEAR SIR,                                    No date.

"In addition to the multiplied favours you have done me, I shall
be much obliged by a sight of the second and third Reports on the
Dignity of a Peer; but fear this letter will not reach you before you
leave London. Your letter of the 13th did not reach me till Friday
evening at a very late hour, as I had been all the week at Heworth, and
Curry (the postman) had brought my letters to this place. The Placita
Coronæ, which you mention as in the Chapter House, are very interesting documents arranged in counties and in separate bags. The Chapter
House is a great repository of curious historical materials, a great part
of which are still unsorted. Among the papers belonging to the Court
of Ward and Liveries are a great number of deeds belonging to estates
which were in Wardship. One document there is intituled Nor-
thumbr. De Juribus et Libertatibus Domini Regis in excessibus Vicecom.
&c. 3 Ed. 2. I wish very much I had put into your hands a catalogue
of the records in various parts of the kingdom respecting Northumberland, which I made out for the purpose of taking with me to London,
&c. We have had very fine weather of late. Most truly yours,

"JOHN HODGSON."

To W. C. TREVELYAN, Esq.

" MY DEAR SIR,                                    Wallington, Friday.

"In passing along the line of the Roman Wall on Monday last
I found a skeleton of an animal about 2½ feet under the Wall, in a
deep scar of diluvial sand. One of the bones I brought away with me,
and if, after knowing to what animal it belongs, I find that it is curious,
I can secure the whole. I did not in my excursion find much that is
new, but at Burdoswald in a part of the wall found a centurial stone
remaining in its original situation and quite perfect: it is in two
lines COH. III. + PRORIAN. There is still a considerable quantity of wall
standing 5 and 6 feet high, and covered with ivy and hazels, very
near its west end. Our new road is getting well forward, and over the
moors has a very imposing appearance. The cut just south of Whelpington is not quite made; but the bridge is nearly finished, and much

carting is every day carried on over it.  In a week's time, if the weather
be good, the whole from Belsay to the Knows will be opened.  Very
little is doing upon the railway between Carlisle and Newcastle.
Believe me to be, my dear Sir, very truly yours,

" John Hodgson."

From EDWARD SWINBURNE, Esq.

" My dear Sir,                                          23 Jan. 1831.

     " I do not know how to advise you with respect to putting this
at the head of your short preface: in some parts it is a failure, as in the
light part of the sky, which was irremediable, as also in the way the two
large ash trees are separated from each other: the boat and figure are stiff,
and so is the water, but there is some pretty work and execution about it.
Is it good enough for so conspicuous a place?  Would it not come better
in a secondary situation in another volume?  This one, you say, will have
a good allowance of decoration.  It has been a little out of Jackson's
line, and I should wish him to appear with more of his usual merit so
foremost in the rank.  You will probably before you get this have seen
a proof of it, which I sent you in the pedigree box to Capheaton.  Yours
truly,

" Ed. Swinburne."

From N. J. WINCH, Esq.

" My dear Sir,                         Newcastle-upon-Tyne, Feb. 27, 1831.*

     " I am now finishing the Flora of Northumberland and Durham
for the Transactions of our Natural History Society, and in the preface
wish to say something respecting Wallis.  Pray can you give me any
information, however slight, about him? (that is, provided you have
no intention of printing the matter yourself,) for it is a pity this part
at least of the kingdom should know nothing about so indefatigable a
naturalist.  Dr. Pulteney, in his Biography, only mentions his work.
My Catalogue will extend to 120 pages, of which twenty alone are

---

* This letter, and the answer which it received, have been in some measure anticipated; see vol. I. p. 193.  Upon consideration, it has been determined to give them a
place at full in their order of time.

printed. Requesting you to excuse the trouble of this application, believe me to be, my dear Sir, truly yours,

"NAT. J. WINCH."

To N. J. WINCH, Esq.

"MY DEAR SIR, Whelpington, 2 March, 1831.

"I venerate the name of Wallis. He was an amiable minded, but highly useful man, and filled his situation in life with zeal and credit. As an author he is remarkable for integrity and simplicity. He never borrows a fact without acknowledging where he obtained it; nor with his subject ever bringing himself into his reader's notice. I know very little about his life. In Hutchinson's History of Cumberland you will find a short account of him; but it is there very erroneously stated that he was born in the neighbourhood of Ireby in that county; whereas in the Preface to his History of Northumberland he expressly says that he received his first breath in the Roman Castrum Alione, or Whitley Castle, in the parish of Kirkhaugh, in this county. After he returned from the South of England, he was a stipendiary curate at Simonburn under the late Dr. Scott, who gradually began to treat him with a harshness and hauteur which his gentle spirit never resented, but which he was far too high-minded to submit to. The Doctor's spaniels were once disturbing to his congregation, and he bid Mr. Wallis 'put them out,' but no notice was taken of the insolent command. After being several years at Simonburn, he removed to Haughton near Darlington, and soon after to Billingham near Stockton-upon-Tees, where he for some time officiated as curate. But blindness and infirmity obliged him to retire from the duties of his profession to the village of Norton, where he died in 1793. I have an octavo tract, entitled 'The Occasional Miscellany, in prose and verse, consisting of a variety of letters, which were originally written to a young gentleman who designed to go into Holy Orders, with a specimen of sacred poetry and sermons. Omne tulit punctum qui miscuit utile dulci.—*Hor*. Vol. I. by John Wallis, A.M. late of Queen's College, Oxford. Newcastle-upon-Tyne. Printed by John Gooding on the Side 1748.' This volume consists of 7 letters on 267 pages, and is preceded by a dedication, ' To Her Grace the Duchess of Richmond and Lennox' on 9 pages. ' The preface written by a friend,' in 20 pages, and the subscribers' names on 18 pages. The 8th letter contains, ' The Royal Penitent, or Human Frailty delineated, in the person of David: a sacred poem,' besides another poem called 'The Royal Penitent's Exhortation.' This on the subject of your letter is the only information I at present can bring to my memory; but if I meet with more before your book is ready to publish, I will not fail to embody it in another letter. From, my dear Sir, &c.

JOHN HODGSON."

To MR. SOPWITH.

" MY DEAR SIR,                                        March, 1831.

" The accompanying architectural drawing has been sent to me by Mr. Peter Nicholson, architect, Morpeth; and I feel myself obliged to have the subject engraved. It is the *Old Bridge* at Morpeth, which was formerly united to the chapel still remaining at its end. The united institution was called the Bridge and Chapel of Morpeth. Part of the chapel is seen through the left-hand arch; and as I have now engravings of all the churches and chapels in Morpeth Deanery excepting this, I am very anxious to have the scenery, houses, trees, &c. seen through the arches or over the battlements of this bridge, added, and the drawing reduced to the common size of such subjects in my book. Mr. Nicholson lives in the Old Gaol, and would shew the point from which the drawing was taken. It is all from actual measurement. Now my object in writing to you is just this: I fear Mr. Nicholson (the engraver) has no person to send to finish the drawing, so that it could be forthwith put into his hands. Will you, therefore, have the goodness to call upon him, and ask him if he can get the drawing completed? and if not, to put it in the hands of some other person to do, as soon as possible, for I could find no person in Morpeth that could make the additions; and when I was there last Friday could not venture to make them myself. This is the last favour I have to ask you for the volume; and any charges you think right to make me liable to in getting it completed I will cheerfully pay. Of course you must understand me as wishing you to employ some person to do me this job, not as going by a side-wind to get you to do the drawing yourself. The frontispiece to Carey's Memoirs has been put into Mr. Collard's hands, and as the book is bad to procure I wish he would keep both it and the engraving as free from dust and soiling as possible, which when you see him pray mention. He need not be in any great hurry about the job.

" J. HODGSON."

To ROBERT MACKRETH, Esq., Newcastle.

"MY DEAR SIR,                                   Whelpington, 23 March, 1831.

"The plates, Langhurst, Nunnykirk, and Lilburne, all got hither safely; for which I feel much indebted to your kindness and excellent intention.

"As you have gone so far about getting ways and means for engraving the portrait, I feel I cannot now stir in it: but when I mentioned to you my wish to have it put into a good hand, that it might come out with the present volume, I had a plan of remunerating myself for the expense. I should have advertised that it might be had at such a price in the advertisement that announced the volume, but I would not have *given* it with the volume. My anxiety to have it published, however, is entirely on your sister's account. She has had a vast deal of trouble with it, and I wish to get it circulated as a specimen of her talents. I have often to write to Mr. Adamson, but do not like to mention the subject to him; therefore, pray do tell me what has been done. You see our plans are virtually the same, only yours is more secure to me. Pray enable it to be well done, and me to give a copy of it to each of my subscribers in the volume next after that in which I am engaged.

"Mr. Swinburne was heard from by his brother Sir John about six or eight weeks since. He was with his brother, General Swinburne, who is Governor of Milan; but there was no account of his coming to England.——

"I shall be under the necessity of sending to press an account of Morpeth Gaol without a syllable from Mr. Dobson, to whose talents I am very anxious to do every justice. He seems to hate pen and ink as much as he loves his pencil and compasses. If you see him tell him what I say, and you will do me a favour, as I have made no minutes about the size, style, or decorations of the building, always expecting a simple statement of facts on these heads from himself.——

                                        "JOHN HODGSON."


To ROBERT MACKRETH, Esq., Newcastle.

"MY DEAR SIR,                                   Whelpington, 8 April, 1831.

"I have this morning been reflecting on the subject I talked about with you yesterday, and I think it best to do in this way: let the portrait be engraved on steel, and each person who wishes to have a proof impression of it pay 1*l*.    This will enable me to send out one impression with each copy of my book, and to reserve the plate for a second edition of the work, if such a demand should ever be made. The proof impressions not subscribed for I could wish to be divided between your sister and myself; and could further wish that not one impression, if possible, should get abroad, but under this arrangement.

"My intention is to write about Tindale Ward in my next volume. I have, therefore, according to your request, sent you a list of all the seats in it I can think of.    When you are making excursions, if you could now and then sketch me a church, it would be doing me a great favour. You know I engrave the churches and chapels, which come under my notice, on wood.

"I think your notice or heading quite proper; though perhaps it might be as well to say, instead of *the express purpose*, 'for the purpose of being engraved for his work,' or, which is better, 'the portrait to be copied from an excellent miniature likeness painted and presented to Mr. H. by Miss H. M., for the express purpose of being engraved for his work.'    But this, and every other part of the affair, I leave to your own kind and judicious management.——

" John Hodgson."

To W. C. TREVELYAN, Esq., 6, St. Andrew's Street, Edinburgh.

"My dear Sir,                    Whelpington, 13 May, 1831.

    "After collecting all the information I can respecting Horsley, the author of the Britannia Romana, I find that very little indeed is known about him.    It is said that he was born of Northumberland parents, at Pinkie House, in Scotland, in 1685.    In 1781 John Horsley of Widdrington, Gentleman, was a trustee for the Presbyterian Chapel of Morpeth; and it is said that John Horsley, the antiquary, was minister of a Presbyterian congregation at Widdrington, before he was called to be minister of that at Morpeth.    In 1729 he published a Memoir and funeral sermon on Dr. Harle, Presbyterian minister at Morpeth in the beginning of the eighteenth century, and from that time to his death at Alnwick.    He also published in the Philosophical Transactions an account of rain in Northumberland observed at Widdrington in the years 1722-1723.    In his sermon on Dr. Harle he speaks of their being relations, and to his dedication of it to Mrs. Harle, who was a Miss Legard of Newcastle, he subscribes himself her affectionate kinsman. Besides publishing his Britannia Romana, he delivered lectures on Natural Philosophy, and his apparatus at his death was purchased by Dr. Caleb Rotherham, of Kendal, and after passing through several hands was deposited in the Library of the Dissenters' Chapel in Red Cross Street, London. I suppose him to have been a kinsman of Robert Cay, who after his death addressed from Newcastle, from 1732—1736, several letters to Roger Gale, Esq.; which are printed in Hutchinson's Northumberland, vol. i. p. 147, 148, 178, and 199; and in some of which Horsley is mentioned. Robert Cay also, in 1753, dedicated Horsley's Posthumous Map to Hugh Earl of Northumberland: and before that, in 1748, voted at the Northumberland Election for lands in North Charlton. This Robert Cay died at Newcastle, 25 April, 1754.

" Then I find published, ' Abridgment of the Public Statutes, by John Cay, Esq., London, 1789.' John Cay, Esq. also, in 1758, published Statutes at large, from Magna Charta to 30 Geo. II. 6 vols. folio, which is a valuable edition on account of its great accuracy; and John Cay, Esq. of North Charlton, voted for the election in 1774. Robert Hodgson Cay, Esq. of North Charlton, trustee of a will in 1802: and at present, John Cay, Esq., of Edinburgh, proprietor of the same place.

" Now my object in addressing this letter to you is to request that you will do me the favour to inquire, by any way that may suggest itself to you, whether Mr. Cay, now of Edinburgh and North Charlton, can give any account of Horsley's parentage, birth, and early education, marriage, &c. &c., and whether Mr. Cay's family have any letters or papers written by him. At any rate, if Mr. Cay's family have a pedigree of their own descent I should be glad to be furnished with it; and if Horsley's father married a sister of Robert Cay, Esq., as I suspect he did, the pedigree may possibly account for his being born at Pinkie House, near Haddington.——John Cay, of North Shields, was also a trustee to the Presbyterian meeting-house at Morpeth in 1721, and Horsley, in his Britannia, speaks of some fact he obtained from his uncle's gardener at Cousins-House, which house is in the parish of Wallsend, and is now called Carville.

" The memoir on Horsley, and an account of the life and writings of Turner, are nearly all that I have to finish respecting Morpeth, but my printers certainly get very slowly forward. An early answer to this would be a great obligation.

" Will you be able to get to the digging at Housesteads in the beginning of next month?  With my best regards to your brother, I am, dear Sir, yours very truly,

" JOHN HODGSON."

To MR. ROBERT WHITE, AT MR. WATSON'S, PLUMBER, HIGH BRIDGE, NEWCASTLE.

" SIR,                                        Whelpington, May 23, 1831.

"  I am much, very much obliged by your notes respecting the neighbourhood of Otterburn, and fully intended answering your letter on the day after I received it, but by some accident shut it up in my book under Otterburn, and forgot where I had put it till I found it there to-day.  I do not know how to account for the difference between the late clerk of Whelpington's account of Percy's Cross and yours.*  He was a mason and worked much for Mr. Ellis at Otterburn, and built Keildar Castle for the Duke of Northumberland; and a man in my own opinion, and indeed in the opinion of every one that knew him, of the strictest veracity.  He was certainly an old man when he gave me the information, which I have printed, and his memory on the subject might not be quite correct.  Do you think that the stone he remembered procuring in Davyshiel Crag, could be put to any use about the House at Otterburn; (he, for instance, made the architrave of the kitchen chimney) and the stone you describe put into the base of the old Cross?  I have printed a very long account of Mitford Castle, which you will be able to see, I hope, in a very short time; but, till it be published, I send you a genealogy of its Lords, which will give you some idea how the property of it descended after the Valence and the Strathbogie families became possessed of it.  You may keep the proof, as it has only been hitherto preserved from being used as packing paper.  I am, Sir, your obliged servant,

" JOHN HODGSON."

To ROBERT MACKRETH.

" Whelpington, May, 1831.

"  ——— I got the inclosed last night, and have sent Mr. Creswell Baker a copy of your Lilburne, with the hopes that he may employ you

---

*  The following is an extract from a note by Mr. White accompanying this letter, for both of which I beg to thank him.  "In 1831, I wrote to Mr. Hodgson on a mistake which I conceived he had made in his History, part II. vol. I., about Percy's Cross, and he replied to it in a letter of which I annex a copy," 7 Mar., 1853.  In his lately published " Battle of Otterburn," Mr. White prints the above letter, and enters fully into the question of the real scene of the battle.

to lithograph the three views of his house which he promised for my work.——We are to have a digging—an antiquarian digging—at House-steads as soon as the weather gets fine. I hope Adamson will go up. The place is on the Roman Wall, and there are some remarkably fine views of basaltic rocks near it, one especially, on the edge of Craig Lough, which would make a most interesting picture. The lakes there would also, from one point or another, form good subjects. Will you make one of the party?

"After my volume is complete and published, I think you might with fair prospect of profit print a set of views to illustrate the work, as far as it is gone, without at all interfering with the embellishments I give. I could point out many passages in the book which would suit such a purpose; as in Part ii. vol. i. p. 167, account of Blackburn Linn. P. 185, Chattlehope Spout, and Babswood Kirk. P. 305, Rothley Crags and Rothley Mill. P. 308, Thrunton Wells. P. 301, Walks at Hartburn. 198, Waney Crags, &c. &c. The forthcoming volume every where abounds with descriptions of scenery.——

"JOHN HODGSON."

The following Circular details the steps which were taken at this period to obtain a portrait of Mr. Hodgson for the forthcoming volume of his History. I have already printed some correspondence on the subject. Other letters will be given hereafter, as it is not without its interest. I will only add, that the portrait was duly executed from the miniature here spoken of, and that after having been published in his History, part II. vol. ii. it adorns the first volume of this Memoir.

CIRCULAR to the
SUBSCRIBERS to Mr. HODGSON'S HISTORY of NORTHUMBERLAND.

"SIR, 31st May, 1831, High Swinburn Place, Newcastle.

"I am directed to inform you that a number of the friends of the Rev. John Hodgson are anxious to testify their regard for him, and the estimation in which they hold his valuable History of Northumberland, by presenting him with an engraved portrait of himself, to be inserted in the forthcoming volume of his Northumberland.

"The portrait is engraving on steel by Scriven, from an excellent miniature likeness, painted and presented to Mr. Hodgson by Miss H. F. S. Mackreth, for the express purpose of being engraved for his work.

" The expense of the engraving amounts to about sixty guineas, and, in order to give as many of Mr. Hodgson's friends as possible an opportunity of subscribing, it has been agreed that the amount of each subscription shall be limited to one guinea, and each subscriber will be entitled to receive a proof impression of the plate, independent of the copy inserted in the work.

" Should you therefore wish to place your name amongst Mr. Hodgson's friends for the above purpose, I am directed to beg the favor of your signifying your intention to me before the 15th of June.    I have the honour to be, Sir, your obedient servant,

" Robert Mackreth, Junr., Hon. Sec."

### To Wm. WOODMAN, Esq.

" My dear Sir,                                        Whelpington, 7 June, 1831.

" The proof is one which I am afraid to put to press without your seeing.    Pray look it over, and write out for each page on a separate piece of paper such corrections as you see are wanted.    I cannot make additions; but whatever observations you send me for each page and column I will endeavour to make the best use of I can.    A great deal of Morpeth is yet to print.    It has risen into a long account, and will be very expensive to me; but on that account I will not shrink from making it as perfect as the nature of my work requires.    Yours, my dear Sir, very truly,

" John Hodgson."

### To the Rev. A. HEDLEY.

" My dear Hedley,                                        Whelpington, 20 June, 1831.

" I find your Gentleman's Magazine has been thoughtlessly kept here for two months.    I think it increases in interest.——Your offer to let me have your printing press has taken such possession of my son John, that I fear he will dread its sincerity till he sees the press.*    You

---

* The press was duly presented and thankfully received by the boy, who speedily set himself to use it in a humble way under his father's guidance.  His first attempt

must not, however, hesitate to rue of your offer, if you think you will
ever turn printer again: but if you send it here I will promise you that
it shall soon be made use of, and that *Whelpington* shall not be long
unknown to book fanciers, as a place with a printing press.——I find I
have omitted to take the height of the walls of the west tower of the
south gateway of Housesteads; should you have an opportunity of
getting it done, you will do me a favour by letting the measurements
be made at two places, thus, [*a drawing with the pen ;*] that is, the
height of the east wall from the ground, and the height of the west wall
from the surface to which we dug. One of the towers of Rutupiæ, or
Richborough, was of solid masonry for many feet upwards. I wish you
could also get me a section of the moulding on the corner cornice-stone,
which you observed lying in front of the station as we came away. I
long to hear of your being at Chesterholm, but not at it as your residence. It must never be anything else but your *Ædes recreandi:* and
as soon as you get to it, and can see me, let me know, that we may have
the excursion to Gillsland. Yours ever, most truly,

" JOHN HODGSON."

### To W. C. TREVELYAN, Esq.

" MY DEAR SIR, Whelpington, 25 June, 1831.

" If I had thought my thanks for the kind and successful services
you have done me in applying to Mr. Cay for information about Horsley
were worth paying the postage of a letter for, you should long ago have
heard from me. Mr. Cay has been at great pains in making researches
and writing letters; and, with a frankness and candour that endears his
disposition to me, has sent me twelve of Horsley's letters to his great-
grandfather, Robert Cay, Esq. on subjects connected with the Magna

at printing appears to have been a morning hymn written by his father, in four stanzas,
for the use of the church choir at Whelpington, accompanied by the woodcut of the
church used in the history. He next set up and struck off a few copies in duodecimo
of the stanzas composed by his father upon the sight of his native country from the top
of Hartside, to be mentioned in a future page. This little book, if it may be dignified
with such a name, consists of four pages neatly folded and stitched, with the title of
" Poetic Trifles, Whelpington, John Hodgson, jun. 1832." With the exception of a
circular or two relative to his father's History, I am not aware of any other performance.
Of the press itself, I find a notice in Hodgson's Journal under the 23rd Nov. 1840,
that it had been lent to a Polytechnic Exhibition at Newcastle, and was returned
" much injured, and great quantities of type lost." See also p. 192, above.

On the 4th of July, 1831, Hodgson paid a visit to Durham, and on the following day we went together in his carriage to the valley of the Tees, that he might inspect the site of the Roman camp at Piersebridge, which he then saw for the first time. He afterwards went to the limestone quarries at Bolam, hard by, to examine the effect of the whin dyke upon a stratum of coal, with which it had come in contact whilst bubbling up in a liquid and burning state from the bowels of the earth. The phenomenon is precisely the same as that which in 1815 he had conducted Sir H. Davy to see at Coaley Hill, near Newcastle. The coal on both sides of the dyke is reduced to a cinder. I well remember an incident in this expedition which reminded me strongly of Mr. Surtees of Mainsforth and his humanity. On our road, in point-ing out the manner in which coach-drivers (the race is now extinct) were in the habit of amusing themselves by lashing road-side birds with the whip, my companion accidentally near Walworth had the mishap to kill a chaffinch, which made him angry with himself, and for a long time afterwards extremely unhappy.


FROM THE REV. A. HEDLEY.


" MY DEAR HODGSON,                Whitfield Rectory, July 10, 1831.

    " To shew my friend John how much I am in earnest about my little printing press, I shall thank you to say to him that I beg his ac-ceptance of it, not as a loan, but as a present; together with the ma-terials belonging to it. I hope he will turn out another Elzeyir, or a Ruddiman at least; or another Neddy Walker would not be amiss; who, I suspect, if not so famous, has died a much richer man than either of the two. You will miss him I fear. But to return to the printing press. I think the best way of your getting it home would be to send your lad and cart for it at once; to come here one day and return the next. This would cost you nothing but the turnpike gates; as I sus-pect the labour of your man and horse for that time will not be of much value. You may send a *largish* sized box for the press to be stowed in, and the cases, with what type there is, I will pack up and send, with the stand, which is a lumbering sort of thing, but may be found useful.——
                                                " A. H."

### To Mr. R. W. HODGSON.

"My dear Richard,        Whelpington, Aug. 12, 1831.

"Pray get the inclosed sent to Mr. Clifford. I wish I could have had time to write some hints to Mr. Hutton about the places where he will find the whin sill: but I really have not time to-night. We are expecting Ned every moment. I know I have notes made at the mines at the foot of Troutbeck, and on the west side of Dunfell. Also at Melmerby. At Huttonshole and Keshgill Linn, near Alston in Gilderdale. From Windylawhill, near Glenwhelt, all along the whin range to Green Leighton, also near Featherstone. The hind at Housesteads will show you how a bed of limestone cuts the whin in a crystaline state, about half a mile west of Housesteads. Look into the limestone quarry near Bekplay, and examine near Barrowsford, where the whin passes the Tyne. The Gunnerton Hills, especially Gunnerton Crag, are extremely interesting. Mr. Charleton's is at least ten miles north of the whin range.——Tell Mr. Hutton that at Mr. Romney's house, on the east side of Little Melfell, greenstone and old red sandstone are in contact, just as they are under Crossfell near Melmerby: and that at Mr. Romney's house there are the finest possible examples how the old red sandstone has been converted into whin. Only there are no limestone nodules at Melmerby in the old red sandstone, as at Ulswater foot and Little Melfell.——A basket of mushrooms for Mr. Whitehead will accompany this.        JOHN HODGSON."

I have already extracted from the following letter the valuable information which it contains respecting Hodgson's own personal history in his boyhood and youth. My extracts will be found in the first chapter of the first volume of this Memoir; but I do not on that account think it proper to omit them in printing here the letter itself of which they form so important a part. Mr. Hutton was the eminent geologist and naturalist already spoken of. In the letter there appears to be somewhat of repetition, and some of Hodgson's geological notions may perhaps now be considered antiquated in character; but at all events it deserves to be recorded in a memoir of its writer.

### To Mr. R. W. HODGSON.

"My dear Richard,        August 18, 1831.

"You tell me that you and Mr. Hutton are about to set off on a geological tour to Brough in Westmerland, and to walk from that place through Whelpington to Holy Island, to investigate the appearances of the whinstone stratum that comes through this district.  This, I suppose, is your first regular attempt to study from nature a science, which of all others, with respect to the planet we inhabit, is in usefulness and grandeur the most interesting.  I will not, however, now expatiate upon its usefulness, but attempt to tell you by what steps I was led to the little knowledge I have of geological subjects; and in doing so I will throw it into a sort of memoir of my acquaintance with rocks of the old red sandstone, and of the trap or basaltic genus, a form which I think will of all others be most interesting to yourself.  For the correctness of what I tell you I must rely on my memory and my minute-books.  And as I have been for many years partially acquainted with some parts of the country through which you intend to pass, especially the country about Melmerby, I will endeavour to weave into my narrative such observations upon it as my memoranda will enable me to make, and have the whole ready by the time you arrive here.  The reward for the labour I am undertaking will be the pleasure it will afford you; for I well know that you will feel gratified to find that I have employed a portion of my time in assisting you in your first entrance into a study which is strongly connected with your interests as a man of business; and cannot fail to lead your active mind into inquiries of deep moment to you as a subject of that POWER, which by natural and uniform processes fitted our globe for the habitation of man, and by similar laws keeps it in perennial youth and activity.

" My attention, my dear Richard, has been insensibly directed to geological subjects from a period which I cannot exactly ascertain.  I was born in a narrow transition valley in the parish of Shap in Westmerland,* and after being a few months old was brought up at Rosgill, a village in the same parish, which is seated on a slope of the croppings of the lowest beds of the mountain limestone.

" These circumstances from my earliest youth made the sight of the transition rocks, and the clay, sandstone and limestone strata, immediately incumbent upon it, familiar to my eye.  Swindale Beck entered the Lowther at Rosgill, and the Lowther ran between the trap and slate system and that of the mountain limestone through the village of Bampton Grange, to the grammar-school of which I was sent at the age of seven, and where my father went to reside four years afterwards. The school had a library belonging to it, and in it I found Whitehurst's Theory of the Earth, which my early imagination delighted to revel in, whenever I could escape from the intricacies of grammar, and the then

* . For the note here appended to the letter, see vol. I. p 3.

to me unknown beauties of the ancient authors of Greece and Rome. At present I have very little recollection of the contents of the book, but it made me fond of searching after different kinds of rocks and organic remains. I had cousins in Swindale, and while I resided at Rosgill used to gather shells of snails—the beautifully banded *helix nemoralis*—on the limestone grounds about us, and carry them to my young friends there, who admired and preserved them as curiosities, because shells of that kind were not found in their own valley, on account, as it was supposed, of its having no limestone in it.

" Swindale to me, wild and craggy as it is, was and continues to be in my remembrance and affections one of the dearest spots on earth. I know every rock and frowning precipice in it, from the Druid's Stone to the black and precipitous front of Wallow Crag.

" When I was at Alston last summer, I went with some friends (Sir J. E. Swinburne, his son-in-law Mr. Bowden, and Mr. Hedley of Chesterholm) to the top of Hartside, to let 'my aching sight' have a view of the 'visions of glory' to be seen from thence. The new road led us in a wrong direction to have a prospect over Lowther and the Shap and Bampton Fells, which I longed most to see; but I ran alone to an eminence, where I got a momentary glance of them; and afterwards wrote the following lines on the occasion.*

" Bampton was a place peculiarly favourable for the study of the mountain limestone formation. The terraced sides and craggy brow of Knipe Scar were well known to the old geologist Woodward, to which he was probably introduced by his contemporary Bishop Gibson, who was born in the contiguous hamlet of High Knipe. Some beds of the limestone there are intimately filled with shells; and I knew quarries near High Knipe that afforded very curious specimens of flint. The limestone stratum called The Clints covered a considerable tract of ground on the top of the Scar, and in it I imagined I could trace how water had gathered into channels and guttered the surface of that remarkable rock before it was cracked into irregular columns in the processes by drying. While I resided at Bampton I also examined with great curiosity similar beds of clint about Hardendale near Shap, and Claythorpe and Burton in Kendal.

* These verses consist of not fewer than twelve stanzas, but as they appear to have been hastily written, and never afterwards revised, they are here omitted. They contain some beautiful ideas and are full of feeling. The scenes of his boyhood and youth, which he so pathetically addresses in these stanzas, he revisited more than once in his declining years. Twice, at least, he fled like the stricken deer, to his native hills and vales in quest of health, but in vain. After Mr. Hedley's printing-press had reached Whelpington, the verses above alluded to gave it its first employment. See above, p. 205.

"I had more delight than dexterity in angling, but my passion for that amusement led me up the sides of all the mountain streams and lakes in the neighbourhood, and familiarized my eye to the appearance of the large tracts of slate and trap rock amongst which the brooks and tarns of the neighbourhood were situated. I had also an uncle by my mother's side, Mr. Robert Rawes, a venerable and highly respected person, who had large quarries of roofing-slate in a mountain valley, which threw its waters into Swindale Beck, and Wrangill at the head of Long Sleddale; and I made frequent excursions to these in search of dendritic impressions. Another of my mother's brothers lived at Seatoller in Borrowdale, and he had a slate quarry on the Castle Crag at the head of Derwentwater; and with him I went to see many curious rocks, quarries, and mines, in that beautiful country, especially the wadmines, the slate-quarries at the head of Buttermere, and the ancient copper-mines worked by a company of Germans at Gold Scalp in Newlands. It was in one of these excursions that I became a frequenter of the museums of Crosthwaite and Hutton, at Keswick, and contributed to them many specimens of minerals and organic remains.

"In these excursions I very well remember coming to the conclusion that the rocks of roofing slate laid in strata passed from mountain to mountain and valley to valley in a nearly direct course, but with considerable variation in thickness and structure: in some places they rive, according to the term of the quarry-men, into thin and highly elastic laminæ: at other places they part by natural parallel faces into slabs of various thickness, which cannot be riven into thinner pieces, not possessing the property which geologists now call the slaty structure. I do not remember the angle at which they lie, but I think it cannot be less than seventy or eighty. The stratum at the head of the valley of Buttermere, just before the road begins to ascend to the gorge into Borrowdale, passes from Eaglecrag on the right through the stream at the bottom of the glen, and up the opposite mountain, one side corresponding with the other with as much regularity as if a mighty gouge had scooped out the hollow of the valley, and had thus disjoined the continuity of the stratum. As far as my memory will assist me in describing its position in a sketch it appeared thus. [*Here is inserted a very neat sketch in pen and ink.*] In Helton-dale beck, between Bampton Waters and Helton mill, there was a hard gravelly rock, which was thickly embedded with greenish or rather ash-coloured sandstones of very various sizes, and worn into roundish, generally reniform, masses, apparently by the action of water. These were much used by carpenters and country people as whetstones for axes and other instruments for cutting wood.

"My father had an uncle who lived in the parsonage-house at Newchurch, and I paid my first visit to him in the summer of 1792 or 1793, and he gave me a copy of Gay, which first introduced me to the 'Rural Sports' of that poet of nature. In this visit I was remarkably struck with the similarity of the rock I saw in Dunmallet and Soulby-fell, at the foot of Ulswater, with that in Helton-dale beck.

"On the 8th of June 1799, when I was nineteen years old, I went to teach the endowed school at Matterdale, which dale, like Newchurch, is a chapelry in the parish of Greystock in Cumberland, and has the two remarkable conical hills in it called Great and Little Mell Fell, which are composed of the same sort of conglomerate rock as that at the foot of Ulswater, and which the country-people there called *roach*. How such mighty quantities and varieties of rolled stones were brought and cemented together was then, and for long after continued, to me matter of wonder and variety of speculation.

"I will now pass over a long period of my life, in which I had gradually acquired as much geological information as to make me an enthusiast on the subject, having read Hutton, Werner, Deluc, and many of the older theorists, especially *Burnet*, whose book is still at least a curiosity which I would not willingly have removed from my shelves; for it will be always valuable for the information it contains respecting the cosmogony of the nations of antiquity; and delightful on account of the eloquence of its style, both in the Latin and English editions. I had also paid great attention to the strata called the coal formation and the carboniferous limestone, and especially to the veins of basalt or trap rock by which they are traversed. Before the terrible accident at Felling Colliery I had visited many of the collieries in the neighbourhood of Newcastle; but that appalling calamity determined me, contrary to the feeling of the coal-owners at that time, to make it as public as I could, and therefore did not, for many weeks after that explosion had in one moment taken away the lives of ninty-one of my parishioners, cease to write notices respecting it in the Newcastle Courant; but also wrote and published a particular account of it and its consequences, and accompanied them with a plan of the mine, and the mode of ventilating it. This I did with the hope of rousing the sympathies of scientific men to investigate the causes of explosions in mines, and finding some mode of preventing them. A part of the work, unknown to myself, was published in the Annals of Philosophy, before the whole of it was ready for sale; and I have been told that it was also published in journals both in France and Germany: so that its circulation in extent exceeded my expectation.

"In the same year (1812) I also read before the Literary and Philosophical Society of Newcastle, ' Some Account of the Strata which form the surface of the Globe;' but as I then imagined that my hearers were indifferent to the subject, in the manner at least that I was able to handle it, I did not finish the essay on the plan I had formed of it; and I have never yet had either leisure or inclination to resume the subject.

"MEMORANDA. Experiments on the coal stratum at Heworth quarry, mentioned in my letter to Sir H. Davy, May 23, 1816.*

"In 1811 I resided at Marsdon some time, and made a collection of the stones I found in the diluvium on the ground, and also of the crystals in the magnesian limestone—as well as of the elastic magnesian limestone, which is laminous, but snaps when the damp is dried out of it. The magnesian limestone opposite the great rock is soft and fit for building purposes."

The following notices are bound up with the letter, of which they appear to be a continuation.

"The old red sandstone district, composed of the beautifully wooded conical hill of Dunmallet, of Soulby Fell at the foot of the lake of Ulswater, and of the two other conical hills called Great and Little Mellfell, had been familiar to me from the year 1794. I resided on the south side of them in 1799 at Matterdale, and the next year just to the north of them at Stainton, at both places in the office of schoolmaster; and from the knowledge then acquired of it, and having frequently asserted, contrary to the opinion of persons conversant with geological subjects, that it dipped under the transition limestone, which stratified upon it in beds parallel to its uppermost surface, I grew from year to year desirous of an opportunity of examining it with some attention; and in 1817 that opportunity was afforded me in a visit to the late Captain Wordsworth, at his seat on Ulswater, in company with my friend and parishioner the late Matthew Atkinson, Esq., of Carrhill near Newcastle. I was not fortunate in weather. From near Christmas 1816 to May 25, 1817, no rain had fallen near Newcastle: but in the morning of Monday the 26th, I set out from High Heworth for Carlisle under exceedingly heavy rain, and from that time to the next November there was scarcely one fair day. The following morning, when I reached Penrith, however, was fine; and the form and colour of the

* Here follow the particulars of the experiments of 1813, printed in vol. I. p. 126.

mountains that environ Ulswater, as I walked by Skirsgill and the beautiful hamlets of Sockbridge and Poolybridge to Captain Wordsworth's, presented them in far more beauty to my mind than I had ever before been able to see them. Many of the Wordsworth family have been domiciled at Sockbridge, and are buried at the neighbouring parish church of Barton.

" The old red sandstone of the Mellfell district is through all that country called *roach* or *roche*, which name retains the Norman form of writing and speaking our word *rock*. Its northern boundary lies along the southern verge of Hutton Moor, and from Penruddock by the Dacre beck to the Eamont; which river and the lower part of Ulswater bound it on the east. On the west it is seen in a small stream that runs by the south side of Soulby fell into Ulswater at Waterfoot, and after leaving this stream, above a place called the Wray, it passes on the west sides of Little and Great Mellfell to the Troutbeck, which stream it is that, I think, bounds it on the west. It is principally composed of nodules of a greenish or bluish-green gritstone, which abound in it from the smallest size to a ton in weight, are all water-worn, but are of the greatest size and quantity in any place that I examined, in the bed of a brook formed about the year 1815 by making a number of open gutters for the purpose of draining the uppermost parts of the hill running into the channel. I am not acquainted with any similar stone *in situ*. I should also observe that these gritstones themselves often assume a conglomerate form; that is, they are composed of water-worn materials, differing very much from each other in substance and texture. The finest of them and most uniform in grit are much in use as whetstones, and when exposed to a white heat become white and crumbling. Equal parts of quick lime and this stone in a powdered state fused into a porous slag in a common wind furnace, 100 grains of it, and 96 grains of carbonate of potash, exposed to a white heat in a smith's forge, very readily melted into a solid dark-green glass; and 10 dwts. and 16 grains of the sand in which it is imbedded, when submitted to a white heat, in which the crucible nearly became invisible in the flames, melted into a black glossy scoria, which while in a fused state was of a thick and tough consistence. Before iron was abundant among our Saxon ancestors, these oblong stones were perhaps formed into *malls*, or, as the name is pronounced here, *mells*, by boring a hole and fixing a handle in their centre; and hence Mell-fells might obtain their name, as the village of Melmerby, in another similar old sandstone district on the eastern side of Cumberland, had its name from being a *by* or village on the *moor* where *mells* were procured. I have, however, in another

place * conjectured that the Mell Fells had their name from being
the Mell or middle hills, for they rise up between the mountain district
to the south and the champaign country to the north, and have cultivated
lands nearly all about them: and if there be any truth in the account
given in Hutchinson's History of Cumberland, that Melmerby had its
name from being the property of Melmor, one of the three sons of one
Halden a Dane, who resided here in the ninth or tenth century, then
all my conjectures respecting the last place at least must go for nothing.†
But besides these grit-stones, many of which bear a striking resemblance
to the war-clubs and mallets of uncivilized nations, the old red sandstone here contains water-worn fragments of numerous other kinds of
rock.    At the highest bridge at Dacre, in particular, I observed that
it contained red and light-blue sandstone, greenish slaty sandstone,
brown porphyry, white quartz, jasper, and nodules of limestone all embedded in a coarse reddish sand, and traversed with strings of sulphate
of barytes.    There is also in the roche, at the middle or foot bridge at
Dacre, a vein of flesh-coloured barytes which crosses the beck in a
zig-zag direction, and is red on its sides, and partly so in its centre, and
also contains rounded ash-coloured pieces of sandstone schist.    This
rock also contains greenish crystals of carbonate of lime dispersed in
it in smallish portions, and often filling up chinks and void spaces
between stones, as if they had formed in them after the rock itself was
formed.    *Limestone* nodules are more abundant in this rock, on the
shore of Ulswater, at the foot of Soulby fell, and in the brook that
runs from Little Mellfell past Wray, than in any other parts of it that I
have examined.    I collected several of them and brought them home
with me to Heworth.    Though their outsides were generally wrinkled
and uneven, probably owing to the unevenness of their temper, yet they
were all polished in the same way that I have seen the Tyne Bottom
limestone done by water running over it, in Gilderdale and at Hutton's
Hole in Howgill, and the black limestone above the trap rock at Keshgill Force near Alston.    Most of them are very hard; some crystalline;
their prevailing colour was darkish-blue, often light-grey or dove-
coloured.    Many of them contained organic remains, and one of that
kind I had sawn into slices of about one third of an inch in thickness
for the purpose of suspending parts of it in diluted muriatic acid,
and ascertaining whether the shells in it were, as they appeared to be,
converted into silex.    Parts of two shells resisted the action of the acid;

* In his derivation of the name of Meldon, in his Hist. of Northumberland, part·ii.
vol. ii. p. 1.
† Hutch. Cumb. i. 217; Burn and Nicholson, vol.    441.

the larger specimen of which was about half an inch broad and nearly perfect, but very brittle. I made accurate drawings of it and several other specimens; but cannot, while I am compiling this paper, lay my hands on them. [*The drawings were afterwards found, and are here inserted.*] The part of the stone nearest the shells dissolved most readily; and the shells themselves had a chalcedonous lustre. Some short time before I visited the district in 1817, Mr. Romney had opened a quarry of greenstone in the channel of a small spring near his house, on the east side of Little Mellfell, for the purpose of building a summer-house with it, and the section of the rock he exposed to view afforded a most decided proof that the greenstone there had been formed by fusion out of old red sandstone, under great superincumbent pressure. The transition from the one form of rock to the other was so gradual and yet so strongly marked, that it was impossible for any one, whose eyes had been accustomed to the marks that fire leaves on rock, to hesitate in concluding that the appearance on the rock here was the effect of great heat acting upon it from below. This is a copy of the section of the quarry which I made upon the spot [*as in a drawing in the margin*]; and the following further description of this quarry I also extract nearly verbally from my minute-book:

| |
|---|
| Surface line. |
| Stratified old red sandstone, no way changed in appearance. |
| Old red sandstone, little changed in form or colour, but rent with perpendicular fissures, the sides of which are glazed and scorious. |
| The green sandstones roasted to whiteness, but still retaining their form. |
| The green grit-stones here half melted, in a state of porcellaneous fusion. |
| The whole here melted into a solid mass, but the forms of each nodule still visible. |
| Crystalline green-stone, without any nodular appearances in it. |

"At Mr. Romney's house the roche has been cut through into trap or greenstone of a very dark and compact kind, from which there is a gradual change upwards till the rock goes into roach, without any marks of fire upon it. The limestone nodules in the intermediate state between perfect roche and perfect greenstone when exposed to the air crumble. The green silicious stones are turned white. Perpendicular fissures too are formed in the roche, and their sides are blistered and glazed like the sides of a furnace. There is much spume-stone, like cinders and scoria, in the middle, and which seems to have parted with some

vapour whilst cooling. Further down, near the pure trap, the no-
dular stones seem to have been only half melted, and thus to have
sunk in their pristine shape into the vitrified mass; they are vitrified, but white. While melting, the rock above has cracked perpen-
dicularly into rude columns; and from this specimen it may be easily
conceived how large masses of superincumbent strata might sink at
various angles, be set on edge, or turned upside down, and force the
liquified sea on which they had floated through the dikes and fissures
formed in this crash of falling. I have before shewn that the stone of
which the roche principally consists melts in a strong heat, and that
the sand in which it is embedded fuses still more readily. Beyond
Mr. Romney's house, in the gorge or pass from Newchurch to Matterdale, the roche pebbles are glazed, as if their outer coat, while hot, had
been slightly vitrified by a vapour of muriate of soda falling upon them;
and in a hollow on the Matterdale side of Little Mellfell there is a sort of
porphyric rock, in a scar, in a decaying and crumbling state, which in the
rounded masses it contains bears the plainest proof of having once been
a bed of conglomerated gravel. Indeed I think it impossible for any
person to study the rocks of this neighbourhood which lie below the
old red sandstone, without being forced to the conclusion that the trap,
porphyry, wacke, and roofing-slate in it, were formed by the agency of
heat out of beds of sandstone or schist that had once been regularly deposited in water; or out of rocks, like the roach of the Mellfells, which
had their origin in some era of our planet when the stratified systems of
sandstone and limestone containing organized animal remains were torn
up and broken by the ocean, and, in its tumultuous tides and waves,
rounded into rough gravel, and again stratified and cemented together
in the form in which we now find them. And this conclusion carries
with it the unavoidable corollary that the rocks thus formed by subterraneous heat are in their present state of newer formation than the
stratified rocks that cover them, and that contain dykes filled with
basalt, which has been forced upwards, and often forms extensive
strata on each side of the dykes.

" That the roche is regularly stratified in beds of very various degrees
in the size of its grit, and that the mountain limestone lies upon it at an
angle of the same inclination as its own dip, there are numerous proofs
in sections of both kinds of rocks exposed to view in the banks or bed of
Dacre beck, which runs upon it from Hutton Moor to its junction with
the Eamont. On the north side of Great Mellfell the roche is in many
places bare and precipitous; and near some springs opposite to the

little hamlet of Troutbeck its grain, though coarse, was thought sufficiently fine to encourage an attempt to quarry it in 1798 for the purpose of building Mr. Hutton's house at        , in Matterdale; but it did not answer the purpose for which it was intended, and the place where the winning was made was in 1817 grown over with turf. The stratified form of the rock may be also seen in scars of it by the sides of Dacre beck, a little below the venerable old mansion house of the Huddlestones at Hutton John, and the little retired village of Hutton; and there are several examples in the same sweet and romantic stream of the mountain limestone putting upon the roche, especially opposite to Penruddook, where there is a little spring with wild mint and cresses growing in it, and the roche upon which the limestone rests suddenly changes from a reddish to a bluish-white colour, and contains calcareous matter. In the bed of the Eamont, opposite Barton Mill, the roche is much finer gritted than any specimens of it I saw about the foot of Ulswater; and in a similar geological position between the transition and mountain limestone rocks there is a bed of coarse old red sandstone, about three or four miles south-east of Ulswater foot in Heltondale beck, between the mill and a farmhouse called Bampton Waters. Kendal Castle is also built upon a small hill of coarse conglomerate, resembling that of Dunmallet.

"In passing over Moor-Duvvoch in 1800 I had observed a stone which I then supposed had some characters upon it with which I was unacquainted. In walking from Askham to Pooleybridge on 8 May, 1811, in company with the Rev. John Collinson, rector of Gateshead, and the late Mr. Matthew Atkinson, I was anxious to have a second sight of it, but sought it in vain. My first excursion from Captain Wordsworth's in 1817 was to examine the junction of the transition and mountain limestone rocks in Ellerbeck and Akebeck brooks, which run into Ulswater from the east of Moor-Duvvoch and the northern limb of Swarthfell. I found in Ellerbeck steatite, and in Akebeck a bed of iron, which is not magnetical *in situ*, but after exposing 100 grains of it to a strong heat it became so, and lost 8 grains in weight. I found no roche here, as on the other side of Ulswater to the east in Heltondale beck, but I suppose it to have been changed into grauwacke, which is there abundant. The beds immediately under the first mountain limestone seemed to be of schist, growing harder and harder as they approached the porphyric and wacke strata. I did not, in this search, forget to look for the stone that attracted my attention in 1800, and reached it soon, when I found it to be a large detached mass of grauwacke, shewing its conglomerate origin in several rings and segments of circles eaten by the weather into its surface as sharply as if they had been cut with a sculptor's chisel; and thus the long-encouraged vision of a Saxon or Latin inscription in Runic, or some other antique characters, vanished in a moment. This stone is upon the side of an old road or cast a little south of the south end of Lord Lonsdale's fir plantations on Moor-Duvvoch.

"On May 30th I examined the limestone, schist, and sandstone beds in the bed and banks of the Lowther near Askham bridge; and walked over the new red sandstone rocks of Whinfield Park to Temple Sowerby. The terrace at Lowther is on the limestone stratum called the Clints, which forms a succession of remarkable escarpments that pass southwards from this place through the bottom of Westmerland, and are called the Scars of Knype, Hardendale, Odendale, and Orton, &c. On the table land on the tops of these scars there are generally large tracts of the limestone still lying quite bare and fissured into a sort of rude irregular columns, which seem to have been formed by the stratum of which they consist being in a state of mud suddenly exposed to considerable heat, probably that of the sun, as the fissures in them narrow downward. When I was a boy at the grammar-school of Bampton, a parish which adjoins that of Lowther, I was familiarly acquainted with the large tract of clints on Knipe Scar, and once examined the very extensive tracts of similar rock about Claythorpe and Burton in Kendal, and then, about the year 1794, used to imagine that I could trace where water had run over the surface and collected together from small branches into very perceptible channels. I have also sometimes thought I could trace upon them prints of the feet of animals, and have heard a strange account of the prints of the feet of men and horses on a similar stratum of limestone near Tebay; and the tale has got itself appended to a tradition that they are the footsteps of warriors who fought and were slain there in a great battle, and buried in some adjoining cairns.

"On the 30th May also Mr. Atkinson took me to Winderwath, that is, *Wine-water-ford*, where on the right bank of the Eden there are thin laminæ and lumps of fibrous white gypsum: and on the next day we went to see a bed of peat-coal, on the right bank of the Eamont, on an estate called Honey Pots, and belonging to Sir Philip Musgrave of Edenhall. It is a little above a very remarkable cavern in the new red sandstone called Isis Parlis or Isan Parlis.* We found a drift made

* "This cave is partly natural and partly artificial, and now most commonly goes by the name of the Giant's Cave. Attempts have been made to connect its history with

into it for several fathoms, but were told it was of so bad a quality as not to be worth working. It rests on the new red sandstone, and has a thick bed of diluvial matter upon it. When dried it is laminous, brown, and cuts easily with a knife. It burns slowly, and its smoke smells exactly like that of peat.[*]

"The mountain limestone begins to be covered with new red sandstone in the bed of the Eamont, a little below Mr. Perkin's house at Skirsgill, where the junction of the two formations is not accompanied with any dike or throw, but the sandstone is deposited in strata at the same angle as the limestone beneath it. While I was on this visit I had a great wish, but no leisure, to examine the edges of the Red Tarn, a mountain lake under Helvellyn in Westmerland, the waters of which run down Glenridden into Ulswater; for in an angling excursion to that lake in 1799 I received an impression on my mind that the shores of that Avernus were set with a pier of basalt with as much regularity as if it had been done by art. I was also for the same cause prevented examining the bed of a sike that runs in the direction of the road from Newbigging to the village of Stainton, because I have an indistinct recollection of having, while I resided as schoolmaster in that village in 1800, seen great quantities of bones in the banks and channel of the

that of the curious monument in Penrith churchyard called the Giant's Grave; but the accounts of it are sadly darkened with traditions and fables. (See Hutchinson's Cumberland, I. 291, 333.) Formerly the openings into it from the river were closed with masonry and an iron grate. The numerous initials cut in the rocks in its sides show that it is much resorted to as a place of curiosity."

[*] "Feb. 18, 1818. Thirty grains of Honeypot peat-coal were put into the head of a tobacco pipe, the whole top of which I luted over very carefully and closely with finely-prepared fire-clay. On applying it to a reddish heat some smoke and filmy bubbles soon appeared at the head of the pipe, and as the smoke increased in quantity and quickness a dark-brown oil came over in quantity scarcely exceeding a drop. The smoke at first extinguished a taper of hemp tar-paper, but soon became inflammable at about an inch from the aperture, exploding in dim bluish flashes. When the smoke ceased the gas burned with a feeble blue flame, which had a speck of more dense light at its apex than itself. The *residuum* weighed 16 grains, so that as $30 : 14 : : 100 : 46\frac{2}{3}$, the loss in 100 grains. This residuum was a fine black coaly matter, which retained the form and strength of the pieces of peat as they were put into the crucible, and marked smoothly on paper, and by pressure under the thumb made a dry squeaking noise like that of very tender charcoal. After being forty minutes exposed to a brisk heat in an open crucible, it was reduced to eleven grains of fine white powder, three grains of which, mixed with an equal quantity of carbonate of soda, and subjected for ten minutes to the heat of a blast furnace, fused into a semi-transparent whitish glass, covered with a dark-brown glaze; but I found it infusible *per se*, and insoluble in nitric, sulphuric, and muriatic acids."

brook after it enters the fields from the road to Newbigging, and that the bones were intermixed with a soil that was intimately filled with the crinoidea or enchrinal fossil, which in Cumberland is called *fairy beads*, and in Northumberland *St. Cuthbert's beads*.

"I left Captain Wordsworth's house in Penrith on Monday the 2d of June, and walked thence to Melmerby, where, I think, I stayed two nights; but my note-book has no dates from May 31 to June 4, on which day I was at Alston. I had often seen the slate and trap rocks in the neighbourhood of Brough, and in May 1811, in company with Mr. Atkinson and Mr. Collinson, was surprised to find, in passing from Dunfell to the village of Milburne, some low ridges of similar kinds of rock, which, to the left of the way I was passing, rose up wildly and romantically into high conical hills, called Dufton-pike and Knock-pike, from the villages situated near them. I did not then ascertain whether a similar but flatter-headed hill called Kandle-pike was a transition slate hill, but was told by Mr. John Atkinson of Temple Sowerby that all the way from Brough-under-Stainmoor, down as far as Melmerby, there was a line of rocks similar to the low slate hills we passed over at Milburne to those of Saddleback and Souter-fell in Cumberland: and I was now anxious to see how these rocks were situated in the neighbourhood of Melmerby with respect to the old red sandstone which I knew abounded in this neighbourhood, for long prior to that time I had seen Foster's section of the mountain limestone of Cross Fell, and in my note-book for May 1811 I had made the following imaginary sections of strata while I was at Kendal, one of which in an abridged form I engraved in a wooden block as illustrative of some geological notions published in the "Picture of Newcastle," in 1812, and now copy both of them here, not because I think them correct, for they are far from being so, but to show what my notions were on the subject at that period. [*Here are two sketches with the pen.*] My notes, however, respecting the slate and trap rocks in conjunction with the old red sandstone of Melmerby are few, and want a map of the ground I went over to illustrate them. The specimens of rock and minerals also which I brought from this place and the Mellfell district were, for want of room in my house here, left in the garret of the house I lived in at Heworth, and most of them afterwards turned to the useful purpose of mending the highways.

"The old red sandstone or roche appears at the first entry into Melmerby beck from the lane which leads to the fells from the village, and is covered with a reddish sort of earth. It dips to the north-east under a

stratum of whitish sandstone which has a bed of limestone upon it.
Where it rises into swells and hills they are rounder than those of the
schist and basalt close up to the first sandstone. A section of the
cropping of the three beds would appear thus [*a drawing*]. In some
places the roche quite up to the bed of fine-grained sandstone is no
otherwise altered, than by being very strongly cemented together. Here
too it is very full of quartz, as may be seen in the fords and beds of the
brooks, especially in a ford a little above the farmhouse called the Gale,
which belongs to Mr. Holmes of Penrith. It also contains great quantities of bluish-green sandstone in rounded masses, as in the Mellfells,
and these are frequently covered with crystals, but of what sort I have
no account; the sandstone between the roche and limestone is close-
grained and of the kind which is sometimes called moorstone. The
lowest limestone is more precipitous than the bed below it, and has a
sort of terrace before it, as if a broad ledge of it had been swept off by
water while the sandstone below preserved its position.

"Besides these rocks, there are here, as on the other side of the
county, great quantities of trap and schist rock, which lie immediately
below the roche, and form to the south a series of hills, the ridges of
which are more rugged and pointed than those of the old red sandstone.
These fire-formed strata and hills are not lavas, but schists and sandstone
strata, indurated or fused. Here the trap and the roche and the schist
and the trap gradate from each other imperceptibly. That is, there is a
space between the roche and the trap that is neither the one nor the other,
but partakes of the nature of both: and so with the slate-rock—then it
loses its slaty texture, and is half trap and half slate, and then distinct
massive whin. The trap also sometimes splits the rock, and has thrown
masses of it each way, upwards over the limestone and downwards over
the new red sandstone, which here comes close up to the foot of the
mountain, and overlies the indurated slate-rocks.

"Have the great veins of the metalliferous limestones been the effect
of the heat which hardened or vitrified the rocks as far as the old red
sandstone? Their sides are frequently, as in Dunfell, covered with a
hard thick scoria, as if the rock on each side of them had been fused by
subterraneous heat; and have the metals with which these dykes are
filled been sublimed in a gaseous form from below? Or are they a
component part of the strata in which they are found, and by some law
of nature traverse through the solid rock that yields, and then, unable
to pass over these clefts and chasms, crystalize on their sides?

"The schist-rock often divides into perpendicular laminæ, and re-

sembles much that of Saddleback and Souter Fell, being hard and black
as the Welsh roofing-slate. It has been partially quarried at one place, a
good way up the mountain side, and on both sides of the brook, probably with the hope of making roofing-slate of it, for which purpose it
is however unfit, as it is not elastic, and refuses to rive like the grauwacke slate. It splits indeed into thin laminæ, but into too small sizes
to be useful to roof with. Frequently it passes by an insensible line
into fine green trap, or very hard passive and porcelain clay, in this
manner [a drawing]. Here too, as in the junction with the secondary
transition rocks, the schists are often glazed with a sort of black iron
polish. Opposite the Gale, steatite is rather abundant in a softish slate-
pencil schist, and I also found some specimens of asbestos in it.

Whelpington, July 30, 1831.


To the Rev. A. HEDLEY.

" MY DEAR SIR,                          Whelpington, 15 Sept. 1832.

    " I have sinned greatly in keeping your Gent. Mags. so long:
but I must console myself with the hope that they will reach you on
some wet day when you cannot get out, and you have nothing new to
read.

    " How do you and Mrs. H. like your new residence? I must con-
trive to get to see you to make a few more observations on Housesteads,
before the weather gets too cold to write at the door: but pray soon
come down here. Mrs. Hodgson and my family are at Newbigging, but
come home on the 23rd.

    " My printers send me four pages in the week now. I would be
satisfied if they would give me eight.

    " Richard, as he cannot well now go to the law, as he wishes, is anxious
to do something to make himself known, and that may introduce him
to employment: and I am recommending him to become editor of a
very interesting record respecting the county: I mean the Great Roll of
the Pipe, which commences in the time of King Stephen. I shall have
it completed soon, to the end of the reign of Henry the Third; a period
of about 120 years, and of great darkness in the annals of Northumberland, upon which this interesting record would rise like a sun. The
portly book called the Testa de Nevill seems to be collections made by
some clerk in the Exchequer from the Aids accounted for in the Great
Roll. With an introduction shewing its nature, and copious indexes to
it, I am sure it would make a most useful book of reference: for it could

not fail of being a constant treasure-house of material for county history. Sir Charles Monck was here a few days since, and was delighted with some specimens of it. He had never heard tell of it.——

" JOHN HODGSON."

### To his YOUNGEST DAUGHTER, AGED FIVE YEARS.

" MY DEAR EMMA, Whelpington, 15th Sep. 1831.

" What a shocking thing! Joe Fenwick's servant came here yesterday, and took the young cat away to the Whitehill. Joe says that your brother John, bad boy! promised to give him it: and as he has had two dead lately he could no longer do without it. I doubt you never now say any lessons; and that when Mr. Mackay comes back you will have lost all your reading: I wish you would come home, for papa is very dull for want of you. He sat alone in the house yesterday from six in the morning to ten in the night, writing all day—and afterwards had very little sleep. I hope you are quite well. Your affectionate papa,

" JOHN HODGSON.

"Do you know that a pretty swallow has just come down the dining-room chimney: but papa has let it out at the window."

### FROM MR. W. MILLER.

" RESPECTED FRIEND, No. 4, Hope Park, Edinb. 17 of 9 mo., 1831.

" I now send proofs of the three plates which I am engraving for thy History of Northumberland, together with the two original drawings by E. Swinburne. Be so good as to look them over, and return them to me along with the drawings and thy remarks, when I will proceed to finish them off. I have forwarded a proof of the plate of Cresswell House to T. M. Richardson, who will of course touch it himself, but I thought it might be well to forward one to thee also, in case thou might have any observations to make. None of the plates are in a finished state, and I send them now, as I have to leave town this evening for about ten days, and as it would probably detain them too long had I kept them for further revisal on my return. I expect to be in Newcastle on my return, probably about the end of next week, and intend calling on T. M. Richardson for the proof sent to him. Were it in thy power to return thy parcel to him in

Newcastle by that time I could get the whole along with me. Is there any likelihood of E. Swinburne's being home soon? I should certainly have been best satisfied had it been possible for him to revise his plates before publication; at the same time I am sure he would not wish the present volume to be published without them, seeing they were so far advanced. I remain, in great haste, thy friend, very respectfully,

"WILLIAM MILLER."

"*J. Hodgson, Whelpington.*"

To ROB. MACKRETH, ESQ.—Whelpington, 28 Sept. 1831.—"If you have not already written to Mr. Scriven, it is perhaps still in good time to do so, for I now recollect having written to him in summer saying that the prospect of the volume being printed off was very distant; but that a great many of my friends having subscribed to the portrait there would be more money than would pay his charge.

"I would really say of Mr. Clarke and his house, if he cannot afford to pay for printing the impressions, let them go. If he reckon his 100 large impressions to give to his friends as presents, the 800 copies he sends to me would cost him little or nothing. I have been for the last twelve days very unwell, and write with difficulty.

"JOHN HODGSON."

Towards the end of September in this year, Hodgson suffered much from a lingering fever; and from the account of this attack, as recorded in his Journal, he appears to have been for awhile in great danger. His illness came upon him as he was returning to Whelpington, from a Visitation at Morpeth, in the company of his friend Mr. Redman, to whom he had given a place in his carriage. The ways were bad, the evening was cold and dark, and they were three hours on the road. After having tried for a few days to shake off the attack, he left home, where he had been for awhile alone, and proceeded to Newbiggin, on the coast, where, to attend the Visitation, he had left his family enjoying the sea breezes and the facilities of bathing. Here he remained for a fortnight under the care of Mr. Salter, a medical gentleman resident at Blyth; but, as no improvement was taking place, nay rather the contrary, his eldest son came to him from Newcastle, and removed him to that place for the advice of Dr. Headlam, who found him " suffering under a low fever, which was fast depriving

him of strength, and undermining his constitution." Under Dr.
Headlam's judicious treatment he by degrees recovered his usual
health and strength; but another dreadful trial was at hand, the
sad particulars of which I transcribe from his Journal.

"Soon after we came hither [to Newcastle on the 4th of October],
my daughter [Jane-Bridget, then in her sixteenth year], who is
with Mrs. T. Smith, at Burdon Place, complained of being languid
and ill. Mr. Murray was consulted, and he recommended Dr.
Headlam to visit her, who on Sunday, October the 16th, ordered
her to be taken to lodgings in the town; and now, Monday the
17th, Mrs. Hodgson is about to remove her to Mrs. Wilkins's in
Lisle Street. On Thursday, the 20th, Dr. Headlam ordered me
home, as I was uncomfortably lodging at an inn; and on Monday
the 24th, to our inexpressible grief, my dear, amiable, excellent, and
highly talented daughter died. On the Wednesday following she
was buried on the south side of the vaulted graves of her dear
departed brother and sister Isaac and Mary."

The monumental plate printed above contains the name of this
other victim of fever. Three children were thus placed side by
side in the earth in the course of twelve months. A fourth was
soon added to the number.

To Robert Mackreth, Esq.—Whelpington, 21 Oct. 1831. I have
got home very well, and feel myself even in the short time since yesterday
much improved. Indeed I was sick of the noisy apartments I had in
Newcastle, and was most glad to escape from them as soon as I could
get leave. I however regret exceedingly I could not see your sister
on the subject of the engraving, which I greatly fear she will never see
finished to her satisfaction. The face seems as if it was stippled. The
addition of a border, however, and all other amendments, I must leave
to herself and to you, and would hope that with your suggestions Mr.
Scriven may yet be able to give it that force, freedom, and expression,
which a master's hand impresses upon its work.——

"John Hodgson."

To Mrs. HODGSON in Newcastle.

" My dear Jane,                    Whelpington, Oct. 25, 1831.

" Your account of dear Jane is indeed most afflicting, and I now
certainly resign my mind to the worst account that can come, though I

Q 2

will not despair of hearing a good report from you or Dr. Headlam to-morrow. Moralists have said that "whatever is is right;" and we know that when afflictions come upon us by fever and infectious diseases they are visitations which no power of our own could avoid. Jane's case, however, seems to be of that kind. As for my own and Margaret Curry's, there can be no doubt we got the infection at New-biggin. Mr. Surtees's family, of Stamfordham, also brought it home with them from the same place before we were there, and have suffered much in it. I have written to Dr. Headlam about myself; and hope he will give me his opinion of Jane. Since I got here my appetite and strength have much improved—but last night I was kept awake by very severe rheumatic pain in my left hip, and got no sleep till after daylight. All the family are quite well, but the house at nights is very lonely and void to me; and most so when I consider the great fatigue and anxiety you have to endure on account of our dear suffering daughter, for whose recovery all my prayers and best wishes are night and day employed. The bread you got Miss Pattison to send came safely, but I have not yet tasted it. That which we get at Philipson's does very well, and there was some of it in the house this morning.

"I do not know what more I have to say. We must wait the issue of events with resignation and patience: for all events are under the direction of a just and merciful Arbiter, into whose protection it is our wisdom and best interest to commit ourselves with cheerfulness and confidence, and under the assurance that, however He deals with us, He consults what is best for us. Ever my, dear Jane, thine, most truly,

"JOHN HODGSON.

" The suffusion you mention must be a suffusion of serum, which I fear is very dangerous."

FROM EDWARD SWINBURNE, Esq.

" MY DEAR SIR,                    London, 7 Decr. (1831.)

"I have received the proofs, and am just finishing my observations on them for Mr. Miller, and will either send them off to-day or to-morrow per coach. What time do you allow him for amendments? I tell him that you will *let him know that immediately*, and whether the titles at the bottom are to be anything else then Edlingham Castle and Belsay Castle.

" I have had an experienced artist's eye for them, and more has been suggested for the improvement of Belsay than perhaps will be attainable on the score of labour and time. The quantum adopted must depend upon those circumstances, and preference in Miller's judgment, if to be limited, in their interest. I have not time to tell you now what they are; more breadth and piquant effect (the latter being also its characteristic), are the objects aimed at.

" The work of this plate is generally inferior to that of Edlingham, which, done *con amore*, shews more of the master's hand,, and the amendments prepared for the latter are very few. I like it very much: but the Belsay will I hope be an interesting plate. I have embodied Miss Swinburne's observations in my notes.

" I have not yet had an opportunity of calling at Mr. Scriven's to see your portrait. It lays rather out of the way for these short days. Engravings on steel are apt to be dark and harsh.

" I have told Miller to return the drawings to you; they are your property. I mentioned the number of impressions as in yours to me. I have been much better lately; I may say well, quite a different being. I must again assure you of my sympathy for your many and heavy afflictions: whatever of this you met with from Capheaton would be given from the heart, proportionate to the esteem and regard I know they have for you.

" I am glad you can give so good an account of Mrs. Hodgson after such visitations; my best regards to her and your son and daughter.

" Edlingham was a better subject for the style of engraving best suited to your work; Belsay has too much work; and, considering the remuneration, and the much more profitable employment of his time, that Miller can, with his merit, give to it, the hand of the assistants must necessarily be more expected in this than in the other. Your attached friend,

" ED. SWINBURNE."

### FROM ROBERT SURTEES, Esq.

" DEAR SIR,                    Hendon, Sunderland, Dec. 10, 1831.

" Were I at Mainsforth I think I could refer to evidence proving that William Bertram married Hawise, daughter of Guy Balliol, who was thus Roger Bertram's maternal grandfather.

" We have been long detained here by Mrs. Surtees's attendance on her mother, who has been in a very weak and dangerous state for many weeks. I shall be at home, I think, for a few days, on this side of

Christmas, and will look for Balliol and Bertram. As soon as ever we are again established at Mainsforth I shall hope to see you, for the purpose of your making a complete inspection of my papers.

"I recollect long ago seeing in a small octavo red paper book containing a very few extracts from deeds of Gosforth, something that is not included in my printed pedigree of Surtees—of a connection, I think, with Bewick, referring to one of the last successive Thomas Surteeses, towards 1500—if you can at any time refer to this I shall feel obliged by an extract from your notes.

"Have you any regular account of the family of Vaux, settled in Northumberland and connected with Swinburne? I have a correspondent, an advocate in Edinburgh, H. S. Vanse, Esq. (which is a Wigtonshire corruption of Vaus), who is very curious on the subject of the spreading house of De Vallibus, Waus or Vaux; and I shall be glad to learn that any new light will be thrown on the name in your future portions. Mr. Vanse has sent me copies of deeds which would go far to prove that Devorguill, relict of John Balliol, remarried John de Vallibus, a Scottish baron, did not this so very far contradict all other evidence of deeds, as well as Wyntown and Devorguill's own seal in widow's weeds to her charter of Balk. Coll. Other Devorguills may have been; but I'll send you the evidence.——Yours very truly,

"R. SURTEES."

### To ARCHDEACON THORP.

"MY DEAR SIR,           Whelpington, 21 Dec. 1831.

"I thank you for the Prospectus of the University of Durham, and heartily congratulate you on its plan being laid and its foundation begun to be formed. You mentioned to me some of your views upon it when I was at Ryton in summer, and I soon after heard the subject mentioned in the College at Durham. You say 'Help us, as we deserve.' You deserve every help, that those who are capable of giving any you may want, can afford—but from one like myself, who never had the advantage of living in a University, you could expect nothing but theory and plans for experiment. I hope you intend that it should grant degrees. Let it have that power, if you go to Parliament for it. If it cannot grant a degree it may overshadow St. Bee's, but it will never grow into a goodly tree. If it has anything more in it of an eleemosynary nature than Oxford or Cambridge, or is intended to have any inferior advantages, excepting oldness of foundation, richness of libraries,

endowment, patronage, and the like, it will never rise to eminence
superior to a Scotch university, or be resorted to by any but poor
scholars, who may wish to qualify themselves to get into Orders and
hold a Curacy.

"Mr. Clayton and Mr. Brown had a meeting about Jarrow and
Heworth, but they have not said to what conclusions they came
respecting it. I was not well enough at the time to meet them, as Mr.
Brown requested, in Newcastle, but I will see Mr. C. on the subject soon
if I be well enough.——

"I am also much obliged for your inquiries respecting my health.
Within the last week I have made more improvement than I had done
since I came from Newcastle in October. But I am shattered in some
respects beyond all hope of recovery.——

"My poor study does not contain books of reference to enable me to
prosecute the work in which I am engaged with the ease and satisfaction to myself and the expedition I could wish—and here I am
overwhelmed with expenses in the education of my family, which I
cannot afford to send to a public school, or sick in seeing some of them,
who are grown up, buried in obscurity for want of society, and unnoticed by such as by some small attention might make the place in a
degree comfortable to them. But I must not venture to write more on
this subject—for I have started a matter which of late has given me
great uneasiness, but of which I will not permit myself to complain. I
am, dear Sir, most truly yours,

"JOHN HODGSON."

To ROBERT MACKRETH, Esq.

"MY DEAR SIR, Whelpington, 23rd April, 1831.

"Mr. Scriven has done wonders to the portrait since I last saw
a proof of it; and the more I look at it the more I admire it. The
work on the face is exceedingly fine, and the drapery and back-ground
boldly and well executed. I could not have thought the border could
have produced so much good effect. Still, however, I would say that
the tint upon the left cheek bone, and that circles the under part of the
left eye, is a little too bright: the under eyelid not sufficiently detached
from the eye, but too much blended with it; and the shadow on the
upper corner of the right side of the mouth hardly finely enough shaded
off: also the point of light upon the turn of the forehead not bright

enough.    These few remarks I make without much consideration.
Perhaps there is more of frown than of contemplation or thought in the
contraction of the muscle over the right eyebrow, but any body will be
able to criticise on the engraving better than I can.    I return the proof,
though I am very desirous of having two or three before the plate is
lettered.    By all means employ Mr. Scriven to superintend the printing,
and let the royal size be on India paper.    I think I mentioned to you the
number of impressions I should want; about 60 royal and 265 demys
for my book; besides a few more on larger paper, and some for your
sister.    But Mr. Scriven would do me a great favour by sending a list of
the number of impressions taken from the plate before it leaves his
hands; and to pack the plate carefully with the impressions, that I may
have it in case of a new edition of my work being called for, for such I
hope will be the case.    I wish the impressions to come here, and I will
send them with the other engravings to the binder when the work is
ready for delivery.    Be so good as to convey my best thanks to Mr.
Scriven for the skill and care he has used in the engraving.    I take the
earliest opportunity of returning you the proof and the miniature, and
pray do what you can to save me a few unlettered proofs, which I want
for a very particular purpose.    I must not, however, ask anything
which would run to an expense which the subscription will not cover.
The subscribers' separate copies, perhaps, had best be upon India paper,
but not of a size greater than would allow them to be packed with the
volume they are intended to be sent out with.    I have not a list of the
subscribers.    Could you favour me with two or three copies, or half a
dozen if you have them, of your circulars about the engraving, to write
lists of the subscribers upon?——

"JOHN HODGSON."

## CHAPTER X.—1832.

### To Mr. WOODMAN.

6 Jan. 1832.*

### To HENRY PETRIE, Esq.

"MY DEAR SIR,                                   Whelpington, 7 Jan. 1832.

"The bearer of this, Mr. Wm. Woodman, is a young Northumberland gentleman who is going to London to qualify as an attorney. His object in being a bearer of a letter to you is to consult you about the charter of Morpeth School, which had got among Lord Widdrington's† papers, and with them was seized at his attainder, and taken from Whitehall to the Tower in 1819.

"I have been once again at Housesteads on the Roman Wall, and had eleven men at work for four days, but made no other discovery than of some hypocausts, which I supposed to have been part of the apparatus of a granary and a kitchen. The sections of the wall I opened in 1830 were very much injured by the frost of the succeeding winter; but still I found no new character of building either in the stones or the Wall. The Wall in this part is standing in many places six feet high from its foundations, faced with freestones on both sides, each stone being about ten inches square, and the middle filled up with rumler work of whinstone and lime: for in this neighbourhood the Wall runs for many miles on the edge of an escarpment of whin or basalt. I hope as soon as spring sets in to go once again, and finish my researches at Housesteads, and to take a good surveyor with me to put all my

---

* This letter having been, by not an unusual mistake upon the coming in of a new year, wrongly dated, has been already printed in p. 192 above. It was written in reality in the year at which we have arrived, and to which it must be considered to belong.

† The rebel earl of 1715.

sketches, plans, and sections, into order for their publication in the
Archæologia Æliana.

" My friend Mr. Hedley has built a house close to his station of Vindolana, or Little Chesters; and in some researches has found several altars
dedicated by prefects of the *Cohors quarta Gallorum*. There have also some
curious inscriptions been found at Caervorran (Magna), all of which I
have promised to go to copy as soon as the weather will allow me to
write and sketch in the open air. This last and the preceding summer
have been very disastrous to my family, and I have been much borne
down with an epidemic fever myself; so that I could not get the papers
about the Roman Wall, of which I promised you a copy, prepared for
the press. I shall, however, in a very short time have some biographical
and other papers ready for begging your acceptance of a copy of each.

" I last night sent to press the Preface and Indexes to another
volume of the Newcastle Antiquarian Transactions, of which Mr.
Adamson will in a short time send a copy to the British Museum.
Yours, dear Sir, most truly,

"JOHN HODGSON."

To Rob. MACKRETH, Esq.—Jan. 7, 1832.—"A new year is a sad time
for exposing poverty. I really have not at present a farthing to spare
for Mr. Scriven. For a long time in summer I had 50*l.* laid up to send
him when he called for it; but many unseen causes have since that
time risen up to wrest it out of my hand. You will however have to
receive the subscriptions for the plate; and if on that security you dare
join me in a note for 40*l.* at Sir M. W. Ridley's bank, and say what it
is for, I will be willing to give my name to it. They will, I am sure
very readily let you have it, but they require two names.*

"JOHN HODGSON."

### To ROBERT MACKRETH, Esq.

" MY DEAR SIR,                    Whelpington, 10 Jan. 1832.

" There is not a stamp of any kind to get here, and, if there was,
I know no more than a child how to draw a bill in the manner you

* It would appear from this letter, and some of the Correspondence by which it is
succeeded, that, as the portrait was progressing in the hands of the engraver, money was
wanted upon account of the work, and that, the subscriptions towards it not having
been received, Hodgson was called upon to advance such a sum as was required. His

mention, and know of no person I could draw it upon.  The only thing
of the kind I know any thing about is a promissory note, by one of
which I got money last summer to pay Mr. Scriven; but urgent
demands upon me from ill health, affliction, and the demands of my
book, compelled me to make use of it above two months ago; and I think
in my last letter to Mr. Scriven I mentioned that I might not be able
to send him money as I had before intimated, but that he must rely on
the subscription, which had to be paid to you.  If I knew how to draw,
and on what kind of a stamp, and any body to draw upon, I would do
it immediately.   I really had forgot that the subscriptions were to be
paid to me.   Nothing depresses my spirits more than to be asked for
money that I cannot pay.  If I could have come to Newcastle some plan
might have been devised.   One thing is certain, that, if I shall have to
collect the subscriptions, I can never do it.  Mr. Scriven shall be paid;
but for me to send about to the subscribers to my book to ask for the
subscriptions for the portrait, is what all my feelings would revolt at.
It is impossible *for me* to accompany the portrait with any intimation
that money will be due for it.    That can be done no way but by your
sending a printed note with each portrait, saying that you request the
subscription may be paid either to you or at the Courant Office.    I
have never employed any person to collect the subscriptions for my
book till long after they were due, the subscribers having generally sent
the charge either to myself or the Courant Office.    Will you have the
kindness to keep me out of this dilemma by your advice.  Mr. Mackay,
my children's tutor, suggests that Mr. Scriven might draw upon me,
which I am willing that he may do, and to settle with him when the
subscriptions to pay his charge are got in.   If Mr. Scriven had the impressions ready for delivery could they not be sent to each subscriber,
or to many of them near Newcastle, before the work is ready, as I see
nothing in your circular about the time of delivering the proofs?  You
see the circular was sent out by you, which makes me think that the
proofs ought to be accompanied with a short notice also from you when
the subscriptions ought to be paid, and I see no person so proper to pay
them to as yourself.    I am not wishing to get trouble off myself and
throw it upon you.   I will take the trouble to pack up all the proofs
with your card about the subscriptions, and to many subscribers write
a note myself, thanking them for the honour they have done me.  I will

letters on this subject, especially that which comes next in the order of time, are very
characteristic of their writer, of his profound ignorance in money transactions, and of
his candour and simplicity in confessing it.

place no trouble upon you but that of receiving the subscriptions and settling the accounts: which if you cannot do, I cannot, on any account, nor know of any one to do so. I write this in haste, and send it by the Chevy Chase inclosed in a letter to Mr. Adamson. Yours truly,

"JOHN HODGSON."

To R. W. HODGSON, NEWCASTLE.

"MY DEAR RICHARD,                                     Whelpington, 11 Jan. 1832.

"I do not like to persecute you with notes of inquiry how you are; but you must allow me to be anxious for you, and sympathise with you when you are unwell. During my indisposition you took much and deep interest for my recovery, which has been slowly but mercifully accomplished. I continued at work, with the intermission of breakfast time, from four this morning to dinner hour at half-past three, and nobody can feel better in health than I do now at six. My prayer to you is, that, if you want assistance, you will allow your mother or me to come down; and that you will do nothing to bring on a further accession of cold, or by any mental excitement enfeeble your body. I hope with Mr. Greenhow you are in safe and skilful hands.——With my best prayers for your recovery, and all our earnest wishes to hear that you are better, I am, my dear Richard, your most affectionate father,

"JOHN HODGSON."

MR. W. MILLER TO EDWARD SWINBURNE, Esq.

"RESPECTED FRIEND,                                     Edinburgh, 11th of 1 mo. 1832.

"I had the pleasure the day before yesterday of receiving thy parcel, containing touched proofs, &c. of plates of Belsay and Edlingham Castles. I think the touches upon them most valuable, and shall have much pleasure in doing my best to give full effect to thy suggestions. I have already proceeded a considerable length with the touches upon the plate of Belsay, and am much pleased with the improving effect they produce. I hope to have both plates completed for printing this week, and the impressions forwarded to Newcastle within about a week after. I have another plate engraving for the volume,—Cresswell House, from a drawing by T. M. Richardson. It is also within about a day's work of being finished.

" Having a payment to make next week, I have availed myself of thy obliging offer to settle with me for the plates, and inclose on the other side a note of account.    The prices charged are what, I believe, was agreed on formerly; and although they do not quite remunerate me so well as many of my works, I could not for a moment think of charging anything for the additional touches, especially considering ' that the plates are an adornation to the work, and that the additional work is so useful.   I shall take care to take off a few proofs of each plate, and forward them to thy address at Capheaton, when the rest of the impressions are forwarded to Newcastle, and shall take the opportunity of inclosing for thy acceptance a proof or two of some of the plates I have recently finished from Turner.    Having removed upwards of a year ago from Buccleuch Place, have the kindness to address to me No. 4, Hope Park, and believe me very respectfully thy friend,

" WILLIAM MILLER.

| 1832, 1 mo. 11. | | | £ | s. | d. |
|---|---|---|---|---|---|
| Engraving Belsay Castle for Hist. of Northumd. | | | 21 | 0 | 0 |
| Copper plate and lettering title | . | . | 0 | 13 | 0 |
| Engraving Edlingham Castle for do. | . | . | 16 | 16 | 0 |
| Copper plate and lettering title | . | . | 0 | 13 | 0 |
| Carriage of proofs from London. | . | . | 0 | 6 | 8 |
| Printing 310 impressions and paper for do. of | | | | | |
| Belsay . | . | . | 2 | 0 | 0 |
| Do.            do.            Edlingham | | | 2 | 0 | 0 |
| | | | £43 | 8 | 8 |

" I am not sure whether or not it was thy intention that I should charge the expense of printing and paper to thy account, but thought it best just to state the expense."

To ROBERT MACKRETH, ESQ.—Whelpington, 13 Jan. 1832.—I have to send proofs, and therefore return the bill by the first opportunity. Thank you kindly for the relief you have given me.  Being so far from my seat of business in such matters I get easily fluttered from apprehension of plans going wrong, which are very apt to do so when they have to be executed by correspondence.    It is bad news you send me about the length of time my book will take in getting printed.  However, be so kind as to thank Mr. Cook for the use he allows to be made of his substantial name.——

" JOHN HODGSON."

From EDWARD SWINBURNE, Esq.

" My dear Sir,                                                14 Jan. 1832.

"I have seen Mr. Scriven twice. The second time he came to me, and brought me an amended proof of your portrait. He has taken *a great deal of pains* with it. It has undergone some improvement about the mouth, but, between ourselves, it never was nor ever can be yours; indeed it was a very difficult task for a person of Miss Mackreth's early practice, so much depending upon expression, and I am sure there was no want of pains on her part. The brows are also softened, and a half-tint thrown on the left cheek (on the right-hand looking at the print,) just under the eye, which softens the shadow under that bone, giving, as you thought, too muscular an appearance; I do not myself think there is that character, nor do I see any of the harshness I expected from a steel plate; it appears to me finely engraved. He has given more breadth of light on the forehead, and intended working on the arms, one of which is thick.

"Jackson put into my hands the little block of the wood-cut of the West Boat at Warden, when I was about to visit the North, to be given to you. It was done in consequence of an arrangement made with him upon some old score between us before I went abroad. I send you a specimen in the pedigree box I brought from Milan, forwarded by waggon to Capheaton. Had I seen it before it was so far advanced, I should have suggested the suppression of some of the lights, but they were cut away. The execution is generally very neat The body and figure are rather heavy; whether he was misled by the original sketch I can't say, for he had mislaid it. What shall I do with it? do you want it immediately? if so, I shall send it you; otherwise keep it till an opportunity offers.

"I have this moment heard from *friend* Miller. He had received the proofs, and very much, he says, approves the touches upon them, and will do his best in giving full effect to the suggestions. He had already worked upon Belsay, and was pleased with the effect produced. He was in hopes both plates would be completed for printing that week, (date of letter 11th of 1st mo.) and the impressions forwarded to Newcastle about the week after. Cresswell House, for Richardson, was also within about a day's work of being finished.

His prices are, he acknowledges, below his usual remunerating ones; I should think considerably so: I find him on this occasion, as on former transactions, extremely liberal, and it gives me great pleasure to learn that the proposed alterations (in Belsay particularly, for there was little to be done in the other) are so much to his satisfaction, and that he sets to work at them so cheerfully.

"I have memoranda by me of Bellingham Church and Dilston; will you be wanting them soon? shall I work them up for you as vignettes? What can I do for you here? If your next volume should not bring you back better than before your outgoings, it will not be for want of good wishes on the part of your ever attached friend,

"EDWARD SWINBURNE.

"I ought to observe that Miller's acknowledgment respecting the prices above mentioned, was not a voluntary on his part unsolicited by something from me."

To ROBERT MACKRETH, ESQ.—Whelpington, 15 Jan. 1832.—"Things done in a hurry are generally ill done. I had proofs last Friday to send by Chevy Chase, and inclosed some letters with them; but inadvertently sealed the one to you without signing the draft. The Chevy Chase is a bad conveyance, as we lie two miles from Cambo, and no attention is paid to forwarding parcels from that place. I hope now you will find the bill quite right, and that you will have no more trouble on the subject.

"Mr. Edward Swinburne says, 'I have seen Mr. Scriven twice. The second time he came to me and brought me an amended proof of your portrait. He has taken a great deal of pains with it. It has undergone some improvement. The brows are softened, and a half-tint thrown on the cheek (on the right-hand looking at the print) just under the eye, which softens the shadow under that bone, giving, as you thought, too muscular an appearance. I do not see any of the harshness I expected from a steel plate. It appears to me finely engraved. He has given more breadth of light on the forehead, and intended working on the arms, one of which is thick.' This you can shew to your sister.——

"JOHN HODGSON."

### FROM MR. W. MILLER.

"RESPECTED FRIEND,       No. 4, Hope Park, Edin. 1st of 2 m. 1832.

"Having completed the printing of the three plates for thy work, I now send the impressions ordered of each, which are— 60 royal and 260 demy: I have also sent three India proofs of each plate, thinking thou mightest wish to have one or two in that state.

" In the accompanying parcel for Edward Swinburne, which I request thy forwarding to Capheaton at thy leisure, I have inclosed five proofs of each, along with a few other proofs I had to send.   Perhaps thou wouldst have the goodness, when forwarding the parcel, to say what it is, in order that it may not be forwarded to him should he still be in London, unless he should write for it.   As the Chevy Chase is the most direct, and appears to be the cheapest way of sending the parcel, I have concluded to send it by that conveyance, and hope it will arrive safe.   Should I at any time be in the neighbourhood of Whelpington, I should have pleasure in availing myself of thy obliging offer and call upon thee—a few years ago I *walked* from the neighbourhood of New-castle through that part of the country into the South of Scotland, and have repeatedly passed it since in the Chevy Chase when going south. I remain respectfully thy friend,

" WILLIAM MILLER.

" I send the plates of Belsay and Edlingham together with the draw-ings.   The plate of Cresswell House is still with me, as I believe Cresswell Baker may require some more proofs from it."

To ROBERT MACKRETH, ESQ.—Whelpington, 3 Febr. 1832.—" By arrangements made with Mr. Cook, while I was in Newcastle, I now find that I have a good chance of getting liberated from the press in a fortnight's time.   Be so good, therefore, as to request Mr. Scriven to use all expedition in sending the proofs for the subscribers to the plate, and for the book, with the plate, as soon as possible, as we wish to have the impression of the book bound and circulated before the end of this month.   You can perhaps also say to Mr. Scriven that if Tho. C. Palmer, Esq., of Bromley, in Kent, has not already got a proof of the plate, I would thank him to send him one.   I saw the miniature of Mr. Adamson yesterday, and think it very like the original.——

" JOHN HODGSON."

To R. MACKRETH, ESQ.—Whelpington, 14 Feb. 1832.—" With this I send you a proof of my Preface, and will thank you to make on a separate piece of paper any corrections in its accompanying Tables of Plates, and to return it by our postman on Thursday, who leaves New-castle a quarter before twelve.

"Did not you mention some plan of Morpeth Gaol which Mr. Dob-son intended to favour me with?   If I were certain of its being printed

in eight or ten days, I could put it into the list of plates.    I write in
haste, and send my parcel through a communication to Mr. Adamson,
and hope you will receive it to-morrow.——

" JOHN HODGSON."

To ROBERT MACKRETH, ESQ.—Whelpington, 18 Feb. 1832.—" I
received your kind letter last night, and have adopted the most of your
suggestions, and requested Mr. Selkirk to send you a corrected copy of the
proofs in time for your returning them to me on Thursday next by our
post.    I find from Mr. Adamson that the Chevy Chase had not delivered
the parcel in which your packet was sent till Wednesday evening.

" I hope you will think I have blotted out all the dark clouds at the
end of the preface.    Perhaps I may have left some, but what picture
will do without clouds?    I assure you that all my labour and no inconsiderable part of my own money are gratuitously presented on my part
to the subscribers to my work.    I wished it to have been of use to my
family, but the volume now about to be introduced to the world will
have a serious contrary effect—and, added to this, my income has been
considerably abridged within the last three years.    For *one series of
Records* I paid last year above 44*l.*, and on Thursday I received the concluding part of it charged to me 51*l.*    But it would be endless to enter
into details of the expenses the book brings upon me.    I know I have
got reputation by it, but still I cannot live upon that.    These were the
fires that raised the clouds you have kindly recommended me to
expunge.* ——

" JOHN HODGSON."

FROM EDWARD SWINBURNE, ESQ.

" London, 25 Feb. 1832,

" MY DEAR SIR,            15, Great Castle Street, Cavendish Square.

" The copy I took of your work was for my friend Mr. Richard
Duppa, whose death I became acquainted with on my return: it had
taken place a very little before.    It has been a great loss to me, for he
was a very good creature, and the friendship was of long standing.

" His library must have been sold, and thus the copy has come into
the hands of Mr. Charnley, and so it is well he is inclined to keep it and

* This is a letter of painful confessions—and yet he persevered in his undertaking
until not merely his purse but his bodily health gave way !

to continue. I am glad you find Jackson's woodcut so eligible by comparison. His powers, when directed in the line he has been more accustomed to, go much beyond that; his execution has, for wood, a wonderful delicacy and neatness. I hope you will find your son's health get gradually stronger; now is the time for care. When I was very young I was thus greeted by an acquaintance on our meeting after a few years separation: ' What, you are alive still !' What would he say now ?

" The cholera, as you see, makes so far but little progress here (I have not seen this day's account); this may induce the family to begin to travel South. It appears to me much too early to form any opinion of its future operations, judging from its irregular proceedings in other quarters. A fine field is open for medical controversies, which have begun with the usual allowance of bold assertions and vituperation. I like better my own present allowance of health. I have had a very kind summons from Nettlecombe, towards which I shall be turning my steps when these winter months are over. I heartily wish you success with your new volume, and a good continuance of your renovated health for future enterprize. If you meet or correspond with Hedley, remember me kindly to him, as now to Mrs. Hodgson and yourself. I repeat, as often as a magpie, can I do anything for you here? Yours, ever truly,

" ED. SWINBURNE.

" A very good account of Emma Wyndham and her baby. Aunt Julia much commends the latter."

To ROBERT MACKRETH, ESQ.—March 16, 1832.—" I will not omit the opportunity of answering your kind letters to-night by the carrier, though I have this morning to be at Capheaton on business which will occupy me the whole day. Thinking you may expect some official letter to request you to convey my thanks to the several subscribers to the portrait, I have inclosed one, in such terms as I can best contrive, in the hurry I am in at present. I hope, however, you will not in printing, &c. exceed the fund you have obtained; though I will most willingly pay for any expense you may think requisite to go into, in order that my sentiments of the honor done me may be properly conveyed to all who have interested themselves in conferring it. I hope, too, that your sister and yourself have secured as many impressions of the portrait as you wish.

" I cannot account for it, but the parcel containing the plate and impressions, that came last night, needed no other announcement that it

came from Newcastle than the great quantity of coal-dust that had insinu-
ated itself through the whole of it—a handful, at least. I suppose it
had come by sea to you, as our postman says it was impossible it could
procure the dust while under his care.——

" JOHN HODGSON."

To ROBERT MACKRETH, Esq.

" MY DEAR SIR, Whelpington, March 16, 1832.

" Your letter of yesterday, with the plate and the impressions of
the portrait, I received last night, and hope you will be able to find
leisure to say to each subscriber, with his proof of it, how sensible I am
of the honor he has done me, and to convey to him my best thanks for
this public approval of the work which the portrait is intended to
accompany.

" I am under the necessity of begging you to grant me this favour,
having already in the commencement of the volume, with which the
engraving is intended to be delivered, printed the list of the sixty-eight
subscribers to it, which you sent to me some time ago, and also noticed
the obligation I owe to them for the distinguished compliment they have
paid to myself and my work.

" You will, I also hope, allow me further to express my very sincere
wish, that the publication of the portrait may in some measure be the
means of procuring to your sister, Miss H. F. S. Mackreth, (the ingenious
artist who painted the miniature from which it is taken,) all the employment she can wish in the beautiful art in which she has so much
pleasure, and in which her pencil is so highly calculated to excel; and
to request that both she and you will accept of my sincere thanks
for the part you have individually taken in procuring me the honor,
which according to your letter has been conferred upon me. From, my
dear Sir, yours very truly,

" JOHN HODGSON."

To MR. McKAY.

" MY DEAR MR. McKAY, Whelpington, 20 March, 1832.

" I have corrected two sheets of the Pipe Roll. I hope for one
sheet every week, but they can allow me only one proof; and if I take
two, that is, a proof and a revise, I can, from the nature of our post, have

R 2

only one sheet printed in a fortnight. I am, however, taking very great care in preparing the manuscript, for I fear all their mistakes originate with it. They copy slavishly every inaccuracy in punctuation, and capital letters and letters imperfectly formed they oftener mistake than give rightly. I now go over a year or two carefully with a pen and a knife, and satisfy myself thoroughly about all the points, capital letters, contractions, and paragraphs, and after that have it slowly and carefully collated with the office copy. John soon fell into the way of transcribing it, from his knowledge of printing and great patience; and it is quite wonderful how accurately and clearly he prepares it for the press.——My dear Sir, you have always our best wishes; and now our kindest remembrances and regards.*——

" John Hodgson."

To HENRY PETRIE, Esq.

"MY DEAR SIR,                                Whelpington, 3 April, 1832.

" I have the pleasure to beg your acceptance of a small volume, part of which will be found in the volume of my History now in the binder's hands,† but the *Addenda* is new matter, only to be found in the impression of 100 copies of the book, of which this is one.

" Sad afflictions and ill-health have prevented my third and last excursion to the Roman Wall. But I am under promise to go to take minutes of the discoveries mentioned at p. 103, and of the operations going on there, and at Caervorran, in about three weeks' time; when I hope to have the advantage of a draughtsman, and to finish my minutes about Housesteads and the Roman Wall. Mr. Hedley, I believe, intends that I should send the account of the altars found at Vindolana, where he has built a neat cottage for his own residence, to Sir John Swinburne, to be presented to the London Antiquarian Society.

" My next volume will commence with the parish of Alston, which, though in the county of Cumberland, is in the archdeaconry of Northumberland, and must consequently be noticed in my work; I will therefore feel particularly obliged by your favouring me with the *tenor* of the charters noticed in the inclosed list. Some of them are mere exemplifications, and in such cases I only wish to know of which.

---

* Mr. McKay had awhile before been appointed to the mastership of the school at Gifford near Haddington.

† Probably the Memoir of Horsley, &c., to be afterwards mentioned.

Those to Nicholas de Veteriponte, 10 Edw. I., and to the Moneyers of Aldneston, in 8 Edw. III., will, I think, be the most interesting, though the whole of them consist of materials that have never appeared in any history of Alston.

"I have printed my account of Morpeth in a separate form from the same in the volume now about to be published, with which I will inclose a copy of it in the parcel to the British Museum, and beg your acceptance of it. The title-sheet of it is not yet printed, or it should have made part of the parcel which contains this letter. I am, my dear Sir, very faithfully, and with much obligation, yours truly,

" JOHN HODGSON.

" I have added to the parcel two antiquarian papers."

To ROBERT MACKRETH, Esq.—Whelpington, 4 April, 1832.—" Your circular letter is very polite and proper.

" Pray give my best regard to your sister, and say that I request she will keep the miniature for any length of time she may please; two or three years, if she wishes.

" I have written to the Tower for a new batch of records to enable me to go on with a new volume; which I shall not, however, commence till I see the one which should be now in the binder's hands fairly into circulation.——JOHN HODGSON."

CIRCULAR TO THE SUBSCRIBERS FOR THE ENGRAVING OF THE PORTRAIT OF THE
REV. JOHN HODGSON.

" The engraving of Mr. Hodgson's portrait from the miniature painted and presented by Miss H. F. S. Mackreth being completed, I have forwarded the plate with the requisite impressions for his volume to Mr. Hodgson, in the names of the subscribers, requesting his acceptance of it as an embellishment to his History of Northumberland, and a public mark of their regard for him individually, and the estimation in which they hold his work.

" I have received an answer from him, requesting me to convey to each subscriber his acknowledgment of the deep sense he has of the honour conferred upon him, and his best thanks for this public approval of the work the portrait is intended to accompany.

" As the expenses of the engraving and impressions must be immediately defrayed, I have to beg you will have the goodness to pay your subscription of one guinea either to me, at High Swinburne Place, or Mr. Cook, the Courant Office, Pilgrim Street, Newcastle, at your earliest convenience.

"I have the honour to be your obedient servant,

"ROBT. MACKRETH, *Hon. Sec.*

"High Swinburne Place, Newcastle."

To WILLIAM WOODMAN, Esq.

"MY DEAR SIR,                    Whelpington, 30 April, 1832.

"I have very great pleasure in sending you a copy of my account of Morpeth.*  It is not yet published, and I hope you will not let it be much seen.

"You will see that it has extended to a greater length than I could think it would when I first began it.  I have not yet got my printer's account of the expense of it, but I inclose with your copy one for the Corporation of Morpeth; and I fear I cannot without loss—seven or eight pounds, at least—send copies to each alderman, as I said to them I hoped I should be able to do.  But do not deliver the corporation copy till you see the volume published; and, in the mean time, pray do me the favour to find out whether or not they would think me departing shabbily from a promise, which I would cheerfully perform if I could well afford, and will perform it if it is expected.  I write this in great haste, to catch the first opportunity of sending your copy. Very faithfully yours,

"JOHN HODGSON."

The opening of the month of May in this year witnessed the publication of another volume of the History of Northumberland, (Part II. vol. ii.) the second of the series dedicated and exclusively confined to parochial history.  It treats of the West Division of Morpeth Ward, as subdivided into the parishes of Meldon, Mitford, Longhorsley, Hebburn Chapelry, and Morpeth;—of the East Division of the same ward, consisting of the parishes of Bothal, Ulgham Chapelry, Woodhorn, Newbigging Chapelry, and Widdrington Chapelry;—of Horton Chapelry in the East Division, and of the parish of Stannington in the West Division of Castle Ward.

* From his forthcoming volume, bound in a separate form.  The price of this portion in its separate state was afterwards fixed at £1 1s.

In pursuance of my plan, and for the reasons so often stated, I scruple not to lay before my readers the Preface with which this volume also was accompanied, together with a list of the subscribers to Miss Mackreth's portrait, which was published along with it, and other details relating to its embellishments. The Preface is, as usual, very characteristic of its writer, and of his feelings as his work was advancing; and the subjoined lists are creditable to those who were able to appreciate and willing to acknowledge the value of his labours, by rendering to him such services and assistances as were in their power.

## PREFACE TO PART II. VOL. II.

" This volume closes the history of one of the deaneries of the archdeaconry of Northumberland, a district which extends throughout the heart of the country, from the border of Scotland on Carter Fell, to the German Ocean; and comprises nearly the whole of Morpeth Ward, and considerable portions of Castle, Coquetdale, and Tindale Wards. I had hoped to complete it in less room; but to keep the work in some degree of uniformity, and to finish the district with the volume, I have been compelled to be at more expense than the impression can repay me, for the great quantity of small types used in the notes, and especially in the pedigrees and Latin authorities, has made it chargeable to me far beyond my first calculations.

" The accompanying list of plates will serve in some degree to show the point of support and patronage to which this work has arrived, and for which the author is indebted, and has now the pleasure of requesting the several contributors of them to accept his best and most grateful thanks; but, besides these, he is under obligations for other gratifying tokens of approbation. Immediately after the publication of the volume of Parochial History which preceded this, it obtained the kind approval of Sir J. E. Swinburne, Baronet, by his becoming a sharer with me in the expenses of printing it: and to himself and family I am indebted for various extracts from manuscripts and rare printed books in the British Museum. The Bishop of Durham has in a very kind manner approved of my labours; and the copious extracts I have made from the minutes of the Parochial Visitations of Dr. Singleton, Archdeacon of Northumberland, and from the books of his predecessors, Mr. Sharp and Drs. Robinson and Sharp, will shew how much this volume is enriched by the free permission given to me to make whatever use of

them I pleased.   Sir Charles M. L. Monck enabled me, while in London
in 1829, to employ the hands of amanuenses in copying several im-
portant papers.    John Hodgson, Esq. M.P. for Newcastle-upon-Tyne,
presented me with a volume of extracts made by himself from the
Sessions Books of Northumberland, and has sent me extracts gleaned from
MSS. in various parts of the kingdom.   From W. C. Trevelyan, Esq., of
Wallington, I have received large collections of materials from Dodsworth's
Manuscripts in the Bodleian Library, and from that of Miss Currer at
Eshton Hall, in Craven; and from his sister, Mrs. Wyndham, a remarkably
correct and copious Index to Ridpath's Border History, all compiled and
written by her own hand.   H. Petrie, Esq., Keeper of the Records in
the Tower, and C. G. Young, Esq., York Herald and Registrar at the
Heralds' College, have cheerfully and gratuitously given me such
assistance as I have solicited from them.    The generous and graphic
hand of Edward Swinburne, Esq., still continues to transfer to my work
views of the scenery of the county, and of the residences of its ancient
barons and gentry, with that happy simplicity and brilliance which so
pre-eminently characterise the productions of his pencil; and to the
zeal and kindness of Mr. Sopwith, surveyor, I am indebted for correct
delineations or engravings of various churches, chapels, and other
subjects, as expressed in the list of plates; as well as for copies of several
interesting papers relative to Northumberland matters, in the Cottonian
Library in the British Museum.    The fine miniature from which the
portrait at the beginning of this volume has been engraved was painted
expressly for it, by Miss H. F. S. Mackreth, at her own particular
request, and gratuitously presented to the author; and after the preface
is given a list of those friends to the work, who have honoured him,
through their secretary Mr. Mackreth, with the finely executed plate and
impressions of the portrait.   John Dobson, Esq. and Robert Mackreth,
Esq. have also, without previously mentioning their kind intentions to
me, interested themselves in embellishing my book, by obtaining for it
the lithographic views of seats now presented to the reader at the
expense of their several proprietors.   Mr. Thomas Bell, land surveyor,
has to all my applications for assistance in genealogical inquiries, paid
early and prompt attention, and it is to him that I am indebted for a
copy of the widely-spreading tree of the Widdrington family, from which
I have drawn the outline of a considerable portion of the Widdrington
pedigree.
    " The active mind and ready pen of Mr. William Woodman, solicitor,
in Morpeth, left me comparatively little to do in searching for materials

for my account of the corporation of that town, in which, however
copious it may seem, I have inserted only a very small part of the information he has given me from the books of the several companies: and
to the Bailiffs and Aldermen of Morpeth my thanks are due, for leave
to copy from the muniments deposited in their town's hutch, the numerous charters and other documents and papers of which the lengthened
'Annals of Morpeth' are principally composed; and finally, to all other
patrons and encouragers of this work by subscribing for copies of it,
my best thanks are due, and hereby most cheerfully and gratefully
rendered.

"I lament that so long an interval has elapsed since my subscribers
received a volume of this work in March 1828.   Many causes have retarded its progress; but none over which I have had a controlling power.
Though much care, expense and labour have been employed in rendering it as correct and perfect as my means would enable me to do, still
it contains many errors and imperfections, the principal of which I have
endeavoured to supply by an appendix of errata and addenda.   Judicious and candid readers, when they consider where and by whom it is
written, will, I doubt not, be tender over its demerits.   It is not, perhaps,
possible, without great facilities in means, books and situation, to go on
rapidly with a work so varied, large, and profitless to its author as this
is; and when I say that one who engages in a performance of this kind
ought to be rich and childless, I beg I may not be considered as doing so in
despondency and complaint, but as apologising for imperfections which
I could not supply.   I rise to this labour every morning with increasing desire to complete it.   It keeps in delightful employment a mind
that finds it as impossible to be idle, as to be soured by disappointment
or insensible to encouragement.   'Periculorum præmia et laborum
fructum contemnere,' is a stoical virtue which I cannot boast of; and
for the distinguished encouragement I have received I feel cheered and
gratified.   With all its imperfections there is, however, one thing which
I can fearlessly venture to say of my book—if it does not spangle with
the bright jewels of genius and wisdom—if it does not captivate with
the charms of ' useful and entertaining knowledge '—if it is not robed
in the elegant and costly attire of oratory—nearly the whole of it is
original, and now for the first time makes its appearance before the
public, and all of it, I hope, in the simple garb of truth.   I have never
yet set down at my loom to weave into the web of any person or family's
history the airy visions of apocryphal ancestry, or the flaring colours
of adulation.   As I have stood by the stream of time, I have perhaps

collected, in their passage down it, many an unimportant fact; but I know that I have suffered many a foul tale of slander and dishonour to glide silently past me, and to sink in its course.　To appetites habituated to riot on the rich luxuriance of novels in the form of melo-dramatic history, I know I am offering tasteless and unexciting food; and I cannot here ask the classical scholar to a rich repast of the history, manners, and literature of the kings and people of a mighty nation; but I invite the ingenuous and curious inhabitants, and especially the young people of the places I have written upon, to partake of aliment calculated, I hope, to make them honest and single-hearted patriots, and keep within them a joyous and imperishable love for the places of their nativity.

J. H.

" Whelpington, Feb. 3, 1832."

*An Alphabetical List of the Subscribers to whom the Author is indebted for the Engraving of the Portrait which fronts the Title-page.*

Adamson, John, Esq., F.A.S., M.R.S.L., &c.
Antiquarian Society, Newcastle.
Atkinson, R. A., Esq., Newcastle.
Beaumont, Thos. W., Esq., M.P., Bywell.
Bell, Matthew, Esq., M.P., Woolsington.
Bentham, Wm., Esq., F.A.S., of Upper Gower Street, London.
Bewicke, Mrs., Close House.
Bigge, Chas. Wm., Linden, Esq.
Birkett, the Rev. James, Haydon Bridge.
Bird, the Rev. Christ. Vicar of Chollerton and Warden.
Brandling, John, Esq., Gosforth.
Brandling, William, Esq., Gosforth.
Buddle, John, Esq., Wallsend.
Brockett, John Trotter, Newcastle, Esq., F.A.S.
Carr, Ralph, of Dunston, Esq.
Charnley, Em., Esq., Newcastle.
Clayton, John, of Newcastle, Esq.
Clayton, Nathaniel, Chesters, Esq.
Clennell, Thos., Harbottle Castle, Esq.
Collinson, the Rev. John, Rector of Gateshead.
Cook, the Rev. Joseph, Newton Hall, Vicar of Shilbottle, &c.
Coulston, Col., Blenkinsopp Castle.

Darnell, the Rev. W. N., Rector of Stanhope.
Davidson, the Misses, Newcastle.
Dobson, John, Esq., Newcastle.
Donkin, Armourer, Esq., Newcastle.
Durham, the Right Rev. the Lord Bishop of.
Ellison, Cuth., Hebburn Hall, Esq.
Ellison, Miss, Newcastle.
Falla, Wm., Esq., Gateshead.
Fenwicke, the Rev. Geo. Ousley, Vicar of Kempston, Bedfordshire.
Fenwick, John, Esq., Newcastle.
Fenwick, Perceval, Esq., Newcastle.
Forster, John, Esq., East Shaftoe.
Haigh, the Rev. Wm., Vicar of Wooler.
Hedley, the Rev. Anthony, Chesterholm.
Hill, George, Esq., Kenton.
Hodgson, John, of Elswick, Esq. M.P.
Kirsopp, John, Esq., Hexham.
Lambert, John, Esq., Alnwick.
Lawson, William, of Long Hurst, Esq.
Literary and Philosophical Society, Newcastle.
Mackreth, Robert, Esq., Newcastle.
Maughan, Nicholas, Newbrough Lodge, Esq.

Monck, Sir C. M. L., Belsay Castle, Bart.
Northumberland, His Grace the Duke of.
Ogle, the Rev. John Saville, of Kirkley, Prebendary of Durham.
Ord, Wm., of Whitfield, Esq., M.P.
Orde, Wm., of Nunnykirk, Esq.
Prudhoe, the Right Hon. the Lord.
Purvis, Thomas, of Plawsworth Cottage and Lincoln's Inn, Esq.
Raine, the Rev. J., Rector of Meldon, and St. Mary South Bailey, Durham.
Ridley, Sir M. W., of Blagdon, Baronet, M.P.
Sharp, the Rev. A., Bamborough.
Silvertop, George, of Minsteracres, Esq. High Sheriff of Northumberland.
Smith, Sir David, of Alnwick, Baronet.

Straker, John, Esq., Jarrow Lodge.
Swinburne, Edward, sen., Esq., Capheaton.
Swinburne, Sir J. E., of Capheaton, Baronet, F.R.S. F.A.S. M.R.S.L., &c. &c.
Surtees, Robt., of Mainsforth, Esq. F.A.S.
Thompson, Benjamin, Esq., Newcastle.
Trevelyan, Sir John, of Wallington, Bart.
Trevelyan, W. C., Esq., Wallington.
Turner, the Rev. Wm., Newcastle.
Vernon, the Hon. G. J., of Sudbury Hall, Derbyshire, Esq., M.P.
Ward, John, Esq., Durham.
Wallace, Albany, Esq., Queen Anne Street, London.
Wallace, the Right Hon. the Lord.

---

## PLATES, VIGNETTES, ETC. BELONGING TO THIS VOLUME.

*₀* The Contributors to whose names an obelisk (†) is attached have presented the Author both with the Plates and the Impressions: and the double obelisk (‡) denotes that the Contributors favoured the Author with the use of the wooden blocks on which the subjects are engraved.

| SUBJECT. | DESIGNED BY | ENGRAVED BY | CONTRIBUTED BY |
|---|---|---|---|
| 184. Woodhorn Church . | T. Sopwith | Isaac Nicholson | The Author. |
| 204. Cresswell Tower, &c. | Ditto | Ditto | Ditto. |
| 205. Cresswell Fossil . | Ditto | Thomas Sopwith | T. Sopwith.† |
| 206. Cresswell House . | T. M. Richardson | William Millar | A. J. Cresswell Baker. |
| 214. Newbigging Chapel | T. Sopwith | Isaac Nicholson | The Author. |
| 222. Widdrington Chapel | Ditto | Ditto | Ditto. |
| 266. Horton Chapel . | Miss Errington | Ditto | Ditto. |
| 279. Stannington Church | T. Sopwith | Ditto | Ditto. |
| 352. Bedlington Church . | Isaac Nicholson | Ditto | Ditto. |
| 355. Remains of a Cross . | Ditto | Ditto | Ditto. |
| 374. Seal of R. de Merlay I. | Rev. James Raine | Ditto | Ditto. |
| 375. Seal of R. de Merlay II. (See also p. 480) | Isaac Nicholson | Ditto | Ditto. |
| 375. Seal of R. de Merlay III. | The Author | Ditto | Ditto. |
| 379. Seal of Willm. Lord Dacre | Isaac Nicholson | Ditto | S. A. P. Æ.‡ (a) |
| 384. Gateway of Morpeth (b) | T. Sopwith | William Collard | The Author. |
| — Arms on Serjeant's Mace, Morpeth | William Collard | Ditto | Ditto. |
| 396. Ulgham Chapel . | T. Sopwith | Isaac Nicholson | Ditto. |
| 426. Morpeth Old Bridge and Chapel | William Collard | Ditto | Ditto. |
| 433. Seal of the Corporation of Morpeth | Isaac Nicholson | Ditto | Ditto. |
| 437. Plan of Northumberland County Goal, &c. at Morpeth | John Dobson | William Collard | C. W. Bigge, Esq. |

## PLATES,

### GIVEN AT THE END OF THIS VOLUME FOR FORMER AND FUTURE PARTS OF THIS WORK.

*₀* The Contributors to whose names (*) is fixed have presented both the Plates and Impressions to the Author ; those with (†) have presented the Impressions ; and those with (‡) the Plates.

| SUBJECT. | DESIGNED BY | ENGRAVED BY | CONTRIBUTED BY |
|---|---|---|---|
| Edlingham Castle . | Edw. Swinburne, Esq. | William Millar | Sir J. E. Swinburne, Bart.* |
| Belsay Castle . . . | Ditto | Ditto | Edward Swinburne, Esq.* |
| Whelpington . . . | Ditto | Ditto | Ditto and others.* |
| Whitfield Hall . . | Ditto | F. C. Lewis | William Ord, Esq., M.P.* |
| Jesmond Chapel . . | J. W. Carmichael | Ditto | James Losh, Esq.* |
| Nafferton Hall . . | Edw. Swinburne, Esq. | Ditto | F. Cholmley, Esq.* |
| Wallington . . . | Mrs. Wyndham | W. H. Lizars | Sir John Trevelyan, Bart.† |
| Aydon Castle . . . | J. Dobson, Architect | Robert Mackreth | Sir Edward Blackett, Bart. |
| Chesters, with Chollerford Bridge in the foreground | Robert Mackreth | Ditto | John Clayton, Esq. |
| Lilburn Tower . . | J. Dobson, Architect | Ditto | H. J. Wm. Collingwood, Esq. |
| Nunnykirk . . . | Ditto | Ditto | William Orde, Esq. |
| Fireplace in Edlingham Castle | W. C. Trevelyan | W. C. Trevelyan | W. C. Trevelyan, Esq.‡ |
| R. Thornton's Tomb . | T. Sopwith | Mark Lambert | T. Sopwith.† |

a Societas Antiquariorum Pontis-Ælii.

b This plate contains the arms on the mace of the Corporation of Morpeth ; and I cannot but express my thanks to Mr. Collard for the care and skill he has employed upon it.

By way of general remark upon this volume of the History of
Northumberland, it must be stated that from its beginning to its
end it is written with great care, and abounds with the most interesting and varied information, especially in the *Notes* and
*Miscellanea* appended to each parish or locality.  Of Hodgson's
method of condensing many valuable historical facts under these
heads a few remarks have been already made.  In this volume he
improves upon his plan, finding a place for numerous pieces of
information not alluded to in his narrative, or serving as its
vouchers.    In the pedigrees also we have the same laborious
detail and lucid arrangement, each link and generation illustrated
by sketches of biography, and authenticated by dates and references.    On some of the pedigrees, however, which appear to
have been put into his hands in a state of comparative readiness
for the press, especially in their earlier links, many remarks
might be made; but it may be as well to defer this subject till we
come to the last volume of his labours, in which there are still
graver departures from truth in the genealogies which, at the
request of individuals, he has unsuspectingly placed upon record
in his pages.

I proceed to draw the attention of the reader to some of the
contents of this volume, the second from its author's pen, as
is above stated, which is exclusively confined to parochial history,
and, with this object in view, it is my intention to be more
copious in my extracts than on former occasions, especially in
descriptions of local scenery, or in the case of subjects peculiarly
indicating the turn of Mr. Hodgson's mind.  In his boyhood and
youth he was an intense admirer of outward nature in its various
phases; and we shall see from this volume that his taste had kept
pace with his years.  We shall see, also, how feelingly he could
meditate upon the apparently trifling subjects which came in his
way—the name of a hamlet, the division of a town-field, or the
stump of an old village cross.

And first of Meldon, with which the volume opens.  From my
connection with this parish, my well-known intimacy with Mr.
Hodgson, and my having devoted much of my time to topographical inquiries, a report appears to have gone abroad that I and
not he was the writer of its history.  This report is sufficiently
contradicted by certain letters which have appeared in the pre-

ceding pages of this volume, but I take the present opportunity of distinctly and personally stating that it has no foundation in truth. Circumstances of a private nature had compelled me to gather together much historical information from the earliest period respecting the parish of Meldon. This information was placed by me in Hodgson's hands, and from it and his own resources, he, and he alone, wrote the history which appears in the volume before us. But to the identification of that notable witch Meg of Meldon as Margaret Selby, the second wife of Sir William Fenwick of Wallington, I certainly do lay some claim. Witch-finders were formerly men of note, and were well paid for their pains. The only reward I have received is the interest which the discovery appears to have excited. After having pointed out to Mr. Hodgson the fact that, by means of the dower of that lady, advanced by her husband in mortgage, the Herons of Meldon, a popular family, were eventually ejected from their ancient estate, he pursued the hint, and was not long in coming to the same conclusion as myself, that Dame Margaret Fenwick was the veritable witch who, if one may jest upon a subject once so terrific, kept the Wansbeck in hot water from her own period till modern times.*

The following is Hodgson's account of this lady and her tricks:—

" MEG OF MELDON.—MEG, or, as some call her, THE MAID OF MELDON, was, according to tradition, a person of considerable celebrity in her day as a witch and a miser; and since her death has continued to be the subject of many a winter evening's ghost tale. That she was *Margaret Selby*, the mother of Sir William Fenwick of Meldon, is, I think plain from the following circumstances. After her death she used to go and come from Meldon by a subterraneous coach-road to Hartington Hall, which was her residence after her husband's death. The entry into this underground way at Hartington was by a very large whinstone in the Hart, called the *battling-stone*, from its being used to beat or *battle*

* From a letter printed above, p. 115, the reader might infer that in Hodgson's opinion it was the wife of Sir William of Meldon, and not his mother, who thus " cast her cantraips " by the side of the Wansbeck. This mistake does not exist in the following extract. The real witch is there correctly pointed out, and, as if afraid of consequences, for in the opinion of the vulgar Meg is still on the move on suitable occasions, it is done by a *query*—" Was this the famous MEG OF MELDON ?" See the Pedigree of Fenwick, p. 17.

the lie out of webs upon it in the bleaching season. Some years since, in repairing Hartington Hall, and removing a thick coat of whitewash from the walls of a room, the stucco-work was found to be ornamented with family pictures, one of which some old persons remembered to have seen before it was covered, and said it was always called Meg of Meldon. Like a picture of the same lady which was at Seaton Delaval in 1810, this was habited in a round hat, with a large brim tied down at each ear, and in a stuff gown turned up nearly to the elbows, with a vandyked sleeve of linen; the whole shoulders were covered with a thickly gathered ruff or frill. Portraits, said to be of her and her husband Sir William Fenwick (senior), are preserved at Ford Castle. The traditional superstitions of the neighbourhood say that, as a retribution for her covetous disposition and practice in unearthly arts, her spirit was condemned to wander seven years and rest seven years. During the season she had to walk her nightly rounds she was the terror of the country from Morpeth to Hartington Hall. The places of her most usual resort were those in which she had bestowed her hoarded treasure — places she always abandoned after her pelf was found and turned to useful purposes. Many nights of watching and penance are said to have been spent over a well a little to the south-east of Meldon Tower, where she had deposited a bull's hide full of gold, which has never yet been discovered, though the present unbelieving generation can never now see the phantom of its departed owner performing its vigils over it. Several large fortunes within the last century are attributed to the discovery of bags of her gold. The most frequent scene of her midnight vagaries was about Meldon Bridge, along the battlements of which she was often seen running in the form of a little dog. But she was Proteus-like, and appeared in a thousand forms, lights, and colours, flickering over the Wansbeck, or under a fine row of beech trees by the river side, in the lane between the bridge and Meldon Park. One of her most favourite forms was that of a beautiful woman. The people of Meldon, however, became so familiarised with her appearance as to say when she passed them, 'There goes Meg of Meldon.' The ceiling of Meldon schoolhouse once gave way with the weight of a bag of her money while the master was out at his dinner, and the varlets, who were fortunate enough to be in, had a rich scramble for it. Another of her haunts was in an ancient stone coffin on the site of Newminster Abbey, where those who had the gift of seeing ghosts have seen her sitting in a doleful posture for many nights together. This coffin was called by the country people *the trough of the Maid of Meldon*, and water found in it was a specific in removing warts and curing many inveterate complaints. Such are the fables with which the calumny of an ignorant and superstitious age aspersed the character and the memory of a person who was probably much more enlightened and virtuous than her credulous contemporaries. So bad a name may not, however, owe all its origin to the wickedness of wondering gossips. If she was, as they say, a pitiless money-getting matron, she could not be a greater curse to her neighbourhood than vain and extravagant mothers are to their own families. The investment of her fortune in the mortgage of Meldon, and the hard case of young Heron being forced to join in conveying the ancient seat and lands of his ancestors to her son, while they tell no good tale either for her or the Fenwick family, were circumstances likely enough to cause a strong popular feeling in favour of the ousted heir, and as strong a hatred to his wealthy oppressors." (P. 11, &c.)

" MELDON.—Its surface, especially in the part called *Meldon Park*, is wavy and bold, and the banks of the Wansbeck, which runs from east to west through it, are fringed with alder, or covered with natural or planted trees, to which much praiseworthy attention has, in latter years, been paid by the proprietors of the estate. This *Park* contains 859 acres on the south, and 108 acres on the north side of the Wansbeck; and extends from the village of Meldon to the northern boundary of the parish: it is surrounded with a stone wall laid in mortar, which, till within the last twenty years, was in many places twelve feet high, but has been uniformly reduced to about five feet. It was probably made by the Radclyffe family.* Deerhorns are frequently found here: one, in particular, remarkable for its size, was turned up by the plough, five or six years ago, in the low wet ground to the south-west of the bridge, and is now in possession of Mr. Wailes, one of the receivers of Greenwich Hospital. The *park-keeper's house*, an old grey building, on the southern bank of the river, though in a low and warm situation, is raised high enough to give its tenant a supervisor's eye over nearly the whole area of the park; and in the arrangement of its chimney tops, and the mullions and weather-mouldings of its windows, was, no doubt, at the time it was built, a crack specimen of the architecture of the seventeenth century." (P. 3, &c.)

---

* Hodgson's conjecture is wrong. The park wall was the work of the Fenwicks, soon after the year 1620.

" RIVERGREEN.—This is one of the lovely and lonely spots with which
the sides of the Wansbeck abound.   The mill, the river, the flowery
haugh, the old orchard and its cosey and sheltered cottage—and all
these girt around with shaggy and wooded banks, and enlivened with
the miller and the woodman's families, form a panorama, which wants
nothing but some such picturesque accompaniments as it once had in
its patriarch Joshua Delaval, and his fourscore goats and sixteen kids,
to make it a subject, by the magic of some master's hand, worthy of
blooming on canvass through the live-long year."  (p. 24.)

The history of Mitford, and its old Baronial Castle, is written
with much spirit, and the descent of its lords carefully traced.  Few
fortresses in Northumberland could tell such a tale as the Castle
of Mitford.   From the earliest Norman, if not from a still more
remote period, its name was famous for centuries, whether it was
in the hands of England or Scotland.   Here William the Lion
resided and dated his charters; here Roger Bertram, in league
with the rebellious Barons of the south, plotted against Henry
the Third, much to his cost; and here, in 1317, were kept for awhile
in durance the kidnapped Cardinals in attendance upon that sad
lack-Latin prelate Lewis Beaumont, Bishop of Durham, whose
gravestone occupies so large a portion of the choir of his cathedral.

Of this castle, still massive in solitary decay, Hodgson has
given the following graphic description.   Its lonely stateliness,
however, can with difficulty be represented by the pen.

"Wallis was mistaken when he said that the CASTLE OF MITFORD
stands ' on a mount, the work and labour, seemingly, of art;' for the
eminence which it occupies is composed of a stratum of coarse yellow
sandstone rock, covered with a natural bed of clay, mixed with sand and
gravel, and about ten feet thick.  This rock has been in ancient times
much worked away on the east and south-east sides of the mount,
probably for stones for building and repairing the castle, as well as for
forming ditches and rocky escarpments to strengthen its out-works·
Mr. Mitford has also of late years procured large quantities of stones for
the foundations and inner walls of his new mansion-house, from a
quarry which has opened a fine section of the south side of the hill, and
is now working within the area of the castle walls.  The form of the
mound is somewhat elliptical, and the great wall of the castle encircles
the whole area of its summit in a line conformable with its brow.  The

*keep* is on the highest point, and at its northern extremity; is five-sided, each side being of different dimensions, and the internal area about 22½ feet square, and divided into two vaulted rooms of good masonry, having a stone staircase leading to them. One of these rooms is supplied with two ducts in its wall, apparently for the purpose of conveying water to it.* These cells are the only remains of the keep, all the upper parts of which, as well as the outside stone staircase, leading to the entrance door into its second story, are destroyed, and nothing now remains of it but the two cells already noticed. The entrance to the little court which surrounded it was from the second court, by a gateway, through a thick barmkin of stone, flanked on the south by a strong semicircular breastwork of earth. This was the strongest part of the fortress, and overlooked *the outer gateway and court*, which stood on the most northerly limb of the hill, and almost close to the Foss-bridge: but all traces of this gateway, and of the walls of the outer court, excepting some lines of their foundations, are now obliterated. The *inner court* occupies the main part of the crown of the hill, is now occupied as a garden and orchard, and measures, in the widest parts about 240 feet, both from north to south and from east to west. This part, with the keep, to the outside of the walls, contains very little more than an acre. The gateway leading to it was on the north-east side of the hill, and the channel five yards long, for the bar of its gate still appears in the wall there. Mr. Robert Tate, when he made a plan and survey of this castle for Sir David Smith in 1810, found a quarry working at the southern point of the inner court; and, in the earth upon its top, saw several graves at about three feet from the surface, each grave being covered, close above the remains, with a few flat stones. None of the interments which he saw had apparently been made in coffins, except one, which was in a coffin of stone. In May 1828, on the place where Mr. Tate marked upon his plan an oblong building ' supposed *the chapel*,' the foundations of a strong wall, buried in rubbish, appeared in the quarry; and behind it, in the natural earth, a grave was exposed, in which bones, mixed with kitchen ashes, were encased in rough masonry; and immediately above them, five human skulls, and other bones, confusedly huddled together, were hanging out of the bank—remains of men who had perished within the castle walls of the

* These were openings for another purpose. Our ancestors had seldom the delicacy to place such conveniences out of sight. At Langley Hall, near Durham, not fewer than three or four were openly accessible from the great hall of the mansion.

Baron of Mitford; but whether they fell in some mutiny of the garrison, or in the fury of an assault, or by the midnight hand of murder, who shall conjecture? All, however, who were buried here, had not lived to become warriors; for, in the autumn of the same year, we found among the rubbish which had fallen from the top of the quarry the jaw-bone of a child, every way perfect, excepting in its wanting the full comple-ment of grinders, and some of its second set of fore-teeth being only just above the bone. How much is there for reflection in the fate and situation of these remains of mortality; and when I suffer imagination, only for a little time, to lift up the curtain of history, and think I see from the opposite bank to the south the armies of Scotland investing the moated plain upon which the fortress stands; when I see showers of arrows and javelins flying round its bulwarks, the neighbouring hamlets and villages wrapped in flames, and hear the clashing of arms and the shouting of the besiegers and the besieged—how grateful it is to gaze again, and see the peaceful scene as it now is—the ruined keep, and its semicircular wall that flanks it on the south, overgrown with trees and weeds; the massive rampart that encased it on the north ' split with the winter's frost,' the rude walls and towers that environed the hill rising in shattered masses among elder-trees and thorns, or shadowed with groups of gigantic ash-trees; the moated and entrenched plain covered with cattle; and, away beyond, the beautiful white walls of the new manor-house, the hoary remains of the old one,* and the venerable church, backed with orchards and gardens, and river banks,—all how lovely and luxuriant! But the account of Mitford Castle must not be borne away in a flood of imagination: history must relate its annals in her own sober language." (P. 56, &c.)

"MITFORD.—The new manor-house, the shell of which was in its progress while the notes and minutes for this account of Mitford were collecting, is a very handsome square edifice, built from designs by Mr. Dobson. The beautiful white sandstone of which its outside walls are built, is obtained from a stratum of rock which forms the bed of the Font for several hundred yards, between the Newton Park and Nun-

---

* The intermediate residence of the owner of the estate, built after the castle had gone to decay, and having originally over its doorway the date of its erection, the year 1637, in raised characters. This date now appears, as I am informed, to be 1037, and it is said that an owner of the mansion, now upwards of a century ago, effected this alteration by chiseling off the upper part of the figure 6, in proof of the antiquity of his family. Surely the family of Mitford of Mitford stood in no need of an assumed antiquity!

s 2

riding estates—a wild romantic spot, where the craggy banks of the
river are deeply browed over with bilberry plants and heath, and all
along on both sides, and especially at a huge projecting rock called
Corby Crag, overhung with ancient woods of oak.  All the quarry gear
was swept away by one of the great floods of this year.  Great praise
is due to Mr. Mitford for choosing a stone for his new residence which
is not only beautiful, but has every appearance of being indestructible
by atmospheric agents.  The site of the house is also well chosen.  It
is on the brow of the northern bank of the river, and overlooks the
plain on which the castle, church, and gardens of the old manor-
house of Mitford are situated, and fine reaches of rich river-side
scenery in the grounds of Newminster Abbey and Morpeth.  This is a
fertile and most delightful place.  (P. 67.)

How seldom have our topographers sate down to prose and
reason in the following quiet and delightful way.

" NEWTON UNDERWOOD.—The second name, *Underwood*, was probably
added after the settlement at Newton Park was formed.  It is perhaps
impossible to ascertain, with any degree of precision, at what period in
the Saxon or Danish age the principal settlements were made in
Northumberland; but the great number of places called *Newton, Newbigging, Newstead*, and the various assarted places under the generic
name of *Riding*" (ridding or clearing) " all over the county, show that
numerous new villages and hamlets were built in it at a very distant
period—a great many of them probably before the Conquest.  Nunriding
certainly had its name after that period.  The Saxon and Danish settlers
founded villages in unfortified places much more extensively than had
been done under the auspices of Rome.  They had their property
marked out by certain metes and bounds, so that each of them distinctly
knew the lands of which he was lord; and where he could allot to a
son, or convey to a servant, any tract of uncultivated land without
the fear of their being interrupted in the possession of it by an arbi-
trary power.  This property in the soil made men patriots—made them
love the place in which they lived.  For who would not draw the sword
and shed his blood in defending the cottage which had sheltered, and
the acres which had fed, himself and his forefathers?  Formerly men
defended every right and custom of their ancestors and place with an
exactness and a pertinacity which are unknown in these times.  They
rode the boundaries of their parishes and manors annually; pulled down

the fences of all encroachments on their commons; and fined the offenders in their courts. This was the cause why the extensive tracts called *commons*, in which not only the tenants had a *common* right of pasturage with their lords, but the different tenants of lordships had a *common* right upon them, were so long in being cultivated. The ridges upon them, which had never been disturbed, and had been held in *common* by various proprietors from the Roman era, where they could not be divided by *common* consent, were left undisturbed by the plough-share till they began to be divided by acts of parliament in the last century. The Saxons and Danes imposed names upon nearly the whole of the villages of this and other counties: when they increased in population the soil became sub-divided, *new* names were imposed, *new biggings* were made, and *new towns* planted. After the Union between England and Scotland, and other causes of quiet and increased industry in the country had increased the population, men withdrew from the protection of castles, fortalices and villages; and waste lands and commons began to be divided, and a new class of names given to new settlements —such as Blink-bonny, Brandy-well-hall, Breadless-row, Click-him-in, Coldknuckles, Delicate-hall, Delight, Fell-him-down, Glower-o'er-him, Maccaroni, Make-me-rich, Mount-Hooley, Philadelphia, Pinch-me-near, Pondicherry, Portobello, Quality-corner, Skirl-naked, and numerous others equally quaint and fanciful."* (P. 68.)

" CAWSEY PARK.—Probably this place was honoured with a chapel on account of the monks of Durham having rested here in their flight from that place, with the body of St. Cuthbert, to Holy Island, in 1069. The monks, in this flight before the arms of William the Conqueror, are said by Symeon, to have rested the first night at Jarrow, the second at Bedlington, the third at Tughall, and to have reached Holy Island on the fourth. Mr. Raine, in his ' St. Cuthbert,' quotes Wessington, who was Prior of Durham from 1416 to 1446, to show, ' that in general, wherever a church was in after days dedicated to St. Cuthbert, the bishop and his clergy had, in their wanderings, visited *that very place*

* He might have added *and foolish.* In giving a name to a new place, especially in the neighbourhood of towns, nothing can exceed the folly which we almost daily witness. Instead of pitching upon some appropriate designation, with an eye to the mode adopted in old times, we seem to hunt studiously for names the only tendency of which is to betray our own ignorance or childish vanity, and to make the places themselves a subject of ridicule in after days. " I know nothing bad of the gentleman (said a lady once in my hearing) except that he has called his new house Rose-bud cottage."

with the body of the saint.'——The quotation is accompanied with a list of the names of many churches in Northumberland, &c. which were thus dedicated to this saint—as Elsdon, Haydon Bridge, and Beltingham, which Mr. Raine supposes to have been resting places of the monks in their first flight with the sacred body from Holy Island into Cumberland (in 868)—As the monks in this flight (1069) are known to have brought with them, not only the body of Saint Cuthbert, but also great store of riches, relics, and ornaments, belonging to his church and shrine, and Bedlington was a good stage, at least eleven miles, from Cawsey Park, it seems probable enough that this was their first resting place on the day in which they travelled from Bedlington to Tughall; and when it is considered in how high veneration the remains of the saint were holden for several centuries, that two great festivals—one on the 20th of March, the day of the vernal equinox, on which the Sun enters Aries, and spring began, in honour of his Deposition—the other on the 4th of September, when the sun was preparing, at the autumnal equinox, to leave our hemisphere, and to commence his march through the six lower Signs of the Zodiac, in honour of his Translation; and when to these considerations we add the accounts of the splendid processions that were made on the days of these festivities, of the great number of the nobility that attended them, and of the intense awe and adoration with which his shrine was at all times approached—we cannot wonder that in commemoration of so great an event as the tutelar deity of the see of Durham having once rested on this estate, its proprietor consecrated it to holy purposes, and ordained that services to God and Saint Cuthbert should be daily said upon it.   But ' Where are now the remains of Saint Cuthbert ?' was a question in legendary lore which no one for the three last centuries, except a succession of three Benedictine monks, to whom the secret of his burial-place was entrusted, it has been said, were able to solve.   These remains for centuries had continued to be the great idol of the church of Durham—a god neither of wood nor stone—no graven image—not the likeness of any thing in heaven, or in earth, or under the earth, made by man's hands — but the body of an ancient anchoret, which, on account of the piety of his life, and the reputed miracles that he wrought after his death, became the object of awe, gratitude, and veneration to the thousands that visited his shrine.   Crowned and mitred heads bowed down to it.   The people were taught to believe that the body was incorruptible, and that its soul, or some divinity which waited around it, was conscious of their wants and wishes, and answered their prayers

by healing their infirmities.  To prevent, as it should seem, the continuance of this corrupt species of worship, the body of the holy man
was ordered by public authority to be decorously buried, which was
accordingly done on the feast of the Epiphany 1542; but, though
several Roman Catholic writers had said that the saint's remains were interred in his shrine, immediately below the place where ' they had rested
in their exalted state,' yet the mystery that time throws over the true
account of such events, and the tale about the Benedictine monks, had
made the matter dubious, till May, 1827, when the Rev. W. N. Darnell,
B.D., prebendary of the church of Durham, in his office of sub-dean
there for that year, having several workmen engaged in repairing the
Nine Altars, employed a party of them to raise the great stone in the
floor of the middle of the shrine, under which ' the constant tradition of
the church ' had stated the remains to lie.  A short time convinced him
that he had hit upon the object of his search, which was carefully and
minutely examined by himself, and other gentlemen, whom he sent for
after the discovery was made, and amongst the rest by Mr. Raine, who,
in his interesting work, entitled ' SAINT CUTHBERT,' has with great industry
and research drawn together a curious and very valuable mass of materials
respecting his life, canonized state, miracles, relics, wanderings, &c., till
his body was recently disinterred and his bones again recommitted to
their ancient resting-place."*   (P. 182.)

COCKLE PARK TOWER (p. 139) may be given as a good specimen of a Border fortress.†  The mullioned window on the right
has lately been removed, and very unwisely inserted in the keep
of Bothal Castle, by way, I suppose, of ornament.  Here resided
a junior branch of the family of Ogle of Bothal, who hesitated
not to murder Philip Green, the Morpeth Tanner, in the reign
of Elizabeth, for presuming to underrate their blood in comparison
with that of the Dacres.

I have spoken of Mr. Hodgson's account of the castle of Mitford.  The same character of laborious accuracy and minuteness
belongs to his description of the castle of Bothal, and his history
of its owners.  His picture of the scenery upon the Wansbeck
at Bothal is also striking and correct.

" The general aspect of the district is bare, its features flat and tame,
but along the banks of the Wansbeck the scenery is rich and various,

* See above, p. 164.              † See the next page.

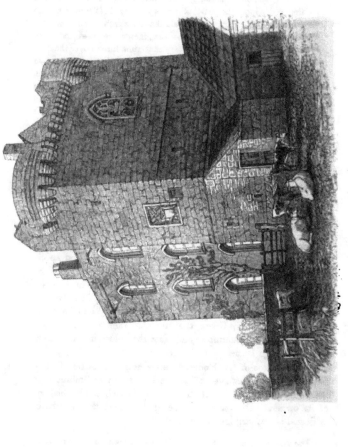

COCKET PARK TOWER

consisting of high banks clothed with woods, and here and there inclosing haughs of uncommon fertility, or of rocks gray with lichens or crowned with gigantic forest trees. Akenside sang of the Wansbeck; but poet or painter has never yet done justice to the ever-varying charms of the course of this lovely stream, from the fountain in the wild moors about the Waney Crags, till, in the lone and sequestered woods of Bothal and Sheepwash, she begins to put on her beautiful and bridal robes before she weds with the ocean."

If Mr. Hodgson had lived in heathen times his deity would most assuredly have been a bright-haired goddess in her garland of water-lilies, presiding over a stream winding its way through such scenery as he here describes. It was his constant habit in his walks and rides to stay for a while and gaze into running water, especially if it was clear and flowing in a pure channel. " It reminds one so of eternity," was his usual expression on such occasions.

" BOTHAL CASTLE," he says, in another place, " stands on the north side of the Wansbeck, between the meetings of that river and Bothalburn. Its site is an oblong knoll, the ascent to the plane of which rises rather abruptly from the river on the east and west, but on the north sweeps gently off from the gateway to the village. The prospect from it extends about half a mile up and down the river, and very much resembles in richness and variety the charming scenery about the castle of Mitford; for the view from the castle here is confined on every side with river banks and rising grounds, but has within it woods and meadows, and arable lands river-laved, and of great fertility, besides orchards and gardens, that only wait for the profits of the Barony being again employed in bidding the vivifying voice of hospitality be heard within the castle walls, to make them as exuberant in ' all kinds of herbs and flowers,' and fruits, and ' licorice very fine,' as they were in the days of Cuthbert Lord Ogle and Queen Elizabeth." (P. 151.)

Of the church of Newbigging, as it then existed, we have a very correct drawing from the pencil of Mr. Sopwith. Northumberland has not much of church architecture to boast of. The chapel of Newbigging is perhaps an exception. As a general remark, it seems apparent that the churches in this county, especially those in places verging towards the Borders of Scotland, were almost in every instance, in addition to their serving as places of divine

NEWBIGGING CHURCH.

worship, fortified places; or, in other words, so constructed that they could hold out for a while against a sudden inroad, until the neighbourhood could be raised and the marauders repelled. In some, as at Ancroft, the tower served as a peel-house, in daily occupation. In others, as at Meldon, the windows were so narrow as not to admit of a man's body. These modes of construction all indicate a liability to attacks of violence, and, in numerous instances, from existing appearances, it is quite manifest that great damage has been done to the fabric by hostile invaders. But, whatever may have been the case in former periods, they have suffered enough, and more than enough, in modern times. Any faint traces of good workmanship which the rough hand of the Scot had spared have in late years, in far too many instances, given way to want of feeling in archdeacons, or parsimony in ignorant penny-saving churchwardens, no superior power thinking it its duty to control either the one or the other. The fine old church of Newbigging has been twice a martyr. About a century ago its chancel roof fell in, and was not replaced; its aisles stood in need of repair, and they were demolished. Such was its state when the sketch of it was made which ornaments Hodgson's History. The remainder of its tale is soon told. A very few years ago a sufficient fund was raised to restore it to its ancient condition; but the attempt ended in placing a new roof upon the chancel of a modern and unseemly kind, and in re-building just so much of the former aisles as might form a mere passage from east to west by the side of the ancient pillars, which had been preserved in the newly-built boundary wall at the time in which it was curtailed of its fair proportions. Other sad mistakes were made, such as the insertion of dormer windows in the roof the nave; and it has come to pass that its later state is, in point of decency and fit arrangement, worse than ever. The church has been originally very remarkable for its architectural features and proportions, which prove that its builder was no man of parsimony or cold calculation. I strongly suspect that its architect was the same man who constructed the priory church of Finchale, with its graceful lancets and mouldings, and perhaps the church of St. Andrew's at Auckland. About the same time that this proceeding was going on at Newbigging, the fine old

chancel of its mother church of Woodhorne, of which also Mr.
Hodgson gives an engraving, was stalled on both sides with what
appear to be old cast-away seats from first-class railway carriages.

Among the Newbigging Miscellanea, Hodgson reprints the
Sonnet addressed to the Moon, which has been already noticed.
It was, as he here informs us, written in 1807, and "was more
suggested to the author's mind by evening sea-side walks at
Newbigging than at any other place."

"Somewhat above twenty years since Newbigging to me was a
favourite spot; and the fine sands of the bay, the long dry moor, and its
bold and rocky shores, can never fail to be interesting resorts to any
that can be gratified with surveying the vastness and admiring the
power and the productions of the mighty deep. The rocks abound
with various sorts of sea-weed—among which at low-water curious and
rare fishes are often found; and the attention of the naturalist would be
highly rewarded by investigating the numerous and beautiful animals
of the molluscous genus, which coat and bespangle the sides of the
rocks and the loose stones in the pools near the margin of the sea at
low-water. (P. 215.)——The rocks on the shore near the church abound
with impressions and casts of trees. One cast in particular, off a head-
land nearly opposite the chapel, is highly petrified, and large lumps of it
are washed on the shore. It is 21 feet long, and has a long rent in the
rock running past one end of it, and filled with coarse sulphuret of iron.
The bait or grain of its wood in some specimens is distinctly seen; but
the greater part of it is amorphous, and covered with beautiful brown
quartz crystal. A similar petrifaction of a tree of the palm genus, in
joints, and of great length, appeared in the freestone quarry at High
Heworth in 1816 and 1817." (P. 541.)

"The Village of Ulgham stands very pleasantly on the south side
of the Line, which runs past it, under narrow and woody banks, and
has the road from Morpeth by Widdrington to Warkworth passing
through the western part of it. It consists of four farm-houses and two
ale-houses, disposed in two rows, and interspersed with very indifferent
thatched cottages with gardens behind, and a wide disorderly street
between them; a few of its cottages have, however, been lately rebuilt in
a good substantial style, and more are now in the same praiseworthy
progress of improvement. Here still remains a sacred and venerable
object of ancient times, a stump of the *village cross,* four feet high, with

steps up to it, once neatly fluted, but now guttered by the weather, and worn into hollows by whetting upon.  The villagers have a vulgar tradition that it was a cross to hold a market at when there was a plague at Morpeth.   But their predecessors, before the fanaticism of the Commonwealth broke off the holy sign that surmounted it, assembled about it in groups in summer evenings; and the only throng that ever gathered about it was on the day of the dedication of their chapel, when the people in the neighbouring villages came to partake of the joy and festivities of Ulgham feast, which is now dwindled into a poor gingerbread fair, and the purposes of its institution forgotten.  The chapel yard and gardens here abound with the garden snail *(helix hortensis)*, a filthy and destructive animal, which ought to be carefully gathered and destroyed."

The history of the splendid old family of Widdrington, and its fall in 1715, is well worked out, (p. 223, &c.), and the account of the last Lord and his fate is told with much feeling.  Of the castle of Widdrington Hodgson is compelled to give such a description only as could be derived from oral testimony or engravings, for in his time not a trace of the ancient fabric remained.  To the story of its demolition he makes allusion, but the following is a fuller, and it is believed a more correct, account of that unhappy proceeding.

Sir George Warren had been for some time in possession of the estate of Widdrington, but had never seen it, or the very characteristic old castle which graced the summit of the hill in its centre.  His attention however failed not to be drawn periodically to bills for repairs of the fabric, laid before him by his steward, and in consequence, in a hasty moment, knowing that the building was in a great measure uninhabitable, and further that there would soon be a still greater call upon his purse for its repair, as it had at that time suffered much from an accidental fire, he ordered it to be at once pulled down as expensive and useless.  His command was complied with; but a while afterwards, upon coming into the North, and being struck with the situation, he requested his steward to give him his notion of the kind of mansion-house which he should build on the top of the hill, to supply the place of that which had been removed, giving him at the same time to understand that he was not inclined to be sparing in the expense.  The steward exhibited a drawing from Buck's View in 1726, but without a name. "That," said Sir George, "is the very kind of house I should like to build." "That," said the steward, "is the very house which by your command I destroyed." The present edifice looks more like a dovecot than a castle. It may be well compared to the *stump* of one of the warrior Widdrington's legs in the ballad of Chevy Chase, pointing upwards. It was built about seventy years ago, and has of course been for a long time uninhabitable.

"PLESSEY.—The most remarkable buildings in this township were the CHURCH and HOSPITAL OF HERFORD BRIDGE. Of these time has left us a few scattered notices in records, but not a trace on the earth of their walls. The field in which they stood was called the Chapel field; and old gardens, and the exact site of the chapel, were described to me by a person born at Plessey, and now 71 years old, and who, as a boy, was present when the stone coffin, now in the walks at Blagdon, was found within the area of the chapel walls. He told me that his mother, hearing of the discovery, ran from the village to the spot, a distance of two or three hundred yards, and was horrified on her first view of it, to see himself rising out of it. She said that ill-luck would attend him through life: and he was certainly in early years seized with pains, which she attributed wholly to his being the first to lie down in that chamber of death, after its cover was removed, and now he is stone blind and has a wooden leg, but cheerful spirits, and religious knowledge and hopes, which make him smile at his mother's prognostications, and attribute his pains and deprivations to their proper causes."

HERFORD BRIDGE.—The northern bank of the river at Herford Bridge is steep and woody, and has its brow crowned with the graceful villa of William Burdon, Esq. and an emerald haugh rich and lovely before it; and I think I can no where find a more graceful place than in "these flowery fields of joy," where the Blythe,

'In notes with many a winding bout,
Of linked sweetness long drawn out,'

steals over his rocky bed, to insert a translation of Dean Ogle's charming ode to this ever youthful and delightful stream. The original, in Latin, must be preserved for the account of Kirkley. The Dean wrote it in 1763, after a long absence from Kirkley, his patrimonial seat and estate. (P. 309.)

O thou ! that murmuring tell'st along
My native fields thy ceaseless song,
And speedest on thy pebbled bed
With the green ocean's waves to wed.
Still through my own beloved meads
Thy never failing stream proceeds :
To me the mind is not the same
Since first upon thy banks I came,
And like another joyous child
The hours in harmless sport beguiled ;
Or heaps upon thy winding shore
Of shining pebbles laid in store ;
Or loved within thy cooling wave
My yet too tender feet to lave ;
Or caught thy fry in fishers' toils
And boasted of my numerous spoils :
So passed my days in labour vain,
Days never to return again.
So late a boy ! to-morrow old !
And so the years on years are rolled ;
Day steals on day with steady feet—
And what, dear stream, with speed more fleet
Than thy loquacious waters sweep
To mingle with the mighty deep ?
But take unto the troubled main,
Take all my grief and all my pain,
And keep, as erst, thy winding ways,
And cheer our house with happy days."

In order that the scholar may put the fidelity of Hodgson's translation to the test, I venture to subjoin the Ode itself, which proves its writer to have been deeply saturated with the proprieties and elegancies of Horace.

### AD BLYTHUM AMNEM ANNO 1763.

Tu qui, strepente subtèr amnis gurgite
    Paterna lambis prædia,
Inter reluctantes lapillos ad mare
    Iter minutum dividens,
Tu, scilicet, per prata, ut olim, volveris ;
    Non ista sed mens est mihi
Olim quæ erat, fluenta cum propter tua
    Securus errabam puer,
Horas inertes, imputandas vix reor,
    Fallens labore ineptulo ;

Seu congerebam flexuoso in margine
    Quos sistit unda calculos,
Pedes lubebat seu magis tenellulos
    Frigente lymphâ tingere,
Aquatiles seu fortè inescarem incolas,
    Opima jactans præmia !
Curis peribant his dies inanibus,
    Nunquam heu reditari dies !
Heri puer eram, cràs futurus sum senex,
    Sic annus annum dimovet,
Et irremisso pede dies urget diem !
    Velociore non quidem
Tuæ loquaces sata per et sylvas aquæ
    Volvuntur in vastum mare.
Quin aufer hinc tecum pelagus in turbidum
    Longè aufer has curas precor ;
Et rite pergas sospitare flumine
    Circumfluo nostram domum.*

" Shotton.—The division of one large town field into various doles or
parcels of land, caused every flat, knoll, marsh, spring, and runner of
water, to have some distinct and appropriate name, which was carefully
preserved as long as the field continued to belong to different proprietors.
This observation is strongly exemplified by different deeds respecting
Shotton, especially by that respecting its chapel: but when a whole
ville became the property of one person, and the old inhabitants had
settled in mercantile towns, or migrated to foreign countries, the boundary stones of their ridges, selions, and acres of land were removed, the
whole field divided into new inclosures with new names, and such old
English sounding names as Lambootefurlong, the Linthaugh, the
Bakestonedene, the Ladyland, and Pilgrim's Well were soon lost and
forgotten.  (P. 316.)

Monastic institutions did not abound in Northumberland.  On
this side of the Border there had been no David of Scotland, no
" fair saint to the crown " to stud the rich valleys of the county
with such well-endowed and graceful edifices as Jedburgh,
Melrose, Dryburgh, and Kelso, which even now, in ruin, are
such splendid objects upon the Tweed.  Of the foundations of
this nature which Northumberland could boast the principal one,
Tinmouth perhaps, when architecturally considered, excepted,

* This Ode was also translated by the poet Bowles with great elegance and
accuracy.

was Newminster, which stood in times of old on the Wansbeck, a mile above Morpeth, in a portion of the county at which Hodgson had arrived in his History, and demanded a notice in his pages. The reader shall judge whether that demand was made in vain.

"I now for the first time in the progress of this work begin to tread upon monastic ground, but no 'ivy-mantled tower' or 'fretted vault' remains as evidence of the style of the buildings that covered it, nothing but the archway of the (north) door of the conventual church; all is green sward, overspreading long lines of walls, and irregular heaps of ruins piled upon the graves of many that were noble, holy, and wise, or covering the dust that once beamed in the eye of beauty, or wielded the sword of the mighty and the brave——but the changes we lament are often the origin of new and better orders of things; subterraneous fire, and the ceaseless motion and varying temperature of air and water, are daily causing catastrophes to man, which keep the world in perpetual youth; and improvements in civilized life rise upon the ruins of institutions that were once considered models of perfection." (P. 403., &c.)

The monks of Newminster were of the Cistercian order. Their house "was the eldest, and, as yet, the only daughter of the mother-church of Fountains," and from her, in process of time, there branched forth three offsets, the monasteries of Pipewell, Sallay, and Roche. Hodgson enters as minutely into the history of the Abbey of Newminster as his information would permit, and gives proof that on the subject of the monastic as well as the other departments of archæological inquiry he could write with ease and fidelity. But since his narrative was compiled the Chartulary of the Monastery, once in the possession of Lord William Howard and afterwards lost, has been recovered, and will soon see the light under the editorial care of the Surtees Society; and many additions will then doubtless be made to a history already replete with interest.

In their choice of a site for their church the monks of Newminster were singularly happy, and Mr. Hodgson is equally happy in its description:

"From the site of Newminster the prospect along the valley of the Wansbeck reaches little more, in its farthest extent, than a quarter of a mile. It seems to be set in an amphitheatre of woods; downwards a part of the houses at Bowle's Green can be seen from the north door of its church; and, upwards, through trees in rich meadows, glimmerings of the ground above Mitford. Where the river juts against its banks sandy scars appear, hemmed with broom and brushwood; in other parts their sinuous sides are cut with courses of brooks, and covered with fine forest trees. Looking to the south, it seems to stand on the chord of a regular semicircle, where the banks, though high, slope gradually off, as if on purpose to admit the winter noon and the summer morning's sun. Its site, however, beguiles imagination more by the charm of loveliness than grandeur; it is the richness of American river-side scenery, in a champaign country, that invites you to linger upon it—fine meadows inclosed by indented diluvial banks of uniform height, with nothing but sky beyond their sylvan brows—no waterfall or glen barred up with walls of everlasting rock or mountain towering above the clouds."

The following is a correct description of the present state of the hill upon which the monastery stood. It is clear that under careful hands Newminster would come forth from the ground like another Jervaux.* The monastery to which I refer was a few years ago a grass-grown mound like Newminster. Now, thanks to its owner, it is one of the glories of Richmondshire.

" Scarcely a stone appears above the ground; but several feet upwards of many of the walls, especially of the chapter-house and domestic apartments, still remain buried in the rubbish of their upper parts. Ivy and roots of trees and grasses wind through the walls of deserted buildings, and as effectually level them with the earth as any labour of man. The church, which has stood on ground considerably higher than the level of the plain which surrounds it, was on the north side of the whole establishment, and consisted of a tower, nave, transept, and chancel, in all about 270 feet long. The cloisters were on the south side of the nave, and apparently about 102 feet from east to west, and 80 from north to south, and had extensive buildings on every side of of them, especially the chapter-house and many others, of very various

* At the same time, unless care be taken of it after the operation, it had better remain in its present condition. Finchale was a few years ago freed from the accumulated rubbish of three centuries, and one consequence has been that mobs of cheap-trippers almost weekly in summer desecrate its sanctity, and carry their abominations so far as literally to hold their dances in the chancel of the church itself.

sizes, on the east and south; from which side, through the cloisters to the north wall of the nave of the church, the ruins cover about 320 feet. Some large ash-trees and hawthorns, and abundance of wake-robin, thrive on these ruins. Under one group of ash-trees, to the south-west of the abbey, a fine spring rises out of a gentle knoll, on which there are traces of much masonry. This water was, probably, con-veyed hither in a covered conduit, as its source must be in higher ground than where it rises; and a narrow march, a sort of natural foss, sweeps between it and the banks, round three sides of the monastery. The common burial-ground has been on the north side of the church. On the west there have been orchards and gardens between the church and some outer buildings; and on the north a gateway on the road from Morpeth to the north door of the church. If the floors of any part of the church, cloisters, or chapter-house remain, interesting inscriptions may still be found. I have seen no remains of mouldings here but such as belong to the architecture of the fourteenth century—to the time of the three Edwards, or somewhat later. Formerly many stones were taken hence for building with in Morpeth." (P. 405.)

To the history of the castle and town of Morpeth Hodgson has devoted not fewer than 165 pages, many of them in very small type, and has handled it in all its bearings with the skill of a workman.* From the space, however, which he found it neces-sary to devote to this borough, he must have seen the utter im-possibility of confining the parochial history of the county to three volumes, according to his original plan. At this rate, Hexham alone, considering the extent and importance of the materials with respect to it and its franchise, preserved in the registers of York and in the public offices, would of itself have occupied at least half a volume, Alnwick another half, and it would be no easy matter even to conjecture the space which would be demanded by Newcastle, ancient and modern, with all its enterprise and com-merce. In addition to those subjects of oppidan interest, which would not admit of undue abridgment or condensation, there re-mained Bamborough, Dunstanborough, Wark, and the other

* In this part of the volume he received very great assistance from his friend and correspondent Mr. Woodman, afterwards Town Clerk of the borough. The letters with which Mr. Woodman has favoured me prove the nature and value of his services in the history of his native town.

great fortresses and castles of the district, to say nothing of monastic, Border, and parochial history.    But, happily for posterity, he persevered in his diffuseness, hoping against hope, for additional patronage and encouragement.

Under Morpeth he has adopted a somewhat novel plan of setting before his readers many facts and circumstances of great interest connected with the town and its neighbourhood, arranged under the heads of MORPETH MISCELLANEA and MORPETH ANNALS. It was for these pages that he compiled the well-known biographies of Gibson, Harle, Horsley, and Turner, which were afterwards published in a separate shape, and became so popular that the little volume in which they are contained is now of rare occurrence.

Horsley's BRITANNIA ROMANA is the storehouse from which succeeding Romanists have drawn the most valuable information. That judicious and painstaking man seems literally to have left no stone unturned in quest of an inscription and the historical facts which it might disclose, and the result of his long-continued labour was the book above mentioned.    Of his personal history nearly everything had been long forgotten, when Hodgson set himself piously to the task of collecting its scattered fragments, which he has thrown together in this his Memoir, the concluding paragraph of which will be read with painful interest when it is understood that its writer was himself at the very time it was penned a living example of the hopeless condition to which Horsley had perhaps been reduced.

" About a year before he died, he told his friend Mr. R. Cay that he was quite wearied out with his attention to his Britannia Romana, which I think he lived to see printed off, but, perhaps, not published.    It had probably injured his health, and when the excitement of going on with it ceased, he lingered and fell—died without seeing how his great work was received by the tyranny of letters, and with the sad reflection that his labours were not only profitless, but might never repay his family the sums he had expended upon them.    One dying under such circumstances is little lamented and soon forgotten.    With himself, his family lose their support, and poverty soon wrings affectionate remembrances for the dead out of the hearts of dearest relatives and friends.    The minister of religion performs the same official rites over his remains that are said over all: but the obsequies of his funeral are not performed with the incense of eulogy, or his memory consecrated and cherished by any account of his life.   No stone tells which was Horsley's grave, nor any parish register that I have seen * where he was buried.   What a lesson to the mind that riots on the hope of posthumous fame !"

No one but a man placed in the same painful position could have written in such a way as this; and there may be others who have spent upon the public time and toil, and the best years of their youth and health, who can bear testimony to the truth of his words.

To the Memoir of William Turner, and an analysis of his writings, botanical and theological, Hodgson devotes several columns in his small type.   From the period of his residence at Lanchester, and perhaps even from his boyhood, he himself had been an ardent botanist, and he enters with great spirit into the nature and character of Turner's works on this subject, taking especial care to extract from them every notice of a local character. In his search after Turner's printed works, all of them now very rare, he was indefatigable.   The British Museum, the Bodleian, and other public libraries, were all of them consulted for this purpose, by him or his friends, and in all probability more information on the subject of Turner and his writings is contained in Hodgson's pages than in any other place.

Of the old house of Hepscot, which is described in the above-mentioned alphabetical condensation of local facts, a tale must be told.   In order to write his account of the place, Hodgson paid it a visit almost before the break of day, on the 9th Dec. 1831, and was seen by the farm servants walking about it, and prying, as it appeared, into holes and corners with which no honest man could, in their opinion, have any thing to do.   Nothing was said on either side, but upon reaching Morpeth to breakfast there was a considerable alarm in the town.   Swing had been seen at Hepscot, and the farmer had sent in a man to announce the fact and put the town on its guard.   " Swing," as my readers will remember, was at that precise time the assumed name of a lawless band in the South

* A notice of Horsley's burial on the 15th of Jan. 1731 has been found in the paris register of Morpeth.

of England, who had for some time indulged themselves in acts of robbery and conflagration.

In recording the establishment of a Mechanical and Scientific Institution in Morpeth in 1825, under the patronage of the Earl of Carlisle and Sir J. E. Swinburne, Hodgson makes the following just and beautiful remarks.

"Mankind may, in conformity to the first divine command, increase and multiply upon the earth; but they can never either subdue it or the natural evils that wait on ignorance till the labouring classes amongst them derive from science artificial means of lessening their labour, till they be taught from infancy to reason and think, to read and search after truth in all its subjects and in the nature of all things; till their minds become active, religious and moral, and till well-instructed industry drives wickedness and misery from the earth, and makes every palace and every cottage the abode of wisdom, happiness, and comfort: and institutions of this kind have a direct tendency to spread these great blessings over the world." (P. 449.)

What progress the Morpeth Mechanics' Institute may have made in bringing about the happy state of things here so admirably described we know not.   It is to be hoped that its efforts have not been altogether unattended with success.   But, most assuredly, three years after the above remarks were committed to paper, it gave painful proof that it was not going the right way to work.   Its members were at that time thinking only of themselves and their own individual amusement and pastime, and not of those who were to come after them.   Probably by this time it may have discovered, however slowly,—better late than never,—that it was established for a very different purpose than that of expending its money chiefly upon works of present gratification.   The following extract from a letter written by Mr. Hodgson to Mr. Woodman on the 12th of March, 1835, tells of the somewhat unusual plan which the Morpeth Mechanics were pursuing in that year " to dispel the natural evils which wait upon ignorance."   " The volume intituled ' Magnus Rotulus Pipæ' which I sent to you, has given such offence to the Mechanics' Institution at Morpeth, that, their secretary tells me, 'the committee have determined upon returning it, let the consequences be what they may.'  I have begged that they will send it back to me, *and let me have the former volumes of the work* at a price equivalent to their condition."

To Hodgson's memorable things connected with Morpeth, I am tempted to make the two following additions from the rich stores of the Consistory Court of Durham.  The first touches upon *diablerie*, and the second gives a good notion of the state of society in Northumberland at that period.  Here is a man roundly stating in his will that he is dying from murder, for no other reason save that he had presumed to express his opinion that the Dacres, at that time Lords of Morpeth, had better blood in their veins than the Ogles of Bothal.

June 6, 1627.—" James Cowle, of the parishe of Morpethe, aged 30 years, a witness, &c. has known the said Sara Hatherik for 8 years, and the said Jane Urwen from his infancy.

" He saith that about two yeares since now last past, a more certaine time he remembrethe not, the said Jane Urwen came to this examinate's house, then situate in Morpeth, aboute some business, in an eveninge, and after some other conference the said Jane asked this examinate how and upon what tearmes he had lett a house and certaine grounds unto Lancelott Hatherick, husband of the said Sara, wherin he satisfied her; whereupon the said Jane Urwen replied and said that the said Lancelott was nought, but, quothe she, his wife, meaninge the said Sara, is worse, for, quothe she, there was a man went in Cotton Wood to seeke his kyne and heard a noyse ther, and there were present she, the said Sara, and her mayd, castinge of clues throughe a ridle of all kindes of coloures, as fast as oates, whereunto this examinate's wife betweene ther conference said, ' Lord, how can that be ?' to whome the said Jane replied and said that she the said Sara Hatherwick was a witche—then and ther being presente this examinate, &c.   (Signed)   JAMES COWLE.

" Dorothy Cowle, wife of James Cowle, of the parish of Morpeth, aged thirty years, a witness, &c. has known Sarah Hatherick for four years and Jane Urwen for the same time.

" She saith that two yeares agoe, a more certaine tyme she remembreth not, the said Jane Urwen came unto this examinate's husband's house, then situate in Morpethe, and after divers speeches, amongest them she the said Jane Urwen told this examinate and her husband, &c. that ther was an honest man told her that he wanted his kyne, and beinge seekinge of them in Cotton Wood, he heard a great noyse ther in a hollinge bushe, where he did see Sara Heatherick and her maid servant sittinge with a ridle betwixt them, and castinge clues as fast as oates; which this examinate much wonderinge att, asked how that could be, whereunto she, the said Jane, replied and said that she the said Sara was a witche; and this examinate askeing where she learned the same, the said Jane replied that she learned it of the Lady Pauncheforde articulate. *(Book of Depositions from 1626 to 1631.)*

" In the name of God, Amen.   The xxth day of Julye, Anno Domini 1583, I, Phillope Grene, of Morpeth, seake in my body butt of good and perfett remembrance.——My body to the garth to be buried in my parishe churche of Morpethe.——Mr. Francis Dacres and Mr. Nycholes Rydlye, to whome I have committed the teuitione of my sonne Richard Greane, trusting they will se hym brought uppe at learning, as my speciall trust is in theym̄; and further I do humble crave of theym that they will se my said wiffe and children maynteaned in lawe, for reformacion of this crewell murder, comitted upon me by Georg Ogle, John Ogle, sonnes to Jaymes Ogle of Cawsye Parke, and Martyne Ogle of Trithlington, Alexander Ogle, Anthonye Mylborne, withe others, whome I fullye charge with my death, haven no cawse agaynst me, but that I compared the Dacres bloud to be as good as the Ogles." *( Orig. Will.)*

FROM THE REV. A. HEDLEY, 22 May, 1832.—" I am delighted with your last volume, as every one else is whom I have heard speak of it.  I am afraid the poor author is the only person who will have reason to be dissatisfied with it, as the expense of printing, &c. must be out of all bounds—beyond what you can possibly receive from the sale, even of every copy."——

FROM EDWARD SWINBURNE, Esq.

" MY DEAR SIR,                                                        1832.

   " I am very much concerned to hear from you that Richard has had a return of his alarming complaint.  If this summer weather has reached you he will, I hope, benefit by it.  My brother has mentioned to me his advice to you about any trial of a continental climate, if you had such in contemplation; and I fully concur with him in his view of the difficulties which the present state of Europe throws in your way.

What do you think of Torquay in Devonshire for the spring months, which are liable to such trying vicissitudes in most parts of the Island? Mr. Thomas Bigge's son, James, has been staying there apparently with good effect during the winter. He was very weak when he left town. He returns in a few days—he has made acquaintances there, and I dare say I could get some introductions for Richard. It is a cheap country —the climate well spoken of; some object to it as relaxing, but mildness is the great object for your son at this season. He might go by day-journeys across the country by Leeds, Sheffield, Birmingham, Gloucester, Bristol, Exeter, whence a coach goes by Teignmouth to Torquay; or come up to London, sleeping at York and Grantham, and so by easy journeys to Exeter. The servant I had when on the continent could go with him, if requisite, from hence, to get him settled at Torquay,—he speaks English enough, and is a good-tempered obliging fellow—and without putting you to any additional expense.

" I thank you for your wild notes * to your dear mountain scenery. I can participate in some of your feelings, from grateful recollections of days and friends gone by, as well as admiration of the country. I wish your portrait had never been taken in hand—it was well meant, nor have pains been spared, but power and practice were not yet acquired; and whatever of failure is in it is unfortunately relieved by the elaborate engraving. I heartily wish you success from your new volume, with all its fine trappings. I fear the panic which is paralysing all good efforts, and driving every thing into the gulph of politics, is increasing not only in this country but in the rest of Europe. My best wishes to Mrs. Hodgson and yours. Where is your eldest daughter? I think I desired you to remember me to Hedley when you communicated with him. Yours ever,

"EDWD. SWINBURNE."

To the Rev. A. HEDLEY.

" MY DEAR HEDLEY,                    Whelpington, 30 May, 1832.

" Richard would write to you saying how much benefit he has received from the Whelpington air and his mother's good nursing. I saw him yesterday, and he continues to improve. Dr. Headlam has examined him; and Mr. Greenhow and he will consult together respecting his case to-morrow. But I hope they will see that occasional visits to this place will be best for him. At any rate I can never now

* Doubtless the stanzas upon the sight of Westmerland already mentioned; see p. 211.

pretend to go from home with him.———* I will, however, if I live, come to see you, and that soon—as soon as you can spare time to go about with me. I understand Col. Coulson wishes me to see his researches at Caervorran as soon as possible, and I am very anxious to put together something about the *Masonry* of the Romans in and near the Wall, for Mr. Petrie. I did not know of Mr. Coulson's wish till yesterday, when Adamson urged me to comply with it next week, if possible. Pray write soon and fix a time.

"I was at a vestry meeting at Jarrow on Monday, and Mrs. Hodgson took Emma at the same time to Dr. Headlam. She had, from a severe cold, shrunk so much as to be scarcely able to walk. And, as she has never been well since she had the scarlet fever, we grew alarmed for her. But the doctor says we have no occasion to be apprehensive for her safety. He told us that his father, when he was about Emma's age, had the scarlet fever, and could never taste flesh-meat of any kind till long after he came to manhood, but experienced no inconvenience in health from it.

"Thinking a parcel will cost you no more than a letter, I send you some proofs. I wish I could have found you any more: but you once in a letter told me that you wished you had not seen a proof of the book till the whole volume was sent to you, and I therefore determined that some considerable part at least should, when it was published, be new to you, and therefore did not think you would want the proofs. They have been, I dare say, made use of in the kitchen, and I cannot find any more than those I send.

"Mr. Brown, of Jarrow, hesitates to sanction on his part the separation of Jarrow and Heworth unless I resign both places, though the Dean and Chapter offer houses and tithes to make Heworth by itself (with the fees and Easter offerings, and an old stipend of 6*l.* 6*s.* 4*d.*) worth 120*l.* a-year. If they were separated I could give the curate of Jarrow 100*l.* a-year, and retain 70*l.* myself: but the Dean and Chapter will not confirm their grant while the livings are holden together.

"Our village news is in a very low current this week. Poor Tommy Philipson's son William, however, is here, wearing fast away in a consumption. Mr. John Clayton sent a will for him to sign last week, and it was executed in due form this morning. You will be agreeably surprised to hear that George Smith's family have exerted themselves

* It is probable that the ill-health of the youth had been brought on by too much confinement. He had gone to business when little more than a boy.

sufficiently this spring to get their half-acre into decent cultivation: they did not however get it sufficiently clear to plant with potatoes till yesterday.

" The portrait is for my God-daughter.

." JOHN HODGSON."

To the Rev. A. HEDLEY —Whelpington, 12 June, 1832.—" We shall be delighted to see you: and, if the weather be dry and the rivers low, I should be glad to have your company to Risingham, to examine again the masonry of the bridge. Pray get for me from your mason the dimensions of some Roman lewis-holes, as nearly as he can remember. He mentioned them to me, but I made no minute about them, and dare not write from memory. I delivered your message at Chollerton, where I was very kindly and very hospitably received: but Mr. Bird said he intended being at Chesterholm on the following evening.—— In turning over some letters I found the accompanying one, which will shew you that the ROMAN WALL has been for some time a subject of mine for a separate publication. My own illness and that of Richard's succeeded each other so closely, that the plan was relinquished from necessity; and piercing misfortunes and troubles have prevented its being resumed and forwarded. My latest plan was to make Annals of the Roman Age in Northumberland, including the accounts of the Pipe Roll for Northumberland to the death of Henry the Third, in one volume of Part One in my book, and sell the copyright of the Roman part of the volume to be printed in a cheap form. Should you undertake the Roman Wall, you must reserve for me the right to quote as much of it as I please. I shall, I hope, make a readable article respecting ROMAN MASONRY."

To J. B. NICHOLS, Esq.

" MY DEAR SIR,                           Whelpington, 24 June, 1832.

" I date at home, but write from it on the only piece of paper I can procure, to say that I have drawn up an account for the wood-cuts you mention,* and will send them and it to 25 Parliament Street, on Saturday next, by the steamer, the King of the Netherlands, from Newcastle. I expect Raine here in about eight days, but fear he will not undertake the task of the review you are so kind as to take an interest in:

* Cuts and extracts from his lately published volume. See the Gentleman's Magazine, October and December 1832.

if, however, he does not consent to mount the judgment seat, and send you copy before the 8th of July, I am sure that one of three or four of my friends will be glad to send you such materials as you may easily select an article from, without applying to a professed reviewer for it.

" The four articles I have sent are almost entirely extracts from my book. I have, however, added some notes, and here and there amended the text. The quotations will be found not to stand in the same order as they are in the book. I will thank you to print the woodcuts on soft paper, and when you have done with them, to send them in Mr. Charnley's parcel, bookseller, Newcastle, from Baldwin's and Co.

" The copy of Part III. vol. i. of my book which I send with the cuts is the only odd one which I have, and I wish it had been in a better condition. It was the subscription copy of the late Ralph Spearman, Esq. of Eachwick Hall, who was an odd antiquary and wrote long notes in his books, and tore the waste paper out of their ends to write odd letters upon. I send some clean prints to replace the dirty ones: and with the use of India rubber and the aid of a London binder I hope you will be able to get the copy put into tolerable order.

" You must not offer to pay me for the books I send; but, lest you should think me extravagant, I shall be glad to accept any work of a similar value published by yourselves, and of which you may have a spare copy. I cannot afford to buy many books that might be useful to me; but if you could let me have any work in my way, for those I have sent, you would oblige me.

" The Addenda to the Memoirs are not in the History of Morpeth, but are original matter. Only 100 copies of them were printed. Yours——
" JOHN HODGSON."

June 28, 1832.—To J. B. NICHOLS, ESQ.—" The accompanying letters * were copied at my request by my amanuensis, from originals which he has had for several months in my house, but has now returned them to their right owner. I did not collate the copy with the originals, but have no doubt of its correctness. If you think them worth insertion in the Gentleman's Magazine you are welcome to do so: if not, be kind enough to return the copy when you have done with the woodcuts. I will thank you not to say by whom they were communicated to you. By putting the poetry into small type they will occupy only little room."

* From Robert Burns to William Cruikshank. See Gent. Mag. Aug. 1832, in which they are printed.

### FROM THE REV. A. HEDLEY.

"Chesterholme, July 1, 1832.

"——— Pray come as soon as you can next week. I am ready for all adventures, and to go any where with you. We shall, if you like, make a foray into Bewcastle, and thence over into Liddesdale and the Tarras, in search of Carey's * camp. I think it must be somewhere between a place called the Side (Jock of the Side) in Liddesdale and Langholm. Mr. Benson of Haltwhistle will be happy to take your duty for a Sunday, and you or I between us could take his place at Greenhead and Beltingham; so do not forget to bring what the Scotch ministers call a *galloping Tom* with you; or two of them will be better. I have a place for your gig, if you choose to drive thus far in it, and we could ride or drive as we find it convenient afterwards. If you come *gig-ways* pray bring with you *Raine's Testamenta*, as I wish to look it through at my leisure."———

### To J. B. NICHOLS, Esq.

"MY DEAR SIR, Whelpington, 6 July, 1832.

"I send you two articles for your Magazine, if you think them worth insertion: if not, destroy the charter, but preserve and return with the woodcuts the poetry and letters of Burns.

"The charge to me for the woodcuts was as follows: Cockle Park Tower 5*l.* 5*s.*; Cresswell Tower 3*l.* 3*s.*; Mitford Church 8*l.* 3*s.*; Newbigging chapel 3*l.* 3*s.*

"Raine has not been here. His visits are very uncertain; and the other sources I expected materials for a review from are at present not open to me. The friend I expected I could have applied to is unwell, and other three abroad, or on rambles where letters to them would have little chance to reach them. I must therefore, I fear, beg of you to put into execution your proposition of the 19th of last month, to "do your best to get it well reviewed in London." I have had many very satisfactory letters upon the subject: and inclose you extracts from those of three gentlemen who are good judges of County History, and men who would not flatter me with any such odious matter—though I am indeed ashamed of transcribing the lavish eulogies of one of them.

* Carey Lord Hunsdon, an energetic warden of the Eastern Marches in the reign of Elizabeth.

" I had been constantly for many years in the habit of reading the Gentleman's Magazine till last Christmas, when the copy I had the perusal of was given up on account of the gentleman who took it having removed from his situation.    This month will commence a new volume of it, and if you will have the kindness to send me a copy in *Baldwin's* parcel to Emerson Charnley, bookseller, Newcastle, and continue to do so monthly, I will feel obliged to you.    Mr. Charnley will account to you for it.    If you can get me into the habit of doing it, and wish me to do so, I could easily send you contributions to the Magazine almost every month, but my difficulty would be the mode of sending the parcel. Would it do to send it from Charnley to Baldwin, or by the steamer in the months it plies in? or could I address any M.P. or office franker? During the time parliament is sitting, John Hodgson, Esq., M.P. 5, Parliament Street, would frank any communication to me; though I suppose your connection with the House of Commons and its committee rooms makes it easy for you at all times to get franks.

"When you have done with the woodcuts I sent, if the volume contains any more you wish to have, they shall be sent, with extracts, &c.

" I have no proofs of the book for your reviewer to cut extracts from, excepting the two I inclose, which, if he thinks fit to quote any passage from the preface, will spare the trouble of transcription.

" I have blotted out the names of the authors of the letters which I had put at the head of the extracts from them, that you may shew them to your reviewer.    They are certainly a few out of many testimonies of the good opinion my friends have given me of the work, and may afford hints to any one whose business it may be to give a *just* account of it.——

" Perhaps you could give some short notice of the little volume of Memoirs which I sent to you.    The Appendix to it, you will see, is not printed in the account of Morpeth, of which I have printed fifty copies with a separate title, dedication, introduction, and indexes; but as you have all the rest which it contains, in II. ii. I did not send it to you.

" I am at present busily engaged in a work on *Mural Fortifications*— the Walls of China; Cæsar's Wall in Helvetia; Hadrian's Vallum and Severus's Wall in England; Antoninus Pius's in Scotland; and that of Probus in Hungary.    But my main business will be with that attributed to Severus, and I hope to succeed in making the whole a popular and readable book.    Mr. Petrie of the Tower encourages me much to go on with the work.    Do you think it possible that I could get the following two works by Doederlin:  1. Schediasma Historicum, Imp. P. Æl.

Hadriani et M. Aur. Probi Vallum et Murus. Norimb. 1723, 4to. 2. De Vallis et Muris Limitum Memoralibus. Joan. Andr. Doederlin: in Antiquitatibus Romanis Nordgaviensibus. Weissenburg, 1731? I have "A Tour along the Devil's Wall" in Bavaria, by J. Andreas Buchner, of Risenberg, as translated by my friend Salvin.

"If you could get a sight of the Archæologia Æliana, they would, as far as you have not noticed the work, afford good materials for a review in the Gentleman's Magazine.

"I have written to-day to Raine on the subject of the review, but fear you will not hear from him upon it. From, my dear Sir, yours very truly,

"JOHN HODGSON.

"P.S.—8 July, 1832. Our carrier late last night brought me your valuable present of books, for which pray accept my best thanks.

" To your copy of Whitaker's Sir G. Radcliffe, you may perhaps be glad to add that Dr. John Radcliffe was a nephew of Col. Thomas Radcliffe, and of Edward, second Earl of Derwentwater. See two letters of his in my Northumberland, II. i. 225, 226.

To the REV. J. RAINE.

"MY DEAR RAINE,                                    Whelpington, 7 July, 1832.

"I had a letter dated 19 June last from Mr. B. Nichols requesting the use of some of my woodcuts for the Gent. Magazine, and that I would ask you to write a review of my last volume. I told him that I expected you here in about a fortnight's time, according to your message by Mr. Burrell at the Visitation, and that I would talk to you on the subject. I have had a second letter from him, and therefore mention the matter to you; but fear you cannot undertake so heavy a task. I expected I could have had one or two friends to have sent them a review, but they are either abroad or unwell. I have however sent him three extracts from letters containing opinions on the work. One of them is from yourself. Mr. N. says he will be glad to receive the review, or hints for that purpose. The scheme is all his own contriving; but, as he has taken some trouble with it, I should like him not to be disappointed. You could therefore, perhaps, send him a letter in a day or two's time, containing such hints as a glance over the book may suggest to you. This would be doing me a service, as I wish to have as many copies of the work sold as I can, to redeem some most unfortunate losses which I have within the two last years been fated to suffer.

"I am busy with a work which will form part of the First Part of my Northumberland, and which is on Mural Fortification: but chiefly on our ROMAN WALL. I wish to make it as readable and entertaining as I can; but some works which would be useful to me in compiling it I fear I shall have great difficulty in procuring. Have you in the Dean and Chapter Library, 1. Jo. Alex. Doederlinus Hist. Imp. P.Æ.C. Adriani, et M. Aur. Probi Vallum et Murum. Norimb. 1723, 4to; or 2. De Vallis et Muris Limitum Memoralibus. Joan. Alex. Doederlin: in Antiquitatibus Romanis Nordgaviensibus. Weissenburg, 1771, 4to. The first work is mentioned by Watt, the second by Fabricius, p. 824. There is also another work on the Hungarian Wall by J. Andreas Buchner; but I think I have extracts from it sufficient for my purpose. Do you know any account of Cæsar's Wall but that in his Commentaries? I can get Hyde on the Chinese Wall.——Most truly yours,

"JOHN HODGSON."


To HENRY PETRIE, Esq.

"MY DEAR SIR,                                Whelpington, 7 July, 1832.

"I have received the Alston documents, and my best thanks are due to you for them.

"I have been again at the Roman Wall, and am now drawing together my materials for an account of it, which I am intending to preface with a succinct account of the Chinese, Helvetian, Hungarian, and Scotch Walls. My difficulty in this sequestered place is in getting the works of those who have written on these various mural fortifications—the main one especially—Doederlin's work on the Hungarian Wall: I have copious extracts from Buchner's Tour along it, and access to all the works on the Wall attributed to Severus. I hope the tract or small volume will not occupy much time. I will endeavour to make the account plain and readable; and give a chapter or two on the masonry of the Wall, the buildings within the Roman fortresses, and the Roman bridges in Northumberland. You must therefore expect from me an account of these things in print (*if I can get any one to print it*), and not in MS., as I promised you three years ago. I have ample materials and numerous sketches and plans for the work; but must still, as soon as possible, go with a prepared note-book to examine the whole line of the Wall more accurately than I have hitherto done.

" I began since I received your last communications to write you something about the masonry and style of the Wall, but find I cannot do justice to the subject in the small compass I was allowing myself to move in. Having a parcel to send to Mr. Nichols (25, Parliament Street), I inclose my first day's work on the subject of the Wall. The three leaves of plans are of buildings I excavated in Housesteads, and of which I cannot now get time to give you a description. My sketches are rude, but I will endeavour to get Mr. Sopwith, a good drawer and surveyor, to go with me along the Wall to get correct views and an accurate survey of the whole line: and leave myself nothing else to do but take minutes of the present state of the two Barriers. Horsley's account is by far the best. Warburton's is a copy of it: and all that Hutton has on the subject is copied from Warburton.

" I think I could put my plan into a popular and interesting form, and offer it to Murray for publication at a low price. My brother, who is an architect in Carlisle, would give me much assistance from his local knowledge of that neighbourhood, and you could have a guess of his ability to do so from his little communications to the Transactions of the Newcastle Antiquarian Society, if you could have time to look into the last volume of them, which I suppose is in the British Museum.

" Can you give me any advice or encouragement in this project? It will be most gratefully received.

" I must beg of you to return the accompanying papers at your leisure in a parcel from *Baldwin's* directed to me here, under cover to E. Charnley, Bookseller, Newcastle-upon-Tyne.

" My health is good at present, and I most sincerely hope that your troublesome companion the gout has entirely left you.

" Will you do me the favour to say to Mr. Bayley that I received his kind letter, for which I am much obliged? In Mr. Lysons's time the communications I had from the Tower were by his own directions obtained entirely from Mr. Bayley, and I considered myself indebted solely to him for them. Mr. Raine told me this was not the case; and, though it was painful to me to know that I had not proceeded rightly, I am sure you will pardon me for this explanation, and for saying how grateful I feel for your kindness and the honour you do me in allowing me to correspond with you. From, my dear Sir, yours most truly,

" JOHN HODGSON."

From the ——— ———————————————————————————————————————————————————————————————————————————————————————————— From the ——— in that part of life as long as his health permitted him to write in a calm and intelligible manner, he began to keep a Journal in the same sense as the work and from this point the task of his biographer's judgment in his researches begins. We can now see what he was doing every day during the rest of his life; the ministerial duties he performed, the visits he paid, the company he met, a journey with a full account of the journeys he took from home, and for what purpose. Along with these matters are supplied numerous indications and remarks of a private nature, in the various subjects of his reading or research, serving as so many illustrations of his own pure and character, which it is the object of these pages to delineate with fidelity.

*1838. July 14. I have kept a Journal in my note-book for Northumberland for the last eight days, but find it inconvenient to mix the hours and materials of that collection with other matters, and therefore now I commence with a Journal of miscellaneous occurrences and matters, with the hope that I may be enabled during the remainder of my life, to carry it on with some degree of regularity. I find, as life advances, necessity for my labours and researches increasing, but my memory is unable to retain many impressions on which it is desirable to me should remain upon it.*

To Mr. Sopwith, July 27, 1842.—I am at present largely engaged in an account of the Roman Wall and have got a great deal done. As soon as the subject is fairly in MS. it is my intention to walk along the line of the white barrier, and add to and correct my written account as I see necessary. I intend also to accompany it with a few good drawings of remains of the Wall, of Roman Altars remarkable for

* The following extract from the Journal of 1838 may have a place here, as still further explanatory of the motives which led to the adoption of a Diary. "1838, 13 July. I began this Journal from the suggestion of the late Mrs. Singleton, of Elsdon, daughter of Captain Grose the Antiquary, and mother of Mr. Singleton, Rector of Elsdon and Archdeacon of Northumberland, and I began it for the purpose of referring to it to see where I had been, and what I had been doing."

their form or workmanship, and one or two plans of stations. Now here is business to engage us upon. The Wall has been four times either geometrically or trigonometrically surveyed, and that which seems now to be wanted is some better finished illustrations of it than have been given. I have obtained a great deal of information about other similar Walls in Hungary, by the Caspian Sea, in China, &c. with drawings to illustrate or confirm my opinions about the Wall of Severus,* and I think I can make an interesting account of it, which will make part of my next volume. Could you spare a few days to accompany me? I will bear expenses, and also be glad to do *considerably* more. I wish for some good sections of the works, accurately measured and neatly drawn. The general form of the works in section is this [*a sketch with the pen.*] I want some of the best altars belonging to the Antiquarian Society drawn and engraved all upon a scale. I have for the last few weeks been working hard on this subject, and think that a few weeks more will enable me to have my MS. in a good state to take it to collate with the subject of it.——

" JOHN HODGSON.

1832, July 30.—" In returning home from Bolam this evening, we observed over the little valley of Kirkharle a luminous appearance, which I took to be that called *Ignis Fatuus* or Will-with-the-wisp. It darted upwards, was for a few moments stationary, kindled and glowed like a radiant star, then grew dull, fell again, and was seen behind the trees, disappeared suddenly, rose again, glittered and glowed as before, and then darted off horizontally, and rose and flickered again in the air as before. These dartings, upwards and downwards and backwards and forwards, we observed for about the space of three minutes; and, though we stood three or four minutes, we could observe no more of its antic corruscations." (*Journal.*)

1832, Oct 12.—" Last night I got the account of my poor dear sister Mrs. Cockburn's death, after a severe and long illness."

* The reader who cares for the Roman Wall and its History, will not fail to note this part of the letter. Moreover, in the pen-and-ink sketch referred to a few lines below, the words "Severus's Wall and Ditch " are written over the wall itself, whilst Hadrian's name stands merely over an outline of the earthworks. Hodgson soon came to a different conclusion. He was then, as he informs Mr. Sopwith, " working hard upon the subject," and the name of Severus soon gave place to that of Hadrian.

FROM HENRY PETRIE, Esq.

"MY DEAR SIR,                                    Tower, Aug. 23, 1832.

        "A variety of occupations has prevented my returning your
papers earlier, and I now do so with very many thanks for the information they have afforded me.   I hope you will proceed with your design,
and publish the result of your labours; but I doubt whether a *cheap*
form will suit your purpose: for I apprehend the purchasers of such
works are generally persons who do not look to a few shillings more or
less.   However, when your plan is matured, let me know what you
purpose doing: and I need hardly assure you that the interest I take in
the author as well as in his researches will insure any aid within my
reach.   The following objects seem worthy of particular attention.

        "To compare very carefully the masonry of the undulating courses
with such as are horizontal in the same neighbourhood, as to kind of
stone, its form and size, mortar facings on both sides, and core of wall;
*a priori* one can hardly imagine them of the same period; masonry of
the stations inside and out, marking how joined to, or inserted into
wall, mortar, core; castella, do. do.   Each portion of walls represented,
of whatever description, should be followed by the spade to the foundations.   Sections of wall and trenches, and cleared out by spade to
original surface.   A square yard or so of masonry represented occasionally according to scale.   Is the surface of south side of same appearance below the bank which backs it as above?

        " Believe me, my dear Sir, yours sincerely,

                                                " H. PETRIE."


To MR. SOPWITH.

"MY DEAR SIR,                               Whelpington, 4 Sept. 1832.

        "My plan is to give a history and description of the Roman
Wall in the beginning of the next volume of my work on Northumber-
land, and to throw off 300 or more copies of it, to be sold separately.
The work will include a chapter on *Mural Fortification*, with two views
of the Chinese Wall, and accounts of it and the Walls of Cæsar in
Switzerland and Probus in Hungary, besides some account of the great
walls in Upper Egypt and on the north-east of the old empire of
Assyria.   Then a chapter detailing the history of each station, from

Wallsend to the sea at Bowness in Cumberland. Another chapter on the construction of the wall, stations, baths and bridges, &c. Another on all the inscriptions, arranged under their proper stations—and all this accompanied with very accurate drawings of the finest altars, sculptures, columns, &c. Extended and foreshortened views of the Wall as it passes on the basaltic cliffs over the forest of Loughs will be a great embellishment. [*A sketch with the pen in illustration.*] I have numerous . memoranda that I have been making for the last twenty-two years of the places I wish to be sketched. I have also in my intention to give an account of the legions and cohorts employed on the line of the wall, with explanations of their standards, seals, &c. which I believe no one has yet attempted, or ever thought it practicable to reduce to certainty the meaning of the various devices on the numerous altars and stones that have been found. About Housesteads and Wall Town there are fine remains of the wall, sections of pieces of which will be found very interesting. Some London friends encourage me much in this very considerable undertaking. The stations in Northumberland *are all done*, and, if the weather takes up, I would instantly take my manuscript to Chollerford bridge, and thence proceed on foot westward to the sea. A horse or gig would be of no use. We could send our things from place to place by a carrier, and hire a man or two to go with us, if we saw occasion. About your remuneration I must not give advice; but, if copies of the work (as many as you may please to be struck off for you on a paper different from my own) would satisfy you, they shall be at your service. You might dispose of some for pay, and give away some to advantage. I will bear our joint expenses. Be so good as let me hear from you on Thursday. Some of the altars belonging to the A. S. at Newcastle will have to be sketched, and some of the collection in the library at Durham; also some of those at the rectory at Ryton, and especially Mr. Hedley's. The whole will make a book that may be sold for 30*s*. or 2*l*. a copy. From yours truly,

" JOHN HODGSON."


FROM THE ARCHBISHOP OF CANTERBURY.

" REV. SIR,                              Addington Hall, Sept. 8, 1832.

" The merits of your History of Northumberland have been mentioned to me in such strong terms by Mr. Edward Swinburne, that I am desirous of possessing a copy of the work; and I shall be obliged to you to direct your agent in London to send one to Lambeth Palace.

On account of the more convenient size of the volume, I prefer small paper. I remain, Rev. Sir, your very obedient servant,

"W. CANTUAR."

To THE REV. A. HEDLEY.

"MY DEAR HEDLEY,                    Whelpington, 25 October.

"I send you the MS. book, Gents. Mag. (four numbers), and the Saxon coins,* the best of which you will find much cleaner than when you saw them first. I do not recognise any of them to be from the same die as any in Ruding, excepting that of Redulf, and, as it is not a fair impression, it is difficult to say whether the one I return and that engraved were from the same die or not. If you can get any more in an oxidated state, you may clean them in one minute by putting them into sulphurous acid. If the acid be sulphuric, add some water to weaken it, and to about two table-spoonsful of it you may put about twenty coins; as soon as the ebullition after adding them to the acid ceases, which will be in about a minute's time, add a quantity of water to the acid, and then clean the coins with a piece of cotton rag. This process will render them legible at once. If any of them have a hard incrustation of red oxide upon them, they should be treated separately with diluted acid laid on with a feather.

"We got to Chollerford about half past six on the day we left the Emerald Gem, and dined at 7 o'clock, and reached home the next day at four.

"Your little altar is very curious. The NO, which seemingly belongs to the first line, is really an appendage of the second, over which it has been placed, as we used to do a syllable for which we had not room, when we learned to write: and then you get quit of the difficulty nostro; and the whole will be DEO NEPTVNO SARABOSINO. Probably the Gallic cohort was from the banks of the Sarabus or Sar.

"With kind regards to Mrs. Hedley, and thanks for her kind hospitality and timely search for things left behind, which I could only thank her for by a wave of my hat, I am, very truly and ever yours,

"JOHN HODGSON."

* Mr. Hedley had doubtless come into possession of some of the 8000 stycas found ten days previously in the churchyard of Hexham. Of these coins Mr. Adamson soon afterwards published a valuable account, with engravings, in the Transactions of the Society of Antiquaries.

Under the date of the 1st of November in this year I find this entry in Hodgson's Journal, "Commenced the Anglo-Saxon History of Northumberland." This compilation was doubtless intended to constitute a portion of the first part of his History of Northumberland, and it appears to have occupied much of his attention in after-periods of his life, as I find numerous entries in his Journal respecting it, and many complaints of his want of books on the subject. The manuscript is before me, and it consists chiefly of chronological facts and arrangements from the ordinary authorities, requiring much additional research and labour before any use could have been made of it for his purpose.

### To ROBERT MACKRETH, Esq.

" MY DEAR SIR,             Whelpington, 21st Nov. 1832.

" I have been endeavouring to make up two royal copies of my book; but find myself unable to so do for want of several plates of that size. Some of them I hope you will be able to furnish me with; as, for instance, one of the Keep of Mitford Castle, one of Remains of ditto, one of Aydon Castle, two of Chesters, and one of Nunnykirk. If you cannot supply the whole of the above in royal size, I hope you may be able to do so in demy; and you will oblige me by sending such of them as you can find to Loraine's, the bookbinder, with this notice upon them, " Plates for end of Part II. vol. 2, of Mr. Hodgson's Northumberland:" and I must further beg the favour of your sending a list of them to me at the same time.

" Respecting my son John, I should really feel very much obliged by your speaking to Mr. Dobson about him, as he wishes to study the profession of an architect or engineer. He is now past eighteen years old, and in good health. When he was a child he became deaf by a violent attack of scarlet fever; but since he was twelve years old his hearing has so gradually improved that no one would now suppose that he had ever been deaf. He has made considerable progress in learning the Latin language, and understands a little of Greek; besides having done a great deal in geometry, logarithms, &c.; but he has had no opportunity of learning planning or perspective. The favour I wish you to ask of Mr. Dobson is, that he would take my son under his tuition, if he could do so conveniently; and if so, on what terms. I think he would find him ingenious: he is very good-tempered and industrious, and I think I could answer for his being very correct and steady.*

"I should also esteem it a very great favour if Mr. Dobson would supply me with a plan of a size suitable for my work of the Roman Bath on Sir Edward Blackett's estate at Halton, and any minutes he may have respecting it. I wrote to Mr. Dobson some time since on this subject, but think that he has either never got my letter or mislaid and forgot it. With kind regards to all the family——

"JOHN HODGSON."

To ROBERT MACKRETH, ESQ. Dec. 28, 1832.—"I am very much obliged to you indeed for the kind trouble and interest you have taken respecting my son. I could speak to Mr. Buddle about him: but am very diffident in such matters. If, therefore, you could mention the matter to him you would greatly oblige me.

"Thank you also for your attention about the prints. I will write to the binder and the carrier next week. Mr. Dobson's plan will be most acceptable to me. I wish to have a good article in my next volume on the subject of Roman Baths.——

"JOHN HODGSON."

* This poor youth lived to die of cholera in June in this present year 1857, at Allahabad, the day after his wife had been snatched away by the same disease. Happily they were childless. We have seen him an amateur printer at Whelpington. He afterwards settled in Newcastle as a civil engineer, and had gone out to India in that capacity under an appointment by Government.

Road-making in Northumberland—Correspondence—Journal—Healeyside—Mounces
—Kielder Castle—Correspondence—Presented to the Vicarage of Hartburn—Cor-
respondence—Agistment Tithe at Whelpington—Journal—Wardrew or Gilsland
—Correspondence — Dr. Murray — Professor Magnusson—Correspondence—
Richardson's Border Castles, &c. —History of Durham Cathedral—Short publica-
tions during the year.

THE following letter, written by Mr. Hodgson in the commencement of the year we have reached, seems worthy of being
reprinted from the newspaper in which it made its appearance.
The day will arrive when the efforts at that time making to open
out a new line of road through an important part of the county
of Northumberland, with which the public in general had previously held but little intercourse, will be read with interest, as
the last attempt at road-making in the district after the old-
fashioned way.  We now construct roads of different materials,
and care not for the obstacles which gave so much trouble to our
forefathers.  The quotation " Per mare, per terras, per flumina
curris," or, better still, *si fas sit*, " Curva recta, aspera plana,"
might with propriety be adopted as a motto for the seal of a rail-
road.

In this year also Hodgson made numerous other communications
to magazines and newspapers, of which an enumeration will be
placed at the end of the chapter.

TO THE EDITORS OF THE NEWCASTLE COURANT.

" GENTLEMEN,

" The rebellion in 1745 was productive of the most beneficial
effects to the kingdom at large.  It extinguished all the hopes of the
house of Stewart, and seated the house of Hanover firmly on the
throne of England.  It gave a tone, and energy, and confidence to the
industry of Britain, which have ever since continued to increase.  Till
then, the Highlands of Scotland were a distinct country from the

Lowlands: but the hopes of the last Pretender were no sooner crushed, than the Highlands were traversed with roads in different directions, and its war-like clans disarmed.   On the borders, between England and Scotland, great plans of improvement were also then formed, and almost immediately put into execution.   In December, 1746, the grand jury, clergy, and freeholders of Northumberland represented to parliament that the high road between Newcastle and Buckton-burn, on the northern boundary of the county, a little to the north of Belford, was the high post road from London to Edinburgh; but, by reason of the many heavy carriages passing upon it, it was become so deep and ruinous, that travellers could not pass along it without great danger; in consequence of which an Act was granted for erecting turnpikes upon it, and collecting tolls at them for the repairs of the road.   This was the first Turnpike Act granted to the county.   In January, 1749, a similar representation was made to the House of Commons of the bad condition of the road between Newcastle, by way of Ponteland, to the Wansbeck, at South Middleton Bridge; and between Newcastle and North Shields; and Acts obtained for the repairs of both of them.   In March, 1751, the counties of Northumberland and Cumberland, in a joint petition, stated, that the road from Newcastle to Carlisle led, for the most part, "through a country uncultivated, and very thinly inhabited;" that it was "frequently unpassable, and at all times very inconvenient, either for troops or carriages: and that it had been found by experience, during the late rebellion, and on former occasions, that travellers and troops could not be properly guarded through the country without a more free and open communication;" and, therefore, concluded with praying that national assistance, and the authority of Parliament, might be given, for laying out, making, and keeping in repair a proper public high road across the island in that direction.   The prayer of the petition was allowed, and various sums granted, from time to time, for completing the road.   In 1751 Acts were also procured for repairing the high roads from Morpeth to the High Cross at Elsdon; from Alemouth, by Rothbury, to Hexham; and from Longhorsley, by Whittingham, to the river Bramish.   Now all this proves that the county at that time was putting forth great exertion.   Within the short space of five years Parliament embodied seven different committees, or bodies of trustees, for improving the roads of Northumberland, all of which, excepting one, that for the road from Morpeth to Elsdon, have, by successive re-enactments, been kept in existence, and in different degrees of activity. Their first powers, however, excepting in the case of the commissioners for the military way from Newcastle to Carlisle, were confined almost entirely to the *repairs* of old lines of road, which, through the agricultural grounds that had recently been in a state of common, were very frequently carried in strange zigzag directions, for the purpose of making the adjoining fields square. Through the ancient inclosed lands these roads were often, and especially in the neighbourhood of villages, extremely narrow, and worn deeply down between high banks by long use, winter rains, and for want of proper repairs; and over the moors and uninclosed lands they ran in straight lines, totally regardless of the steepest hills and deepest valleys. Experience gradually proved that comparatively little good was done to travellers, and in expediting mails and couriers, by making a road firm and smooth, while its line was crooked where the form of the country allowed it to be straight, and it was carried in a direct line over the top of a hill when it might have been formed along its side, at the same or nearly equal distance. After the mails were carried by coaches, these inconveniences were more than ever felt; and though the commissioners for the most-frequented of these roads have, from time to time, been obtaining enlarged powers to widen, straighten, cut down banks, and avoid steep hills, it has not been till within the last few years that they have formed extensive plans of improvement. Large sums of money are now expending on the roads through Alnwick to Berwick, and on that through Longhorsley by way of Wooler to the Tweed at Coldstream Bridge. I am led to these representations by a letter you have given in your paper of the 19th instant, from the Scotsman newspaper, respecting the improvements carrying forward by the commissioners of the Ponteland road, on the Chevy Chase line of communication between Newcastle and Edinburgh; and think it may be of some use in quickening the public mind to the encouragement of public works, by pointing out how slow the progress of improvement of roads in this county has been, in a slight sketch of the history of the Ponteland trust from its auspicious commencement in 1749 till the sudden start it began to make towards perfection within the last three years. The first Act for it passed the House of Commons on March 8, 1749; and was for erecting turnpikes on the road between the Cowgate, on the west boundary of Newcastle Town Moor, and the river Wansbeck, at South Middleton; and with the tolls levied at such gates repairing the road. This Act was for twenty-one years, which period was extended for five years by the Broad Wheel Act of 28 George II. The petition for its renewal in 1775 states, that the commissioners had at that time completed the road; that they had expended upon it 2,800*l.* of money, borrowed upon the security of the tolls, of which sum they had repaid 200*l.*; but that 2,600*l.* of it, besides ' a considerable arrear of interest, still remained due.' It also states, that 1,000*l.* of that sum belonged to the Infirmary of Newcastle. In 1797 the Act was again renewed; and the road extended at its north end from South Middleton Bridge to the Alemouth turnpike road, near Wallington Bridge. A fourth Act for it was obtained in 1818; and in 1830 all the money due from it, except the 1,000*l.* belonging to the Infirmary of Newcastle, being paid off, its tolls exceedingly low, and its revenues in a very flourishing condition, its commissioners thought themselves fully justified in undertaking some great improvements upon it; and an Act was accordingly obtained with powers much higher than any of the former; for it not only provided for keeping it up from the Cowgate to the Alemouth Road at Wallington, and to straighten it and carry it on better levels in two places, between Higham Dykes and Belsay, but to make an entire new branch from it at Belsay Fir Plantation, past Harnham, Capheaton, Kirkharle, Littleharle, and Whelpington, and over the moors by Raylees and Monkridge into the Redesdale turnpike-road at Otterburn. This improvement had been rendered almost indispensable by the trust on the road over Harwood from Morpeth to Elsdon having been lost about seven years since, and the extreme steepness and bad state of the road on Elsdon Banks. Of this new branch, a great part of it, from Belsay Fir Plantation to about a mile beyond Whelpington, is now completed and open to the public; and contracts for finishing the whole of it have been entered into. A committee, too, in the course of next month, will be formed for carrying it over the moors from Whelpington to Otterburn, and it is expected that the whole will be completed in the course of the ensuing year. Nearly 8,000*l.* have already been expended upon it; and, from correct calculations, it is known that the remaining portion will be completed for something less than 5,000*l.* The tolls in their present state, and with one gate still wanting on the line, are in such a flourishing state as to leave no doubt of their producing a revenue not only capable of keeping the whole of the road under the trust in excellent repair, and of paying the interest of all sums required to complete the meditated improvements, but to allow of a sinking fund for the gradual repayment of the sums borrowed.

" To persons accustomed to travel from Belsay to Otterburn, and to contend with the steep hills, and be retarded by the vexatious turns in the old road, the view of this new line will be matter of rejoicing and

the most agreeable surprise.  The levels along it are beautifully preserved, and, though its line is slightly serpentine, it is exceedingly
direct.  It sweeps, as Mr. Sopwith, its surveyor, in his report to its first
promoters, well observed, through ' a succession of hollows admirably
adapted to make it easy and picturesque.'

"It may not be without its use also to remark, that new lines and
branches of well-engineered roads, like the one I have been describing,
offer great conveniences and means of improvement, not only to the
places through which they pass, but to districts at considerable distances
from them.  They train the population on each side of them into
a knowledge how to construct their parish . roads properly at the least
expense; and excite in them a desire to keep them in good repair.  An example of this kind is no where more wanted than in several of the central
parts of Northumberland, and in the districts skirting its moors, where
the most shameful want of public honesty, with regard to keeping the
highways in repair, prevails.  Here and there, where a turnpike road
passes through a township, or an active and right-minded proprietor
resides, the statute work is often well and honestly done, but in general
very little is done.  A spade or a hammer in many townships is never
lifted—nor a farthing of money ever expended.  All this sloth and
unjust appropriation of public labour and money would soon be corrected if more roads had turnpikes upon them, or one or more parishes
were thrown into districts for the maintenance of their highways, instead
of that great public charge being left, as it very commonly is, to single
townships, which are often single farms, and the occupiers of which
erroneously think that the justice they refuse to the public is a benefit
to themselves; whereas the treachery which is always lying in wait to
catch an advantage from the highway, poor rate, or revenue schedule,
loses gold for want of employing that time in honest and profitable
labour, which it spends in plotting how it may successfully evade the
payment of a copper farthing.                          V. W."

"24th January, 1833."

To the Rev. J. Raine.—Whelpington, 30 Jan. 1833.—" You would
get my note, saying it was not in my power to go with you to Mr.
Gilly's at Norham.  It was very mortifying not to be one in the excursion.  But I am under the necessity of quietly denying myself many
little trips to see my friends, which would be exceedingly agreeable to
me.  The Archdeacon of Durham asked me to visit him during his residence at Durham; but I am not worth the freight of being carried to
any distance from home.

" Your old preceptor has got magnificently rewarded for his Greek.*
It is gratifying to see a frank and hearty soul like Tate rewarded for a
life of great usefulness and labour, and cheerful to reflect that that
reward in him will not fill him with cold sulky pride, but with joyful-
ness and generosity.——JOHN HODGSON."


### To MR. SOPWITH.

" MY DEAR SIR,                                  Whelpington, 20 Feb. 1833.
    " I did not till last night recollect to give you some information
which, if you are not already possessed of it, may be of considerable use
to you.  De Gallois,† the engineer under the French government for
mining purposes in the great coal district in the neighbourhood of St.
Etienne, resided with me at High Heworth for nearly a year, in 1816
and 1817; and he told me that there was not only an accurate map
of all the surface of that remarkable coal formation, but also plans of all
the workings in it, and sections, both from north to south and east to
west, of all its strata that had been sunk or bored through.  I know
that the workings there are very extensive; and that the coals are now
taken on railways from them both to the Rhone and Saone.  Lyons is
supplied with them; and it affords iron for the forges, &c., of St.
Etienne.  Probably you may get this series of mineralogical surveys
from Paris by some house in London.  I think they are on a considerable scale; but I have no minute about them, and cannot tell you their
price.  I have always understood that the privileged inhabitants in the
Forest of Dean are very jealous of their rights, and not over good to
manage.  It is a very interesting district.  Its Styre cyder is reckoned
uncommonly fine; but no beverage of that kind can be taken without
great caution.——Yours very truly,

                                        " JOHN HODGSON."


### FROM THE REV. EDWARD BIGGE.‡

" MY DEAR SIR,                                  Newcastle, Feb. 27, 1833.
    " When we last met at Capheaton you expressed a wish to have
some MSS. relating to Northumberland copied, which are in the Bod-

    * Lord Grey, as Prime Minister, had conferred upon Mr. Tate a residentiary stall
in the Cathedral of St. Paul's, after a long and eminently successful career as Master
of Richmond School.
    † See Vol. I. p. 197.
    ‡ Here is another gentleman offering his services as a copyist.  Mr. Bigge was of
the family of Linden, a Fellow of Merton College, Oxford, and the first Archdeacon of

leian or the Ashmolean Museum. I am going to Oxford about the 13th of March, and shall be very happy to undertake the work for you; and I think I may possibly get access to those MSS. at Baliol College which the liberal master refused to let you copy.* If you can let me know the titles of the MSS. and how you wish them to be written out, before the 13th, I will do my best to get it done as soon as possible.—— Yours very truly, • "EDWARD BIGGE."

1833, 9 April.—" Susannah went from home for the first time for further education, namely, to get lessons in Italian, drawing, and music, in Newcastle, and to board with Mrs. Rawes."†—*Journal.*

11 April.—" Emma found a butterfly in a semi-torpid state, and, as I was stepping from a chair upon the sideboard to put the little creature in safety from spiders on a picture-frame, the chair-bottom fell in with a crash, and I tumbled on the sharp edge of it, and hurt my right side very much."—*Ib.*

13th April.—" From the effects of the fall I had on Thursday, forced to say that duty to-morrow would be done here, in the afternoon only, by Mr. Redman. Mr. Carfrae bled me yesterday, which was the first time of my life that I had blood let."—*Ib.*

15 May.—" Dined with Mrs. Smart at Heworth. Immediately after dinner it began to thunder and lighten, which was continued without intermission, peal after peal, and flash after flash, so quickly and constantly that any interval between them was scarcely perceptible. The hail and rain accompanying this very awful storm were heavy at times, but in no great quantity. While attending a funeral at the chapel the storm began to abate, but still the lightning through the large windows flickered in that great cage of light with an effect that to me was perfectly unique, and grand beyond all I had ever conceived.

Lindisfarne, an appointment which he did not long hold, dying in the prime of life and at the commencement of a career of usefulness. That the obsolete name of Lindisfarne should have been injudiciously revived when this change took place has been a subject of surprise and regret to all those who are acquainted with the name and the history of Holy Island.

  * See Vol. I. p. 374.

  † This amiable girl, then in her sixteenth year, must have left home under a bad omen. She too caught a fever and died.

The storm continued to roll around at a distance till nine, and then approached High Heworth again for about a quarter of an hour in the direction from Sunderland. It was now become dusk, and the lightning, darting in angular lines out of a thick black cloud, was of the bright colour of hot melted silver."*

I proceed with my extracts from the Journal upon a somewhat larger scale. Hodgson is again surveying the county, and we have another visit to Mounces and its neighbourhood, with a peep into the poetic ground of Scotland.

1833, 28 May.—" HESLEYSIDE.—A grove of horse-chestnuts in full flower and great beauty, each flower as large as ever I saw them in Kent.

" MOUNCES.—Reached Mounces about five. The trees in great beauty; though the ash and some of the poplar species are only just bursting into leaf. Dog-mercury very abundant under trees near the house. The ground exceedingly dry, and the river and brooks quite low."

May 29th.—" Honeysuckle in full blossom. Apple-trees against a south wall, with abundance of fruit fully set. The trees with smooth bark and in great health. This morning grey, calm, and warm. The cuckoo singing on every side, and the air full of the song and joy of multitudes of other birds. Shrubs of sweet briar perfume the air. The lilac gorgeous, gooseberry leafed, currants with fruit set. Sweet-briar wild on the haughs above Wellhaugh. Top of Lauriston Fell. Hermitage's grey towers,† in an untried country; but here and there clumps of trees and plantations of firs, &c. by the Liddel side. Hills above Hermitage Castle of wild variety of outline. Solway Firth glistening in the west, but the day rather hazy.

" Bradby and Gombury with trees about them, over Hermitage, seem in the slate and porphyry country.

" Limekiln Edge, a          formation, which runs from the limestone stratum at Dinley Byres across the Liddel to the limekilns in the brow of the hill in the direction towards Hawick. The same bed traverses the Bewcastle district, and consequently belongs to the Crossfell

* This storm will be long remembered in the North of England. There was not a house in Durham in which the windows looking towards the south were not almost entirely destroyed.

† In Scotland, the Hermitage Castle of Sir Walter Scott.

system. In descending towards Willowbog in our way back I found pieces of the black flint in the breays of the road, 200 feet or more above the level of the brook. The flint is indeed of very various shades. It is in the brook and its banks in the Lewis-burn above the junction of that stream with the Oakenshaw burn at the Forks. The coal only eighteen inches thick. Sir John gets for tolls about 60*l.*, colliery 150*l.*, estate of Mounces 1800*l.* a-year. It was never more than 1500*l.* a-year. The coal has a tender clay-stone roof. The road is made chiefly of sandstone; it runs and winds in sweet and easy lines, and is well engineered. WELLHAUGH, the haugh on which the house stands, runs up behind it to a narrow point, from which the prospect reaches up the Tyne beyond the grounds of Lewis-burn, and is closed majestically with the bold sweeping outline of Bewshaugh. The Tyne sweeps up the east side of the haugh, and has a Dutch dyke upon its brink to defend the land from its ravages; and between it and the dyke its margin is now hemmed with bird-cherry, alder, and other low trees, and the earth beautifully bespangled with trollius europæus (globe flower) and purple orchises; and before the place where I am sitting the Gowan-burn enters the Tyne through winding banks hung with fine birch and alder woods, and having great haughs between them. The house of Gowan-burn stands further up, on a knoll not seen from this place. Then at the turn where the river begins to run to the south the prospect extends for a mile over a broad haugh, with the river on the right and old woods, and on the left the wild woods of Hawkhurst: and in the distance Mounces rises tufted and bosomed in trees and woods that creep up the rising ground and fill up the cleugh of Leplish ground, the whole backed with pasture-ground in this form [*a sketch with the pen.*]

" The coal of the Lewisburn ground is beautifully covered with the prismatic colours  A pit is worked in the Lewisburn above the Forks in a twenty-inch seam, and has a stone roof. But query? in so far as respects the roof.

" May 30th. —KIELDER CASTLE. —The Tyne comes out of Deadwater through narrow haughs edged with carexes and spotted with sedges (iris tuberosa), and has steep woody banks on both sides, especially the left, thick with old alders and thorns and birch and oak, twisted and bent into every form that time and rough winds and a high climate could throw them. Their old stems are matted with moss, and their boughs are hung and fringed with lichens; while the young trees dart up among them straight and smooth barked. Thrushes, blackbirds, and numerous other songsters, the cuckoo, the lark, the red-breast, and many others, with their whirring and chirping and whistling notes, mix the harmony into melody.   Under the trees primroses and speedwell, and by the river sides symmachia nemorum, &c. &c.   On the east and on the left bank of the Kielder the mountain side is traversed with the memorials of two old marches or fences of earth.

" On the south from the castle, the ground slopes swiftly in bright green turf off to the Kielder, which has old thorns, interspersed with other trees, on each side: especially on the west it is rich with sycamore, the straight leaders of which are exceedingly rich and luxuriant among the foliage of the old natural wood.

" The Tyne after it comes out of Deadwater becomes animated, and runs with gentleness of joy in the summer months through haughs sheltered with woody banks and cheered along its course with the woodland choir.   Vigorous spruce rise up in the wood west of the castle, and on the left bank of the Tyne by the winding road from the castle to the ford over the Kielder; and opposite the castle an oldish wood of spruce and Scotch fir frowns over it.   About the castle many very fantastic old thorns and birch trees.   The south wall of the garden, which is on the haugh on the river bank of the Kielder, just above its junction with the Tyne, seems old, and has largish sycamore about it. Is it the site of Burtreehaugh ?   Tree-peony beautiful in it, and plenty of rhubarb.   The Tyne from leaving the Kielder through the haugh is thickly shaded with alder, and a chain bridge over it and the Kielder.—— Carexes and meadow-sweet rise underneath hazels, the roots of which are perfumed with sweet woodruff (asperula odorata), which grows here plentifully.   The old birches have on their crooked stems great hunches and wens bearded with young shoots, as ragged and bushy as a Jew's beard.   [*A sketch of the castle and neighbourhood.*]   Kielder Castle has an amphitheatre before it, and a haugh below hung round with wood. The distance is closed with the benty sward of the southern limb of Bewshaugh.   It is a sweet seclusion in balmy and delicious air, ' far from the madding crowd's ignoble strife;' a place to hide oneself in from the avarice and cant and humbug of that cruel and hard-hearted monster called civilized life.   Its towers are grown grey, and never now with the sun upon them seem harsh among the great variety of green in the trees around, and the colours of the bent and heathery mountains behind them.——The early red orchis very fine between the river and the road in the haugh below Bewshaugh.   One I plucked had a thyrn of flowers 7½ inches long from the bottom of the lowest petal or floweret foot-stalk to the top of the highest, and 58 flowerets in all.   Stumps of fir-trees still sticking up in the Howlet moss, which is full of them, as found in cutting open drains.——

"MOUNCES.—May 31. This is a breathless warm morning. But still at six the coolness from the dew tempers the air, which is balmy and delightful. Swallows of the four species numerous about the place. The eaves-martin very plentiful. The swift least so; indeed I have seen none, but am told there are several. The sand-martin in places very numerous, especially in a sandy scar not far from the Willow crag on the north side of the new road. The weather is so dry that the martins can get no clay of a proper consistence to build their nests. What they get is so sandy that it falls as soon as it is dry. Hawthorn in full blossom all about Hesleyside: the perfume delicious. The whole country-dale most charming. Several new houses building. Falstone most lovely haughs."

To MR. SOPWITH.—1 June, 1833.—" I think that one or more of my notes to you must not have reached you, as I am sure that in one I mentioned the subject of your being elected a member of the Society of Civil Engineers, and congratulated you on the distinguished honour that body had conferred upon you. Long may you live to enjoy the reflexions of self-respect which unsolicited reward for useful services raises in well-regulated minds. Praise in print is often a matter of mere moonshine and quackery, which the world gives and takes as a matter of course: and it is so often daubed on by the hands of mere selfishness and flattery that there is more honour in being without its whitewash than with it: but to be selected by Mr. Telford as one proper, on account of talent and acquirement, to be elected a member of the body of English Civil Engineers, cannot fail to lead to honourable and useful distinction.

" Sir J. E. S. talks of getting you to make some Surveys and a mining report about Mounces; but when he may determine to do so I cannot tell. Think on, and talk to me about it when you come hither. I mentioned to him your book of Isometrical Surveying: you should send him a prospectus of it as soon as you can.——

" JOHN HODGSON."

To MR. SOPWITH.—25 June, 1833.—" Pray accept of my best thanks for your very neat and curious little volume respecting Alston and its neighbourhood. I have sent a short notice of it to the (Newcastle) Journal, having had occasion to write to that office this morning. I did not venture to send a long article, fearing that they might not have room

for it. . It is very respectably printed, and the copy you have sent is
exceeding neatly bound.   I dare not venture to say when I shall be in
Newcastle.——

                                                "JOHN HODGSON."

In the beginning of the month of July in this year, when
Hodgson was, as usual, deeply occupied in his parochial duties
and upon the History which had so long engaged his attention, an
event occurred which materially affected him and his family, and
led to his removal from Whelpington to Hartburn, where, after a
residence of upwards of ten years, his mortal remains now rest in
peace.

The circumstances in which at this time he was placed were
such as in many respects to make a change welcome.   The sad
years of 1830 and 1831, and the loss of three of his children, had
given him a blow from the effects of which he was daily labouring,
and so far was he from having cast off the consequences of his
own serious attack of illness in the latter of the above years,
brought on doubtless in a great measure by affliction, that his
health was daily becoming more feeble and uncertain.   His years,
as it was remarked, were beginning to tell upon his personal appearance, and he seemed to be becoming an old man before his time.
Another subject had for a long time been giving him much
anxiety.   He still held the benefice of Jarrow with Heworth, to
which he was becoming yearly less able to pay that attention
which such a responsibility demanded.   This cure, as we have
seen, he had wished to resign at once, but having been solicited to
retain it awhile longer, he had complied with the request.   He
soon, however, repented him of his determination.*

But, in addition to feeble health and the effects of affliction and
bereavement, coupled with a sense of responsibility which he was
not able to satisfy in a conscientious manner, there were other
causes in operation to render him but little at ease in his circumstances and feelings.   His History of Northumberland had not met

* "1832, Oct. 29.  Population of Jarrow 3,598 ; of Heworth 5,424.  Receipts of
incumbent; Lough House 55l. 3s. 4d. ; Garden at Jarrow 10l. ; Dividend of Stock
2l 6s. 8d ; Easter Offerings 19l. 6s. 8d. ; Pensions, &c. 13l. ; Fees 100l. 7s. 1d.
Total present income 200l. 3s 9d. ; Disbursements to the two curates 145l. 3s. 2d.
leaving for incumbent 55l. 0s. 7d."  Journal.

with the encouragement which he had reasonably expected. The copies which he had sold were not numerous, and for many of that few their purchasers had neglected to make due compensation. He had published a circular delicately alluding to this omission, but in many cases it had not been attended to, and again he was beginning to feel straitened in his means, a grievous addition to the other causes which were pressing so heavily upon his body and mind.

In this state of things, on the 5th of July the vicarage of Hartburn, a few miles lower down, upon the Hart, became vacant by the death of Mr. Davison,* its aged incumbent, and Hodgson lost no time in consulting Archdeacon Thorp, who had for a long period been his friend, with respect to the propriety of his becoming a suitor to the Bishop of Durham for the vacant living. The Archdeacon's advice was in favour of the application, and there is reason to believe that he did more than merely confer with Hodgson on the subject. The request was granted, and the vicar of Whelpington † became vicar of Hartburn, vacating the former benefice and that of Jarrow with Heworth. In due time he was collated and inducted,‡ but he did not take up his residence upon his new preferment till the following spring, much work being required in the vicarage house and glebe buildings, which from long neglect were scarcely in a tenantable condition. It may be stated that in point of income the living of Hartburn was considerably superior to that of Whelpington, but then, such were the outlays and expenses which Hodgson was compelled to

* Soon after Mr. Davison's death Mr. Hodgson communicated to the Gentleman's Magazine a short memoir of him, which is written with much kindly feeling. " Mr. Davison was (says he) a gentleman of mild disposition and elegant manners; in the pulpit he was remarkable for his melodious tones of voice, and his graceful and winning mode of delivery; and in his social habits full of frankness and friendship. He was very rarely during the latter part of his life seen from home, confining himself almost wholly to his sequestered and delightfully situated vicarage house, on the romantic banks of the Hart, or within the limits of his parish, which, however, is very exten. sive." *Gent. Mag., Aug.* 18, 1833.

† The gross receipt of the living of Whelpington in 1832 was 301*l*. 1*s.* 4½*d.*

‡ He was instituted on the 24th of October, by Mr. Ekins, rector of Morpeth, under a commission from the Bishop, was inducted by his friend Mr. Redman, vicar of Kirkharle, on the 26th, and he read in on the following Sunday, the third of November.

incur, in putting the house and other buildings into decent repair, that he soon found himself a loser by the change. He received no dilapidations from the representatives of his predecessor, having himself to satisfy a demand of this nature at Whelpington, and he died at the very time when he was beginning to shake off his incumbrances and the living was beginning to be in an improved state under the Act for the Commutation of Tithes.

In accepting this preferment Hodgson, whilst he gained new friendships, together with considerable advantages in being nearer a post town, and in enjoying greater facilities in his communication with the Newcastle libraries and the press, did not turn his back upon his friends in the neighbourhood of Whelpington. Hartburn is the adjoining parish on the east. The houses of Capheaton and Wallington were still at an easy distance. One of his nearest clerical neighbours was still his countryman Mr. Redman, the aged vicar of Kirkharle, a gentleman of whom more will be said in a future page, and he came into close contact with Mr. Meggison, vicar of Bolam, for whom he had long entertained a high regard.

For the reasons above stated the reader will consider the subject of our memoir as resident at Whelpington until the spring of 1834, and we may now proceed with his history in this locality.

To Mr. SOPWITH.—13 July, 1833.—" A great digging is to commence at Housesteads on the 15th instant, of which I had no regular notice till Thursday night, and no positive commands as Secretary of the Antiquarian Society to be there till yesterday: I intend to be on the ground about eleven o'clock, and shall have my quarters at Chesterholm. If you could make it convenient to be one night from home, say on Tuesday or Wednesday, all I can want you could then, I think, do for me. You will be near the most spirited subjects for views both of the wall and the precipices called the *Devil's Teeth*, of which I want sketches. But I must not press you to come.——

" JOHN HODGSON."

To Mr. P. MACKAY, Gifford near Haddington.

" MY DEAR SIR,                                        Chesterholm, 17th July, 1833.

" Mr. Sopwith is going hence to-day to Whelpington in his way to Edinburgh, and I send this note with him to say that Capheaton school is vacant, and that I want a master for it.    Hedley recommends one who *can teach Mr. Wood's plan.*    One that had a natural gentleness of temper with a love of his profession, and would be orderly, and teach the children good principles of religion and morality and good manners, would be most acceptable at the place: but the emolument is indifferent. A house to live in, if wanted, a garden, and the school-room you know. These are free, besides something, I do not know what, for assisting me as clerk once a fortnight; but this would not be required from one otherwise well qualified for the situation.    Then the late master, when he attended well to the school,. had about forty scholars, at an average of about a pound a scholar, by the year; but latterly, from his neglecting his duty, that number was reduced one third or one fourth at least.    Nothing but reading, writing, and arithmetic has been of late taught in the school.    But *I think* (I have no positive orders to say that it would be the case), Mr. Tone's boys (three of them) after Christmas would attend a master that could teach Latin and the mathematics.    I wish you could recommend me a person.    I have been inundated with applications: those that are fit for it have better situations.    You know the order of the place, and the sort of person and qualifications wanted.    Pray help me if you can.    I would have written to Professor Pillans: but the situation is too poor for one of his pupils.    You know the kindness of the Capheaton family.    But that must not be holden out as a lure to serve instead of emolument.    I write in great haste.

 "John is with me at a *howk* in Housesteads.    We do not expect to go home till Saturday.

 " I left all well at home.    Pray write to me soon about the school, *which is vacant,* and a master wanted.    Most truly——

" JOHN HODGSON."

In the beginning of August, 1833, Mr. Hodgson felt himself called upon to take a step which gave him great pain, but a sense of duty, under the peculiar circumstances of the case, induced him to comply with a recommendation made to him by an eminent solicitor in Newcastle, who had for many years been his friend and a great promoter of his topographical researches.

The circumstances were these.    The agistment tithe of the parish of Whelpington belonged to the vicar, but none had been paid for some length of time.    The amount of this tithe, as by far the greater portion of the parish was in grass, was considerable. Lord Tenterden's Act for the Commutation of Tithes was coming

into operation, and the time had arrived when, according to the
Act, the claim should be made, or the right lost for ever.    Mr.
Hodgson saw at once the propriety of the advice he had received,
and upon returning home from Newcastle he made known his
determination to his parishioners in a circular in the following
terms.

"In order to prevent the permanent loss to the Living of Whelpington
of the tithes of agistment, I have felt it my duty to file a bill in the
Exchequer, for the establishment of a right which is too clear to admit
of question, as I am advised.    As far as I am personally concerned, I
take this step with reluctance, because my wish is to live at peace with
my parishioners; but after full consideration of the matter I felt that I
could not act otherwise.    Will you have the kindness to intimate, either
to myself or to Messieurs Clayton of Newcastle, my solicitors, to what
professional man the process of the Court (which as a necessary matter
of form must be issued) may be sent on the part of yourself and your
tenants, in order that personal service may be dispensed with?

"I have only to add that I do not wish to precipitate your decision,
whether or not you will resist the claim; I will wait any time you think
necessary to enable you to consider the matter fully; and all the information I possess is open to your inspection."

No sooner, however, had Hodgson issued this circular than his
heart failed him—not from any doubt as to the result of his claim,
nor from any indifference to the rights of his benefice or the
interest of his successors, but from the positive distress and misery
of mind which came upon him from the feeling that there might
be an interruption of the harmony in which he had lived for ten
years with his parishioners.    In his Journal he calls the issuing
of the circulars "a horrible duty," and the day "a painful one."
There are those who may be of opinion that it was not only justi-
fiable, under the circumstances of the case, but a positive obligation;
and that if any thing *horrible* was connected with the transaction it
would be more naturally on the part of those who, having long
held unjustly—Sir H. Spelman would have used a stronger term
—what did not belong to them, might be inclined to resist any
attempt to recover to the vicarage what was withheld from it by
no better title than that of strength of arm.    At all events Hodg-

son had hardly made the claim before he abandoned it—and thus purchased peace at the expense of his successors, by establishing the non-payment of agistment tithe in this parish for ever. " For your sake, and your sake only, (writes his solicitor when all was over,) I regret the addition to the income of the Living of Whel- pington. For your successors I care nothing. The case was so clear, that I feel satisfied all parties would have struck within six months."

But where during these proceedings was the patron of the Living? Surely as the temporary possessor of this right for the good of the church, in his capacity as a trustee for the time being, it was his duty in this and every similar case, during the Commutation process, to have been on the alert *ne quid ecclesia detrimenti caperet.* The absence of the duly constituted autho- rities on such occasions, and of the countenance and assistance which would have accompanied their presence under a sense of duty, was deeply felt in every diocese of the kingdom.

Aug. 22, 1833.—To Mr. J. G. Nichols.—" I have not been able to send you another paper for the Collectanea,* but will endeavour to give you one before the end of the year. Perhaps you could return me the ' List of the Clergy who assisted the Bishop of Durham in his diocese in Queen Elizabeth's time', which I sent for the Collectanea, and which from its plan and unique nature I value highly. I inclose for you a short account of my late aged neighbour the Rev. T. Davison, Vicar of Hartburn, which I hope you will think acceptable for the Magazine."

Wardrew or Gillsland Wells.—3 Sept. 1833.—" I reached this place *(from surveying the Roman Wall westwards )* after seven last night in rain up the valley of Gillsland. The potato tops all destroyed by a strong hoar frost that came on with the full of the moon the preceding night. There indeed was snow on the high lands last Saturday morning, that is on Tindale Fell.

" The Spa of sulphur water is rather agreeable than otherwise; it is diuretic. At six in the morning great numbers of persons, chiefly labouring people, are thronging about it. It is situated close upon the

---

* On the 8th of January in this year Hodgson had communicated to the Collectanea Topographica, a paper entitled " Collections respecting the Monastery of Jarrow, &c." The second, on the same subject, bears date on the 20th of November.

right bank of the Irthing, which is here a black, wild, and raving stream
in floods.    Its bed is exceedingly rough, with large masses of square
sandstone and limestone.    Its sides flanked with lofty and steep scars,
fringed and eye-browed with wild natural wood, interspersed with firs
and larches.    The strata, which are sandstone, a thick bed of limestone
and beds of schist alternating, are extremely regular, but the schist beds
being soft crumble away with the action of the weather and the mad
force of the river, and thus undermine the beds of harder rock.    Jetties
or binks of hard rock here and there protrude from the line of the perpendicular scars, and are covered with grass or wild plants or luxuriant
shrubs, or young trees—for it seems that their bed is never permitted
to stand long enough to allow them to grow old.    This is immediately
above the Spa, i. e. just on both sides of it: but below, and on a
covered seat where I am walking, a large mass of rock overhangs the
walk, and has its brow wreathed and crowned with the odd fantastic
roots of large ash and birch and other trees [*a large and neat drawing with the pen.*]    This is a grand place.    The scenery very much
resembles that of the Alne below the cupola bridge, but it is not so
high, and the strata have perhaps larger beds of schist.    The spa issues
out of a schistose bed.    The house of Wardrew crowns the opposite
bank; but is not seen from the walks about the well.    The left bank is
more wooded, and both more so downwards.    Upwards two white
cottages are seen, but the reaches of the view are short, and the river
makes quick turns.    It is now, in a dampish morning, a sad midgey
glen; wild plants, meadow-sweet, hind or raspberry bushes, foxbells,
scabious, strawberry, wake-robin, rushes and carexes, bilberry, &c. &c.

" The house here called the Shaws is the property of Major Mounsey,
who has filled it with pictures in oil and in print.    The oil paintings
that I have seen have little merit: many of them are, bad: some in oil
apparently are originals, but most of them copies, dry hard things, fit
only for farm houses, where the eye of art has not become a tenant, or
for village alehouse signs where picture has not been studied.    Major
Mounsey has a large collection of agates, and two tables inlaid with
agates, bloodstones, oriental crystals, &c. &c.    Also a collection of old
paintings in his own cottage, and a large one at Carlisle.    He retains in
his house an artist and a lapidary.

" 4 Sept.—The light this morning at six shines on the scar to the
right of the line that slants over the Shaw, and is very bright, flowing
over a part of the river, and under the clump of ash and larch trees on
the right, and catching on their boughs.    This morning is exceedingly

cold, still, however, many invalids at six are flocking to these healing waters, and great quantities of them are taking away water in earthen and glass bottles to be distributed over the country. Much of it is also used for tea and culinary purposes. It is certainly a weak water."
(*Journal.*)

### FROM THE REV. A. HEDLEY.

"Sept. 4, 1833.

" ———Your description of Chesterholme is so *John Wilson-ish* that it would seem to have mistaken its way to Sylvanus Urban instead of Blackwood.* Mrs. Hedley threatens to send you in a bill for *wine and cake*, should your account of us tell upon the curiosity of the public; and there are already symptoms that this may be the case. You have

---

* Hedley is here alluding to a very remarkable communication addressed by Hodgson to the Gentleman's Magazine, under the title of "Scenery and Antiquities of Northumberland," and printed in the Supplement to vol. ciii. pt. i. p. 594. I have longed much to transfer the whole of this paper to my pages, but a few extracts must suffice. " Akenside has sung, and some few writers have described, the beauties of the Northumberland glens and valleys; but no author has ever yet done justice to the ever-varying, the wild and lovely scenery of the river Tyne, and its two arms, and numerous tributary streams. A master amateur artist has, indeed, sat on all their banks, and transcribed their rocks, and trees, and castles, and brown waters, and foaming lins, and purple air, into his enchanted portfolios; and who is there in Northumberland who has not seen the scenery of the Tyne, and the crags, and the cranes (?) and the heathery banks, and the yellow foam of the waterfalls of the Lewis and Oakenshaw burns rise under the magic pencil of Swinburne, and glowing on the walls of the mansions of his friends. I too have been an adorer of nature on the banks of this river, and have wandered upon them early and late, and have gone up almost all her wild burns to their sources. I have gathered plants, and sought for fossils and minerals, and traced the strata of the mountains up the dark waters of the Kielder, and over the lines of the Lewis and Oakenshaw burns, and collected the beautiful ebon-coloured and agatized flints which abound in the banks and beds of these streams. I have traversed the marble and basaltic floors of Gildurdale-beck, sought out the wild haunts of the rapid Thornhope, and the headlong Knar; and seen the wild flowers, the mosses and marcantias, on the brows, and the stony channels of the oak and alder-shaded sides of Glendue and Glencoyn, near Lamley, and the choice retreats of nature about Featherstone Castle; but none of the water nymphs or elves of Northumberland has a lovelier or a more classic range of scenery to rove in than the *Chineley burn*. She collects her waters from streamlets that rise beyond the famous Roman barriers— the Dyke of Hadrian, and the wall of stone attributed to Severus." He proceeds to describe at considerable length the scenery upon Brooky burn, Kuag burn, and Bardon burn, and arriving at Mr. Hedley's newly erected house of Chesterholme, is very diffuse in its praise.

unfortunately made one great mistake.    I had by no means the distinguished honor of being an 'intimate friend' of Sir W. Scott, and was never but once at Abbotsford."*

On the 12th September in this year there died in Newcastle Dr. John Murray, a medical practitioner of great skill and a gentleman of considerable literary attainments, with whom Hodgson had been long intimately and professionally acquainted.    Dr. Murray had been for thirty-three years surgeon to the Newcastle Dispensary, and in the first report of that institution published after his death " his talents and merits in the faithful discharge of his professional duties, his numberless acts of beneficence and private charity towards the poor, and his constant endeavour to promote the essential objects of the department he so ably upheld," are duly recorded with gratitude.    Of this gentleman also Hodgson communicated a short memoir to the Gentleman's Magazine; and from Miss Pattison, who was, I believe, a niece of the deceased, he received soon afterwards the following valuable presents, which he has gratefully recorded in his Journal.

" 1833, Oct 22.—Miss Pattison gave me a MS. History of Newcastle in four large folio volumes    Geographia Antiqua.    The first volume of Jones's Index to Records in the Exchequer.    (I had the second volume.) Description of the Cathedrals of York and Canterbury, and a collection of printed music for Miss Hodgson.

" 1833, Sept. 30.—Miss Pattison gave me a copying machine; Madox's History of the Exchequer, his Firma Burgi and Baronia, also Chalmers's Caledonia, Horsley's Britannia Romana, and Kennet's Register."

* After having stated in the narrative of his paper that Mr. Hedley " was an intimate friend of the Great Talisman of Romance," Hodgson has a note as follows.    " Mr. Hedley, in one of his visits to Abbotsford, was pressed to stay some time longer than his invitation extended to; but, knowing that much company was expected on the day he should have left, he endeavoured to obtain his release, through fear of crowding the house.    " Take ye no heed of that; ye shall be comfortably lodged, and incommode nobody," was Sir Walter's reply.    After the whole of the party had retired to rest, the baronet took a lantern and conducted Mr. H. through an open court into a passage which led to a snug suite of sleeping apartments, and said ' Ye see, Maister Hedley, this is over my stables—a hundred years since I would ha' trusted never a Northumberland borderer to sleep me near my horses.' "

FROM PROFESSOR FINN MAGNUSON.*

" MY DEAR SIR, Copenhagen, 14 Sept. 1833.

" I regret very much that I not can, in correct or rather tolerable English, express my due thanks to you for your honoured letter of 25 Juny past, and your kind present of the History of Morpeth, as a very evident proof of your celebrated learning and industry. As I received the said letter and parcel was Capt. Gronbeck's vessel departed from hence; and now he is again preparing for a tour to Newcastle. What I have could do for you in procuring Danish books concerning the History of Northumberland is indeed nothing; as few or no Danish works are translated in Latin. Of Icelandic works many yet are thus published, but only few of them illustrate that matter particularly. What I have could procure of this kind I send by the present opportunity.——The said books contain particularly remarkable accounts of the Northumbrian king (or English Vice-Roi in York), Eirch or Eric Blodoxe (Bloodax, *sangui-securis*); of Snorronis Shurlæi Historia Regum Norwegiæ, vulgo Hks or Heimekringla, edita Haviniæ in 6 tomis in folio, T. 1; and Mr. Wheaton's History of the Normanns (which work I not possess). In the great work Langebeck Scriptores Rerum Danicarum medii ævi, T. 7 or 8 in folio, are perhaps some small notices on Northumberland to be found, but probably not of any important value. Saxo Grammaticus (of whose Historia Danica Bishop Müller prepares a new edition) I not need to name.

" I am so free to beg your acceptance of a trifling Latin brochure of my own, in some way illustrating the mythology and the arts of our forefathers; and of Professor Rafn's last improved edition of the Death Song of Ragnar Lodbrok, as a small token of my high esteem, and have the honour to remain, my dear Sir, your obedient and humble servant,

"FINN MAGNUSON."

TO THE REV. J. RAINE.

" MY DEAR RAINE, Whelpington, 5 Oct. 1833.

" I fear that before I can tell you you will have heard that Hartburn has been offered to me. Most heartily do I wish that your suit about Meldon was at an end before I go to the preferment which

* President of the Royal Society of Antiquaries of Copenhagen.

seems to await me; and that you and Mrs. Raine and family could come to visit us in our new residence.

"I have seen the house and find heavy dilapidations: but have no doubt that I shall soon put the whole premises into good tenantable repair. The situation is delightful.

"The Bishop has not yet written to me on the subject, but I expect will do so soon. The communication I had was through Mr. Archdeacon Thorp.——

"JOHN HODGSON."

To JOHN CAY, Esq. Advocate, Edinburgh.

"MY DEAR SIR,                              Whelpington, Oct. 31, 1833.

"Many of the papers * are very curious, and the material of an history of about 44 Northumbrian parishes has, I have no doubt, many savoury antiquarian morsels left in it, in spite of the banquets which its four-footed admirers have made off it. When I can return it to you I cannot possibly fix a time; but you may depend upon my taking every care of the whole contents of your parcel and returning it in the same form as I received it.

"Your other promised communications I shall look for with great interest. They may be addressed to me at this place, which I hardly expect to leave this winter; as there is a curate and his family in the house at Hartburn, and the parts which he does not occupy are in such indifferent repair that they will take much time to put them right. Possibly at some time you may meet with the remainder of the MS. History of Northumberland; and if so, pray let me have the use of it. I wish I was a little nearer you to assist you in sorting the masses of papers which you speak of: but hope when you meet with any on the subject of Northumberland you will lay them aside, and allow me a sight of them. Very trivial hints often lead to important discoveries: and be assured that your very kind, courteous, and interesting communications so far from . . . . me confer on me the greatest obligations. Believe me——

"JOHN HODGSON."

* The papers left behind him by Horsley, of which mention has been made above, and of which Hodgson obtained the inspection through Mr. Cay's kind instrumentality. See a subsequent letter in this year.

To the Rev. DR. ROBINSON.*

"My dear Doctor,  Whelpington, near Newcastle, Nov. 1, 1833.

"It gives me I assure you very great pleasure to receive your letter of the 28th of last month: and I am equally delighted at the opportunity of reassuming our correspondence.

"The bill you mention may be paid at any time to any agent of Messrs. Blackwell and Co., proprietors of the Newcastle Courant.

"The bookselling trade is now so much altered that I really fear that a County History commenced at present would have very little chance of paying the expenses of getting it up. If indeed you could condense all your information respecting Westmerland into a thick imperial octavo, and sell it for about 2l., I think it very probable that a very great number might be sold: but people now like to see a book before they buy it, and are shy in giving in their names as subscribers: and to begin to print such a work without subscribers would require very considerable capital to procure the information, assistance, and embellishments necessary to insure its sale. Of my own book I have, I dare say, made very little, and with the last volume been at considerable loss; but I am afraid to examine its accounts, which I have not balanced for the last two years. My copy of Burn's Westmerland shall be put into the hands of a bookbinder and forwarded for your inspection. It has many loose papers in it; and having been long used, and only in boards, it has too much of the point of beauty, and is in too frail a condition, to travel without some new covering.

"Alice de Romley is a lady with whom I have had a long acquaintance.———[A long statement respecting her, with a pedigree.]———I wish I could have answered your queries more satisfactorily than I have; but I have given them all the little attention in my power, and am——

"John Hodgson.

"The Rev. John Robinson, Clifton, Penrith."

The same Mr. T. M. Richardson, the well-known artist, who had in the year 1819 solicited the aid of Hodgson's pen in a contemplated publication on the Architectural Antiquities of Northumberland, is again anxious to publish some of his very beautiful sketches of Castles, &c. on both sides of the Border, and it ap-

* Who, as it appears, was meditating a History of Westmerland. No one could be better qualified to give information on such a subject than Hodgson.

pears from the following letter that Hodgson had again expressed his readiness to revise such descriptions of the subjects to be engraved as might be submitted to his inspection. It is much to be regretted that this second attempt was not more successful than the first. After two parts had been published it was discontinued for want of encouragement, although the subjects were well selected, and executed in a very bold and effective way. The castles represented, as plates of an imperial quarto size, are Alnwick, Carlisle, Fast Castle, Thrave Castle, Durham Castle and Cathedral, and Bothal Castle, with beautiful etchings as vignettes of the Birks Tower, the famous Arch in Durham Castle, and the Tower of Burradon. The specimens of Richardson's powers of sketching and engraving (for the large views are all of them by himself), are most striking, and his name ought to have been a sufficient guarantee for that to which so many unworthily look before they hold out a helping hand to such meritorious undertakings, *the getting something for their money.* I find in Hodgson's Journal various notices of his having duly performed his part in this undertaking.

FROM MR. T. M. RICHARDSON.

" DEAR SIR,                      Newcastle, Nov. 25, 1833.

" I feel particularly obliged by your kind offer of assistance, and gladly avail myself of it. Without such assistance we should be in very great difficulty, as Mr. Sopwith has so many engagements at present as to render it impossible for him to do it. Before receiving your note I had drawn up the manuscript I now send you, which I had determined to submit to your notice, wishing you to make any alteration you think necessary; for, as I have remarked in my address, writing is most assuredly not my profession.

" The descriptive parts of the pictures I should like to remain in substance as they are; the language to be altered in any way you may think proper. That part is from my own observation. The parts borrowed are mentioned as such. I thought of adding to the description of the Gate of Carlisle a poem inserted in the Border Antiquities, called " Carlisle Yetts." That, I think, added to what I have sent, would be long enough. To the description of Alnwick Castle must be added some history. I have sent a printed copy of Alnwick, which was for a work

I began to publish some years ago: it contains some original information about the family which was sent by Sir David Smith, Bart., and I cannot now recollect what part it is. The whole of our letterpress for each subject *must not* occupy more than two pages, the size of the printed copy sent. To the description of Fast Castle I should like the quotations to remain, if you think well of it; but I leave the whole to yourself. The description of the Birks is to have a vignette at the head of the page.——I fear the proofs will do little in giving you an idea of the work, they are so bad, having none that were printed in London.—— I beg to remain, dear Sir, your obliged servant,

"T. M. RICHARDSON."

To THE REV. J. RAINE.

"MY DEAR RAINE,                    Whelpington, 25 Nov. 1833.

"I see your 'Lytel Boke'* is published, and promise myself great gratification in reading the copy which Richard tells me you have kindly requested him to forward to me. The one which accompanies this note was left to the management of the Courant Office in adjusting the part containing the Memoirs † out of a quarto into its present size, and you will perceive that the beginning of each life should have had some alterations and additions to make them intelligible. They were first printed in an account of Morpeth; and when they escaped out of that locality should have had another 'habitation and a name' conferred upon them. Since I printed them I have got several more interesting MSS. by Horsley from Mr. Cay. One an interesting personal research into the effects of a thunderstorm near Barnard Castle, on September 19, 1729. Another 'An Essay on Cairns and Tumuli.' Besides a MS. history of 48 parochial districts in Northumberland, written by some other hand in 1733. The rats unfortunately have had a relish for the literature of the history, and have feasted rather greedily upon it. But though parts of it are thus made unintelligible, others are not so much mutilated but their lost members may by a little exercise of sagacity be readily restored.

"You will have been told that my successor in this place is the Rev.

---

* A Brief Account of Durham Cathedral, &c.
† Of Horsley, &c. from his History of Morpeth.

VOL. II.                    Y

W. Waldegrave Parke, of Addington, near Maidstone.* He is brother of Mr. Parke, rector of Elwick Hall.

" Have you any historical fragments about Alston and Garrigill? I have a bad copy of a sort of award made on the part of the Bishop of Durham, by Mag. H. de Stanbir', between the inhabitants of Gerard's Gill and Sir H. Chaplain of Aldeniston, but my abstract of it has no date, and I know not where to refer for anything about this Master H. of Stanbir'. As Alston is in the Archdeaconry of Northumberland, I must give a sort of a sketch of its history. None of your recently discovered *mining records* relate, I suppose, to that parish. It is a barren district, but you can perhaps give me something to fertilize and give a greenness to its history. I have much from the Tower respecting its ancient mines, and many hints in the Pipe Roll respecting them. One Erkenbald, at an early period, occurs as owing to the Treasury 2,154l. for the rent of them.

" 26 Nov. I have got your Durham Cathedral. It is a very pretty book, and its tale is told in such plain ungarnished words as will make it both attractive and useful. Facts are the things which a traveller wants when he visits the palaces and castles and churches of former ages ; and because he has generally little time to spare, such facts are most acceptable to him when they are briefly and simply narrated in the manner you have done. But where, my friend, is your little Table of Contents or Alphabetical Index, which would in an instant, by your own fireside, or in the evening at your inn, transport you at once into any part of the cathedral you please ? One might have been made in an hour : and if you could have found no other place for it it might have been printed on the back of the second title-page; or, which would have been better perhaps, on the second page of ' St. Cuthbert,' which might have followed p. viii. of Preface.

" We have lost our Whelpington post, after it had run, as is well known, for upwards of a century; and now I have a bag twice a week in and out by the Chevy Chase coach from the Courant Office—where you have had your work got up much better than your humble typographers in Durham could have done it.        J. H."

Mr. Hodgson's minor publications during this year, in addition to those already mentioned, were:—

* This gentleman, upon seeing the wild district in which Whelpington was situated, declined to accept the living.

On the Druidical Temple at Shap in Westmerland. *Gentleman's Magazine*, 1833.

Jan. 16. Sent a paper on the Old Red Sandstone of Melfells, &c., to Mr. Hutton, for the Natural History Society of Newcastle.

On Inscriptions on Babylonian Bricks. *Gentleman's Magazine*, Jan. 1833.

On the Phrenology of the Middle Ages, *Ib.* Feb. 1833.

On the Roman Station Vindolana, *Ib. Supp.* pt. i. 595.

May 17. Wrote to the *Newcastle Courant* about Nightingales, and also on Mr. Tindale's death, and the new road to Otterburn.

June 25. For *Newcastle Journal* an account of Mr. Sopwith's Guide to the Alston Mining District.

July 8. For *Saturday Magazine*, an Account of Our Lady's Well at Halystone, with a sketch, by desire of the Committee of General Literature and Education.

Aug. 6. To the *Antiquarian Society, Newcastle*, on the progress of researches at Housesteads, with plans, &c.

Nov. 20. To *Newcastle Courant*, on the road hence to Edinburgh.

———— Collections respecting the Monastery and Parish of Jarrow, dated 20 Nov. See *Collectanea Topographica et Genealogica*, vol. II. p. 40, in continuation of a paper on the same subject published in the same Collection, p. 66, and dated on the 8th of January preceding.

In the same publication I find by his pen, but written probably in the following year, " Charters respecting the Gospatric and other Northern families," and also " Charters respecting the Monastery of Finchale."

FROM the period of his induction to the living of Hartburn until he took up his residence in the parish, Mr. Hodgson's Journal abounds with entries of his proceedings in his endeavours to put the house into a fit state for the reception of his family. The numerous journies which he took to the place for this purpose, and the operations in which he was engaged, are all duly recorded. But there are other entries of a graver kind, illustrative of his private thoughts and devotions. He thus begins the year 1834—

1834, Jan. 1, Whelpington.—" O God Almighty! grant that this may be to myself, my family, my parishioners, and all the Christian world, the beginning of a new and more holy life than any of us have hitherto led; and that the Gospel of thy Son may spread over all heathen lands, and produce in them a rich harvest of holiness and happiness; which prayer I offer up in the name of thy dearly beloved Son Jesus Christ."

To WILLIAM DICKSON, Esq., ALNWICK.*

" DEAR SIR,                                        Hartburn, 6 Jan. 1834.

" As I wish to collate some parts of the printed edition of the Pipe Roll before I publish it, with the office copy, I will thank you to return it, directed to me here to the care of Dr. Hedley, Morpeth, who will send it to me by a person that comes hither every Friday. The volume which will contain it is all ready for publication but one leaf.

* Here is a new correspondent. Mr. Hodgson had, however, for some time been, to his great advantage, personally acquainted with Mr. Dickson, a solicitor at Alnwick of high honour and reputation, and a gentleman who has long occupied no inferior position in the school of inquiry into the History of Northumberland. He has been for some time Clerk of the Peace for the County.

I had intended to have given with it a history of the Roman and Saxon era of Northumberland, including a history of the Roman Wall, and of Mural Fortifications generally, and had prepared the whole for the press to publish as Part I. of my book; but before I had done with the printing the Pipe Roll I found the expense of obtaining the office copy, preparing it for the press, printing, &c., so very great, that I was forced to abandon my plan, and make it a volume, with some history of the Roll, and a few other unpublished records.

"I saw a pedigree of the Forsters in MS. at Mr. Raine's, ready to be printed in his North Durham, which will give you the full history of that family. The common statements are all very incorrect, especially respecting the connection of Forster the Warden of the Marches with General Forster and Lady Crewe.——Very faithfully yours,

"JOHN HODGSON."

In the autumn of the preceding year, during one of his numerous expeditions along the line of the Roman Wall, for the purposes of his History, Hodgson had observed the bones of an animal imbedded in the earth, and partly exposed to view, in a piece of broken ground, immediately above which stood a portion of the Wall. This was an object which could not fail to engage his attention, as he saw at a glance that, to whatever animal these remains had belonged, they had been deposited in the place in which they were making their appearance before the Romans had constructed their line of demarcation. He, therefore, took possession of one or more of the bones, and, upon returning home, having through a common friend consulted Dr. Knox, an eminent anatomist in Edinburgh, and having his own previously formed opinion on the subject confirmed by such high authority, he on the 17th of January in this year presented the remains of the animal to the University of Durham, along with following explanatory letter, addressed to the Warden:—

To THE VENERABLE ARCHDEACON THORP, WARDEN OF THE UNIVERSITY OF DURHAM.

"MR. ARCHDEACON,                    Whelpington, 17 Jan. 1834.

"With this I have the pleasure of sending you the remains of a skeleton which I mentioned to you in September last, and which you did me the favour to say you would be glad to accept as a present to the Museum of the University of Durham.

"The history of their discovery is briefly this. In autumn last I found it necessary for certain historical purposes to trace the line and examine the state of the Roman Wall, from Thirlwall Castle, in Northumberland, to Bowness on Solway Frith; and observed in the deep hollow lane which leads from the ford over the King to the village of Walton, that the foundations of the Wall were exposed in the brow of a high sandy scar on the north side of the road, but did not alight to examine them. On my return, however, a few days afterwards, I was induced to ascertain with care the mode of the construction of these foundations, and whether they were really a part of the Roman Wall or of some other building; and, in scrambling up the sandy bank of the lane, was surprised to find a great number of bones disposed in their natural order, and sticking out of the brow of the bank about two feet below the lowest stone of the Wall; for a very slight inspection convinced me that the masonry I had alighted to examine was true Roman work. I was particular in observing the posture of these organic remains, and the kind and appearance of the materials in which they were imbedded. The animal to which they had belonged had fallen upon its right side, and its ribs, by binding together the sand that was amongst them, had kept it from falling, and thus had formed a protuberant spot on the face of the scar; or, rather, they formed a sort of shelf in the sand, in the back part of which the vertebræ of the animal laid in a sort of arc, the outside of which inclined against the crumbling brink of the scar. Their lair had not the slightest appearance of having been artificially formed for the purpose of interring the animal of which they were the remains; but, on the contrary, the sand amongst its ribs, and above, below, and on each side of them, was so entirely without intermixture of materials differing from those of the whole face of the scar, that no one acquainted with geological appearances could for a moment hesitate to conclude that the animal to which they belonged, and the stratum of sand in which they were found, were both deposited at the same period of time; and that the whole material of the scar below the Roman Wall is a genuine geological *diluvium*. It is material to be explicit on this point. The sandbank under consideration is formed principally of the *detritus* of the red sandstone of Cumberland, and resembles those of the hills about Brampton and the Couran Hills near the Gelt. But it also contains rocky materials essentially different from any rock found *in situ* to the east of the western margin of the new red sandstone of Cumberland, and to the east between it and the German Ocean, or any way for a very great distance to the north or south of it. In fact, one piece of porphyry and another of greenstone, such as belong to the western mountains of Cumberland from Warnell Fell to Keswick, were found imbedded in this bank, close to the remains of the skeleton; and numerous other pieces were sticking out of the brow of the scar or lying amongst the fallen sand in the slope below, among which we also picked up a handsome agate and a piece of rich red jasper. The country all around Walton has blocks of granite, porphyry, greenstone, and of other primary rocks thrown over the ground, not only in any route from this place to Bowness, but to the east of it along the banks of the Irthing and the Tippal as far as Haltwhistle. Indeed the face of the country all the way from Solway Firth to the German Ocean bears indubitable proofs of having been swept over by a heavy and rapid current of water, coming in a westerly or north-westerly direction. This current, I apprehend, entered the site of our island at the great opening between the Criffell Hills and Warnell Fell, and was again confined in its progress eastward by Tindale Fell and the ridge above Bewcastle; but kept its deepest and longest course through the gorge of Glenwhelt and the valley of the Tippal into the Tyne. For on the plain of Cumberland about Bowness, Drumbugh, and Brough-upon-Sands, the walls of the fields and houses are very commonly founded on erratic blocks, brought from the west, and found gradually lesser in size and quantity as far as the eastern sea. Boulders too of the new red sandstone abound all the way up the Irthing, and as far as the banks of the Tyne, about Haltwhistle. About Horsley-on-the-Tyne rounded blocks of Cumberland porphyry abound. I have also seen large pieces of grauwacke from the same county among the diluvium exposed in digging the foundations of houses about Swinburne Place, in Newcastle; and specimens of every variety of Cumberland primary rock occur in the diluvium in the banks of the Tyne between Newcastle and the sea. In short, it may be laid down as a positive rule that between the two seas, in the directions of the Tyne and the Irthing, each succession of diluvium, whether sand or gravel hills, or clayey deposits, embedded with large erratic blocks, has been formed of materials found in strata to the west of it; while there is no instance of one piece of rock being found, even at the very short distance of a few yards, to the west of the place where it is found *in situ:* and this is, perhaps, the most conspicuously verified in the case of the whin formation that runs obliquely out of Cumberland by Glenwhelt and the

Roman Wall through Northumberland to the Farne Islands. Not a
fragment of the rock is to be found scattered over the surface of the
country, or embedded in the diluvium to the north side of its line
of bearing, while the whole country, from its western escarpment to the
sea, is strewn with its ruins. It is otherwise with the *alluvium*, or
river-borne sands and gravel. They are carried downwards in the direction of the stream that bears them, in whatever direction the course
of the stream may be. Thus rolled pieces of lime and sandstone found
*in situ* in the upper parts of the river King may be found in the gravel
in the bed and banks of that river where it is crossed by the road from
Lanercost to Walton, and in the meadows about its junction with the
Irthing; but no such rolled materials are found in the sandbanks
which contain the bones under consideration, and which, as well as I
can guess from memory, for I made no minutes respecting its height on
the spot, is at least 50 or 60 feet above the level of the King and the
nearly contiguous river the Irthing. All the loose rocky materials
found in them and on the surface of the adjacent country in every direction above the banks of these rivers, have been transported by an
ocean current from the west, and form, as I said, real and genuine
diluvium; consequently all other substances found naturally embedded
amongst them must be considered as coeval with them in respect to the
period of their being deposited in their present positions: and these are
arguments which have brought me to the conclusion that the Walton
Lane bones, which I now beg the favour of your presenting to the
Museum of Durham University, are real diluvial remains, and consequently that the animal to which they belonged perished in the waters
of the last great ocean current which swept across this part of the
island, which current, I apprehend, was the same as the Deluge of
Noah.

 " At the time of finding these remains, it was inconvenient for me to
take them up and remove them, for part of my tour had to be made on
foot; I therefore drew the outermost bone of the rack or vertebræ
from the sand, and brought it away with me, under the supposition,
both from its position and form, that it was the atlas of that part of the
animal, and the most likely of any of the remaining bones to identify it
with the genus or species, to which it belonged; for of the head or
horns, or other strongly characteristic bones, I could see no trace.
Lest, however, I should run into any absurd conjectures in this matter,
by the favour of a friend the specimen was submitted to the inspection
of Dr. Knox, and that eminent anatomist gave it as his opinion that it

was 'the *vertebra dentata*, or second cervical vertebra, of a deer or animal of the deer kind, rather larger than the usual height of our red deer;' but qualified his opinion with a wish that all the bones were sent to him, but above all the bones of the head and horns, to render his opinion unquestionable.

"To myself the locality of the remains of the skeleton seemed to confer upon them considerable curiosity and interest. The Romans had built their famous Wall over them, and their preservation made it probable that other coeval organic remains might be found in the diluvial sandhills and strata that cover the natural rock of the surrounding country. These considerations, in addition to the interest Dr. Knox took in them, induced me to request the gentleman who accompanied me in my tour at the time of their discovery to get every bone of them, and fragment of bone, carefully taken up and sent to me. This he obligingly did, taking away, as he observes, every piece he could find. They consist almost entirely of the back bone and the ribs. Of the former you will find twenty-two of the thirty-three joints of which the vertebræ of the stag genus are formed. The greater part of them are very entire; of three only the spine or part of the spine or blade of the joint remains, and of one, or perhaps two, of the neck bones only a fragment. The ribs I have not had leisure to class or examine. Only one of the shoulder blades was found, and no part of the bones of the leg, but a small portion of a canon or shank bone. These, I apprehend, had fallen out of the sandbank long ago; and no one deeming them of any curious importance they had rolled down into the roadway below their ancient tomb, and, after having for some thousand years escaped destruction by the waters of the Deluge, been ground to dust under the wheels of carriages. Fortunately some parts of the skull were rescued, and the largest of them (a part of the *os frontis*, or outer bone of the brow above the eyes, five inches across, and with part of the vitrea, or bone of the brain-cells, still attached to it), by the flatness of its outer table proves it to belong to an animal of the *cervus* tribe, and thus confirms the accuracy and sagacity of Dr. Knox's opinion.

"That the subject the remains of which have occasioned these remarks was wafted from some country to the west or north-west of the spot where they were found, with my present information on such matters, does not to me seem to admit of dispute. Where that country was, whether now sunk in the ocean, or a part of the green island of Erin, I will not conjecture; but I trust that if the fact of their discovery should become generally known it will awaken the curiosity of the

country where it was made, and lead to other and more interesting
geological discoveries.——I have the honour to be, dear Mr. Archdeacon, very truly yours,

                                    "JOHN HODGSON."

The two following letters would appear to savour too strongly
of the present period, when testimonials are almost as common as
teapots. Twenty years ago they were more rare, and therefore
the more acceptable. Now-o'-days a testimonial is almost becoming a bye-word. In how many instances are they suggested
by the would-be recipient himself, or proceed from some obse-
quious friend and flatterer, who has a private object in view.
Twenty years ago there might be in the teapot a flavour of sincerity, and in the creamjug somewhat of the milk of kindness.

TO THE REV. JOHN HODGSON.

"REV. SIR,                              Heworth, Jan. 21, 1834.

    "At a meeting of the parishioners of the chapelry of Heworth,
when your letter was read communicating to the chapelwardens your
resignation of the living of Jarrow-with-Heworth, it was immediately
resolved to enter into a subscription for the purchasing a piece of
plate to present to you, as a token of their esteem and respect for your
long and valuable services. Your friends in Jarrow having joined us
in this testimony, we have now the pleasure to forward you a silver tea
service, and, in our official capacity, to convey to you the deep sense of
the many obligations we lay under for your great public services; and,
however we may regret the separation that has taken place, we rejoice
in your temporal advancement, and sincerely hope that those Christian
virtues that have rendered you so amiable and respectable here may be
duly appreciated by your future parishioners. Wishing you health,
happiness, and prosperity, with long life to enjoy the humble tribute of
our respect, we are, Rev. Sir, your obedient humble servants,

                    "M. NESBIT,  }
                     T. MURRAY,  } Chapelwardens for Heworth."

TO MESSRS. NESBITT AND MURRAY, CHAPELWARDENS OF HEWORTH.

"GENTLEMEN,                          Whelpington, 22 January, 1834.

    "I have this morning received your letter, and with it the
service of plate which the parishioners of Jarrow and Heworth have

been pleased to confer upon me, and which I accept as a very gratifying token of their approbation of my services during the period of my incumbency. I believe that I expressed to you at the time I resigned the living that I did so with mingled sensations of pleasure and regret; for I felt delighted with the prospect that the spiritual welfare of the parish would be essentially promoted by my giving up a charge in which I had for some years past been unable to take any active and efficient part; but I also felt regret that a long and amicable connection of upwards of a quarter of a century was thus rather suddenly severed.

"I beg, gentlemen, the favour of your presenting my best thanks to the parishioners of Jarrow and Heworth for the valuable testimony of esteem and regard with which they have honoured me; and of your assuring them that I shall always entertain the greatest friendship and respect for them, and ever feel a deep and affectionate anxiety for all their best interests, both spiritual and temporal.

"I also beg the favour of your accepting my very sincere acknowledgments of the obligation I feel to yourselves for the friendly trouble you have taken in this affair, and that you will believe me very truly and respectfully yours,

" JOHN HODGSON."

Hodgson's next letter is upon a painful subject. Let it be enough to say here that it refers to the death of our common friend Mr. Surtees, which took place on the 11th of February preceding.

To THE REV. JAMES RAINE.

"MY DEAR RAINE,            Whelpington, 17 Feb. 1834.

"An honourable and a great spirit has fled from amongst us. I have for the last two years, from week to week, been promising myself the pleasure of spending a few days at Mainsforth; and it was certainly neither indolence nor selfishness, but a much harder master than both, which kept me a prisoner here, and from the ever joyous and delightful society of Surtees. I wish I could have written some tribute to his memory, but my feeble spirit is unable to encounter so great a task. When I received your brief announcement of his death I was laid up of a cold at Capheaton; and Captain Blackett, who was there, Mr. Edward Swinburne, and myself, were all equally astounded at the news. They all soon afterwards left me to myself, and went to walk; and in the first moment of my loneliness the following lines started from me; to further exertion on the subject I was unable to bear—

> Spirit of glory! through the beams of day
> Heav'n-ward * I see thee speeding on thy way,
> Chasing the setting sun's unstayed career,
> And riding on his rays, unknown to fear;
> ' Thy chariot and thy horses both of fire,'
> From earth with speed of rapid light retire;
> Now on the solar disc effulgence shed,
> And bear thee to the mansions of the mighty dead.

"I needed not to have sent you a few dull lines to prove to you that my estimation and regard for Surtees were exceedingly high, but they have fallen from my pen; and the only request I have to make of you respecting them is, that you will shew them to nobody. Now, when I think of it, pray tell me how far he has advanced in printing another volume. If it would pay you for doing so, you should go on with the work.

"Your brother John mentioned to me a work on Sabaism, or Palestine, or some other interesting subject, lately published, and of which he thought he could procure me the loan for a few days. Pray tell him this, and how much I should be gratified by his writing to me.

"Have you made any inquiries about lodgings and a tutor for my son, who is now fast recovering?† I think I mentioned to you that he is a sprightly and a spirited boy, but with a mind unable to bear any cold or harsh treatment; and, as I fear he is backward in his learning, it is of great moment that he get the assistance of some clever and gentle spirit as a tutor, to help him forward in his school exercises, and to get his whole attention to bear for a while on that point, for he has got too much into the habit, and indeed delight, of reading whatever entertaining works in the form of romance or history fall in his way. You will oblige me by writing soon on this subject, and saying whether you would advise him or not to enter at the school before Easter, or the week after Easter, which indeed will be as soon, I dare say, as he will be able to move from home. I should hope that one of the students at the University might be prevailed upon to become his tutor.——

"JOHN HODGSON."

* " Onward " in a later copy.

† William, his youngest son, then in his thirteenth year. The boy had been chiefly educated at home, but he had been for awhile at school at Gifford, with Mr. Mackay, and afterwards at Morpeth under Mr. Rapier. The youth came to Durham, but he soon was laid in his grave.

When he was upon the point of quitting Whelpington for his new preferment, it was officially announced to Mr. Hodgson that he had been elected an honorary member of the Royal Society of Northern Antiquaries of Copenhagen. For this mark of distinction he was doubtless indebted to his correspondent Dr. Finn Magnussen.

"1834. March 16, Sunday, Whelpington. — Blessed Sunday.— On which I intend, God willing, to preach from the second lesson, ' Except a man be born of water and the Spirit he cannot enter into the kingdom of heaven.' O! that I may feel increase of grace in my soul above the measure of affliction and worldly trouble which is poured into it."— (*Journal.*)

Hodgson's farewell sermon at Whelpington was preached on the 23rd of March, 1834, from Phil. iv. 7, and on the 28th (Good Friday) he began to officiate at Hartburn, and along with his family took up his final residence there on the 5th of April following.*

"1834. 28 March.—I preached at Hartburn, ' I came down from Heaven not to do mine own will, but the will of Him that sent me.' The congregation consisted only of ten persons, besides the clerk and myself. In the parish of Whelpington I saw no persons at work; the congregation was good, and the communicants about twenty-five or twenty-six. In my way to Hartburn I saw about Cambo, and all the way to church, persons following their ordinary employment; and, as the clerk had omitted to tell Mr. Chesters that the Sacrament of the Lord's Supper was usually administered as on this day, there was no Communion. At Cambo I saw one man killing a pig, and the blacksmith's shop was open. Jesus Christ, thy blood was shed and thy hands and feet wounded with great nails as on this day !"—(*Journal.*)

* One of Hodgson's last visits before his departure from Whelpington was paid to an aged man in humble life, who had been a friend of his father, and who having migrated in early life into Northumberland, and having sojourned for a while at Whitfield, had found his way to Little Harle Newhouses in his parish:

"1834. 4 April.—Called on William White, an aged and venerable man, in declining health, at Little Harle Newhouses. He was a friend of my father, and is now, I think he said, 94 years old."—(*Journal.*)

A few words must now be devoted to a brief account of the parish of Hartburn, of which Mr. Hodgson had become the vicar in the preceding year, and in which he now comes to reside.

In point of surface the parish of Hartburn extends over a tract of about 60,000 acres, and is divided into not fewer than twenty-seven townships, many of them at a great distance from the parish church, and some of them extending far to the north-west, over much high and wild moor land, in the direction of Elsdon and Rothbury. Like that of Kirkwhelpington, its population, amounting in 1831 to 1,440, consists almost entirely of families employed in agriculture. Its three pure streams, the Wansbeck, the Hart, and the Font, are not defiled by machinery of any kind: nor is coal mining carried on to any extent within its limits. In the character of its surface, also, it resembles that of Whelpington; especially in its higher parts. In the lower portions of the parish the soil is of a richer kind; and the scenery, especially upon the banks of its streams, of which more will be said here-after, infinitely superior to any natural beauties at Whelpington, and, indeed, in this respect it is superior perhaps to any other locality in the whole county of Northumberland.

By an arrangement, far from unusual in the north of England, the church of Hartburn is placed nearly at the extreme eastern verge of the parish, in a low warm spot, far away from the winds and storms which sweep over the high ground of the district in the months of winter and till the end of April. That its founder was influenced " dulcedine loci," and was a man of taste, may be inferred from the choice which he has made of a site in every respect so remarkable; the inconveniences of which, in a spiritual point of view, would soon cease to be felt, in consequence of the numerous chapels which became by degrees scattered over the upper parts of the parish at an early period.

The church and vicarage house of Hartburn, in point of situation in a scene of picturesque beauty, have only two rivals in the whole diocese of Durham, and these are, Mitford, a few miles lower down, in the same vale of the Wansbeck, and Winston on the Tees, both, like Hartburn, in the patronage of the see of Durham. The church and parsonage-house at Winston stand boldly upon a lofty brow, overhanging the river and its streams,

and looking over a rich tract of country, with the well-wooded
valley of the Tees in the foreground; the sprightly village of
Gainford, in its lowly nest by the river, and the spires of Coniscliffe
and Darlington on the east; the bowers of Wycliffe, the birth-
place of the Reformer, and Rokeby, the theme of poets, with
Barnard Castle, the cradle of kings, on the west, and the proud
towers of Raby on the north; and, moreover, the fine old timber
by which the parsonage-house is surrounded grows upon the
glebe land, and is in consequence safe from the scrieve of the
woodman. Mitford, again, is of a different character, but extremely beautiful in its situation—low, warm, and quiet, and out
of the world, as it were, and yet possessing all the advantages of
a moderately but not densely peopled neighbourhood. Here
meet the two bright streams of the Wansbeck and Font, which at
their junction, and far above it and below, are most remarkable
for their beauty. In front of the house and church, the latter of
an Early-Norman date, with a spacious chancel of Early-English,
and grey with lichens and moss, stands the massive old weather
and Scotch beaten castle of Mitford, an extensive ruin of the
Norman period of architecture, which, from having been very
frequently a bone of contention between the two kingdoms, has
perhaps a greater abundance of historical associations connected
with its name than almost any other fortress in Northumberland.*
But here, it is not so at Hartburn, the vicar is poor indeed.
His endowment consists merely of a money payment, fixed so long
ago as the year 1307, when it was a fit compensation for what it
purported to be rendered as an equivalent, but now utterly
unsuited to the wants and prices of the day. He has no acres
of glebe to look upon from his window, and, consequently,
no stately tree which he can call his own. Hard-hearted, however, will he be who shall ever suffer a woodman's axe to rob
this fair scene of its charms. At present, happily, there is no
ground for fear. The family of Mitford is deeply sensible of the
beauties by which it is surrounded.

But if the glebe house of Mitford has a junction of two streams
at its door, so has Hartburn. The latter stands upon a tongue of
of land, surrounded by high ground, in just the situation to have

* See above, p. 257.

been pitched upon by our church or abbey-building ancestors; a castle might have stood here in perfect security, but a church had taken possession of the site before the castle-building period of our history.    Immediately behind the church and vicarage-house there runs, at the foot of a steep precipice, over masses of rock which have been falling from the crag for ages, the sparkling rivulet of the Hart, alive with trout, and reflecting in its pools the wing of the king-fisher and water-ousel.    In front there is a hollow and well-planted dene, of great depth, through which runs a lively little brook, capable of making a considerable noise in wet seasons.    Still further to the south, at the distance of a few fields, there flows gently, through meadows and pastures far-famed for their rich-ness, the Wansbeck, with which Hodgson had held daily inter-course at the foot of his garden at Whelpington for the ten preceding years of his life; and now he had, as it were, descended with its stream to a new habitation, in which it was again to be his companion.    With the Wansbeck, of which I am writing, about a mile below Hartburn, the Hart unites its waters within the park wall of Meldon, after flowing from the church down-wards through a deep channel over a rocky bed, richly fringed with native timber, among which the yew and holly are conspicuous. But the chief beauty of the Hart must be sought for from the church upwards, where, for about a mile, it closely imitates, upon a somewhat reduced scale, the character of the far-famed Greta at its junction with the Tees at Rokeby.    And here the Vicar of Hartburn walks in his own glades, under the shadow of his own rocks and stately trees, " the monarch of all he surveys " on the southern bank of the stream.    Never was there a fairer or more favourable spot for meditation, for botanical research,—the wood abounding with curious plants—or for the amusement of angling, a pursuit to which Hodgson had been so passionately devoted in his youth.

Mr. Hodgson had written and printed his description of the Hartburn Wood before he became its owner;* and therefore he cannot be accused of having painted its beauties in partial colours or with a pencil prejudiced in its favour.    " The glebe lands," says he, " contain about 100 acres, and have their northern boundary

* See Part II. vol. i. p. 301.

along the bank of the Hart, hemmed with a thick and thriving wood, which owes much of its beauty and variety to the care and bounty of Dr. Sharp,* who also formed a walk along it, and cut a grotto of two rooms in the rock, and made a covered way from it to the river for the convenience of bathing. This in Roman days would have been " antrum Pani Nymphisque sacrum." Here the trees of the larch and pine genus have risen to a giant size; the jetties of grey crag are fringed with fern, wild grasses, and shrubs, and the river's ever-varying and everlasting song " imposes silence with a stilly sound."

The Hartburn woods are well known in the southern district of Northumberland, and are much frequented by parties of pleasure, able to appreciate their charms. Happily they are not within the reach of cheap trips by land or water, or their high repute might occasionally render them a nuisance to their owner, to say nothing of the sad Sunday desecrations which he might be compelled to witness. It would be no easy task to describe the proceedings of a mob vomited forth from a Shields steamboat on a Sunday morning, in the glades of the Coquet near Warkworth and its Hermitage, or on the sacred ground of Farne or Holy Island.

A few words of the character of the timber upon the glebe at Hartburn, and the size to which some of it has attained.

* Dr. Sharp, who was also Archdeacon of Northumberland, Prebendary of Durham, and Perpetual Curate of Bamborough, was a considerable benefactor to his successors in the vicarage of Hartburn. He not only planted the banks of the Hart with the timber, which after the lapse of a century has some of it reached so remarkable a size, but he built much to the glebe house, especially two very large rooms, a dining and drawing-room, in which it was his delight to entertain his neighbours with musical performances, with the assistance of the Durham choir, many of whom he invited to visit him at stated periods. He himself was a musical performer of considerable attainments. His favourite instrument was the violincello; and in the ecstacy of enjoyment he would throw off his coat, and fiddle among baronets and squires, and their lady wives and daughters, in his shirt sleeves, till, as my informant, a singing man, who had often been present on such occasions, once told me, he was black in the face.—Dr. Sharp lived in a period of high punctilio and form. Upon one occasion at Bamborough, when he was about to preach, the beadle's staff was reported to be missing. The doctor, however, could not preach without the usual stately ceremonial of a dual procession, and he had recourse to an impromptu and ingenious device to meet the difficulty. He made the sexton shoulder the vestry poker, and march before him in state to the door of the pulpit.

Mr. Hodgson had not been long settled in his new preferment before he was requested by Mr. Loudon to furnish him with the measurements of some of his principal trees for the " Arboretum Britannicum;" and here are the notes made in his Journal upon which his reply to this request was founded, together with the reply itself, which furnishes some curious particulars of other trees, communicated at the same time, but not noticed by Mr. Loudon in his book.[*]

"1835, June 15.   Measured the following trees in the vicarage wood.

"POPULUS ALBA.—The white poplar.   Girth, at a foot from the ground, 8 ft. 4½ in. ; height 82 ft.

"PINUS LARIX.—The larch.   Of these only two large ones in the wood; the larger of which is of the following dimensions: girth 12 ft. height 89 ft.; spread of its branches from side to side 47 ft.; without branches for about 50 ft.   On good soil.   Situation sheltered and shaded by a sloping bank, covered with forest trees to the south-west.

"PINUS PICEA.—Silver Fir.   Of these two large ones remain, with a clear space between them of 11 ft. 9 in.   Formerly there were two more of the same in a quadrangular clump, and about 9 ft. from each of the two remaining, and 12 ft. from each other.   One of them at a foot from the ground is 11 ft. 9 in. in girth, 98 ft. high, and spreads over a diameter of 40 ft.   The other is about 96 ft. high, and 10 ft. 4 in. in girth.   Both of them are bare of branches for 50 ft., or more, on the side on which the two grew that were felled.   Near them are four thriving plants of different growth, which have apparently sprung up naturally.   Both the large ones are forked at about 50 feet from the ground.

"QUERCUS ROBUR.—The oak.   Girth 10 ft. at a foot from the ground; height 74 ft.; spread in diameter 59 ft. 8 in.   Situation sheltered from the west and south-west, and on a strong clayey soil.

"June 20.—Other trees for Mr. Loudon.—THUJA.—One 3 ft. girth; 32 ft. high; 17 ft. spread.   Another 2 ft. 11 in. girth; 35 ft. high; 14 ft. spread.

---

[*] Mr. Loudon notices only the silver firs and the oak.   One of the former he represents to be 138 feet high.   This is probably a misprint, as it contradicts the account in the Journal.   There is another evident mistake in his book.   Hodgson's "Two Queens," he prints " Nod Queens."   The oak is noticed in his vol. iii. p. 1840, and the firs vol. iv. p. 2338.

" TAXUS.—Yew. Girth 6 ft. 5 in. Trifid at 2 ft. 5 in. from ground,
and one branch 3 ft. 9 in., the other 3 ft. 5 in., and the third 2 ft. 10 in.;
the three together 6 ft. 1 in. Height 38 ft.; spread 39 ft.

" SPANISH CHESTNUT.—Girth 7 ft. 8 in.; spread 40 ft.; height 46 ft.

" ASH, on west side of churchyard. Girth 17 ft. 4 in.; height about
60 ft.; spread 80 ft.

" June 22.—Finished the account of trees in the wood here for Mr.
Loudon, and sent him (to be returned) a copy of the foolish poems I
wrote at Lanchester, as he requested."

### To MR. LOUDON.*

" SIR,                                                    June 1835.

" I have great pleasure in endeavouring to give you the most
correct information in my power on the subjects of your inquiries.
The ' Return Paper ' I have filled up with dimensions, &c. which have
been very carefully taken.

" The vicarage wood here was planted, according to the best information I can obtain, by Dr. Sharp, grandson of Archbishop Sharp, a
few years after he became incumbent of Hartburn, in 1749. It is
situated on the right bank of the Hart, which forms a principal branch
of the Wansbeck, and as it passes through the wood runs for the
greatest part of the way in a south-east direction. All the trees of
which I have given you the dimensions are sheltered by high banks,
which slope gradually down to the river, and grow, as I would guess,
at somewhat less than 380 feet above the level of the sea.

" 1. There are several white poplars in the hedges in the vicarage
farm, but none of them to be compared in size or beauty to the one
of which I have given you the dimensions; which for      feet above the
ground is without branches, and has a smooth neutral tinted bark of a
greenish cast, and in outward appearance gives the promise of cutting
up into clean planks; the trunk, to near the head, from the commencement of the branches, is quite straight and clean barked as below.

" 2. The soil upon which the oak grows seems to be a good loam at
the surface, but the substratum is moist; and a little below it there is
an outburst of water, which has rendered the ground a little swampy.
Its early growth has been much favoured by the ground to the south-
west rising rather abruptly, and sheltering it from the strongest prevailing winds.

* From the rough draft.

z 2

"3. Thuja. I found one of the three of these trees, and which was the largest, quite dead when I came here last year, and apparently from the branches of an oak tree overshadowing it. Out of its trunk I have had four panel-bottomed and backed chairs constructed, and which, though substantially built, are very remarkably light.

"4. The silver firs are here, for their superior height to the trees around them, called 'The Two Queens.' Five seedlings of different growths have sprung up near them, and are thriving well. The distance between them is only eleven feet nine inches. About . . . years since there were four of them in the same clump; two of which were cut down and sold to the Plessy Colliery. Both of the two remaining ones are without branches for 50 feet upwards, on the side on which the two grew that were felled. Both of them are forked, or divide into two heads at between 40 and 50 feet in height, and this is the general character—(I mean that of being forked or dividing into two or more grains)—of all the silver firs I have seen. They thrive well in the woods about Inverary Castle.

"5. The larch is very straight, and for want of room has not thrown out branches till it has outstript in height the trees around it. This tree, wherever it is planted in soils and situations suited to its vigorous growth, and is not stinted for room, throws out mighty branches horizontally to the ground. One in the lawn of the vicarage house of Stamfordham has had its top, at about a middle period of its growth, blown off, and consequently not attained a great height—as well as I could guess from memory not above 50 feet: but its arms are like trees, and in its whole appearance it resembles much the drawings I have seen of foreign specimens of the cedar-larch, or cedar of Lebanon. All that Pliny, all that Dr. Anderson, all that all writers say of its beauty, durability, and excellence, is not half enough."

I must not omit to add that there runs through the parish of Hartburn another charming rivulet, with its attendant rocks and woods, the Font; which, as has been stated above, joins the Wansbeck at Mitford, and helps to give a name to that place of old renown and well-known beauty.

The parish church of Hartburn, the mother of so many daughters, is large and stately. It is of the Early-English period, retaining no trace of the earlier fabric by which it must have been preceded. Its spacious chancel, the work doubtless of the monks of St. Alban's, gives no indication of want of taste or liberality in its builders. The lancets of this part of the fabric are of a good character, especially those in the eastern wall. In the body of the church, the sash windows, which had been thrust into the openings nearly a century ago, after the fashion of Northumberland, were during Hodgson's incumbency removed. Better would it have been if they had been suffered to remain, until there was a feeling in the parish to supply their place with something in a better style than the unfortunate attempts at architecture by which they have been succeeded. The tower is remarkably good in its proportions and execution; and its base mouldings, which Hodgson laid bare and made visible, as they ought to be, are correct and elegant. On the western face of this tower there is an instance of a large window having its tracery carved in one stone. There are other examples of this kind in the county. The window here is an insertion at a later period, and its tracery is of the Perpendicular character.

Here again is a parish despoiled of its rights. The monastery of St. Alban's had at an early period become possessed of the advowson; but they did not long content themselves with the unprofitable privilege of merely presenting an incumbent.

About the year 1250 they obtained to themselves and their successors an appropriation of the principal part of the tithes arising in the parish; and, in consequence, at the Dissolution of Monasteries there came into the vale a lay impropriator, with a grant from the crown in his hand, to take possession of what had been originally dedicated by the founder of the church, in the most solemn way, to Almighty God for ever. He contemplated in his day of devotion the sacrilegious intrusion of neither monk nor layman. We know from history that the one did not thrive upon his ill-gotten goods; and neither, in many most striking instances, has the other. Sir Henry Spelman's History of Sacrilege is, in its *facts*, one of the most striking books with which the reader of history can possibly become acquainted, and daily additions might be made to its pages. Attempts have been made from time to time by zealous churchmen to recover such property for the purposes to which it was dedicated, under imprecations which it is awful to read, upon those who should in after times pervert it to secular or profane uses; but efforts of this kind will probably never be successful until the church itself, I mean the clerical holders of impropriations, shall set the example.

It must not be denied that the monks of St. Alban's did much towards the due performance of divine service in the parish of Hartburn, in co-operating to carry the ministrations of religion to the very homes and doors of its widely-scattered population. Well had it been if the example had been followed by those by whom they were succeeded under the fiat of spoliation. The endowment of the vicar could not of course be touched by any act of the crown; but not so, as it appears, the stipends of the chaplains who were at that time officiating in the outposts of the parish. The chapels within the parish of Hartburn were not fewer than eight in number, Netherwitton, Nunnykirk, Temple Thornton, Middleton, Shafto, Cambo, Hartington,* and Green-leighton. In all these places, duly set apart for God's service, with the exception of Netherwitton, the voice of religion ceased to be heard almost immediately after the Dissolution, and from that time till our own days the parish church, and the above excepted chapel, were the only places of divine worship in the parish in conformity with our established religion. In presenting Mr. Hodgson to the benefice, arrangements were made by the patron that the chapel of Netherwitton should become a separate benefice with an endowment of its own. In 1842 the chapel of Cambo was rebuilt by Hodgson's exertions upon a somewhat different site, and duly severed, and endowed chiefly out of the income of the vicarage; and thus there are now three officiating clergymen in the parish. At one time there were not fewer than nine, perhaps more, as there were chantries in the mother church. And yet this is the period in our history to which we are apt to look back with an eye of pity, and praise ourselves for our superior intelligence and liberality, and congratulate ourselves upon our freedom from error, and from the pernicious influences of superstition or a mistaken creed. But, if error was taught in those days, there was a well-meant earnestness in its dissemination, which we surely

---

* From a note in his Journal of the 7th June, 1841, Hodgson appears to have satisfied himself that to the chapel of Hartington there were attached not fewer than 70 acres of land, which, if such was the case, are now lost for ever to the purposes for which they were appropriated.

should run no risk in imitating, with the full light of sacred truth before us, and every obligation, sacred and secular, to urge us to the performance of so holy a work.

In his various removals from place to place after his first settlement in the county of Durham in the year 1800, Hodgson had been fortunate in finding in each new habitation in its turn subjects for antiquarian investigation. Next to the due and conscientious discharge of his ministerial functions, and his duties as the father of a family, in this pursuit he had taken, as we have seen, from his youth upwards, an infinite delight. Here at Hartburn he found, as at Whelpington, upon the hills and eminences in his parish, the camps and entrenchments of a people who had flourished long, probably, before the period of Roman sway in the north of the island; and at Angerton there was discovered in 1842 the grave of a British lady of rank, of which he has left a full account in his Journal, to be noticed hereafter. "At the head of the vicarage wood the ground is bounded by an old, hollow, thorny lane used as a bridle-way: it is part of the Roman road called the Devil's Causeway, and at this place is known by the name of Harpeth as it passes the Hart."* Thus did he write in 1827, before the commencement of his incumbency at Hartburn. After that event had taken place, he investigated more minutely the passage of this road across the stream; and was delighted to find in the rock, over which the water flows, distinct traces of the bridge which had afforded a pathway for the traveller.

"1834, Aug. 18.—I have ascertained to a certainty that the Watling Street, a famous Roman Road, went down the hollow way into the wood, and crossed the Hart just below the grotto by a bridge of timber, a double row of square holes still remaining in the bed of the Hart for fixing it in, thus." (*A sketch is here inserted.*)

On the summit of the hill which faces the little inn at Meldon Park corner, he discovered the lines of a Roman summer camp; so levelled however by the plough as to afford no certain proof of its extent. These traces are now still more flattened by the sock and coulter, and in truth are scarcely visible. In addition to these matters of antiquarian interest, the peelhouses and decayed

* Hist., Pt. II., vol. i. 1827.

chapels in his parish afforded him further subjects for inquiry.
In his own vicarage-house there was an old place of strength of
the former character, which he repaired, and, by means of door-
ways which he opened in its massive and well-grouted walls,
made useful for domestic purposes.  An upper room of this
building he converted during his last and long illness into a temporary study, which served also for a bed-room; and here he
died.

Before Hodgson could take up his residence at Hartburn the
repairs of his future place of residence occupied much of his care
and thought.  The fabric was, as has been stated, in an almost
uninhabitable condition.  The farmhouse and its out-buildings
were also in a bad state; and to these he was compelled to direct
his immediate attention.  The garden wall, by the side of which
runs the public road, was nearly level with the ground, and the
garden itself was squalid and overrun with weeds.  Fences to the
wood in many places there were none; and, in short, he found
everything in such a condition as to cause him much anxiety, and
call repeatedly for his superintendence before his final departure
from Whelpington.  The dilapidations had been duly valued,
and he repaired and restored in hope of receiving the sum agreed
upon by arbitration, but, to his most serious inconvenience and
sorrow, when the time for payment arrived he was informed that
no effects could be found.  To add to his distresses he had been
called upon for dilapidations at Whelpington, notwithstanding
the money he had laid out there upon the vicarage house and its
premises.

From this period Hodgson began to be oppressed with pecuniary difficulties, and no long time had passed over his head in
his new preferment before he began to regret bitterly that by the
acceptance of the living he had put himself into so painful a situation.  The income of the benefice was, it is true, considerably
above that of Whelpington, but one expense had fallen upon his
shoulders after another, and he saw no reasonable prospect of being
able for a length of time to extricate himself from their accumulated pressure.

It is pleasing to see from his Journal how Hodgson began to
occupy his time in his new residence.  His History and his wood,

next to his parochial duties, afforded him comfort under the painful circumstances in which he was placed. He had been called to a holy work, and he performed it in Christian earnest. If trials were thrown in his way, he possessed a mind capable of valuing them at their true worth, and of patiently comprehending their object. With the great works in which he was engaged in his thoughts, and the handiwork of nature around him, he could see flowers in his way, as well as thorns; and could thankfully gather them and refresh himself with their fragrance.

"1834.—6 Ap.—HARTBURN.—Sunday.—A most charming morning, but the ground white before sun-rise with hoar frost. Daws and rooks in abundance about the tower of the church, in the rocky scar of the garden, and the great trees about it. Starlings, blackbirds, and thrushes, in great numbers.

"8 Ap.—Mr. Spencer Trevelyan showed me two spikes of flowers which he plucked near the bottom of the vicarage wood to-day, and which I took to be a species of orobranche. The flower was of a pale blush colour, with small pink spots, the spike not more than three or four inches long. It grows on sycamore roots. The weather has been for near a month dry and cold, and, though the wood wind-flower and prim-rose are abundant, the spring has made no advance. Neither Smith nor Hooker notices any orobranche that flowers before July. Sent speci-mens of it to Richard (*his son*), and Mr. Hutton.—14th Ap. The orobranche in the wood is much injured this morning by the frost, which was a white hoar on the grass and thin ice on the water. The orobranche is turned black, as far as it has risen above the dry leaves, below them uninjured. Mr. Robertson, in a note to Richard, says the plant which I took for an orobranche is luthæa squamaria, a plant of the natural order Orobranchæ, and a very singular order it is."

On the 18th of April, 1834, Mr. Hodgson obeyed the sum-mons of the writer of this Memoir, and attended a meeting at Durham for the purpose of founding a society in honour of his late friend Mr. Surtees of Mainsforth, whose death had caused him so much grief and affliction. At first he did not augur well of the continuance or utility of any such society, but before his death he saw cause to alter his opinion, having derived much ·benefit from its publications. This was the first institution of the kind established in England, and its success was such that its plan was imitated, and its rules in general more or less adopted by numerous other bodies of men who associated themselves together for literary purposes. A bare enumeration of the publishing societies which were soon afterwards established in imitation of that founded in honour of Mr. Surtees's memory, and in accordance to its plans, would occupy more of space than can be devoted to it. The Surtees Society was the mother of them all, and she has long outlived many of her daughters, who seem to have fallen away, some from mismanagement and others from want of the fostering hand of public patronage. Among the latest letters which Hodgson wrote was one to Mr. Petheram, the bookseller (4 Dec. 1843), in which he takes care to praise the Surtees Society, and speaks of its having led the van and set the example to so many others.

Before his departure from Durham on that day he was tempted to be present at a scene to which he had long been a stranger. When he was a child, the blows he received from having trod upon a duck prevented him from being present at the races upon Knipe Scar. Here he has no swelled face to prevent him from refreshing his memory with such a scene, but his conscience would not permit him to enjoy the sight.*

Soon after the establishment of the Surtees Society Hodgson communicated to the Newcastle Courant the following account of it, and of the objects which it had in view, giving at the same time a sketch of the character of Mr. Surtees himself, and a few remarks upon the suitableness of such an institution in honour of the name and memory of his friend. His picture is highly drawn, and his colours perhaps too vivid, but it is essentially correct.

"That an intellectual monument should be reared in memory of the mind of Surtees is a subject of just exultation: for that mind was of vast dimensions, and contained machinery which has executed work of ex-

* "1834, April 18.—At meeting at Durham for founding the Surtees Society.— Before we came from Durham Mr. Brockett wished to see one heat at Durham races, and I accompanied him, Adamson, and Allan to the ground, but did not find myself comfortable in mixing with the crowd and contemplating it in its present state of mind, and as a multitude of immortal beings."—(Journal.)

quisite beauty and lasting material. It was highly poetical; bright with wit as the light of morning; benevolent as spring; full of veneration for everything that was good, and especially for God; daring and determined, and hence a fearless advocate of truth and justice, and of large improvements in our civil and religious institutions. His great work, in its plan, unfolds the boldness of his conception; in the extent to which he carried it, his perseverance in purpose; in the great sums he expended in publishing it, his disinterestedness, and the abundance of his affection for his native county. It abounds with vigorous writing, abhorrence of tyranny, admiration of high-minded principles, clear insight into and forcible delineation of character; proofs of extensive reading, and a highly-stored memory. It has in it a playfulness and joy in wit and language that never frown nor tire; and, though a lynx-eyed critic may discover in its pages the carelessness of genius in accurate attention to detail, yet it abounds with imagery as finely drawn and sweetly touched as ever glowed on poet's page or painter's canvas. His character was all original—owed nothing to timid imitation: but drew all its traits out of an endless ingenuity of imagination; that had a treasure-house of thought to work in, in which nothing but the most humane and charitable, natural and straight-forward and honest principles, were deposited. The destitute deplore his loss, for his sympathy was no less lively with the afflicted than his joy was overflowing with the happy. Of antiquity he was an empassioned adorer, but no idolater. His views into ancient times were all intellectual: his mind could not bow down to customs and institutions and things whose only claim to attention was that they were old; but he loved to martial nations and and families, and individuals of past ages, in array before him, and weep or rejoice over them, according to their several conditions and capabilities of happiness or misery. And great minds have rejoiced in similar retrospects into the history of man. When Cicero began to think about antiquity his mind was presented with a vision, increasing in splendour from his own to the time of the creation, and over that period he saw beings of immortal essence and ineffable beatitude moving in light more glorious than his bodily eyes had ever seen. ' Antiquity,' he exclaims, ' approaches very nigh to the Gods.' He saw through a sun-glance, over the troubled sea of civilised life, into the calm and balmy days of the golden and patriarchal ages, and beyond them was blessed with a view of beings supreme in intellectual power, and living in air and light that preserved them in perpetual youth. Antiquity is

the temple in which all the ideas of our mortal veneration are en-
shrined, and in which we bow down in adoration to the great Architect
of the Universe; for it is in this temple that the Jew and the Christian
have laid up the sacred books of their religions, and beside them
deposited for the use of posterity the commentaries and expositions
that learned men, from time to time, have written upon these sacred
oracles.  Here too are kept all that the philosopher has unfolded of the
laws of nature, all that the historian has recorded of the mighty, and
the wise, and the good, that have lived and done their part well upon
earth; and before the altar of this temple it is that the philosopher and
the scholar still constantly stand feeding and increasing the flame of
knowledge, which has often been dim, but never extinguished, from the
day on which the mind of man first began to throw its light upon the
earth, to the bright noon of intellectual day in which we now live.

"The Catalogue of the Surtees Society enumerates his Grace the
Duke of Buccleuch and Queensberry as its president, a list of fifteen
eminent literary characters in different parts of the kingdom as its other
officers, and considerably upwards of an hundred more of ordinary members, distinguished as promoters and patrons of ancient English literature, or as friends and admirers of the lamented individual to whose
memory their labours are intended to be a monument."

But another grievous trial arrives.  A fourth child, a beloved
daughter, who had reached her seventeenth year, and had come
home from school unwell, is summoned to her grave.  A fifth,
his eldest daughter, sickens, but her father's prayers for her recovery are mercifully heard.  She is still alive,— a mother and a
widow.

"1834, 2 May.  On my return home from visiting the parish, I
found Susannah up, but beginning to grow comatose.  Sent for Mr.
Saunders and Dr. Hedley, but all their joint exertions and skill were
not permitted to save her, for she expired about half-past six on the 3d.

"O God! we beseech Thee to calm our afflictions, and make us resigned to this most heavy visitation.  In the midst of life we are in
death; of whom may we look for succour but of Thee, O God!

"I feel a sort of melancholy satisfaction in having committed (what I
had often thought) a good deal of extravagance in having a very accurate likeness of my dear departed daughter taken last year by my friend

Nicholson of Edinburgh. It is now all that is left of mortal semblance
of one that so lately was the loveliest and the sweetest among many.
I shall gaze upon it with grief tempered with pleasure; and her mortal
remains shall go to the graveyard of Whelpington, to lie side by side
with the ashes of her once beautiful brother, and two amiable and most
affectionate sisters. Mary was taken away in the simplicity of innocent childhood; and had presentiments of being soon carried up to
heaven. Isaac was highly talented, and I had intended that his abilities
should be employed in the service of the altar. Jane I hoped to have
employed in copying the scenery of Northumberland into my book;
but as that expectation was not permitted to be realised, Susannah took
lessons to be able to fulfil the same intentions. She had finished one
etching; but the eye that I hoped would have gazed long on the beauties of Hartburn has closed, after seeing them only a few times.

"1834, May 6. In the afternoon the remains of my most dear
daughter Susannah were interred on the right side (south) of the remains of her sister Jane, in a grave about 7 ft. deep, and walled on the
side as high as the coffin, and then covered with large flagstones.
Edw. Swinburne, Esq., &c. &c.—

"SUSANNAH ALIA FILIA PERQUAM PIA ANNOS JAM SEPTEMDECIM NATA
APUD HARTBURN V. NON. MAII ANN. M'DCCCXXXIV. MORTI INOPINATÆ OCCUBUIT
HICQUE ETIAM SUBTUS TUMULATUR.

"1834, May 13. Opened the doorway from the vaulted keep of the
old parsonage tower of Hartburn to the back-kitchen, by which the
vault is made use of, both as a common and coal-cellar, and a covered
passage between the two kitchens.*

"1834, May 24. Wrote to Mr. Richardson to get the etching of the
great doorway of Tinmouth Priory Church by my late most dear
daughter Susannah burnished, and a score of impressions stricken off on
India paper to distribute among her friends.

"1834, May 31. Elizabeth seriously ill. My prayers to Almighty
God to spare my child's life.

"O God! the blessed Gospel of thy miracle-working Son Christ, the
Saviour of the world, has smoothed human life and diffused over the
world science that works miracles. O grant that my child's medical
advisers may be agents in thy hand to restore her health."

---

* They who know what it is to have been in affliction will not be surprised at this
proceeding at such a time. It is well with the mind when it has resolution to turn
itself away, even for a moment, from its woes.

"MY DEAR SIR,  Elsdon Castle, May 3, 1834.

"First to gratitude and then to business. Have the goodness to convey to Mrs. Hodgson our best thanks for her gingerbread, which our whole party pronounced excellent. I shall prize very highly your memoranda of Percy Papers; and as both the Duke and Lord Prudhoe have a laudable curiosity on these subjects, I trust that they will commission me to get a complete copy of them all on their account; at all events I shall endeavour to persuade them when I see them in London. With regard to your derivation of ' Elsdon' (although still retaining a prejudice in favour of the royal Ella, who, I find upon the authority of J. Major, a person cited by Lambard, and with whom you are better acquainted than myself, was frequently the origin of local names, as Ellescroft, near York, &c.), I prefer the 'Hill of the Waters' to the more ingenious, but perhaps less satisfactory, 'Hill of Decision.' The Westmerland word and game would require equally an explanation to the southern reader, to whom I trust your book will penetrate, and he might pettishly, though certainly unjustly, complain of the ' obscurum per obscurius.'——Before this parish had a hearse at their disposal the bodies of the deceased parishioners were carried to the grave on poles resting on men's shoulders; these poles were the perquisite of the rector, and were called 'pikehandles,' a custom rising rather from the nature of his residence in a fortalice in an unquiet country than from any ecclesiastical claim. The old tower was, I apprehend, built and maintained for secular purposes; and when it passed into the hands of the rector the custom passed with it. All traces of it are now obliterated; but in 1762, when Bishop Dodgson was appointed, it continued in force, although beginning to be treated with negligence on the part of the rector, and with evasion on the part of the parishioners. Perhaps the memory of so trifling a circumstance may be worth a transient notice.——

"THOMAS SINGLETON."


FROM EDWARD SWINBURNE, ESQ.—9 May, 1834.—" I was in hopes that I could have contrived yesterday to have driven round by Hartburn to Cambo to meet the coach hither, to inquire after you and yours, after the awful ceremony I had witnessed, and during which I was edified in no small degree by your firmness and your resignation; and the trial must have been rendered more severe by the situation in which your amiable daughter's mortal remains were committed to the earth, close to the memorial of your previous domestic calamities: I did not husband my time well enough, and I was obliged to proceed direct to my destination. I am sorry my present movements to the South will for some time put it out of my power personally to assure yourself and Mrs. Hodgson, as well as your children, of my sympathy. May you be long without a renewal of these chastening visitations.—ED. SWIN-BURNE."

FROM EDWARD SWINBURNE, Esq.

" MY DEAR SIR,        Alston, 16 May, 1834.

" The weather has been very favourable for my objects in this direction. I set out on Monday, and proceeded to Featherstone. I found many objections to the view of the castle from the north-west. The gateway is but a mass of ivy; the old tower itself has little to re-commend it; the features of the dwelling part are much concealed by luxuriant ivy, and a general view from that point greatly obstructed by trees. After looking at the castle from other points, I had about fixed upon the south-west, at some distance, including the whole range of the body of the castle, with the old tower and part of the woody hill to the east, when I was informed by a person, a bailiff I apprehend of Lord Wallace's steward, that it was near to the spot which Lord Wallace himself thought was the most favourable point, as also Miss Carlisle. This determined me to draw it from thence. It looks very shewy and important, which has evidently been the object of the many decorative additions made to it. Lord Wallace will probably be pleased with the choice which he was too delicate to urge me to. I want to see Hedley at his very pretty little oasis at Chesterholme, where he is doing a great deal well, with present and promise of future good effect. I hope you will be able to go and see him there and refresh your harassed spirits. The place, as all this country, is advancing rapidly with this genial spring to the period of its greatest annual beauty. The carriage road from Haltwhistle to Eels Bridge is very inconvenient; all hilly and some of it very steep, part of it bad.——I was too limited in point of time to stop at Knarsdale Hall, which is within a walk of Featherstone Castle, but I made a memorandum of the new church, which I think will be sufficient for you. It is hideous. Why adopt that meagre Gothic, with its broad, flat, unmeaning mullions? I have also got Kirk-

haugh from the south-east, shewing the east window, with its little
remnant of Gothic. Alston is so choked up with buildings that I have
only got a sketch of it from a distance, viz. from the bank near the
Lowbyer Inn, including a small part of the town; it has indeed no
peculiar feature. I have also a memorandum of Garrigill Church,
which is ugly enough. It is a curious mining place, which I should
like to have seen with you. The limestone bed of the river, so dark in
colour, is remarkable. The river is there a very scanty stream, and
fully impregnated with the scourings of the minerals.

" Allow me to renew the offer I made you when you were leaving
Whelpington. Should your considerable expenses make the accommodation desirable it would be, as before, without inconvenience to me.

" What a profusion of wild flowers adorn all the banks of the rivers
hereabouts. The ash trees are the only drawbacks from the beauty of
the scenery, everything else is resplendent with youthful animation.
My kindest regards to all your family, to whom and to yourself I renew
my assurance of heartfelt sympathy.

" EDWARD SWINBURNE."

" To THE REV. J. RAINE.—20 May, 1834.—My place is looking very
beautiful; rejoicing in all the luxuriance of youthful life; on which
every time I stir from my door or gaze out at a window, I look certainly
with pleasure, but it is a pleasure mingled with mournful and melancholy feelings. The workmen about me are beginning to fall off.
Yesterday I had only six. Next week I hope to have fewer; and in the
course of three weeks to get as much done in the inside of the house as
will give us in a comfortable way all the accommodation we shall want
for some time. The expense is overpowering. My life must be long
spared to allow me to remove the load that has been laid upon me.

" J. H."

To EDWARD SWINBURNE, Esq.

" MY DEAR SIR,                                          Hartburn, 20 May, 1834.

" I am writing in a hurry under cover to London, to request a
favour of Mr. Bowden, and will not fail to answer, though briefly, your
very kind notes from Penrith.

" About the Views you have taken far too much trouble. It is gratifying, however, to me to know that you have had fine weather, and it
is not the Mitford sketches over again. It was fortunate that you met

with Lord Wallace's bailiff, and learnt not only the most favourite, but the most imposing, view of Featherstone. Hedley has given me an account of your excursion, and invited me and Mrs. Hodgson to go thither; but that I cannot at present. Mr. Wearing came to his new residence at Netherwitton on Tuesday; and I must now use my exertions to get his part of the house put into order.* The kitchen he occupied *must be* nearly all rebuilt. The workmen are at it. The *front wall* is proceeding with; and will be in a great state of forwardness by this week's end. But applications for *money on account* come so much thicker than I expected, that I begin to feel a good deal worried with the work I must do; and on that account will no longer refuse to accept your kind offer, so often and so handsomely made, to accommodate me with 100*l.* for a short time; but that time, I fear, I cannot promise to be shorter than my next tithe-rent day. When this note falls into your hand you can, however, mention to me whether it will be convenient to you to accommodate me for that length of time or not.

"I have written to Raine on the blank part of the letter, which I think exceedingly proper; you have been a large contributor to the work. I fear the projected Society will never thrive.† The letter to Richardson shall also be forwarded this evening.

"Mrs. Hodgson bears her mighty loss with great fortitude. My dear Sir, the spring around is in all the pride and luxuriance of loveliness and beauty; and, though it has pleased God to make us mourners, yet we can gaze on His glorious works with pleasure and delight: though neither my wife nor myself have been in the wood since our loss, and our pleasure in this situation has something of a sombre cast thrown over it, which mingles it with a regret and melancholy that make us

* Mr. Wearing had during the lifetime of the previous incumbent been curate of the parish of Netherwitton, a chapelry within it, and had resided in the vicarage house with Mr. Davison. Netherwitton now becomes a separate benefice, and Mr. Wearing is its first incumbent.

† Mr. Swinburne had been solicited to join the Surtees Society, then in the course of formation, and had declined. He had contributed many beautiful drawings to Mr. Surtees's History of Durham. The THIRTY-FOUR volumes already published by the Society are the best answer to Mr. Hodgson's fears. They touch upon every topic of archæology connected with the province over which they extend, and are well known and much consulted by those who wish to obtain genuine information on the various subjects which they embrace. Besides, the Surtees Society was the first institution of its kind in England, and if it has been productive of no other good, it has at all events conferred a great boon upon the kingdom, by setting an example which has been imitated to a very great extent for similar useful purposes.

sorrowful, but do not extinguish the power of rejoicing in the mercies and favours which Providence has still reserved to us.   My dear Sir, ever yours most truly and gratefully,

"JOHN HODGSON."

On the 25th of June Hodgson left home upon a short tour into Scotland in company with Lady Decies of Bolam, and Miss Brown, the governess of his daughter.   It is much to be regretted that the Journal which he kept during this expedition cannot at the present time be found.   From a letter, to be noticed hereafter, it appears to have extended to 228 pages,* and to have contained numerous sketches of various objects of interest which came in his way.   The book was presented by him to Lady Decies, as a record of their expedition, and where it is now cannot be ascertained.   The following letter will detail the route which the travellers followed, and I have again to express my regret that I am deprived of this important record of Hodgson's thoughts and feelings on the occasion, and his observations upon a country with which he had been previously so little acquainted.

To MR. R. W. HODGSON.

" MY DEAR RICHARD,                            Hartburn, 9 July, 1834.

" Will you be so good as to put a seal into the inclosed, and give it to Mr. John Clayton, who will perhaps say more to you on the subject than he could have time to write to me.

" We got from the Highlands on Saturday evening.   I will give you our route:—

" June 24. To Edinburgh.

" 25. To Kirkaldy, Cupar, St. Andrew's, Dundee.

" 26. To Forfar, Brechin, Lawrence Kirk, Newhaven, Aberdeen.

" 27. To Kintore, Inverary, Hew of Garry, Strath Boyce, Huntly. Keith, Fochabers, Elgin, Forres, Nairn, Inverness.

" 28. At Inverness, a great meeting of thousands of persons, preparatory to Sacrament next day.   Sketches about the place; and visited the vitrified fort of Craig-Phadric.

* The following letter, however, mentions only 140.   He had doubtless enlarged the volume with recollections soon after his return home.

"27. Sunday. Was present in the afternoon at the administration of the Presbyterian Sacrament in the open air, before an assembly of thousands, grouped circularly before four tables. The preaching and service all in Gaelic, under a burning sun, and with the broad Firth of Moray before us, and beyond the blue and snow-crowned head of Ben Nevis in the distance. This was a most remarkable spectacle.

"30. Embarked in the Rob Roy steamer up Loch Ness, to Falls of Foyers and Fort Augustus. Loch Oish in Glengarry's country, and the great mountains of Strath Glass. Then Loch Lochy, with Ben Nevis in full sight—snow-capped—and above 4,000 feet high. Then Inverlochy Castle and Fort William.

"July 1. Embarked again in Rob Roy from Fort William on Loch Eil. Passed the north of Loch Levin into Loch Lennhe. Islands of Storma and Lismore. Mull before us at a distance, but towering into the clouds. Dunstaffnage Castle. Then the island of Ke-ora, Dunolly Castle, and Oban, where we landed, and at 12 A.M. took a stage coach, which took us up the left bank of Loch Etive, past Dunstaffnage Castle, by Taynalt, up Glen Nent, passed the bare granitic head of Ben Cruachan, to the great inland lake of Loch Awe, which we crossed by a ferry to Senachan, and thence went to Inverary.

"July 2. Crossed from Inverary over Loch Fine to St. Catherine, and thence, in a coach and four driven in great style, through the narrow pass of Glen Beg, by Mony Brechin Bridge, into Glen Goyle, to Loch Goyle head, where we took our passage in the St. Catherine steamer down to Loch Goyle and Loch Long into the Firth of Clyde, and to Glasgow.

"July 3. From Glasgow to Lanark and the Falls of the Clyde. To Carnwath, Currie, and Edinburgh.

"July 4. All day at Edinburgh, in the Society of Arts, Royal and Antiquarian Societies, Parliament House, Advocates' Library, and the Record Office, with Mr. Thomson the keeper of which I dined.

"July 5. From Edinburgh to Hartburn.

"The minutes and sketches of this tour occupy 140 closely written pages in my note-book; but are not of much moment, as we went on wings.

"We are all well. William and Robert Hodgson from Carlisle have been here since the day after I set out on my journey.

"When are you coming? I wish you would bring John Wylam or Mr. Bourne with you, or both of them together.——Your most affectionate father, "JOHN HODGSON."

2 A 2

" Dear Sir,                                    London, July 7, 1834.

    "In the 'Inquisitiones Nonarum,' published by the Record
Commissioners, the county of Northumberland amongst others is wanting.  In arranging the documents in the Exchequer this has lately been
found, and the Commissioners have been good enough to furnish me
with a transcript, from which I have made a copy, which I send here-
with.  I am also getting a copy made of the Parliamentary Survey of
Church Livings made in the time of the Commonwealth, so far as
regards Northumberland, which I will send you in a few days.  The
latter record is of the greater value, as the ' Valor Ecclesiasticus' of
Henry VIII. for Northumberland is not in existence; all that we know
of being the ' Summa Valoris,' published in the last volume of the
Valor.  In a former volume of your History you have printed the
Northumberland part of Pope Nicholas's Taxation; and if the ' Nonarum Inquisitiones' and the Parliamentary Survey were published, we
should then have a complete set of the Ecclesiastical Surveys relating to
Northumberland.  If you think it desirable to have these documents
printed as an Appendix, either to the forthcoming or any succeeding
volume of your history, I shall be most happy to pay for the printing
of the requisite number of copies of them as my contribution towards
your valuable work.  The Nonæ which I send include several parishes
out of the county, viz. the whole of North Durham, and Aldston and
Denton in Cumberland.  It would, however, undoubtedly be desirable to
publish them entire, as it would then form a complete supplement to the
the publication of the Record Commission.  I am, dear Sir, very
truly yours,

                                    " John Hodgson."*

    " 1834, 25 Aug.—Knaresdale. A population here savage and cunning,
unbenefited yet by civilisation or religion; but the rising generation

---

    * Between our Mr. Hodgson and Mr. Hodgson of Elswick, afterwards Mr. Hodgson
Hinde, there had for some time existed an intimacy, and a kindred feeling in the county
of Northumberland and its history.  They do not, however, appear to have had much
epistolary correspondence with each other before this period.  The above letter will
inform the reader of the able and zealous person to whom he is now introduced, and
when he shall be given to understand that Mr. Hodgon Hinde is at the present time
strenuously engaged in completing one volume at least of the first part of Hodgson's
unfinished History of Northumberland, he will, with the above letter before him, at
once come to the conclusion that the undertaking is in the most able hands.

are being regularly instructed. The cultivated land is broadest on the banks of the Knar; less so on the Thornhope; and the Mill-burn moor comes down nearly to the inn, brown and bristling with heather.

" Ah Lord God! that creatures of thine can traverse and live upon this beautiful earth and not see all the wonders with which it abounds, and the traces of the labours of the races of men that fed upon its bounty, where they now till it and live upon it little more thankfully than the cattle that assist them in their labours.

" Nature here frowns, but not austerely, in her high mountain brows; but her feet and her footstool are lovely."—(*Journal.*)

" 1834, Nov. 28.—In returning from Durham to Newcastle by coach this morning, I walked out of the town a short way, and was taken up by the coach.

" Yesterday as I walked past the east end of the cathedral I was struck with the mightiness of the mass of the tower, and the grandeur of the mind that designed it, and the command of means there must have been to finish such a work. To be sure, the whole building was the work of successive ages, and each part frequently of many years, and of more than one episcopate.

" This morning, a little after eight, the sun was up, and a pale mild light showed the beauty of the fine new broad road,* its two footpaths and walls winding off and disappearing between green banks to great advantage. The meadows too on the left beautifully tossed up into wavy forms, green as in May, pastured upon by groups of cows and sheep, and alive with the jocund and responsive voices of several parties of boys playing at cricket and other games; browed and hemmed with old brushwood and young plantations and hedges, all just now gilded with the sweet light of one of the most lovely November mornings that I ever saw; these all opened in me a fountain of joy and gratitude, which, however I may have been scowled upon by pride or sneered at by scorn, will I hope still continue to pour from my soul a stream of pleasure, which the keenest winds of adversity and persecution can never dry up —which contempt cannot blow out of its bed, and will always be too warm for neglect to freeze."—(*Journal.*)

" To THE REV. J. RAINE.—Hartburn, 8 Dec. 1834.—You mentioned Newminster Chartulary as a fit subject for the Surtees Society press.

---

* A new road from Durham for a mile in the direction of Newcastle, to avoid the steep street of Framwellgate.

I have got a sight of it, and have negotiated, as far as I can at present, for a copy of it. In a fortnight's time I can tell you the result of my diplomacy in this matter. It is a small quarto of about 150 folios; but parts of it have had gallic acid spread over them to bring up the writing, and they are now nearly defaced. It has marginal references on the side, in the handwriting of the celebrated William Howard (Belted Will); and you will see that I mentioned it in a note under Blakemoor in my last published volume, as well as the Lawson MS., which I shewed you in the Durham Library, with a view of identifying the handwriting of it with that of the Philosopher Harrison. To-day I have had an intimation that my woodcuts will be done in time for my volume now in the press being published before the close of the year."

Mr. Hodgson does not appear to have devoted much time during this year to magazines or periodical publications, save that he contributed a report on Housesteads to the Antiquarian Society of Newcastle, and to the Newcastle Courant a notice of the Brief Account of Durham Cathedral.

Death of Mr. Hedley—Publication of Part III. vol. III.—The Northumberland Pipe
Rolls—Correspondence—Journal—Commencement of a new Volume of History—
Journal—Visit to Carham—Minor Publications.

In the beginning of the year 1835, before Hodgson had resided
twelve months at Hartburn, he found himself oppressed with
difficulties, the result of expenses incurred in his History and in
taking possession of his new preferment. " Your mother," writes
he to his son Richard on the 13th of January, " I think, makes
improvement. The time of year for her is bad, and there is no
doubt the miserable state of our affairs is a heavy pressure upon
her. What we are to do I cannot tell.——To part with my books
would be to part with my life, for without some literary employment I fear I could not live."——I willingly omit the greater
portion of this letter, as its only tendency would be to give great
pain to any reader in possession of a feeling heart.

To add to Hodgson's affliction, the hand of death, in the opening
of this year, interrupted the faithful and affectionate intercourse
which had so long existed between him and his friend Mr. Hedley.
This sudden and melancholy event took place on the 17th of
January from the effects of a cold caught in superintending the
workmen who were engaged in disinterring the *rudera* of the Roman station of Vindolana, within which Hedley had built a house
for his future residence.

That Hodgson deeply felt his loss during the remainder of his
life is certain, and how thoroughly he understood the merits and
excellences of this gentleman may be gathered from the memoir
of him which he soon afterwards placed upon record in the volume
of his History upon which he was then entering.* Hedley's
epitaph at Beltingham is also by his pen; a brief but comprehensive sketch of the life and character of his friend.

The early Pipe Rolls for the county of Northumberland have

* Hist. Part. II. vol. iii. p. 330, &c. See also Gent. Mag. for October 1835 for
another short memoir from Hodgson's pen.

been frequently mentioned in the preceding pages, and we have seen with what anxiety Hodgson could write about them to his friends, and have moreover heard many grievous complaints of the large sum of money which he had paid for a transcript of those valuable documents. After having entertained various plans for their publication, many of which are above alluded to, he at last determined to send them forth to the world as the concluding volume of the third part or division of his History, and in the beginning of the year at which we have arrived the book made its appearance accordingly under that title,* and gave additional proof of the determination of its editor to shrink from no labour or expense in carrying out his great undertaking. But a few words must be said of the Pipe Rolls themselves.

Of the counties of Northumberland and Durham, as they are now bounded, no mention is made in the Domesday Survey of 1085. Of Cumberland and Westmerland portions only are described in that record. It matters not here to enter into the causes of these omissions, which are so serious a hindrance to the local historian. In the other counties of the kingdom we can ascertain not only the names of the landholders at the above period, but, in general, those of their Saxon predecessors, together with the other minute and varied information of a statistical nature for which this record is famous. In Northumberland, however, and the other districts so circumstanced, we are obliged to begin our inquiries at a later date, and take our commencement with the Pipe Rolls, which "are returns made into the Court of Exchequer from year to year by the sheriffs of the county, who acted as the king's bailiffs, and occasionally by other persons who had to account to the king for any portion of the royal revenue." Surely no stinted thanks are due to one who, as far as Northumberland is concerned, has placed those records before us in their integrity, illustrating as they do a long period of time of which we have almost no other history. If Mr. Hodgson had done nothing more for Northumberland than print those documents, he would

---

* In addition to the number required for his History, he printed 100 copies for general sale, with a copy of his portrait, an appropriate title, and a dedication to the Bishop of Durham. It was this additional number which afterwards hung so heavily upon his hands.

have laid the county under the greatest obligations. The value of
his services in this single act of labour and cost may not now,
perhaps, be appreciated as it deserves, but the time will probably
arrive when people will wonder at the patience which could drudg-
ingly correct the proof sheets of such complicated transcripts, and
admire the resolution of the man who, for the sake of the public
and posterity, could, at whatever cost and labour, give perpetuity
by means of the press to such singularly valuable historical documents, which had previously existed in the original only, liable
daily to destruction from fire or other casualty.

The obligations which in the matter of these Rolls Hodgson
owed to his namesake Mr. Hodgson, (now John Hodgson Hinde,
Esq.,) are duly acknowledged in the Preface. Mr. Hinde has
since that time conferred upon the public an additional favour by
editing for the Society of Antiquaries of Newcastle such Pipe
Rolls for the reigns of Henry I., Richard I. and John, as refer to
the counties of Cumberland and Westmerland, and to the county
Palatine of Durham whilst in the hands of the crown from time
to time in vacancies of the see. To this volume he has prefixed
an introduction abounding with very valuable information respecting the North of England during the above reigns, and from an
earlier period. With Mr. Hodgson's Pipe Rolls, and those of Mr.
Hodgson Hinde before him, if the local historian is unable to quaff
the "integros fontes" of Domesday, he may at least reach the
source of other minor streams of great purity which spring up at
no great distance, and drink of their waters before they have
become perturbed by the defilements of fable.

The other documents in Hodgson's volume are all of them
extremely valuable, and they will save many a weary hour of
anxious search and investigation to him who shall have courage
and encouragement to complete the task to which one man has
already devoted a life shortened by its severity.

If the author were to assume to himself the right to give an
opinion upon the merits of this book, he would have no hesitation
in setting it above any other of Mr. Hodgson's volumes in point
of perpetual utility, as the genuine and only source of that portion
of our Northumbrian History which extends from the Conquest
over the two following centuries. In every county that is

the darkest of our historical periods, even with Domesday to help us, but Northumberland has no Domesday to boast of.

Mr. Hodgson has prefixed to this volume a long Preface, of which the following is an extract, omitting much of a technical nature descriptive of the Rolls themselves, their history and uses.*

"Anxiety to supply, as much as possible from authentic sources, the information respecting Northumberland wanting in the Domesday Survey of England in the time of William the Conqueror, induced the editor of this volume, in 1830, to request Mr. Adamson of Newcastle to apply at the Court of Exchequer in Somerset House, for a copy of the Rotuli Annales, or Pipe Rolls, from their commencement in 1131, only forty-five years after the Domesday Survey was finished, to the end of the reign of Henry the Third in 1272.——After terms were agreed up·n for fees, transcribing and examining, the task of making a full copy was undertaken by William Foxton, Esq., and by him completed in 1832; and the interval between that year and the present has been occupied in preparing them for the press, and conducting them through it. Since the office copy was procured, the only two original Rolls that were then missing have been found, and a copy of them forwarded to the editor by John Hodgson, Esq., M.P. for Newcastle; and with the Northumberland portion of the *Liber Niger* appended to this printed series. By the unremitting and intelligent zeal of the same gentleman in procuring materials for this work, and at his expense, I am also now enabled to add to this Preface the Northumberland *Nonarum Inquisitiones* which were supposed to be lost; the *Summa Valoris*, printed in the 'Valor Ecclesiasticus' of Henry VIII., and the *Ecclesiastical Survey* of the same county in 1650; and, as a fit companion to these, I have added the *Feodary's Book* of Northumberland freeholders and their lands in 1568.'

"I was," he adds, in a preliminary notice, "reluctant to add another to the two volumes of records I have already given, because I feared that, in its present form, its contents might not be acceptable to many who kindly contribute their patronage to this work by subscribing to it; but I was encouraged to do so by the hope that, even as it is, it will be kindly received by others, and be gratifying to all, when the numerous personages of its masked pages begin to appear in their full English

---

* In his Preface, p. lxxii., Hodgson speaks of a membrane of the "Valor Ecclesiasticus" of Hen. VIII., the only portion of that Survey referring to Northumberland which has been seen in modern times, and which was then missing. It has not since been found.

costume, in the history of the places where they resided, and where the
drama of their lives was performed. To myself it has been heavily
expensive; and censure can hardly be severe in scrutinizing the motives
that have given to the public a work which cannot fail to confer considerable advantage on historical literature, but on which the editor's
time and labour have been gratuitously bestowed. I will add that it is
certainly the last volume of its kind that I shall offer to the public, and
that the Parochial History will now be carried forward with all the
speed that my means and leisure will allow. To be brief is now also
more in my power, since the materials of this volume will permit me to
write with greater certainty and confidence than I could without them,
for doubt and uncertainty are great multipliers of words; but much
brevity cannot be expected where the subject teems with topics of the
highest local interest and curiosity; and of these Northumberland, for
the last seventeen centuries, has yielded a most abundant harvest, little
of which has hitherto been reaped and gathered in for the benefit or
amusement of its present or future generations.

" Hartburn Vicarage House, Dec. 16, 1834."

I throw into a note a few further particulars respecting this ill-
fated, but most useful publication.*

Hodgson's Correspondence proceeds as usual, and continues as
interesting as before,† but my space is beginning to be contracted,

* " To Mr. J. G. Nichols, 7 Nov. 1835.—The notice of the Pipe Roll (Gent. Mag.
Oct. 1835) was very kind and hearty : but you are far from right when you intimate
my ample means to obtain copies of Public Records. No man can hardly be less able.
I assure you the expense of the Pipe Roll has been a *real affliction* to me. I printed
100 copies of it and the Preface, with a distinct title-page, " The Great Roll of the
Pipe, &c. for Northumberland," with a dedication to the Bishop of Durham, which I
have not yet offered for sale. My friend and namesake the late M.P. for Newcastle
sent a copy of it to Mr. Cooper of the Record Commission, and I have given four copies
of it away. Bound in cloth, with the portrait of myself, I thought they should sell at
2l. 2s. I send one copy as a specimen, and would be glad to know if you would take
the whole or a part of them, and at what price."——Mr. Nichols, in reply to the question
in the latter part of the above extract, declined to purchase the impression, but was of
opinion that probably the Record Commission might take it and make it one of their
publications, but upon application being made they also, through their secretary Mr.
Cooper, declined to comply with the request.

† I may mention in particular the names of Mr. J. Hodgson Hinde, Mr. E. Swinburne, Mr. Dickson, Mr. Woodman, Mr. John Thompson, and Mr. Sopwith, as
correspondents interesting themselves in behalf of his History.

and a place can be given to such materials only as more peculiarly
refer to the subject of my Memoir and his own personal history.

The communication of a Manchester newspaper at this period
led to the following entry in Hodgson's Journal, and the renewal
of his acquaintance with one of his Sedgefield scholars, whom he
had lost sight of for thirty years.*   The youth had thriven in the
world, and the way in which he addresses his former master in a
letter written a while afterwards, is much to his credit.†

"1835, Jan. 17.   A newspaper sent from Manchester with the
synopsis of the poll there.

|  | Plumpers. | Splits. | Total. |
|---|---|---|---|
| Thompson | 115 | 3241 | 3356 |
| Philips | 150 | 3013 | 3163 |
| Braidley | 1231 | 1304 | 2535 |
| Wolseley • | 24 | 559 | 583 |

" This paper was addressed to me here, and in the same ink and handwriting there was on the side of Mr. Braidley's speech ' Mr. Braidley, a
scholar of Mr. Hodgson's at Sedgefield.'  He was a son of Benjamin
Braidley of that place, and the fourth in the call-roll when I left that
place on account of ill-health in April 1804."

"Feb. 13, 1835, Gateshead Park.

" FROM MISS ELIZ. COOKSON.‡—MY DEAR SIR,—As I am going from
home for a couple of months, I return you the old papers, which I have

---

* See vol. i. p. 16.

† In a letter to Hodgson dated on the 18th of May, 1835, Mr. Braidley thus writes
to his former master.  " It would give me great pleasure to see you once more.  The
scenes of my early days pass rapidly before my view at this moment.——My own outset in business was as an apprentice to an Irish linen merchant.  Subsequently I
entered into the business of cotton manufacturer, and my present firm is Braidley and
McClure.  Within the last eight years I have had six of hard official and responsible
public duty to perform, first as Overseer and Sidesman ; second as Churchwarden ;
third as High Constable of the Town ; after, in the succeeding two years (an un-
precedented thing) Borough Reeve of the Town, and last year High Constable of the
Hundred of Salford, a population of 700,000 souls."  How popular he was as the
Conservative Candidate for Manchester in 1835 may be seen above.  " I sent you
(says he) a paper with the particulars of our last election.  The Roman Catholics,
Dissenters, and Radicals are too strong here."  Mr. Braidley talks much in his letter
of his former schoolfellows and their subsequent history.

‡ Upon Hodgson's taking up his abode at Hartburn, he found the father of this
lady, an old friend from the neighbourhood of Newcastle, building for himself a

had much pleasure in copying, but I find some of the writing I cannot make quite out. However I have done my best, and when I return to Meldon I hope you will again employ me.——I am, dear Sir, yours most truly,

"ELIZTH. COOKSON."

"1835, Feb. 17.—Finished Calderwood's History of the Reformation in Scotland, which, as it was written by one of the Reformers, and at the request of the General Assembly, may be considered a faithful exposition of the doctrines and discipline of the Kirk up to the time of the death of James the First. The Scotch reformers, no doubt, began their preaching in a land in great comparative darkness in the knowledge of the Gospel. The country was poor and warlike. Arms had made it fierce and contentious; and the church here, as in other parts of Europe, was more a system of idolatrous forms and superstitions than a body quickened by the Holy Spirit of God. As the glory of God can only be spread by the knowledge of Him through the great mass of mankind, in His intense regard for the happiness of man, so it is abated by that knowledge being kept from the multitude; and greatly to be feared that when the teachers of the Gospel are not zealous of spreading it widely and clearly among their flocks, it is known only to them in a mere formal way. Having eyes to see it, they see it not. To know God in revelation and nature, in the gracious revelation of His will, in the Bible, and in the wonders of His wisdom in the Book of Nature, to exult in this knowledge, and delight to live according to its instructions, and spread it far among mankind, and see others rejoice and glorify their Maker in its light—this is happiness indeed, and doing the work which the pastors of Christ's Church were sent to do. But little of this had been done when the Reformation began: and when a few bold and intrepid spirits, born among a people bred in arms and contention, began to unfold to the people the Love of God, in sending His Son to be a ransom for the sins of men; and the glorious light of the Gospel began

mansion-house at Meldon, a mile and a half to the east of his vicarage. Mr. Cookson had long resided at Gateshead Park, near Heworth, and upon purchasing Meldon he thus wrote to the new vicar of Hartburn. " It appears to me as if my family were fated to pursue you, as I first followed you to the county of Durham, and shall to Northumberland, where I hope, when my house is finished, we shall be good neighbours. It is not, however, my intention to follow you to your bishopric, as I trust to make Meldon my place of rest." Here is another lady-contributor to the History of Northumberland.

"1835, May 19. Dined at Meldon for the first time, Mr. Cookson having first come to reside there on the 9th inst."—(Journal.)

to shine into men's hearts, they grew indignant that this knowledge had
been hidden from them; and the preachers, taking advantage of this
indignation, stirred them up to overthrow from its lowest foundations
the system of the Church as then established and administered.  The
work these reformers undertook to do they did vigorously; but still they
did it injudiciously and fiercely.  They did not cleanse the temple with a
bunch of *small* cords and with mildness and love; but they drove the
priests out of their cathedrals and churches, and the monks out of their
abbeys and priories, with thongs steeped in the pungent and galling
waters of vengeance; and consumed their dwelling-houses with fire, and
broke down all their carved work with axes and hammers.  The nobles
and barons of the country, too, came with great zeal in many parts to
their assistance, and repaid themselves bountifully for their zealous co-
operation by appropriating to themselves the lands and teinds of the
churches and monasteries.  The opposition of the monks and clergy
was like men throwing water into the mouth of a flaming volcano.
The more they did the faster they hastened their own ruin.  They had
not eyes to see nor heads to know the day of their visitation; and therefore sudden destruction came upon them unawares.  Some, however,
saw, and stood as mediators between the parties, so that civil war did
not ensue.  But how moving was it to see the beautiful Mary insulted
with the brutal tyranny and coarse language of those overheated and
ambitious men!  A woman who forgets and forsakes the religion that
has been instilled into her early mind, cannot but be an object of pity
under all circumstances.  But in an age when faith in certain forms and
ceremonies, and that saw all the doctrines it was taught at a far and
awful distance, and through awful and appalling spectacles, when there
was little general knowledge even in the highest orders of society—in
such an age, and with such a faith, to suppose that a woman of the
highest rank and the greatest beauty was all at once to cast away the
prejudices of her education, and become a convert to the doctrines of
persons who derided and insulted what she considered true, awful, and
sacred, was unreasonable and monstrous.  The work they went to
do was a good one.  Reform was wanting; but they did not go to it in
a mild and Christian manner: and the temper that planned and carried
forward the Reformation of Scotland has never left the land; for a
polemical spirit still pervades it and rankles at its heart; breeding
animosities and divisions in its own church, and keeping red the coals
of hatred against all that name the name of Christ but themselves."—
(*Journal.*)

"1835, 11 March.—Circumstances put the human mind every day into a variety of conditions—they often allow it to be bold, full of ideality, keen in research, patient of labour, panting to do public good, to bring the mass of mankind into a good moral condition.   But—that sad *but!*—there is so little αγαπη, so much ερως, so much selfishness, that no man of small means and large demands upon him can honestly give largely and freely his time and powers to the inconsiderate, the ungrateful, and the unsteady public, and yet he ventures sometimes to do much to raise past generations into importance, from a desire to make the present have veneration for their forefathers—for who is not desirous and compassioned to fill his children with all the knowledge and the experience he has obtained, often obtained with great labour, and under trying difficulties and afflictions."—*(Journal.)*

To H. PETRIE, ESQ.—"Do you think that any London publisher of credit would encourage me to prepare my manuscript on the Roman Wall for the press?"—Mr. Petrie in reply.—28 March, 1835.—" I have waited until I could furnish you with the result of my inquiries on the subject of publication with respect to your account of the wall.   This, I am sorry to say, is anything but encouraging; the demand for similar works, however interesting or well executed, being so extremely limited that such an undertaking by a bookseller seems utterly hopeless.   Still I trust you will gratify us by the result of your examination in some shape; and should you determine on a subscription for that purpose, I need hardly add that I shall be happy to promote it by every means in my power."——

From SIR C. G. YOUNG.—" 28 Mar. 1835.—Our poor friend Surtees has paid the debt of nature since I last heard from you, to my grief, as well as that of all his friends.   He was a noble spirit, and his Durham a charming book.   In addition to such a text, what delightful notes; and, independently of the legendary lore, what expression of life they embody."——

"1835, 10 April.—Planted July flowers in the wood, four silver firs by the river edge, and three scions of the great poplar on the west side of the garden.   Also planted some kernels of horse-chestnut which I found in the wood, where that sort of kernels are a favourite food of slugs, which feed upon them under layers of dry leaves."—*(Journal.)*

" 1835, Ap. 12.—Mr. ———— came to Hartburn last Tuesday to ask if I had any objection to Mr. ————'s meeting me at ———— to-day, as he had ascertained Mr. ———— was anxious to do.   I made no objection, and said, though Mr. ———— had done all he could to annoy me, and gratify his own avarice, I had no other feeling for his taste in doing so than that of extreme pity. For what feeling but that of pity can one have for a mind that, to compass an avaricious end, will fawn on you with one hand and persecute you with another; who has no courage to do what is right, but what rage excites and hirelings at law, to execute, and where sincerity and honesty are of no further use than what a man of the world can put them to, in accomplishing selfish ends? These are the money which hypocrisy brings into the market to purchase favour and good opinion with, but of which it knows no other use. But smiles on some faces are only the lights which display the broad features of knavery through their thin mask of cunning."—(*Journal.*)

"1835, 25th and 29th April.—Botanical reading. Tournfort and Turner's Herbals. Hooker and Smith's Floras. Mr. Trevelyan called and requested me to show him *Lathræa Squamosa,* which he says grows on the roots of different kinds of trees, and is found in the wood of Roadley Lake.

> Some soils there are where poisonous plants delight
> To grow, and few and feeble are the herbs
> That rise around them. Cities too there are
> So rank in moral odour that, from age
> To age, they cast the pestilential breath
> Of mischief round so strongly, that the air
> Of joy and social harmony and mirth,
> Which virtue loves to live and thrive amongst,
> Is foul and tainted."—(*Journal.*)

On the 8th of May Hodgson again took up his pen and proceeded in his great undertaking, having given to himself the short rest of a few months only, during which he had been moving from place to place in quest of information. Domestic difficulties and public neglect only served as excitements to new but fruitless labours. He had set himself a work, and he was determined to finish it.—"1835, May 8. Began Pt. II. vol. iii. of my History of Northumberland." He had barely finished this volume when his pen refused to proceed, and thus this became his last effort in behalf of Northumberland.

"1835, 31 May.—Sunday.—Rifle no tomb, disturb not the remains nor insult the memory of the dead. John xiv. 19. Sermon on the invisible as well as visible church of Christ—its spiritual and temporal existence. The Jews could not see Christ; and when they crucified him, they thought they were putting out of existence some inconsiderable person, a poor enthusiast or cunning impostor—but He triumphed over death and the malice of his enemies, and when He ascended led captivity captive. So His church: wicked men think when they see the temporal existence of the Church, as upheld by the State, they see it all; and if they succeed in destroying it nothing of it will remain —but even in its humiliation it will rise up triumphantly before its enemies, for its Great Head in Heaven will always continue with it, even unto the end of the world."—*Journal.*

" 1835, 10 July.—Something to be done about better psalmody in the Church. The English people, as they acquire leisure and conquer the difficulties of their climate by improved roads and agriculture, will gain a taste for elegant acquirements and amusements. As soon as the mass of the people begin by general systems of education to be accustomed to these improvements, musical instruments will be found in every cottage; and music will soothe and enchant the cradle. Thousands whose voices would every Sabbath-day have joined in praising God, if music had formed one of the charms and amusements of their infant ears, are now dumb and dull when the voice of thanksgiving is raised."
—*Journal.*

On the first of June Hodgson left home to pay a short visit to his friend John Hodgson Hinde, Esq. at Carham. He travelled by the Chevy Chase coach to Jedburgh, where he was met by his friend; and the two afterwards devoted a few days to a Survey of the Northumberland side of the Tweed, especially in the neighbourhood of the Cheviot Hills, which are most of them remarkable for their old British settlements. Hodgson's notes made on this expedition are numerous and valuable.

" 1835, 24 Nov.—Very unwell in the afternoon. Every day I lament that I was ever tempted to plunge myself into the difficulties into which I have fallen in coming from Whelpington to this place. Richard and Isabella came here this day (25th), and on entering the ford at Angerton, their horse turned furious, plunged forward, reared, broke the shafts of the gig, fell on its knees, and was almost instantly drowned. I thank God neither of them was killed. Isabella jumped into the water and was able to get out. Richard endeavoured to unloose the trapping in vain, from the depth of the water, as the river was high; he had no knife in his pocket."

2 B

To THE REV. J. RAINE, Dec. 19, 1835.—" I wish that any kind person who is fond of parochial history would take two or three wards of the county out of my hands.——I wrote as little as I well could respecting Bedlington, considering the nature of its situation; and the errors I committed respecting its church must be attributable chiefly to an omission of looking into the authorities in the second volume of Records. But my feelings have so often been cauterised with notices of my blunders and omissions that they are now sear and cicatrized against all such observations.——I can most cordially sympathize with your friend Dunham. I have a history of the ROMAN WALL nearly ready for the press, and neither dare print it in my own book nor can I get a London bookseller to undertake it; though the filthy thing that Hutton wrote on the subject went through two or three editions."

" 1835, 23 Dec.—At Capheaton.—I began to talk with Mr. Wilkinson,* the traveller in Egypt, on the pretensions of the Theban Magi to converse with spirits; but he said the subject was not agreeable to reflect upon and he did not like to talk about it. Mr. Wilkinson said it was a delightful employment to make accurate maps, and that he had made an extensive survey of the country about Thebes, besides his engraved plans of the remains of that celebrated city and the adjacent country, but that he could get no one to undertake to publish his map, which he, however, gave to Arrowsmith the map-publisher."

In the course of the year 1835, Hodgson communicated to the Gentleman's Magazine an account of a MS. in his possession containing medical receipts, &c. &c. compiled chiefly in the latter part of the reign of Queen Elizabeth, and continued by various hands. The book appears to have belonged to a person of the name of Emmanuel Potter, and is a compilation of great curiosity and interest. It is now the property of the author.† He also published in the same repository (Oct.) a short memoir of his friend Hedley, and reviews of the two first publications of the Surtees Society in the Newcastle Courant, and wrote an account of Naworth Castle for Mr. M. A. Richardson's Border Castles, &c.

---

* Sir Gardner Wilkinson.
† For Hodgson's account of this MS. see Gent. Mag. July and Aug. 1835.

" 1836, Jan. 30.   Read Lord Ripon's address for 1835 to the Royal
Society of Literature.   His account of Coleridge very interesting.   I
am myself persuaded that the mechanical philosophy with which Dr.
James (? Samuel) Clarke, and others, treated Christianity was very de-
teriorating, very chilling to the warm spirit of our blessed, our heart-
stirring, our life-giving religion.   That system of reducing all things
to demonstration, as in mathematics and science, cannot, I constantly
feel, account for trains of thought which often marshal themselves
before my mind.   At a very early period of my life I felt for a long
time an involuntary consciousness that all my thoughts were known
not only by the Creator of the Universe, but by many with whom I had
to associate—that God had given that faculty to them and not to me
and others, and hence my inferiority in intellect, and especially in
moral attainments.   I never could for years dispossess myself of this
notion, nor ever reveal it to any one; for while it haunted me I could
well enough see the probability of its being a mere delusion.   It had,
however, great power over my thoughts—used to create in me a dread
and fearfulness of going into the presence of men of birth, talents, and
attainments—even while a counteracting and impatient thirst for knowledge impelled me to seek their company."—*Journal.*

" 1836, Feb. 6.—You say you were baptized and confirmed into the
Church of England—which is made up of a great many churches, of
which Hartburn is one.   But you must consider that Hartburn Church
is not the building in which we assemble, but the people that assemble
in it, and, strictly, of them only such as are in communion with it by
partaking of the Holy Communion of the Body and Blood of Jesus
Christ.   Come, therefore, I beseech you to that blessed rite, and let our
church be a large one here, walking in brotherly love; and a joyful
one in Heaven, where, if we do our part here on earth, we may all hope
to meet in God's good time."—*Ib.*

If my space had sufficed, I should have gladly inserted in this portion of my Memoir a long letter, addressed by Hodgson in this year to the Commissioners on Public Records, with respect to the utility of their publications. That utility had been called in question in Parliament, and certain queries had in consequence been addressed by the Commission to literary men, especially to those engaged in topographical pursuits, in order to obtain such answers as might meet the objections which had been brought forward against the Commission and its operations. Hodgson's answers, the rough copy of which he has carefully preserved, are full and minute, and are justly in favour of a renewal of the Commission, which had afforded such valuable information touching the early part of our national history to those who, like himself, lived at a distance from the public repositories in which the records themselves are preserved.*

" 1836, July 12. Went to Durham. At the meeting and dinner of the Surtees Society. Slept at Mr. Raine's at Crook Hall. I mention here that Mr. Townsend, at the Society's dinner, eulogised my Northumberland highly, so much so as to distress much more than gratify me: for, though some may cheer me with speaking well of my labour, yet the general feeling towards me is pity for so laborious and unprofitable a work, and the opinion of it that it is too long and minute; and while I hear once of any excellence that it contains, I hear twenty times of its errors and omissions. Personal eulogium at public meetings is nothing more than giving an expectation of much to be returned, and therefore thickly laid on. ' Claw me and I will claw thee.' "—Ib.

" 1836, 15 Sept. Returned Douglas's ' Peerage of Scotland,' to —— which I had borrowed for information about the Kings of Scotland. Mr. —— bought it to assist me in compiling the pedigree of the —— family given in Part II. vol. i. of my Northumberland, when that volume was nearly ready for the press. The volume would have been complete without the half-sheet which contains the pedigree, for printing which so much as ' thank you ' was never spared me. So much for Scotch pride and generosity!"—Ib.

* Hodgson's answers were, I believe, printed by the Commission as testimonials in its favour.

On the 29th of September Hodgson was one of a party, who, with Sir J. E. Swinburne, the President, at its head, made a progress to Auckland Castle, to confer upon the Bishop of Durham a patent of honorary membership in the Society of Antiquaries of Newcastle.

"1836, Dec. 28. The four inscriptions of Platorius Nepos. As usual every day, much lost time in Gruter and other authors to illustrate the subject. Minute investigation useless in a poor collection of books; for I constantly find in large libraries subjects well and largely treated upon, and my notes wretchedly lean. All this is lonely and useless research.—My wife and children!—The satellites of Cancer and Capricorn curious, and especially the domiciles of the twelve signs to the seven planets. Be brief. There is no end of these mystic signs and symbols. Best to say 'Deny thyself, take up thy cross.' Teach the Christian year. The heathen year to some might be progress in spiritual perfection, much self-denial, great abstraction of thought—to another class some glances into the beauties of natural religion; to the lowest, genii of woods and rivers, intelligences in all the forms that imagination, craft-believing benevolence and superstition could form them into. How painful it is to read the authors half-heathen half-Christian, as Julius Firmicus, Lactantius—and the exemplifiers of Sabaism, Porphyry and Macrobius. While I have written the Borcovicus account my little library of books only gave me imperfect glances into heathen theology, and the account of the Mithraic cave in the first part of the Archæologia Æliana is a poor affair. Mr. Raine shewed me a work in Latin on the subject some four or five years since in the D & C. Library at Durham, which, had I seen it in 1822, would doubtless have spared me much useless toil. My candle however lights only a very small circle of books, and I find myself often trying to illustrate subjects which have been before investigated by telescopic and microscopic minds."—*Journal.**

"1837, Feb. 15. Remember under the Inscriptions, &c. on Ambo-

---

* Hodgson contributed during this year—

An Account of Naworth Castle for Mr. Richardson's Border Castles.

A Letter in the Dialect of the Shetland Islands, with an explanatory column in English. (Gent. Mag. Dec. 1836.)

Notes upon Ross's Preliminary Essay to his Pictorial Account of Newcastle.

Newcastle Charters for the *Collectanea Topographica et Genealogica.*

glanna, to notice the Sacella in the Roman camps, in which the tutelary deities were venerated.—The eagles and other ensigns among the soldiers were chiefly venerated here—also say something of this kind—the elevation of the serpent in the wilderness was the type of an event which from the moment of its occurrence on Mount Calvary to the last day in the world cannot be too vividly kept in view by every individual of each successive generation of mankind.  It was the policy of the old religion not to vulgarise its doctrines, precepts, and mysteries by committing them to writing.  They thus overawed the mind—they were never nearly approached or intimately known to any but the priests.  All the initiated had neither leisure nor opportunity to examine narrowly the machinery of their spectacles.

" As experience teaches us. and we daily feel, that the Deity, who is invisible to us, conducts the material world by a process which is eternal, so we feel from the intellectual processes of our own minds that they also are essences and intelligences which are eternal."—*Journal.*

" 1837, 17 March.  O for time to write upon the origin of parish churches in England.  Gibbon was certainly right when he said that ' the conquest of Britain reflects less glory on the name of Cæsar than on that of Gregory the Great.'[*]  Instead of six legions, as Gibbon also observes, only forty monks were sent on this conquest, and in less than two years he announced to the Bishop of Alexandria the baptism of the King of Kent and ten thousand of his subjects.   In this wretched place for literary inquiry I am not, however, nearer than about twenty miles of access to a book on Church Antiquities, Bingham, or any other.  The Ordo Romanus, as established by Gregory, is the tribunal to appeal to on these matters, and our own Domesday the only authentic record of churches prior to the time of its compilation."—*Ib.*

" 1837, 24 March.  Good Friday.  Only eight communicants!  When shall I ever rouse this parish out of its slumbers?"—*Ib.*

" 1837, 8 May.  Account of the Corbridge silver dish.  It is pure Sabaism — the sun at the autumnal equinox, after he has slain the swift deer with golden horns and brazen feet, and the commencement of the hunting season and the rains.  The Gentile priests allegorised every thing, the months and seasons; and these allegories they applied mystically to man's present and immortal condition   They wrote down in

* Gibbon, viii. 167.  Ed. 1790.

words none of their mysteries, but symbolised them all. Pity it is that
the concluding six books of Ovid's Fasti are lost. Then to explain
this I want the astronomical works of Aratus and Hyginus, and the
modern guides, Winckelman and Montfaucon. The old Gentile faith was
however liable to be affected by fashion. A legend will not be told
exactly in the same way by Homer and Hesiod, Aratus and Hyginus,
Ovid and Cicero, Virgil and Theocritus, and Porphyry or Macrobius;
while all of these authors may be agreed in the identity of the different
symbols and the exact portion of the sun's annual labour to which they
refer. The account I have written of the Corbridge dish will, I fear,
add only another to the many accounts that have been given of it.
What Ceres shall be now found to recover the lost Proserpine of Ovid?
The age may be that of the Antonines."—*Ib.*

" 1837, June 21. Answered Mr. Lambert's second application that
I would write for him a history of St. Nicholas's Church in Newcastle—
that I had not leisure."—*Ib.*

" 1837, 30 June. Science guided by the Gospel will subdue the
world. Grace will become so highly acquainted (*sic*) with the laws of
nature as to civilise all lands, and fill them with people capable of con-
verting all the productions of nature to their advantage."—*Ib.*

To Mr. JOHN THOMPSON.—July 1, 1837.—" The Roman Wall is not
done. It has been a weary work during a long and weary winter."

FROM MRS. SURTEES.— " Mainsforth, July 14, 1837.—Dear Sir, I lose
no time in assuring you that a long absence from home has been the
cause of my not attending to your wishes long ago; but the book and
your kind note never got into my possession till last night, when I spent
the evening at Crook Hall, and there I found your parcel. I will forward the volume of Northumberland as you wish to Charnley's, and I
am happy in having an opportunity of again thanking you for your
kind and quite unmerited attention to me. I never had met with (till
a short time ago) your beautifully written paper on the Surtees Society,
where my lamented husband's character and feelings are so delicately
and strikingly drawn. All who knew Mr. Surtees must value the
memorial, and think the picture executed by a masterly hand. The
feelings expressed of his character accord exactly with my own. I have
begged Mr. Raine will get me a collection of sheets printed, that I may

give pleasure to those who loved Surtees. I hope this is not taking a liberty with your pen, but as the paper was circulated in a newspaper I trust I shall not err in gratifying my wishes; however let me know if you have the slightest objection. I hope you enjoy good health, and have delight in your arduous undertaking. I should be glad to hear that no domestic sorrows come nigh your dwelling. Should you at any time be in Durham, and feel a wish to see poor old Mainsforth again, I need not say how it gladdens my heart to see a friend that poor Surtees loved. The house, and all things, are strangely altered, the object of attraction is removed, and I have now nothing to induce a visit but the memory of the past, and a hearty welcome. You perhaps know that as soon as a short memorial is written of Surtees (which is to be appended to the last volume, all that he finished of the county will be given to the public. I had hoped to have met with Mr. Edward Swinburne in town, but he did not arrive before I left. I wished to have known about some engravings done by Miller in Edinburgh; but now I must write to him myself. Perhaps you could tell me where Mr. Swinburne is at this present time, for he knows what subjects were executed for Durham. Pardon the trouble I am giving you, and believe me, with kind regards to your family, your obliged friend, ANNE SURTEES."

In the beginning of August in this year Hodgson again suffered much from his old complaint, and, by the advice of Doctors Headlam and Hedley, proceeded for a while to Gilsland, from which place he returned to another scene of affliction. The Durham school-boy has gone home to enter upon his eternal holy-day.

"1837, 8 Sept.—My dear William last night was seized with acute inflammation in his liver, and severely leeched in the night. 9. William still alarmingly ill. 11. Dr. Hedley gives me almost no hope of William's recovery. 12. A little better this afternoon. 16. William's symptoms returned alarmingly. 18. Richard John, and T. Pearson came to see dear William in his last struggles with death. His dear innocent spirit fled from the boundaries of this world at twenty minutes after eleven.

NATE, VALE, INGENUE PRÆSTANS, PIETATE, PUDORE,
ET PLUSQUAM NATI NUMINE, CHARE, VALE.

But I will not irreverently here adopt the whole of Bishop Lowth's beautiful epitaph on his daughter, though my most dear departed son excelled not only in great personal handsomeness, but in elegant manners, high mental talent, and deep affection for his parents, his brothers and sisters, and unaffected piety to God.

" 21 Sept.—The remains of my most dear and affectionate son William were buried in the churchyard here, close under the middle window of the east end of the chancel. The grave is in the rock, and nearly six feet deep; but the remains are inclosed in a wall covered with two layers of smooth flat stones. Mr. Rapier read the service."—*Journal.*

To Sir J. E. Swinburne.—" Hartburn, 31 Oct., 1837.—On my return home on Friday I found Mr. Carlyle's transcript of the letter respecting the ' Kepe Wall ' and your kind note inquiring after my health. While I was at Gilsland I got stronger on my legs, but grew every day thinner; and on the day I left the place unfortunately got hot, fatigued, and wet, which brought on cold and a most painful attack of dyspepsia, from which I could get no relief till this morning. Now I am quite at ease and feel as well as I ever was, and hope that no sickening circumstance may come to put me wrong again. Both Dr. Hedley and Dr. Headlam recommended me to go to Gilsland. Indeed I had not had Dr. Headlam's advice had I not fainted for some time at my daughter Pearson's from excessive pain; and my son Richard brought him to see me. Certainly I have great cause to be thankful that he was consulted, for for the last two months I have been a severe sufferer.———"

" 1837, Dec. 7.—The charge against old men for being covetous may be correct, and the vice natural. Experience has proved to them the difficulty of supporting life creditably without being rigidly provident, and the passion of selfishness, when once permitted to get dominant in the human mind, while it indulges itself in providing against want, extinguishes all feeling for character, all notions of equity, all affection for others.

" In the company of a person whose wealth gives him great command over the happiness of the people amongst whom I live, I would be respectful and avoid familiarity—if he was tyrannical, or ignorant, or avaricious, or profligate, honour or comfort from his presence I could not receive. These are only to be had from the just, the benevolent, the well-informed, and the virtuous; and self-respect or comfort will always be enjoyed in such company whether they be wealthy or not."—*Journal.*

" 1837, 12 Dec.—The immortality men covet in the memory of posterity is too frequently grasped at by violent and mischievous hands, and loss of reputation assigned as its reward. The coronet that was

gained by exciting a dangerous mob to menace the seat of government
can never sooth the fevered head that obtained it, or honour the brows
of its posterity.   The jewels that his own prince and a mighty poten-
tate of the North encircled it with may blaze in the sight of ignorance,
and dazzle the eyes of the wearer, but no light will beam from them
into the meridian sun of impartial history."—*Journal.*

" Philosophy has not been apt to prescribe abstinence and self-denial
against the malady of sin: but consult Porphyry ' De Abstinentia;'
which author, however, though a great enemy to Christianity, was
perhaps more indebted to it for settled notions on good morals than to
his favourite Platonic Philosophy.   Consult also Jamblicus and Proclus."
—*Ibid.* *

1838.—A letter from the Rev. W. N. Darnell, Rector of
Stanhope, on the 10th of January, on a matter of pedigree, in his
capacity as one of the trustees of Lord Crewes's Estates, contains
the following kind expression of interest in Hodgson's welfare.
" It is a long time since we have crossed each other, and the old
link of the Trevelyans seems almost broken.   I should be glad to
hear something of you, and something good, if possible; for you
have had many difficulties to contend with in life, and have made
a noble resistance to them."   In his reply Hodgson notices this
part of Mr. Darnell's letter in the following affecting way.   What
a pity that such a man should have had such confessions to make,
and that too in the sixtieth year of his age !

"I feel obliged by your inquiries after my welfare.   My removal
hither was a great pecuniary misfortune.   The place had been long
under sequestration, and the buildings were ruinous.   Though the case
was tried in Chancery, I could not get a penny out of the sum secured
on my predecessor's life, by way of remuneration for dilapidations; so
that, if I be permitted to live, I shall for many years be in a worse
pecuniary situation than I was before the late bishop prefered me to this
sequestered but agreeable situation.   Contingencies and heavy afflictions
have also added to my embarrasments: and the hardest thing of all is
that my work, instead of bringing me profit, is now attended with loss-

---

* In 1837 Hodgson wrote or contributed—Notice of Roman Coins found at Borcum
in Northumberland (Gent. Mag. Dec. 1837).   Names of Pilgrims admitted into the
English College at Rome—*Collectanea Topographica.*   Report on the publications of
the Record Commissioners.

Many subscribers are dead, and not a few never pay me for it. The work, however, is occupation, and I go on with great cheerfulness, and hope to have another volume out in a few months time. My health during the year has had several hard shocks, though, thank God, it is now pretty well. I wish I could have given you a better account of myself." *

"1838, Feb 21.—For the spiritual meaning of John xix. 23 and 24 respecting Christ's garments, remember the interpretation of Theophylact in Joh. p. 404. The niceties of theology can be no more seen by an unobservant mind than the beauties of grammar by an unlettered hind. This is a beautiful subject."—*Ibid.*

"1838, 3 Mar.—I forgot to notice that the Hart yesterday broke up the ice that had bound it in fetters since the beginning of January, and that it bore it down with great majesty and grandeur. The channel of the stream was quite full, and the noise of the breaking up in the pools so loud as to send me out of my study, to see what had happened. Much timber was borne down with the ice."—*Journal.*

"1838, 18 March.—Sunday, Rom. xii. 3.—Our churches have not increased in comfort in proportion to our notions of comfort. Our forefathers were hardy because their habitations were cold. In the churches they were better sheltered than in their own shiels. The wintry tempest howled in tremendous wrath over them and their dwellings. The houses of Wes^d. (? Westmerland) were Norwegian; their scales the shiels of this county. They rested on beds of heath, and chaff and leaves, and indeed still do. They had their long nights of revelry and ease. The poor laid up for winter. They were careful, like the provision-ant. Now, every man lives on his yesterday's earnings: and when labour ceases in winter he has to seek food and firing from his parish, and the churches are too cold for him. O that we had the hardy bodies and the warm hearts of our forefathers! I have yielded to agitation. But is there not a grandeur in the worship of this season? Let us look to the joy, the glad tidings of great joy, that should animate all of us on the day of the Nativity of our dear Lord: then, with Stephen, we see Heaven opened, and Jesus sitting at the right hand of God: then the day of the

* In the course of the following year, doubtless through Mr. Darnell's kind representations, the trustees of Lord Crewe's Estate made a grant of 50l. towards the sum which Hodgson had been obliged to expend upon his vicarage house.

beloved Apostle John the Evangelist, and the favoured-with visions and
revelations in Patmos.  O, ye Innocents, that sing the new song before
the throne, and follow the Lamb whithersoever he goeth!  Who shall feel
his heart chill and cold when he casts his mind eighteen centuries back
and (sees) Herod's soldiers slaughtering all the children of Bethlehem
and in all the coasts thereof, from two years old and under?  Open next
the page of English History, on the 29th of December, and read there
the deed done by Hugh de Morville, before the great altar of the church
of Canterbury, and the monarch of the land barefooted, on his way to
atone in penance for the atrocious murder.

"Begin with St. Thomas's eve, day, &c., and introduce cheerfulness,
the love of spring, the sunshine of summer, the golden harvest of autumn,
into the heart and countenance.

"Man fixes his abode, and nature makes him love the place of his
nativity, and the storms of winter as well as the bounties of summer.
His contrivance, if I may not say his providence, is unceasingly called
into action.  Apprehensions of want make him labour and give him
forethought; but the birds fly to countries abounding in food; not till
that food, however, fails them here.   The lark and the thrush do not
migrate, unless frost and snow fetter the earth and deprive them of food."
—*Journal.*

" 1838, 25 Mar.—Sunday, Mr. ———— preached here.  In his sermon,
to show the value of the human soul in the sight of its Creator, he used
the illustration that it was more estimable than the earth or planets, or
the sun itself.   The sermon in fact was good, very eloquent in parts;
but certainly had too much of " breaches " in it; and the assertion, so
often made and so severely reprehended, that the happiness of a human
soul is of far more consideration than the existence of the sun—or, in
other words, that God had rather see the extinction of the sun out of the
universe, than a human soul fall into perdition, is a proud and rash conception, unwarranted by Scripture, and repugnant to all analogy.  ' When
I consider the heavens, the work of thy hands,' &c."—*Ibid.*

To MRS. HODGSON.—29 Ap. 1838.—" My very dear Jane, you would, I
think, be scarcely past Bolam yesterday when the spirit of our dear
young neighbour departed from amongst us, and a more amiable and
guileless one it has not left behind it.  He is, I firmly trust, in conscious
happiness.  The storm-shaken tent he left untenanted will be gathered
up and committed to the earth to-morrow, but, ruined as it is, it was

once, I thoroughly believe, a tabernacle and a temple in which his soul did service to his Creator."*

To Mr. John Thompson.—"29 May, 1838.—The History of the Roman Wall is all now at press, and that of Wall-town was sent yesterday.†"

To Mr. Sopwith.—"May 29, 1838.—I have done with the Roman Wall, and am now again at the Parochial History of Northumberland, of which I sent yesterday in the Roman Wall my account of the township of Wall Town.——If I had five heads and ten hands I do not think I could get out the volume now printing, before the meeting of the British Institution at Newcastle in August, and I will not spoil the volume by being driven to finish it in over great haste, though I have been much pressed to have it out at that time.     John Hodgson."

To the Rev. J. Raine.—"Hartburn, June 16, 1838.—I am contemplating a drive into Newcastle early on Monday morning, and I have taken my leave of the study of Roman Antiquities, I hope for life.——I am wanting much to get the volume published which is now in press, and I have still 80 or 90 pages of the history and all the indexes to write, so that I could not this summer expend more time out of my study.—— Since a little time after I saw you in Newcastle at Christmas, my health has been better than for the last thirty years or more.——   J. H."

In June 1838, Hodgson made one in the proceedings upon the opening of the Newcastle and Carlisle railroad, and he wrote to his wife an amusing letter for which room cannot be here found, descriptive of the event and its numerous mishaps.

To Mr. Mackay.—"29 June, 1838.—I have little to tell you about: my literary labours do not make rapid progress. The account of the Roman Wall is however done, and the Parochial History again proceeding. Indeed, I have so much manuscript at press as to allow me to

* Thomas, second son of Thomas Bewick, the tenant of the glebe, in the 34th year of his age.

† On the topographical subjects connected with this volume, Mr. Hodgson's letters to Mr. Thompson are numerous, and the information which he received in reply copious and accurate. The above letter proceeds to put various questions, which evince his confidence in the zeal and intelligence of his correspondent.

meditate a fortnight's ramble among the Lakes of Westmerland.  Miss
Manners is with us, and she and Mrs. Hodgson are to be my companions.——I hope to take the Isle of Man into our tour.——We have
engaged a governess for Emma.  We wish much to have her educated
at home: for I have a great horror of boarding-schools, and great contempt for the education generally given in them." *

"1838, 14 July.—Want of sleep since I left home (for Nunwick,
Houghton Castle, &c.) and desire to obtain the information I wanted,
have left me languid and sleepy and dissatisfied with myself.  I have,
however, answered some letters, and much in papers that have been
laid upon my table during my absence, and have seen all the people in
the village to-day.  I began this journal from suggestions of the late
Mrs. Singleton of Elsdon, daughter of Mr. Grose the antiquary, and
mother of Dr. Singleton, rector of Elsdon and Archdeacon of Northumberland; and began it only for the sole purpose of referring to it (to see)
where I had been, and what I had been doing.  How few of broad daylight thoughts, of early morning dreams, a man puts into a journal of
this kind!  Kind! how much might be written on that one word, how
much of delight, how much of pain and sorrow, how much of judicious
joy?  The globe that I live upon, and the infinitude of globes and systems of        that I see in the heavens around me, and the thoughts
and contemplations of my own faculties, bring me back to the old and
wise exclamation, 'Lord, what is man, that thou art mindful of him?' &c."

"1838, 20 Aug.—Came to Newcastle to-day to attend the meeting
of the British Association for the Advancement of Science.  Dined with
Mr. Hodgson Hinde,  Lord Dungannon, Mr. King, Mr. Raine, Messrs.
Richard and Thomas Hodgson, &c. &c. of the party.  I felt disinclined
to go to the evening meeting and the mayor's ball.——
  "Mr. G. Stephenson, the engineer, was at Mr. Hinde's dinner.  He said,
in an argument with Mr. Orde of Nunnykirk, that there was no difficulty
in making locomotive engines, such as he built, to go 100 miles an

---

* Surely the time is not far distant when the system of education pursued in our
female boarding-schools will undergo a thorough revision.  In most of them the poor
girls are little better than slaves, set to a daily task of the most spiritless and talent-
quelling labour, in acquiring a parrot sort of acquaintance with matters utterly useless
in after-life.  Many of them, too, it is much to be feared, are seminaries in which
education is embittered and debased by low sectarian notions of religion.

hour—that there was no such thing as taking fire by friction—that the
motion of a steam-engine was like that of the earth, propelled round the
sun by the united action of the sun and moon—that he could make a
railway in a straight line from London to Newcastle that would run the
distance in an hour—that the Carter Fell was solid whin—and at the
promenade in the evening he swelled to a great size when he told me of
his grand reception in the Netherlands—that an engineer was a good
business, but that no one again would make as much of it as he had
done. Mr. Orde was beginning, after dinner, to whet his teeth to
encounter him, but the company rose. He talked nonsense—though
naturally he is clever and clear-headed. At the promenade he also
told me that his son and he made an inclined plane in their works to
ascertain why the railroads did not rust, and on laying silk on the line
after it had been used that it all 'brizzled up,' and he was then assured
that they were electrified. Who does not know that heating iron makes
it magnetic, and that the constant use of rails keeps them from rusting?

"1838, 25 Aug.—Went this morning to Chesters. Mr. Nath. Clayton said he received the rudiments of his education in grammar from
the Rev. Mr. Fisher of Kirk Oswald, and that his master at Harrow,
when he was coming home after his first half-year there, said to him,
'Tell the old gentleman that he has had a young bear to teach, but has
taught him well.'"

"1838, 26 Aug.—Sunday.—Took the whole of the service at Hums-
haugh. Sermon 1 Cor. ii. 2. 'For I am determined,' &c. Written on
the occasion of the meeting of the British Association."

"1838, 17 Sept.—Dined at ———. In the evening —— talked most
foolishly, ignorantly, and dogmatically, on religion—that religion could
nowhere flourish without the protection of the State, and that in all its
forms it was a mere State engine—and that one religion for that purpose
was as good as another. It was impossible to argue with him. He is
ambidexter, fighting first on one side and then on the other. I con-
tended that religion would exist and flourish, even without State protection, though I questioned that States could long exist without the aid
of true religion. He spoke most disparagingly of the Bible—that the
Old Testament was so absurd that it required imbecility to believe
it, and that the New was fabricated from a mixture of Judaism with the
religions of Greece and Rome which prevailed in the time of Augustus,

and he brought forth repeatedly, with a sort of sneering triumph, the opinions in Virgil's Pollio—

" Ultima Cumæi venit jam Carminis ætas ;
Magnus ab integro sæclorum nascitur ordo.
Jam redit et Virgo, &c."

and the line

" It was expedient that one man should die for the people."—

that in the compliments to Cæsar and the absurd flattery that was bestowed upon him the Christian religion had its origin."

" 1838, 18 Sep.—This is the anniversary of the death of my most dear William, and I had the melancholy duty this morning to perform of meeting my most amiable son John at Belsay Bar, to take him home, at Dr. DeMey's request, to resuscitate his health, which he has injured by too severe attention to his business and studies."

CHAPTER XV.—1839.

Mr. Redman—Attack of Illness—History, Part II. Vol. III.—The Roman Wall.

To THE REV. J. RAINE.—Hartburn, Ap. 17, 1839.—"My work is progressing slowly, though I really work hard at it. Haydon is finished, Newbrough nearly ready for the press, and Wardon, concerning which there seems little to say, will finish the volume, which, I fear, will see jocund June far spent before it makes its appearance. I, my wife and daughter, are all quite well, anxiously invoking spring from her southern climes, and gratified should we be, if, with the cuckoo and swallow, she would bring you to see the primroses blooming on our banks, and the trees bourgeoning in our lovely woods.——As soon as my present volume is finished I hope to take up my quarters at Hexham and Dilston for a week or a fortnight, to reconnoitre in that neighbourhood for a new campaign. Cast about in your mind if you could not spare time to be aid-de-camp to me for a few days.—J. H."

1839, May 20.—"Went to Kirkharle to call upon my dear friend Mr. Redman,* before he left his house in the evening, on his way to his retirement (at Hartley Cottage) near Kirkby Stephen in Westmerland,

* The name of the Rev. Thomas Redman, one of Hodgson's nearest clerical neighbours whilst he resided at Whelpington, has been often mentioned in these pages. With this gentleman, who was still a neighbour, although now at a somewhat greater distance, Hodgson had kept up a friendship; but at the period at which we have arrived Mr. Redman began to feel the hand of old age, and, with the consent of the Bishop of Durham, retired to his native county of Westmerland to reside with his relations. He was born in 1761, and was now, therefore, in the 78th year of his age; but he continued to live on, in a happy state of quiet repose, till the year 1855, when he died, at the great age of 94, having been a clergyman in the diocese of Durham for upwards of seventy years. He was a gentleman of peaceful unassuming manners, and if, in mental powers and acquirements, not a Hodgson, yet a man who by long and quiet observation had gained an extensive acquaintance with the world and its ways, and his stock of learning was by no means inconsiderable. For some years before his death, it was his daily habit during his retirement to walk a mile, to a wood near his house, and cut a pea-rod, which he brought home in his hand and laid up till it was wanted, thus combining a useful object with the exercise which was necessary for his health, and which in all probability added to his days. Hodgson bade him farewell on the 20th of May upon his leaving Kirkharle; but Mr. Redman will again cross our path when it is beset with troubles.

and requested him to be the bearer of a parcel containing an engraved copy of my portrait, and a letter, to the Rev. John Bowstead, rector of Musgrave, my respected preceptor."—*Journal.*

But we are now drawing near to the dimness of an evening sun setting in trouble, and to the shades of a long and gloomy twilight.

Before the end of the month at which we have arrived, that active and powerful faculty of memory, which had so long sate firmly upon its throne in the midst of trials and afflictions, became enveloped in obscurity; now and then emerging from the clouds which overshadowed it, and manifesting itself in its former energy and strength, but soon again disappearing from view, and threatening to take its departure for ever. The earthly tabernacle of this mental faculty was at the same time shattered and rent, and the whole man became an object of pity and commiseration. So much for mortality, and the mental and bodily endowments with which it disports itself, when it pleases Almighty God to give the word, and call upon tribulation to do its work in purifying the heart!

Hodgson had commenced on the 8th of May, 1835, the volume of his History to which he was now putting a finishing hand; and from that time, as might be proved from his Journal, he had devoted to it his daily energies to a degree still more intense and dangerous to himself than on former occasions. No day passed over his head without an effort to complete his undertaking. In truth the publication of such portions of his Journal as refer to the engagements of his pen during the progress of this volume would not fail to excite a surprise that his feeble constitution should have held out so long and so well under such exertions. Let me, in proof of this opinion, set before my readers his proceedings from the commencement of the month of August in this year (1839), until the 20th of that same month, on which day he was struck down by the blow under which he never ceased to labour until he was released from his troubles by the hand of death.

On the 1st of August, and for several days afterwards, he was employed in putting together some very important additions, by way of Appendix to that volume of his History which had so long and so intensely occupied his mind, and which was now printed,

and nearly ready for publication. The bulk of the book had been long finished. That part of it devoted to the ROMAN WALL had been completed and fairly out of his hands so long previously as the 29th of May in the preceding year * (1838); the concluding parochial history had all of it passed through the press; and on the day first mentioned he records in his Journal the finishing of the Taxation of 1254 (Appendix, p. 422). On the following day he prepared for the printers the Schedule of Procurations in 1317, commencing at p. 426, and supplied to him by the author. On the 3rd he was occupied on the same subject, and on a sermon to be preached on the 4th, on the text 1 Kings xxii. 8. On the 5th he finished his account of the Procurations in 1317. On the 6th he began to prepare a list of *Addenda et Corrigenda* to the volume at large, printed in the Appendix at p. 430, &c. The 8th and 9th found him occupied on the same subject, and especially upon *Corrections to the Wall*, which engaged his attention till the 13th, when he states in his Journal of that day that his Appendix to his account of the Wall was finished. I must add that on the 11th, which was the 11th Sunday after Trinity, he preached from 2 Kings v 12; and, on the same day in the school room at Cambo, from Psalm xix. 12. On the 14th he resumed the Appendix, &c. to his book, which was finally completed on the following day, and which afterwards passed through the press from the original copy in his own neat hand, ready drawn up for that purpose. On the 18th he preached at Hartburn from Mark vii. 37, but it does not appear that he took any part in the Divine Service at Cambo in the afternoon. On Monday the 19th he wrote a few letters to his friends, and afterwards he began to draw up an account of a remarkable Roman Altar, dedicated to the Roman deity Silvanus, and preserved in the Rectory at Stanhope. On the following day it is recorded in his diary that at an early hour he " finished and forwarded to press for the Gentleman's Magazine the letter on the altar Silvano," &c.†
And here begins a long and affecting blank in his Journal.

It appears from a letter written by him to Sir J. E. Swin-

* See above, p. 381.
† See Gent. Mag. for October, 1839.

2 c 2

burne, to be noticed hereafter, and from the statements of his family, that, in the afternoon of the same day, he began to compile an index for his forthcoming volume, and that, having become fairly worn out with the toil, he fell asleep on his chair, and upon awakening was found to be labouring under an attack of illness of the most serious and alarming kind, suffering greatly from bodily pain, deprived apparently of his powers of memory and vision, and unconscious of the lamentations of those around him.

After a few days, however, he began to recover his sight, and recognise the different members of his family, but for many weeks his bodily sufferings were almost daily of the most acute kind. Excruciating pains in his head, and the agonies of almost continual spasms, proceeding from an obstruction of the passage into the larger intestines, were his daily torments. The torpor under which he laboured was also great, and, what was, apparently, to himself the most severe affliction of all, he constantly laboured more or less under an almost total inability to comprehend what was said to him,* or to express his wants in words, so as to give a name to objects quite familiar to him, or to ideas which he seemed perfectly to apprehend. Against these infirmities it was very painful to witness his struggles in his fruitless efforts to understand or make himself understood by his family. Now and then he could read a few words, or write what his lips refused to enunciate, but even these were efforts the exercise of which speedily reduced him again into a state of helpless inability. During all this time, however, it was a great comfort to those around him to observe that his powers of mind were still in a sound state, even when his bodily sufferings were the most severe, and his inability to comprehend others or express his own thoughts in words or in writing the most manifest and distressing. I am informed by one of his medical advisers that " this cerebral affection was no doubt the result of close and intense application to the subject of his laborious inquiries."

* One single proof may be given of the state to which, in this respect he was reduced. When his medical adviser desired him to shew his tongue, the words conveyed no meaning to his ear, but when his friend set the example he instantly complied with the request.

In this sad condition he continued for several weeks, in general in an improving state, and not unfrequently able for a few minutes to hold conversation with his friends in an intelligible way, but always making numerous mistakes in his words, conscious all the while that his tongue was not doing its duty, but bearing with patience the melancholy state to which he was reduced. In his short walks or drives, when writing materials were not at hand, his method was to catch the shape of the word he wished to make use of by writing with his finger upon the palm of his left hand, or with the end of his stick upon the ground, two or three of its opening letters.

After a lapse of three months, during which Mr. Hodgson had been, and continued to be, at intervals a great sufferer, but had perfectly recovered his sight, and had, upon the whole, regained somewhat of strength, although his powers of memory, or rather of enunciation, continued in the same imperfect state, he left home by the advice of his medical friends, to try the effects of a warmer climate during the winter. But before we proceed to accompany him it may be advisable to devote a few paragraphs to that volume of the History of Northumberland which had reduced its author to his present unhappy condition.

This volume had been printed, the whole of it, under Hodgson's own eye and care, with the exception of the few pages of Additions and Corrections above alluded to, which, however, had been drawn up by his own pen, and were ready for the press, and with the further exception of a Preface and Index, for the former of which a few hints only were found among his papers.

As Mr. Hodgson's ultimate recovery was held to be extremely doubtful, and delay appeared to be inexpedient, the task of introducing this volume to the public was willingly undertaken by the writer of these pages, and his first care was to see that its author's own *Additions* and *Corrections* were faithfully printed according to his directions, adding at the same time a few of his own, chiefly of a typographical nature, which had met his eye in turning over its pages. The Preface which he placed at the head of the volume was chiefly of an explanatory nature, but in addition to his own statements he deemed it his duty to introduce such *memoranda* as Hodgson had committed to paper in explanation of his feelings and sentiments respecting the volume itself. Those *memoranda* are here reprinted, and from them we may gather what the preface would have contained if it had received the finishing hand of the author of the volume. They are indeed most characteristic of their writer.

" A work of        years cannot fail in finding its author in various moods for writing—at morning vigorous and confident; towards evening languid and diffident," &c.

" This volume, like the rest, has been sent to the press in small portions.   No parish—no part of the Roman Wall—perfected.   Hence *Corrigenda, Addenda,* and long trains of inaccuracies."

" It was never either expected or desired that either these Volumes or Prefaces should administer to the amusements of refinement that can allow no fact or tale of by-gone days to be admitted into its presence if elegance and pleasure do not accompany them.   The severities are here mingled with the amenities of life; and, if the plumed and jewelled diadem cannot cast its eye without disdain over the pictures here presented, the sober eye of rural contemplation may not refuse to gild them with its sunny smile of passing approbation."

" I have lived to write scarce a third of what I contemplated; friends that I wished to have pleased have gone to the grave.   If I ever had any ambition to gratify the great, or obtain the patronage of the noble, visions so vain neither flatter my day-thoughts nor my dreams.   I have raised persons and families from oblivion, while the genealogies of the great interest myself no more than those of the poor.·   But the genealogies of the poor are soon forgotten, because their deeds are seldom interesting enough to become matter of history; while few of the names of the great in their generation could have little more written under them than the record of their vanity—nothing to keep a grateful remembrance of them on earth—nothing of their love to the souls of men—nothing about their zeal for the Church of Christ "

" Topographical inquiry, as it discovers truth, gives the same kind of delight as science feels when new arrangements of form and matter present themselves before her.   Our theological studies in these days, at every step we take mortify and humiliate the soul, as we behold the prostration and ruin of the doctrines and knowledge of the Ancient Church, and even the fallen condition of man's knowledge in the tenets of the Reformed Episcopal Churches.   Who now accounts of Baptism as the holy thing it is?   The Eucharistal sacrifice is banished from the altars of our churches. Confession of sins is forgotten as a doctrine and a duty; marriage made a civil contract, men now not knowing that they ought to love their wives as their own bodies—even as the Lord the Church. Who knows now deeply about any of these doctrines, or keeps the fasts or festivals of the Church? and who in the latter days of his life, in endeavouring to illuminate his mind with the knowledge of the glorious things of God, does not bitterly lament that he was born in times when these things were not only not taught but known and practised only by those who adhered to the ancient faith, mingled as it is with ingredients taken from the altars of the Gentile religion. But in raising towns and families from their ashes, and sketching them in durable words and panoramic detail, the mind feels gratified with its own reproductive powers, and hopes that it has prepared intellectual feasts for good men for ages yet to come—filled again our woods and and the borders of our streams with the Dryads and Naiads of ancient times—our mountains with the elk and the stag and the furious wild boar—our plains with brave Brigantes, mingled with the lordly Roman," &c. &c.

" Though veneration for the opinions and remains of the works of men who lived in times far past, and especially of those who first drank of the fountain of human time, be a passion strongly implanted in a large proportion of mankind, yet cupidity comes, in aid of vanity, to figure in fashionable life, and the desire to procure artificial wants extinguishes in the vast mass of men all ancestral pride, all curiosity to know the history of their own race, all wish to be acquainted with the opinions and doctrines that relate to his origin and future destination. Every man is naturally ignorant, and, whether in rude or polished society, cannot be instructed in the wisdom of past ages intuitively. To be wise from the experience of our forefathers requires each successive generation to be dipped in the pure unadulterated stream of antiquity. Without we be baptized there, the secret books of our religion are sealed secrets, and all history barbarian darkness."

" If any man envy me the honour or the profit of this undertaking, if he find he can sit in the chair I have occupied, I shall cheerfully resign it to him: I would gladly be remunerated for what I have spent and done, but I would most gladly relinquish my labours to any one who is ambitious to prosecute them."

" The constant apprehension of writing too much is as constantly counterbalanced by apprehension of disgust for negligence or contemptuous brevity. While I can have little fear of offending the inhabitants of a place on the Tyne for a detailed account of the annals of their own village, they may be apt to blame me for diffusiveness which may delight the villagers on the Tweed."

" To give the work in a less form than I am doing it would be little better than the skeleton histories of the county that have been already published. To print in large type might be agreeable to persons who had rather have a work in ten or twelve volumes than in eight with four times the information. My alternative is to endeavour to finish the work in the same manner as the latter part of this volume is printed."

" I have sketched out an extensive plan, and feel myself daily more able to fill up and finish its details, but want other hands to fill in the outlines. My pecuniary resources will not allow me to keep an amanuensis. Every line and letter, from notes to indexes, have to go to press in my own handwriting—and then there is the immense loss of time in researches; whereas, if each clergyman would send me extracts from his parish registers respecting all families that have been eminent in the county, or by connection with it, and all families allow me a free use of their papers for genealogical purposes and the history of their own or other families that have lived upon their estate, or even allow me at home, the use of the abstract of their deeds, I might progress in my work with reasonable speed."

" Now in this work, if I be taunted with the motive of approbation for my object, I will not permit my mind to feel the sting. For whose approbation do I seek? Not the world's, not the praise of the vain, the novel reader—but I seek the approbation of good men. Next to heaven, the earth we live upon, and the men that have lived upon it, demand our veneration. Where do the ashes of saints lie whose bodies were temples of the Holy Ghost?" &c.

" I began this work with the hope that some profit might arise to educate and maintain my children, and also with some confidence in my own powers, that I might set the history of the county in a more clear light than preceding historians had done. I was fully aware of many deficiencies in myself to undertake the work, but I had some confidence once that I would try to do it well. I have lived to see that works of this kind are not suited to the times I live in, perhaps to any time. It is not profitable to me—it is not suited to my profession. I ought to do my duty in my profession—to take up night and day to do it well. —Well, no; but as well as good intentions, holy zeal, every thought and faculty of my mind, fully exerted, could do it."

" The account of the Walls in Britain occupy many pages in this volume—but a full account of them has been given, with the aid of small type, in a comparatively small space. In the process of writing and sending the manuscript to the press as it was written, new thoughts arose, as might be reasonably expected, when truth not theory was the object of inquiry."

" Though my volumes increase I study brevity. On the Roman Wall I have omitted much that I would have liked to have said."

" In the Roman part I have suppressed many quotations made from Vegetius, Hyginus, A. Marcellinus, and other authors, respecting their border fortifications and modes of constructing their chesters, anxious to give all possible local information, but refraining from burdening my account with information applied to similar works as well as these."

" On the Roman Walls I have written much that few will read. Above a hundred years have elapsed since the subject has received from any one but Gough's clever hand a general review. Warburton's VALLUM ROMANUM is a reprint from Horsley. It is curious that Horsley's work seems unknown to continental antiquaries. Bertram, in his Richard of Cirencester, had not seen it, nor do I see that Orel quotes it."

" As all the Roman antiquities treated of in this work relate either to the Barriers or Stations connected with them, they ought to have formed one chapter or portion of the work, and might now be easily put into proper form and corrected."

" The very low state of antiquarian feeling in Northumberland in 1726, may be inferred from the fact that the only subscriber to Gordon's ' Itinerarium Septentrionale, or Journey through most of the Counties of Scotland and those of the North of England' was ' The Honourable Sir John Swinburne, Bart.' and yet it was this curious work that roused the antiquarian genius of Horsley, and afforded a plan for the foundation of his ' Britannia.' "

" Give an article on the SPELLING of places, to show that ancient spelling was uniform as to the meaning of names, though with much variation in letters."

" Another article on pedigrees."

" I would beg of good minds to think of the value of pedigrees recorded in England to families that have settled under English colonization in various parts of the globe. They can come back with affectionate minds to revisit the place where their ancestors lived."

" The day is past, except for the day, to publish apocryphal pedigrees.

Ingenuity cannot hide an obscure origin, nor a distinguished descent be concealed.  Truth is sought for ingenuously and successfully.  The works that parliament has edited have opened sources of information which the craft of forgers never suspected to exist.  Families that for centuries have sunk into obscurity may now trace their descent from distinguished ancestry, and new ones, stung by envy, may rake out of the ashes of oblivion lists of long forgotten names to add consequence to the pride of poverty and decayed gentility.  Oh, I have often heard, with a heart burning with indignation, but muscles motionless as a statue, the sneer that vulgar envy has thrown upon a pedigree which for centuries back could connect itself with the solid and enduring links of truth and honour, but only in later years had its lines of descent emblazoned with gold and jewelry.  What family in Britain has not enriched itself by commerce or trade, or married to children of these prolific and splendid mothers?  ' The family of the Aces never kept a carriage till they married a daughter of the Deuces the bankers.'  To which a wise man, cherishing natural affection for the welfare of his ancestors that have been removed from the earth may say—I only want to know who were my forefathers, that I may mourn or rejoice over the history of their whole line, and hope their eternal state may be glorious.  For what virtuous man can look over even the dates of the birth and marriage and death of his direct line of ancestors, and their children of each generation, with a mind unmoved by a multitude of contending affections?  the hope excited by the birth of a firstborn child, &c. &c.? the joy at the prospect of a son or daughter being happy in marriage?  the affliction, however smothered from the eye of the unfeeling world, at the death of a beloved child?  Then watch the storm that rises over a mortgage, and the family desolation to the third or fourth generation that marks its course?  Then, what is the folly and the malice that casts its sneers on the generation of a family that inherits from a female parent and takes her ancestral name!  It is still the same in blood.  The Queen takes a partner to the throne.  Are their posterity less royal because their father of the second or any other generation had his crown only by marriage and not by inheritance?  Is the ducal honour lessened because it was won from the affection of a wife?"

" In a pedigree, watch over its members the movement that a mortgage makes—its post effects, afflictive restlessness—then deadly torpor.  Take lessons of prudence from them.  Commerce creates unsteadiness."

" Mr. Swinburne.  His overflowing love."

" Sir J. E. S. has enabled me to have the honor of adding to my name

in the title-page of this work the initials M.R.S.L. without expense to
myself as long as I may be permitted to conduct it.   And to his brother
I am indebted for munificent assistance in lightening the encumbrances
with which my preferment to this place have unfortunately fettered
me."

"I mention as a fact that, except for the kindness of Sir J. E. Swinburne and his brother Mr. Edward Swinburne, this volume could never
have made its appearance.  For the generosity of friendship, the incense
of gratitude is the only offering I have to make, and I now make it upon
the most public altar."

My prefatorial remarks were concluded by the following feeling
verses addressed by Alexander Gill, master of Westminster
School in 1635, to his friend " Mr. John Speed, being very
sicke."  They are copied from the introductory verses to Speed's
Maps of England, &c. with one or two slight alterations.

> "Great love and little skill may cause me to mis-say,
> But certainly this sickness cannot make thee die :
> Though cruell symptomes and these thirty yeares assay
> For thy deare country doth thy health and strength decay.
> Yet, sith thy toylsome labour and thy industrie
> Is for thy countries sake, her fame on hie to raise,
> She shall thy temples crowne with everlasting bayes ;
> And, in despite of death, shall cause thy memorie
> To live in endless fame with all posteritie."

ALEXANDER GILL, to *his friend* MR. JOHN SPEED, *being very sicke.   Introductory verses to Speed's Maps.*

The volume itself contains a detailed account of the early
Lords of the upper region of Tindale, with the history of the
parishes of Alston, Kirkhaugh, Knaresdale, Lambley, Whitfield,
and Haltwhistle.   And here, under Haltwhistle, Hodgson introduces his readers to the ROMAN WALL, to which he devotes not
fewer than 173 pages, chiefly in the small type used for notes
in his previous volumes.   To this long account of the Wall it
is my intention to return by and by.   At page 323 he re-assumes
the parochial description of the district, and proceeds with the
history of Haltwhistle, and that of Wardon, with their respective
chapelries, which, with an appendix of additional matter and corrections, &c. completes a volume of 526 closely printed pages.

Of the merits of this volume in a topographical point of view I
forbear to dwell at large, for want of room.   I would only state,
in general terms, that it is, if possible, superior to its predecessors
in fullness of information and accuracy of detail.*  I cannot, how-

* There is, however, a subject in connection with this and the former volumes of the
History of Northumberland, to which I am under a promise to call the attention of my
readers.

The families in the county of Northumberland who can establish a well-founded
claim to a genealogy ascending above the Union of the Crowns of England and Scotland in 1603 are few, and of that few a small number only are connected with those
portions of the county which Hodgson lived to describe.  When a pedigree of this
description came in his way, to such an extent did he carry his respect for ancient
descent, when graced with generous and manly deeds, that his blood seems to have
warmed within him as he took up his pen to record the name and fame of its members.
Witness his pedigrees of the old Lords of Redesdale and Tindale, of Swinburne, Trevelyan and Blackett, Ogle, Bertram, Widdrington, Dacre, and a few others, upon
which he has bestowed the most painful research and the most scrupulous investigation
of authorities.  But he was not always upon his guard against imposition, when
occupied with graver matters than the unedifying search after grandfathers and grand-
mothers notable only for their acres and gold, whose names live only in title-deeds or
parish registers.  To apocryphal pedigrees he too readily, but most unsuspectingly,
afforded a place in his pages.  In the simplicity and honesty of his heart he gave
others credit for the same qualities, but in many instances he was deceived.  It would
be no difficult matter to point out in his book pedigrees supplied by others in which
old exploded absurdities are revived, and a long list of ancestors, beginning at the Conquest, is studiously put forward without a tittle of evidence, or even of possibility, in its
favour.  To spring from an ancestor *who came in with William the Conqueror*, has long
been the pet ambition of our country squires.  Perhaps it may be new to them to be
told, upon the authority of Thierry, that, with very few exceptions, the Conqueror
was followed over chiefly by the very persons from whom they would *rather not descend*,
the vagabonds and outcasts of Normandy.  But it is not only in their early generations
that some of Hodgson's pedigrees are undeserving of credit.  Three families, at the
fewest, have engrafted themselves upon ancient and knightly stocks, from a mere similarity of name.  Another is made to spring lawfully from a knight who most assuredly
had no son to transmit his name and blood.  One usurps not only the name but the
arms of an ancient family, with which it never had the least connection; and there are
other vainglorious assumptions of so palpable a nature as to excite a surprise that
Hodgson's attention was not at once indignantly arrested when they met his eye.
How could a gentleman be living in 1374, and leave a son to die in 1587?  Contradictions of this nature might be gathered together in numbers.  One pedigree of high
pretension Hodgson had the good luck to examine and reject at once.  In this case the
progenitor, as usual, came in with the Conqueror, but in his account of the family
he only took up the line with the commencement of authentic evidence, failing however to expose an assumption of name to which it was not entitled.  To another pedigree he gave a place in his book upon solicitation, although it had no natural or
ancient connection with the county, and after having taken much trouble upon the

ever, refrain from expressing my regret that its author should
have disfigured his pages by mean engravings of some of the
most wretchedly designed and miserably constructed churches
which have been built by modern hands.  It would have been a
charitable deed to have left them to fall quietly at no distant day,
and leave no memorial behind them.*

We may now devote a few words to the History of the
ROMAN WALL, which forms so prominent a feature in the volume
before us, and so fully, and for ever, establishes Hodgson's fame
as the discoverer of what had been so long forgotten, the name of
the emperor under whose auspices this mighty barrier was
constructed.  Before Hodgson's time all had been doubt and difficulty for ages.  Henceforward Hadrian and Hodgson may well be
spoken of together in connection with the Wall—the one as its
builder, the other as the restorer to him of the mural † crown
which had fallen from his head, and had been for many centuries
worn by one who had no just claim to the distinction.

In the course of the preceding pages, and especially during the
period in which Mr. Hodgson was actually engaged in writing
his History of the Wall, much has been printed relative to his
plans and proceedings with regard to it.  As the treatise advanced in his hands, and he was beginning to foresee the conclusions at which he should arrive, and their certain tendency to

subject was never thanked for his pains.  Even empty thanks would have been a boon
in comparison with the ungrateful return which he in reality received.  What a pity
that there was then no " Burke's Commoners " as a suitable receptacle for such home-
spun webs of fiction as some of those to which I have alluded—a book in which no one
can be put out of countenance by his neighbour.  The Empress Catherine at one time
constructed a gorgeous edifice, but it was of ice, which melted away when exposed to the
light and heat of the sun.

* The minor subjects which occupied Hodgson's pen in 1839 were the following :

An Account of a Roman Altar found at Hardriding in Northumberland.  Gent.
Mag. Aug. 1839.

An Account of a Roman Altar at Stanhope in the county of Durham.  Ibid. Octob.
1839.

A Circular to be issued by the Society of Antiquaries of Newcastle, on the Pipe Rolls
of Westmerland, Cumberland, and Durham.

† Among the Romans themselves this word, when designative of a mark of honour,
had a different meaning.  There is no fear, however, of its being misunderstood in the
sense in which I use it, and we cannot have a more appropriate term.

remove for ever the doubts and difficulties which had so long
existed upon the question, he made various attempts to embody his
essay in a publication to be solely devoted to the subject.  But,
as his Journals and letters prove, every discouragement was
thrown in his way; and he was eventually, but most reluctantly,
compelled to crowd his long narrative, with all its reasonings and
disquisitions, into a volume of his parochial history, compressed,
by means of type of a diminutive size, into a space utterly unworthy of its author and his undertaking.  From the year 1810
scarcely a summer had passed over his head without a visit to the
Wall.  In divers years, with not many intervals, he had traced its
course from sea to sea, carefully noting its character and
features of interest.  His Note Books, all of them dated, are full
of memoranda and sketches made upon the spot from year to year;
and the result of all these personal investigations and laborious
inquiries, for want of means of his own, and from a lack of that
patronage and encouragement for which he could not beg, but
which might have been so fitly bestowed, he was at last obliged
to leave behind him in the shape and place in which we find it, for
others in process of time to fuse into a more convenient shape, to
stamp it with the catchword of popularity, and give it currency.

The plan which Hodgson adopted in presenting to his readers
the result of his labours is as follows:

As an introduction to the subject more immediately under his
attention, he gives notices of the history, structure, &c. of the
Medean Wall, the Bosphorian Barriers, the Phocian and Lace-
dæmonian Walls, the Caspian, Caucasian, and Syrian Gates,
the Wall of Mount Libanus, the Wall between the Piræus and
Athens, the Chinese Wall (with engravings), the Wall of Probus,
and the Gate of Denmark.  The general character of the Roman
Barriers in Britain next engages his attention, and under this
head we have a careful examination of the various historians who
have written upon the subject.  He then proceeds to give an
account of the Stations at a greater or less distance from the Wall
attributed to Agricola, and then the Wall itself with its accompaniments forms the subject of a long history in great detail, proceeding from Station to Station, and noting every inscription or

artistic fragment found in each, from time to time, illustrated by numerous plans and engravings on wood or copper.

The reader will not have failed to observe, from divers letters and expressions in the preceding part of our Memoir, that, up to a certain period, Hodgson, as it appears, was not free from the received notion that Severus and not Hadrian was the builder of the Wall. We may now see that, after a careful sifting of historical evidence, and above all, perhaps, by a minute investigation with respect to the Wall itself and its collateral fosses and road-way—want of room obliges me to omit his arguments—he arrives at a different conclusion.

" In the progress of the preceding investigations I have gradually and slowly come to the conviction that the whole barrier between the Tyne at Segedunum and the Solway at Bowness, and consisting of the vallum and the murus, with all the castella and towers of the latter, and many of the stations on their line, were planned and executed by Hadrian; and I have endeavoured to show that, in this whole, there is an evident *unity of design* and a fitness for the general purposes for which it was intended, which, I think, could not have been accomplished, if part of the vallum had been done by Agricola, the rest of it by Hadrian, and the murus with its castella towers and military way by Severus." (p. 309.)

Again—

" We have thus found both probable and conclusive evidence that the Wall and all its members were planned and constructed by Hadrian; and evidence equally strong that five of the stations next to the Wall on the south, and three next north to it, were in existence, if not built, in that reign. But in support of Spartian's assertion that Severus drew a murus from sea to sea, and that this was the highest honour of his name, and procured for him the title of Britannicus, no corresponding testimony occurs in any other ancient writer on the exploits of Severus, nor has inscription been found to corroborate it. Indeed the historians of his own time mention the barriers which he passed on his march into Caledonia as fortifications familiarly known: and even Spartian himself speaks of the *murus at the vallum*, not as anything new, but apparently to distinguish the works of Hadrian on the confines between the Brigantes and the Meatæ (the Wall in question) from those of Antonine on the southern boundary of Caledonia (between the Firth

of Forth and the Clyde), where there was a vallum but no murus."
(p. 315.)

The following extract must conclude my notice of Hodgson's
labours on the subject of the Roman Wall, with which his name
is now inseparably connected.

" The extreme length to which the preceding account has been carried
forbids any extended view or recapitulation of the subject. When I
first began to prepare it for the press, &c. I hoped that less than one
hundred pages of the small type in which it is printed would have contained the whole. Much curious material and many views and illustrations of the subject that were presented to my mind, during the many
months that it has occupied my attention, have been suppressed. I
have especially curbed the rein of fancy and exuberance in explaining
the great number of inscriptions that have come within the plan of my
inquiry; and, if heavy charges of prolixity and book-making be brought
against me, I can defend my minuteness and anxiety to omit no information that the intelligent inhabitants of any particular part of these
famous fortifications may expect to find here, only by saying, that, if
my inquiry had been printed in the large type of the text of this work,
it would have contained little more than one-third of the information it
embodies in its present form, and been attended with less labour and
expense to myself somewhat in the same ratio: but, if I could have
afforded to give a volume of 1,200 instead of 400 pages for the sum
these are sold at, it should have been done, rather than any materials or
illustrations should have been suppressed which in my own estimation
were curious at present, in time might become important, but eventually
might sink in the river of oblivion."*    (p. 305.)

---

* In 1851, eleven years after the volume containing Mr. Hodgson's treatise on the
ROMAN WALL had issued from the press, there was published a work on the same subject, with the following title, "The Roman Wall, an Historical, Topographical, and
Descriptive Account of the Barrier of the Lower Isthmus, extending from the Tyne to
the Solway, deduced from numerous personal surveys, by the Rev. John Collingwood
Bruce, M.A." &c. In the preface to this volume acknowledgments are made of the
high patronage which its author had enjoyed, and which, it may be remarked in passing,
Mr. Hodgson had looked for in vain. The Duke of Northumberland had presented to
the work such woodcuts as Mr. (now Dr.) Bruce thought it necessary to use in the way
of illustrations. Messrs. Clayton, Fenwick, and Kell were liberal contributors of embellishments; and, in short, great encouragement appears to have been given to the
undertaking. The subscribers to the work were upwards of 300 in number. Dr. Bruce
states in his title-page that his publication was " deduced from numerous personal

surveys," a mode of expression from which his readers might not unnaturally infer that he had derived little or no assistance from previous writers on the subject. It is probable, however, that Dr. Bruce did not intend the words which I have quoted to bear this construction; as in the course of his book he frequently, with due acknowledgment, avails himself of the labours of preceding writers, and, in particular, he thus speaks of Mr. Hodgson and his Treatise : " Hodgson paid great attention to the Wall and its antiquities. The last published portion of his History contains a vast mass of learned information on the subject. It is, perhaps, enough for the present author to say, that, had not Horsley and Hodgson cleared the way before him, he would never have adventured to write a book upon the Barrier of the Lower Isthmus. Though he cannot be a Horsley or a Hodgson, he hopes he will never prove a Warburton." * (Edit. 1, p. 107.) It has, however, been observed that Dr. Bruce is not always careful to pay a seemly tribute of acknowledgment to such previous authors as he occasionally takes for his guides, and charges have been brought against him under this head with respect to Mr. Hodgson, in particular, some of which might, perhaps, to a certain extent be substantiated. But then it must be remembered that in travelling over the same ground it is not always easy to avoid treading in the footsteps of those who have gone before us—nay, indeed, it may be impossible; especially if the path be one which has been made smooth and passable by their labours. Under such unavoidable difficulties, however, any direct transcript of even a single line would seem in justice to have called for as direct an acknowledgment. But, whatever may be the want of references, here and there, in Dr. Bruce's book at large, it must, I think, be admitted that his tacit appropriation to himself of one, at least, of Mr. Hodgson's discoveries, the most brilliant of them all, and that which does the highest credit to his powers of patient investigation, appears to be manifest in his chapter on "The Question, Who built the Wall? discussed." In describing station after station, and in giving the reading of one inscription after another, there may be no particular field for originality of thought or display of ability. To make a book on those subjects the measuring-chain and the pencil of the draughtsman are the chief requisites. But Mr. Hodgson aimed at something of infinitely higher interest than any such mere mechanical and patchwork details as those of which I have spoken, when he brought his mind to bear upon one subject, in particular, of the greatest historical importance—that upon which the very Wall itself, with all its accompaniments, depended—a subject which had been for many generations a matter of doubt and dispute; and, by dint of patient research and thought, fairly settled it for ever, rendering all subsequent inquiries with reference to it utterly needless. When, therefore, the reader of Mr. Hodgson's Memoir is informed that in Dr. Bruce's book there is a chapter headed, "The Question, Who built the Wall? discussed," and has been given to understand, as abovementioned, that that self-same question had been already fully discussed and satisfactorily answered by one in whose

* Warburton, it will be remembered (see vol. I. p. 191, of this Memoir), was the person who, soon after the publication of Horsley's " Britannia Romana," including his History of the Wall, in 1732, dishonestly copied nearly the whole of it into a small quarto, to which he gave the title of " Vallum Romanum," &c., under the pretence, as he states in his preface, " that all books hitherto published relating to the Picts Wall are in large unwieldly folio volumes, and intermixed with matters quite foreign to my purpose or intention, which is no more than to provide a pocket companion," &c. (Pref. p. vii.)

history he has, perhaps, so far taken an interest, he will probably come to the conclusion that, in this matter, there was no field even for the semblance of a new discussion,
much less for any laboured display of learned investigation. Mr. Hodgson had proposed this very question to himself many years before Dr. Bruce had turned his attention
to it, and, by a process of legitimate reasoning, with the best historical authorities and
the Wall itself and its accompaniments before him, had satisfactorily restored to the Emperor Hadrian the honour of which he had been so long deprived. And yet Dr. Bruce,
professing in the very opening words of his chapter on the Builder of the Wall, to
enter upon what he calls "a region of speculation," goes over the self-same ground,
with a considerable shew of research, and an apparent affectation of originality, and
proceeds upon the very same authorities, and in the very same order, (not scrupling to
appropriate to himself many of Mr. Hodgson's translations of them without acknowledgment,*) until, by the same course of reasoning, he comes, as it were *proprio Marte,*
to Hodgson's previously arrived at and well-known conclusion, as the result of his own
personal and unaided investigation. It must be admitted that upon two occasions,
in the course of his disquisition on the builder of the Wall, Dr. Bruce does certainly bring
Mr. Hodgson before his readers, but it is in a very remarkable way. The passages referred to are these: † "Thus, as Hodgson, who powerfully supports the view here
taken, remarks," &c. Again: "Mr. Hodgson, who has written so much and so ably
upon the Roman Wall, long ago, and at great length, advocated the view now given.
His testimony is valuable. He says, 'In the progress,'" &c. quoting the passage
printed above, p. 399, the very passage, be it remarked, in which Mr. Hodgson
announces *his* discovery. It will probably appear to the reader that there is something of a very novel nature in this mode of reasoning, and a somewhat unnatural inver-
sion of terms. Every one has heard the old saying of "putting the cart before the
horse." Dr. Bruce appears to me to have yoked his argument in a similar way.
Ought he not to have expressed himself in some such words of acknowledgment as
these? "This was Mr. Hodgson's view, as is amply proved in his History, and that
view I also entertain. The discovery was *his,* and the result of my inquiries confirms
it. Let me repeat what I have said elsewhere, 'I may not be a Horsley or a Hodgson,
but I hope I shall never prove a Warburton.'" It must be again remarked that Mr.
Hodgson had most satisfactorily settled this very question in 1837. Why did Dr. Bruce,
in 1851, deem it necessary to enter upon it again, terming it, as he does, "a region of
speculation," when, in truth, nothing whatever had been left for him to speculate
upon, or display his learning; and why did he think it enough to pay Hodgson the
empty compliment of merely calling him in as a witness of some sort of authority,
upon a "*view*" upon which he himself had been laboriously bestowing a needless
parade of argument, as if it were not Hodgson's ground upon which he was treading,
step by step, with Hodgson for his guide, and the question were one still open for investigation? Surely all this needless discussion might have been spared, and the

---

* See pp. 351, 352, 353, and 354 of Dr. Bruce's second edition, and Hodgson,
pp. 163, 164, &c. In p. 164, Hodgson states that he had copied from Horsley's
translations the passages of which he avails himself in Herodian and Xiphiline, but
Dr. Bruce makes no reference either to Horsley or to Hodgson for his transcripts of
them.

† Second edition, p. 365 and p. 368.

fullest and most unequivocal admission of Hodgson's discovery might have been made
as an act of justice to his memory. His friends would then have had no reason to
complain of the apparent unfairness of a new and somewhat ostentatious disquisition,
detracting from the few and hardly-earned honours of one to whom they look back
with reverence.

I much regret that upon the subject of Dr. Bruce's publication I cannot yet lay
aside my pen.

My attention has been directed to a remark in the preface to Dr. Bruce's first edition,
which is reprinted in his second, that Mr. Hodgson's " mind, at the time his work was
in preparation, was bending under the weight of his ill-requited labours," and that, no
doubt as a consequence, " he has failed to present his ample materials to the reader in
that condensed and well-arranged form which distinguishes his previous volumes, and
without which a book on antiquities will not arrest the attention of the general reader."
It is very greatly to be regretted, for the sake of Dr. Bruce as well as for the sake of
Mr. Hodgson's surviving family, who have suffered most acutely from the former of these
insinuations, that he should have sent forth to the world a statement which was not only
utterly groundless, but which had such a manifest tendency to depreciate Mr. Hodgson's
labours, and, as a natural consequence, to exalt his own, in the estimation of the public.
In truth, his object in thus alluding to Mr. Hodgson's state of mind seems hardly capable
of being misunderstood, for the words by which it is followed up are a conclusion from
his premises in direct favour of his own attempt to supply such defects in Hodgson's
book as had been occasioned by the mental infirmity of its author. That his words are
not only capable of the above construction, but that it was actually and publicly put
upon them immediately afterwards is proved by a review of his book in the Archæo-
ological Journal, a work of extensive circulation (Vol. viii. p. 104, 1851), in which the
same incorrect statement is repeated in somewhat different and, perhaps, more delicate
terms, and that too as a direct argument in favour of Dr. Bruce's publication. The
words of the Reviewer are these : " The account of the Wall to which we allude, prepared by the Rev. John Hodgson, was unfortunately produced without his personal
care or final revision."[*] But further. It has been reported, in favour of Dr. Bruce's
book, and in depreciation of that of Mr. Hodgson, that the personal acquaintance of
the latter with the Wall was limited, confined to a few visits only, preparatory to his
History. These two objections—the first referring to that tender and delicate subject
the state of Mr. Hodgson's mind—so hastily here called into question—and the
second to his limited acquaintance with the Wall, are both of them capable of
being disposed of in the most satisfactory way, not by mere arguments or assertions,
but by facts. The second shall have the first notice. It has been already remarked
that Mr. Hodgson's acquaintance with the Wall commenced in the year 1810, when
Dr. Bruce must have been still a child, and it must be repeated that from that time he
visited it, or portions of it, nearly once a year, and frequently twice or thrice, especially from the commencement of his residence at Whelpington in 1823 down to the

---

[*] In proof that I am justified in drawing the above inference, the Reviewer goes on
to say, in the following page, " Mr. Bruce has now supplied a desideratum in Antiquarian Literature, by producing a treatise in which he has happily combined much of
the information gathered by previous writers with a mass of original and personal observations."

year 1838, frequently tracking its course from sea to sea, and crowding his Journal with sketches and measurements in illustration of its peculiarities. My vouchers for these statements are his Minute Books themselves, which have all of them been preserved, and which are still more explicit with respect to the other equally groundless assertion, from which inferences have been drawn, and are still brought forward, in disparagement of his book—I mean that his mind was " bending," and that, his work was unfortunately produced " without his personal care or final revision." It appears from his Journal that he began to write his History of the Wall on the 27th of July, 1836; from which date the progress of his pen on the subject may be traced almost daily until the 22nd of May, 1838; on which day I find the following entry, " May 22nd, 1838.* Sent the last copy *(or portion of manuscript)* on this long and unprofitable subject to press." It may be worth while to note, in passing along, (so minute are his Journals in the information they afford,) that the precise intermediate period between 1836 and 1838, in which he was beginning to arrive at the conclusion which will hand his name down to posterity, I mean that Hadrian was the constructor of the Wall, was on the 29th and 30th of November, 1837. Now with respect to Hodgson's state of mind during this period of two years, it might, perhaps, be enough to refer to his book itself, in which the most inquisitive eye can detect no failure of his reasoning powers, but, on the very contrary, the most careful detail of facts, followed up by the most discriminating and judicious weighing of evidence; and, as the result of such pains-taking investigation, conclusions arrived at, and committed to paper, in the most legitimate and lucid way. Surely in all this there is enough of proof that Mr. Hodgson's mind was *not* in a " bending " state when he was preparing his History of the Wall. But if any further evidence should still be wanting, I have other vouchers, and Mr. Hodgson himself shall be the first witness to be called for that purpose: He thus writes (p. 392 above) with respect to his future proceedings, after having finished his History of the Wall, and the volume in which it is contained : " I have sketched out an extensive plan, and *feel myself daily more able to fill up and finish its details,* but want other hands," &c. I now ask permission to place Dr. Bruce himself in the witness-box. In his Treatise on the Wall Mr. Hodgson made one grand discovery, at which he arrived, as is proved by his Journal, in November 1837, when he had been engaged for nearly a year and a half upon the subject. In comparison with the importance of this conclusion all the other parts of his essay are as nothing, the mere ordinary warp and woof of compilation. Now that grand discovery Dr. Bruce at once adopted—it is in truth the most important part, the very gem of his book; nay, he did more than this—he twice called upon Hodgson himself as a voucher for its soundness, and by implication for the soundness of mind of its author—and, by so doing he not only confirmed the mental capacity of him to whom he appealed, and in whose footsteps he was treading, but gave the strongest possible testimony in contradiction of his own assertion to the contrary.

Enough, and perhaps more than enough, has been said of the state of Mr. Hodgson's mind during the time he was engaged upon the Roman Wall and its History. But, as the body has much to do with mental labour, a few words may be devoted to that subject. With reference to Mr. Hodgson's general state of bodily health during the two

---

* See also above, p. 381, for four distinct confirmations of this date, as that of the completion of his labours on this subject.

years of his engagement upon the Wall, his Journal contains few complaints. He suffered occasionally from indigestion and headache, but his attacks were not more numerous or more severe than they had been for several years. Happily, with regard to his condition in this respect during a very important period of his undertaking, I mean from January to May in 1838, during which time he was putting a finishing hand to his labours, an engagement which would naturally call for all his energies of body and mind, nothing can be more decisive than a few words from a letter addressed by him to the writer of this Memoir on the 16th of June, 1838, a few weeks after his task was completed. "Since I saw you at Newcastle, at Christmas, my health has been better than for the last thirty years or more." (P. 381, above.) Need one word more be said against the unjustifiable assertion, contained in Dr. Bruce's Preface, that, whilst Mr. Hodgson's book was in preparation, his mind was bending under the weight of ill-requited labours?

There is still another subject which calls for a few words before I conclude my remarks upon the statements and inferences against Mr. Hodgson's publication on the Wall, which I have thought it my duty to notice. Somewhat must be said in proof that his History of the Roman Wall did, in reality, receive the final revision of its author, whatever may have been for any object asserted to the contrary—and here again I have only to refer to his Journal. When, in 1832, the aged daughter of Captain Grose, and the mother of Archdeacon Singleton, prevailed upon him to keep a daily record of this nature, neither he nor she could foresee how useful it would eventually become for other purposes than those for which it was recommended. The reviewer of Dr. Bruce's book, in the Archæological Journal in 1851, was pleased to assert that Mr. Hodgson's account of the Wall "was unfortunately produced without his personal care or final revision." With respect to the personal care here spoken of, enough, and to any candid reader more than enough, has been said in the preceding pages, and especially in the opening paragraphs of these remarks, which have already extended to too great a length, but which could not, in justice, have been compressed into a more limited space. I have now simply to deal with what has been called the "final revision" of its author, by which can only be meant the putting to the book a finishing hand before its publication. Now against this final assertion, equally as presumptuous and groundless as those which have already been disposed of, what can be so decisive as the following short and pithy entries in the authority referred to?

1839.

Aug. 6. *Addenda et Corrigenda.*

„ 7. Appendix of *Additions and Corrections* again.

„ 8. More of *Addenda* about the *Roman Wall.*

„ 9. Camps beyond the Wall on the sea-shore from Walker by Plessey, &c.*

„ 10. *Additions and Corrections about the Wall.*

„ 13. *Appendix to Account of Wall finished.*

---

* My other extracts from the Journal, as above, refer only, in a general way, to the additions and corrections in which Hodgson was then daily engaged. Here, happily, is an entry relative to a definite and specific subject—the stray camps north of the Wall along the coast, with a distinct mention of places. Now if the reader will just turn to Hodgson's volume, and to p. 440 of its Appendix, he will find there the very result of this day's labours. The reviewer will perhaps admit that this savours somewhat of a revising care, even if it stood alone, against his assertion.

Up to this period Mr. Hodgson had enjoyed his usual health, and it was not till a whole week after the last of the above entries had been made, and he was beginning to labour upon an Index to his book, that he was seized with the serious illness under which he afterwards continued more or less to labour. The *Additions and Corrections* above spoken of, all of them in his own clear and distinct handwriting, are now upon my table, feelingly calling upon me to do an act of justice to their compiler ; and it only remains for me to state, once more, that they were most carefully and conscientiously printed in the appendix to his volume from this, the very copy which he had prepared with his own pen for that purpose. I am here making no new statement or telling a new tale. The circumstances under which in 1839 it became my duty to act a friendly part, in seeing these self-same additions and corrections duly printed, were sufficiently detailed in the preface to the volume itself, of which they form a part. But it is more than probable that the reviewer did not, in his candour and impartiality, deem it his duty to look at Mr. Hodgson's book at all.    He had a purpose to serve. He had learned his lesson from an assertion in Dr. Bruce's preface, and poor Hodgson's book was to be sacrificed, by whatever means.*

For this long note I offer no apology.  In making the above statements I have had no other object in view than the doing an act of justice to the meritorious but ill-requited labours of my friend.  It must be honestly admitted that Hodgson's History of the Wall is, from the circumstance of its being mixed up in a large volume with other matter on a different subject, and crowded into so many notes, as it were, in a small type, in some measure an inaccessible book, but ill-arranged and unreadable are terms which have been applied to it with great injustice.  The circumstances under which it made its appearance were those of necessity and not of choice.  To its author no one held out a helping hand.  If he had enjoyed the high and substantial patronage with which Dr. Bruce was favoured, his treatise would have been published in a separate shape, and then all that would have been required for many a long year would have been, for the benefit of his family, a few additions, after Dr. Bruce's own plan, of such discoveries as had been made from time to time after its publication, and there would have been no necessity, real or pretended, for any new survey of ground already examined, for any new disquisition upon points which no longer admitted of doubt or dispute, or for any unjustifiable assertions and arguments in favour of the necessity of such proceedings.

---

* In the various reviews of Dr. Bruce's book which I have had an opportunity of seeing, Mr. Hodgson's treatise is either not mentioned at all, or it is brought forward chiefly for the purpose of evincing the superior character of that by Dr. Bruce. The Literary Gazette (April, 1851) expresses its superlative pleasure with the chapter headed "The Question, who built the Wall? which is very sensibly and logically discussed." Even the Gentleman's Magazine speaks slightingly of its old friend and correspondent, and describes his work as expensive, and almost as little known as the remains of which it treats. (Feb. 1851, p. 148). Again, in p. 151, it appears to ascribe to Dr. Bruce the credit of having so weighed the testimony of ancient writers as to have of himself come to the conclusion that the Vallum and Wall are to be ascribed to the genius of Hadrian. In a long and laudatory review of Dr. Bruce's Book in the Edinburgh (July, 1851) Hodgson's name is, I believe, never once mentioned. No review of Dr. Bruce's second edition has fallen in my way, with the exception of one in the Gentleman's Magazine, in which also Mr. Hodgson's name does not occur.

SINCE the above remarks were in type there has appeared the supplementary volume to Mr. Hodgson's History of Northumberland, of which I have above spoken (p. 356,) undertaken by John Hodgson Hinde, Esq. at the request of the Society of Antiquaries of Newcastle. In his preface to this volume Mr. Hinde gives full credit to Mr. Hodgson for the "clearness and ability" of his views respecting the Roman Wall; but, deeming it necessary that more should be said on the subject, he has admitted into his pages another long disquisition from the pen of Dr. Bruce, in a chapter of thirty-two quarto pages, under the title "When and by whom was the Roman Wall built?" In this second inquiry I again find but little mention made of Mr. Hodgson and his discovery, except in the following passage, near its beginning: "Another opinion has been entertained, and at this Mr. Hodgson arrived during the preparation of his last volume: it is that the whole of the works, with the exception, perhaps, of a few of the stations, which may have been erected by Agricola, are the work of Hadrian." Of Mr. Hodgson we hear no more, save an occasional reference to his book on a point of minor importance; but there follow the same list of authorities, and the same line of reasoning as before, more laboriously discussed, and, it may be, more judiciously handled. The volume before me is professedly supplementary to Mr. Hodgson's History, which was left imperfect at his death. But, at any rate, there was no deficiency in his work upon the subject of the builder of the Wall, and it really does appear to me that not only might much of this chapter have been spared and room gained for other subjects of real necessity and utility, but that, in such portions of it as time had rendered necessary, there ought perhaps to have been a more distinct recognition of the foundation upon which it rested.

But let me turn to a more agreeable subject, and express my most anxious wish that Mr. Hodgson Hinde may be induced and encouraged to proceed with the important task which he has so kindly undertaken. I am reminded in every page of his performance of the gratification with which such a publication would have been welcomed by his departed friend. It is an historical essay of the very highest rank and character, in which ancient Northumbria, in all her members and dynasties, is made to stand fairly before us, from the period of the Roman conquest down to comparatively modern times. The remarkable features in the volume are the caution by which Mr. Hinde's pen is guided, his intimate acquaintance with the best historical authorities, and his judicious arrangement of their testimony so as to weave for posterity a web of genuine history. His chapter on Northern Tenures is in many of its parts not more novel than valuable. His delicacy in dedicating the volume "To Richard Wellington Hodgson, Esq. as a supplement to his father's labours, and as a token of regard for his memory," is gratefully acknowledged, and it will hereafter be duly appreciated in that Northumberland with which the name of Hodgson is for ever inseparably connected, and which now, with this proof of his ability before her, looks to Mr. Hodgson Hinde as the "alter ab illo" to lay her under additional obligations.

## CHAPTER XVI.—1839, 1840, 1841.

### The Isle of Wight—Extracts from Letters and Journals—Returns to Hartburn—Extracts from Letters and Journals.

WE may now resume our subject. On the 21st of November, 1839, Hodgson took his leave of Hartburn for the winter, by the recommendation of his medical advisers, and means were not wanting to meet the necessary expenses of the journey. His circumstances were well known to his friends, and no one was better acquainted with them than he who had, from the kindest and purest of motives, for so many years held out to him a helping hand in his pursuits and afflictions. A munificent gift of money found its way from Capheaton to Hartburn, in this his present time of need, the acceptance of which was requested in the most delicate terms; and thus Hodgson had, like the swallow, wings wherewith to fly from the severities of a Northumbrian winter to a southern sun and a more genial air. He was accompanied by Mrs. Hodgson, by Emma his youngest daughter, now Mrs. Kennicott, and also by Miss Brown, who has been already mentioned. His intention was to proceed at once to the southern coast of France, the climate of which had been recommended; but, by the advice of Dr. Holland, a physician who was consulted in London, this plan was abandoned, and the party became temporary settlers in the Isle of Wight.

It has been already observed, that from the day of Hodgson's attack, on the 20th of August, 1839, till the 21st of November, there is a melancholy blank in the Journal of which I have so often availed myself. On the latter day it re-commences, but it far too frequently gives indications of great bodily pain, and, in many of its entries, of that defective state of memory under which its writer never afterwards ceased more or less to labour. Of its numerous mistakes in words and names some appear to have been corrected afterwards, when he had the temporary ability so to do; others remain; and the Journal itself, and the few letters which he wrote after this period, may in general terms be said to be full of woe. Now and then he brightens up, in the absence of pain, and now and then there are indications that he was in full possession of his powers of memory; but, in a general way, no other conclusion can be come to, than that the very contrary was in both respects the case. At all times, however, both Journal and Letters breathe the spirit of patient resignation, and a due acknowledgement of the Hand from which cometh affliction.

My task is now to glean from Hodgson's journals and letters, from 1839 until he was removed from the world, such extracts as illustrate the conclusion of his now painful history. Those of them which I find uncorrected by himself or his family, will crave the aid of my pen; but no liberties shall be taken with the sense or meaning of the matter with which I shall have to deal. And here I would beg of those of my readers who have no heart of sympathy, and no feeling for suffering humanity, to close the book. I have a picture to draw which to one who reads for amusement will have no charms.

It has been stated that, in the first instance, Hodgson sought for health in the Isle of Wight. A brief preliminary sketch may here be given of his subsequent movements. After his return home in May, 1840, he paid numerous visits in the course of the year to Newcastle, Durham, Tynemouth, Hexham, and Newbigging. In 1842 he proceeded to Harrogate, by medical advice, and on his return diverged at Darlington, and visited his old friend Mr. Redman, at Hartley Cottage, near Kirkby Stephen, on his road to Shap Well, a mineral spring not far from the place of his nativity. He visited Shap again in 1843, and again in 1844; frequently, moreover, during these latter years spending a day or two with his friends at Newcastle or Durham. In truth, for the few concluding years of his life, there was about him a restlessness, which appears to have made him impatient of home, and anxious for a change of place. It was his habit to walk into the house of a friend when he was least expected, and his quiet and composed demeanour under his sufferings in body and memory made him always an object of the most sincere sympathy and commiseration.

I now proceed with my promised extracts from his letters and journals, with an occasional paragraph of my own in the way of explanation, and again I must remind my reader that the noblest feelings of the heart are those excited by a sense of sympathy and humanity.

A pleasing sonnet upon the occasion of Mr. Hodgson's departure from home must not, however, be overlooked. It proceeded from the pen of Mr. Robert White, who has been more than once mentioned, and who still bears witness to the kindnesses of his friend, and the sincerity with which he himself thus prayed for the restoration of his health.

ON THE REV. J. HODGSON'S DEPARTURE TO THE SOUTH OF ENGLAND IN 1839.

> Behold Northumbria drooping and in tears!
> Dark lowering clouds shadow her visage fair:
> Why should she grieve? The fleeting lapse of years
> Can furrow not her cheek, nor blanch her hair;
> Yet has she cause of sorrow. He whose care
> For years has been to rear a pillar high,
> And grave thereon her story, doth repair
> In quest of health beneath a warmer sky.
> And she indeed may mourn, for never eye
> Gloated like his o'er all her ancient lore,
> Or who beside could better testify
> What she is now, and what she was of yore?
> Watch him, ye heavenly Powers! where'er he roam;
> Bind up his nerves, and guide him safely home.

The first extract which I make from Hodgson's Journal shall be in the precise words in which I find it, that the reader may be enabled to form a correct notion of the state to which he was reduced. There runs through the whole passage a beautiful train of thought, but it is very piteous to see the difficulties under which its writer was then labouring, and the mistakes which he has made in committing his ideas to paper.

" 1839. Dec. 7. Cowes.—The rocks that God has fixed into the hills, and his works that man has planted in his fields, still, as I did in my ardent youth, still now I love to search and gaze among—to venerate the ancient oaks and clay of the streams and fields of Medina; but the elasticity of my mind is gone; the strength of my frame is fled: my words have lost their sprightly names; I cannot collect them into multitudes of names; I cannot paint my soul into beautiful lines and flowers. The child of poesy does not visit me and carry me through wilds that cities love to live among, and are fast filling the earth.  Still, however, I love to see oranges, though not exuberant in size, growing in the midst of December in the gardens of Wight.   Man is restoring to her some of the pristine beauties of the garden of her ancient Father, the glories that he has obscured.

" 1839, Dec. 9.—Wrote (rode) by the side of the Solent to Gurnard's Bay, were (where) the land near a limekiln is sliding into the side of the sea.   The apple trees near the houses sadly stunted, and yellow with lichens.   The beautiful plant I saw on Friday last in a shrubbery at East Cowes is the *arbutus uva ursi*, which grows even in Northumberland, as I think, in the open air, at Cresswell.*

" 1839, Dec. 11.   To-day I was all day confined by a cold.   The east wind harsh and impetuous.   Remember the names of Great and Small Mel-fell, in Cumberland, and Mel-don, in Northumberland. Mel-fell is, I think, the name of a conical hill in Westmerland: and if I be ever to read clearly again, let me try what is the true origin of Melmerby.

" 1839, Dec. 12.   In (the) introduction to a volume of my sermons,† show that the churches of Northumberland were built in the main cross roads of that county, and that they were built for the purpose of civilizing the country.   The town people the first Christianized. ' But see if some account of this is not inserted in my Northumberland.

" Dec. 12.   My head to-day very much deranged.   Walked about half a mile with great unpleasure.   The wind, however, to the south. The fields near West Cowes deeply green."

" Dec. 15.   Cowes.—Another blessed Sunday, whose services I have not been able to visit since the 20th of August.   My head in good state all day."

Mr. Hodgson's first letter after he was settled at Cowes was, as might have been expected, addressed to Sir J. E. Swinburne, and it must not be withheld from my readers.   No liberty has

---

* This entry I also give as it is written, with the exception of the two explanatory amendments.  It will be seen from this and the preceding extract, written at an interval of two days only, how Hodgson's memory fluctuated in its powers.

† This is the only reference which has occurred to me of any intention on Hodgson's part to publish a volume of Sermons.

been taken with it save that of correcting its mistakes in spelling. It is valuable for my purpose, as its writer makes some affecting statements explanatory of the origin and nature of his attack, and also gives some interesting information respecting the last volume of his labours.*

"To Sir J. E. Swinburne.—Cowes, 28 Dec. 1839.—My dear Sir John,—Ever since I went from Hartburn I have been very desirous to do my duty to write a note to you of words, however short; but, till about a week ago, my eyes and memory have so little improved that I have been afraid of writing an intelligible word.   Now, I am sure you will be very greatly gratified to hear that I can with some assurance say that my mind begins to prove better, and it is very gratifying to myself to hear from my son, Mr. John, that my last volume of Northumberland is all at the press, if not all published.   When I was in August last suddenly interrupted from my labours, the whole of the book was finished, with the exception of the preface, contents of the parochial history, and an alphabetical account of the names of places, persons, subjects, and the Roman Wall—with the commencement of the work which (which work) I was in the first day so perplexed, that immediately after my return from it I fell asleep, and awoke unable to remember very few words respecting the names of persons and places. From some hasty minutes of my own, Mr. Raine, who kindly and voluntarily came to see me, offered to write the preface, which I regret was not finished in that just and proper form it was my intention to finish, so well as I wished.   When Mr. Raine came I could not read a word I had written; but the minutes I am mentioning he has selected, and submitted, as I understand, to the inspection of my son Mr. Richard. The contents of parishes were written by John, and of the Roman Wall by myself, some weeks before my misfortune.   With all the care my friends and myself have been able to finish the work, I am sensible it can never be able to the munificent and gratifying favours you have bestowed upon me.   My words, however imperfect, must be written quickly or not at all; and here I am wishful to add, that, when my friends recommended me to go to France or Italy, Mr. Richard procured an account of my state from Dr. Hedley, of Morpeth, and procured also Dr. Headlam's advice to consult Dr. Holland to recommend me his assistance.   I, however, took Dr. Hedley's statement to Dr. Chambers,

---

* I print from a rough copy or draft.  It may be doubted whether the letter was sent in Hodgson's own hand.

who unfortunately was so much employed that he could not see me. Dr. Holland, however, was greatly and very kindly attentive to me; and for several reasons recommended me not to go to France, but to spend the winter, at least, in the Isle of Wight, or about Torbay or Bath. To this place he recommended us to visit first; and, a day after, we came here, where we have continued since. At first we had very cold but not freezing weather, and my head still continued very bad. The south and west winds have improvement, and as my improvement has begun will now I hope continue. My party are all very well. Our house is very convenient and of reasonable price, and our attendant attentive and quiet. To correct this hasty note I am sorry I am unable, but hope you will be able to understand my general meaning. Mrs. Hodgson and my daughter desire to be very gratefully remembered to yourself, Miss Swinburne, and your brother Mr. Edward, and to themselves and yourself I am, my dear Sir John, ever very gratefully and truly yours,

JOHN HODGSON."

"1840, Jan. 2.—Cowes.—To MR. JOHN HODGSON, jun.—To the tediousness of complaint in my eyes and head for two or three days, I have been troubled with toothache, which also torments my ears, but our very beautiful weather touches as tenderly as it can to a bruised heart, and this trouble will I trust be transient.——I know there are many things respecting the volume which I ought to mention, but all knowledge about them is absent at present, and I will not now inquire into them.

"Jan. 3.—I wish that my overstretch of mind and memory on Aug. 20 in last year may be permitted to recover, for me to do my duty at Hartburn. Certainly I find myself both in my eyes and memory a little more clearly to-day than I was a month since.

"Jan. 18. Mr. Swinburne, of Capheaton, and his brother Captain Swinburne came to us from Bonchurch, and Captain S. most kindly invited us to go to his house till we could get conveniently accommodated with lodgings at Bonchurch or Ventnor. They were the first old friends who had cheered us, whom we had seen since we left the North in November last, and certainly, after so long absent, the sounds of so great and excellent friends to me were most grateful and exhilarating.——

"Jan. 18. To-day I wrote a letter to my son John, and another to the Rev. J. Raine, my first letter to him since my illness in August last.

"To the Rev. J. Raine.—Cowes, Isle of Wight, 18 Jan. 1840.——
My health and memory have of late (been) beginning to improve: and I
have been wandering through the country among the oldest churches to
four or five miles.* On Friday next we go to Bonchurch in this island,
where we expect to continue for a month or six weeks. If, however,
I should find lodgings at Ventnor, your note will find me under the
care of Captain Swinburne,† of East Dene, Bonchurch.

"The short note I have written to you I dare not examine. I am
still also unable to read without very great difficulty.——

"Pray speak softly over my words, they have lived in the storms
and come to the door of a *friend* to listen to his old accustomed
soothings.                                                    J. H."

"To the Rev. J. Raine.—Feb. 7, 1840.—Cliff House, Bonchurch.——
Oh that I might speak the words and see the sights that once could
gladden ! My estate, however, is not in the pitiable way in which you
saw it. I was at service at Bonchurch on (Sun)day last, and much
delighted with attending it. All the prayer and duty I could understand in some little state, but the sermon was beyond my reach.——I
have written you a long word, and when I began the first I thought I
could not write more than half a dozen words. Certainly at times my
eyes and memory are much better than they were when your brother
and yourself came to cheer me in my lone but not desponding state.——
                                                              J. H."

"To Mr. John Hodgson, junior.—Bonchurch, Feb. 20, 1840.—My
eyes and my memory are so exceedingly imperfect that I cannot read

* One of Hodgson's amusements was to visit the island churches within his neighbourhood, and make notes, in a somewhat unintelligible style, of their peculiarities. His
Journal is about this period full of architectural sketches, many of them in a rough
way, and many of them by the elegant pen of Miss Brown. He also superintended the
transcript of a Guide to the Island, and illustrated the copy with such drawings or
engravings as fell in his way.

† A son of his friend Sir J. E. Swinburne, whom he found residing upon the
Island, and from whom he received much kind attention. On the day on which this
letter was written, Capt. Swinburne, as is above stated, accompanied by Mr. Edward
Swinburne his brother, (Hodgson's old friend,) called upon him, and kindly offered him
the use of his house till he could procure more convenient lodgings. For thirty long
years Hodgson had enjoyed an unbroken series of kindnesses from the family of Swinburne, and here it is again providentially at hand when he was far from home, to cheer
him in his loneliness and affliction. The soothing presence of Mr. Edward Swinburne
under such circumstances would be most gratefully welcomed.

half a dozen words of writing together without great patience and time; so that, if I do not very greatly improve, I never can be able to read either the lessons or to preach.   Still, however, I could be of great use in visiting the sick and paying attention to the parish—so that I should hope I may procure a good curate; and a good preacher will be indispensable.——But, as my health certainly improves, I think I ought to hear the nightingale before I go homewards, and to allow the cuckoo and the swallow to throw green grass and leaves over the fields and hedges at Hartburn."

On the 11th of March, Mr. Hodgson and his family took their departure from the Isle of Wight, and upon reaching London Dr. Holland, who was again consulted, found him " materially improved," but considered it " of great importance, seeing the causes which have led to his malady, that he should not be engaged in any serious or laborious avocations for some months."   He did not limit his patient to any one place of residence, now that the severity of winter had passed by, but recommended " the same general plan of management as essential to the complete establishment of his health."   After a short time, therefore, Mrs. Hodgson and her family returned to Hartburn by sea, whilst her husband remained to spend a few weeks with his relations the Palmers and Raweses, at Beckenham, in Kent, and, during his abode there, he paid a short visit to the British Museum, to see, for the first time, the lately published volume of his history.   The visit, however, was a melancholy one, as the excitement was too great for him to bear.   " Yesterday," says he, on the 25th of March, in a letter to the author, " I saw at the Museum a copy of my book, but I could not read a word about it."   He also, on the 26th, attended a meeting of the Society of Antiquaries, under the care of Mr. John Gough Nichols, " but " says he in his Journal " I could understand but little on the subject."

" To Mrs. Hodgson.—Clay Hill, Beckenham, April 8, 1840. —I wrote to you a note on Sunday, and directed it to the care of John or Richard.   For my life I could not think of the name of Tom's house or John's office; but to-day I will direct to you to the care of Tom at the Quayside—but I should have thought his name, without the place, was quite sufficient.   Raine sent me a note this morning, and, if I be well to-morrow, I shall go to see him in the Court of Serjeants' inn, in Chancery Lane, as he says he has much to say to me."

" 1840, April 19.   Still I cannot read any sort of book, and with great difficulty read a whole (word) as I write it; that is, to read a few lines either of books or writing troubles me very much."

" April 26.—As a new æra to my memory at Church I quote the text for the sermon this morning at Bromley.  Psalm xvi. 10 and 11. ' Thou wilt not leave,' &c."   [The two verses are written with accuracy.]

May  3. — " Second Sunday after Easter.   At church at Bromley I thought I understood the service and sermon better than I had ever done since I have been unwell.   The sermon was on Genesis xix. 26. ' And his wife,' &c."

" May 4.—To-day I told Mrs. Palmer my wish to return to Hart-burn to-morrow.   To mention this I did painfully, for, though I wish to go home, I have been most kindly and hospitably, and indeed benevolently, received by her and my other cousins, Miss Rawes, and their brothers, Mr. and Mrs. William Rawes.   In Mrs. Palmer's house my health has been for the last six weeks exceedingly improved, and I hope that God will pour blessings over her head for her benevolent attentions to me."

After the departure of Mrs. Hodgson to the North, Hodgson soon became impatient of being so far from his family and his home, and on the 7th of May he unexpectedly arrived at Hart-burn, by way of Preston, Carlisle, and Newcastle, apparently in better health than might have been expected.   After a day or two, however, his journey began to tell upon him, for on the 12th, in rising from bed, he fell into a fainting fit, which lasted for a quarter of an hour; and what added to the affliction, he had, when attacked, fallen upon his breast against the edge of a chair, an accident from which he suffered much for several days.   After a copious bleeding, however, he again slowly rallied, and began to arrange his papers,* and amuse himself in his wood and in

* It appears from his Journal, that he had hardly become settled at home, before he began to arrange in parishes and townships his collections for the unpublished portion of his History of Northumberland.   As soon as this employment, which occupied him for several months, was finished, the papers, &c. were bound up in volumes in his own house under his immediate superintendence, and by means of outside lettering were rendered easy of access to future inquirers.

nailing the fruit-trees in his garden. But his power of memory and conversation still continued defective. " My speech (writes he,) fled in literary labour, and I do not feel the loss dishonourable."

" To THE REV. J. RAINE, May 19, 1840.—My health begins to change, and I think for the better, as my fits of pain are, I think, not so frequent, long, and painful; but I am very weak, and my legs dry and withered as old sticks."

" July 10.—I have for six years observed a sort of diminutive birch in the vicarage wood, the leaves of which (have) red botryodinal spots on the outside: on the inside green as usual: the tree is small. It seems to be of the kind by botanists called *Betula nana:* only a part of the leaves are blotched with a red colour, which under a microscope are of the form which mineralogists call *botryodinal,* and very beautiful. I shewed them to Mr. Cookson, of Meldon Park, in 1835, who supposed that their deep red blotches were caused by insects; but his opinion was merely by guess and without microscopic enquiry. By the single lens which I have I can see that numerous minute insects traverse through its hills and valleys, but I am unable to see that its blotched colours are caused by larvæ of insects.——This birch is not the genus called *nana,* but probably a variety of the common or white birch— *betula alba.".* [In this extract the editor has not found it necessary to alter a single letter.]

" To THE REV. J. RAINE, July 15.—I ought, for very many accounts, to have written to you for nearly two months since; and yet there are very many reasons why I should still continue not to write a word. Since I came home from Beckenham, in the beginning of May, you have not received a note from me; but still my sight and memory are very imperfect, and my head subject to almost constant pain. I will not, however, delay a moment longer to say to you that instead (in spite) of all my present suffering and infirmity I am very much better than I was when I first returned home, and ought to be full of lively and very great thankfulness for so great a blessing. The note I am writing to you I could perhaps read; but will not venture to search for redundances and errors. How is Mrs. Raine, and all your dear children? I long much to go to Durham and to see you all, and to hear how your brother and his family are at Blyth. He wrote to me two letters, soon after he did me the great favour of visiting me during my illness in

autumn last, and it grieves me to say that I have answered neither of
them. Pray, in your next letter to him, give my very kind remembrance to him, and say that if he again favours me with a note I will
endeavour to read it and answer it myself."

" 1840. 26 July.—6 Sunday after Trinity. I read the Lord's prayer,
the collect, and the ten commandments of the Holy Communion, but
from the imperfect state of my eyes did not dare to read any more."[*]

" Aug. 13.—Went with Mrs. H. and Miss Pearson, by Meldon Park
corner, to River Green Hall, to see there Guy Stoker, a poor old
decayed man, who was once my tenant near Stamfordham. He says
he is eighty-two years old. He lives with a son and daughter, who
support him. After seeing him we went to the delightfully situated
place of River Green Mill, and by the woods and winding north side of
the Wansbeck to the Morpeth road, nearly a mile east of Throphill.
Reve-howe—I am glad, in the sad wreck of my memory, to remember—
the ancient name of the place called Rivergreen. I had not before
this evening driven along the lonely and charming road from Rivergreen Mill to the Throphill lands."

" 20 Aug.—It is just one year to day since I became so unwell
in my sight and memory; of which sad calamity, however, am thankful
that I am so much better, and that my bodily health continues generally
so very well."

It is pleasing to see with what brightness the flame of Hodgson's antiquarian zeal could still burn when once again kindled.
On the 14th of August he goes, along with his very kind
neighbour Mr. Cookson, of Meldon Park, to inspect the foundations of a chapel, or hermitage, which the latter had found upon
his estate, in the wood on the north side of the Wansbeck, near
the Holy Well, and he inserts in his diary pen-and-ink sketches
of its ground plan, and the mouldings of parts of its masonry.
On the following day a remarkable grave was found in his
churchyard, and this also formed a subject for his pen and his
observations.

---

[*] This was his first attempt at taking a part in the church service since the
beginning of his illness. He never afterwards ventured to do more than to read the
communion service, or that of a marriage or burial.

" 1840. Sep. 23.—In my garden.   Still heavy showers, which deter
the harvest.     But wet or fair, while my head is well, I am thankful
that in my study or my garden, or about other parts of my house, I can
always find plenty of employment."

" Sep.  29.—Restitched  and  interleaved  an  old  book  of  cookery
intituled ' The Queen-like Closet,' in which my grandmother Elizabeth
Hobson, and her sister Mary, have in two different places written their
names.   Their memories are very dear to me."

On Saturday the third of October, Hodgson paid an unexpected
visit to Crook Hall.     On the next day he attended Divine
Service at St. Mary's in the South Bailey, and was a partaker of
the Holy Communion; but on the following morning he was
seized with an attack of illness which was somewhat alarming, and
which continued over Tuesday.   On Wednesday, however, being
in an improving state, and resolving to return home, he was
accompanied to Newcastle, whence he proceeded to Morpeth to
consult Mr. Hawdon, his medical adviser.

" To THE REV.  J.  RAINE.—Hartburn, Oct.  9,—Since I came
home I have been constantly confined to my bed till to-day; but hope
I am recovering, and by to-morrow to take some exercise.—Mrs.
Hodgson begs both to Mrs. Raine and yourself her very great kindness
and thanks for your attention to me.——                 J. H."

" Oct.  22.—Opened the hall door-way of the old rectory house
of Hartburn—the door-way had been burnt severely by fire; probably
in the time of Edw. I. or Edw. II,, when the Scotch made their severe
inroads into Northumberland."

" Dec.  19.—As tools are the instruments of workmen, so names
(words) are the tools of speakers and writers.   When they lose the
memory of names their speech and words are dumb and silent—as a
joiner's hands without tools are useless."

" To THE REV.  J.  RAINE.—Hartburn, 23 Dec.—For four or five
days I have had great pain in my head, but Mr. Hawdon promises
to give me relief in a few days' time.—I was walking in my garden last

2 E 2

night when the clock of Meldon hall struck eight, as loudly and clear as if I was standing below its tower; and soon after, a cloud cleared away from the east, and on the north shewed on each side of the hemisphere the most beautiful streamers I ever saw. Darkness moved rapidly with embattled spears on both sides of his warriors: while the brazen armour moved for battle, the champions walked in clouds. We never saw a sight so beautiful. I have made a blotted note about a glorious subject. ——"*

" To the Rev. J. Raine.—1841, Innocents' Day.—How am I to thank you for the comfortable house you have prepared for us at Durham?† but I am sure you will think it best for me to hybernate in my own hive, for what can I want there in winter? If a sunny day makes me frisk about my garden, as soon as a cloud darkens I fly into my cell, and have all the warmth and honey that I want."——

" 7 Jan. I have to-day, for the first time since I have been unwell, been able to remember the name of Hildebrand, the vigorous Pope Gregory the Seventh. I wish I was able to read my dear friend Mr. Bowden's ‡ work respecting the time and exertions of that bold and powerful man. I saw, when I was last at Capheaton, that Mr. Bowden's book was published, but unable to read a word respecting it."

" Feb. 18. Wrote a letter to Mr. J. T. Brockett, to thank him for (his) proposal for a plan to get the remaining part of the parishes of Northumberland finished.§ The meeting thought my plan impracticable. But it would take five vols. instead of two, as I thought. I proposed to publish them in double columns and small letter, as I had

* There is in the Gentleman's Magazine for Feb. 1841, a paper by Hodgson on certain Roman altars and coins found at Risingham. This paper was his only literary production in 1840.

† The author had recommended Hodgson and his family to spend a few weeks in Durham during the severity of winter, and had obtained permission for them to reside in one of the University houses.

‡ This gentleman had married a daughter of Sir John E. Swinburne, and had written a life of the Pontiff here spoken of.

§ This entry refers to a communication made to him by Messrs. Brockett and Adamson, on behalf of the Society of Antiquaries of Newcastle, who had expressed a wish to print at their expense the remainder of the History of Northumberland, provided it could be compressed into two volumes. The author happened to be present at the discussion; and upon his stating that four or five, at least, would be required, the design was abandoned.

done the Roman Wall, and think two volumes as thick as that of II. ii.
in small letter and double columns, would complete the work."

"1841, 27 Feb.  Had a long insensible fit to-day.  Twelve leeches
on my temples."

"11 March.  All day from seven in the morning to eight in
the evening in the open air.  Fox hunters often in our sight.  Two
foxes started on the Hart bank, opposite to High Angerton, and three
opposite to the grotto in the vicarage wood.  One of the three last was
chased so urgently along the north side of the Hart that he took
security among the slipped rocks in front of the vicarage garden.  Very
greatly against my wish the hunters threw down my slidden rocks, till
they unkennelled the fox, but though he wanted in many a form to take
shelter among the rocks and trees, he was taken within sight of the
house.  The sight of men, horses, and dogs, all urgent for the chase,
was very animated.  The whole village and school and hunters were on
the banks of the brook.  The women and children among the trees in
my garden.  Men, huntsmen, and dogs in the churchyard.  The smiths,
carpenters, and country people digging down the slidden ground, and
the gentlemen with fine horses waited and watched the work on the
left side of the brook, and on its woody banks.  Warm sunny day."

"April 21.  Poesy was my most early adoration.  My head is
broken; my language lost; my ears hear, but I understand not.  Still
however my soul hears the song of poesy.  I hear it in the four
winds; in the four voices of the year; in day and night; in the morning
and the evening.  It is in the brooks, in the fields, in the woods and the
gardens."——

"May 3.  God's will is improving man and things gradually.  My
short view wants to improve Northumberland.  Greater patriots—
greater men—all improving for the whole world, and God for all."

"May 7.  Sorted several woodcuts for Mr. Richardson's 'Table
Book.'  I fear that his book is very injudiciously collected, but I cannot
read it.  I hope that I am assisting one that is amusing and innocent.
England, I should say Britain, seems to fear that her learning is hastening
to an end, and, fearful of her death, is exerting all her power to
publish all her learning; as fruit-trees, when injured or growing old,

blossom more gloriously, when they begin to wither, than when they flourished."*

1841, May 24. "Mild west wind. Warm and dry. Apple trees blossom in great glory. All day in the garden, or selecting stones in the river for the wood-walk near the school house. Till half-past nine breaking stones for the garden walks. These rolled masses gathered from my garden, or from the heaps of rubbish thrown against the tower of the church wall, reprove me (*not*) for doing them any injury; they chide me for no idleness, no usefulness, no mention that my head is in pain, my brain in distress. I can muse upon them as I break them, and consider how many thousand ages they have rolled in rivers or by the sides of the sea; how many more ages they have reposed in the earth; and now I am breaking them—a restless busy man, that must soon, must soon be silent, and not disturb man or break the fragments of the broken earth any more. But I rejoice that, as I break them, I can find myself happy, and even on earth be at rest; can forget the idle, and the hard-hearted and the wicked; be happy, and find a time, and many times and places, 'where the wicked cease from troubling and the weary are at rest.'"

"May 29. Very rich mild weather. Anxious to think as little as I can; to sit or lie in the warm sun; to bask like an animal; or to crawl out of the scorching sun and lie under the shadow of a tree. Thought in my study distresses the brain."

"June 6. Trinity Sunday. At church, and communicated, but in heavy distress of pain."

The following kind and complimentary letter proves the estimation in which Hodgson was held by the University of Durham. The degree was conferred at the appointed time,† and the gratifi-

* This was one of Hodgson's frequent subjects of meditation. I have repeatedly seen him muse over a common garden-weed, and its struggle, when pulled up, to form a premature flower and produce seed if it came in contact with the least moisture. "as if (said he) it was the only plant in the world of its kind, and the continuance of its species depended upon it alone."

† "1841, Aug. 1.—Read Communion service before sermon. First time I had my M.A. hood on." That hood, by the gift of Mrs. Hodgson after Mr. Hodgson's death, now every Sunday brings back the remembrance of him to one who wears it for that purpose. The scarf which he wears at the same time is a part of the mourning, as it

cation which he derived from the honour, is briefly but feelingly
described in the subjoined extract from his Journal.    It was my
fortune to sit next him in the common room, after dinner in the
Hall; and it was very affecting to witness his anxiety to say a
few words after his health had been proposed by the warden, who
had for many years been one of the kindest of his friends.    He
had hardly risen from his chair to return thanks before his memory
forsook him and he sat down in silence.

FROM ARCHDEACON THORP, WARDEN OF THE UNIVERSITY OF DURHAM.—
" College, Durham, June 15, 1841.—My dear Hodgson, The University
propose to confer upon you the degree of M.A. on the 23rd instant.
Our Convocation will be at *one* o'clock on that day, and it will be well
to have you here the evening before    You will breakfast with me on
Wednesday the 23rd at nine o'clock, and dine in the hall at five, if it
suit you to stay over the day.    It is a real pleasure to me to make this
communication, and I am, dear Hodgson, your sincere friend,

CHA.*THORP."

" 22 June.    Came by Morpeth to Durham."

" 23 June.    To-day I had the honour of having the degree of M.A.
conferred upon me at the convocation of the University.    Professor
Chevallier made an address on the subject, in words of praise, and
*(blank)* which I had not expected.    Among the objects he noticed
the different knowledge required to write a County History, and the
attention I had taken to understand the cause of the accidents which
happen in collieries, and the subject I submitted to Sir Humphry Davy.
I wish my wife and children had heard his speech!    It would have
gratified them greatly.    I smothered my own feelings as well as I could.
Praise from friends or individuals may be suspected of flattery or adulation, but thanks of a public body ought not to be suspected of praise
that should not be gratified.    After the Convocation dined at the hall.
Sat between Collinson and King.    Collinson said Chevallier should have
been told that in building the chapel of Heworth I had renewed ancient
church architecture in the North, and Raine that my monument to Dawes
and my memoir to him had made him a monument (*to be remembered*)
at Heworth."

is called, in which he followed another friend, Mr. Surtees, of Mainsforth, to his grave.
It may, perhaps, be considered a childish affectation to mention these things,—but he
has his own opinion upon the subject.

" 1841, Jul. 1.   Again employed in the weary work of subscriptions to my History of Northumberland still owing to me."

"July 7.   Rode for two or three hours to-day without fatigue. Delighted again to call at the houses of my parishioners."

" July 11.—Lord Howick lost his election to day.   Ossulston 1,216, Cresswell 1,163, Howick 1,101.   At this I shall rejoice if I find the Tories do their part well, and labour for the public good, and especially labour for the good of good men."

" Hartburn, 26 Aug.—I am going to get them (Emma, his daughter, and Miss Brown, her governess) to finish the picture of Pliny the younger, his mother, and their Spanish friend, at the second morning of the great eruption of Vesuvius, in A D. 79, which I was beginning to paint in 1810, when I was engaged to write my account of Northumberland in the Beauties of England and Wales, and never painted afterwards."*

" Sept. 4.—Mr. Brockett, in the first edition of his Glossary, says ' The elucidation of language,' &c., and then begins, ' First impressions and early associations are difficult to remove.   In our youth we are instructed to regard the Greeks and the Romans,' &c.   Are not these ' First impressions,' &c. in Mr. Brockett's Preface taken from the Preface and the first words of Bosworth's ' Elements of Anglo-Saxon Grammar?' who says ' Early associations and impressions are seldom entirely removed.   From our youth we have been taught to look upon the Greeks and Romans as the most learned and polished people.   In the same proportion as we have admired and revered the Greeks and the Romans, we have been led to disregard and despise the Goths for raising the standard of liberty upon the ruins of the Roman empire,' &c.   Certainly it would have been far more noble to quote these genuine words than to copy them almost slavishly, and without referring to Bosworth's book—printed in 1823, Brockett's in 1825."

" Sept. 4.—At four John and I set off from Newbigging to New-castle.   John was driver, and immediately drove straight forward from the road into the Stakeford.   Horse and gig were almost instantly

* About this period Hodgson was much occupied in scraping off the whitewash of many years from the walls of his church, in removing rubbish from its walls, &c.

nearly floating, now wading, now swimming.  The kind horse took the
water like a spaniel.  Fortunately John bent his direction to the right
and we were soon mid-wheel high and a little more till we got to the
other side.——At Hartford Bridge we got dry shoes and stockings, and
in that state came to Newcastle.——Our bags and their contents were
soaked in salt water.  John's dressing case and my new box have without the use of keys opened their contents.  Their paste and glue are dissolved.——While we were in the river I continued very cool and without
fear; but our danger was so great that for thinking of it I could not
sleep till after two o'clock."

"1841, 8 Sept.—James Potts, of the Light Battalion, killed at Sala-
manca, 22 July, 1812.  His wife buried him in a field, on an open and
exposed place, and, having no instrument to cover his body, collected
earth and stones in her lap to build his grave—raised a barrow to him
—as in Homer's time, in honour of the mighty dead."

"To the Rev. J. RAINE. — Hexham,* 6 Sept.—I have been here
a week, confined almost constantly to house or bed by indisposition
and bad weather.  I have seen nothing, and, till to-day, unable to say
when you might expect to see me.  Pray write to me at the Post
Office, Hexham, whether you could meet me here on Thursday, and at
what hour, and I will be at the station to meet you.——The "Black
Book" I have had, but after I copied a part of it I dare not collate it:
doing so hurts my head."

"Sept. 25. — Drove Mrs. H., Emma, and Miss Brown, to New-
biggin, where Mr. Woodman had taken lodgings for us. —— 26.
Sunday.  Not at church to day.  Very much distressed—my head
broken.  Wandered along the sea-side banks.  The head to the south

* He had left home in quest of materials for another portion of his History, with
which he was still anxious to proceed, and had visited several places in North Tynedale
for that purpose.  His Journal contains many very interesting entries and sketches
made during this visit.  It was upon this, or a former occasion, that he heard a derivation which much amused him.  The public road near Simonburn climbs up a steep
elevation called Lincoln Hill.  "Pray (said he to a man who was driving a cart upon
the spot), can you tell why this place is called Lincoln Hill?"  "Why, sir, if you
please, (said the man,) it's because we *links on* at the bottom, to get up the hill, and takes
off at the top."  The man was doubtless right in his account of the real origin of the
name.  It carries with it a reason, but not *so* many of the modern appellations which
one daily hears.

side of the bay is much fretted by the sea, and has an old quarry on the side next to the Spital brook. The fretted rocks at the narrow point of the head are grey with ancient lichens. Not a vestige now remains of Newbiggin Hospital."

"To the Rev. J. RAINE.—Newbigging Baliol, Morpeth, 27 Sept. 1841.—I wish I could have been able to be present at the anniversary of the Surtees Society, but on Thursday I am engaged to be at the meeting of some friends for laying the foundation stone of Cambo Chapel.*—Mr. Hawdon has ordered both Mrs. Hodgson and myself to Newbigging.——I wish I could have had an opportunity of seeing the Bishop *(at the meeting of the Surtees Society)* for a few minutes. I wrote to him on the 24th of June last, but he has not answered my note, and took no notice about it at the Visitation. It was about the chapel of Cambo that I wrote to him.—I fear that I have offended his lordship by my letter. I know that I wrote to him briefly, and in a headache, but in the fewest words that I could, that I might not trouble him with useless numbers. If I could any way avoid to offend him (it) would be my most anxious study; but still my head is not in a state to write anything well, and most of all able to suffer distress from fear that I have offended one human being.—If you can, pray try to get an opportunity of soothing a broken reed: strong again it never can be, but soft words are good for aching brains. I was very unwell while at Hexham; and when I got better could learn little about its church.——I was also a few hours at Dilston, and found some account of the chapel and mill of Temple Thornton; but my head ached so much that I could not read the Greenwich Hospital papers, and Mr. Grey directed some minutes to be copied which are curious. Here I am, without books; and as the morning is thick, and the sea cannot be seen, I have written a note to you, dark, however, I am sure, as the Scottish mist that is enveloping us from the beauties of Newbigging Baliol.          J. H."

"27 Sept.—Mr. Murray Aynsley called on Saturday on Mr. Woodman, and 'in reply,' as Mr. W. says, 'to my application for the payment of 2l. 2s., returned the last volume of your History. He is legally bound to keep it and pay for it; but I suppose you will not be inclined to litigate the question? I therefore allowed him to leave it.'†—

---

* A chapel of ease which he was beginning to build in his parish. See hereafter.

† I am told that upon being informed by Mr. Woodman that the returned volume would be gladly taken back by its author, as in a very short time, instead of being

In my account of Whelpington, when he found I wrote his pedigree only through that of the Aynsleys of Little Harle, he got me to print four additional pages of his descent through the Murrays; but, though my book was perfect without those star-pages, he never thanked me for the trouble. He bought Wood's Scottish Peerage to enable me to write the pedigree of the Murrays, and I thought he intended me the book for the trouble; but he sent a note requesting me to return it. I made much new matter to the pedigree."

"1841, Oct. 23.—At Morpeth. Mr. Woodman gave me 30*l.* amount of Northumberland payments. People would not pay by (notwithstanding) my application."

"7 Nov. Sunday.—Very thankful that I was able to go to church to-day and remain during service without pain."

"20 Nov.—Called on Mr. Joseph Cookson, now at Meldon Park; an amiable charmingly-minded gentleman; sweet in his manners to his gentle wife, and kind to a mind like mine that kindness can do good for."

"9 Dec.—Called on John Brown, of High Angerton, one about my own age, and feeble now like myself; but, till a few months since, never had a headache. But I wish he could dream like me, and think of flying over rivers, and hearing music over lakes, and think his soul in the milky way—though every day my head by the slightest thoughts and words is often distracted."

"18 Dec.—To-day began to make a new catalogue of my books, Northumberland and Antiquarian. The next to be Poetry; but the sound of the poet and of music to me is now brought low, and all their sons and daughters are silent and dead, and nothing is heard as in the night, but the murmur of the brooks and the voice of the sea."

"22 Dec.—A letter from Mr. Macaulay, Albany, London, respecting the history and character of Sir John Fenwick of Wallington."

"1842, Jan. 11.—Wrote about Jacobite poems to Mr. Macaulay."

merely worth its publication price of two guineas, it would sell for at least five, the repudiator would fain have retained it. This however he was not permitted to do.

I proceed with my extracts from Mr. Hodgson's Journal, Letters, &c., according to the plan adopted in the preceding chapter. My task is drawing rapidly to its termination, and, with the exception of an occasional departure from home in search of health, or a visit to a relation or friend, there is not much of variety in my materials or in the life which is waning away. Hodgson had been long neglected by the world. It must be the peculiar happiness of a man of his simple character and of his acquaintance with the world and its vanities to depart in peace, with no complaint upon his tongue, and no feeling of disappointment in his heart.

"1842, Feb. 18. Desired Mr. Milnthorpe, Mr. Cookson's gardener, to get me eighteen apple trees and six pear trees, to make the orchard greater in the garden; also thirty black Italian poplars, fifty spruce firs, and ten larches, to plant in the wood."

"Feb. 24. Began to arrange in yearly order Mr. Swinburne's drawings engraved for my History. Feb. 25th. Pasting in guarded books Mr. Swinburne's drawings."

As it was impossible for Hodgson to be idle, I find him engaged in the opening of the year 1842 in drawing up a descriptive catalogue of his printed works and manuscript collections respecting the History of Northumberland, which he proposed to publish in parts, from time to time, in proof of what he had already done, and of the extent and importance of his unpublished

materials on the subject. To the account of his printed works he
appended an occasional extract from a private letter or a review
in their favour. Of this catalogue the first part was published in
March in this year, with a title and advertisement as below, from
which the object which he had in view will be ascertained; and
it will further be seen how intent his mind still was upon the
subject by which his health had been destroyed. By the advice
of a friend, however, who was fearful of the consequences of such
an arduous undertaking to one already broken down by literary
labour, the design was abandoned, and Hodgson continued to
work at the easier task which he had commenced in 1840, the
arrangement of his manuscript collections in local order. This
undertaking he happily completed, and his papers relating to any
parish or township in the county may now be found in a moment.
In a letter addressed by him on the 2d of April to the author,
who had ventured to give him the above advice, he thus writes,
" I have been saying to some of my friends that I will endeavour
to bind all my papers into volumes, number them with order, and
do nothing more. But a catalogue, such as I planned, would be
very interesting. Even the British History of Northumberland,
the names of all its places, arms, bronze implements, and cairns
and clay urns, would, in methodical order, bring to life the days
of full two thousand years."

" A Catalogue of Printed and Manuscript Works, on Northumberland and Miscellaneous Subjects. By the Rev. JOHN HODGSON, M.A.,
M.R.S.L., &c. Newcastle: for the Author. 1842.

" ADVERTISEMENT.—After fighting a long time with difficulties in
writing a History of Northumberland, the author was suddenly conquered
and carried out of battle, and is now, in that, as in every other kind of war,
completely " hors de combat;" but he hopes, that as he kept his arms,
he may, as an old soldier, be allowed to re-temper and re-polish them,
stamp them with his own signature, and prepare young historians to
fight in the field, till the difficulty be overcome.

" The testimonies for Printed Books in this catalogue, are selected principally in favour of those that are for sale; of which it is of importance
to one that has to dispose of them, that their reputable character should
be labelled in established and distinct words. But the list and credit of
those that are out of print will also be noticed, that they may raise their

voice in favour of their brethren, who are 'still standing idle in the market,' and each desirous of obtaining a shelf in some honourable library: for the copies of 'Northumberland,' that were subscribed for, were offered by mistake at much too low a price, and, therefore, caused very great loss: but the remaining part, it is hoped, will be taken at the sums for which they are charged in the Catalogue.*

" But the Manuscript Books are the part of this Catalogue for which the author's mind feels the deepest interest. The printed books have been before the public. The numerous manuscript volumes and papers he has compiled and collected respecting Northumberland are confined to his study. He is, therefore, anxious that this *Descriptive Account* of them may be perused by competent judges of historical subjects; for he thinks they would recommend the whole collection to be deposited in some Antiquarian Library. Of the Catalogue itself, he certainly cannot promise that he can make it fit for a lady's boudoir; but he hopes he can still, by extracts and anecdotes taken from each volume, and in every parish in the county, make the book a fit companion for his preceding volumes on Northumberland, and proper for a gentleman's library; though he cannot publish it for less than 30s. royal, and a *guinea* demy quarto for each copy, which will be printed in size and pages as nearly as possible to that of his parochial volumes: but if orders for subscriptions, sufficient to pay the expense of the work, be not early forwarded to the author, he will proceed no further with it than the present specimen of its type and mode of printing.

" An alphabetical list of the subscribers who assisted the author in the expense of the six published volumes will be printed at the end of the Catalogue, which is recommended as a suitable appendix to them, and a valuable *key* to vast materials for completing the whole work of the History of Northumberland:—to compose which, besides thirty-two years' collections of general manuscript books on the subject, he has

---

* For a few copies of Part II. vol. iii. he had in the preceding year printed a new title, calling it " The Roman Wall and South Tindale," &c. with a " Synopsis of Contents," wishing them to be sold as a separate and perfect work. " 1841, June 14. Wrote a new title-page for II. iii., and four lines as a motto. I could not find a good one out of any author; and, as I am unable to read much for one, I fixed the Roman and Saxon age as the ground of the motto, and sent it to the press." — *Journal.* The lines are these :—

" Rome's armies rise; and Thirlwall's line of towers
And castles planned by Hadrian's mighty powers:
The land of Saxon settlers ; daughters born,
And glorious sons of England's early morn."

thick folio volumes and a closet of papers for each parish, and a ' General Index ' of contents for every township and principal family in the county; so that there is ample opportunity for making the Catalogue a *Compendium of the History of Northumberland.*

" For the use which will be made of the names and letters of some departed friends, and living patrons and fellow-labourers in the historical vineyard of Northumberland, it is hoped that the author's pride and vanity will not be visited with heavy condemnation. The selections from records and papers may gratify and amuse, but will disturb no man's pride or jealousy; for they are all oaks dry and stunted by the storms of centuries, or leaves that the winds of many winters blew into dens and caves, and did not sweep down the river of time to sink and perish in the sea.

" *Hartburn Tower, Morpeth, March 18th,* 1842."

" From EDWARD SWINBURNE, Esq. to MRS. WYNDHAM. — 32, Great Castle Street, 14 May, 1842.—I saw not long ago, when at Hartburn, a nice letter of yours, as to head and heart, to dear Mr. Hodgson. He was pretty well at the time, but his health varies sadly, and his memory is proportionably affected. In that respect he was then in rather an improved state. Of the soundness of his views, in all respects, I can see little, if any alteration; the activity of his mind is, as it used to be, without limits. It is, however, distressing to see him stopt and puzzled in his communications by the injury done to his once fine memory; though he bears it with great equanimity, and his cheerfulness under so afflicting a change is very consoling."

" 1842.—May 13.—Blessed and beautiful weather. The first day, this year, I heard a cuckoo, the sweet sound of balmy and benevolent weather."

" May 14.—Read the order of burial for a child at (from) North Middleton, and did-it quite correctly and with little difficulty."

" May 23.—Mr. Tone told me that an ancient grave had been found in the Broomhouse sandpit to-day, and I went there in the afternoon, and found Mr. Gardner and Mr. Waterson, the inspector for building,* at the remains. The two uppermost stones, before I went there, had been removed, and the third of them so much broken down at the west

* The new mansion house at Angerton.

end that the bones had been removed and some parts of the grave examined. I then measured it. *(Two sketches with the pen, and measurements.)*  The stones were all of them rough flags, of the same kind as are naturally found in the rocky banks on the side of the Hart, from High Angerton to Broomhouse.   No mark of tool is seen on any of them.   They are generally about five feet high(?)   Each side or corner of this grave was intimately closed with soft dark-blue clay, such as is found by the side of the Pow-burn, on the north side of the Angerton meadows; and this had been done as if to prevent the sand from oozing into the grave and filling it up.   It was still soft, and fit to cover or plaster upon, as on the day on which it was first made.   But a brown sandy soil of earth, for about four or five inches thick, had covered the bottom of the grave and oozed with water through the sides of the upper stones, and in these [it] were found two thigh-bones, *(os femoris,)* both broken, one at both ends, the other at the lower end, and only 14½ inches of it remaining; one leg-bone, *(or tibia,)* both ends remaining, and 14 inches long; each patella; a fibula, the lower end broken, only seven inches remaining; one arm *(os humeri)* or shoulder-bone, the lower end broken, only eleven inches remaining; one *os ilium* or *pelvis*, broken; one *os calcis*.   (June 19, Mr. Hawdon says that of these bones my account is right, and [that they are] those of a woman.)   All these antiquities from 1 to 6 *(of which there are neat sketches in Indian ink)* were found in the grave opened to-day in the Broomhouse sandpit.   1. Is a knife of bronze, [*more probably the head of a spear,*] the blade much oxidated by time, and, when I saw it, broken into four parts, but the handle end and its three copper rivets or nails are covered with an only very thin film of rust; 2 and 3, an ear-drop and seven flat beads made of slaty coal, of which there is abundance on each side of the Hart and among its gravel.   Eight beads were found; but one was broken, which I readily split, to find of what mineral substance it was made: 4, 5, 6, two sharp knives and a light hammer of flint, probably fixed in wooden handles.   The bones preserved were imbedded with sandy earth, and all the implements found among them are now in my possession.   But the man who first opened the grave put into his pocket three teeth, which he gave me afterwards, and took with him a small piece of flint, which he threw away as useless and incurious.\*"

---

\* Hodgson has noted that an account of this discovery was sent by him to the New-castle Courant, but that many errors had been committed by the compositor.

The reader must not, with the above extract before him, conclude that Hodgson's health was at this period in a more satisfactory state than usual. His Journal gives painful testimony to the contrary. If this faithful record should prove, that with him there was *nulla dies sine nota*, it proves but too generally that there was also no day without great bodily pain. Towards the end of May, however, being in a somewhat better condition, he made a short progress into the north-western parts of the county, visiting the castles of Elsdon, Harbottle, the old church of Halystone, &c. &c. His Journal contains many interesting notices of his proceedings on this occasion, and many neat illustrative sketches by Miss Brown.

July was to him a month of almost uninterrupted suffering; but again he rallied, and on the 12th of August departed from home for Harrogate, by the recommendation of his medical advisers, Dr. Headlam and Mr. Hawdon. His state of health, as the reader has been informed, had been much worse than usual towards the end of the preceding month, and, now that he had to a certain extent recovered his strength, it was hoped that this step might be of advantage to him. Having reached Harrogate he states, on the 18th, that he felt himself better than he had been for many weeks, but on the 20th he was again " in distressing pain," which continued over the following day; and on the 22nd he quitted Harrogate and proceeded to Hartley Cottage near Kirby Stephen in Westmerland, the residence of his old friend Mr. Redman, from which place he took his departure on the 26th for Shap Wells, a place not far from Swindale, where he was born, and very near to Bampton, where he was educated. His Journal here contains many entries of interest, such as a description of a British circle of stones, of a Roman camp, of Shap Abbey, &c. The numerous notes made during this visit to Shap, descriptive of the remarkable scenery and antiquities of that place and neighbourhood, are not less interesting than those of which the reader has had so many specimens in the preceding parts of this memoir; and now that Hodgson was, as it were, at the very home of his childhood, they contain many affecting allusions to former days. " Rosgill is just about as it was sixty years ago." " Bampton Grange bright with its white houses and rich orchards." " At the north-east corner of the school the pier of the church-cross is now the turning post of the wicket to the entrance to the school." But even Shap, with all its touching associations, could not long detain him. He was sore stricken, and he was restless. The visitors in the hotel appear to have treated him with feeling kindness. One of them lent him a horse, to explore the scenes of his boyhood; but, having been from the 9th to the 12th of September again a great sufferer from internal pain, he fled on the 13th to Carlisle, to his brother's, and on the following day to Newcastle, and so to his home at Hartburn.

"Oct. 2, 1842.—Could not go to church. Educate the people well. It is a work of love. God's great work to man."

"14 Nov. 1842.—To Mr. Petheram.—If you should hazard to print in your catalogue any of the books noticed in my 'Specimen,' the only thing about the matter I am desirous of knowing is, what *per cent.* I ought to pay you for the sums you receive. The scarce book No. 3 Roman Wall, &c., has been nearly all taken by friends to whom I had sent copies of the 'Specimen.' As I am now again in good health, but read and write very badly, it would amuse me to exchange a few of my own works for books published in your catalogue."*

"Dec. 2, 1842.—I have spent a very happy visit to[at]Acton,† though sorry that I cannot understand the interesting historical information told me respecting Northumberland. O that I was well enough to copy many papers that he shewed me!"

"Dec. 23, 1842.—A day of great pain, but read the service for the burial of Anne Robson of Newham."

"To Mrs. Wyndham.—Meldon Park, Morpeth, 30 Dec. 1842.—While Mrs. Hodgson, Emma, and I have been staying all night here, and before breakfast be ready, and indeed my candle is a good deal brighter than the orient light of morning, I cannot refrain from endeavouring to express my best thanks to you for your very kind letter of Saturday last. My

---

* Mr. Petheram consented to this arrangement, and he has favoured me with a sight of Hodgson's letters selecting such books as he wished to have in exchange. They are thirteen or fourteen in number, and extend to the year 1844.

† The residence of John Hodgson Hinde, Esq.

health, indeed, as some good friend has been telling you, is very much improved; and the only blessing I seem to be in want of is, that I could again fluently read the words I wish to write, and see and understand how to correct the errors I make in my notes, and put all sentences in proper form and position.   But, indeed, I am very thankful for the improvement that has been given to me; and now begin to entertain a hope that ere long I may be able, not only to read the prayers of the Church, but at times to write and read a short sermon.*"

" 1843, Jan. 5.—Sir J. E. Swinburne told me that if my health had been as good as it was four years since, the present bishop of Durham, as he had mentioned, would have made me archdeacon of Northumberland or Lindisfarne."†

In the beginning of the year 1843, an arrangement was made for the tithes of the parish of Hartburn under the Commutation Act, by which the value of the benefice was considerably increased; and it is probable that if Hodgson had lived for a few years longer, under this improved state of things, he would have escaped from the difficulties under which he had long laboured.   The sum agreed upon, however, was not the real value of the tithes.   The landowners made an offer of three-fourths of the amount, and the Bishop of Durham, the patron of the living, consented to the arrangement.

" 1843, 1 Feb.—This drawing I made in 1817 of a shell which I found in a blue limestone boulder in the old red sandstone between Dacre Fell and Ulswater.   I brought home several other limestones.   The shell was in silex, and I intended to separate several others with acids, but about that time I began more regularly than before to investigate the History of Northumberland, and that wish soon employed all my other literary researches."

" 1843, Feb. 13.—At Capheaton.   Found dear Edward quite well

* In 1842 Hodgson communicated to the Gent. Mag. (Dec.) a letter on a Roman altar found at Olenacum or Old Carlisle, another on Roman altars of iron, and to the Gateshead Observer a third on the names of places in the Vale of Whittingham.

† I give this entry as I find it in the Journal, and cannot refrain from thinking that there must have been some mistake in the matter.   Most assuredly the appointment would not have been to Hodgson's advantage in any one point of view, and it is equally certain that he was, by his habits and feelings, utterly unfit for the office.

again and joyous. Sir John as full of sport as ever, and Miss Swinburne mild and good as a May morning."

" To MR. McKAY.—Hartburn, Morpeth, 22 Feb. 1843.—My dear Sir. I must not allow you to think that I am intending to forget you; but am going to endeavour, under my own hand and seal, to assure you that both Mrs. Hodgson, Emma, and myself still very often talk about you, and that in these long and dark and wet days and nights we would be often very glad to hear your cheerful conversation, to talk again about long past days at Whelpington, and the pleasure you are enjoying at your own fireside.

" I cannot write a long letter to you; but I am sure you will be glad to hear that my health, since I came from Shap, has so much improved that in bodily health I am now as well as I have ever been for many years. My eyes and memory have also much improved, though I am still unable to read any part of my duty, excepting for the burial of the dead or marriages. However, I am slowly compiling a little book on a religious subject, which I intend to print and distribute for the use of my parishioners.* The History of Northumberland is nearly still; and about my garden and the undercliff on our side the burn and the wood, you must come to see at your next opportunity, which I must beg will be as soon as you possibly can. The chapel at Cambo is done, and has duty doing usually in it in the afternoons. Everybody praises its beauty, and it is well attended. The school here will have my next summer's work to repair; indeed I feel [fear] nearly to rebuild; all of it is in such wretched order and inconvenient. The worst work, however, which I have to do, is to repair the ancient tower of my house: as it at present appears in the roof anything but an old fortress. Its tiles must, as soon as I am able, be stripped away and Welch slates be donned upon the tower's neck and head, which I hope will make them look very kindly and courteously upon my people, and the travellers, as they pass along the road.

" My dear Sir, if I cannot write to you a good letter and put all its words in good grammatical order, I am sure you will find that I am cheerful; and with best regards from Mrs. H. and Emma, I assure you that I am always yours very faithfully,

" JOHN HODGSON."

* He alludes here to a Book of Family Morning and Evening Prayers, which he had begun to compile, chiefly from the Prayer Book, a few weeks before the date of this letter, and at which he laboured for a few weeks, but was obliged to lay it aside.

" To W. C. TREVELYAN, Esq.—Hartburn, Morpeth, 25 Feb. 1843.— My dear Sir, since I received your inquiries about my health, congratulations about my tithes, and accounts of your late interesting journey over the Alps to Rome, and especially through a considerable part of Greece, the weather has been either so cold, or so dark, with drizzling rain, that I have been unable to write even a short note to you, as you requested I would. To-day, however, the morning begins to brighten, and I will endeavour to thank you, as I most cordially do, for the interest you take about my health, which I have very great thankfulness to be able to tell you has within the last three or four months improved very considerably, though still I read very badly, and am almost more difficult to talk than to write.

" How I wish I could have been with you when you were in Bœotia! For, if I had been there, I might have had an occasion of going from the Gulf of Crissus to Thermopylæ and examining the Phocian Wall. When I was at school at Bampton, forty-three years since, Professor Carlyle, then Chancellor of the Diocese of Carlisle, was anxious that I should go with him as his secretary, in the expedition he made with Lord Elgin, as Ambassador to the Ottoman Court. I ardently wished to have been able to go; but instead of sailing through the Hellespontus, and seeing Hæmus and Rhodope on the right of the Propontis, and Caucasus and Taurus on the left, I was content to become in that year (1799) the schoolmaster of Matterdale in Cumberland. It was, however, very curious that, four years after, the professor was appointed chaplain of Bishop Barrington, and I had to be examined by him at Newcastle for deacon's orders; after which he put into my hands two very ancient manuscript copies of the Greek Testament, and begged me to collate them with Wetstein's copy. He had several other copies, which he purchased in different Grecian monasteries. I thought our friendship was going for some time to be firmly fixed; but he died at Newcastle before I could be ordained. Your letter about Greece reminds me of these circumstances, but my head, I fear, will not allow me to write another paragraph to you. I must not, however, omit to beg you to say to Sir John, your father, that I am very much delighted that his health has improved so much as you have told me. But I should beg that, in future, he will endeavour to have his carriage driven more carefully than it has frequently been; for, though he has never yet had his bones broken by falling, he has often been overturned in imminent danger; and has as much occasion to take care about his carriage as I have to be tender in treating my brain.          " JOHN HODGSON."

"1843. March 24.—Dusted my books in the library, and removed part of my MS. books into the tower closet, which room during this winter has been my study."

"To the Rev. J. Raine.—Hartburn, Ap. 19, 1843.—For a long time I have been fondly indulging myself with the hope that the first morning after Easter Tuesday was past, I would put on wings and fly to Durham. But, though Ceres this morning has found her beautiful daughter, and all life seems to be teeming with joy, I cannot take my car and come to you. Our good friend Mr. Edward Swinburne has flattered us with the hope that, if to-day should continue fine, he would come in the afternoon and stay with us till Thursday or Friday, so that Purvis and a servant went to the market at Morpeth instead of me. The proper names, I used formerly to see so well, still float like sunbeam motes before my eyes, and will not appear in their wonted form. I have a hundred things to tell you which I have not words to write."

"1843, 17 May.—From the library windows this evening my garden, the church, fields, and trees around seemed more charming than I ever thought them before. The light that was upon them, the gean trees in full blossom, the apple trees just beginning to burst into flower, the new walk and terrace wall in the middle of the garden, and the whole scene, seemed to me the most beautiful place I ever saw."

"1843, 7 June.—A fine morning, and a west wind; cool, but fanning sweetly before the rising sun. I hope now that for a few months the north winds that blow upon the graves of men, and the east wind, that chills us with death, will sleep in their own chambers."

"1843, 9 June.—All yesterday [well] and all night enjoyed quiet and blessed sleep. When Ferdinando Galiani, who wrote on Vesuvius, &c., presented some curious minerals to the Pope, he said 'Beatissime Pater, fac ut lapides isti panes fiant.' Was he poor when he said this?"

"1843, 19 June—At six, in a very cold morning, came by Morpeth to Newcastle, and then to Durham. Dined and had tea with Mr. Raine. At night to attend the Architectural Society of Durham, at the Castle, the Warden in the chair. Mr. Thompson read a paper on Magdalen Chapel in Gilesgate; Mr. Greenwell a description of the church of Lanchester; and Mr. Raine a history of the different æras of the cathedral of Durham. 20. Went to the cathedral church. Queen's accession to the throne. The dean preached a sensible, useful, and patriotic sermon. Spent the afternoon at Mr. Raine's. 21. At the Convocation dined at the hall. The meeting very agreeable to me. The Dean very gracious to me. The Warden, as always, very kind and attentive to me. 22. Breakfasted with the Warden. Dined with Raine. Got to Newcastle by five."

" 1843, 23 June.—Spent the day at Tynemouth with Tom and the children. In the colliery villages the gardens generally very much improved within the last twenty years. Even potatoes planted with manure on heaps of small coals. Nature creates aristocracies for noble purposes."

After having taken measures for the re-building the parish school at Hartburn, Hodgson determined to pay another visit to the neighbourhood of his birth-place. Swindale and its associations were the subject of his thoughts by day and his dreams in the night season; and, although a year had not elapsed since his former visit, he was impatient for a renewal of the pleasure which it had afforded him. His companion was the Rev. J. H. Newton, a clergyman who had been engaged in the duty at Cambo; and the two reached Shap Well on the 11th of July. Hodgson suffered much from the journey, and on the following morning he was in a deplorable state. But in a day or two he gained somewhat of strength, and drove or rode in quest of objects, the recollection of which was endeared to him by the long acquaintance of sixty years. He sought the old Shap Thorn, but no trace of it could be found. A party of Ordnance surveyors had felled and burnt it. In the old cairn on the Crosby-Ravensworth road he was more fortunate. But again he began to be impatient. " I intended this morning (writes he on the 20th) to go by places of my night and my day dreams—Rosgill, Bampton, and Haweswater—to Penrith; but it was then wet, and now at mid-day more so." He had purchased a pony at Shap, and on this animal he rode to Carlisle, and from Carlisle he returned by railway to the station nearest to his house. This, however, was not his last visit to the blue hills and delightful valleys of his native Westmerland. One more will claim to be recorded, and then—all is over.

" 1843, 26 July.—Hartburn.—Mr. Bates of Milburn, his mother and eldest sister, came here to tea to-day.  I love them because they are relations of Mr. Ellison of Hebburn."

" 1843, 27 July.—I am very unwilling to begin to write, especially letters.  Words will not fluently come out of my mind, and even the most abundant words that can be found are very unable to describe the thoughts that fill the mind, especially intellectual thoughts.  I can see and admire the beautiful furniture that adorns the earth, but how imperfectly can I write in words the gardens, trees, and fields that I see through the window before me."

The new chapel of Cambo has been often mentioned in the preceding pages.  The original chapel having been suffered to fall into decay soon after the Reformation, Hodgson had not been long settled at Hartburn before he began to take measures for the spiritual advantage of this remote part of his parish.  In 1837 considerable progress had been made in raising the necessary funds for the construction and endowment of a new edifice, and towards both purposes Sir John Trevelyan of Wallington, the owner of the chief portion of the district of Cambo, was a liberal contributor.  The foundation-stone of the chapel was laid by Lady Trevelyan on the 30th of September 1841, the schoolroom having been previously licensed for divine service, and as soon as it was finished, the same licence was on the 1st of Jan. 1843, extended to the new structure, which was at length duly consecrated by the Bishop of Durham, on the 17th of August following, (1843,) Mr. Hodgson's contribution to its endowment having been the vicarial tithes of three townships, which he gave up for himself and successors for ever.  He himself was present at the consecration, but was not able to take any official part in the ceremony.*

" To Mr. McKay.—Hartburn, 2 Oct. 1843.—I was able to be at the holy communion at Hartburn church, and to attend evening service at Cambo yesterday.  Two or three days will carry up all our harvest."

* A minute account of the consecration was written by Mr. Hodgson for the local newspapers, with a list of subscriptions, &c.

"This morning I am expecting a bookbinder to repair my shattered library, and gild them with proper titles. My books may be repaired a little, from the labour they suffered on Northumberland. My memory cannot. Four years, however, since, as I told you, I was almost momentarily, but in sleep, deprived of the power of speaking or writing the names of persons I loved most dearly; and now ought to be thankful that I can write a letter to my friends, and to assure them that I still love them as well as I did when I was better able to be delighted with their company, and mingle with the pleasures of social life.

"I know you will pardon me for this brief and, I fear, almost [un]intelligible letter. But I must not deprive myself of assuring you that I esteem you much; and that I have bodily health quite sufficient to give me very great enjoyment in seeing the beautiful world in which we live, the affectionate kindness which I enjoy, and the hopes I have of that kingdom which I believe, but have not seen.—Dear Mr. McKay, yours ever very faithfully,                    JOHN HODGSON."

"1843, Nov. 4.—This is my 64th birthday, and I thank my Creator that my health is so good as it is."

"To the REV. J. RAINE.—Nov. 20, 1843.—My health keeps me in so much pain that I am unfit to be at any place but home. I have for many months been very desirous of going to Newcastle on business, but have not courage to do so. I am never well when I am there. But I still hope for better health, and when that happy time may come certainly I must endeavour to be over again at Durham. Still there is no answer to my letter to Miss Atkinson of Temple Sowerby.

"Did you ever see in the library of the Literary and Philosophical Society of Newcastle a thick folio, closely written, a 'Life of Mr. Ambrose Barnes, Alderman of Newcastle.' He was son of Mr. Theophilus Barnes, of Startforth on the Tees, near Barnard Castle. The author's preface is addressed 'To my honoured friend Sir Theodore Talbot,' and signed 'your honour's humble devoted servant, M. R. June 19, 1716.' I have several extracts from it, and, though it is full of religious stuff, it contains a great deal of curious local history, especially about Newcastle, the great plague, &c. Some extracts from it were some years since printed in the Newcastle Courant, but the editor of the pamphlet made it as dry as tharm. I had the MS. at Whelpington, and intended to have printed all the historical parts that were interesting; but why the copy was not finished I cannot tell, and the extracts that were copied I cannot read.   But it seems to contain a great deal of family history, anecdotes, &c., and these I think, free from religious weeds, might be made a pretty garden flower border to your Surtees Society.   When you get to London pray write to me.   A friendly letter does me a power of good.—J. H."

" 1843, Dec. 19.—Men generally are obstinate in proportion to their ignorance.   Common sense is the best sense.   All say this, but how few, except in trade, speak and practise from real experience ?   More than half the conversation we hear has as [little] real sterling truth as the aerial hen-scratches we see in the clear blue sky."

"1843, Dec. 29.  Newcastle.—Called on Mr. John Fenwick about my Memoir on the late Mr. Hedley.  He wished I would myself prepare it for the press.   I said I would be glad to do so.   It is now some six years since I put a note on the name of [my] dear friend in [my] Northumberland History.   I hope when I return to Hartburn my memory will remember some other words worthy of his name."*

" To the REV. J. RAINE.—Eldon Street, Newcastle, Dec. 30, 1843.—I have for many weeks been sadly disordered, but Dr. Headlam has attended me here for about a week, and I am getting pretty well.— J. H."

Mr. Hodgson's last literary labour was the revising or rather rewriting as it were, a MS. Glossary of North Country Words, which he had begun to compile at an early period of his life, and had enlarged from time to time, as he had had opportunity.   On the 4th of Jan. in this year, (1844,) he was requested by Mr. W. E. Brockett, who was preparing a third edition of his father's publication on the same subject, to lend his aid in making it more perfect, and with this request he readily complied.   His first step was to revise the former collection above spoken of, contained in an octavo volume of upwards of 200 pages, (from which he

---

* I find a few memoranda among Hodgson's papers indicating an intention to enlarge his Memoir of Hedley, as it appeared in his History (Part II. vol. iii. p. 331) but no further steps were taken in the matter.

When the above note was made Hodgson was in Newcastle, where for several days his life was in imminent danger, from an attack which was more violent than usual. He had gone thither to spend his Christmas with his children.

had previously made many contributions to Mr. Brockett's first edition,) and for this purpose he adopted a volume of the folio size, adding to it many new words and explanations. With this task he amused himself from January to June, at his leisure hours, interweaving in his pages numerous local stories, legends, traditions, &c. &c. by way of illustration. He had finished the letter P when illness compelled him to seek aid once more at Shap Wells in June, and no further progress was made in the undertaking.* He appears, however, to have communicated to Mr. Brockett, after his return home, such words, under the letters A and B, as suited his purpose, and was proceeding to carry out his promise, when Mr. Pearson's death, and his own sad attack in September, compelled him to lay aside his pen.

" 1844, Jan. 27.—Read much in ' Blackmore's Creation,' in which I can see little about the beauty of outward nature. Indeed it is a dry philosophical poem. I read it many years since, but could never admire its beauty or its use. Very few people have ability or time to read it. Indeed, if I had to give a lecture on Natural Theology or endeavour to improve Paley's inimitable [work] on that subject, I might be inclined to quote many melodious and forcible lines from Blackmore's ' Seven Books demonstrating the Existence and Providence of a God.' "

" To THE REV. J. RAINE.—Hartburn, 29 Jan. 1844.—I was very sorry to find that you were not well enough to be in Newcastle on the second of this month, and that I was not in our lodgings when you came there on the Thursday following. Indeed I had a week before promised, if I was able, to spend a day with my brother at Carlisle, as I had not seen him for above four years, on my way to the Isle of Wight. But I was very ill the night I was at Carlisle; and nearly all the time I was in Newcastle; but now I have had eight days free from pain, and have slept more quietly than I have done for above two months before. Indeed all the time I was in Newcastle I was in Dr. Headlam's care, and now think I am enjoying great benefit by his advice. Mr. Meggison was here to-day and rejoiced me by saying he had seen you about a

* I cannot refrain from expressing an opinion that the publication of this volume by a judicious hand, imperfect though it be, would be well received, especially in the Northern counties of England. It affords much curious local information in illustration of the words which it contains, and is something of a very different character from any compilation of a similar kind with which I am acquainted.

week since in Newcastle, and that you were looking well and in great
spirits.   God Almighty keep them up, for one opposed as you have
been must have supernatural aid to support him.——Mr. Woodman
to-day tells me that the Courant gets slowly forward in printing your
Records for the Lords.   I should like to have a copy of them.——On
Nov. last, the 29th, I received rather a long letter from Mr. John
Richard Walbran, of Ripon, respecting the Baliol family of Barnard
Castle.   I was very unwell at the time, and could with great difficulty
read his letter; but, ill as I was, I endeavoured to write a sketch of the
pedigree of the early Baliols, and, if he wished, would be glad to investigate the history more.   But he has never answered my letter.   He
says ' Mr. Raine has kindly noticed from your Pipe Rolls (A 68) Eustace
heir of Barnard: 1 John.   Is there reason to suppose he was his son!'
He also says ' In preparing for publication a brief History of the Barony
of Gainford and Barnard Castle, I have had reason to investigate the
very confused pedigree of the Baliols.'   Pray tell who this Mr. Walbran
is, and why you may suppose he has not answered my letter.*   I
should be sorry to suppose that I wrote anything to offend him.   I did
not write to him till Dec. 4.

" J. H."

" 1844, Feb. 18.—I read the funeral service for a burial to-day and
went through the duty better than I could have expected, but grew
very ill in the evening and in the night."

" To the Rev. J. Raine.—Hartburn, 22 Apr. 1844.—I dare say that
our schoolmaster had given you a correct account of my health.   Since
October last I have had almost constant and distressing pain.   I can
seldom get to my garden, though my fruit trees, all planted by myself,
are in beautiful blossom, and the whole of the garden trim and beautiful as any modest lady would array herself for a drawingroom.   The
only amusement I have is adding memorandums to [my] Northumberland books.——As far as l can understand, the case of Mr. Pearson is
as bad as it can be.   My dear Hilda says that the medical gentleman
they have at Torquay says he is so weak that he cannot get to New-

* Mr. Walbran had been absent in London, pursuing his inquiries on the subject of
his intended history.   Upon his return he made his peace with his correspondent.
Would that this gentleman would finish the book alluded to !   One part only is before the
public, and it is the most perfect specimen which has ever issued from the press of a
compendious account of a district which, like that of the Barony of Gainford, teems
with interest.   In truth, I say it advisedly, it has no rival in our minor topographical
publications.

castle in less than eight days—that he must go to bed in a steam-vessel
from Torquay to Southampton; thence to London by railway, and from
London to Newcastle by steamboat.

" JOHN HODGSON."

The Shap Wells and their salutary power again came into
Hodgson's mind, and, urged probably by a still stronger motive,
another sight of the scenes of his boyhood, he paid a final visit to
those localities, to refresh his memory and rejoice his eyes with
sights which he was to see no more.   He left home on the 27th
of June accompanied by his youngest daughter, but he had
another companion who was becoming daily more decisive in its
attacks upon him and giving him daily warning that his end was
at hand.   And yet he could still record in his diary the names of
the flowers which were blooming in his walks, and reminding
him of bygone days when they shed their fragrance upon his boyhood.   Such was the strength which at this time his malady had
gained over his constitution that in general he was confined to his
bed; but during his short intervals of ease he mused, as usual,
among the Druidical stones mentioned upon a former occasion; and
moreover his Journal proves that nothing escaped him in his walks
which had a tendency to soothe his mind.   He met at the Well
other branches of the family of Rawes, his relations, who were
very attentive to him and his daughter in accommodating them
with the use of a carriage to visit several places of interest in the
neighbourhood.   At Shap he examined the parish register and
made numerous extracts relative to his family and relations.

With respect to this final visit to Shap, and the scenes of his
boyhood, I have been favoured with the following affecting
account by Mrs. Kennicott, his daughter, who, as I have said, was
his companion on the occasion.

" I shall never forget how alarmed I was at his being so excited
when we paid a visit to Bampton (where he had been a school-boy)—
how he ran up the steps of the old church and gave the bells a peal
which he had so often rung in his youth, and then took me to the pew
where he used to sit and shewed me his initials which he had himself
cut when a boy in the church—and how when we got to the brow of
the hill above Haweswater tears filled his eyes; for he could then see

Swindale his native valley, and Rosgill in the distance. We called upon a very distant relation, a Mr. Hodgson, vicar of Bampton, a plain simple country clergyman, and also Mrs. Hudson, a cousin, a very old lady, who lived in the village of Shap. We went and stayed a day and a night with Mr. Rawes, of Kendal, since dead.

In this way Hodgson continued to occupy himself for upwards of a month, until on the 30th of July he turned his face homewards. At Hartburn, however, affliction of another kind was ready to receive him. Mr. Pearson, the husband of his eldest daughter, had returned from Torquay in a hopeless state of consumption, and had come to Hartburn to die in peace. He lingered however till the 22nd of August, on which day his afflicted wife became a widow with four children, and she and they still live to lament the loss of a husband and a father.

This was Hodgson's last visit to Shap; and thus the cords one after another are broken by which we are bound to the earth.

"1844, Aug. 24.—I was able to walk in the churchyard to-day, and in Hartburn Wood, for several hours."

"1844, Aug. 26.—My sons Richard and John, and Mr. Bourne and Mr. Calvert, nephew of Mr. Pearson, came hither to take the remains of our dear son-in-law Mr. Pearson to his grave in the Jesmond Cemetery near Newcastle."

"1844, Sep. 3.—I was well enough to attend morning prayers and the holy communion to-day."

Hodgson's bodily health during the whole of the preceding spring and summer had been in a truly pitiable state. His Journal is little more than a record of painful days, spent chiefly in bed, or of thankfulness for any brief interval in his sufferings. Expressions of impatience or complaint there are none. All is peaceful resignation, and in his hours of sunshine such reflections as the following, after an attack of more than usual severity:—"April 18. I have had a blessed night of repose, and have been able to walk for an hour in the garden. Weather beautiful. Fruit trees on the walls getting into full blossom." He must have well known that his death was approaching; and how often, in those his solitary walks in his garden, must he have cast a quiet eye of resignation over its eastern wall upon the venerable tower of his church and the rude and moss-grown gravestones in his churchyard! My next extract from his Journal will prepare the reader for the end.

"1844, Sept. 5.—I was struck with a paralytic stroke, and deprived of the use of my left side. Mr. Hawdon was sent for, but, being absent, his assistant Mr. Kilby, came and bled me in the right arm and ordered me to be leeched and blistered.

His right hand and arm being happily not affected by this sad attack he continues to make entries in his Journal from day to day as usual, only his memoranda are more brief and incorrectly written, and his writing occasionally less legible. But he appears to have been deeply aware of the change which was at hand. He had long made an upper room of the old vicarage tower his bedroom, and occasionally his study. He now hastens to put it into a decent state, that he might breathe his last in it. A new window is made in the north wall, paint and plaster are applied where necessary, and in this room he took up his abode on the 28th, having on the 26th bid a final farewell to his son John, who was proceeding to Silesia as an engineer, in partnership with the Messrs. Hawthorns of Newcastle, under whom he had learned his art.

" To THE REV. J. RAINE.—Hartburn, 8 Sept. 1844.—My dear Raine, you will be sorry to learn, as much as I am, that the        of the
        have decided the law against the rector of Ford. I am sure you will be grieved that I, on Tuesday last, had a severe paralytic affect [attack], and consequently am unable to write to you about ————, and to write to you very badly in my bed. Pray give me soon a short note. Yours truly,

" JOHN HODGSON."

" Sept. 23.—Came again into the tower-room."

" —— 30.—Mr. Hawdon visited me, my spasmodic pains being very severe."

" Oct. 9.—Found several copies [corrected by himself into plants] of woody nightshade on the Thornton road to Witton, and planted them in the garden here as a pleasant hedge-shrub."

"Oct. 26.—Saturday.—The weather still very fine. I fear I must give up to write notes to my Journal as my memory gradually decreases."

"To the Rev. J. Raine.—Hartburn, 13 Nov. 1844.—The very kind note I received from you last week compels me to endeavour to write a few lines to you.——As to myself, I am now walking up and down stairs without my stick, and often beginning to visit my improving school, and all my cottagers, somewhat as formerly; but cannot forget to tell you that most afflicting spasms are visiting me daily, and requiring the nightly use of anti-spasmodic drops, morpheum, &c. &c. At present, too, my daughter Emma, and all Mrs. Pearson's children, with myself, have lately made my house a perfect hospital, while my wife is the nurse of us all; but, thank God, still toiling away in good spirits and perfect health. Now, as you know there is no end of writing, this to-day must conclude my (I fear rather dolorous) epistle, though I would be glad to write more cheerfully than my account has fallen into; and to assure you, with my best regards to Mrs. R. and your family, that I am always your most sincere friend,

"JOHN HODGSON."

"To the Rev. J. Raine.—9 Dec. 1844.—A month since you said 'Give me a line now and then, as it may amuse you to write to an old friend;' and for several mornings before I rose I thought as soon as I was dressed I would write to you; and arranged in thoughts the subjects I would tell you, and had sketched the letter in paragraphs and words; but as soon as I begun to see and think upon the mighty subjects of the real world, its interests, and its troubles, the ideal visages of the mental world, that I had been engaged with, vanished away; my sad pains began, and threw me on my couch, and a word was not left to tell you. However on a brighter day than I usually have, I may tell you that about a fortnight since——— You know I am unable to read what I have written to you, and therefore cannot correct my errors. Yours ever,                                               "J. H."

CHAPTER XVIII.—1845.

Journal.—Letters—Last illness—Death—Conclusion.

Mr. Hodgson's Journal is now beginning to exhibit no doubtful indications that a change was approaching. Up to the end of November in the preceding year, (1844,) it contains entries made from day to day, without interruption; but most of them give token of an unsteady hand and a shaking pen. In December they stop at the tenth, on which day a visit from his "amiable friend" "Mr. John Thompson, the botanist of Crowhall," is recorded. In January, 1845, there is only one memorandum, and that on the last day of the month. Christmas, that holy time of joy, must have been therefore to poor Hodgson a season of uninterrupted pain and trial, the day of the schoolmaster to prepare him for those joys "in the Highest" of which the blessed angels sung on the morn of the Nativity. In February I find no trace of his pen whatever. In March he has made one single entry; in April three; the last of which refers to three letters written on that day, the first to his brother Christopher, at Carlisle, the second to his (Christopher's) son Robert, and the third to his own son John, in Silesia; and here terminates the faithful record which has so long been my guide in tracing the bright and gloomy days of my friend. In his case the very reverse of the poet's observation had been for many a long year but too painfully true:—

"Si numeres anno soles et nubila toto,
Invenies nitidum saepius isse diem."

But let no one think that, even in the midst of his severest afflictions, he was without his comforts and consolations. We have already had before us numerous proofs of the way in which he could think and reflect, and soothe his pains by holy thoughts and pious resignation, but I have gathered from his Journal for the present page a few more extracts, which still further shew

VOL. II.          2 G

what those comforts and consolations were, and which, in truth, render him an object of envy rather than of commiseration. Such subjects of deep and pious contemplation had been the matter of his daily thoughts, from his youth upwards; and it is a happy thing for my purpose that he has occasionally, as it were by accident, committed a few of them to paper, in illustration of his devout feelings, and of the general tenor of his mental intercourse with that Heavenly Father, to whom, wherever he was, and whatever he did, he always looked up with profound self-abasement and sincerity of heart.

"1840, Sep. 27.—O that I may long to live and adore in the Church. the type of the first admittance and the last approach to the merciful and glorious God, through Jesus Christ! O that I may die daily! O that I may not be buried in Egypt! "Bury me not, I pray thee, in Egypt," but bury me "in linen clothes, with spices, as the manner of the Jews is to bury." I would have my dead body be carried from the north and darkness to the altar of Christ, and then from it borne through the southern door of light into my church's garden, and in that garden to be buried in "a new sepulchre where never man was laid " *

"1840, Aug. 3.—Few people have ability to see the secrets of God's nature; or the glorious powers and treasures of the sun; the infinite young beauties of spring, the bright joys of summer," &c.

"1841, 4 Mar.—Once again at church. Blessed Sunday, and beautiful weather."†

"1841, May 22. Drive to Morpeth; my ears still in pain. Can talk little; but the year is bursting forth into great beauty; and, though I cannot hear the voice of man, I can, and do, rejoice in the beauty of the silent and glorious works of God. Cædmon spoke in his poetry the deep words of God, and the sweet words of Christ; and Milton raised his

* These references to Egypt as the type of sin, and to the north side of the church-yard as expressive of darkness, will be easily understood by those who are acquainted with the beautiful system of symbolical representation which prevailed in the early centuries of the Church. Again, when Hodgson expressed a desire that his body should be carried to the altar, he was referring to a goodly custom still in use in many old north-country churches, the placing the coffin in the chancel, during that part of the funeral ceremony which is performed in the church.

† He had not been at church during the whole of the preceding winter, by order of is medical adviser.

" pealing organ" to the same high and extatic height. In this world they
both brought all heaven before their eyes. Now, I can no longer listen to
their voice or read their "service high and anthems clear." I cannot
sing in the songs of the Church, yet, while I can see the young and beautiful year, mighty blessings are left to me."

"1842, 29 May.—At St. Nicholas' church, Newcastle. O the de-
lightfulness of the service! Delicious to hear the voices of the sons of
music! The house of God when glorious and full of joy is indeed delightful. O that I could again join in the service and live for ever in the
house of my God.
" All men wishful to be good are God's agents, and history in its voice
applauds their names. Davy was a glorious priest of God."

" 1842, 6 Nov. New sets of morning prayers. Must I venture to
print a set for every day next year, both for morning and evening?"

" 1842, 21 Dec.—Dear John came here in the evening to spend new
year and a few other days. The weather for several days had been
warm, but windy; and with the new moon the weather grew calm, the
sky clear, and the air frosty. We have had a blessed year. May God
have the kindness to send us another, and many years, of happiness
and plenty."

"1843, Jan. 22.—Third Sunday after Trinity (Epiphany). Man is
full of ignorance and sin, and the more he improves in knowledge, the
more he becomes conscious of his ingratitude to God. Humble me, O
Lord, and improve me in the knowledge of my sinfulness."

" 1843, 25 Jan.—Let me never forget the blessed state of health I
have enjoyed for several days past. 26. I pray God that Mr. Edw.
Swinburne's health may be again restored. He suffers much."

"1843, 19 Feb. Not at church. Sexag. Sunday: very few at church
indeed. I could not go thither. O that I might be permitted to pray
and speak again in the house of my God! O that I could bring forth
fruit with patience!"

" 1843, Apr. 21.—It is just 20 years to-day since Mr. Redman inducted
me into the church of Whelpington; and I feel great thankfulness to my

2 G 2

merciful Father, for having for so many years spared the life of such
vile earth and miserable sinner as I feel myself, one of the deepest sin-
ners. O spare me, good Lord, spare thy servant whom thou hast re-
deemed with thy precious blood, and be not angry with me for ever!

"1843, 6 May.—Cuckoo heard, but not a swallow yet. Pain of mind
is the penalty of sin. O. D. O. M. Jesu. O that my mind could be
blessed with the bright knowledge of truth, and an ardent zeal and
desire to pursue it!"

"1843, 4 June. Whitsunday.—He who wishes to go to the Holy
Communion with a meek and lowly heart, should especially abstain from
food till he has ' eat of that bread 'and drunk of that cup,' in remembrance of his Saviour's death. When the stomach' is full the head
cannot see clearly into heavenly things."

"1843, 18 June. First Sunday after Trinity.—' Beloved, let us love
one another, for love is of God, and every one that loveth is born of
God and loveth God,' &c. From the beginning to the end of the epistle
all amazingly beautiful. It is a halo of love around the light of God.

"1843, July 20.—The star we live in is the Temple of God; and to
know and admire his works is to serve and adore him."

"1843, 24 July.—O that I could deplore my manifold sins and
wickedness, and rouse myself up to fight the good fight it is my duty to
do! But I fear the night of my life is too far spent to allow me to give
any vigorous effort to rise up in the armour of light. Oh glorious
light, the light of my God and my Saviour, be bright, and do not darken
my soul in eternal death!"

"1844, 11 Feb.—Mr. Hawdon came to see me to-day—orders me
more blue pill; but thinks I will be soon well again. But when shall
I be able to print my projected Book of Morning and Evening Prayers?
If I should be allowed to do so, I seem to think it would improve my
mind, preserve many thoughts that float across my soul, steady them,
and give them something more than a shadow and a name."

"1844, 21 Feb.—Mr. Hawdon was again here to-day and encourages
me with the hope that my health will soon grow better. Mrs. H. in a

letter tells us that Tom and Hilda with her infant child have fixed to go to London to-morrow to consult Dr. Holland or Dr. Clark, and go from thence to Torquay; also that on Friday she will bring their three other children to Hartburn. God Almighty bless them all, and assist me to give them all the happiness that my Almighty Father may allow me to give them!"

Having finished the repairs and alterations in the tower-room above mentioned, Hodgson sent for the village carpenter to give certain directions rendered necessary by its situation. "When I am dead," said he, "you will find it difficult to convey my coffin through the narrow passage which leads into the house itself: have ready, therefore, against the time it may be wanted, an inclined plane made of boards, which may rest at one end upon the sill of the window and at the other on the ground. By this contrivance you will avoid all the trouble of the narrow passage and staircase." The parish clerk was next sent for, and to him directions were given as to the precise spot in the churchyard in which this poor suffering but patient man wished to be buried. "At the east end of the church the rock comes near to the day. Remove the thin soil which covers it, and make a deep cavity in the sandstone, and there let me lie in peace." It is not common for dying men to trouble themselves with such matters as these, or have the heart and grace to look upon them with a firm and fearless eye. There are those who would have expressed somewhat less of surprise if a detail had been here given of the making of a will and the settlement of worldly affairs. But Hodgson had no such subject to divert his departing thoughts. He had nothing to leave, except a good and holy name, and he had no trustees to appoint for the benefit of his wife and children save ONE, to whose blessed care he confided them in his heart, without the formalities of pen and paper. He knew in whom he had trusted, and he continued to rely upon the same gracious Being for those whom he was leaving behind him.

He could still, however, write a letter now and then to a friend; and it is a consoling thought to the author that he was one of those who were so reckoned and remembered.

"To the Rev. J. Raine.—Hartburn, 7 Jan. 1845.—My dear Raine. How must I find any kind congratulatory words for the letter you sent me on Christmas last and the present new year. I fear I think of nothing but the old and common words of the time of year, but I can beg you and your family to accept my best wishes for health and blessings for the ensuing and many new years, and a rapid and happy escape out of the law's entanglements and delay. Emma and Mrs. Hodgson preserve their usual good health, but I must not omit to mention to you that of late I have been exceedingly afflicted with severe fits of spasm; indeed reduced into a very weak state; and very seldom endeavour to write a word of any kind, chiefly because I am so very unable to read what I write. Of late, however, we have had two fine January days, and I have endeavoured to give you my best thanks for your last letter, and to assure you that I am always your most sincere friend,                                "John Hodgson."

"To the Rev. J. Raine.—Hartburn, 11 March, 1845.—My dear Raine, I believe I wrote a note to you in January last; but since that time I have been indeed so very unwell as to be utterly unable to write to you, as you kindly requested me to do. I have been afflicted with pain or been so very weak as to be unable to walk: indeed the harsh weather we have had for these two months has kept me a very great time to bed; and the pain that has been afflicting me for above fifty years, and every year increasing more, has since December last confined me almost entirely to my bedroom. I have indeed for above six weeks been daily expecting to send a note to you stamped HARTBURN, as we have requested Lord Lonsdale to fix a post office at this place and another at Cambo: indeed his lordship has made my servant Purvis to be almost immediately post-messenger from Meldon Park Corner to Cambo. I may also tell you that the magistrates of Northumberland have, in consequence of an indictment, ordered their surveyor general of bridges to examine the present state of Hartburn Bridge and the roads at each end of it; in consequence of which he was last week with two assistants examining the best method of doing so, which we understand is thought to build an entire new bridge in a new situation; which we expect to be commenced in the beginning of this summer. My pains have commenced and send me to bed, so that I cannot write another word. With best regards to Mrs. R. and your family, yours most affectionately,

                                "John Hodgson."

On the 10th of April Hodgson wrote another short letter to the author in a trembling hand, and without much connection in its matter or arrangement. This letter turns chiefly upon a subject in which the latter was deeply concerned, and which had for several months excited the greatest interest at Hartburn, especially in Hodgson himself, who, in the weak state to which he was reduced by his bodily infirmities, must have suffered greatly from his anxiety. "My sight," says he, at the bottom of the first page, "is so bad that I cannot turn my paper. Your old friend Hodgson"—and these were his last words to me.

During the following month of May he was in general in a better condition than usual; but with June came a return of his malady in a more severe form than ever, and in the middle of the month a happy release from his earthly sufferings.

The pen of an affectionate daughter, now Mrs. Kennicott, shall describe the closing scene. She and her mother were the only two of the sufferer's family who were present at his last moments upon earth, and with her painful but faithful narrative I presume not to meddle. She shall close the eyes of her father.

"Our dear father was quite confined to his room for at least a week before his death. His sufferings were very great, from the commencement of the last attack of spasm; and for about the last three days he was quite paralysed in his body and lower limbs. There appeared no dimness of memory; and he liked my poor dear mother and myself to sit as usual with our work beside him. He became much worse on the second day, when we went for Jane Gibson; and Mr. Hawdon came in the afternoon. It is quite impossible for any one to know the amount of my father's sufferings: he was so very considerate for the feelings of those about him that he never fully expressed what he himself felt. He sometimes gave vent to the most piteous groans, and then I believe his sufferings were awful, but that was about four days before his death. About ten P.M. he asked to see Purvis, who came much affected to his bed side, when he immediately held out his hand and mentioned his name, but that was all he said—and frequently during the night he recognised dear mother and myself, and always very affectionately pressed our hands, and sometimes uttered our names *very low*. He was then too weak to speak much, and before that his pain was much too severe to allow him to talk. I well remember the last Sunday he spent in this world—how he had the morning service read to him by my dear mother, and frequently asked for chapters to be read from the Bible, especially out of the Psalms. Neither my mother nor I were in the room when he died; for my poor mother became hysterical, and Mr. Hawdon, who was most kind, and had remained all night in the house, insisted upon her being removed from the room. He also took me out soon afterwards, I think about five A.M.; and he died about half-past six. Jane afterwards told me that he as it were slept away. We all know that he bore his afflictions with truly Christian resignation, humbly trusting in the merits of our blessed Saviour for salvation in a better world."*

Having been born in the year 1779, he was now in the 66th year of his age. He died on Thursday the 12th of June, 1845, and on the Tuesday following his remains were deposited in his churchyard in the place which he had appointed, beneath the eastern lancets of the chancel.

* A post-mortem examination confirmed the opinions of Mr. Hodgson's medical attendants. He was found to have been labouring under three distinct diseases. First, an enlargement of the heart. Secondly, a cerebral affection, the result of long and severe mental exertion, under which his brain was gradually becoming soft and unable to perform its functions, and hence the failure of his memory, or rather of the ability to express himself in the language which his mental powers suggested, but to which his tongue refused to give a correct utterance. Under this affliction he might eventually have been reduced to a state of childhood. His third disease proceeded from a torpid and irregular action of the larger intestines, taking its origin in his sedentary habits, and in the end terminating in a stricture of the ilio-colic valve, which had so far closed up the passage that there were extracted from it many pellets of lead or shot, which had been unable to pass away and were remaining to increase the obstruction. His food, whatever it was, and of which he in general almost feared to partake, had long been of the simplest kind, and had been minced into the smallest fragments to promote its digestion. The shot however had escaped the edge of the knife. But another discovery was made of a still further and more deadly obstruction. On the colon there was found a formation, the nucleus of which resembled a steel pen, and which must have caused immense pain when any thing of a solid nature came in contact with it. His family, however, had no recollection of having heard him say that he had ever accidentally swallowed any such substance. From this combination of internal obstructions proceeded the violent spasms under which he had for so many years suffered, and eventually his death. Under the disease of his brain he might for some time have lived a helpless life, but he had more powerful enemies to contend with, and he was conquered. Some very extraordinary cases of cerebral affection, resembling that under which Mr. Hodgson laboured, are recorded in Abercrombie's " Treatise on the Diseases of the Brain."

HARTBURN CHURCH.

It was not necessary to follow Mr. Hodgson's directions respecting the lowering of his coffin from the tower-room, by means of an inclined plane of timber, as a window was easily removed, and space was thus obtained to turn the coffin in the passage.  An oblong gravestone, ornamented with a cross after the old fashion, was soon afterwards placed over his grave, upon which, along with his own, was recorded the name of his son William, who had been buried near the place in 1837; and, in addition to a memorial window, a monument is now in preparation, to be erected in the chancel of the church, in the back of one of the sedilia, in commemoration of him and the other members of his family, who had died before him, or have since departed from the world.*  Among the latter is his affectionate and widowed wife, who after his death resided in Newcastle, and, dying there of the cholera morbus in 1853, reposes in the same grave with her husband.   The inscription is as follows:

* Mention has been frequently made of the different members of Mr. Hodgson's family.   Their names are as follows.  One son and two daughters are now the only survivors of nine children.

1. Elizabeth Hilda, born in 1811 ; married in 1835 to Thomas Bourn, son of John Brooksbank Pearson, Esq.  Mrs. Pearson became a widow in 1844, with four children.

2. Richard Wellington, born in 1812, married in 1835 to Isabella, daughter of George Straker, Esq. and has one son and four daughters.

3. John, born in 1814, married in 1846 to Mary Ann, daughter of William Hawthorn, Esq.  This amiable couple died of cholera morbus at Allahabad in the East Indies, she on the 19 June 1857, and he on the following day.  He had previously been a civil engineer in Silesia, and was, at the time of his death, in the service of the East India Railway Company in that capacity.  They were in the fort of the above mentioned place during the late rebellion, and their death was hastened by the scarcity and badness of the provisions to which they were reduced.  Happily they died a natural death.

4. Jane Bridget, born in 1816, died in 1831.

5. Susannah, born in 1817, died in 1834.

6. Isaac, born in 1819, died in 1830.

7. William Wilson, born in 1821, died in 1837.

8. Mary, born in 1825, died in 1830.

9. Emma, born in 1826, married in 1846 to the Rev. Benjamin Centum Kennicott, incumbent of All Saints Monkwearmouth, and has a numerous family.

IN CŒMITERIO, QUOD EXTRA, JACENT SEPULTI JOHANNES
HODGSON, A.M. HUJUS ECCLESIÆ VICARIUS, CUI PLURIMUM DEBET
NORTHUMBRIA. QUALIS ERAT TESTATUR VITA IN PUBLICUM EDITA.
OBIIT XII. JUNII ANNO SALUTIS MDCCCXLV. ÆTATIS SUÆ LXV.

JANA BRIGIDA UXOR AMANTISSIMA DECESSIT E VITA APUD
NOV. CASTR., MORBO CHOLERÆ CORREPTA, SEP. XVII. ANNO
MDCCCLIII. ÆT. LXVIII.

GULIELMUS WILSON FILIUS OB. XVIII. SEP. A.D. MDCCCXXXVII.
ÆT. XVI.

---

FILIUS ET FILIÆ SEQUENTES APUD WHELPINGTONIAM IN DOMINO
DORMIUNT:

ISAACUS, OB. SEP. XXVII. A.D. MDCCCXXX. ÆT. XI. MARIA, OB.
EODEM DIE ÆT. V. JANA BRIGIDA OB. OCT. XXVI. A.D.
MDCCCXXXI. ÆT. XV. ET SUSANNAH OB. III. MAII A.D. MDCCCXXXIV.
ÆT. XVII.

---

JOHANNES FILIUS SECUNDUS CUM UXORE MARIA ANNA MORBO
CHOLERÆ SUCCUBUERE INFRA MŒNIA CIVITATIS ALLAHABAD
IN INDIÆ ORIENTALIS PARTIBUS. ILLE XX JUN. MDCCCLVII. ILLA
PRIDIE. ILLE XLIII. ANNOS NATUS. ILLA XXXIII.

---

IN VITA CONCORDES. IN MORTE DISJUNCTI. DISSIPATOS CON-
GREGABIT ET AD VITÆ SEMPITERNÆ SOCIETATEM CONVOCA-
BIT ILLE QUI EST RESURRECTIO ET VITA ET CUI SIT GLORIA IN
ÆTERNUM. "VENIO CITO. AMEN! VENI, DOMINE JHESU!"

Of the numerous notices of Mr. Hodgson's death which appeared
at the time in the public magazines and newspapers, want of room
compels me to notice one only: another touching sonnet by the
kind-hearted Mr. Robert White, written with a sorrowing pen.

SONNET ON THE HISTORIAN OF NORTHUMBERLAND.

Amongst the number who for honours strive
Throughout Northumbria's bounds, by hill or wave,
Exists there one whose glory shall survive,
When he hath passed the portals of the grave?
Say, from before Time's scythe, with ardour brave,
Has he retrieved such trophies, that his name
Posterity shall gratefully engrave
Within the dome of all-enduring Fame?
Yes, Hodgson, such renown thy merits claim:
Northumbria's faithful chronicler art thou,—

Thy page to future ages shall proclaim
What can of her be known, and she thy brow
With never-fading leaves may now entwine—
Her immortality is wreathed with thine!

It must be further added that in a pleasing collection of biographical notices entitled "The Worthies of Westmorland,"
published in 1850, in two volumes 12mo, by George Atkinson,
Esq. barrister-at-law, a niche is assigned to Mr. Hodgson, and a
few pages are devoted to his memory.  Mr. Atkinson is a member
of the family of Atkinson of Temple Sowerby, with which
Hodgson had been long intimately acquainted, and the short
memoir to which I allude is written with a gentlemanly feeling,
and a strict regard for truth in its account of the leading features
of the character and history of its subject.*

* Notwithstanding his limited means, Hodgson had gathered together a considerable
number of books on various subjects.  Many of them he had picked up at book
stalls in Newcastle during his residence at Heworth: a few, those chiefly of value, had
been presents to him from his friends.  The whole, with the exception of his manuscript collections, were sold by auction at Hartburn soon after his death, and the price
which they fetched was more the result of respect to his memory than of their intrinsic value.

With respect to his manuscript collections, all of them put into order by his own
hands awhile before his death, the following particulars may be placed upon record for
the encouragement of those who may hereafter take it into their heads to gather
together materials for a County History.

"Statement submitted to a meeting held at Alnwick Oct. 16, 1845, the Right Hon.
Lord Prudhoe in the chair, and afterwards circulated.

"The late Mr. Hodgson of Hartburn, whose History of the County of Northumberland, so far as he had an opportunity of carrying it, reflects so much credit on his
talents, industry, and judgment, in addition to the published volumes, has left
behind him an immense mass of materials for the completion of the work.

"It is a matter of the deepest interest to the landed proprietors and others connected with the county, that means should be taken to secure the safe custody of the
MSS., and if possible the ultimate completion of the work.

"To carry out the first of these objects it is proposed to raise by subscription the sum
of 500l."

But Northumberland, true to its apathy, cared not for poor Hodgson or his papers.
This sensible appeal, originating in the kindness of Mr. Hodgson Hinde, was only able
to produce the miserable sum of 165l.; and the manuscripts are now where they
ought to be, in the hands of the eldest son of their compiler; who, whilst he affectionately sets upon them the value which they justly deserve, knows at the same time
how to estimate the regard in which his father's labours are held in that county to

It is probable that those of my readers who have perused the preceding pages of this memoir with attention have formed to themselves a somewhat correct idea of the general character of its subject. It is not unusual, however, for a biographer to sum up, to a certain extent, the substance of his narrative at its close, and to supply such omissions as may be necessary, in completion of his undertaking. With this custom, so far as it is recapitulatory, it is perhaps unnecessary in the present case to comply. I have endeavoured to set Mr. Hodgson before the world from his boyhood upwards, chiefly from the delicate touches of his own modest but graphic pen, not only as an historian, a clergyman, and the father of a family, but as a proficient in the various branches of science and literature to which, in the outset, I reported him to have been attached, and to his own pen, in these respects, I must leave him. The short space which I have left to myself will, perhaps, be better devoted to a few personal recollections of such points and features in his character as have not necessarily been treated upon already; and, in supplying those details, it is not my intention to follow any particular order; but, after the fashion of the painter, to dash them in, here and there, as they occur to my mind, in the way of so many random finishing touches to my picture.

And first of his personal appearance, and general demeanour when alone or in company.

In personal appearance Mr. Hodgson was above the middle size, tall and erect, at no period of his life stout in figure, but

which he devoted his energies for thirty years, and his life in the end. The subscribers to the 165*l.* were the following:—

| | £ | | £ |
|---|---|---|---|
| Lord Prudhoe | 10 | Mr. H. Hinde | 10 |
| Sir J. E. Swinburne | 10 | Mrs. Hodgson | 10 |
| Mr. Edw. Swinburne | 10 | Mr. Bigge | 10 |
| Mr. B. Creswell | 10 | Mr. J. Clayton | 5 |
| Mr. Ord (Whitfield) | 10 | Bishop of Durham | 10 |
| Mr. Burdon | 10 | Rev. W. N. Darnell | 10 |
| Mr. Dixon Dixon | 10 | Sir W. C. Trevelyan | 5 |
| Mr. Peareth | 10 | Sir M. W. Ridley | 5 |
| Mr. Dickson (Alnwick) | 10 | Mr. Charles Ord | 10 |

daily acting in his intercourse with the world. But then, in all
this, there was in his case no sacrifice of independence, no indication of subserviency or flattery, things which of all others he
detested from his heart, no concealment, nor any semblance of a
thought inwardly entertained to which he was hesitating to give
utterance. All with him was fair and candid and open, and at
the same time it was quiet and unassuming, respectful and sincere.
The maxim of the heathen that a man ought so to talk and act
as if his most secret thoughts were visible to the world, was in
Hodgson's case fully acted upon, not merely to the letter, but in
the spirit, without the least taint of hypocrisy or dissimulation.
In mixed companies he manifested no anxiety or ambition to take
a prominent part in conversation, and to the ordinary topics of the
day he paid little or no regard, but on subjects of interest his
powers of attention were very remarkable, and a smile of pleasure would creep over his face when he was enabled to add to his
stock of knowledge in any of the various departments of science
with which he was more or less acquainted, or on any other subject
in which he took an interest. And then again, if his anxiety to
learn was great, his pleasure in communicating information to
others from the various storehouses of his memory was still
greater, and I have, in the course of my memoir, already remarked that in such cases, with a few friends around him, he
would talk for any length of time on a favourite topic, and
delight his hearers with the rich treasures of his mind. (vol. i. p.
138.) It was enough for him to have a text upon which to dilate,
and hearers, not only willing to listen, but thankful for the information which he could afford. He seldom laughed aloud;
even in his happiest moments his countenance had more in it of
gravity than mirth; but his smile, in which he was not backward
to indulge, was singularly captivating, and his eye could in a
moment assume a striking brightness, and take its place among
the other expressive features of his face, giving a confirmatory
character of placid benignity to the whole. I have already intimated that in his words he was hesitative and slow. Such, however, was not the case when a subject was started in which he
took a more than usual interest, and in which, as the saying goes,
he was at home. He then would speak fluently, but still slowly,

and his grave and earnest manner of expressing his sentiments
seldom failed to command great attention.   His attempts at
speaking in public were generally failures, the simple circumstance of being obliged to rise operating upon his natural diffi-
dence, and acting as a bridle to his tongue.   Upon one occasion,
at a meeting of the Society of Antiquaries of Newcastle, a subject
was brought forward in its turn upon which he had certain
verbal statements to make, of importance to the business of the
day, but, in order to obtain them, the difficulty under which he
generally laboured in making a set speech being well known, he
was requested to keep his seat; and the result was most satisfactory.   His hearers were delighted with the lucid arrangement of
his arguments and the captivating simplicity of his words.

In his family demeanour Mr. Hodgson's quiet and composed
affection for those around him was most conspicuous, but this
affection by no means manifested itself in tolerating self-will or in
countenancing pernicious indulgence.   Upon this subject, however, it is not necessary to dilate.   I have already placed upon
record such letters from him to his wife and children as render
him an admirable pattern of imitation to every husband or father
of a family.   It is scarcely possible to overrate the hearty kindness or anxiety of his feelings, when he takes up his pen to write
to his wife or a child, and the good and touching advice which
he gave to them when absent he took especial care to enforce
upon them when present, not only by precept, but by example.
Professing, as I have done throughout this memoir, to keep his
character as a husband and a father especially in view, for the
credit, may I not add glory, of his name, it has been a source of
no small gratification to me to learn that my well-meant efforts
in this respect have been attended with a result which I could
scarcely have anticipated.   His letters to his wife and children,
especially those from London in 1819 and 1821, in the first
volume of this memoir, have, in the opinion of those whose
judgment may not be doubted, most fully answered the purpose
for which I ventured to bring them before the public, and no
other proof would appear to be required, on my part, that Mr.
Hodgson was a truly kind and affectionate husband and father

Neither is it necessary to give any further description of him as a friend. In this respect also he has drawn his portrait with his own pen, in the numerous letters which I have placed before my readers.

Somewhat must in the next place be said of Mr. Hodgson as a duly ordained minister of God's Holy Word and Sacraments. He had been well schooled among the thousands of Jarrow and Heworth, for a period not far short of twenty years, and had become practically and thoroughly acquainted with his duties as a parish priest. The way in which he had acquitted himself in that laborious parish, amid trials and difficulties of the most severe kind, and the personal privations to which he for so long a period was compelled to submit, have been already touched upon in an earlier page. I would only remark here that the experience which he had there acquired in his daily labours for the good of his people, was of the greatest use to him in the less toilsome cures of Whelpington and Hartburn. With a diminished population, his exertions for the temporal and spiritual welfare of his flock were not relaxed in proportion to his diminished responsibility, and he was encouraged to persevere in the habits he had formed, not merely because it was his duty, but because he had a more reasonable hope of witnessing the fruit of his labours. In his peculiar temperament and character, as a grave serious man upon all ordinary occasions, he was doubly so when engaged in the work of his Master. His mode of reading was solemn and dignified, and his preaching remarkable for its earnestness and its adaptation to the understandings of those whom he was addressing. In expatiating upon the high and holy doctrines and duties of Christianity, he would frequently lay aside the notes which he had before him, and launch out into an extempore address, which from the earnestness of his words, the eagerness of his face, and the flashing brightness of his eyes, giving token in himself of the most thorough conviction of the worth and pleasantness of godliness, readily found its way to the hearts of his hearers. I have given a few extracts from his sermons,* and I can never forget his

---

* In my notices of Mr. Hodgson's sermons I confined myself to those only which had been printed, or preached upon public occasions. Of the latter, one preached at a visitation held in 1830 by the Rev. W. N. Darnell, B.D., as Official to the Dean and Chapter of Durham, and containing the following striking passages, escaped my attention in its order of time:—

grave dignity in the pulpit, or the anxiety, evinced by every motion of his body and every cadence of his deep-toned and

"It is cheerful and gratifying to hope that the Church of God, in this our beloved land, is awake, and sees the polished swords of infidelity, and the poisoned darts of dissent and heresy, that are pointed against her. There is now, indeed, come unto her a day of visitation ; but it is not hidden from her eyes ; and who does not see her rising up, in the mightiness of her youthful strength, and calling upon ten thousand watchers and warriors to gird themselves in the panoply of Christian armour, and go forth with the sword of the Spirit, which is the everlasting and irrefragable word of God, and fight against the champions of infidelity, and convince all gainsayers, and put to silence the ignorance of foolish men.——

"While, however, we contemplate all this progress of civilization and all this march of intellect, that, in the memory of many of us, have brought refinement, science, and extensive general knowledge within the reach of all ranks of people, let us not suppose it to be all the result of mere human contrivance, and a foundation upon which some mighty structure of human greatness and happiness is to be founded. All this array is making under special plans of Providence, but cannot be permanent unless it be cemented by that order which nothing but religion can impart to it. Wealth begets leisure ; and wealth and leisure, if not under the guidance of piety and the curb of a steady and firm government, have not only a natural tendency to luxuriate in corruptions of refinement and knowledge, but nurse up on every side sure and cruel agents of destruction. Wealth, like the timid deer starting at the rustling of the leaves of the forest, may, at any distant sounds of war, rise from her splendid halls of commerce in our land, and on strong pinions flee away to shores where the billows of organized and agitated discontent beat less furiously. Want of use, from commercial embarrassment, may stiffen into masses of rust all the looms and wonderful machinery by which we manufacture clothing and multitudes of comforts and infinities of luxuries for the whole world, and then, in this condition—with an un-settled poverty and avarice storming us without, and exasperated wretchedness fighting within, where in a few years would be all our boasted palaces, our arts, sciences, schools, and places of public amusements—what are all these luxuries to a man or a nation that has to eat its bread by the sweat of its brow ? I will not, however, darken the conclusion of this discourse with any foreboding apprehensions that such a storm of calamity is preparing to burst over us ; that the couch of wealth has become so luxuriously wicked, or the throne of intellect so daring and blasphemous, that the red-hot thunderbolts of Heaven are preparing to be thrown against them : but would encourage the hope, and pray for its realization, that God, from the increasing piety, learning, and zeal for his word in our nation, is daily multiplying agents of his will, ready to do his work, not only with scrupulous attention to order and discipline, but fearlessly and efficiently ready to spend and be spent for the salvation of the souls committed to their care, and ready to carry abroad the glad tidings of the Word of Everlasting Life among all nations and kindreds of the earth. For I am persuaded that, as long as this world swings beneath the blue and starry vault of Heaven, God will neither permit one iota or one tittle of His word to pass away, nor that word to be left without an able and efficient succession of ministers, apostolically ordained, to open and unfold to His Church the wonders which it contains."

earnest voice, that his words should not fall upon his congregation in vain. His peculiar opinions, opinions at which alone a man like him, who knew the early history of the Church, its sad fallings off in modern times, and the necessity for new life and vigour in its members and ministrations, could arrive, may be gathered from the preceding pages, and they need not be repeated here. His parochial visitations, which were regular, and no mere matter of dry formality, were continued to the very end of his life. Long after his maladies had compelled him to cease from any public duty in his church, he would go from house to house in his parish, and set before his people a living pattern of the beauty of holiness.

Much has been already said of the History of Northumberland, and care has been taken to place before the reader a brief review of each volume, and, in particular, those portions of each in which its author speaks, as it were, for himself, and details his feelings and views and objects from time to time, as the work was advancing in the press. I refer to his prefaces, every one of which, even the shortest, has much in it in illustration of the peculiar character of its writer, of his candour and frankness, his exalted but just notions of the utility of such publications, and his deep devotion to the subject in which he was engaged. If by any means a kindred feeling could have been excited in those for whose use he was so painfully employed, his labours might have eventually become more profitable to himself, and more creditable, I do not mean to himself, for that would have been impossible, but to the county by which they had been patronized. This great task was the subject of his daily thoughts and labours, in spite of every discouragement. He was an early riser, and not unfrequently in the summer months the break of day found him at his undertaking. In winter he would kindle his fire and light his lamp at an early hour, and still his work was the same. In preparing his History he was remarkable for the various little devices to which he had recourse to lighten his labours. He had what he called pigeon-holes, labelled with the names of townships, for loose papers, and portfolios for documents of a larger size, under the same arrangements. His materials were in general collected in thin pocket-books of an octavo size, closely ruled, in order that no room might be wasted; and when five or six of those could hold no more they were bound up in one volume, which passing into the hands of his assistant writer, who was generally the tutor in his family, or those of Mrs. Hodgson or some of his children, was returned to him with the advantage of an excellent index of men and places.    This was a process which all his volumes of collections of whatever size were compelled to undergo.    Nay even to such printed books as he found of use in the way of reference, such as Brand's Newcastle, Wallis's and Hutchinson's Northumberland, Ridpath's Border History, Randall's Northumberland Churches, &c., indexes were made for his use; and not unfrequently his lady neighbours, the Miss Swinburnes and Trevelyans, rendered themselves singularly useful in this department.*    I have elsewhere spoken of the care which he took in so arranging his copy, especially that of his pedigrees, as to give the least possible trouble to the compositors.    His practical knowledge of the printing press and its operations was the result of personal experience in the office of his friends the Akenheads, whilst he resided at Gateshead, in 1807 and 1808, and it saved much trouble both to himself and others.    A pot of paste made by his own hands, having in it a small quantity of acetate of lead, to prevent its giving birth to book-worms, and a brush made also by himself from the bristles of one of his own swine, stood daily at his elbow, and with these materials it was his custom to unite together the fragments or portions of his history, as he was preparing it for the printer.

I proceed to certain features in Mr. Hodgson's character of a more general nature, with which it may not be uninteresting to posterity to be acquainted.

Of his qualifications as a man of business, there are certain indications in the preceding pages, and one, in particular, which which will save me the trouble of any detailed recapitulation. " I know no more than a child how to draw a bill in the manner you mention, and know of no person I could draw it upon.——

* See part II. vol. I. p. vii. for a grateful acknowledgement of thanks to the above ladies for having assisted in transcribing for the purposes of his History not fewer than seven quarto volumes of Northumberland wills, administrations, and marriage bonds lent to him by the author.

If I knew how to draw, and on what kind of stamp, and any body to draw upon, I would do it immediately." (p. 235.)

And yet there were subjects infinite in number and variety upon which Mr. Hodgson could look with a practical eye.

To almost every single product of the earth he could assign its use, present or probable in coming time, and few things annoyed him more than to see land in a bad state of cultivation, when means and materials were at the very door of the sloven who occupied it, to put it into a different condition. A favourite topic of meditation was the time when even the highest of the Northumbrian hills would wave with timber, and on its sides rich meadows and pastures and cornfields would laugh and sing in luxurious vegetation. In his reading also he suffered nothing of a practical nature to escape him, especially upon subjects of a domestic nature. In books illustrative of machinery and its powers he took a peculiar pleasure, and spared no time in making himself thoroughly acquainted with the various principles which they developed, and the intended movements of the diagrams with which they were accompanied; but he was equally interested in subjects of a more humble and homely nature. Books of cookery, in particular, never failed to engage his attention; not that he was an epicure, in any sense of the word, his delight being always in food of the simplest and most ordinary kind, and that too in moderation; but he studied the art of cookery from a conviction that it might be greatly simplified, and rendered infinitely less expensive to families of slender means. He knew well "all the simples of a thousand names— telling their strange and vigorous faculties." (Comus, 627.) I have heard him repeatedly and learnedly expatiate upon the nutritious qualities and properties of plants and herbs upon which we are apt to tread as so many worthless weeds, and express his regret that they were no longer used, especially by needy persons, for the kind purposes for which they were intended. Often did he try to convince his own family of the truth of his speculations in those respects, and many a mess did he make, with the "More-tum" of Virgil in his hand, from the various products of the earth which were within his reach in his garden or in the fields. He would steal into the kitchen, after the dinner for the day had

been arranged, and, abetted by a "neat-handed Phillis," who
doubtless laughed in her sleeve as she was acting under his
directions, a dish was unexpectedly produced at dinner, instead of
the one which had been ordered; but his "herbs and other
country messes" were in general pronounced unsavoury by all
except himself, and were sent out "porcis comedenda," like the
pears in Horace.  The same principle induced him to insert in
his History of the County, and that too in the gravest and most
didactic way (II. ii. 458), a plan for making foot-mats from the
carex or sedge which grows by the sides of its streams, and this
is not the only piece of advice of a similar character to be found
in his pages.

I have, in a preceding paragraph of these conclusions, remarked
upon the devoted feeling with which Mr. Hodgson prosecuted
his great design, notwithstanding the difficulties which he had to
encounter, and I may be excused for again reverting to the
subject, in order to state that it was not only occupation to his
pen but to his poetical thoughts and feelings.  It may not be
too late to touch briefly upon the intense hold which from time
to time the county of Northumberland and its inhabitants, its
mountains and its streams, its history and its legends, had
in this point of view gained upon his heart.  Northumberland was
to him the scene, as it were, of a great romance, connecting itself
with the earliest times and coming down to the present day.  He
thought of it by day and he dreamt of it by night.  He could at
any time, in imagination, raise from their graves the men of a
village or district who had flourished in times of old, could
clothe them with flesh and blood, and array them in the peculiar
habiliments of their period, whether of war or peace; could
expatiate upon their peculiar employments in the different
seasons of the year, upon the amount of their knowledge of
whatever kind, especially upon their skill in agriculture, upon
the precise portions of their townfields which were then in inclosure, and upon the extent of their commons and wastes; their
habits too, and amusements, their joys and sorrows, he could with
ease set before his mind—the various kinds of food upon which
they must have lived, the wild animals with which they must
have had to contend, and the diseases to which they must have

been liable. Such subjects as these afforded him endless themes of musing and meditation, and happy was the hearer who had an opportunity of listening to him on such occasions when his tongue gave expression to his thoughts. In His history there are numerous outbreaks of this nature, to some of which allusion has been made in their places.

Mention has been made of Hodgson's kindness to animals. This feeling was not confined to the narrow circle of his own farmyard or fields. To see a living creature in pain was evidently a source of pain to himself, and, on the contrary, its apparent comfort and happiness gave him unfeigned pleasure. In his walks and rides nothing connected with natural history escaped his notice. I have seen him stop and watch the movements of a butterfly with great attention, and I have heard him expatiate in admiring terms upon the beauty of a clear running stream and the various lessons which it can teach.

There was one point in Mr. Hodgson's character which must be reverenced, because it was the result of thought and conviction. For works of fiction of a peculiar class he entertained a dislike amounting almost to an abhorrence. For instance, he never could bring himself to read more than a page or two of the Waverley Novels. It was not that he underrated the high talent which they developed, or the moral lessons which they tended to inculcate, but he dreaded the effects which such half-historical half-imaginative publications would produce upon the minds of their readers. He had through life been an historian in the legitimate sense of the word, and he held, no doubt with much reason on his side, that there should be no compromise, open or disguised, between genuine history and poetical embellishment. The Waverley Novels, therefore, and other modern publications of their class, were not admitted at Hartburn.

Thus have I performed the affectionate duty to which at the grave of my friend I silently pledged myself as we were placing his body in the earth. How I have executed my task I pretend not to judge or express an opinion. This is a subject which must be left to my readers, and to a better tribunal still, to which Mr. Hodgson might have been otherwise unknown—to posterity. It has been my aim, as I stated in the outset, to catch the tone and spirit of his own biographical essays; and if I have in any respect departed from the pattern which I set before me, it has been, I trust, rather in the length to which my memoir has extended, than in any other deviation. For the size of my book, the nature of its contents must plead my apology. What have I printed which is not essentially necessary to my undertaking? What lines have I marked upon my canvas, what colours or tints have I used, which do not harmoniously combine to render perfect the portrait of such a man?

---

WESTMINSTER: PRINTED BY J. B. NICHOLS AND SONS, 25, PARLIAMENT STREET.

# LIST of WORKS in GENERAL LITERATURE

PUBLISHED BY

## Messrs. LONGMAN, BROWN, GREEN, LONGMANS, and ROBERTS,

39, PATERNOSTER ROW, LONDON.

## CLASSIFIED INDEX.

# NEW WORKS and NEW EDITIONS

PUBLISHED BY

### Messrs. LONGMAN, BROWN, GREEN, LONGMANS, and ROBERTS,

PATERNOSTER ROW, LONDON.

---

**Miss Acton's Modern Cookery for Private** Families, reduced to a System of Easy Practice in a Series of carefully-tested Receipts, in which the Principles of Baron Liebig and other eminent Writers have been as much as possible applied and explained. Newly-revised and enlarged Edition; with 8 Plates, comprising 27 Figures, and 150 Woodcuts. Fcp. 8vo. 7s. 6d.

**Acton's English Bread-Book for Domestic Use,** adapted to Families of every grade: Containing the plainest and most minute Instructions to the Learner, and Practical Receipts for many varieties of Bread; with Notices of the present System of Adulteration and its Consequences, and of the Improved Baking Processes and Institutions established Abroad. Fcp. 8vo. price 4s. 6d. cloth.

**Aikin.—Select Works of the British** Poets, from Ben Jonson to Beattie. With Biographical and Critical Prefaces by Dr. AIKIN. New Edition, with Supplement by LUCY AIKIN; consisting of additional Selections from more recent Poets. 8vo. price 18s.

**Arago (F.)—Biographies of Distinguished** Scientific Men. Translated by Admiral W. H. SMYTH, D.C.L., F.R.S., &c.; the Rev. BADEN POWELL, M.A.; and ROBERT GRANT, M.A., F.R.A.S. 8vo. 18s.

**Arago's Meteorological Essays.** With an Introduction by BARON HUMBOLDT. Translated under the superintendence of Lieut.-Colonel E. SABINE, R.A., Treasurer and V.P.R.S. 8vo. 18s.

**Arago's Popular Astronomy.** Translated and edited by Admiral W. H. SMYTH, D.C.L., F.R.S.; and ROBERT GRANT, M.A., F.R.A.S. In Two Volumes. Vol. I. 8vo. with Plates and Woodcuts, 21s.

**Arnold.—Poems. By Matthew Arnold.** Third Edition of the *First Series*. Fcp. 8vo. price 5s. 6d.

**Arnold.—Poems. By Matthew Arnold. Second** Series, about one-third new; the rest finally selected from the Volumes of 1849 and 1852, now withdrawn. Fcp. 8vo. price 5s.

**Lord Bacon's Works. A New Edition,** revised and elucidated; and enlarged by the addition of many pieces not printed before Collected and Edited by ROBERT LESLIE ELLIS, M.A., Fellow of Trinity College, Cambridge; JAMES SPEDDING, M.A. of Trinity College, Cambridge; and DOUGLAS DENON HEATH, Esq., Barrister-at-Law, and late Fellow of Trinity College, Cambridge.— The publication has commenced with the Division of the *Philosophical Works*, to be completed in 5 vols., of which Vols. I. to III. in 8vo, price 18s. each, are now ready. Vols. IV. and V. are in the press.

**Joanna Baillie's Dramatic and Poetical** Works: Comprising the Plays of the Passions, Miscellaneous Dramas, Metrical Legends, Fugitive Pieces, and Ahalya Baee. Second Edition, with a Life of Joanna Baillie, Portrait, and Vignette. Square crown 8vo. 21s. cloth; or 42s. bound in morocco by Hayday.

**Baker. — The Rifle and the Hound in** Ceylon. By S. W. BAKER, Esq. New Edition, with 13 Illustrations engraved on Wood. Fcp. 8vo. 4s. 6d.

**Baker. — Eight Years' Wanderings in Ceylon.** By S. W. BAKER, Esq. With 6 coloured Plates. 8vo. price 15s.

**Barth. — Travels and Discoveries in** North and Central Africa: Being the Journal of an Expedition undertaken under the auspices of Her Britannic Majesty's Government in the Years 1849—1855. By HENRY BARTH, Ph.D., D.C.L., Fellow of the Royal Geographical and Asiatic Societies, &c. Vols. I. to III., with 11 Maps, 100 Engravings on Wood, and 36 Illustrations in tinted Lithography, price 63s.—Vols. IV. and V., completing the work, are in the press.

**Bayldon's Art of Valuing Rents and** Tillages, and Claims of Tenants upon Quitting Farms, at both Michaelmas and Lady-Day; as revised by Mr. DONALDSON. *Seventh Edition,* enlarged and adapted to the Present Time: With the Principles and Mode of Valuing Land and other Property for Parochial Assessment and Enfranchisement of Copyholds, under the recent Acts of Parliament. By ROBERT BAKER, Land-Agent and Valuer. 8vo. 10s. 6d.

B 2

A Month in the Forests of France. By the Hon. GRANTLEY F. BERKELEY, Author of *Reminiscences of a Huntsman.* 8vo. with 2 Etchings by John Leech (1 coloured). [*Nearly ready.*

Black's Practical Treatise on Brewing, based on Chemical and Economical Principles: With Formulæ for Public Brewers, and Instructions for Private Families. New Edition, with Additions. 8vo. 10s. 6d.

Blaine's Encyclopædia of Rural Sports; or, a complete Account, Historical, Practical, and Descriptive, of Hunting, Shooting, Fishing, Racing, and other Field Sports and Athletic Amusements of the present day. New Edition, revised by HARRY HIEOVER, EPHEMERA, and Mr. A. GRAHAM. With upwards of 600 Woodcuts. 8vo. 50s.

Blair's Chronological and Historical Tables, from the Creation to the Present Time: With Additions and Corrections from the most authentic Writers; including the Computation of St. Paul, as connecting the Period from the Exode to the Temple. Under the revision of SIR HENRY ELLIS, K.H. Imperial 8vo. 31s. 6d. half-morocco.

Bloomfield. — The Greek Testament, with copious English Notes, Critical, Philological, and Explanatory. Especially adapted to the use of Theological Students and Ministers. By the Rev. S. T. BLOOMFIELD, D.D., F.S.A. Ninth Edition, revised. 2 vols. 8vo. with Map, price £2. 8s.

Dr. Bloomfield's College and School Edition of the *Greek Testament:* With brief English Notes, chiefly Philological and Explanatory, especially formed for use in Colleges and the Public Schools. Seventh Edition, improved; with Map and Index. Fcp. 8vo. 7s. 6d.

Dr. Bloomfield's College and School *Lexicon* to the Greek Testament. New Edition, carefully revised. Fcp. 8vo. price 10s. 6d. cloth.

Bourne. — A Treatise on the Steam-Engine, in its Application to Mines, Mills, Steam-Navigation, and Railways. By the Artisan Club. Edited by JOHN BOURNE, C.E. New Edition; with 33 Steel Plates and 349 Wood Engravings. 4to. price 27s.

Bourne's Catechism of the Steam-Engine in its various Applications to Mines, Mills, Steam-Navigation, Railways, and Agriculture: With Practical Instructions for the Manufacture and Management of Engines of every class. Fourth Edition, enlarged; with 89 Woodcuts. Fcp. 8vo. 6s.

Bourne. — A Treatise on the Screw Propeller: With various Suggestions of Improvement. By JOHN BOURNE, C.E. New Edition, thoroughly revised and corrected: With 20 large Plates and numerous Woodcuts. 4to. price 38s.

Boyd. — A Manual for Naval Cadets. Published with the sanction and approval of the Lords Commissioners of the Admiralty. By JOHN M'NEILL BOYD, Captain R.N. With Compass-Signals in Colours, and 236 Woodcuts. Fcp. 8vo. 10s. 6d.

Brande.—A Dictionary of Science, Literature, and Art: Comprising the History, Description, and Scientific Principles of every Branch of Human Knowledge; with the Derivation and Definition of all the Terms in general use. Edited by W. T. BRANDE, F.R.S.L. and E.; assisted by Dr. J. CAUVIN. Third Edition, revised and corrected; with numerous Woodcuts. 8vo. 60s.

Professor Brande's Lectures on Organic Chemistry, as applied to Manufactures; including Dyeing, Bleaching, Calico-Printing, Sugar-Manufacture, the Preservation of Wood, Tanning, &c.; delivered before the Members of the Royal Institution. Arranged by permission from the Lecturer's Notes by J. SCOFFERN, M.B. Fcp. 8vo. with Woodcuts, price 7s. 6d.

Brewer. — An Atlas of History and Geography, from the Commencement of the Christian Era to the Present Time: Comprising a Series of Sixteen coloured Maps, arranged in Chronological Order, with Illustrative Memoirs. By the Rev. J. S. BREWER, M.A., Professor of English History and Literature in King's College, London. *Second Edition,* revised and corrected. Royal 8vo. 12s. 6d. half-bound.

Brodie. — Psychological Inquiries, in a Series of Essays intended to illustrate the Influence of the Physical Organisation on the Mental Faculties. By SIR BENJAMIN C. BRODIE, Bart. Third Edition. Fcp. 8vo. 5s.

Bull. — The Maternal Management of Children in Health and Disease. By T. BULL, M.D., Member of the Royal College of Physicians; formerly Physician-Accoucheur to the Finsbury Midwifery Institution. New Edition. Fcp. 8vo. 5s.

Dr. T. Bull's Hints to Mothers on the Management of their Health during the Period of Pregnancy and in the Lying-in Room: With an Exposure of Popular Errors in connexion with those subjects, &c.; and Hints upon Nursing. New Edition. Fcp. 8vo. 5s.

# ALPHABETICAL CATALOGUE

of

**Buckingham.—Autobiography of James** Silk Buckingham: Including his Voyages, Travels, Adventures, Speculations, Successes and Failures, frankly and faithfully narrated; with Characteristic Sketches of Public Men. Vols. I. and II. post 8vo. 21s.

**Bunsen. — Christianity and Mankind,** their Beginnings and Prospects. By CHRISTIAN CHARLES JOSIAS BUNSEN, D.D., D.C.L., D.Ph. Being a New Edition, corrected, remodelled, and extended, of *Hippolytus and his Age*. 7 vols. 8vo. £5. 5s.

*⁎* This Second Edition of the *Hippolytus* is composed of three distinct works, which may be had separately, as follows:—

1. Hippolytus and his Age; or, the Beginnings and Prospects of Christianity. 2 vols. 8vo. price £1. 10s.
2. Outline of the Philosophy of Universal History applied to Language and Religion: Containing an Account of the Alphabetical Conferences. 2 vols. 8vo. price £1. 13s.
3. Analecta Ante-Nicæna. 3 vols. 8vo. price £2. 2s.

**Bunsen. — Lyra Germanica: Hymns for** the Sundays and chief Festivals of the Christian Year. Translated from the German by CATHERINE WINKWORTH. Third Edition. Fcp. 8vo. 5s.

*⁎* This selection of German Hymns has been made from a collection published in Germany by the Chevalier BUNSEN; and forms a companion volume to

**Theologia Germanica:** Which setteth forth many fair lincaments of Divine Truth, and saith very lofty and lovely things touching a Perfect Life. Translated by SUSANNA WINKWORTH. With a Preface by the Rev. CHARLES KINGSLEY; and a Letter by Chevalier BUNSEN. Third Edition. Fcp. 8vo. 5s.

**Bunsen. — Egypt's Place in Universal** History: An Historical Investigation, in Five Books. By C. C. J. BUNSEN, D.D., D.C.L., D.Ph. Translated from the German by C. H. COTTRELL, Esq., M.A. With many Illustrations. Vol. I. 8vo. 28s.; Vol. II. 8vo. 30s.

**Burton (J. H.)—The History of Scotland** from the Revolution to the Extinction of the Last Jacobite Insurrection (1689-1748). By JOHN HILL BURTON. 2 vols. 8vo. 26s.

**Bishop S. Butler's General Atlas of** Modern and Ancient Geography; comprising Fifty-two full-coloured Maps; with complete Indices. New Edition, nearly all re-engraved, enlarged, and greatly improved. Edited by the Author's Son. Royal 4to. 24s. half-bound.

Separately { The Modern Atlas of 28 full-coloured Maps. Royal 8vo. price 12s. The Ancient Atlas of 24 full-coloured Maps. Royal 8vo. price 12s.

**Bishop S. Butler's Sketch of Modern and** Ancient Geography. New Edition, thoroughly revised, with such Alterations introduced as continually progressive Discoveries and the latest Information have rendered necessary. Post 8vo. price 7s. 6d.

**Burton.—First Footsteps in East Africa;** or, an Exploration of Harar. By RICHARD F. BURTON, Captain, Bombay Army. With Maps and coloured Plates. 8vo. 18s.

**Burton. — Personal Narrative of a Pil**grimage to El Medinah and Meccah. By RICHARD F. BURTON, Captain, Bombay Army. *Second Edition*, revised; with coloured Plates and Woodcuts. 2 vols. crown 8vo. price 24s.

**The Cabinet Lawyer: A Popular Digest** of the Laws of England, Civil and Criminal; with a Dictionary of Law Terms, Maxims, Statutes, and Judicial Antiquities; Correct Tables of Assessed Taxes, Stamp Duties, Excise Licenses, and Post-Horse Duties; Post-Office Regulations; and Prison Discipline. 17th Edition, comprising the Public Acts of the Session 1857. Fcp. 8vo. 10s. 6d.

**The Cabinet Gazetteer: A Popular Expo**sition of All the Countries of the World: their Government, Population, Revenues, Commerce, and Industries; Agricultural, Manufactured, and Mineral Products; Religion, Laws, Manners, and Social State; With brief Notices of their History and Antiquities. By the Author of *The Cabinet Lawyer*. Fcp. 8vo. 10s. 6d. cloth; or 13s. bound in calf.

"The author has neglected no modern sources of information, and all his short, succinct, and neat descriptions of the different places are quite conformable to present knowledge. Sarawak, for example, in Borneo, is not omitted, and of San Francisco there is quite a detailed description. The work is compiled with considerable care, and in the 912 pages | that it contains there is a vast amount of geographical and topographical information pleasantly condensed. The *Cabinet Gazetteer*, though not intended to supersede more elaborate works, will, to some extent, have that effect; but it will be sure to find a large and permanent circulation of its own."

ECONOMIST.

**Calendar of English State Papers, Do**mestic Series, of the Reigns of Edward VI., Mary, Elizabeth, 1547—1580, preserved in the State Paper Department of Her Majesty's Public Record Office. Edited by ROBERT LEMON, Esq., F.S.A., under the direction of the Master of the Rolls, and with the sanction of Her Majesty's Secretary of State for the Home Department. Imperial 8vo. 15s.

**Calendar of English State Papers, Do**mestic Series, of the Reign of James I., 1603—1610 (comprising the Papers relating to the Gunpowder Plot), preserved in the State Paper Department of H.M. Public Record Office. Edited by MARY ANNE EVERETT GREEN, Author of *The Lives of the Princesses of England*, &c., under the direction of the Master of the Rolls, and with the sanction of H.M. Secretary of State for the Home Department. Imperial 8vo. 15s.

D 3

**Calvert. — The Wife's Manual; or,** Prayers, Thoughts, and Songs on Several Occasions of a Matron's Life. By the Rev. W. CALVERT, M.A. Ornamented from Designs by the Author in the style of *Queen Elizabeth's Prayer-Book.* Second Edition. Crown 8vo. 10s. 6d.

**Carlisle (Lord).—A Diary in Turkish and** Greek Waters. By the Right Hon. the EARL OF CARLISLE. Fifth Edition. Post 8vo. price 10s. 6d.

**Catlow.—Popular Conchology; or, the** Shell Cabinet arranged according to the Modern System: With a detailed Account of the Animals, and a complete Descriptive List of the Families and Genera of Recent and Fossil Shells. By AGNES CATLOW. Second Edition, much improved; with 405 Woodcut Illustrations. Post 8vo. price 14s.

**Cecil. — The Stud Farm; or, Hints on** Breeding Horses for the Turf, the Chase, and the Road. Addressed to Breeders of Race-Horses and Hunters, Landed Proprietors, and especially to Tenant Farmers. By CECIL. Fcp. 8vo. with Frontispiece, 5s.

**Cecil's Stable Practice; or, Hints on Training** for the Turf, the Chase, and the Road; with Observations on Racing and Hunting, Wasting, Race-Riding, and Handi-capping: Addressed to Owners of Racers, Hunters, and other Horses, and to all who are concerned in Racing, Steeple-Chasing, and Fox-Hunting. Fcp. 8vo. with Plate, price 5s. half-bound.

**Chapman. — History of Gustavus Adol-** phus, and of the Thirty Years' War up to the King's Death: With some Account of its Conclusion by the Peace of Westphalia, in 1648. By B. CHAPMAN, M.A., Vicar of Letherhead. 8vo. with Plans, 12s. 6d.

**Chevreul On the Harmony and Contrast** of Colours, and their Applications to the Arts: Including Painting, Interior Decoration, Tapestries, Carpets, Mosaics, Coloured Glazing, Paper-Staining, Calico-Printing, Letterpress-Printing, Map-Colouring, Dress, Landscape and Flower-Gardening, &c. &c. Translated by CHARLES MARTEL. Second Edition; with 4 Plates. Crown 8vo. price 10s. 6d.

**Connolly.—History of the Royal Sappers** and Miners: Including the Services of the Corps in the Crimea and at the Siege of Sebastopol. By T. W. J. CONNOLLY, Quarter of the Royal Engineers. *Second* revised and enlarged; with 17 co-'ates. 2 vols. 8vo. price 30s.

**Conybeare and Howson.—The Life and** Epistles of Saint Paul: Comprising a complete Biography of the Apostle, and a Translation of his Epistles inserted in Chronological Order. By the Rev. W. J. CONYBEARE, M.A.; and the Rev. J. S. HOWSON, M.A. *Second Edition,* revised and corrected; with several Maps and Woodcuts, and 4 Plates. 2 vols. square crown 8vo. 31s. 6d. cloth.
*\** The Original Edition, with more numerous Illustrations, in 3 vols. 4to. price 68s.—may also be had.

**Conybeare.—Essays, Ecclesiastical and Social:** Reprinted, with Additions, from the *Edinburgh Review.* By the Rev. W. J. CONYBEARE, M.A., late Fellow of Trinity College, Cambridge. 8vo. 12s.

**Dr. Copland's Dictionary of Practical** Medicine: Comprising General Pathology, the Nature and Treatment of Diseases, Morbid Structures, and the Disorders especially incidental to Climates, to Sex, and to the different Epochs of Life; with numerous approved Formulæ of the Medicines recommended. Vols. I. and II. 8vo. price £3; and Parts X. to XVIII. 4s. 6d. each.
*\** Part XIX., completing the work, is nearly ready.

**Cotton. — Instructions in the Doctrine** and Practice of Christianity. Intended chiefly as an Introduction to Confirmation. By G. E. L. COTTON, M.A. 18mo. 2s. 6d.

**Cresy's Encyclopædia of Civil Engi-** neering, Historical, Theoretical, and Practical. Illustrated by upwards of 3,000 Woodcuts. *Second Edition,* revised and brought down to the Present Time in a Supplement, comprising Metropolitan Water-Supply, Drainage of Towns, Railways, Cubical Proportion, Brick and Iron Construction, Iron Screw Piles, Tubular Bridges, &c. 8vo. 68s. cloth. — The SUPPLEMENT separately, price 10s. 6d. cloth.

**The Cricket-Field; or, the Science and** History of the Game of Cricket. By the Author of *Principles of Scientific Batting.* Second Edition, greatly improved; with Plates and Woodcuts. Fcp. 8vo. price 5s.

**Crosse.—Memorials, Scientific and Li-** terary, of Andrew Crosse, the Electrician. Edited by Mrs. CROSSE. Post 8vo. 9s. 6d.

**Cruikshank. — The Life of Sir John** Falstaff, illustrated by George Cruikshank. With a Biography of the Knight, from authentic sources, by ROBERT B. BROUGH, Esq. Royal 8vo.—In course of publication monthly, and to be completed in 10 Numbers, each containing 2 Plates, price 1s. The first 6 Numbers are now ready.

**Lady Cust's Invalid's Book.** — The Invalid's Own Book: A Collection of Recipes from various Books and various Countries. By the Honourable LADY CUST. *Second Edition.* Fcp. 8vo. price 2s. 6d.

**Dale.** — The Domestic Liturgy and Family Chaplain, in Two Parts: PART I. Church Services adapted for Domestic Use, with Prayers for Every Day of the Week, selected from the Book of Common Prayer; PART II. an appropriate Sermon for Every Sunday in the Year. By the Rev. THOMAS DALE, M.A., Canon Residentiary of St. Paul's. Second Edition. Post 4to. 21s. cloth; 31s. 6d. calf; or £2. 10s. morocco.

Separately { THE FAMILY CHAPLAIN, 12s.
{ THE DOMESTIC LITURGY, 10s. 6d.

**Davy (Dr. J.)** — The Angler and his Friend; or, Piscatory Colloquies and Fishing Excursions. By JOHN DAVY, M.D., F.R.S., &c. Fcp. 8vo. price 6s.

**The Angler in the Lake District:** Or, Piscatory Colloquies and Fishing Excursions in Westmoreland and Cumberland. By JOHN DAVY, M.D., F.R.S. Fcp. 8vo. 6s. 6d.

**Delabeche.** — Report on the Geology of Cornwall, Devon, and West Somerset. By SIR H. T. DELABECHE, F.R.S. With Maps, Plates, and Woodcuts. 8vo. price 14s.

**De la Rive.** — A Treatise on Electricity in Theory and Practice. By A. DE LA RIVE, Professor in the Academy of Geneva. Translated for the Author by C. V. WALKER, F.R.S. *In Three Volumes;* with numerous Woodcuts. Vol. I. 8vo. price 18s.; Vol. II. price 28s. — Vol. III. is in the press.

**De Vere.** — May Carols. By Aubrey de VERE, Author of *The Search after Proserpine,* &c. Fcp. 8vo. 5s.

**Discipline.** By the Author of "Letters to my Unknown Friends," &c. Second Edition, enlarged. 18mo. price 2s. 6d.

**Dodd.** — The Food of London: A Sketch of the chief Varieties, Sources of Supply, probable Quantities, Modes of Arrival, Processes of Manufacture, suspected Adulteration, and Machinery of Distribution of the Food for a Community of Two Millions and a Half. By GEORGE DODD, Author of *British Manufactures,* &c. Post 8vo. 10s. 6d.

**Estcourt.** — Music the Voice of Harmony in Creation. Selected and arranged by Mary Jane Estcourt. Fcp. 8vo. 7s. 6d.

**The Eclipse of Faith;** or, a Visit to a Religious Sceptic. 8th Edition. Fcp. 8vo. 5s.

**Defence of The Eclipse of Faith,** by its Author: Being a Rejoinder to Professor Newman's *Reply;* Including a full Examination of that Writer's Criticism on the Character of Christ; and a Chapter on the Aspects and Pretensions of Modern Deism. Second Edition, revised. Post 8vo. 5s. 6d.

**The Englishman's Greek Concordance of** the New Testament: Being an Attempt at a Verbal Connexion between the Greek and the English Texts; including a Concordance to the Proper Names, with Indexes, Greek-English and English-Greek. New Edition, with a new Index. Royal 8vo. price 42s.

**The Englishman's Hebrew and Chaldee Concordance of the Old Testament:** Being an Attempt at a Verbal Connexion between the Original and the English Translations; with Indexes, a List of the Proper Names and their Occurrences, &c. 2 vols. royal 8vo. £3. 13s. 6d.; large paper, £4. 14s. 6d.

**Ephemera's Handbook of Angling;** teaching Fly-Fishing, Trolling, Bottom-Fishing, Salmon-Fishing: With the Natural History of River-Fish, and the best Modes of Catching them. Third Edition, corrected and improved; with Woodcuts. Fcp. 8vo. 5s.

**Ephemera.** — The Book of the Salmon: Comprising the Theory, Principles, and Practice of Fly-Fishing for Salmon: Lists of good Salmon Flies for every good River in the Empire; the Natural History of the Salmon, its Habits described, and the best way of artificially Breeding it. By EPHEMERA; assisted by ANDREW YOUNG. Fcp. 8vo. with coloured Plates, price 14s.

**Fairbairn.** — Useful Information for Engineers: Being a Series of Lectures delivered to the Working Engineers of Yorkshire and Lancashire. With Appendices, containing the Results of Experimental Inquiries into the Strength of Materials, the Causes of Boiler Explosions, &c. By WILLIAM FAIRBAIRN, F.R.S., F.G.S. *Second Edition;* with numerous Plates and Woodcuts. Crown 8vo. price 10s. 6d.

**The Fairy Family: A Series of Ballads** and Metrical Tales illustrating the Fairy Mythology of Europe. With Frontispiece and Pictorial Title. Crown 8vo. 10s. 6d.

**Flemish Interiors. By the Writer of** *A Glance behind the Grilles of Religious Houses in France.* Fcp. 8vo. 7s. 6d.

B 4

**Forester.—Travels in the Islands of Cor-**
sica and Sardinia. By THOMAS FORESTER,
Author of *Rambles in Norway*. With numerous coloured Illustrations and Woodcuts,
from Sketches made during the Tour by
Lieutenant-Colonel M. A. BIDDULPH, R.A.
Imperial 8vo.                    [*In the press.*

**Garratt.—Marvels and Mysteries of In-**
stinct; or, Curiosities of Animal Life. By
GEORGE GARRATT. *Second Edition*, revised
and improved; with a Frontispiece. Fcp.
8vo. 4s. 6d.

**Gilbart.—A Practical Treatise on Bank-**
ing. By JAMES WILLIAM GILBART, F.R.S.,
General Manager of the London and Westminster Bank. *Sixth Edition*, revised
and enlarged. 2 vols. 12mo. Portrait, 16s.

**Gilbart. — Logic for the Million: A**
Familiar Exposition of the Art of Reasoning.
By J. W. GILBART, F.R.S. 5th Edition;
with Portrait of the Author. 12mo. 3s. 6d.

**The Poetical Works of Oliver Goldsmith.**
Edited by BOLTON CORNEY, Esq. Illustrated
by Wood Engravings, from Designs by
Members of the Etching Club. Square
crown 8vo. cloth, 21s.; morocco, £1. 16s.

**Gosse. — A Naturalist's Sojourn in**
Jamaica. By P. H. GOSSE, Esq. With
Plates. Post 8vo. price 14s.

**Green.—Lives of the Princesses of Eng-**
land. By Mrs. MARY ANNE EVERETT
GREEN, Editor of the *Letters of Royal and
Illustrious Ladies*. With numerous Portraits. Complete in 6 vols. post 8vo. price
10s. 6d. each.—Any Volume may be had
*separately* to complete sets.

**Mr. W. R. Greg's Essays on Political**
and Social Science, contributed chiefly to the
*Edinburgh Review*. 2 vols. 8vo. price 24s.

**Greyson. — Selections from the Corre-**
spondence of R. E. H. GREYSON, Esq.
Edited by the Author of *The Eclipse of
Faith*. 2 vols. fcp. 8vo. price 12s.

**Grove. — The Correlation of Physical**
Forces. By W. R. GROVE, Q.C., M.A.,
F.R.S., &c. *Third Edition*. 8vo. price 7s.

**Gurney.—St. Louis and Henri IV.: Being**
a Second Series of Historical Sketches.
By the Rev. JOHN H. GURNEY, M.A., Rector
of St. Mary's, Marylebone. Fcp. 8vo. 6s.

**Evening Recreations; or, Samples from the**
Lecture-Room. Edited by the Rev. J. H.
**···Y**, M.A. Crown 8vo. 5s.

**Gwilt's Encyclopædia of Architecture,**
Historical, Theoretical, and Practical. By
JOSEPH GWILT. With more than 1,000
Wood Engravings, from Designs by J. S.
GWILT. Third Edition. 8vo. 42s.

**Halloran.—Eight Months' Journal** kept
on board one of H.M. Sloops of War, during
Visits to Loochoo, Japan, and Pootoo. By
ALFRED L. HALLORAN, Master, R.N. With
Etchings and Woodcuts. Post 8vo. 7s. 6d.

**Hare (Archdeacon).—The Life of Luther,**
in Forty-eight Historical Engravings. By
GUSTAV KÖNIG. With Explanations by
ARCHDEACON HARE and SUSANNA WINK-
WORTH. Fcp. 4to. price 28s.

**Harford.—Life of Michael Angelo Buon-**
arroti: With Translations of many of his
Poems and Letters; also Memoirs of Sav-
narola, Raphael, and Vittoria Colonna. By
JOHN S. HARFORD, Esq., D.C.L., F.R.S.,
Member of the Academy of Painting of
St. Luke, at Rome, and of the Roman Arch-
æological Society. With Portrait and
Plates. 2 vols. 8vo. 25s.

**Illustrations, Architectural and Pictorial, of**
the Genius of Michael Angelo Buonarroti.
With Descriptions of the Plates, by the
Commendatore CANINA; C. R. COCKERELL,
Esq., R.A.; and J. S. HARFORD, Esq.,
D.C.L., F.R.S. Folio, 73s. 6d. half-bound.

**Harrison.—The Light of the Forge; or,**
Counsels drawn from the Sick-Bed of E. M.
By the Rev. W. HARRISON, M.A., Domestic
Chaplain to H.R.H. the Duchess of Cam-
bridge. Fcp. 8vo. price 5s.

**Harry Hieover.—Stable Talk and Table**
Talk; or, Spectacles for Young Sportsmen.
By HARRY HIEOVER. New Edition, 2 vols.
8vo. with Portrait, price 24s.

**Harry Hieover.—The Hunting-Field.** By HARRY
HIEOVER. With Two Plates. Fcp. 8vo.
5s. half-bound.

**Harry Hieover. — Practical Horsemanship**
By HARRY HIEOVER. *Second Edition*; with
2 Plates. Fcp. 8vo. 5s. half-bound.

**Harry Hieover.—The Pocket and the Stud; or,**
Practical Hints on the Management of the
Stable. By HARRY HIEOVER. Second
Edition; with Portrait of the Author. Fcp.
8vo. price 5s. half-bound.

**Harry Hieover.—The Stud, for Practical Pur-**
poses and Practical Men: Being a Guide
to the Choice of a Horse for use more than
for show. By HARRY HIEOVER. With 2
Plates. Fcp. 8vo. price 5s. half-bound.

**Hassall.—Adulterations Detected; or,** Plain Instructions for the Discovery of Frauds in Food and Medicine. By ARTHUR HILL HASSALL, M.D. Lond., Analyst of *The Lancet* Sanitary Commission, and Author of the Reports of that Commission published under the title of *Food and its Adulterations* (which may also be had, in 8vo. price 28s.) With 225 Illustrations, engraved on Wood. Crown 8vo. 17s. 6d.

**Hassall.—A History of the British Fresh** Water Algæ: Including Descriptions of the Desmideæ and Diatomaceæ. With upwards of One Hundred Plates of Figures, illustrating the various Species. By ARTHUR HILL HASSALL, M.D., Author of *Microscopic Anatomy of the Human Body, &c.* 2 vols. 8vo. with 103 Plates, price £1. 15s.

**Col. Hawker's Instructions to Young** Sportsmen in all that relates to Guns and Shooting. 10th Edition, revised and brought down to the Present Time, by the Author's Son, Major P. W. L. HAWKER. With a Portrait of the Author, and numerous Plates and Woodcuts. 8vo. 21s.

**Haydn's Book of Dignities: Containing** Rolls of the Official Personages of the British Empire, Civil, Ecclesiastical, Judicial, Military, Naval, and Municipal, from the Earliest Periods to the Present Time. Together with the Sovereigns of Europe, from the Foundation of their respective States; the Peerage and Nobility of Great Britain; &c. Being a New Edition, improved and continued, of Beatson's Political Index. 8vo. 25s. half-bound.

**Sir John Herschel.—Essays from the** *Edinburgh* and *Quarterly Reviews,* with Addresses and other Pieces. By SIR JOHN F. W. HERSCHEL, Bart., K.H., M.A. 8vo. price 18s.

**Sir John Herschel.—Outlines of Astro-** nomy. By SIR JOHN F. W. HERSCHEL, Bart., K.H., M.A. New Edition; with Plates and Woodcuts. 8vo. price 18s.

**Hill.—Travels in Siberia. By S. S. Hill,** Esq., Author of *Travels on the Shores of the Baltic.* With a large Map of European and Asiatic Russia. 2 vols. post 8vo. 24s.

**Hinchliff.—Summer Months among the** Alps: With the Ascent of Monte Rosa. By THOMAS W. HINCHLIFF, of Lincoln's Inn, Barrister-at-Law. With 4 tinted Views and 3 Maps. Post 8vo. price 10s. 6d.

**Hints on Etiquette and the Usages of** Society: With a Glance at Bad Habits. New Edition, revised (with Additions) by a Lady of Rank. Fcp. 8vo. price Half-a-Crown.

**Holland. — Medical Notes and Reflec-** tions. By SIR HENRY HOLLAND, Bart., M.D., F.R.S., &c., Physician in Ordinary to the Queen and Prince Albert. Third Edition. 8vo. 18s.

**Holland.—Chapters on Mental Physiology.** By SIR HENRY HOLLAND, Bart., F.R.S., &c. Founded chiefly on Chapters contained in the First and Second Editions of *Medical Notes and Reflections* by the same Author. 8vo. price 10s. 6d.

**Hook.—The Last Days of Our Lord's** Ministry: A Course of Lectures on the principal Events of Passion Week. By the Rev. W. F. HOOK, D.D. New Edition. Fcp. 8vo. price 6s.

**Hooker.—Kew Gardens; or, a Popular** Guide to the Royal Botanic Gardens of Kew. By SIR WILLIAM JACKSON HOOKER, K.H., &c., Director. New Edition; with many Woodcuts. 16mo. price Sixpence.

**Hooker. — Museum of Economic Botany;** or, a Popular Guide to the Useful and Remarkable Vegetable Products of the Museum in the Royal Gardens of Kew. By SIR W. J. HOOKER, K.H., &c., Director. With 29 Woodcuts. 16mo. price 1s.

**Hooker and Arnott.—The British Flora:** comprising the Phænogamous or Flowering Plants, and the Ferns. Seventh Edition, with Additions and Corrections; and numerous Figures illustrative of the Umbelliferous Plants, the Composite Plants, the Grasses, and the Ferns. By SIR W. J. HOOKER, F.R.A. and L.S., &c.; and G. A. WALKER-ARNOTT, LL.D., F.L.S. 12mo. with 12 Plates, price 14s.; with the Plates coloured, price 21s.

**Horne's Introduction to the Critical** Study and Knowledge of the Holy Scriptures. *Tenth Edition,* revised, corrected, and brought down to the present time. Edited by the Rev. T. HARTWELL HORNE, B.D. (the Author); the Rev. SAMUEL DAVIDSON, D.D. of the University of Halle, and LL.D.; and S. PRIDEAUX TREGELLES, LL.D. With 4 Maps and 22 Vignettes and Facsimiles. 4 vols. 8vo. £3. 13s. 6d.

\*\*\* The Four Volumes may also be had *separately* as follows :—

Vol. I.—A Summary of the Evidence for the Genuineness, Authenticity, Uncorrupted Preservation, and Inspiration of the Holy Scriptures. By the Rev. T. H. Horne, B.D... 8vo. 15s.

Vol. II.—The Text of the *Old Testament* considered: With a Treatise on Sacred Interpretation; and a brief Introduction to the *Old Testament* Books and the *Apocrypha.* By S. Davidson, D.D. (Halle) and LL.D. ............... 8vo. 25s.

Vol. III.—A Summary of Biblical Geography and Antiquities. By the Rev. T. H. Horne, B.D. ......... 8vo. 18s.

Vol. IV.—An Introduction to the Textual Criticism of the *New Testament.* By the Rev. T. H. Horne, B.D. The Critical Part re-written, and the remainder revised and edited by S. P. Tregelles, LL.D. ............... 8vo. 18s.

B 5

**Horne.** — A Compendious Introduction to the Study of the Bible. By the Rev. T. HARTWELL HORNE, B.D. New Edition, with Maps and Illustrations. 12mo. 9s.

**Hoskyns.**—Talpa; or, the Chronicles of a Clay Farm: An Agricultural Fragment. By CHANDOS WREN HOSKYNS, Esq. Fourth Edition. With 24 Woodcuts from the original Designs by GEORGE CRUIKSHANK. 16mo. price 5s. 6d.

**How to Nurse Sick Children:** Intended especially as a Help to the Nurses in the Hospital for Sick Children; but containing Directions of service to all who have the charge of the Young. Fcp. 8vo. 1s. 6d.

**Howitt (A. M.)**—An Art-Student in Munich. By ANNA MARY HOWITT. 2 vols. post 8vo. price 14s.

**Howitt.**—The Children's Year. By Mary HOWITT. With Four Illustrations, from Designs by A. M. HOWITT. Square 16mo. 5s.

**Howitt.**—Tallangetta, the Squatter's Home: A Story of Australian Life. By WILLIAM HOWITT, Author of Two Years in Victoria, &c. 2 vols. post 8vo. price 18s.

**Howitt.**—Land, Labour, and Gold; or, Two Years in Victoria: With Visit to Sydney and Van Diemen's Land. By WILLIAM HOWITT. 2 vols. post 8vo. 21s.

**Howitt.**—Visits to Remarkable Places: Old Halls, Battle-Fields, and Scenes illustrative of Striking Passages in English History and Poetry. By WILLIAM HOWITT. With about 80 Wood Engravings. New Edition. 2 vols. square crown 8vo. price 25s.

**William Howitt's Boy's Country Book:** Being the Real Life of a Country Boy, written by himself; exhibiting all the Amusements, Pleasures, and Pursuits of Children in the Country. New Edition; with 40 Woodcuts. Fcp. 8vo. price 6s.

**Howitt.**—The Rural Life of England. By WILLIAM HOWITT. New Edition, corrected and revised; with Woodcuts by Bewick and Williams. Medium 8vo. 21s.

**Huc.**—Christianity in China, Tartary, and Thibet. By M. l'Abbé Huc, formerly Missionary Apostolic in China; Author of The Chinese Empire, &c. 2 vols. 8vo. 21s.

**Huc.**—The Chinese Empire: A Sequel to Huc and Gabet's Journey through Tartary and Thibet. By the Abbé Huc, formerly Missionary Apostolic in China. Second edition; with Map. 2 vols. 8vo. 24s.

**Hudson's Plain Directions for Making Wills** in conformity with the Law: With a clear Exposition of the Law relating to the distribution of Personal Estate in the case of Intestacy, two Forms of Wills, and much useful information. New and enlarged Edition; including the Provisions of the Wills Act Amendment Act. Fcp. 8vo. 2s. 6d.

**Hudson's Executor's Guide.** New and improved Edition; with the Statutes enacted, and the Judicial Decisions pronounced since the last Edition incorporated, comprising the Probate and Administration Acts for England and Ireland, passed in the first Session of the New Parliament. Fcp. 8vo. [Just ready.]

**Hudson and Kennedy.**—Where there's a Will there's a Way: An Ascent of Mont Blanc by a New Route and Without Guides. By the Rev. C. HUDSON, M.A., St. John's College, Cambridge; and E. S. KENNEDY, B.A., Caius College, Cambridge. Second Edition, with Two Ascents of Monte Rosa; a Plate, and a coloured Map. Post 8vo. 5s. 6d.

**Humboldt's Cosmos.** Translated, with the Author's authority, by MRS. SABINE. Vols. I. and II. 16mo. Half-a-Crown each, sewed; 3s. 6d. each, cloth: or in post 8vo. 12s. each, cloth. Vol. III. post 8vo. 12s. 6d. cloth: or in 16mo. Part I. 2s. 6d. sewed, 3s. 6d. cloth; and Part II. 3s. sewed, 4s. cloth.

**Humboldt's Aspects of Nature.** Translated, with the Author's authority, by MRS.SABINE. 16mo. price 6s.: or in 2 vols. 3s. 6d. each, cloth; 2s. 6d. each, sewed.

**Humphreys.** — Parables of Our Lord, illuminated and ornamented in the style of the Missals of the Renaissance by HENRY NOEL HUMPHREYS. Square fcp. 8vo. 21s. in massive carved covers; or 30s. bound in morocco by Hayday.

**Hunt.** — Researches on Light in its Chemical Relations; embracing a Consideration of all the Photographic Processes. By ROBERT HUNT, F.R.S. Second Edition, with Plate and Woodcuts. 8vo. 10s. 6d.

**Hutton.**—A Hundred Years Ago: An Historical Sketch, 1755 to 1756. By JAMES HUTTON. Post 8vo.

**Idle.**—Hints on Shooting, Fishing, &c., both on Sea and Land, and in the Fresh-Water Lochs of Scotland: Being the Experiences of C. IDLE, Esq. Fcp. 8vo. 5s.

Mrs. Jameson's Legends of the Saints and Martyrs, as represented in Christian Art : Forming the First Series of *Sacred and Legendary Art*. Third Edition, revised and improved ; with 17 Etchings and upwards of 180 Woodcuts, many of which are new in this Edition. 2 vols. square crown 8vo. 31s. 6d.

Mrs. Jameson's Legends of the Monastic Orders, as represented in Christian Art. Forming the Second Series of *Sacred and Legendary Art*. Second Edition, enlarged ; with 11 Etchings by the Author, and 88 Woodcuts. Square crown 8vo. price 28s.

Mrs. Jameson's Legends of the Madonna, as represented in Christian Art : Forming the Third Series of *Sacred and Legendary Art*. Second Edition, revised and improved : with numerous Etchings from Drawings by the Author, and upwards of 150 Woodcuts. Square crown 8vo.          [*Nearly ready.*

Mrs. Jameson's Commonplace-Book of Thoughts, Memories, and Fancies, Original and Selected. Part I. Ethics and Character ; Part II. Literature and Art. *Second Edit.* revised and corrected ; with Etchings and Woodcuts. Crown 8vo. 18s.

Mrs. Jameson's Two Lectures on the Employment of Women.
1. SISTERS *of* CHARITY, Catholic and Protestant, Abroad and at Home. *Second Edition*, with new Preface. Fcp. 8vo. 4s.
2. *The* COMMUNION *of* LABOUR: A Second Lecture on the Social Employments of Women. Fcp. 8vo. 3s.

Jaquemet's Compendium of Chronology : Containing the most important Dates of General History, Political, Ecclesiastical, and Literary, from the Creation of the World to the end of the Year 1854. Edited by the Rev. J. ALCORN, M.A. *Second Edition*. Post 8vo. price 7s. 6d.

Lord Jeffrey's Contributions to The Edinburgh Review. A New Edition, complete in One Volume, with a Portrait engraved by Henry Robinson, and a Vignette. Square crown 8vo. 21s. cloth ; or 30s. calf. —Or in 3 vols. 8vo. price 42s.

Bishop Jeremy Taylor's Entire Works : With Life by BISHOP HEBER. Revised and corrected by the Rev. CHARLES PAGE EDEN, Fellow of Oriel College, Oxford. Now complete in 10 vols. 8vo. 10s. 6d. each.

Johns.—The Land of Silence and the Land of Darkness. Being Two Essays on the Blind and on the Deaf and Dumb. By the Rev. B. G. JOHNS, Chaplain of the Blind School, St. George's Fields, Southwark. Fcp. 8vo. price 4s. 6d.

Johnston.—A Dictionary of Geography, Descriptive, Physical, Statistical, and Historical : Forming a complete General Gazetteer of the World. By A. KEITH JOHNSTON, F.R.S.E., F.R.G.S., F.G.S., Geographer at Edinburgh in Ordinary to Her Majesty. Second Edition, thoroughly revised. In 1 vol. of 1,360 pages, comprising about 50,000 Names of Places. 8vo. 36s. cloth ; or half-bound in russia, 41s.

Kemble.—The Saxons in England : A History of the English Commonwealth till the Norman Conquest. By JOHN M. KEMBLE, M.A., &c. 2 vols. 8vo. 28s.

Kesteven.—A Manual of the Domestic Practice of Medicine. By W. B. KESTEVEN, Fellow of the Royal College of Surgeons of England, &c. Square post 8vo. 7s. 6d.

Kirby and Spence's Introduction to Entomology ; or, Elements of the Natural History of Insects : Comprising an Account of Noxious and Useful Insects, of their Metamorphoses, Food, Stratagems, Habitations, Societies, Motions, Noises, Hybernation, Instinct, &c. *Seventh Edition*, with an Appendix relative to the Origin and Progress of the work. Crown 8vo. 5s.

Mrs. R. Lee's Elements of Natural History ; or, First Principles of Zoology : Comprising the Principles of Classification, interspersed with amusing and instructive Accounts of the most remarkable Animals. New Edition ; Woodcuts. Fcp. 8vo. 7s. 6d.

Letters to my Unknown Friends. By a LADY, Author of *Letters on Happiness*. Fourth Edition. Fcp. 8vo. 6s.

Letters on Happiness, addressed to a Friend. By a LADY, Author of *Letters to my Unknown Friends*. Fcp. 8vo. 6s.

L.E.L.—The Poetical Works of Letitia Elizabeth Landon ; comprising the *Improvisatrice*, the *Venetian Bracelet*, the *Golden Violet*, the *Troubadour*, and Poetical Remains. New Edition ; with 2 Vignettes by R. Doyle. 2 vols. 16mo. 10s. cloth ; morocco, 21s.

Dr. John Lindley's Theory and Practice of Horticulture ; or, an Attempt to explain the principal Operations of Gardening upon Physiological Grounds : Being the Second Edition of the *Theory of Horticulture*, much enlarged ; with 98 Woodcuts. 8vo. 21s.

Dr. John Lindley's Introduction to Botany. New Edition, with Corrections and copious Additions. 2 vols. 8vo. with Six Plates and numerous Woodcuts, price ?'
B 6

## LARDNER'S CABINET CYCLOPÆDIA

Of History, Biography, Literature, the Arts and Sciences, Natural History, and Manners.
A Series of Original Works by

| | | |
|---|---|---|
| SIR JOHN HERSCHEL, | THOMAS KEIGHTLEY, | BISHOP THIRLWALL, |
| SIR JAMES MACKINTOSH, | JOHN FORSTER, | THE REV. G. R. GLEIG, |
| ROBERT SOUTHEY, | SIR WALTER SCOTT, | J. C. L. DE SISMONDI, |
| SIR DAVID BREWSTER, | THOMAS MOORE, | JOHN PHILLIPS, F.R.S., &c. |

AND OTHER EMINENT WRITERS.

Complete in 132 vols. fcp. 8vo. with Vignette Titles, price, in cloth, Nineteen Guineas.
The Works *separately*, in Sets or Series, price Three Shillings and Sixpence each Volume.

*A List of the* WORKS *composing the* CABINET CYCLOPÆDIA:—

---

**Linwood.—Anthologia Oxoniensis, sive**
Florilegium e Lusibus poeticis diversorum
Oxoniensium Græcis et Latinis decerptum.
Curante GULIELMO LINWOOD, M.A., Ædis
Christi Alumno. 8vo. price 14s.

**Lorimer's (C.) Letters to a Young Master**
Mariner on some Subjects connected with
his Calling. New Edition. Fcp. 8vo. 5s. 6d.

**Loudon's Encyclopædia of Gardening:**
Comprising the Theory and Practice of Hor-
ticulture, Floriculture, Arboriculture, and
Landscape-Gardening. With many hundred
Woodcuts. New Edition, corrected and
improved by MRS. LOUDON. 8vo. 50s.

**Loudon's Encyclopædia of Trees and**
Shrubs, or *Arboretum et Fruticetum Britannicum* abridged: Containing the Hardy Trees
and Shrubs of Great Britain, Native and
Foreign, Scientifically and Popularly Described. With about 2,000 Woodcuts.
8vo. 50s.

**Loudon's Encyclopædia of Agriculture:**
Comprising the Theory and Practice of the
Valuation, Transfer, Laying-out, Improvement, and Management of Landed Property;
and of the Cultivation and Economy of the
Animal and Vegetable Productions of Agriculture. New and cheaper Edition; with
1,100 Woodcuts. 8vo. 31s. 6d.

**Loudon's Encyclopædia of Plants:** Comprising the Specific Character, Description, Culture, History, Application in the Arts, and every other desirable Particular respecting all the Plants found in Great Britain. New Edition, corrected by MRS. LOUDON. With upwards of 12,000 Woodcuts. 8vo. £3. 13s. 6d.—Second Supplement, 21s.

**Loudon's Encyclopædia of Cottage,** Farm, and Villa Architecture and Furniture. New Edition, edited by MRS. LOUDON; with more than 2,000 Woodcuts. 8vo. 63s.

**Loudon's Self-Instruction for Young** Gardeners, Foresters, Bailiffs, Land Stewards, and Farmers; in Arithmetic, Bookkeeping, Geometry, Mensuration, Practical Trigonometry, Mechanics, Land-Surveying, Levelling, Planning and Mapping, Architectural Drawing, and Isometrical Projection and Perspective. 8vo. Portrait, 7s. 6d.

**Loudon's Hortus Britannicus; or,** Catalogue of all the Plants found in Great Britain. New Edition, corrected by MRS. LOUDON. 8vo. 31s. 6d.

**Mrs. Loudon's Lady's Country Companion;** or, How to Enjoy a Country Life Rationally. Fourth Edition, with Plates and Woodcuts. Fcp. 8vo. 5s.

**Mrs. Loudon's Amateur Gardener's** Calendar, or Monthly Guide to what should be avoided and done in a Garden. 16mo. with Woodcuts, 7s. 6d.

**Low's Elements of Practical Agriculture;** comprehending the Cultivation of Plants, the Husbandry of the Domestic Animals, and the Economy of the Farm. New Edition; with 200 Woodcuts. 8vo. 21s.

**Macaulay.—Speeches of the Right Hon.** Lord Macaulay. Corrected by HIMSELF. 8vo. price 12s.

**Macaulay. — The History of England** from the Accession of James II. By the Right Hon. LORD MACAULAY. New Edition. Vols. I. and II. 8vo. price 32s.; Vols III. and IV. price 36s.

**Lord Macaulay's Critical and Historical** Essays contributed to The Edinburgh Review. Four Editions, as follows:—

1. A LIBRARY EDITION (the Eighth), in 3 vols. 8vo. price 36s.
2. Complete in ONE VOLUME, with Portrait and Vignette. Square crown 8vo. price 21s. cloth; or 30s. calf.
3. Another NEW EDITION, in 3 vols. fcp. 8vo. price 21s. cloth.
4. The PEOPLE'S EDITION, in 2 vols. crown 8vo. price 8s. cloth.

**Macaulay.—Lays of Ancient Rome, with** Ivry and the Armada. By the Right Hon. LORD MACAULAY. New Edition. 16mo. price 4s. 6d. cloth; or 10s. 6d. bound in morocco.

**Lord Macaulay's Lays of Ancient Rome.** With numerous Illustrations, Original and from the Antique, drawn on Wood by George Scharf, jun., and engraved by Samuel Williams. New Edition. Fcp. 4to. price 21s. boards; or 42s. bound in morocco.

**Mac Donald. — Poems. By George** MAC DONALD, Author of Within and Without. Fcp. 8vo. 7s.

**Mac Donald.—Within and Without: A** Dramatic Poem. By GEORGE MAC DONALD. Second Edition, revised; fcp. 8vo. 4s. 6d.

**Macdonald. — Villa Verocchio; or, the** Youth of Leonardo da Vinci: A Tale. By the late MISS D. L. MACDONALD. Fcp. 8vo. price 6s.

**MacDougall.—The Theory of War illus-** trated by numerous Examples from History. By Lieutenant-Colonel MACDOUGALL, Superintendent of Studies in the Royal Military College, Sandhurst. Post 8vo. with 10 Plans of Battles, price 10s. 6d.

**M'Dougall.—The Eventful Voyage of** H.M. Discovery Ship Resolute to the Arctic Regions in Search of Sir John Franklin and the Missing Crews of H.M. Discovery Ships Erebus and Terror, 1852, 1853, 1854. To which is added an Account of her being fallen in with by an American Whaler, after her abandonment in Barrow Straits, and of her presentation to Queen Victoria by the Government of the United States. By GEORGE F. M'DOUGALL, Master. With a coloured Chart; 8 Illustrations in tinted Lithography; and 22 Woodcuts. 8vo. price 21s. cloth.

**Sir James Mackintosh's Miscellaneous** Works: Including his Contributions to The Edinburgh Review. Complete in One Volume; with Portrait and Vignette. Square crown 8vo. 21s. cloth; or 30s. bound in calf: or in 3 vols. fcp. 8vo. 21s.

**Sir James Mackintosh's History of England** from the Earliest Times to the final Establishment of the Reformation. Library Edition, revised. 2 vols. 8vo. 21s.

**Macleod.—The Theory and Practice of** Banking: With the Elementary Principles of Currency, Prices, Credit, and Exchanges. By HENRY DUNNING MACLEOD, of the Inner Temple, Esq., Barrister-at-Law. 2 vols. royal 8vo. price 30s.

**Macnaught.—The Doctrine of Inspiration**: Being an Inquiry concerning the Infallibility, Inspiration, and Authority of Holy Writ. By the Rev. JOHN MACNAUGHT, M.A. *Second Edition,* revised. Crown 8vo. price 4s. 6d.

**M'Culloch's Dictionary, Practical, Theoretical,** and Historical, of Commerce and Commercial Navigation. Illustrated with Maps and Plans. New Edition, corrected to the Present Time ; with a Supplement. 8vo. price 50s. cloth ; half-russia, 55s.

**M'Culloch's Dictionary, Geographical,** Statistical, and Historical, of the various Countries, Places, and principal Natural Objects in the World. Illustrated with Six large Maps. New Edition, revised; with a Supplement. 2 vols. 8vo. price 63s.

**Maguire.—Rome; its Ruler and its In**stitutions. By JOHN FRANCIS MAGUIRE, M.P. With a Portrait of Pope Pius IX. Post 8vo. price 10s. 6d.

**Maitland.—The Church in the Cata**combs : A Description of the Primitive Church of Rome. Illustrated by its Sepulchral Remains. By the Rev. CHARLES MAITLAND. New Edition ; with several Woodcuts. 8vo. price 14s.

**Out-of-Doors Drawing.— Aphorisms on** Drawing. By the Rev. S. C. MALAN, M.A. of Balliol College, Oxford ; Vicar of Broadwindsor, Dorset. Post 8vo. 3s. 6d.

**Mrs. Marcet's Conversations on Chemis**try, in which the Elements of that Science are familiarly explained and illustrated by Experiments. New Edition, enlarged and improved. 2 vols. fcp. 8vo. price 14s.

**Mrs. Marcet's Conversations on Natural Phi**losophy, in which the Elements of that Science are familiarly explained. New Edition, enlarged and corrected ; with 23 Plates. Fcp. 8vo. price 10s. 6d.

**Martineau.—Endeavours after the Chris**tian Life : Discourses. By JAMES MARTINEAU. 2 vols. post 8vo. 7s. 6d. each.

**Martineau.—Hymns for the Christian Church** and Home. Collected and edited by JAMES MARTINEAU. *Eleventh Edition,* 32mo. 3s. 6d. cloth, or 5s. calf ; *Fifth Edition,* 32mo. 1s. 4d. cloth, or 1s. 8d. roan.

**Martineau.—Miscellanies: Comprising Essays** on Dr. Priestley, Arnold's *Life and Correspondence,* Church and State, Theodore Parker's *Discourse of Religion,* "Phases of Faith," the Church of England, and the Battle of the Churches. By JAMES MARTINEAU. Post 8vo. 9s.

**Maunder's Scientific and Literary Trea**sury : A new and popular Encyclopædia of Science and the Belles-Lettres ; including all branches of Science, and every subject connected with Literature and Art. New Edition. Fcp. 8vo. price 10s. cloth ; bound in roan, 12s. ; calf, 12s. 6d.

**Maunder's Biographical Treasury; con**sisting of Memoirs, Sketches, and brief Notices of above 12,000 Eminent Persons of All Ages and Nations, from the Earliest Period of History : Forming a new and complete Dictionary of Universal Biography. Ninth Edition, revised throughout. Fcp. 8vo. 10s. cloth; bound in roan, 12s. ; calf, 12s. 6d.

**Maunder's Treasury of Knowledge, and** Library of Reference. Comprising an English Dictionary and Grammar, a Universal Gazetteer, a Classical Dictionary, a Chronology, a Law Dictionary, a Synopsis of the Peerage, numerous useful Tables, &c. New Edition, carefully revised and corrected throughout : With Additions. Fcp. 8vo. 10s. cloth ; bound in roan, 12s. ; calf, 12s. 6d.

**Maunder's Treasury of Natural History;** or, a Popular Dictionary of Animated Nature : In which the Zoological Characteristics that distinguish the different Classes, Genera, and Species, are combined with a variety of interesting Information illustrative of the Habits, Instincts, and General Economy of the Animal Kingdom. With 900 Woodcuts. New Edition. Fcp. 8vo. price 10s. cloth ; roan, 12s. ; calf, 12s. 6d.

**Maunder's Historical Treasury ; com**prising a General Introductory Outline of Universal History, Ancient and Modern, and a Series of separate Histories of every principal Nation that exists ; their Rise, Progress, and Present Condition, the Moral and Social Character of their respective Inhabitants, their Religion, Manners and Customs, &c. New Edition ; revised throughout, with a new GENERAL INDEX. Fcp. 8vo. 10s. cloth ; roan, 12s. ; calf, 12s. 6d.

**Maunder's Geographical Treasury. —** The Treasury of Geography, Physical, Historical, Descriptive, and Political ; containing a succinct Account of Every Country in the World : Preceded by an Introductory Outline of the History of Geography ; a Familiar Inquiry into the Varieties of Race and Language exhibited by different Nations; and a View of the Relations of Geography to Astronomy and the Physical Sciences. Commenced by the late SAMUEL MAUNDER ; completed by WILLIAM HUGHES, F.R.G.S., late Professor of Geography in the College for Civil Engineers. *New Edition;* with 7 Maps and 16 Steel Plates. Fcp. 8vo. 10s. cloth ; roan, 12s. ; calf, 12s. 6d.

Melville. — The Confidence-Man: His Masquerade. By HERMAN MELVILLE, Author of *Typee*, *Omoo*, &c. Fcp. 8vo. 5s.

Merivale. — A History of the Romans under the Empire. By the Rev. CHARLES MERIVALE, B.D., late Fellow of St. John's College, Cambridge. 8vo. with Maps.
Vols. I. and II. comprising the History to the Fall of *Julius Cæsar*. Second Edition..........................28s.
Vol. III. to the establishment of the Monarchy by *Augustus*. Second Edition ........................14s.
Vols. IV. and V. from *Augustus* to *Claudine*, B.C. 27 to A.D. 54...........................32s.

Merivale.—The Fall of the Roman Republic: A Short History of the Last Century of the Commonwealth. By the Rev. C. MERIVALE, B.D., late Fellow of St. John's College, Cambridge. New Edition. 12mo. 7s. 6d.

Merivale.—An Account of the Life and Letters of Cicero. Translated from the German of ABEKEN; and Edited by the Rev. CHARLES MERIVALE, B.D. 12mo. 9s. 6d.

Merivale (L. A.)—Christian Records: A Short History of Apostolic Age. By L. A. MERIVALE. Fcp. 8vo. 7s. 6d.

Miles.—The Horse's Foot, and How to Keep it Sound. *Eighth Edition*; with an Appendix on Shoeing in general, and Hunters in particular, 12 Plates and 12 Woodcuts. By W. MILES, Esq. Imperial 8vo. 12s. 6d.
*** Two Casts or Models of Off Fore Feet, No. 1, *Shod for All Purposes*, No. 2, *Shod with Leather*, on Mr. Miles's plan, may be had, price 3s. each.

Miles.—A Plain Treatise on Horse-Shoeing. By WILLIAM MILES, Esq. With Plates and Woodcuts. Small 4to. price 5s.

Milner's History of the Church of Christ. With Additions by the late Rev. ISAAC MILNER, D.D., F.R.S. A New Edition, revised, with additional Notes by the Rev. T. GRANTHAM, B.D. 4 vols. 8vo. price 52s.

Montgomery.—Memoirs of the Life and Writings of James Montgomery: Including Selections from his Correspondence, Remains in Prose and Verse, and Conversations. By JOHN HOLLAND and JAMES EVERETT. With Portraits and Vignettes. 7 vols. post 8vo. price £3. 13s. 6d.

James Montgomery's Poetical Works: Collective Edition; with the Author's Autobiographical Prefaces, complete in One Volume; with Portrait and Vignette. Square crown 8vo. price 10s. 6d. cloth; morocco, 21s.—Or, in 4 vols. fcp. 8vo. with Portrait, d 7 other Plates, price 14s.

Moore.—The Power of the Soul over the Body, considered in relation to Health and Morals. By GEORGE MOORE, M.D. *Fifth Edition*. Fcp. 8vo. 6s.
"It shows that unless the inward principle be disciplined, purified, and enlightened, vainly must we look for that harmony | between mind and body so necessary to human enjoyment.....We would say, Read the book." ATHENÆUM.

Moore.—Man and his Motives. By George MOORE, M.D. *Third Edition*. Fcp. 8vo. 6s.

Moore.—The Use of the Body in relation to the Mind. By GEORGE MOORE, M.D. *Third Edition*. Fcp. 8vo. 6s.

Moore. — Memoirs, Journal, and Correspondence of Thomas Moore. Edited by the Right Hon. LORD JOHN RUSSELL, M.P. With Portraits and Vignette Illustrations. 8 vols. post 8vo. price 10s. 6d. each.

Thomas Moore's Poetical Works: Comprising the Author's recent Introductions and Notes. The *Traveller's Edition*, complete in One Volume, printed in Ruby Type; with a Portrait. Crown 8vo. 12s. 6d. cloth; morocco by Hayday, 21s.—Also the *Library Edition* complete in 1 vol. medium 8vo. with Portrait and Vignette, 21s. cloth; morocco by Hayday, 42s. — And the *First collected Edition*, in 10 vols. fcp. 8vo. with Portrait and 19 Plates, price 35s.

Moore. — Poetry and Pictures from Thomas Moore: Being Selections of the most popular and admired of Moore's Poems, copiously illustrated with highly-finished Wood Engravings from original Designs by
C. W. COPE, R.A. F. R. PICKERSGILL, R.A.
E. C. CORBOULD, S. READ,
J. CROPSEY, G. THOMAS,
E. DUNCAN, F. TOPHAM,
BIRKET FOSTER, H. WARREN,
J. C. HORSLEY, A.R.A. HARRISON WEIR, and
H. LE JEUNE, F. WYBURD.
Fcp. 4to., printed on toned paper, and elegantly bound. [*Nearly ready*.

Moore's Epicurean. New Edition, with the Notes from the collective edition of *Moore's Poetical Works*; and a Vignette engraved on Wood from an original Design by D. MACLISE, R.A. 16mo. 5s. cloth; or 12s. 6d. morocco by Hayday.

Moore's Songs, Ballads, and Sacred Songs. New Edition, printed in Ruby Type; with the Notes from the collective edition of *Moore's Poetical Works*, and a Vignette from a Design by T. Creswick, R.A. 32mo. 2s. 6d —An Edition in 16mo. with Vignette by R. Doyle, price 5s.; or 12s. 6d. morocco by Hayday.

**Moore's Lalla Rookh: An Oriental** Romance. With 13 highly-finished Steel Plates from Original Designs by Corbould, Meadows, and Stephanoff, engraved under the superintendence of the late Charles Heath. New Edition. Square crown 8vo. price 15s. cloth ; morocco, 28s.

**Moore's Lalla Rookh.** New Edition, printed in Ruby Type; with the Preface and Notes from the collective edition of *Moore's Poetical Works*, and a Frontispiece from a Design by Kenny Meadows. 32mo. 2s. 6d. —An Edition in 16mo. with Vignette, 5s. ; or 12s. 6d. morocco by Hayday.

**Moore's Irish Melodies. A New Edi-**tion, with 13 highly-finished Steel Plates, from Original Designs by

| | |
|---|---|
| C. W. COPE, R.A. | D. MACLISE, R.A. |
| T. CRESWICK, R.A. | J. E. MILLAIS, A.R.A. |
| A. L. EGG, A.R.A. | W. MULREADY, R.A. |
| W. P. FRITH, R.A. | J. SANT, |
| W. E. FROST, A.R.A. | F. STONE, A.R.A.; and |
| J. C. HORSLEY, | E. M. WARD, R.A. |

Square crown 8vo. price 21s. cloth ; or 31s. 6d. handsomely bound in morocco.

**Moore's Irish Melodies,** printed in Ruby Type; with the Preface and Notes from the collective edition of *Moore's Poetical Works*, the Advertisements originally prefixed, and a Portrait of the Author. 32mo. 2s. 6d.— An Edition in 16mo. with Vignette, 5s. ; or 12s. 6d. morocco by Hayday.

**Moore's Irish Melodies.** Illustrated by D. Maclise, R.A. New Edition ; with 161 Designs, and the whole of the Letterpress engraved on Steel, by F. P. Becker. Super-royal 8vo. 31s. 6d. boards ; £2. 12s. 6d. morocco by Hayday.

**Moore's Irish Melodies, the Music with** the Words ; the Symphonies and Accompaniments by Sir John Stevenson, Mus. Doc. Complete in One Volume, small Music size, convenient and legible at the pianoforte, but more portable than the usual form of Musical publications. Imperial 8vo. 31s. 6d. cloth ; or 42s. half-bound in morocco.

**Moore.—The Crosses, Altar, and Orna-**ments in the Churches of St. Paul's, Knightsbridge, and St. Barnabas, Pimlico : A concise Report of the Proceedings and Judgments in the Cases of Westerton v. Liddell, Horne, and others, and Beal v. Liddell, Parke, and Evans ; as heard and determined by the Consistory Court of London, the Arches Court of Canterbury, and the Judicial Committee of H.M. Most Hon. Privy Council. By EDMUND F. MOORE, Esq., M.A., Barrister-at-Law. Royal 8vo. price 12s. cloth.

**Morell.—Elements of Psychology: Part** I., containing the Analysis of the Intellectual Powers. By J. D. MORELL, M.A., One of Her Majesty's Inspectors of Schools. Post 8vo. 7s. 6d.

**Morning Clouds.** [A book of practical ethics, in form of letters of counsel, encouragement, and sympathy, specially addressed to young women on their entrance into life.] Post 8vo. price 7s.

**Moseley.—The Mechanical Principles of** Engineering and Architecture. By H. MOSELEY, M.A., F.R.S., Canon of Bristol, &c. Second Edition, enlarged ; with numerous Corrections and Woodcuts. 8vo. 24s.

**Memoirs and Letters of the late Colonel** ARMINE S. H. MOUNTAIN, C.B., Aide-de-Camp to the Queen, and Adjutant-General of Her Majesty's Forces in India. Edited by Mrs. MOUNTAIN. With a Portrait drawn on Stone by R. J. LANE, A.E.R.A. Post 8vo. 8s. 6d.

**Mure.—A Critical History of the Lan-**guage and Literature of Ancient Greece. By WILLIAM MURE, M.P. of Caldwell. Second Edition. Vols. I. to III. 8vo. price 36s. ; Vol. IV. price 15s. ; Vol. V. price 18s.

**Murray's Encyclopædia of Geography ;** comprising a complete Description of the Earth : Exhibiting its Relation to the Heavenly Bodies, its Physical Structure, the Natural History of each Country, and the Industry, Commerce, Political Institutions, and Civil and Social State of All Nations. Second Edition ; with 82 Maps, and upwards of 1,000 other Woodcuts. 8vo. price 60s.

**Neale. — The Closing Scene ; or, Chris-**tianity and Infidelity contrasted in the Last Hours of Remarkable Persons. By the Rev. ERSKINE NEALE, M.A. New Editions. 2 vols. fcp. 8vo. price 6s. each.

**Oldacre.—The Last of the Old Squires.** A Sketch. By CEDRIC OLDACRE, Esq., of Sax - Normanbury, sometime of Christ Church, Oxon. Crown 8vo. price 9s. 6d.

**Osborn. — Quedah ; or, Stray Leaves** from a Journal in Malayan Waters. By Captain SHERARD OSBORN, R.N., C.B., Author of *Stray Leaves from an Arctic Journal,* and of the *Narrative of the Discovery of the North-West Passage.* With a coloured Chart and tinted Illustrations. Post 8vo. price 10s. 6d.

**Osborn.—The Discovery of the North-**West Passage by H.M.S. *Investigator*, Captain R. M'CLURE, 1850-1854. Edited by Captain SHERARD OSBORN, C.B., from the Logs and Journals of Captain R. M'Clure. Second Edition, revised ; with Additions to the Chapter on the Hybernation of Animals in the Arctic Regions, a Geological Paper by Sir RODERICK I. MURCHISON, a Portrait of Captain M'Clure, a coloured Chart and tinted Illustrations. 8vo. price 15s.

**Owen. — Lectures on the Comparative** Anatomy and Physiology of the Invertebrate Animals, delivered at the Royal College of Surgeons. By RICHARD OWEN, F.R.S., Hunterian Professor to the College. Second Edition, with 235 Woodcuts. 8vo. 21s.

**Professor Owen's Lectures on the Comparative** Anatomy and Physiology of the Vertebrate Animals, delivered at the Royal College of Surgeons in 1844 and 1846. With numerous Woodcuts. Vol. I. 8vo. price 14s.

**Memoirs of Admiral Parry, the Arctic** Navigator. By his Son, the Rev. E. PARRY, M.A. of Balliol College, Oxford ; Domestic Chaplain to the Lord Bishop of London. Third Edition ; with a Portrait and coloured Chart of the North-West Passage. Fcp. 8vo. price 5s.

**Dr. Pereira's Elements of Materia** Medica and Therapeutics. *Third Edition*, enlarged and improved from the Author's Materials, by A. S. TAYLOR, M.D., and G. O. REES, M.D. : With numerous Woodcuts. Vol. I. 8vo. 28s. ; Vol. II. Part I. 21s. ; Vol. II. Part II. 24s.

**Dr. Pereira's Lectures on Polarised Light,** together with a Lecture on the Microscope. 2d Edition, enlarged from Materials left by the Author, by the Rev. B. POWELL, M.A., &c. Fcp. 8vo. with Woodcuts, 7s.

**Perry.—The Franks, from their First** Appearance in History to the Death of King Pepin. By WALTER C. PERRY, Barrister-at-Law, Doctor in Philosophy and Master of Arts in the University of Göttingen. 8vo. price 12s. 6d.

**Peschel's Elements of Physics. Trans-**lated from the German, with Notes, by E. WEST. With Diagrams and Woodcuts. 3 vols. fcp. 8vo. 21s.

**Ida Pfeiffer's Lady's Second Journey** round the World: From London to the Cape of Good Hope, Borneo, Java, Sumatra, Celebes, Ceram, the Moluccas &c., California, Panama, Peru, Ecuador, and the United States. 2 vols. post 8vo. 21s.

**Phillips's Elementary Introduction to** Mineralogy. A New Edition, with extensive Alterations and Additions, by H. J. BROOKE, F.R.S., F.G.S. ; and W. H. MILLER, M.A., F.G.S. With numerous Wood Engravings. Post 8vo. 18s.

**Phillips.—A Guide to Geology. By John** PHILLIPS, M.A., F.R.S., F.G.S., &c. Fourth Edition, corrected to the Present Time ; with 4 Plates. Fcp. 8vo. 5s.

**Phillips.—Figures and Descriptions of the** Palæozoic Fossils of Cornwall, Devon, and West Somerset ; observed in the course of the Ordnance Geological Survey of that District. By JOHN PHILLIPS, F.R.S., F.G.S., &c. 8vo. with 60 Plates, price 9s.

**Piesse's Art of Perfumery, and Methods** of Obtaining the Odours of Plants : With Instructions for the Manufacture of Perfumes for the Handkerchief, Scented Powders, Odorous Vinegars, Dentifrices, Pomatums, Cosmétiques, Perfumed Soap, &c. ; and an Appendix on the Colours of Flowers, Artificial Fruit Essences, &c. *Second Edition*, revised and improved ; with 46 Woodcuts. Crown 8vo. 8s. 6d.

**Captain Portlock's Report on the Geology** of the County of Londonderry, and of Parts of Tyrone and Fermanagh, examined and described under the Authority of the Master-General and Board of Ordnance. 8vo. with 48 Plates, price 24s.

**Powell.—Essays on the Spirit of the** Inductive Philosophy, the Unity of Worlds, and the Philosophy of Creation. By the Rev. BADEN POWELL, M.A., F.R.S., F.R.A.S., F.G.S., Savilian Professor of Geometry in the University of Oxford. Second Edition, revised. Crown 8vo. with Woodcuts, 12s. 6d.

**Pycroft's Course of English Reading,** adapted to every taste and capacity : With Literary Anecdotes. New and cheaper Edition. Fcp. 8vo. price 5s.

**Raikes.—A Portion of the Journal kept** by THOMAS RAIKES, Esq., from 1831 to 1847 : Comprising Reminiscences of Social and Political Life in London and Paris during that period. Vols. I. and II. (*Second Edition*), post 8vo. 21s. ; Vols. III. and IV. with *Index*, completing the work, price 21s.

**Reade. — The Poetical Works of John** Edmund Reade. New Edition, revised and corrected ; with Additional Poems. 4 vols. fcp. 8vo. price 20s.

**Dr. Reece's Medical Guide:** Comprising a complete Modern Dispensatory, and a Practical Treatise on the distinguishing Symptoms, Causes, Prevention, Cure, and Palliation of the Diseases incident to the Human Frame. Seventeenth Edition, corrected and enlarged by the Author's Son, Dr. H. REECE, M.R.C.S., &c. 8vo. 12s.

**Rich's Illustrated Companion to the** Latin Dictionary and Greek Lexicon : Forming a Glossary of all the Words representing Visible Objects connected with the Arts, Manufactures, and Every-Day Life of the Ancients. With about 2,000 Woodcuts from the Antique. Post 8vo. 21s.

**Richardson. — Fourteen Years' Expe-** rience of Cold Water : Its Uses and Abuses. By Captain M. RICHARDSON, late of the 4th Light Dragoons. Post 8vo. with Woodcuts, price 6s.

"The first object of Captain Richardson's book is to extend the use of the cold-water cure to the humbler classes, by a simpler mode of treatment. This simplicity principally consists in the substitution of wet bandages covered by dry bandages for the wet sheet and other processes of established hydropathy. Captain Richardson considers the bandage not only more beneficial medically than the sheet, but much more easily applied, while it does not interrupt a man's avocations, but can be worn even at work. The general expositions are followed by directions for the treatment of diseases under the Captain's system." SPECTATOR.

**Horsemanship ; or, the Art of Riding** and Managing a Horse, adapted to the Guidance of Ladies and Gentlemen on the Road and in the Field : With Instructions for Breaking-in Colts and Young Horses. By CAPTAIN RICHARDSON, late of the 4th Light Dragoons. With 5 Plates. Square crown 8vo. 14s.

**Household Prayers for Four Weeks ;** With additional Prayers for Special Occasions. To which is added a Course of Scripture Reading for Every Day in the Year. By the Rev. J. E. RIDDLE, M.A., Incumbent of St. Philip's, Leckhampton. Crown 8vo. price 3s. 6d.

**Riddle's Complete Latin-English and** English-Latin Dictionary, for the use of Colleges and Schools. New and cheaper Edition, revised and corrected. 8vo. 21s.

Separately { The English-Latin Dictionary, 7s.
{ The Latin-English Dictionary, 15s.

**Riddle's Diamond Latin-English Dictionary.** A Guide to the Meaning, Quality, and right Accentuation of Latin Classical Words. Royal 32mo. price 4s.

**Riddle's Copious and Critical Latin-** English Lexicon, founded on the German-Latin Dictionaries of Dr. William Freund. New and cheaper Edition. Post 4to. 31s. 6d.

**Rivers's Rose-Amateur's Guide ;** containing ample Descriptions of all the fine leading varieties of Roses, regularly classed in their respective Families ; their History and Mode of Culture. Fifth Edition, corrected and improved. Fcp. 8vo. 3s. 6d.

**Dr. E. Robinson's Greek and English** Lexicon to the Greek Testament. A New Edition, revised and in great part re-written. 8vo. price 18s.

**Mr. Henry Rogers's Essays selected from** Contributions to the *Edinburgh Review*. Second and cheaper Edition, with Additions. 3 vols. fcp. 8vo. 21s.

**Dr. Roget's Thesaurus of English Words** and Phrases classified and arranged so as to facilitate the Expression of Ideas and assist in Literary Composition. Sixth Edition, revised and improved. Crown 8vo. 10s. 6d.

**Ronalds's Fly-Fisher's Entomology:** With coloured Representations of the Natural and Artificial Insect, and a few Observations and Instructions on Trout and Grayling Fishing. *Fifth Edition*, thoroughly revised by an Experienced Fly-Fisher ; with 20 new coloured Plates. 8vo. 14s.

**Rowton's Debater: A Series of complete** Debates, Outlines of Debates, and Questions for Discussion ; with ample References to the best Sources of Information. New Edition. Fcp. 8vo. 6s.

**The Saints our Example. By the Author** of *Letters to my Unknown Friends*, &c. Fcp. 8vo. price 7s.

**Scherzer.—Travels in the Free States of** Central America : Nicaragua, Honduras, and San Salvador. By Dr. CARL SCHERZER. With a coloured Map. 2 vols. post 8vo. 16s.

"Central America is not an inviting place for the lounging traveller. The roads are bad ; there are no inns; food is scarce ; the people are dishonest ; scoundrels swarm ; neither life nor property is safe. Dr. Scherzer travelled with guides of doubtful fidelity, was forced to keep his hand on his gun and revolver, sometimes compelled to eat a few black beans or starve ; now groping at night through a forest, now escorted by barefooted soldiers with helmets of pasteboard and tinsel ; now swinging in a hammock in a filthy hovel ; now receiving the President of a State by the light of a candle stuck in a bottle. Altogether having a hard and hazardous life of it. But he does not complain. A cheerier and braver traveller seldom has made his way in outlandish tracks far beyond the limits of the civilised world. The Central American question will probably endow Dr. Scherzer's book with an additional attraction." GLOBE.

**Dr. L. Schmitz's History of Greece, from** the Earliest Times to the Taking of Corinth by the Romans, B.C. 146, mainly based upon Bishop Thirlwall's History. *Fourth Edition*, with Supplementary Chapters on the Literature and the Arts of Ancient Greece ; and illustrated with a Map of Athens and 137 Woodcuts, designed from the Antique by G. Scharf, jun., F.S.A. 12mo. 7s. 6d.

**Scrivenor's History of the Iron Trade,** from the Earliest Records to the Present Period. New Edition, corrected. 8vo. price 10s. 6d.

**Sir Edward Seaward's Narrative of his** Shipwreck, and consequent Discovery of certain Islands in the Caribbean Sea. Third Edition. 2 vols. post 8vo. 21s.—An ABRIDGMENT, in 16mo. price 2s. 6d.

**The Sermon in the Mount.** Printed by C. Whittingham, uniformly with the *Thumb Bible*; bound and clasped. 64mo. 1s. 6d.

**Sewell.—Amy Herbert.** By a Lady. Edited by the Rev. WILLIAM SEWELL, B.D., Fellow and Tutor of Exeter College, Oxford. New Edition. Fcp. 8vo. price 6s.

**Sewell.—The Earl's Daughter.** By the Author of *Amy Herbert*. Edited by the Rev. W. SEWELL, B.D. 2 vols. fcp. 8vo. 9s.

**Sewell. — Gertrude: A Tale.** By the Author of *Amy Herbert*. Edited by the Rev. W. SEWELL, B.D. Fcp. 8vo. price 6s.

**Sewell. — Margaret Percival.** By the Author of *Amy Herbert*. Edited by the Rev. W. SEWELL, B.D. 2 vols. fcp. 8vo. price 12s.

*By the same Author, New Editions,*

Ivors. 2 vols. fcp. 8vo. price 12s.
Cleve Hall. 2 vols. fcp. 8vo. price 12s.
Katharine Ashton. 2 vols. fcp. 8vo. price 12s.
The Experience of Life. Fcp. 8vo. price 7s. 6d.
Laneton Parsonage: A Tale for Children, on the Practical Use of a portion of the Church Catechism. 2 vols. fcp. 8vo. price 12s.
Readings for Every Day in Lent: Compiled from the Writings of BISHOP JEREMY TAYLOR. Fcp. 8vo. price 5s.
Readings for a Month preparatory to Confirmation: Compiled from the Works of Writers of the Early and of the English Church. New and cheaper Edition. Fcp. 8vo. 4s.

**Bowdler's Family Shakspeare: In which** nothing is *added* to the Original Text; but those words and expressions are *omitted* which cannot with propriety be read aloud. Illustrated with Thirty-six Vignettes engraved on Wood from original Designs by

| | |
|---|---|
| G. COOKE, R.A. | T. STOTHARD, R.A. |
| R. COOKE, | R. THOMSON, R.A. |
| H. HOWARD, R.A. | R. WESTALL, R.A. |
| H. SINGLETON, | R. WOODFORDE, R.A. |
| R. SMIRKE, R.A. | |

*New Edition*, printed in a more convenient form. 6 vols. fcp. 8vo. price 30s. cloth; separately, 5s. each.

*⁎* The LIBRARY EDITION, with the same Illustrations, in One Volume, medium 8vo. price 21s. cloth.

**Sharp's New British Gazetteer, or Topographical Dictionary of the British Islands** and Narrow Seas: Comprising concise Descriptions of about Sixty Thousand Places, Seats, Natural Features, and Objects of Note, founded on the best authorities. 2 vols. 8vo. price £2. 16s.

"We have already had occasion to mention this book, and a careful examination of its contents has convinced us of its great value. The remarkable clearness with which its condensations and abbreviations are made appears to us its most admirable feature. We have no book of similar bulk in the language containing anything like the amount of information of various kinds so well arranged and so easily accessible as in this new gazetteer. Every article bears the mark of studied, careful, and exact compilation. It comprehends both the topography and the hydrography of the United Kingdom, and is constructed on the plan of facilitating reference by bringing together as many articles as possible under distinct heads....All the positions have been retaken from the maps; and not only the county but the quarter of the county given in which a name might be looked for. We must, in short, repeat with a liberal acquiescence what Mr. Sharp himself remarks of his five years' diligent labour, that it will be found to comprise, in a clear and legible type, more substantial information, collected from original sources, and put into a convenient form, than the bulkiest of its class." EXAMINER.

**Short Whist; its Rise, Progress, and** Laws: With Observations to make any one a Whist-Player. Containing also the Laws of Piquet, Cassino, Ecarté, Cribbage, Backgammon. By Major A. New Edition; to which are added, Precepts for Tyros, by Mrs. B. Fcp. 8vo. 3s.

**Sinclair. — The Journey of Life.** By CATHERINE SINCLAIR, Author of *The Business of Life*. New Edition. Fcp. 8vo. 5s.

**Sir Roger De Coverley. From the Spectator.** With Notes and Illustrations, by W. HENRY WILLS; and 12 Wood Engravings from Designs by F. TAYLER. Second and cheaper Edition. Crown 8vo. 10s. 6d.; or 21s. in morocco by Hayday.—An Edition without Woodcuts, in 16mo. price 1s.

**The Sketches: Three Tales.** By the Author of *Amy Herbert, The Old Man's Home*, and *Hawkstone*. The *Third Edition*; with 6 Illustrations in Aquatint. Fcp. 8vo. price 4s. 6d. boards.

**Smee's Elements of Electro-Metallurgy.** Third Edition, revised, corrected, and considerably enlarged; with Electrotypes and numerous Woodcuts. Post 8vo. 10s. 6d.

**Smith (G.) — History of Wesleyan Methodism:** VOL. I. Wesley and his Times. By GEORGE SMITH, F.A.S., Member of the Royal Asiatic Society, &c.; Author of *Sacred Annals, or Researches into the History and Religion of Mankind*, &c. Crown 8vo. with 8 Facsimiles of Methodist Society Tickets, price 10s. 6d. cloth.

**Smith (G. V.)—The Prophecies relating** to Nineveh and the Assyrians. Translated from the Hebrew, with Historical Introductions and Notes, exhibiting the principal Results of the recent Discoveries. By GEORGE VANCE SMITH, B.A. Post 8vo. with a Map, price 10s. 6d. cloth.

**Smith (J.) —The Voyage and Shipwreck** of St. Paul : With Dissertations on the Life and Writings of St. Luke, and the Ships and Navigation of the Ancients. By JAMES SMITH, of Jordanhill, Esq., F.R.S. Second Edition ; with Charts, Views, and Woodcuts. Crown 8vo. 8s. 6d.

**A Memoir of the Rev. Sydney Smith.** By his Daughter, LADY HOLLAND. With a Selection from his Letters, edited by MRS. AUSTIN. New Edition. 2 vols. 8vo. 28s.

**The Rev. Sydney Smith's Miscellaneous** Works : Including his Contributions to The Edinburgh Review. Three Editions :—

1. A LIBRARY EDITION (the Fourth), in 3 vols. 8vo. with Portrait, 36s.

2. Complete in ONE VOLUME, with Portrait and Vignette. Square crown 8vo. price 21s. cloth ; or 30s. bound in calf.

3. Another NEW EDITION, in 3 vols. fcp. 8vo. price 21s.

**The Rev. Sydney Smith's Elementary** Sketches of Moral Philosophy, delivered at the Royal Institution in the Years 1804, 1805, and 1806. Third Edition. Fcp. 8vo. 7s.

**Snow.—A Two-Years' Cruise off Tierra** del Fuego, the Falkland Islands, Patagonia, and the River Plate. A Narrative of Life in the Southern Seas. By W. PARKER SNOW, late Commander of the Mission Yacht Allen Gardiner; Author of "Voyage of the Prince Albert in Search of Sir John Franklin." With 3 coloured Charts and 6 tinted Illustrations. 2 vols. post 8vo. 24s.

"A Robinson-Crusoe style of narration, and a kind of rough and picturesque treatment, sustain the interest of the nautical descriptions more than might be supposed ; the wild and violent weather of the Falkland Islands, with the dangers of their navigation and the peculiar character of the River Plate, have a novelty beyond the common run of voyaging. The adventures in Tierra del Fuego are very interesting." SPECTATOR.

**Robert Southey's Complete Poetical** Works ; containing all the Author's last Introductions and Notes. The Library Edition, complete in One Volume, with Portrait and Vignette. Medium 8vo. price 21s. cloth ; 42s. bound in morocco. — Also, the First collected Edition, in 10 vols. fcp. 8vo. with Portrait and 19 Vignettes, price 35s.

**Select Works of the British Poets; from** Chaucer to Lovelace inclusive. With Biographical Sketches by the late ROBERT SOUTHEY. Medium 8vo. price 30s.

**Southey's Correspondence. — Selections** from the Letters of Robert Southey, &c. Edited by his Son-in-Law, the Rev. JOHN WOOD WARTER, B.D., Vicar of West Tarring, Sussex. 4 vols. post 8vo. price 42s.

**The Life and Correspondence of the late Robert** Southey. Edited by his Son, the Rev. C. C. SOUTHEY, M.A., Vicar of Ardleigh. With Portraits and Landscape Illustrations. 6 vols. post 8vo. price 63s.

**Southey's Doctor, complete in One** Volume. Edited by the Rev. J. W. WARTER, B.D. With Portrait, Vignette, Bust, and coloured Plate. Square crown 8vo. 21s.

**Southey's Commonplace-Books, complete in** Four Volumes. Edited by the Rev. J. W. WARTER, B.D. 4 vols. square crown 8vo. price £3. 18s.

Each Commonplace-Book, complete in itself, may be had separately, as follows :—

FIRST SERIES—CHOICE PASSAGES, &c. 18s.
SECOND SERIES—SPECIAL COLLECTIONS. 18s.
THIRD SERIES—ANALYTICAL READINGS. 21s.
FOURTH SERIES—ORIGINAL MEMORANDA, &c. 21s.

**Southey's Life of Wesley ; and Rise and** Progress of Methodism. New Edition, with Notes and Additions. Edited by the Rev. C. C. SOUTHEY, M.A. 2 vols. 8vo. with 2 Portraits, price 28s.

**Spottiswoode. — A Tarantasse Journey** through Eastern Russia, in the Autumn of 1856. By WILLIAM SPOTTISWOODE, M.A., F.R.S. With a Map of Russia, several Wood Engravings, and Seven Illustrations in tinted Lithography from Sketches by the Author. Post 8vo. price 10s. 6d.

**Stephen.—Lectures on the History of** France. By the Right Hon. SIR JAMES STEPHEN, K.C.B., LL.D., Professor of Modern History in the University of Cambridge. Third Edition. 2 vols. 8vo. price 24s.

**Stephen.—Essays in Ecclesiastical Bio-** graphy ; from The Edinburgh Review. By the Right Hon. SIR JAMES STEPHEN, K.C.B., LL.D., Professor of Modern History in the University of Cambridge. Third Edition. 2 vols. 8vo. 24s.

**Stonehenge.—The Greyhound : Being a** Treatise on the Art of Breeding, Rearing, and Training Greyhounds for Public Running ; their Diseases and Treatment : Containing also Rules for the Management of Coursing Meetings, and for the Decision of Courses. By STONEHENGE. With Frontispiece and Woodcuts. Square crown 8vo. price 21s. half-bound.

Stow. — The Training System, Moral Training School, and Normal Seminary for preparing Schoolmasters and Governesses. By DAVID STOW, Esq., Honorary Secretary to the Glasgow Normal Free Seminary. Tenth Edition; with Plates and Woodcuts. Post 8vo. price 6s.

Strickland. — Lives of the Queens of England. By AGNES STRICKLAND. Dedicated, by express permission, to Her Majesty. Embellished with Portraits of every Queen, engraved from the most authentic sources. Complete in 8 vols. post 8vo. price 7s. 6d. each. — Any Volume may be had *separately* to complete Sets.

Memoirs of Rear-Admiral Sir William Symonds, Knt., C.B., F.R.S., late Surveyor of the Navy. Published with the sanction of his Executors, as directed by his Will; and edited by J. A. SHARP. 8vo. with Plates and Wood Engravings.
[*In the press.*

Taylor. — Loyola: and Jesuitism in its Rudiments. By ISAAC TAYLOR. Post 8vo. price 10s. 6d.

Taylor. — Wesley and Methodism. By ISAAC TAYLOR. Post 8vo. Portrait, 10s. 6d.

Thacker's Courser's Annual Remembrancer and Stud-Book: Being an Alphabetical Return of the Running at all the Public Coursing Clubs in England, Ireland, and Scotland, for the Season 1856–57; with the *Pedigrees* (as far as received) of the DOGS. By ROBERT ABRAM WELSH, Liverpool. 8vo. 21s.
*⁎* Published annually in *October.*

Thirlwall. — The History of Greece. By the Right Rev. the LORD BISHOP of ST. DAVID's (the Rev. Connop Thirlwall). An improved Library Edition; with Maps. 8 vols. 8vo. price £3. — An Edition in 8 vols. fcp. 8vo. with Vignette Titles, price 28s.

Thomas. — Historical Notes relative to the History of England; embracing the Period from the Accession of King Henry VIII. to the Death of Queen Anne inclusive (1509 to 1714): Designed as a Book of instant Reference for the purpose of ascertaining the Dates of Events mentioned in History and in Manuscripts. The Names of Persons and Events mentioned in History within the above period placed in Alphabetical and Chronological Order, with Dates; and the Authority from whence taken given in each case, whether from Printed History or from Manuscripts. By F. S. THOMAS, Secretary of the Public Record Department. 3 vols. royal 8vo. price £2.

Thomson's Seasons. Edited by Bolton CORNEY, Esq. Illustrated with 77 fine Wood Engravings from Designs by Members of the Etching Club. Square crown 8vo. 21s. cloth; or 36s. bound in morocco.

Thomson (the Rev. Dr.) — An Outline of the necessary Laws of Thought: A Treatise on Pure and Applied Logic. By WILLIAM THOMSON, D.D., Provost of Queen's College, Oxford. *Fourth Edition*, carefully revised. Fcp. 8vo. price 7s. 6d.

Thomson's Tables of Interest, at Three, Four, Four-and-a-Half, and Five per Cent., from One Pound to Ten Thousand, and from 1 to 365 Days, in a regular progression of single Days; with Interest at all the above Rates, from One to Twelve Months, and from One to Ten Years. Also, numerous other Tables of Exchanges, Time, and Discounts. New Edition. 12mo. price 8s.

Thornbury. — Shakspeare's England; or, Sketches of Social History during the Reign of Elizabeth. By G. W. THORNBURY, Author of *History of the Buccaneers*, &c. 2 vols. crown 8vo. 21s.
" A work which stands unrivalled for the variety and entertaining character of its contents, and which well deserves a place on the library-shelf, by the side either of the historians of England or the prince of dramatists."
JOHN BULL.

The Thumb Bible; or, Verbum Sempiternum. By J. TAYLOR. Being an Epitome of the Old and New Testaments in English Verse. Reprinted from the Edition of 1693; bound and clasped. 64mo. 1s. 6d.

Bishop Tomline's Introduction to the Study of the Bible: Containing Proofs of the Authenticity and Inspiration of the Scriptures; a Summary of the History of the Jews; an Account of the Jewish Sects; and a brief Statement of Contents of several Books of the *Old Testament*. New Edition. Fcp. 8vo. 5s. 6d.

Tooke. — History of Prices, and of the State of the Circulation, during the Nine Years from 1848 to 1856 inclusive. Forming Vols. V. and VI. of Tooke's *History of Prices from* 1792 *to the Present Time*; and comprising a copious Index to the whole of the Six Volumes. By THOMAS TOOKE, F.R.S. and WILLIAM NEWMARCH. 2 vols. 8vo. price 52s. 6d.

Townsend. — Modern State Trials revised and illustrated with Essays and Notes. By W. C. TOWNSEND, Esq., M.A., Q.C. 2 vols. 8vo. price 30s.

# COMPLETION

### OF

# THE TRAVELLER'S LIBRARY.

*Summary of the Contents of the* TRAVELLER'S LIBRARY, *now complete in* 103 *Parts, price One Shilling each, or in* 50 *Volumes, price* 2s. 6d. *each in cloth.—To be had also, in complete Sets only, at Five Guineas per Set, bound in cloth, lettered, in* 25 *Volumes, classified as follows:—*

## VOYAGES AND TRAVELS.

### IN EUROPE.

A CONTINENTAL TOUR ........ BY J. BARROW.
ARCTIC VOYAGES AND } BY F. MAYNE.
   DISCOVERIES
BRITTANY AND THE BIBLE ...... BY I. HOPE.
BRITTANY AND THE CHASE .... BY I. HOPE.
CORSICA ................ BY F. GREGOROVIUS.
GERMANY, ETC.: NOTES OF } BY S. LAING.
   A TRAVELLER
ICELAND .................... BY P. MILES.
NORWAY, A RESIDENCE IN .... BY S. LAING.
NORWAY, RAMBLES IN .... BY T. FORESTER.
RUSSIA ........ BY THE MARQUIS DE CUSTINE.
RUSSIA AND TURKEY .. BY J. R. M'CULLOCH.
ST. PETERSBURG ........ BY M. JERRMANN.
THE RUSSIANS OF THE SOUTH, BY S. BROOKS.
SWISS MEN AND SWISS } BY R. FERGUSON.
   MOUNTAINS
MONT BLANC, ASCENT OF ...... BY J. AULDJO.
SKETCHES OF NATURE } BY F. VON TSCHUDI.
   IN THE ALPS
VISIT TO THE VAUDOIS } BY E. BAINES.
   OF PIEDMONT

### IN ASIA.

CHINA AND THIBET........ BY THE ABBE' HUC
SYRIA AND PALESTINE.......... "BÖTHEN."
THE PHILIPPINE ISLANDS, BY F. GIRONIÈRE.

### IN AFRICA.

AFRICAN WANDERINGS........ BY M. WERNE.
MOROCCO ................ BY X. DURRIEU.
NIGER EXPLORATION.. BY T. J. HUTCHINSON
THE ZULUS OF NATAL .... BY G. H. MASON.

### IN AMERICA.

BRAZIL .................. BY E. WILBERFORCE.
CANADA ................ BY A. M. JAMESON.
CUBA .................. BY W. H. HURLBUT.
NORTH AMERICAN WILDS .... BY C. LANMAN.

### IN AUSTRALIA.

AUSTRALIAN COLONIES ...... BY W. HUGHES.

### ROUND THE WORLD.

A LADY'S VOYAGE.......... BY IDA PFEIFFER.

## HISTORY AND BIOGRAPHY.

MEMOIR OF THE DUKE OF WELLINGTON.
THE LIFE OF MARSHAL } BY THE REV. T. O.
   TURENNE         COCKAYNE.
SCHAMYL .... BY BODENSTEDT AND WAGNER.
FERDINAND I. AND MAXIMI- } BY RANKE.
   LIAN II.
FRANCIS ARAGO'S AUTOBIOGRAPHY.
THOMAS HOLCROFT'S MEMOIRS.

CHESTERFIELD & SELWYN, BY A. HAYWARD.
SWIFT AND RICHARDSON, BY LORD JEFFREY.
DEFOE AND CHURCHILL .... BY J. FORSTER.
ANECDOTES OF DR. JOHNSON, BY MRS. PIOZZI.
TURKEY AND CHRISTENDOM.
LEIPSIC CAMPAIGN, BY THE REV. G. R. GLEIG.
AN ESSAY ON THE LIFE AND } BY HENRY
   GENIUS OF THOMAS FULLER } ROGERS.

## ESSAYS BY LORD MACAULAY.

WARREN HASTINGS.
LORD CLIVE.
WILLIAM PITT.
THE EARL OF CHATHAM.
RANKE'S HISTORY OF THE POPES.
GLADSTONE ON CHURCH AND STATE.
ADDISON'S LIFE AND WRITINGS.
HORACE WALPOLE.
LORD BACON.

LORD BYRON.
COMIC DRAMATISTS OF THE RESTORATION.
FREDERIC THE GREAT.
HALLAM'S CONSTITUTIONAL HISTORY.
CROKER'S EDITION OF BOSWELL'S LIFE OF
   JOHNSON.

LORD MACAULAY'S SPEECHES ON PARLIA-
   MENTARY REFORM.

## WORKS OF FICTION.

THE LOVE STORY, FROM SOUTHEY'S DOCTOR.
SIR ROGER DE COVERLEY .... } FROM THE
                SPECTATOR.
MEMOIRS OF A MAITRE-D'ARMES, BY DUMAS.
CONFESSIONS OF A } BY E. SOUVESTRE.
   WORKING MAN ..

AN ATTIC PHILOSO- } BY E. SOUVESTRE.
   PHER IN PARIS
SIR EDWARD SEAWARD'S NARRATIVE OF
   HIS SHIPWRECK.

## NATURAL HISTORY, &c.

NATURAL HISTORY OF } BY DR. L. KEMP.
   CREATION
INDICATIONS OF INSTINCT, BY DR. L. KEMP.

ELECTRIC TELEGRAPH, &c. BY DR. G. WILSON.
OUR COAL-FIELDS AND OUR COAL-PITS.
CORNWALL, ITS MINES, MINERS, &c.

## MISCELLANEOUS WORKS.

LECTURES AND ADDRESSES { BY THE EARL OF
                   CARLISLE.
SELECTIONS FROM SYDNEY SMITH'S
   WRITINGS.
PRINTING ...................... BY A. STARK.

RAILWAY MORALS AND } BY H. SPENCER.
   RAILWAY POLICY ..
MORMONISM .. BY THE REV. W. J. CONYBEARE.
LONDON .................. BY J. R. M'CULLOCH.

The Traveller's Library being now complete, the Publishers call attention to this collection as well adapted for *Travellers* and *Emigrants*, for *School-room Libraries*, the *Libraries of Mechanics' Institutions*, *Young Men's Libraries*, the *Libraries of Ships*, and similar purposes. The separate volumes are suited for *School Prizes*, *Presents to Young People*, and for general instruction and entertainment. The Series comprises fourteen of the most popular of Lord Macaulay's *Essays*, and his *Speeches* on Parliamentary Reform. The department of Travels contains some account of eight of the principal countries of Europe, as well as travels in four districts of Africa, in four of America, and in three of Asia. Madame Pfeiffer's *First Journey round the World* is included; and a general account of the *Australian Colonies*. In Biography and History will be found Lord Macaulay's Biographical Sketches of *Warren Hastings*, *Clive*, *Pitt*, *Walpole*, *Bacon*, and others; besides Memoirs of *Wellington*, *Turenne*, *F. Arago*, &c.; an Essay on the *Life* and Genius of *Thomas Fuller*, with Selections from his Writings, by Mr. Henry Rogers; and a history of the *Leipsic Campaign*, by Mr. Gleig, — which is the only separate account of this remarkable campaign. Works of Fiction did not come within the plan of the TRAVELLER'S LIBRARY; but the *Confessions of a Working Man*, by Souvestre, which is indeed a fiction founded on fact, has been included, and has been read with unusual interest by many of the working classes, for whose use it is especially recommended. Dumas's story of the *Maître-d'Armes*, though in form a work of fiction, gives a striking picture of an episode in the history of Russia. Amongst the works on Science and Natural Philosophy, a general view of Creation is embodied in Dr. Kemp's *Natural History of Creation*; and in his *Indications of Instinct* remarkable facts in natural history are collected. Dr. Wilson has contributed a popular account of the *Electric Telegraph*. In the volumes on the *Coal-Fields*, and on the Tin and other Mining Districts of Cornwall, is given an account of the mineral wealth of England, the habits and manners of the miners, and the scenery of the surrounding country. It only remains to add, that among the Miscellaneous Works are a Selection of the best Writings of the Rev. Sydney Smith; Lord Carlisle's *Lectures and Addresses*; an account of *Mormonism*, by the Rev. W. J. Conybeare; an exposition of *Railway management and mismanagement*, by Mr. Herbert Spencer; an account of the Origin and Practice of *Printing*, by Mr. Stark; and an account of *London*, by Mr. M'Culloch.

"If we were called upon to lay the first stone of a Mechanics' Institute or Book-Society's Collection, it should be composed of the hundred and two parts of the *Traveller's Library*. It is the best Shilling Series extant. Here are Mr. Macaulay's best writings, the anthologia of Sydney Smith, some admirable literary essays by different authors, several excellent volumes of science, narratives of travel in eight European, four American, four African, and three Asiatic countries, and examples from the works of Souvestre and Dumas. Bound together, they form twenty-five convenient volumes, which any society of a hundred and five members may possess, upon payment of one shilling each. An association of this kind, formed in every small town, would thus create sufficient basis for a free library upon a modest scale. Good books are *not* beyond the reach of working men, if working men will combine to obtain them."                               LEADER.

☞ The *Traveller's Library* may also be had as originally issued in 102 parts, 1s. each, forming 50 vols. 2s. 6d. each; or any separate parts or volumes.

**Trollope.—Barchester Towers.** By Anthony Trollope. 3 vols. post 8vo. price 31s. 6d.

"*Barchester Towers* (a kind of sequel in continuation of Mr. Trollope's former novel *The Warden*) does not depend only on story for its interest; the careful writing, the good humour with a tendency often to be Shandean in its expression, and the sense and right feeling with which the way is threaded among questions of high church and low church, are very noticeable, and secure for it unquestionable rank among the few really well-written tales that every season produces."                  EXAMINER.

**Trollope.—The Warden.** By Anthony Trollope. Post 8vo. 10s. 6d.

**Sharon Turner's Sacred History of the World**, attempted to be Philosophically considered, in a Series of Letters to a Son. New Edition, edited by the Rev. S. TURNER. 3 vols. post 8vo. price 31s. 6d.

**Sharon Turner's History of England** during the Middle Ages: Comprising the Reigns from the Norman Conquest to the Accession of Henry VIII. Fifth Edition, revised by the Rev. S. TURNER. 4 vols. 8vo. price 50s.

**Sharon Turner's History of the Anglo-Saxons**, from the Earliest Period to the Norman Conquest. Seventh Edition, revised by the Rev. S. TURNER. 3 vols. 8vo. 36s.

**Dr. Turton's Manual of the Land and Fresh-Water Shells of Great Britain.** New Edition, thoroughly revised and brought up to the Present Time. Edited by Dr. J. E. GRAY, F.R.S., &c., Keeper of the Zoological Department in the British Museum. Crown 8vo. with Coloured Plates. [*In the press.*

**Dr. Ure's Dictionary of Arts, Manufactures, and Mines**: Containing a clear Exposition of their Principles and Practice. Fourth Edition, much enlarged; most of the Articles being entirely re-written, and many new Articles added. With nearly 1,600 Woodcuts. 2 vols. 8vo. price 60s.

**Van Der Hoeven's Handbook of Zoology.** Translated from the Second Dutch Edition by the Rev. WILLIAM CLARK, M.D., F.R.S., &c., late Fellow of Trinity College, and Professor of Anatomy in the University of Cambridge; with additional References furnished by the Author. In Two Volumes. Vol. I. *Invertebrate Animals*; with 15 Plates, comprising numerous Figures. 8vo. 30s.

**Vehse.—Memoirs of the Court, Aristocracy, and Diplomacy of Austria.** By Dr. E. VEHSE. Translated from the German by FRANZ DEMMLER. 2 vols. post 8vo. 21s.

Von Tempsky. — Mitla: A Narrative of Incidents and Personal Adventures on a Journey in Mexico and Guatemala in the Years 1853 and 1854: With Observations on the Modes of Life in those Countries. By G. F. VON TEMPSKY. Edited by J. S. BELL, Author of *Journal of a Residence in Circassia in the Years 1836 to* 1839. With Illustrations in Chromolithography and Engravings on Wood. 8vo.     [*In the press.*

Wade. — England's Greatness: Its Rise and Progress in Government, Laws, Religion, and Social Life; Agriculture, Commerce, and Manufactures; Science, Literature, and the Arts, from the Earliest Period to the Peace of Paris. By JOHN WADE, Author of the *Cabinet Lawyer,* &c. Post 8vo. 10s. 6d.

Waterton. — Essays on Natural History, chiefly Ornithology. By C. WATERTON, Esq. With an Autobiography of the Author, and Views of Walton Hall. New and cheaper Edition. 2 vols. fcp. 8vo. price 10s.

Waterton's Essays on Natural History. Third Series; with a Continuation of the Autobiography, and a Portrait of the Author. Fcp. 8vo. price 6s.

Webster and Parkes's Encyclopædia of Domestic Economy; comprising such subjects as are most immediately connected with Housekeeping: As, The Construction of Domestic Edifices, with the Modes of Warming, Ventilating, and Lighting them—A description of the various articles of Furniture, with the nature of their Materials—Duties of Servants—&c. New Edition; with nearly 1,000 Woodcuts. 8vo. price 50s.

Weld. — Vacations in Ireland. By CHARLES RICHARD WELD, Barrister-at-Law. Post 8vo. with a tinted View of Birr Castle, price 10s. 6d.

Weld.—A Vacation Tour in the United States and Canada. By C. R. WELD, Barrister-at-Law. Post 8vo. with Map, 10s. 6d.

West. — Lectures on the Diseases of Infancy and Childhood. By CHARLES WEST, M.D., Physician to the Hospital for Sick Children; Physician-Accoucheur to, and Lecturer on Midwifery at, St. Bartholomew's Hospital. Third Edition. 8vo. 14s.

Willich's Popular Tables for ascertaining the Value of Lifehold, Leasehold, and Church Property, Renewal Fines, &c. With numerous additional Tables—Chemical, Astronomical, Trigonometrical, Common and Hyperbolic Logarithms; Constants, Squares, Cubes, Roots, Reciprocals, &c. Fourth Edition, enlarged. Post 8vo. price 10s.

Whitelocke's Journal of the English Embassy to the Court of Sweden in the Years 1653 and 1654. A New Edition, revised by HENRY REEVE, Esq., F.S.A. 2 vols. 8vo. 24s.

Wilmot's Abridgment of Blackstone's Commentaries on the Laws of England, intended for the use of Young Persons, and comprised in a series of Letters from a Father to his Daughter. 12mo. price 6s. 6d.

Wilson (W.)—Bryologia Britannica: Containing the Mosses of Great Britain and Ireland systematically arranged and described according to the Method of *Bruch* and *Schimper;* with 61 illustrative Plates. Being a New Edition, enlarged and altered, of the *Muscologia Britannica* of Messrs. Hooker and Taylor. By WILLIAM WILSON, President of the Warrington Natural History Society. 8vo. 42s.; or, with the Plates coloured, price £4. 4s. cloth.

Yonge.—A New English-Greek Lexicon: Containing all the Greek Words used by Writers of good authority. By C. D. YONGE, B.A. *Second Edition,* revised and corrected. Post 4to. price 21s.

Yonge's New Latin Gradus: Containing Every Word used by the Poets of good authority. For the use of Eton, Westminster, Winchester, Harrow, Charterhouse, and Rugby Schools; King's College, London; and Marlborough College. *Fifth Edition.* Post 8vo. price 9s.; or with APPENDIX of *Epithets* classified according to their *English* Meaning, 12s.

Youatt.—The Horse. By William Youatt. With a Treatise of Draught. New Edition, with numerous Wood Engravings, from Designs by William Harvey. (Messrs. LONGMAN and Co.'s Edition should be ordered.) 8vo. price 10s.

Youatt. — The Dog. By William Youatt. A New Edition; with numerous Engravings, from Designs by W. Harvey. 8vo. 6s.

Young. — The Christ of History: An Argument grounded in the Facts of His Life on Earth. By JOHN YOUNG, LL.D. Second Edition. Post 8vo. 7s. 6d.

Young.—The Mystery; or, Evil and God. By JOHN YOUNG, LL.D. Post 8vo. 7s. 6d.

Zumpt's Grammar of the Latin Language. Translated and adapted for the use of English Students by DR. L. SCHMITZ, F.R.S.E.: With numerous Additions and Corrections by the Author and Translator. 4th Edition, thoroughly revised. 8vo. 14s.

[*October* 1857.

PRINTED BY SPOTTISWOODE AND CO., NEW-STREET SQUARE, LONDON.

www.ingramcontent.com/pod-product-compliance
Lightning Source LLC
LaVergne TN
LVHW012208040326
832903LV00003B/187